Female Voices of the North II.

Wiener Texte zur Skandinavistik (WTS)

Band 3

Wiener Texte zur Skandinavistik

herausgegeben von Robert Nedoma (Wien) und
Sven Hakon Rossel (Wien)

Band 3

Praesens Verlag
Literaturwissenschaft | Sprachwissenschaft
Musikwissenschaft | Kulturwissenschaft

Wien 2006

Female Voices of the North II

An Anthology

Edited by Inger M. Olsen
and Sven Hakon Rossel
in collaboration with Monica Wenusch

Gedruckt mit Förderung
des Bundesministeriums für Bildung, Wissenschaft und Kultur, Wien
bm:bwk
des dänischen Ministeriums für Wissenschaft, Technologie und
Entwicklung, Kopenhagen
FILI (Finnish Literature Information Centre), Helsinki
NORLA (Centre for Norwegian Literature Abroad), Oslo
sowie
des Svenska Institutet, Stockholm

Bibliografische Information Der Deutschen Bibliothek

Die Deutsche Bibliothek verzeichnet diese Publikation in der Deutschen
Nationalbibliografie; detaillierte bibliografische Daten sind im Internet über
<http://dnb.ddb.de> abrufbar.

ISBN 3-7069-0155-2

© 2006 Wien | *Praesens Verlag*
http://www.praesens.at
eMail: edition@praesens.at

Contents

8

Introduction

Women writers were overlooked, if not deliberately ignored, until the 1970s. It is not for this introduction to grapple with the reasons. Instead, the contributors to this anthology and their literary companions of the past illuminate the solitary and often painful journey to recognition of person, intelligence and wit in writing by strong-willed women. Therein the reader will find many of the repressions they endured were subtle and others overt.

The vanguard of the women demanding to be heard in literature came from the Nordic countries of Europe. They were successful, but mostly they have not been heard in English. Thus, an anthology of Nordic female writers in English, or, for that matter, any non-Nordic language, is overdue. Taking the artistic and thematic variety of this vein of literature into consideration it is *long* overdue.

The selection process of this anthology was difficult, considering the avalanche of polished material that has accreted downstream in time, unseen, through the years. With this difficulty in mind we have attempted to cover various chronological stages in literary development while keeping in mind that – these volumes are in no way complete or comprehensive.

The first volume of the anthology, *Female Voices of the North I* from 2002, included texts from Denmark, the Faroe Islands, Greenland, Iceland and Norway before 1814. The present volume includes texts from Finland, Norway (post 1814) and Sweden as well as an entire collection of Sami poetry.

In regard to the selections included here – presented in chronological order – there is an introductory essay that places the writer in question in a literary, historical and/or social context. This is followed by the text proper both in the original language and in an English translation varying in length and sometimes may be only an excerpt according to a decision made by the contributor.

The presentation concludes with a list of major primary works and a selective bibliography. The editors adhere and subscribe to theoretical diversity and thus have not prescribed any specific methodological approach as it would limit the readability of the essays. Notes regarding the fictional texts will be found mainly under the English translation.

It is our hope that the presentation of the fictional text in the original language, as well as in the English translation, will make this anthology attractive to both undergraduate and graduate instruction in Scandinavian programs, Comparative Literature programs and women's programs as well.

We would like to thank our contributors for their cooperation, encouragement and good spirit throughout the sometimes difficult editorial process and we thank authors, translators and publishers for giving their permission to use the texts included in this anthology. We also extend our gratitude to the Danish Ministry of Science, Technology and Innovation, Copenhagen, Svenska Institutet, Stockholm, NORLA (Centre for Norwegian Literature Abroad) and the Finnish Literature Information Centre, Helsinki for financial support.

Special thanks go to Monica Wenusch, Vienna, for her editorial assistance and to Norman A. Olsen, Longview, Washington, USA for his assistance in readying the manuscript for printing – his linguistic and stylistic expertise as well as sound judgments have been invaluable.

Inger M. Olsen   Sven Hakon Rossel
Longview   Vienna

Saint Birgitta of Sweden:
A Visionary Female Voice of the Middle Ages

MONICA WENUSCH (UNIVERSITY OF VIENNA)

During her lifetime Birgitta Birgersdotter – St Birgitta of Sweden – became one of the most intriguing and charismatic figures in Europe, a woman who achieved respect and recognition. She was a woman who experienced a worldly life and a life dedicated to God and spirituality. Not only her deep faith, but also her progressive ideas and the will to make a change and to reform, as well as her sense for reality and pragmatism make Birgitta an outstanding figure of the time. She was a gentle, yet strong-willed and successful woman with an impact, in her time as well as today, more than 700 years after her death.

Birgitta's lifetime (1303-73) covers a major part of the 14th century; contemporary mystics such as Meister Eckhardt (1260-1328) and Heinrich Seuse (1295-1366) as well as Katharina of Siena (1347-1380) could be mentioned. Church politics of this period were determined first by Pope Clement V and his moving from Rome to Avignon in southern France in 1309 in order to find a safer place to live, and then by the Western or Papal Schism (1378-1417), that is the split within the Catholic Church resulting from the papacy's return to Rome in 1378. Secular politics were marked by the Hundred Years' War between England and France which broke out in 1339. Christianity had been introduced in Sweden in the early 11th century, approximately 300 years before Birgitta's birth, and thereby the country was ecclesiastically brought under the authority of Rome. Sweden at the time meant the regions Svealand and Götaland in central and southern Sweden respectively; as well as the west of Finland which was ruled by Sweden. However, there were close political, cultural and religious relations between the Nordic countries. Sweden was a society that did not institute a general legal system until the mid-14th century and the first Swedish university in Uppsala was not founded until 1477. Furthermore, society at the time – both secular and sacred – was strictly hierarchically structured.

Birgitta was born into this environment as a descendant of a highly renowned Swedish family with a reputation for strict devotion to the Church
and piety. Her father was a powerful and influential figure in Swedish
society, a distinguished so-called law man (i.e. a local judge). He held one
of the most prestigious offices in the land. Her mother was a noblewoman,
related to the royal family. Due to this family background Birgitta represented the traditional aristocracy of Sweden. Her upbringing and education
in this environment – by and among the leading figures in politics, legislation as well as the Church – meant that Birgitta was perfectly prepared for
the life she was supposed to lead.

In addition to these circumstances Birgitta was a deeply religious, uncompromising and strong willed woman – even though physically slender
and small. Her contemporaries report she was always a gentle and friendly
woman, with a smile on her face. Nevertheless, she did not hesitate to touch
upon controversial issues for example within the Church or in society.
Apart from that, she showed a strong interest in people's everyday life, an
interest that exerted a deep effect on her and she never closed her eyes to
social or political issues.

Birgitta knew at an early age that she had a religious calling. She received her first visions at the age of seven. When she was ten years old she
heard a sermon on the passion of Christ. That night Christ appeared to her
as if he had just been crucified and to her question who had done this to
him, Christ answered, "Whoever despises me and spurns my love does this
to me."[1] From that day on, the Passion of Christ affected Birgitta so much
that she hardly could think of it without weeping. This revelation became a
great influence throughout her whole life and the theme constantly recurs in
her revelations.

However, Birgitta was not able to follow her call immediately because
her father had determined that his daughter – at age fourteen – should be
given in marriage to the five year older Ulf Gudmarsson (1298-1344) who
also became a law man and – to Birgitta's luck – turned out to be a distinctly pious man. Together they had eight children. One of the daughters,
Saint Katarina (1331-1381), who later accompanied her mother on her
many journeys, on which Birgitta proved to be an untiring pilgrim, is the
best known of them. Two of the other children died at an early age, a fact
that must have had a major influence on Birgitta's Christianity which was
focused on the motherly love of the Virgin Mary and on the idea of a
mother's suffering through her child's suffering. In a revelation Birgitta
meets Mary – the *mater dolorosa*, the grieving Mother – who describes her
sufferings when seeing her son, Jesus Christ, being crucified and tortured.
In general, the Virgin Mary takes a major part in Birgitta's revelations

---

[1]   See Morris, 37.

focusing on God's mother also as the Mother of Mercy and as a role model and example to humanity. Already at this point in her life Birgitta's strong social consciousness was evident. Among other things, she took care of and helped troubled women, for instance women who had been ostracized by society or had children out of wedlock.

Together with her husband, Birgitta went on several pilgrimages, including one in 1341 to Santiago de Compostela in Spain. Ulf died shortly after their return, and some time after his death Christ appeared to Birgitta and told her that he had chosen her to be his bride.[2] From now on she devoted herself totally to God and religion. One could state that Birgitta in the first half of her life lead a life that more or less was expected of a noblewoman of the time. That is, she married and had an extended family with a range of commitments. Now, she was ready to dedicate the other half of her life to spirituality and her faith. Finally, in 1346, Birgitta received a revelation telling her to go to Rome,[3] where she – apart from travels – should remain until her death after her return from a pilgrimage to the Holy Land at the age of 70 in 1373. Furthermore, Birgitta had been anxious to have her Order, the Birgittine Order,[4] officially approved. That was the reason, why she went to Rome. She had written down the rules of the Order exactly as she had received them from Mary in a revelation, telling her the Order to be a convent of both nuns and monks, yet separated from each other, but subordinate to an abbess. This concept of a double monastery was a sensation for the Middle Ages.[5] However, the Order, *Ordo Sanctissimi Salvatori* (The Order of the Most Holy Saviour), was not approved until 1370 by Pope Urban V, who included a number of changes concerning the rules. The convent should be established in Vadstena, by the Lake Vättern, where the royal family owned a castle. In 1346 the palace was bequeathed to Birgitta

2 See also *Revelaciones* V 11, I 32.
3 See *Revelaciones* IX/*Extravagantes* 8.
4 The Birgittine Order, *Ordo Sanctissimi Salvatoris*, was founded about 1346, although the mother house at Vadstena at Lake Vättern, Sweden, was not begun until 1369. On August 5, 1370, Pope Urban V approved the Birgittine rule but required the use also of the so-called Augustinian rule, a number of general precepts for monastic life. The modern Sisters of the Most Holy Saviour of Saint Birgitta, founded at Rome in 1911 by Mother Elisabeth Hesselblad, were recognized by the Holy See on September 12, 1942, as an offshot of the ancient order.
5 For further information see Morris 160ff.
Birgitta writes that Virgin Mary after her Son's death and resurrection so to speak received the status of a queen and became both head and queen over the twelve apostles and the other apostles, hence, she argues, the first Christian community was a matriarchate. Men resp. the apostles had practical tasks like spreading the word and administering the sacraments and were headed by Peter, while Mary is both the earthly and heavenly example above all others due to her virtue of her absolute love and her identification with her Son's sufferings. This is a reason why her Order should be led by a woman.

for conversion to a monastery but construction work for the church did not start until 1369.

Birgitta's image of herself was that of Christ's bride, which meant and means being united with Christ in a life-long, sacramental relationship. Due to this mystical marriage God was speaking to her. The visions she received tackled a variety of issues and matters. One can find accounts on the life and death of Jesus Christ, accounts of the Virgin Mary, saints and much more and on secular matters as well. However, her revelations also contain frightening depictions of hell and purgatory with picturesque descriptions of methods of torture and punishment. It may come as a surprise that the smiling, pious woman had such cruel ideas, but an explanation can be found in the fact that punishment should stress the seriousness of sin. It should help to understand the meaning of sin, the sin which in Birgitta's mystical dimension meant that Christ is being crucified again and again with every time a sin is committed, i.e. that Christ suffers in eternity for all the sins in the world. Birgitta did not see herself elevated above guilt and punishment, since she was convinced that during her marriage she had been too worldly, voluptuous, vain and sensual, a thought which caused her pain. This is an issue thematized in the revelations as well.

In fact, Birgitta was a very complex woman. Strong-willed and gentle at the same time. She showed a fearless nature, when it came to denunciation of unacceptable conditions, abuse of power and sins; she made them a subject of discussion, no matter who or what was concerned. She did not leave herself out either, and was critical towards herself as well. However, she also sought to make political statements with her revelations, supported by letters and other means of written documents. Through her texts she criticised both ecclesiastical life in Rome and life at the royal court.[6] She was brave enough to criticise corruption within the Church, the worldly and licentious life of clergymen, cardinals and even the pope, but did not leave out secular rulers. All that was done with total absence of opportunism. She was anxious that the papal seat which since 1305 had been in Avignon, in the south of France, should be reestablished in Rome. Thus it was a wide range of concrete issues and matters of her contemporary society which Birgitta discussed in her revelations.

***

In all, Birgitta received about 700 revelations, *Revelaciones celestes* (Divine Revelations). These are visions from God, Jesus Christ, the Virgin Mary as well as from other saints which contain accounts and commentar-

---

[6]   Birgitta's critical comments on the royal court date back to her time at the Swedish court in Stockholm in the mid 1330s, when she was appointed as mentor and governess to the new queen, Blanche of Namur. See for example *Revelaciones* VIII, 10-12. Birgitta left the court after five years.

ies, but also advice and admonitions on how to lead a proper life, and show-ing the consequences of disobedience or compliance. Birgitta – with her theology that was practical and focused on deeds – valued the responsibility of humans and the ability to choose that which is right. She believed that one makes a decision freely, and consequently – depending on whether the choice had been good or evil – angels or demons would come along in order to execute consequences of the choice in life. Naturally, the good choice is always a life in Christ's succession.

Birgitta received her revelations in Swedish and in general wrote them down in her native language in order later on to have them translated into Latin by clergymen, i.e. her confessors. Sometimes they were directly translated from her oral presentation. This translation was then read to Birgitta so that no word might be omitted or changed. The first printed edition of Birgitta's revelations was published in 1492 in Lübeck, Ger-many. From a stylistic point of view, the extraordinary departure from the norm in Birgitta's writing is found in her very personal and unconventional style. In general, she prefered to learn from life and actual deeds more than from tenets and books. According to that, she stresses her statements and comments not so much with quotations from the Bible or the Church patri-archs – which was common use in the Middle Ages –, but by using exam-ples mostly taken from nature and people's everyday life.

Birgitta prefers concrete representations to theoretical and abstract theo-logical discussions, a fact that results in a unique freshness and immediacy of her texts and demonstrates the author's talent for depicting situations taken from her own everyday experiences. Birgitta uses images, draws comparisons and parallels and does not hesitate to use, for instance, images from the biological life of a woman and touches upon issues and details such as delivery, nursing etc. No topic is too delicate for her. This method of composing and designing a text gives an insight in the life and work of the Middle Ages, of for example farmers and workmen, but also and not at least of women. Nevertheless, the descriptions of ordinary people and lives are used primarily in order to focus on spiritual matters and to depict con-crete experiences as parables for divine issues which thereby stand out vividly. The description of a worldly marriage can, for example, lead to a depiction of the spiritual relation between God and the soul or between Christ and the Church. In several revelations, marriage is an important issue. A traditional hierarchy like virginity, marriage and widowhood is represented as three virtuous and worthy states with the condition, however, that they are accompanied by spiritual purity, using Mary as an example.[7] However, worldly and spiritual life are frequently compared with each other.

---

[7] See, for instance, *Revelaciones IX/Extravagantes* 20-21.

The narrative of the Nativity where the physical side of Mary giving birth to Christ is described, and the narratives of the Passion of Christ are some of the most renowned of Birgitta's revelations. They are striking with a detailed, intensive, realistic, almost naturalistic style. The specific (and sanguinary) depictions of Christ's crucifixion and the tortures he goes through, together with the account of his mother's, Mary's, suffering are outstanding and deeply moving, not at least because of the eyewitness perspective the accounts are presented in.

***

Of course, Birgitta's life and work has always been criticized and opposed. Doubts were raised whether her visions were reliable; some of her contemporaries would have loved to see her burnt as a witch and heretic. As late as in the 20th century August Strindberg portrayed Birgitta in the beginning of his play *Folkungasagan* (1901; The Saga of the Folkungs) as a power-hungry, overbearing, pietistic old woman, full of cruelty, malice and arrogance and sees her as an unruly, domineering and (in a negative sense) emancipated woman.

Whatever one might think of such a description, Birgitta undoubtedly stands out as an emancipated woman of remarkable willpower and nature, especially considering the time she lived in, in which she had a voice that was heard and even respected, probably also feared by those being criticized. It is with good reason Saint Birgitta was appointed one of Europe's patrons in 1999 and that her Order still exists all around the world. Furthermore, Birgitta was the only woman in the 14th century to be canonized. Her revelations give evidence to a deep spirituality and belief in God, a true will to reform and a warm interest in people and society. Ideas and images of the Middle Ages emerge through her revelations, issues that are not hidden in the style of her texts which like the contents testify to Birgitta's strong sense of reality and always sharp and observant eye linked with a clear female voice which managed to make itself be heard.

Revelaciones

Excerpta

Relevaciones liber VII, 21

Cum essem ad presepe Domini in Bethleem, vidi quandam virginem pregnantem pulcherrimam valde, indutam albo mantello et subtili tunica, per quam abextra eius carnes virgineas clare cernebam. Cuius vterus plenus et multum tumidus erat, quia iam parata erat ad pariendum. Cum qua senex quidam honestissimus erat et secum habebant ambo vnum bouem et asinum. (…) portauit ad virginem candelam accensam fixitque eam in muro et exiuit extra, ne partui personaliter interesset. (…) Cumque (…) omnia sic parata essent, tunc virgo genuflexa est cum magna reuerencia, ponens se ad oracionem, et dorsum versus presepe tenebat, faciem vero ad celum leuatam versus orientem. Erectis igitur manibus et oculis in celum intentis stabat quasi in extasi contemplacionis suspensa, inebriata diuina dulcedine. Et sic ea in oracione stante vidi tunc ego mouere iacentem in vtero eius, et illico in momento et ictu oculi peperit filium, a quo tanta lux ineffabilis et splendor exibat, quod sol non esset ei comparabilis. Neque candela illa, quam posuerat senex, quoquomodo lumen reddebat, quia splendor ille diuinus splendorem materialem candele totaliter annichilauerat. Et tam subitus et momentaneus erat ille modus pariendi, quod ego non poteram aduertere nec discernere, quomodo vel in quo membro pariebat. Verumptamen statim vidi illum gloriosum infantem iacentem in terra nudum nitidissimum. Cuius carnes mundissime erant ab omni sorde et immundicia. Vidi eciam pellem secundinam iacentem prope eum, inuolutam et valde nitidam. Audiui eciam tunc cantus angelorum mirabilis suauitatis et magne dulcedinis. Et statim venter virginis, qui ante partum tumidissimus erat, retraxit se et videbatur tunc corpus eius mirabilis pulchritudinis et delicatum. Cum igitur virgo sensit se iam peperisse, statim inclinato capite et iunctis manibus cum magna honestate et reuerencia adorauit puerum et dixit illi: "Bene veneris, Deus meus, Dominus meus et filius meus!" Et tunc puer plorans et quasi tremens pre frigore et duricia pauimenti, vbi iacebat, voluebat se paululum et extendebat membra, quereus inuenire refrigerium et matris fauorem. Quem tunc mater suscepit in manibus et strinxit eum ad pectus suum, et cum maxilla et pectore calefaciebat eum cum magna leticia et tenera compassione materna. Que tunc sedens in terra posuit filium in gremio et recepit cum digitis subtiliter vmbilicum eius, qui statim abscisus est, nec inde aliquis liquor aut sanguis exiuit. Et statim cepit eum inuoluere diligenter, primo in panniculis lineis et postea in laneis et stringens corpusculum, tibias et brachia eius cum fascia, que suta erat in quatuor partes superioris panniculi lanei. Postea vero inuoluit ligando in capite pueri illos duos panniculos lineos, quos ad hoc paratos habebat. Hiis igitur completis intrauit senex, et prosternens se ad terram genibus flexis adorando eum plorabat pre gaudio. Nec tunc in partu virgo illa immutabatur colore vel infirmitate, nec in ea defecit fortitudo aliqua corporalis, sicut in aliis mulieribus parientibus fieri solet, nisi quod venter eius tumidus retraxit se ad priorem statum, in quo erat, antequam puerum conciperet. Tunc autem surrexit ipsa, habens puerum in vlnis suis, et simul ambo, scilicet ipsa et Ioseph, posuerunt eum in presepio et flexis genibus adorabant eum cum gaudio et immensa leticia.

Relevaciones liber VII, 15

Ad montem Caluarie dum essem mestissima plorans, vidi Dominum meum nudum et flagellatum ductum per Iudeos ad crucifigendum. Qui diligenter ab eis custodiebatur. Vidi quoque tunc foramen quoddam excisum in monte et crucifixores in circuitu paratos ad operandum crudelitatem. Dominus autem conuersus ad me dixit michi: "Attende tu, quia in isto foramine petre infixus fuit pes crucis mee tempore passionis." Et statim vidi, qualiter ibi crux eius a Iudeis figebatur et firmabatur fortiter in foramine petre montis cum lignis confixis cum malleo valentissime circumquaque, vt crux solidius staret, ne caderet. Cum igitur crux ita solide firmata esset ibidem, statim adaptabantur tabule lignee in circuitu stipitis crucis per modum graduum vsque ad locum, vbi pedes eius crucifigi debebant, vt possent per illos gradus tabularum tam ipse quam crucifixores ascendere et super tabulas illas apciori modo stare ad crucifigendum eum. Post hec autem ascenderunt ipsi per illos gradus, ducentes eum cum irrisione et vituperio maximo. Qui gratanter ascendens velut agnus mansuetus ductus ad immolandum, cum esset iam super tabulas illas, non coactus sed statim voluntarie extendit brachium suum et aperta sua dextera manu posuit eam in cruce, quam illi seui tortores immaniter crucifixerunt, et perforabant eam clauo per illam partem, qua os solidius erat. Tunc eciam trahentes cum fune vehementer manum eius sinistram cruci affixerunt eam simili modo. Deinde extento corpore vltra modum in cruce posita fuit vna tibia eius super aliam et sic iunctos pedes affixerunt in cruce duobus clauis, et in tantum extenderunt illa gloriosa membra in cruce vehementer, quod quasi omnes vene et nerui eius rumpebantur. Quo facto coronam de spinis, quam deposuerunt de capite eius, cum crucifigeretur, iterum imposuerunt et aptauerunt capiti suo sanctissimo. Que tam fortiter pupugit reuerendum caput eius, quod oculi sui repleti fuerunt illico fluente sanguine, aures quoque obstruebantur et facies et barba quasi tegebantur et intincta erant illo roseo sanguine. Et statim illi crucifixores et milites amouerunt velociter omnes tabulas illas, que adherebant cruci, et tunc remansit crux sola et alta et Dominus meus crucifixus in illa. Cumque ego repleta dolore respicerem crudelitatem illorum, vidi tunc matrem eius mestissimam in terra iacentem et quasi trementem et semimortuam. Quam consolabantur Iohannes et alie sorores eius, que tunc stabant non longe a cruce ad eius partem dexteram. Dolor igitur nouus compassionis illius sanctissime matris in tantum transfixit me, quod quasi senciebam, quod cor meum pertransibat quidam gladius acutus importabilis amaritudinis. Surgens tandem tunc illa eius mater dolorosa, quasi exinanita corpore, respexit ad filium suum, et sic sustentata stabat a sororibus, tota stupore suspensa et velut mortua viuens, gladio doloris transfixa. Quam cum Filius respexisset et alios amicos plorantes, voce flebili commendabat eam Iohanni, et bene cernebatur in gestu eius et voce, quod cor ipsius ex compassione matris penetrabatur acutissima sagitta doloris immensi. Tunc autem oculi eius amabiles et decori apparebant semimortui, os eius erat apertum et sanguinolentum, vultus pallidus et submersus totusque liuidus et intinctus sanguine, corpus quoque totum erat quasi liuidum et pallidum et languidum valde ex continuo fluxu decurrentis sanguinis. Cutis eciam et caro illa virginea sanctissimi corporis eius ita delicata et tenera erat, quod ex modica percussione illata signum liuidum exterius apparebat. Aliquando vero conabatur ipse extensiones facere in cruce pre amaritudine nimia, quam senciebat, intensi doloris acutissimi. Nam quandoque dolor de membris eius et venis perforatis ascendebat ad cor et vexabat eum crudeliter intenso martirio, et sic mors eius prolongabatur et dilatabatur cum tormento graui et ingenti amaritutdine. Tunc igitur ille anxius pre nimia doloris angustia et vicinus iam morti ad Patrem clamauit alta voce et flebili dicens: "O Pater, quare dereliquisti me?" Habebatque tunc labia pallida et linguam sanguinolentam, ventrem submissum coherentem dorso, ac si nulla intus habuisset viscera. Secundo quoque clamauit iterum cum anxio dolore maximo: "O Pater, in manus tuas commendo spiritum meum." Et tunc caput eius erigens se aliquantulum statim inclinauit se et sic emisit spiritum. Que tunc mater eius videns contremuit pre immensa amaritudine, volens cadere in terram, nisi quod sustinebatur ab aliis mulieribus. In illa igitur hora manus illius aliquantulum se retraxerunt a loco perforacionis clauorum pre nimio pondere corporis, et sic corpus eius quasi sustentabatur a clauis, quibus pedes crucifixi erant. Digiti autem et manus et brachia magis iam extenta erant quam ante, spatule vero et dorsum eius quasi stringebantur ad crucem. Tunc denique circumstantes Iudei irridentes clamabant contra matrem eius multa dicentes. Alii namque dicebant: "Maria, iam mortuus est filius tuus", alii vero dicebant alia verba irrisoria. Et sic stantibus turbis in circuitu venit vnus accurrens cum furia maxima et infixit lanceam in eius latere dextro tam vehementer et valide, quod quasi per aliam partem corporis lancea voluit pertransire. Quod cum extraheretur lancea de corpore, statim habundanter exibat de vulnere illo cum impetu quasi quidam fluuius sanguinis, ferrum vero lancee et aliqua pars haste rubicunda exibat de corpore et intincta sanguine. Que videns mater ita vehementer contremuit cum amaro gemitu, quod bene cernebatur in eius facie et gestu, quod anima eius tunc penetrabatur acuto doloris gladio. Hiis autem expletis cum turbe multe recederent, deposuerunt Dominum quidam amici eius. Quem tunc pie mater recepit inter sua brachia sanctissima et reclinauit eum sedens in genu totum dilaceratum, vulneratum et liuidum. Quem lauabant cum lacrimis ipsa et Iohannes et alie mulieres plorantes. Et tunc tersit eius mater mestissima cum lintheo suo totum corpus eius et vulnera clausitque eius oculos deosculando eos et inuoluit eum in sindone munda. Et sic duxerunt eum cum planctu et dolore maximo et posuerunt eum in sepulchro.

Relevaciones liber IX/Extravagantes, 20

Filius Dei loquitur: "(…) tres ordines sunt, qui michi summe placent, scilicet virginitas, viduitas et coniugium, ideo hii tres ordines preferendi et honorandi sunt pre omnibus, tum quia magna puritatis et honestatis habent insignia, tum quia mater mea hos tres ordines in se compleuit. Fuit enim purissima virgo in partu et post partum, fuit et vere mater et virgo, fuit et vidua post ascensionem meam, corporali presencia mea viduata. Propterea cum ellgenda est abbatissa, vna, que est de aliquo istorum trium ordinum, eligatur. (…)"

Relevaciones liber IX/Extravagantes, 21

Christus dicit, quod abbatissa debet esse virgo munda et probata atque moribus exemplaris, et quod in defectu huiusmodi virginis potest assumi in abbatissam humilis et probata vidua.

Ihesus Christus loquitur: "Pulchra coniunccio et decens confederacio est, vt virgo presit virginibus. Nam inter omnia primatum tenet ipsa mundicia carnis et mentis, de qua et per quam ego Deus incarnari volui. Verum quia mater mea virgo fuit et mater, sed non ideo mater quia cognita viro, sed afflata spiritu patris et mei genuit me verum Deum et hominem, ideo hic nouus ordo dedicandus est matri mee. Et quecumque preesse debet virginibus eius, necesse est et laudabile, vt sit virgo et munda et probata moribus et in virtutibus exemplaris. Si vero virgo talis in congregacione non fuerit, que officium virginis matris mee implere potuerit, non displicet michi, si onus humilitatis assumat humilis et probate vite vidua, quia accepcior est michi humilis vidua quam virgo superba. Ergo si Deo placuerit exaltare humilia et efferre viduitatem ex necessitate, non derogatur ex hoc laudabili consuetudini virginum, quia Deus omnia humilia exaltare dignatur. Quid enim humilius fuit et est matre mea? Quid vero est, quod humilitas perfecta non meretur? Propter humilitatem quippe factus sum ego, Deus et Dei filius, verus filius virginis. Et sine humilitate non est via in celum."

Revelaciones liber IV, 86

Mater Dei loquitur dicens, quod ipsa est similis flori, a quo apes trahunt dulcedinem (…).

Mater loquitur: "Ego sum regina et mater misericordie. Filius meus creator omnium tanta circa me dulcedine affectus est, quod omnium, que creata sunt, spiritualem michi dedit intelligenciam. Ideo ego simillima sum flori, de quo apes maxime trahunt dulcedinem, a quo, quantumcumque colligitur, nichilominus ei dulcedo remanet. Sic ego omnibus graciam impetrare possum et ego semper habundo. Verum eciam electi mei similes sunt apibus, quia tota deuocione circa honorem meum afficiuntur. Ipsi enim quasi apes habent duos pedes, scilicet continuum desiderium augendi honorem meum (…). Habent eciam duas alas, scilicet reputando se indignos laudare me, secundo obediendo omnibus, que sunt ad honorem meum. Habent eciam aculeum, qui si defecerit eis moriuntur. Sic amici Dei habent tribulaciones mundi, que ante finem vite propter virtutum custodiam non auferuntur ab eis, sed ego habundans consolacione consolabor eos."

Relevaciones liber III, 32

Mater loquitur ad sponsam dicens: "Quidam querens lapides repperit magnetem quem eleuans manu propria custodiuit in thesauro suo et per eum deduxit nauem ad portum tutum. Sic filius meus multos querens lapides sanctorum me specialiter elegit in matrem sibi, ut per me homines reducerentur ad portum celi. Ergo sicut magnes attrahit sibi ferrum, sic ego attraho Deo dura corda. (…)"

Relevaciones liber VI, 111

Quod obediencia prefertur castitati et introducit ad gloriam.

"Quid times? Eciam si decies comederes in die propter obedienciam, non tibi imputabitur in peccatum. Nam virginitas meretur coronam, viduitas appropinquat Deo sed obediencia omnes introducit ad gloriam."

Revelaciones liber VI, 120

Caritas comparatur arbori, de qua omnes virtutes procedunt, inter quas obediencia primatum tenet.

Christus, filius Dei, loquitur: "Sicut arbor habet multos ramos, hii autem, qui sublimiores sunt, plus recipiunt de ardore et vento, sic est eciam de virtutibus. Caritas quippe est quasi arbor, de qua omnes virtutes procedunt, inter quas primatum tenet obediencia. Pro qua ego ipse Deus subire crucem et mortem non dubitaui. Ideo obediencia est michi placita sicut fructus suauissimus, quia sicut pax pacatissima, sic et homo ille est michi amicissimus, qui se ex humilitate aliis subicit et velle suum totum ponit ad manus aliorum. (…)"

Revelations

Excerpts

Translated by Monica Wenusch

Relevations, book VII, chapter 21

When I was at the manger of the Lord in Bethlehem, I saw the most beautiful pregnant Virgin in good health, wearing a white shirt and a plain tunic through which I clearly discerned her virginal flesh. Her womb was firm and widely swollen, since she was ready to give birth. With her was a certain most honorable old man, and with them were both an ox and a mule. (…) He brought a lit candle to the Virgin, fixed it on the wall and went outside so that he would not be present in person. (…) And when all had been prepared, the Virgin knelt down with great reverence in order to pray, and she turned her back toward the manger with her face, in fact, lifted to heaven, toward the east. Thus, with raised hands and intent eyes toward heaven she stood as if elevated in an ecstasy of contemplation, inebriated in divine sweetness. And as she so was standing thus in prayers, I saw what was lying in her womb move and at once, in a moment and in the glimpse of the eye, she gave birth to a son from whom such an ineffable light and splendor went out that the sun could not be compared to it. It was not the candle that the old man had placed there, that reflected light, since this divine splendor totally repealed the material splendor of the candle. And then, the way of giving birth was so sudden and momentary that I could not notice or discern, how or in which part of the body she was giving birth. But, at once, I saw this glorious Child lying on the earth, naked and beautiful. His flesh was most clean without any dirt and uncleanness. I also saw the afterbirth lying next to Him, fallen down and very neat. I also heard the gentleness and great sweetness of the wonderful chant of the angels. And at once, the Virgin's womb that before the birth had been most swollen retracted and her body then appeared wonderfully beautiful and delicate. When the Virgin felt that she now had given birth, she at once, with bowed head and joined hands, adored the boy with great dignity and reverence and said to Him, "Be welcome, my God, my Lord and my Son!" And then the boy, crying and, as it were, trembling from the cold and the hardness of the floor where He lay, rolled a little and extended His limbs, seeking to find refreshment and the Mother's favor. Then the Mother took Him in her hands and held Him tight to her breast, and with her cheek and breast she warmed Him with great joy and tender motherly compassion. Then, sitting on the earth, she put her Son in her lap and with her fingers she took His umbilical cord which at once was cut off so that no kind of liquid or blood was flowing. At once, she began to wrap Him diligently, first in small linen clothes and then in woollen ones, wrapping the little body, His legs and arms, with a ribbon that was sewn into four parts of the outer woollen cloth. Later, in fact, she wrapped and tied on the boy's head those two pieces of linen clothes which she had ready for that purpose. As these things were accomplished, the old man entered and throwing himself on the floor, he adored the child, kneeling, and crying for joy. The Virgin had not changed in color or infirmity at the birth, neither was she failing anything in bodily strength as it usually happens with other women giving birth, with the exception that her swollen womb retracted to the prior state in which it had been before she conceived the boy. Then she arose, holding the boy in her arms, and both together, that is she herself and Joseph put Him into the manger and on their knees they adored Him with delight and immense joy.

Relevations, book VII, chapter 15

While I was at Mount Calvary, most mournfully wailing, I saw that my Lord, naked and tortured, had been led by the Jews to the crucifixion. He was strictly guarded by them. Then I also saw that a hole had been made in the mount and that the crucifiers stood in a circle, ready to fulfil the cruelty. But the Lord turned to me and said to me, "Be attentive, for in this hole in the rock the foot of the cross was fixed at the time of the passion." And immediately I saw how the cross was raised there by the Jews, fastened firmly in the hole in the rock of the mount, it was fixed with wood, most firmly fixed with a hammer all around, so that the cross might stand solidly and would not fall. After the cross had been fastened so solidly there, at once, wooden planks were placed around the trunk of the cross in order to form steps to the place where His feet should be crucified, to allow the crucifiers but also Himself to ascend the cross by those plank steps so that they, in this more convenient way, could stand in order to crucify Him. After this, they ascended on these steps, leading Him with greatest derision and reprimanding. He ascended gladly, like a lamb led to be sacrified. As He already was standing on these planks, He – not forced to it but of His free will – extended His arm, opened His right hand and placed it on the cross. His wild torturers crucified the hand horribly and pierced it with a nail in that part where the bone was more solid. And then, they drew His left hand vehemently with a rope and fixed it to the cross in a similar way. Then, as the extended body was fixed on the cross beyond measures, they placed one of his shins over the other and then joined them on the cross by fixing them with two nails. They extended those glorious limbs on the cross so vehemently that nearly all His veins and sinews were bursting. After having done that, they put back the crown of thorns, which they had taken off His head when He was crucified, placing it on His most holy head. The crown pricked His head so severely that His eyes were filled with flowing blood, also His ears were obstructed and it was as if His face and beard were covered and dipped in this rose-red blood. And at once, those crucifiers and soldiers rapidly removed all the planks which were fixed to the cross, and then the cross stood alone and grandly, and my Lord was crucified upon it. And then I, full of sorrow, saw their cruelty, I saw His most mournful Mother lying on the earth as if trembling and half-dead. John and those others, her sisters, consoled her, who then did not stand far away from the cross on its right side. But then the new sorrow of the compassion of this most holy Mother transfixed me, so that I felt as if the sharp sword of unbearable bitterness went through my heart. Then, finally, his sorrowful Mother arose, as if her body was exhausted, she looked back at her Son, and like that, she stood supported by her sisters, totally paralyzed with suspense and like dead yet alive, transfixed by the sword of sorrow. When the Son saw her and the other wailing friends, He commended her with moving voice to John, and one could clearly see in His gesture and voice that His own heart was penetrated with the sharpest arrow of immense sorrow out of compassion for His Mother. But then His kind and beautiful eyes appeared half-dead, His mouth was open and full of blood, and His face pale and sunken and totally livid and immersed in blood, also all of His body was as if blue and pale and very weak from the continuous flow of blood. Also his skin and the virginal flesh of His most holy body were so delicate and tender that, after He was hit with a moderate blow, a livid mark appeared on the surface. But from time to time He tried to stretch on the cross due to the tremendous bitterness of the intense and most acute pain that He felt. And at times the pain ascended from his limbs and perforated veins to his heart and tortured Him cruelly in an intense martyrdom. Thus, His death was prolonged and delayed with severe torment and immense bitterness. Then, frightened by the tremendous distress of pain and already near to death, He in a high and tearful voice cried to the Father, "O Father, why have you forsaken me?" Then, He had pale lips and a bloody tongue, His abdomen was sunken and adhered to His back as if He had no viscera within. Also a second time He exclaimed again in the greatest pain and anxiety, "O Father, in Your hands I commend My spirit." And then His head, raising itself a little, immediately bowed. And thus He sent forth His spirit. His Mother, seeing that, trembled at that immense bitterness, she would have fallen onto the earth if she had not been supported by the other women. Then, in that hour, His hands moved a little from the place of the nail holes due to the exceeding weight of the body, thus His body was as if supported by the nails with which his feet were crucified. His fingers, though, and His hands and arms were already more extended than before, while His shoulder blades and the back were as if tightened to the cross. Then, at last, the Jews who stood around cried out in derision against His Mother, saying many things. "Mary, now your Son is dead", others, in fact, said other mocking words. Thus, while they stood around in crowds, one man came running with the greatest fury, and infixed a lance in His right side, so violently and vehemently that it was as if the lance would pass through the other side of the body. As the lance was removed from the body, at once a flow of blood, as it were, with force streamed out of the wound in abundance, in fact, the iron blade of the lance and some part of the shaft came out of the body red and stained with blood. The Mother, seeing this, trembled so immensely with bitter sighing that it clearly could be seen in her face and gesture that her soul then was being pierced by the sharp sword of sorrow. When all this was accomplished, they were receding in large crowds, and certain of His friends took down the Lord. Now, the Mother received Him into her most holy arms and, sitting, she laid Him on her knee, Him who was torn all over, wounded and livid. She herself, John and the other weeping women washed Him in tears. Then, with her linen cloth, the most mournful Mother wiped all of His body and the wounds and closed His eyes, kissing them. And thus, they led Him away with wailing and the greatest sorrow and placed Him into his sepulchre.

Relevations, book IX/Extravagantes, chapter 20

God's Son speaks, "(…) there are three states I think highest of, namely virginity, widowhood and marriage [with God]. Those three standings must be preferred and honored above all, since they are signs of high purity and dignity and My Mother integrates those three states within herself. She had been the purest virgin at the time of My birth and after My birth, she had been a true mother and virgin, she had been a widow after My ascension, since my physical presence was stolen from her. Therefore, when an abbess shall be elected, it shall be one that emerges from one of these three states (…)."

Relevations, book IX/Extravagantes, chapter 21

Christ tells that an abbess has to be a pure and recognized virgin and an example in virtues, and that a humble and recognized widow can be chosen as abbess, when there is no such virgin.

Jesus Christ speaks, "It is a good combination and a proper confederation that a virgin is to be head of the virgins. For of all things, purity of the flesh and mind has to be preferred, from which and through which I, God, sought to be made flesh. But since My Mother was a virgin and a mother at the same time, however mother not due to her being sexually recognized, but because she was breathed upon by My and My Father's spirit, she has born Me, I, who am true God and true man, therefore is the new Order [of Saint Saviour] dedicated to My Mother, and it is necessary and laudable that whoever is chosen to be head of the virgins is a pure, in her habits recognized virgin and an example in virtues. But when such a virgin should not be found in the community who is able to fulfil My virgin Mother's commitment, I do not disapprove, if instead of a distinguished virgin a humble widow of recognized conduct takes over the task of humility. When then it pleases God to elevate the humble and to elevate widowhood out of necessity, it would not take anything away from the virgins' laudable habit, since God considers it worthy to elevate all the humble. What has been more humble than My Mother? But what can be found, that would not deserve the total humility? For humility's sake, I, God and Son of God, became the virgin's true son, and without humility, there is no way to heaven."

Revelations, book IV, chapter 86

The Mother of God tells that she is like a flower from which sweetness is drawn by the bees (...).

The Mother speaks, "I am the queen and Mother of mercy. My Son, the creator of all things, is affected by so many sweet feelings to me, that He of everything that is created has given me the spiritual intelligence. Therefore I am very much similar to a flower, out of which the bees particularly draw sweetness, how much there may be collected from it, nevertheless there will be left enough of this sweetness. Like this, it is possible for me to obtain mercy for everyone and always to have enough of it. But also my chosen ones are similar to the bees, because with full devotion they are connected to my honor, since they have two feet like the bees, namely the wish to continuously increase my glory (...); they also have two wings, namely that they consider themselves unworthy to praise me, on the other hand they are obedient to me in everything concerning my honor. They also have a sting and die, when they lose it; like this, God's friends have sorrows in the world, which are not taken from them until the end of their days in order to put their virtues to the test, but I who disposes over consolation am going to comfort them."

Relevations, book III, chapter 32

The Mother speaks to the bride [Birgitta], "A certain man who looked for stones found a magnet. He lifted it with his own hand and placed it safe in his vault. With this magnet, he led his ship in the safe harbor. Like that, my Son, as He looked for many holy stones, has chosen just me as His Mother, so through me mankind should be led to the heavenly harbor. So like the magnet attracts the iron to itself, I attract the hard hearts to God. (…)"

Relevations, book VI, chapter 111

Why obedience is anticipated by chastity and leads to glory.

[Christ speaks,] "What do you fear? Even if you would eat ten times a day, but would do that in obedience, it would not be credited as a sin. Thus virginity deserves the crown, widowhood brings you closer to God, but obedience leads everybody into glory."

Revelations, book VI, chapter 120

Love is compared to a tree from which the virtues procede, of which obedience takes the first place.

Christ, God's Son, speaks, "Like a tree has many branches, yet those being higher receive more sun and air, so it is with the virtues. Because love is like a tree from which all virtues procede, of which obedience takes the first place, the obedience for which I, God, did not hesitate to bear the cross and death. Therefore, obedience pleases me like the sweetest fruit, because that is the most peaceful peace, thus I think highest of that man who out of humility subordinates himself to others and who puts all his wanting in other's hands. (…)"

Primary Works

Revelaciones (http://www.umilta.net/bk.html)
Book I, Magister Mathias. Prologue; Birgitta of Sweden. Revelaciones I.
Book II, Revelaciones II (1492).
Book III, Revelaciones III: The Book for Priests 1349-1373 (1492).
Book IV, Revelaciones IV: Miscellany.
Book V, Birgitta of Sweden and Magister Mathias. The Book of Questions.
Book VI, Revelaciones VI: Miscellany (1492).
Book VII, Revelaciones VII: The Book of Pilgrimage 1372-1373.
Book VIII, Revelaciones VIII: The Book of Politics (1492).
Book IX, Revelaciones IX: Extravagantes.
Book X, Revelaciones X: The Book of the Rule.
Book XI: Revelaciones XI: The Book of the Angel.
Book XII: Revelaciones XII: Four Prayers.
Book XIII, Alfonso of Jaén. Epistola solitarii, Revelaciones XIII: Preface to Book VIII.

Selected Bibliography

Heliga Birgitta – budskapet och förebilden: Föredrag vid jubileumssymposiet i Vadstena 3-7 oktober 1991. Alf Härdelin and Mereth Lindgren, eds. Stockholm: Kungl. Vitterhets Historie och Antikvitets Akademien, 1993.

Holböck, Ferdinand. *Gottes Nordlicht: Die hl. Birgitta von Schweden und ihre Offenbarungen.* Stein am Rhein: Christiana-Verlag, 1988.

Jørgensen, Johannes. *Den hellige Birgitta af Vadstena,* 1-2. Copenhagen: Gyldendal, 1941-43; Eng. edition *Saint Bridget of Sweden* 1-2. Ingeborg Lund, tr. London: Longmans, Green & Co., 1954.

Morris, Bridget. *St Birgitta of Sweden.* (*Studies in Medieval Mysticism* 1.) Woodbridge: Boydell Press, 1999.

Norén, Kjerstin. "'Sjælen er af langt bedre natur end kroppen': Om Birgitta af Vadstena." *Nordisk Kvindelitteraturhistorie* 1. Elisabeth Møller-Jensen, ed. Copenhagen: Rosinante/Munksgaard, 1993.

Sjöberg, Nina. *Hustru och man i Birgittas uppenbarelser.* Uppsala: Uppsala Universitet, 2003.

The Self-Fashioning of
Hedvig Charlotta Nordenflycht

PETRA BROOMANS (UNIVERSITY OF GRONINGEN)

It is difficult to know how to begin to write about Hedvig Charlotta Nordenflycht (1718-1763), an intelligent woman who had to establish a writer's
identity in a time when writing was not a common occupation for women.
She was, anyway, the first Swedish woman to earn a living through writing.
Known as the Sappho of the North, alias the Shepherdess of the North, alias
the Sorrowing Turtle-Dove, alias Uranie, she created several writing nom
de plumes to meet the expectations in her time and how a woman should be
raised and of what kind of activities a woman should be allowed to undertake as an adult. During the whole of her writing career she was in dialogue
with other, mostly male, writers, rulers and benefactors to explain and to
defend her own writing and ask for support in order to live and to write.
Nordenflycht seems to have been aware of the importance of shaping her
personal and literary image. Posthumously and in general, the image of
Hedvig Charlotta Nordenflycht in literary history has become that of the
Sorrowing Turtle-Dove or the Nordic Sappho, due mostly to her unfortunate love life and the love poems she wrote. Shortly after her death there
were controversies about how she should be remembered, and even today,
in Swedish literary history, the debate of how we should classify Nordenflycht continues. How Nordenflycht wanted herself to be seen and the image she preferred to last forever are questions before us here.

How did Nordenflycht, who regarded it as one of her tasks to write for
the nation, manage her self-fashioning as a woman and as an author?

The term self-fashioning was coined by the new historicist, Stephen
Greenblatt. In his study, *Renaissance Self-Fashioning. From More to
Shakespeare*, he discusses the way artists and writers designed "the forming
of a self".[1] According to Greenblatt, self-fashioning happens almost always
in the language itself. When it comes to literature, the self-fashioning can

---

[1]   Greenblatt, 2.

be acted out by the protagonist or by the writer in how he/she manifests him/herself.

Greenblatt does not seem to differentiate between the real author's life and the fictional protagonist's life. In the act of self-fashioning, there always occurs submission to "an absolute power or authority situated at least partially outside the self".[2] He mentions several possible authorities; God and institutions like church or court. An institution such as the benefactor can be added to this list. Greenblatt connects "authority" with the "threatening other" or the Alien. The "alien" can be the figure in the painting, or with respect to literature, the "I" in the literary text, which becomes an alien twin to the artist/writer, frozen in a constructed world.

For women writers like the British Margaret Lucas Cavendish (1623-1673), literary self-fashioning in the 17th century was important, since the ways in which these authors constructed themselves, and women as a whole, were crucial to the reception of these works and their authors by the public.[3] The construction of the self often served a carefully disguised purpose which lay outside the narrative of the work and in the socio-political climate of the author. According to the study, *Marketing the Author. Authorial Personae, Narrative Selves and Self-Fashioning, 1880-1930*, the authors in this period wanted to control "their public image by creating a self that would help them to do just that".[4] The social, economic and cultural changes in society were the reason for their self-invention. They can be seen as figures in transition from one era to another. In the life and works of Nordenflycht, these mechanisms can be traced as well. Nordenflycht tried continuously to invent a new self in a transitional period in Swedish history, the so called *Frihetstiden* (the Age of Freedom from 1719-1772), to improve her position in the literary and social circles, and also in order to survive financially. She was confronted by "positive" as well as "negative" authorities. It is obvious that Nordenflycht created several images to adapt herself to the expectations, not only of authorities, but also to her own goals and in what she believed in: as love poet (Sappho), as a scholarly poet (Aspasia or Uranie) and as a national/political poet (Svea).

Even today one instrument to construct a self, an identity, is to write an autobiography. Nordenflycht wrote one 1745, when she was 26. In it she tells about her development as a writer. This endorses Greenblatt's observation that the artist or writer constructs a self by means of language (a performative act) and by representing the self before an audience (theatrical).

Hedvig Charlotte Nordenflycht was born in Stockholm on 28 November, 1718, as the youngest of eight children. In her autobiography, written on request of senior government official, A.A. von Stiernman (1695-1765),

---

[2] Greenblatt, 9.
[3] Garnett, no pages.
[4] Demoor, 6.

who wanted to write a book on Swedish women scholars, Nordenflycht states that as a child she showed a strong interest in reading and that she craved knowledge, more than her parents approved of. She could read before she was five years of age and her parents allowed her to learn Latin and German together with her brother. Her brother, though, was often in Uppsala so Hedvig Charlotta could not study on a regularly base. Her parents developed the opinion that she should not study so much; she had to train herself in normal women domestic work.[5] So she read secretly, hiding her books under her apron. To describe oneself as a young girl with an eagerness to read in a reluctant environment seems to have been a way of self-fashioning for intellectual women of the time. The Norwegian translator, Birgitte Lange, who in 1747 translated Don Antonio de Solis' book on the conquest of Mexico, *Historie om Conqvêten af Mexico* from 1684, also described herself as a young girl who wanted to read but was trapped in a conflict between her longing for learning and the traditional occupations for women.[6]

In this autobiography, Nordenflycht depicts the child Hedvig Charlotta as a thinking child with an intellectual hunger and a child who could not find answers to philosophical questions, "Everything was a mystery to me. A desire, wanting to know the connection of everything, gave me a restless that was unusual."[7]

What did Nordenflycht read? She mentions François Fénelon's *Les aventures de Télémaque* (1699), Swedish poets, German itineraries and abstracts from history books among others. After her death all her books were sold and in the auction catalogue we can see which books she had and (probably) had read.[8] In the sonnet "To my books" (Til mina böcker) she depicts her books as reliable, silent and calm friends: she feels safe with them. In books it is possible to wander through "the theatre of Nature" and one can find "One's self, and all that waits for Mankind's study's there".

Nordenflycht writes that, as a child, she almost could have become a "Sceptica" if a tutor, Johan Tideman, had not rescued her and guided her in her search for wisdom and insight. She got from him the belief in "dygd och vishet" (virtue and wisdom).[9] The story of her childhood Nordenflycht presents a "romantic" mode of emplotment,[10] a plot that can be observed in many accounts in literary history. In Nordenflycht's account the heroine is obstructed in her aim of gaining knowledge by her environment, but succeeds in the long term. It is the story of a girl unwillingly learning women's

---

[5] Kruse, 21.
[6] Steinfeld, 29.
[7] *Skrifter* 5.
[8] Kruse, 383-394.
[9] Borelius, 13.
[10] See e.g. White.

domestic duties, actually not allowed to read philosophical books and rescued by a "prince" who taught her and who was meant to become her husband, the wish of her father when he died in 1734. Johan Tideman was not
a handsome young man, but Nordenflycht felt genuine friendship and took
a liking to him. However, Tideman became ill and a year later he died in
1737 and was mourned by Nordenflycht who was only 18 years old.
Though Nordenflycht had written poems before, she now wrote poems with
an intense sorrow. Tideman had been her "mentor",[11] her helper in her aim
to learn and to be able to use her intellectual abilities and was now dependent on herself.

Nordenflycht continued to write occasional poetry, but very soon, after a
year, she met Jacob Fabricius (1703-1741) and fell in love with him. Nordenflycht wanted to learn French and through her nephew and friend, Carl
Klingenberg (1708-1757), the 35 year old minister Fabricius became her
teacher. This love and the loss of it would, according to Kruse, who in 1895
wrote the first PhD-thesis about Nordenflycht, not only make her a poet,
but also for the rest of her life rob her health and her mental balance. As
Kruse writes, an "unsatisfied passion" would, at last, "destroy the powerless
barriers" of Nordenflycht's mind and "bring the poetess to despair and an
early death".[12]

Why had the love of Nordenflycht for Fabricius such an impact? First of
all the couple had to overcome several difficulties in order to marry. Fabricius had to have enough income to maintain a household and when Fabricius was appointed as a minister in Karlskrona, the two could marry in
May, 1741. They settled in Karlskrona. But after only seven months, Fabricius fell seriously ill and passed away in the same year. This was a tremendous shock for the young Nordenflycht, who was only 23 years old when
she lost her husband. She moved back to Stockholm. Shortly after she settled in a little cottage in the countryside on Lidingö, just outside Stockholm.
There, isolated, she wrote about her grief caused by the death of her beloved husband. As Borelius wrote, at that time women were not individuals
but family members. Nordenflycht, however, had a rich and strong personality and became the most pronounced subjective interpreter in Swedish
literature in those days. Even Borelius, one of the first women scholars who
wrote about Nordenflycht, regards her deep sorrow as a great impetus to her
writing. Writing poetry became the author's expression and life's goal.[13]
The volume from 1743 containing nine poems on Fabricius bore the title
Den Sörgande Turtur-Dufvan (The Sorrowing Turtle-Dove).

---

[11] Hedvig Charlotta Nordenflycht, "Brev till kansli-rådet och ridd. Hr. A.A. von
Stiernman". *Skrifter* 9.
[12] Kruse, 26.
[13] Borelius, 76.

In the meantime, the young widow had to find out how to obtain income and she did that by continuing to write occasional poetry. She also continued to plead, as she did as a child and young girl, for her right to know, to learn and to write. Nordenflycht searched and found other mentors, male and female, and communicated with them. That Nordenflycht was not only a love poet, but also a scholarly and political poet is showed by the encounters she had with antagonists and "negative" authorities like Olof von Dalin (1708-1763), the leading figure of Swedish enlightenment, and Jean-Jacques Rousseau. Many of these encounters concerned Nordenflycht's status as a poet and the question whether or not a woman was capable of writing great poetry.

An important example for Nordenflycht in her struggle for the right to use her brains as a woman was the Dano-Norwegian Ludvig Holberg (1684-1754), whom one could regard as a "positive" authority. She got inspired by his poem "*Zille Hans Dotters Gynaicologia eller Forsvars Skrift for Qvinde-Kiønnet*" (The Gynaeceum of Zille Hans Daughter's Defense of Womankind) from 1722, in which Holberg wrote about women's right to use their brains. In her autobiography, Nordenflycht stated that she corresponded with Holberg, but literary historians assume that it was rather a one-way correspondence as there are no letters left. However, by writing to Holberg she formulated herself in matters of women of letters and philosophical questions. Nordenflycht became also known in Denmark when the first volume of *Qvinligt Tankespel* (Feminine Play of Thoughts) from 1744 was translated into Danish in 1746 with the title *Qvindeligt Tanke-Spill af en Hyrdinde i Norden* (Feminine Play of Thoughts by a Shepherdess from the North).

Holberg's essay collection *Moralske Tanker* (1744; Moral Thoughts) and works of many other poets of the Enlightenment, such as Alexander Pope, can be found in Nordenflycht's library. In her poems, she uses her knowledge of the ideas of these European authors whom she regarded as inspiring. About the nature of human being, she reflected in the short, somehow sarcastic poem, "Ängslig Kunskap, swåra Rön" (Anxious Knowledge, hard Results) in which she referred to writers and scholars as Holberg, Alexander Pope and Despréaux (i.e. Nicolas Boileau), who "laugh at a creature they call human". Man can achieve much, but he is not able to know himself. One can reflect on nature and creatures, but human nature is "Anxious Knowledge, hard Results".

Borelius states that Nordenflycht's manifestation to the public in 1743-1744, when she started to use her full name, raised a more clear awareness of herself being an author: "The consciousness to be a woman and a writer goes hand in hand by Hedvig Charlotta Nordenflycht".[14] The "poetic calen-

---

[14]   Borelius, 99.

dar" (Stålmarck) *Qwinligit Tankespel* (1744-50; Feminine Play of Thoughts) was dedicated exclusively to women: Margareta Beata Cronstedt (1689-1772) and Ulrica Tessin (1711-1768). In *Feminine Play of Thoughts*, Nordenflycht published her first feminist poem in 1744: "Fruentimbers Plikt at upöfwa deras Wett" (Women's Duty to Exercise their Brains). Nordenflycht was of the opinion that women not only had the right but also the obligation to use their intellect.

"Om skaldekonstens nytta i ett väl inrättat land" (Thoughts upon the Usefulness of Poetry in a well-appointed Land) was the introductory poem of the 1744 volume. In this Nordenflycht expresses her consciousness as a woman and as an author. This is reflected in this poem's statements about the meaning of being Swedish and the meaning of poetry for the nation. Nordenflycht dedicated "Thoughts upon the Usefulness of Poetry" to Carl Gustaf Tessin (1695-1770), the husband of Ulrica Tessin, who had helped Nordenflycht financially. He also can be regarded as a "positive" authority. Tessin was the leading man of "the Hats", a political faction during the Age of Freedom, their rivals were "the Caps". It is likely that Nordenflycht sympathized with the Hats, partly due to her connections with Tessin. In her poem, Nordenflycht argues that poetry in Sweden has to regain the high status it once had and that poetry and history had to be regarded as twin genres:

> What would our world now know of all the many heroes,
> Of all their acts in times long gone, no Poet there?
> For History and Poetry are comrades with us.

But history only says how everything hangs together, whereas poetry shows "how the human will brings it about". It is a poet's duty to tell about the brave deeds of one's ancestors, to be a great patriot like the person to whom the poem is dedicated, Tessin, and to honor the country "by carving worthy Names in undecaying Cedar."

***

Nordenflycht propagandized poetry for the nation and was aware of what patriotism could mean for her acceptance as a writer. She could and should honor her nation. It was her Swedishness and her sense of public responsibility that made her think so.[15] In Sweden, poetry is not regarded as useful, writes Nordenflycht in her introduction to *Feminine Play of Thoughts*, but to be able to compete with other nations, it should be. Nordenflycht refers to John Milton and Pope in England and Boileau in France and to Torquato Tasso in Italy. They got the same appreciation as, for example, scientists such as Isaac Newton and Galileo Galilei. Nordenflycht suggests that if the Swedish men do not want to write poetry, then they should leave it to the

---

[15]   Borelius, 100.

women so that Sweden could compete with other nations which had out-standing women writers. Nordenflycht refers here to two French women writers, Anne Dacier and Madeleine de Scudéry, and to the Dutch Anna Maria van Schurman.[16] Nordenflycht had texts by all three women in her home. It is possible that these women writers served as so-called role models for Nordenflycht. Borelius speaks of Nordenflycht's sisterhood and of what kind of women Nordenflycht was searching for. According to Borelius she preferred intellectual friendship and found this, amongst others, in her contact with the above-mentioned Norwegian writer and translator Birgitte Lange, who had translated a Spanish history on the conquest of Mexico. Lange was, like Nordenflycht, an intellectual who had a writer's desk as a working place. The fourth and last volume of *Feminine Play of Thoughts* for the years 1748-1750 contains a poem dedicated to Birgitta Lange.

In the 1750s, Nordenflycht was very successful. She got a state pension in 1752, actually quite unusual for a woman writer, and she became the leading figure in the literary society "Tankebyggarorden" (The Order of the Builders of Ideas). On the other hand, she was confronted with catastrophes, such as a great fire in Stockholm in 1751 which destroyed her house and her manuscripts. In 1757, her friend Carl Klingenberg, who had become very important for her and who was also her lover, died. In the poem "Klagan" (The Complaint), she grieves about the death of "My help, my comfort in all need".

Furthermore, Nordenflycht still had her conflicts with Olof von Dalin. Scholars like Sven G. Hansson, who wrote about Nordenflycht's relationship to Dalin,[17] and Torkel Stålmarck have observed that Nordenflycht had become more radical and uncompromising at that time than when writing to Holberg in the 1740s.[18] She also got involved in an international debate about women writers. Rousseau, whom she first regarded as a kindred spirit, had disappointed her with his statements in a comment on an article by Jean le Rond d'Alembert in the French *Encyclopédie* about the plans to open a theatre in Geneva. Rousseau writes that women have destroyed the theatre and that they do not understand art at all, women lack talent and a deep emotional life. This was an attack on the heart and mind of Nordenflycht and in 1759 she wrote "The Woman's Defence". This poem came as an introduction to the second part of *Witterhets arbeten* (Literary Works) from 1762, but it had already been circulated earlier. The version of 1762 was an introduction to a large catalogue of famous women, which had to show that women could compete with men in every area: in war and peace,

---

[16] Borelius, 101.
[17] See bibliography.
[18] Stålmarck, 161.

in the public and scholarly sphere and in religion. The first Nordenflycht mentions is Sappho.

Witterhets arbeten (1759-62) was the reedited and extended version of *Våra Försök* 1-3 (Our Experiments), published in 1753-56 by the "Tanke-byggarorden". At the time of her polemic against Rousseau, Nordenflycht was already the leading member and only female member of "Tankebygga-rorden". This club was founded in 1753 as a counterpart of the "Vitterhets-akademien" (The Royal Academy of Letters, History and Antiquities), established in the same year by queen Lovisa Ulrika (1720-1782) and in which Nordenflycht's rival Olof von Dalin was the leading man. Actually, Nordenflycht was disappointed that she was not allowed to be a member of the queen's academy. Furthermore, it could have been Dalin who had seen to it that Nordenflycht's poem which she had sent to the academy for a contest disappeared. Nordenflycht got her "own" academy anyway. The two other leading members of "Tankebyggarorden" were Gustaf Philip Creutz (1731-1785) and Gustaf Fredrik Gyllenborg (1731-1808). They admired Nordenflycht and supported her, but she also offered them help and guidance. Nordenflycht was the most successful of the members of the society and gathered many young male authors in her salon. One of the young, new members, was Johan Fischerström (1735-1796). Fischerström was very impressed by the Swedish Uranie (see above). In his short biogra-phy of Nordenflycht, he recalls, twenty years later, the first time he met her, in 1761, and expresses his gratitude that he could participate in this society. But, alas, those happy moments would never come back, as he noted.[19] Fischerström admired Nordenflycht, but she loved him deeply. Her poem "Öfver en hyacinth. Til - - -" (On a Hyacinth. To - - -) is regarded as one of her finest poems and as a reflection on her love for Fischerström and his rejection of it.

> No clear dislike toward it I bear.
> I see in your heart, too, that cooling:
> It has to be whate'er is there.

Scholars such as Stålmarck observe that these kinds of poems about love and the metamorphoses of love are quite common in Nordenflycht's work and that she could have written these poems also before she met Fischer-ström.[20] However, the deep feelings Nordenflycht had for the much younger Fischerström were the starting point for some of the most popular love poems in Swedish literature. The feelings of admiration that Fischer-ström had for Nordenflycht were genuine, but after he noticed that her feelings were more than friendship he got cautious, and it became clear to

---

[19] Stålmarck, 185.
[20] Stålmarck, 188.

Nordenflycht that she had to abandon her pursuit. In "On a Hyacinth. To
- - -", Nordenflycht describes her resignation.

It is suggested by Johan Hinric Lidén (1741-1793) that Nordenflycht's
unhappy love for Fischerström caused her early death, but this is not certain.[21] After some other misfortunes, she got seriously ill. According to
Stålmarck, there is nothing that indicates that Nordenflycht got ill because
of the fact that she tried to commit suicide by drowning herself in a lake.
Nordenflycht probably died of cancer.[22] Fischerström writes in his biography that he still gets tears in his eyes when thinking of Nordenflycht and
her last days. He saw to it that her selected works got published posthumously in 1774.[23]

**

When Nordenflycht passed away, she was a famous and beloved writer. In
the journal *Svenska Mercurius* (The Swedish Mercury), Carl Cristoffer
Gjörwell (1731-1811), who was a central figure in Stockholm's intellectual
life, remarked that she got herself an immortal name by her genius and
outstanding literary works. In the next edition of the journal, Nordenflycht's autobiography was published. It was almost not published, and here
we see the first controversy and the making of a writer-image. Stiernman,
who never finished his book on Swedish women scholars, had sent the
autobiography to Gjörwell, but when Gjörwell discussed the matter with
Creutz and other friends of Nordenflycht, he decided not to publish the
document. Creutz and the other friends wanted to honour their friend with a
panegyric in another style.[24] Nordenflycht had written her autobiography at
a time when she was very religious and apparently this side of her personality in a certain period of her life did not fit their image of her. Stiernman,
however, got outrageous and forced Gjörwell to publish it, or threatened to
do it himself. Creutz and Gyllenborg wrote their panegyric as well and
Gjörwell published in another number of *Svenska Mercurius*. Thus, at the
moment of her death, there already existed controversies around the image
of Nordenflycht.

Kruse devotes the last chapter of his study from 1895 to the importance
of Nordenflycht in literary history, the contemporary and posthumous es-
teem, and translations into Danish and German. He notes that Nordenflycht's contemporaries were not able to see the real Nordenflycht.[25] According to Kruse, Nordenflycht's nature is like Rousseau's: "The centre of
her being is emotion. This powerful and deep emotion is her life's joy and

---

[21] Stålmarck, 197.
[22] Stålmarck, 197.
[23] Kruse, 323.
[24] Kruse, 311.
[25] Kruse, 319.

sorrow."[26] He describes Nordenflycht as a lonely heroine who was not able to endure the fact that Fischerström did not love her: "The fire in her soul was extinguished; the strings of the instrument broken. She had to die."[27] This romantic picture of Nordenflycht can be seen against the backdrop of the period of new romanticism in Sweden at the end of the 19th century. Regarding her importance for Swedish literary history, Kruse is quite clear: he regards Nordenflycht as the most gifted author of her time and that her influence was greater than Dalin's. Nordenflycht is a transitional figure, she connects the old and the new and can be regarded as the link between Lasse Lucidor (1638-1674), Jakob Frese (1691-1729) and the early romantic writer Bengt Lidner (1757-1793).[28]

In Swedish literary history, there is, even today, an ongoing debate about the place of Nordenflycht. Borelius observed it already in her study from 1921. According to Borelius, literary historians did create a biased image of Nordenflycht and even P.D.A. Atterbom (1790-1855) was not free from disfigurement. In *Nordisk kvinnolitteraturhistoria*, Birgitta Holm gives a survey of the various Nordenflycht images in Swedish literary history. Holm remarks that there is apparently something provocative in Nordenflycht's self-esteem that so many critics, both male and female, wanted to diminish the importance of her authorship or made her into a lovesick fool. But, friend or enemy, nobody denies that there are moments of genuine poetry to be found in her work.[29] Many literary historians are, like Kruse, of the opinion that Nordenflycht's influence on Swedish literature was more substantial than Dalin's. Göran Hägg wrote in his literary history from 1996 that the male authors in Nordenflycht's time, including Dalin, were not more original than she was.[30] In a comment on J.H. Scheffel's portrait of Nordenflycht, Hägg writes that scholarly rationality and poetic emotion still went hand in hand at that time, but that they are no longer male domains. The portrait reflects, according to Hägg, an admiration for the female genius' conquest of both domains.[31] Maybe this was an image Nordenflycht wanted to last?

***

Literary historians are eager for clear outlines and simple classifications. Some authors do not fit into a box. Hedvig Charlotta Nordenflycht is an example of this phenomenon. Nordenflycht was an all-round author. The "I" in Nordenflycht's texts is not a frozen "I", but fluent and transparent, hard to fix. Regarding women writers Greenblatt's definition of self-

---

[26] Kruse, 313-314.
[27] Kruse, 316.
[28] Kruse, 318.
[29] Holm, 393.
[30] Hägg, 144.
[31] Hägg, 143.

fashioning is complicated. As Demoor writes: "Women authors seem to have experienced a need to construct different selves".[32] That Nordenflycht created different writer images has also to be seen against the backdrop of the political situation in Sweden, the Age of Freedom. On the other hand, Nordenflycht is remembered as the Sappho of the North because she made her breakthrough as a love poet and by that means her public self-image and her characterisation in Swedish literary history was created; "once a 'persona' was created, it was all but impossible to change or replace it."[33] And that was Nordenflycht's problem because, despite her ambitions, her playing with different identities, and her fight for the right to be a writer, an intellectual (Aspasia), her self-fashioning was a failure. One of the interesting sides that contemporaries and posterity did not want to see was her aim to fashion herself as a woman writer who was capable of conquering another male domain, by becoming a "Writer of the Nation". The Sappho of the North never became a "Svea" in Swedish literary history.[34]

Utvalda dikter[35]

Skönhet en bräcklig glans

En blomma rinner up ur mul,
Af wäder blåuuu hon omkul,
Ell' wissnar hon och får sit slut,
När Sommartiden lupit ut:
Så är det ock med skönhets prakt,
Hon äger ej fulkomlig mackt:
Hon lider oundwiklig nöd,
Af siukdom, ålder, tid, och död.
En skönhet är allena til,
Som ewigheten gilla wil:
En ren, en klar, en helgad siäl,
Hon wäxer til, och prydes wäl
Af himlaprackt, en skönhets skrud,
Som gör, at hon behagar Gud.

---

[32] Demoor, 10.
[33] Demoor, 15.
[34] I thank my colleague Alan Swanson for the inspiring conversations about Nordenflycht and his translations of the selected poems.
[35] *Samlade skrifter*, published by Hilma Borelius och Theodor Hjelmqvist. *Svenska författare*. Svenska vitterhetssamfundet 11. Stockholm: Albert Bonniers Förlag, 1924-1938.

Den tysta kärleken.
(Werser för musicalisk composition efter begäran)

Jag älskar, döljer lågan:
Jag nöjes af plågan:
Jag lider:
Jag qwider:
Älskar utan hopp:
I twiksam fruktan kämpar:
Med qwafda suckar dämpar
Den smärta,
Mit hjerta
I tysthet fräter op.
O aldraljufsta börda!
O söta kärleks qwal!
At hemligt kunna wörda
Sit höga wal.

Aria.
(Werser för musicalisk composition efter begäran)

Skall jag dölja i mit bröst,
Alla plågor, som sig qwälja?
Får jag ej, bland oro, wälja
Den, at ta i klagan tröst?
Ack! så sluten tyst i Eder,
Ömme tankar! hwad Er qwal;
Men, min ögon, Er jag beder,
Röjen ej en sorgsen själ.

Ängslig Kunskap, swåra Rön

Despreaux, Pope och *Holberg* le
Åt et djur, de Menska kalla,
Som i Wetenskaper alla,
Hinner långt, och ljus kan ge;
Men sig sielf ej mäktar känna.
Ack! det är ej under wärdt:
Roligt är, at tankan spänna
För et mål, som är en kärt:
At betrakta Gräs och Djuren,
Ger ens möda nöjsam lön;
Men den menskliga naturen,
Ängslig Kunskap, swåra Rön.

Tankar om skaldekonstens nytta i et wäl inrättadt land

Mån Himlen gåfwor ger, at man skal dem förspilla,
Mån icke alt är gjordt til wissa ändamål?
Mån icke hwart et ting kan brukas wäl och illa,
Och ingen sats så sann, som icke ändring tål?
Naturens skatter ä förgäfwes ej beskärde,
Och missbruk af en sak betar ej sakens wärde.

Fast Skaldekonsten war i forna tider skattad
För Gudars egit Språk, och Snillegåfwors pragt,
Har nya tider gjort dess styrka så afmattad,
At hon med all sin höjd är fallen i föragt:
Det tyks, hon borde dock sitt rätta wärde winna,
Se'n forna *Barbari't* i Norden syns förswinna.

Men hon har öde, likt de gamla rätta dygder,
Ju mer wår nya werd tyks blifwa klok och slug,
Jo mera saknas det, i wåra Swenska bygder,
Som påfölgd wara bör på uplyst wett och hug:
Wår ärlighet tar af, alt som wår finhet ökas,
De sanna dygder fly, när med *chimérer* spökas.

Men rot til det förtryck, som Skaldekonsten hotar,
Är mäst det felsteg, som *Poëten* sjelf begår:
Med nedrigt ändamål han så sin ära motar,
At sjelfwa konsten til sin höghet lida får:
När Skalden obetänkt sig låga ämnen wäljer,
Och Ärans Lagerblad, som kram, för winsten, säljer.

Alt, hwad af nedrig drift och grofwa syften smakar,
Förlorar wärdet sitt, och tappar snart sin glans.
Den som på *Helicon* hos Song-Gudinren wakar,
Har nog belöning af hwar enda Ärekrans,
Som han, til dygdens låf och prydnad, sammanknyter,
At honom skydd och hägn af dygden aldrig tryter.

Det är en ädel winst, sin hand til nytta läna:
En wärdig Skald är den, som brukar gåfwan rätt:
Hans mål är aldramäst, at Efterwerden tjena
Med det, han prisar dygd på et behagligt sätt:
Han målar hennes Folk i ärans höga tempel:
Der stå de i sin pragt, til annat Folks exempel.

Hwad hade werden nu af många hjälte-dater,
Som fordom skedt, om ej *Poëter* warit til?
Historien, *Poësien,* de äro ju kamrater,
Som bägge til et gagn och syfte tjena wil:
Den ena säger blott, hur saken sammanhänger,
Den andra med sin kraft sig in i wiljan tränger.

Så är då Skaldens plikt, at sjunga Dygdens Ära,
Uphöja gåfwors dyrd, til Skaparns wälbehag,
Berömma dråpligt Folk: åt Hjältar Offer bära,
Ja, sätta stora werk för werden i en dag;
Man kalle denna konst onyttig, öfwerflödig;
Der en *Trajanus* är, blir *Plinius* straxt nödig.

Hur mången ädel dygd är lagd i glömskans dimma,
Som kunna tjena til et Efterwerdens bloss?
Om den war rätt bekant, och fått i ryktet glimma?
Så gagnar ju en Skald til tids och lasters tross.
Han bör berömma Dygd med alraljufsta stämma,
I högsta ordaprål; men aldrig Sanning skämma.

Han bör den frihet ha, at högt få dygder prisa,
Och skildra laster af i deras wärsta färg;
På det han bägges art så lifligt må bewisa,
At lasten nödgas fly; men dygden bli som bärg.
Det witsord bör han sig bland sina Landsmän skaffa,
At ingen honom kan för nedrigt smicker straffa.

Då tjenar han til gagns, och Skaldekonsten blifwer
Båd' nyttig, angenäm oeh nödig för et Land:
Ju mera Folket högt på Dygdens trappa klifwer,
Ju flera syslor får hans Sannings-wähnta hand,
At prisa, muntra up, de wärdas låf utföra,
Hwart enda dråpligt werk på jorden ewigt göra.

Hans sysla är då det, at Ärans Folk afmåla;
Men det är klagan wärdt, han råkar stundom för
Så fina sinnen, som sit egit låf ej tåla:
Til råga på all dygd, man stora hjertan hör
Begära tystnad, när *Poëten* wil försöka,
At fylla up sin plikt, och äre-offer röka.

Du Ljus, som så i glans bland Swenska ljusen lyser,
At på en stråle kan du kännas grant igen!
Förlåt, jag säger ut den wördnads eld, jag hyser:
Jag går ditt bud emot; men lyder dig dock än:
Du kan befalla mig, at ej ditt låf förklara;
Men aldrig hindra mig, at ewigt tacksam wara.

Jag är så full af nit, jag måste få berömma
Et Ädelmod, som blott i Dig sin like har:
Med Nådegåfwor wil Du twinga mig, at gömma
Din äresol, som dock för werden är så klar:
Wälan! jag tiga wil; hon kan sig dock ej dölja:
Du är Dig altid lik, hon måst Dig altid följa.

Fast Skalder ej få lof, Ditt wärda Låf at sjunga,
Så länge ljudet kan Din fina öron nå,
Har Ryktet längesen med Swensk och Utländsk tunga
Beskrifwit hwad Du är, och hwad Du kan förmå
Til Swerjes pris och gagn. Du är til fullo ädel,
Et skydd för sann förtjenst, et Himlens Nåde-Medel.

Som Du lyser nog, och ej behöfwer läna
Af andra något sken, så lyda wi din lag;
Men, Store *Patriot!* at Efterwerden tjena
Det lär ej wara mot Din wilja och behag?
Kan någon lyklig Skald till fullo Dig beskrifwa,
Så kunde det *modell* för stora *Stats*-Män blifwa.

Om jag så tjenlig hand til denna syslan hade,
Som själen min är full med undran på Din Dygd,
För alla tider jag en präktig målning lade,
Som skull' til skugga ha den undrans wärda blygd,
Du har för egit ros: Den enda dunkla strimma
Skull göra, at din bild i dubbel skönhet glimma.

Men at berömma Dig, skall bli de Skalders göra,
Som ega gåfwor, at Din gåfwor rättlig se:
Då skal den senre werd, när hon Ditt låf får höra,
Besanna hwad jag sagt, min sats det wits-ord ge,
At Skalde-konsten är et Rikes gagn och heder,
Som trycker stora Namn i oförwansklig Ceder.

Skönhets beskrifning

Fyra sköna färgors Glans
Lyser i dit ansikt blida:
    När Naturen dig en krans
Utaf skönhet wille wrida,
    Tog hon fyra blomsters färg,
    Blandad' i din märg,
    Befalte tidens ärg,
Skulle dem, för all ting, skona;
    Ty de wäxt på dygdens berg.

De snöhwita liljors blad
Breddes öfwer hela kroppen;
    Men bekommo högsta *grad*
I den lysand' anlets toppen.
    På den skära ådergrund,
    Dina kinder rund,
    Och din ängla mund,
Syns den högsta rosen-färga,
    Som kan skådas någon stund.

Dina ögons klara sken
Feck den mörkblå himla-glansen:
Ack! dess färga är så ren,
Lyser mäst i hela kransen:
Öfwer de *Tourcoser* blå,
Ser man stråkar twå,
Lik halfmånar gå,
Swarta, som en färgad Sabel,
I det hwita *marmor* stå.

Ack! Naturen har på dig
Gjort en underbar *Chattering:*
All sin konst tog hon til sig,
När hon gaf dig den föräring,
Och, at sätja din person,
Uppå skönhets Thron,
Noga jemkad' hon
Dine strek och *lineamenter,*
I en liuflig *Proportion.*

Til mina böcker. Sonnet

Du wishets samling, du förnuftets bästa föda,
Du ledsna stunders bot, du ädla sinnes ro!
Hur' trygg kan jag, bland Er, I stumma wänner, bo,
Som synas utan smink, och winnas utan möda?
I warnen ej af agg, med smickran ingen döda:
Man, utan fara, kan pa orden Eder tro.
För den, hwars tankar hälst pa kunskapswägen gro,
Ert bästa sällskap städs af nöjen öfwerflöda.
Hwad ljufwa tidsfordrif formån I icke ge?
Man sanning får hos Er beprydd och uptäckt se:
Kring werldsens skådoban naturen genomfara.
Sig sielf, och alt hwad är for menn'skjo-ljus beredt:
Kan någon lust emot så rena nöjen swara,
Som kraft och näring ger åt hjerta och åt wett?

Klagan

Så är det enda från mig tagit,
Som jag af jordiskt alt begärt:
Mit lif, jag som en börda dragit
Och tusend plågor hjertat tärt:
En Wän, war lämnad til min stöd,
Min hjelp, min tröst i all slags nöd,
Som mig förkjusat werldsens plågor.
Nu är mit ankar slitit af,
Nu slåss mit skepp af tusend wågor,
Och mägtar dock ej gå i qvaf.

Du känsla, som min plåga wåller,
Ach! dåmna bårt, du mer ej tål:
Du kraft, som lifvet sammanhåller,
Et olycks lif, et sorgers mål,
Försvinn och stadna i dit lopp
Och lät en sansning höra opp,
Hvars ömhet ingen kan uttala.
Du känsla och du tankefart,
Skall ej en söt, en cwig dwala,
Försätta dig i lugnet snart.

Öfver en hyacint. Til - - -

Du rara ört som ej din like
I färg, i glans, i täckhet har,
Bland all din slägt i *Floras* rike
Din fägring mäst mit öga drar:
På dina blad Naturen spelar,
I konst, i prakt hon yttrar sig,
Den fina balsam-lukt du delar,
Förnöjer och förtjusar mig.

Med trogen omsorg jag dig skiöter,
En lindrig luft du andas får,
En häftig ihl dig aldrig möter,
För heta, köld du säker står.
Et lifligt väder på dig fläktar,
Som tränger genom blad och knopp
Och när af värma du försmäktar
En kylig flod dig friskar opp.

Men liksom du min hydda pryder
Och dig i all din täckhet ter,
En grym förvandlings lag du lyder
Du vissnar, dör och fins ej mer.
Du hastigt all min möda glömmer
Och ledsnar vid min ömma vård,
Bland ringa stoft din fägring gömmer,
Du är ju otacksam och hård?

Men skall jag på en blomma klandra,
Det veka väsen klaga an,
Dess öde är at sig förandra,
Hon måste vara som hon kan.
Hon är et gräs, hon skal förfalna,
Jag intet agg til henne bär.
Så ser jag ock dit hierta kallna
Det måste vara som det är.

Selected Poems

Translated by Alan Swanson

Beauty a Fragile Ray

A flower reaches out from earth,
By wind she's blown, now this way, that,
Or shrivels when she's reached her end,
When Summer's time has run its course:
And so it is with beauty's blaze,
She does not own its power complete:
She suffers need she can't evade,
Of illness, age, of time and death.
A beauty is but simply that
Eternity allows to be:
A pure, transparent, blesséd soul
She grows into, and robed, as well,
In heaven's glory, beauty's dress,
She, thus arrayed, then pleases God.

Silent Love

I love, and hide its fire:
Its torture I enjoy:
I suffer:
I burn:
Love without hope:
In doubting fear I fight:
With stifled sighs I crush
That pain.
My heart
In silence churns.
O, sweetest burden!
O sweet love's agony!
To worship in secret
One's utmost choice.

Aria

Shall I hide within my breast,
All the torments that assail me?
May I not, from out the tumult,
Choose but one to soothe my cry?
Ah! then shut so still within you
Gentle thoughts! all that which hurts;
But, mine eyes, I softly pray you
Not betray a sorrowful soul.

Anxious Knowledge, Hard Results

Despreaux, Pope and *Holberg* laugh
At a creature they call human,
Which in Learning, Art, and Science
Much achieves, and light can shed;
But cannot himself control.
Ah! 'tis not worth e'en a thought:
Better 'tis to spend a moment
For an end which pleases one:
Contemplating Field and Creatures,
Well rewards the work it takes;
But of human nature only
Anxious Knowledge, hard Results.

Thoughts upon the Usefulness of Poetry in a well-appointed Land

Should Heaven give her gifts for us but to misuse,
Is everything not made to fill a certain end?
Can not each thing be used to good or evil purpose,
No sentence e'er so true whose meaning can't be bent?
In vain we try to shield the treasures that are Natures,
But misuse of a thing does not destroy its virtue.

In ancient times, though Poetry was greatly treasured,
The language of the Gods, the Genius' special gift,
We see in modern times its strength attenuated,
And fallen from her heights, of all her pow'r bereft:
It seems to me she ought to see her worth rebated,
Since *Barbarism's* Northern hold has now abated.

But 'tis her fate to be like that of ancient virtues,
The more our modern world doth wise and clever seem,
The more our Swedish homeland lacks that honest vesture
Which from enlightened law and mem'ry ought to come:
Our honesty declines when elegance is lurking,
The truest virtues flee when modern ghosts' are spooking.

But at the heart, however, of that cloud which threatens,
The errors of the Poet most endanger skaldic art:
For lowly ends, he so prevents his glory: fame now beaten,
That art itself must suffer, lowered in defeat,
When, thus unthinking, Poets choose a lowly subject
And sell the laurel wreath for profit, market's object.

Everything which reeks of base desire and baser purpose
Gives up it sheen and loses soon its inner worth.
The poet who attends on high the poet's goddess
Receives his due in every laurel wreath he weaves

In praise of Virtue and of Virtue's honor, knowing
That Virtue her protection never ceases showing.

It is a noble gain to make one's handwork useful:
A worthy Poet's one whose gifts are rightly used:
His goal above all goals is, first, to serve the Future
By praising duty in a manner made to please:
Her People he envisages in Honor's temple,
In glory dressed, to serve for others as example.

What would our world now know of all the many heroes,
Of all their acts in times long gone, no Poet there?
For History and Poetry are comrades with us
Who but one goal and purpose here together serve:
The one says only how the matter hangs together,
But how the human will brings it about, the other.

It is the Poet's work to sing of Virtue's honor,
Our given gifts to praise, unto the Maker's grace,
And honor to our People give: to Heroes offer
A tribute; clearly show the world our mighty acts;
And should one say this art's unneeded, void of meaning;
Where *Trajan* is, a *Pliny*'s needed for his singing.

How many noble virtues lie in dim forgetting,
Which could be useful to a future world as light
If they were rightly known, and in their fame were shining?
Thus should a Poet serve, despite the times and vice.
His voice should sing in words of highest tone of Virtue,
With sweetest harmony, and never Truth besmirching.

He ought to have that freedom, too, that, Virtue praised,
He then may paint in colors harsh the worst of Vice;
And, having both their kinds so well delineated,
That Vice is forced to flee and Virtue's mountain-fast.
This judgement he deserves to have among his landsmen,
Of flatt'ry's bragging tongue none may accuse him.

In such a way he serves a need, and Art remains
Both useful, sweet and necessary for a land:
The more of Virtue that a People seek to claim,
The more there is to do for his most-truthful hand,
The worthy much to praise, to honor and encourage,
And every valiant deed on earth record and burnish.

His work is, then, to paint a People wrapped in Honor;
But this is worth remark, he sometimes comes across
Such sensibilities which cannot take such color:
But far above that virtue, there are greater hearts
Which call for silence when the *Poet*, thus beginning
To do his duty, consecrates his praise by singing:

Thou Light, which so in brilliance Swedish light enlightens,
That by one ray alone we recognize 'tis you!
Excuse me, loud I speak of worshipful effulgence:
I go against your order to offer what is due:
You may command me always not to sing your praises;
But can't prevent me being thankful for your graces.

I'm filled with eagerness, I must all honor render
A true Nobility, which you its likeness finds:
By gracious gifts you would attempt my work to hinder,
To hide that noble sun, whose clarity remains:
So be it, then! I'm dumb. And yet it won't stay hidden:
You are Yourself the same; it follows you unbidden.

Though Poets you forbid to sing your worthy praises,
As far as sound can travel so to reach your ears,
So Fame long since, in Swedish and in Foreign voices,
Has described what You can do and what You are
For Sweden's praise and gain. You are completely noble,
A shield of service true, to Heaven's grace enable.

Since You now shine enough and need not ever borrow
Some light from yet another, so we heed your law;
But, Mighty *Patriot!* to serve what comes tomorrow
Is not, nor cannot be against your will and vow?
Could any happy Poet paint your life completely,
Then, that would serve as *model* for a Statesman fully.

Had I but such a hand to do a task so worthy,
For wonder at Your Virtue compasses my soul,
I would for ever make a painting of such beauty,
Whose undercoat would bear the burden of your zeal,
Itself a hidden rose: This single, covered, lining
Would thus display an image twice as beauteous shining.

But so to praise You ought to be the Poet's doing,
Who gifts possess Your own gifts rightly to discern:
Thus shall a later world, Your praises later hearing,
Acknowledge what I've said, my judgement rightly tuned,
That Poetry exists to do a Country honor
By carving worthy Names in undecaying Cedar.

Description of Beauty

Ah! Four lovely colors' Sheen
Shine from out your face so gentle:
    And when Nature would a wreath
Of her beauty 'round you settle,
    Colors took from flowers four
    Blended deep within,
    Commanded patient time
Should, above all, well protect them
    For they grew on Virtue's mount.

Lily petals, white as snow,
Spread about all o'er your body,
    But achieve their greatest show
On your forehead's shining beauty.
    And upon that limpid background,
    Cheeks of white so round,
    On your angel's mouth,
Comes the highest rosy color
    To be seen from far around.

And your glowing eyes so clear
Darkest blue received from heaven:
    Ah! its color is so pure
It shines brightest of those given:
    Over these turquoises blue
    Curving eyebrows, two,
    Just as half-moons so,
Black, as dark as painted sable,
    Through the chastest *marble* show.

Ah! how Nature has in you
Made a color-scale endearing:
    All her art she brought to show
Now ennobled in your bearing,
    And, on Beauty's throne to sit,
    Placed yourself, to set
    All things now just right,
All your lineaments and features
    In *Proportions* of delight.

To my Books. Sonnet

Assembled wisdom, offspring of the brightest Future,
The cure of tedious hours, for noble thoughts a balm,
How safe with you I feel, you silent friends, and calm,
Who are but what you are, who come in simple vesture.
You do not warn by hate, by flatt'ry no-one killing,

Without a risk, one can upon your words rely.
For him whose thoughts would most the way of learning try
Your good companionship bids pleasure overwhelming.
What pleasant way to while away the hours it gives.
Yet Truth is there, its beauty often open lies:
Throughout the theatre of Nature one may wander.
One's self, and all that waits for Mankind's study's there:
Can any pleasure match the pleasure of pure wonder,
Which strength and nurture give to heart and mind, thus, here?

The Complaint

And thus that thing is taken from me,
The only thing of earth I wished:
My life is but a burden for me,
My heart a thousand ills has worn.
A Friend was given as my stead,
My help, my comfort in all need,
Who trolled away all earthly sorrow.
My anchor now is cut away,
My ship beset in wat'ry furrow,
And yet must e'er be under weigh.

O feeling which my sorrow causes,
Ah! pass away, endure no more:
O strength which all of life encloses,
Unhappy life, by sorrows torn,
Be gone and cease to hold your sway
And let a consciousness give way,
Whose tenderness is past all saying.
O feeling, yes, O thought so swift,
Shall not eternal, sweet, forgetting
Conduct you soon to calmer rest.

On a Hyacinth. To - - -

O rarest plant, which has no equal,
In color, brilliance, none so fair,
'Mongst all the flow'rs in *Flora's* temple
Your beauty most my eye draws there.
Upon your petals, Nature, playing
In Radiance, Art, expression leaves,
Your waft of balsam soft exhaling
Enraptures and possesses me.

With faithful care, your needs I nourish,
None but the mildest air you breathe,
No tempest ever shall you ravage,

From heat and chill protected be.
May none but mildest breezes wafting
Force their way through leaf and bud,
And when the warmth at last is wearing,
May coolest waters lift you up.

But just as you my hut enliven
And show your beauty far and near,
A fearful law of change encroaches,
You wither, die, and are no more.
In haste my care is all forgotten,
You weary at my tender ward,
Your beauty you in dross keep hidden,
You are unthankful, cruel, and hard.

But why should I reproach a flower,
Its simple essence calumnate?
Its fate has only change to offer,
To be whatever is its state.
'Tis but a plant and for decaying,
No clear dislike toward it I bear.
I see in your heart, too, that cooling:
It has to be whate'er is there.

Primary Works

Den sörgande turtur-dufwan, eller Åtskilliga bedröfweliga sånger, under wackra melodier sammansatte och samlade af en medlidande åhörare, 1743.
Qwinligt tankespel. Af en Herdinna i Norden, 1744.
Qwinligt tankespel för åhr 1745, 1745.
Den frälsta Swea i fem sånger, 1746.
Qwinligt tankespel för åren 1746 och 1747, 1747.
Qwinligt tankespel för åren 1748, 1749 och 1750, 1750.
Konung Carl Gustafs tog öfwer Bält 1658, 1754.
Andelige skalde-qwäden af H.C.N., 1758.
Utvalda arbeten. J. Fischerström, ed. Stockholm: Lars Kumblin, 1774.
Samlade skrifter, published by Hilma Borelius and Theodor Hjelmqvist. *Svenska författare*. Svenska vitterhetssamfundet 11. Stockholm: Albert Bonniers förlag, 1924-1938.
Skrifter. Torkel Stålmarck, ed. *Svenska klassiker*, published by the Swedish Academy. Stockholm: Atlantis, 1996.

Selected Bibiography

Borelius, Hilma. *Hedvig Charlotta Nordenflycht*. *Svenska kvinnor II*. Uppsala: J.A. Lindblads förlag, 1921.

Demoor, Marysa, ed. *Marketing the Author. Authorial Personae, narrative Selves and Self-Fashioning, 1880-1930.* Houndmills, Basingstoke, Hampshire and New York: Palgrave Macmillan, 2004.

Garnett, Mariah. "Self-fashioning", The Book of the Tenth Muse. Stephanie Merrim and Kerry Smith, eds. http://www.brown.edu/Departments/Comparative_Literature/10th_muse_book/mariah_self_fashioning.html.

Greenblatt, Stephen. *Renaissance Self-Fashioning. From More to Shakespeare.* Chicago & London: University of Chicago Press, 1980

Hansson, Sven G. *Satir och kvinnokamp i Hedvig Charlotta Nordenflychts diktning. Några konflikter, motståndare och anhängare.* Stockholm: Carlssons, 1991.

Holm, Birgitta. "En siäl som fint och starkt och ömt och häftigt känner". In: *Nordisk kvinnolitteraturhistoria. I Guds namn 1000-1800,* Höganäs: Wiken, 1993, 391-400 (Ruth Nilsson wrote the last part of this chapter, 401-404).

Hägg, Göran. *Den svenska litteraturhistorien.* Stockholm: Wahlström & Widstrand, 1996.

Kruse, John. *Hedvig Charlotta Nordenflycht. Ett skaldinne-porträtt från Sveriges rococotid.* Lund: Gleerupska Universitets-Bokkandeln, 1895.

Nordenflycht, Hedvig Charlotta. *Skrifter.* Torkel Stålmarck, ed. With an introduction of Sture Allén. Stockholm: Atlantis, 1996.

Steinfeld, Toril. "Fra salmeoversettelser til det borgerlige familiedrama". In: *Norsk kvinnelitteraturhistorie. Bind 1 1600-1900.* Oslo: Pax Forlag A.S., 1988, 28-40.

Stålmarck, Torkel. *Hedvig Charlotta Nordenflycht – Ett porträtt.* Stockholm: Norstedts, 1997.

White, Hayden. *Metahistory. The Historical Imagination in the Nineteenth-Century Europe.* Baltimore/London: The Johns Hopkins University Press, 1973.

Fredrika Bremer:
Passionate Promoter of Peace and Women's Rights

ANN-CHARLOTTE GAVEL ADAMS (UNIVERSITY OF WASHINGTON)

Fredrika Bremer (1801-65) was an international celebrity in her day. This is surprising considering that she was a petit, well brought-up, unmarried woman, raised in a very rigid upper-class family in Sweden, a country at the periphery of Europe, where women had no legal rights and no access to higher education. They could neither run a business nor manage the money they might have brought into the marriage. How did Fredrika Bremer break out of those restraints to become a world-famous author and a pioneer in the work for women's rights in Sweden? To be sure, she was an unusual personality, intellectually curious, and engaged in all the social and political questions of her time. She was also exceptionally determined and passionate about the issues she was concerned with, and unafraid and outspoken. But was that enough? What were the key events that brought her this fame and recognition?

Fredrika Bremer was born in 1801 in Åbo (Turku), Finland, the second daughter of Carl Fredric Bremer and Birgitta Charlotta Hollström. Fredrika and her older sister Charlotte were to have three more sisters and two brothers, but only Charlotte and Fredrika lived until old age. The family was native Swedish speakers, and Finland was still under Swedish rule at the time. The Bremers were very well to do. In 1804, Carl Fredric Bremer sold the family business and moved his family to Sweden. This was just in the nick of time. In 1809, Sweden was forced to cede Finland to Russia.

After the family's arrival in Sweden, Carl Fredric Bremer purchased Årsta Castle, about 20 miles south of Stockholm. There are several accounts of the rigid and harsh upbringing of the Bremer children. The father Carl Fredric was very authoritarian and had an unpredictable temper. Young Fredrika experienced her home as a prison, and she sank into a depression. In her posthumously published autobiographical sketches *Sjelvbiografiska anteckningar, bref och efterlemnade skrifter* (1868; Eng. tr. *Life, letters, and posthumous works of Fredrika Bremer,* 1976), she describes the depressing environment of her home as "non-life" where she grew increasingly numb at the realization of the restrictions of women's lives. She was envious of the men, hearing them express ideas and passions, and seeing courage and enterprise in their eyes. One feeling did not turn numb, and that was her pain, it grew sharper and sharper for every day.

In the winter of 1826, Fredrika was given her first chance of escape from the restrictive and increasingly meaningless life she was leading. When the family moved to Stockholm for the winter, Fredrika was allowed to stay behind at Årsta Castle to care for her younger sister Agathe who was suffering from scoliosis. Fredrika suddenly had the freedom to dispose of her own time as she wanted. She was a talented painter and she painted miniature portraits, which she sold. She spent her first own earnings on the poor in the cottages around Årsta Castle. Then – in 48 hours – as "drifven af något oemtoståndligt" (*Fredrika Bremers Brev* 2, 131; "driven by something irresistible"), she sat down and wrote her first short novel, *Axel och Anna* (Axel and Anna). It was written in form of a correspondence between two lovers. In a letter she wrote that the novel "dansade ut ur mitt hufvud eller mitt hjerta" (*Fredrika Bremers Brev* 2, 131; "danced out of my head or my heart"). *Axel and Anna* was published together with a couple of other shorter stories, anonymously, under the title *Teckningar utur Hvardagslifvet* (Sketches from Everyday Life) in 1828. Fredrika's youngest brother August brought it to the attention of the publisher Palmblad in Uppsala. The novel and stories were very well received and sold out quickly. In 1830 and 1831 two additional collections were published under the same title. Readers were curious who the author of these witty and realistic stories might be. In 1831, the secret was revealed and Fredrika Bremer was awarded the small gold medal from the Swedish Academy for her writing. Her father had died the previous year – without learning about his daughter's publications and now Fredrika, at the age of 30, had the experience of a new sense of freedom and a budding independence.

Fredrika's older sister, Charlotte, was the only Bremer child to marry. In 1831, she married a deputy judge, Peter Quiding, in Kristianstad in the south of Sweden. In their home, Fredrika meet Per Johan Böklin, a principal at the school in the city and a minister. He became her tutor and a very important person in her life. Fredrika came to consider him her best friend on earth, both spiritually and intellectually. She moved in with her sister and brother-in-law and for the first time in her life she had a room of her own. She now understood that it was her vocation and calling to be a writer. She was happy and felt it was the beginning of a new life for her. She wrote to her mother that she planned to study to become an author. She embarked on studies of religion and philosophy, and had daily discussions of her readings with Böklin. The close intellectual friendship between the two developed into warmer feelings, and Böklin proposed marriage. Fredrika declined with the motivation that her writing was more important than marriage. Their friendship prevailed even after Böklin later married another woman.

Bremer worked for two years on her next book, which was published under the title *Presidentens döttrar* (Eng. tr. *The President's Daughters*, 1843) in 1834. Many of the intellectual ideas from her discussions with Böklin re-emerged in fictional form in the novel: The need for better education of young girls and more freedom for the married woman. Bremer was here cultivating the seeds that came to fruition in her later writings.

In 1839, *Hemmet, eller Familjesorger och Fröjder* (Eng. tr. *The Home: or Family Cares and Family Joys*, 1843) was published. This novel became her greatest success to date. Her intent with this novel was ambitious: to eradicate the prejudice that a woman's only goal and fulfillment was marriage, and that an unmarried woman was a lost human being without a cause. She wrote for the woman who was single, like herself. *The Home* was translated into seven languages, and Bremer was on her way to becoming an international celebrity. In 1844, she was awarded the large gold medal of the Swedish Academy, for having "befrämjat den Svenska Vitterhetens namnkunnighet i främmande länder" (Burman, 2001, 243; "promoted the visibility of Swedish literature and learning in foreign countries").

In the 1840s, Bremer became more popular and better known abroad than in Sweden. She turned her focus to the societies of the New World. She had read Alexis de Tocqueville's *De la Démocratie en Amérique* (1835), and Harriet Martineau's *Society in America* (1837) and wanted to see for herself this experimental but promising social utopia. In a letter to Böklin in 1845, she wrote: "Du har anat rätt min afsikt med min resa till nya verlden. Det är dess penater jag ville se, det är dess qvinnor jag ville känna" (You have correctly guessed my intention with my journey to the New World. I want to see their idols, I want to learn to know their women). The United States was also an important market for Bremer. By the time she set foot on the North American continent in 1849, at least nine of her books had been translated to English and published in the United States.

Bremer had corresponded with several admirers in America and acquired many supportive friends there, foremost among them a young landscape architect, Andrew Jackson Downing (1815-52), who sent her an invitation. In her response, Bremer expressed her eagerness to see the New World and learn to know the society: "In many of these sferes methought I see the Idea – the sun of intellectual life – clearing up, making its way to earthly reality, and transforming chaos into harmony and beauty." (*Brev* 1, 201)

Bremer's letters to her sister Agathe from America were clearly written to be published, and with an international readership in mind. In 1853-54 they were published as *Hemmen i den nya verlden* 1-3 (Eng. tr. *Homes of the New World* 1-2, 1854).

She had arrived in America with the intention to study the position of women and homes of the New World, but was immediately thrown into a roiling social life that broadened her focus considerably. Her letters seem equally concerned with nature, weather, food that was too rich and not least the many noble and handsome men she encountered. She was invited to meet with the important cultural personalities on the American scene, among them Henry Wadsworth Longfellow, who had been to Sweden a decade earlier and had an interest in Scandinavian literature and Ralph Waldo Emerson. She was also confronted with other issues than the ones she had expected, i.e. slavery and the position of the Indians. Last, not least she was invited to tea at the White House with President Zachary Taylor on July 3, 1850.

Bremer traveled from New York and Boston in the northeast to the Carolinas and Georgia in the south, which she found too hot. She continued west to Chicago, which she found to be horrible and ugly, with an air like 'a cloud of dust' (*Homes of the New World* 1, 606). She visited Swedish settlers in Pine Lake, Wisconsin. In St Paul, Minnesota, a town "thronged with Indians" (*Homes of the New World* 2, 26), she was the guest of the governor Alexander Ramsey. She traveled south on the Mississippi river by steamer and arrived in New Orleans on Christmas Eve 1850. There she attended a slave auction, which she reported on in very matter-of-fact style in her letter home. Her next stop was Havana, Cuba, where she, to her surprise, encountered a fellow Swede, the soprano Jenny Lind, with whom she had a congenial meeting. On September 13, 1850, Bremer returned to Sweden on the S/S Atlantic, after eleven months of crisscrossing the New World. Upon her return, she learned that her sister Agathe, the addressee of her letters, had died.

For all the things she found wrong with America, the slavery, the position of the Indians, the heat and the too rich food, Bremer was very hopeful when it came to the position of the women. She felt that the women's movement had begun there in a very promising fashion and that it was supported by open-minded and noble men. The ideas she absorbed in America had the most impact on her later novels.

In August of 1854, Bremer published "An Invitation to a Peace Alliance" in the London newspaper *The Times*. The event instigating this article was the Crimean War, which began in January 1854. The so-called "Eastern Question" had escalated to a full-fledged conflict between Russia on one side and Turkey, supported by England, France and Sardinia on the other. The article was a passionate appeal for international solidarity between all women of the world with the goal of "peace, love and well-being":

Sisters (...) among the ancient kingdoms of Asia, of the steppes of Siberia, or in the Imperial cities of Russia; sisters of the western countries of Europe (...) and you, sisters in that vast new land beyond the Atlantic Ocean (...) and you, Christian women among the nations of Africa; Christian women in the isles of the South Sea; mild, loving sisters, all over the earth (...) give us your hands! May the earth thus become encircled by a chain of healing, loving energies, which neither ocean nor event, neither discord nor time, can interrupt. (Burman, 362)

The opinions of her article varied widely. An editorial in *The Times* ridiculed the appeal as "the mere illusion of an amiable enthusiast" (Burman, 362) and wondered what might become of the *homes* if women would organize into charitable associations (Burman, 363). But Bremer also heard from many sympathizers, among them the Finnish author Zacharias Topelius.

In March of 1855, after her mother's death, Bremer confided in Böklin that she was now working on a novel, *Hertha* (1856; Eng. tr. 1856), containing the first fruits of her observations and experiences in the New World, but transposed to the Swedishness of her own soul. The novel was to center on a woman, and her development. As the novel progressed from the winter of 1855 to January 1856, Bremer became more open about its polemical nature and her intentions to expose the patriarchal oppression of women. In a letter to her close friend, the Danish writer Hans Christian Andersen in May of 1855, she wrote that the noble souls she had encountered in America had given her courage to express fully what she herself had felt so strongly and clearly, and that it would be a critique of the oppressive patriarchal conditions in her own country and elsewhere.

The title and name "Hertha" did not appeal to Mary Howitt, her English translator, nor to Böklin, who pointed out the association to the old Norse fertility goddess Nerthus, who was celebrated with sexual orgies. But Bremer persisted: "The name has a certain power in its sound and also in the feeling it conveys by its correspondence to the name of the earth." (Burman, 386)

In the first chapter, the characters and setting of *Hertha* seem to set up a conventional, realistic novel of the time with a bourgeois upper middle-class family consisting of a patriarchal and domineering father with grown daughters living at home, neither married nor able to make their own living by a profession. Although there is an inheritance from their deceased mother, it is controlled and squandered by the father. One of the daughters, Hertha, is outspoken but disillusioned about the injustices in her home and against women in society. At a gathering in the local society, she speaks out about the humiliating condition where women have to marry in order to be financially secured. She continues and asserts that she would find it more honorable for a woman to work and contribute to the support of her family and the man she loves. Returning to her home, a depressing, run-down manor house, she is scolded by her father for being late. Going to bed, she takes opium drops to fall asleep – and dreams. The chapter "Hertha's Dream" presented below, in an abridged version, outlines the oppression of women in the patriarchal societies in all the corners of the world, in a style that seems almost cinematic.

At the end of the chapter, the flame in Hertha's heart turns her into a flaming torch. She wakes up and finds her paternal home on fire. The novel is a flaming appeal to women and men all over the world to stand up and demand rights for women.

The novel received much attention in the press, and got both positive and negative reviews. In 1858, a year after the publication of *Hertha,* a law was passed in Sweden, giving married women the right of majority at the age of 25. Whether Bremer's novel had had any impact on the public opinion or the law makers is still debated by scholars. Bremer herself thought so. To her American friends, the Springs, she wrote:

> You will be glad to know of a measure which it is probable that this book and its earnest appeal has influenced, nam. the proposition of our King Oscar to the diet of Sweden at its opening last October that Women in Sweden would be declared of Majority at the age of 25 years. This measure will certainly pass, as the public mind, now, is well prepared to understand its bearing and wisdom." (Burman, 392-93)

Herthas dröm

Kapitel fem ur *Hertha*

Det syntes henne att hon var en själ, nyss född på jorden. I gråstensberget vilade hon som i sin vagga. Hon såg sig själv såsom hade kroppen varit en genomskinlig, eterisk form för själen; och in i själen såg hon klart hjärtat, med dess underbara system av kamrar och ådror, genom vilka livet pulserade på röda, varma vågor, och djupt därinne brann en låga, som än steg, än sjönk, än syntes dunklare, än klarare, men tydligt strävade uppåt, såsom sökte den en friare rymd.

Det var morgon och solen gick glödande upp. Hon gladde sig åt solens ljus och drack leende dess skål ur små bägarlavar med purpurkanter, som stodo omkring hennes vagga, fulla av daggens klara droppar. Hennes hjärta klappade av längtan till ljuset och livet. Från sin lilla vrå i gråstensbergets famn, där hon låg på mjuk mossbädd, såg hon himlen klar över sitt huvud och såg vitt ut över jordens berg och dalar. Hon såg ett högt, härligt grönskande träd, vars grenar räckte vitt omkring över jorden och ända upp i himlen; de voro fulla av sköna, glänsande frukter, och ur trädets krona hörde hon röster viska:
"Lyssna till det trädets susning
Vid vars rot ditt bo är fästat!"

En klar källa sprang sorlande upp nära vid det höga trädets fot. Hon såg tre sköna, allvarliga kvinnor hämta vatten ur källan och begjuta trädet, som därvid tycktes grönska allt friskare. Svanor med glänsande fjädrar simmade sjungande i källan. Hertha såg människor komma och gå under trädets skygd, plocka av dess frukter och sedan jublande

frambringa ädla och sköna skapelser, som de kallade sina verk. Hon såg härliga gestalter, stolta byggningar och de mest smakfulla prydnader framstå under deras händer; hon såg dem glädja sig över sina verk och åter och åter hämta krafter till nya av det härliga trädets frukter. Med klappande hjärta frågade hon:
"Vilka äro dessa?"

En röst svarade: "Dessa äro vetenskapernas och de fria konsternas dyrkare, och de som i skydd av livets och frihetens träd ägna sig åt de yrken, som förädla och glädja människornas hjärtan." Flera av dessa män tycktes ägna en särskild hyllning åt kvinnan. De avbildade hennes gestalt på mångahanda vis, de diktade sånger och höllo vackra tal till hennes ära, påkallande henne att försköna och lyckliggöra jorden.

Hertha kände lågan i sitt hjärta brinna högre och högre och den ingav henne att tänka: "O! att jag finge såsom en av dessa arbeta i det härliga trädets skugga, njuta av deras frukter och glädja människors hjärtan!"

Vid det hon så tänkte, såg hon framblicka ur himlen over sig ett ansikte av oändligt majestät och oändlig faderlig huldhet, och ovillkorligt såg hon upp till detta och bad:
"Fader: Låt mig arbeta och glädja mig, som dessa mina bröder."

Det härliga, milda ansiktet log och svarade: "Gå, min dotter!"

Hertha lämnade då glad sin vrå i urbergets famn och vandrade mot det sköna trädet. Men det var mer avläget ifrån henne än hon trodde, och många hinder mötte under vägen; men hon övervann dem, skyndade modigt framåt, ty alltid hörde hon den friska källans sorl och suset från det mäktiga trädets krona. Nu såg hon det på närmare håll, men då blev hon varse, att det omgavs av en mur, som alldeles hindrade henne att komma det nära. Där voro flera portar på muren med åtskilliga namn av akademier och skolor. Portarna syntes på avstånd vara öppna, men så fort hon nalkades för att ingå genom dem, fann hon dem stängda. Hertha klappade på och bad om inträde. Men dörrväktarna svarade henne:
"Här få blott män fritt ingå och utgå. Vi ha ej rum för kvinnor i våra lärosalar, och de ha intet att göra där!"

Hertha svarade ödmjukt: "Jag vill lära att skapa det ädla och sköna såsom mina bröder; jag vill ej göra intrång hos någon, utan tåligt arbeta och lära, på det jag måtte en gång kunna vederkvicka människohjärtan. Därför låt mig även få plocka av det stora världsträdets frukt."

Då svarade man henne med hårdhet: "Gå, den frukten är ej för dig. Vänd om till din vrå i berget och lär dig att koka eller spinna. Det hör dig och dina gelikar till. Ni ha ej lott med de fria."

Nu hörde hon innanför portarna röster, som sade: "Släpp den unga kvinnan in, hon bör även få njuta av trädets frukter." Men den andra sade: "Nej!" Och det blev ett stretande med portarna, ty somliga ville öppna dem men andra strävade emot. De senare blevo de starkaste och portarna förblevo stängda.

Bedrövad, men ännu icke modfälld, gick Hertha vidare, sökande någon port, genom vilken hon kunde ingå.

(...) Genom en hög gallerport såg hon den klara källan och de sköna kvinnorna, som vaktade den, och bad:
"Räck mig en dryck vatten att läska mig med. Jag försmäktar av törst ..."

Då sågo de på henne, de sköna allvarliga kvinnorna, med blickar av djupt medlidande och svarade:
"Det är oss förbjudet!" Och den äldsta av de tre nornorna tillade:

"Det vilar en fördom,
en gammal förbannelse
över ditt kön
i grönskande Manhem.

Förr än den löses,
får du ej dricka
av Urdakällan;
källan som giver nytt liv!"

Den stränga nornan Verdandi talade nu och sade:
"Den är ej för den svaga.
Den är blott för *den hjältemodiga*,
den starka i viljan,
och för den, som redligen kämpar.
Hon ensam är värdig."

Men den yngsta av de tre såg med en blick full av eld på Hertha och sade:
"Sälla äro de som hava fått *syn*,
som kämpa i tro och i hopp!
De bli välkomna.
De skola segra!"

Hertha förstod ej nornornas ord. Hon förstod blott, att *hon* ej var värdig att dricka av den livgivande källan, att de hade avvisat henne.
(...) Men icke länge satt hon så. Hennes själ uppreste sig, hon mindes nornornas ord vid urdabrunnen, "den är blott för de hjältemodiga och den som redligen kämpar!" Och det grydde henne en mäktig vilja att befria sig och sina bundna själssystrar. (...) "Jag vill redligen kämpa!"
Då flammade lågan i hennes hjärta högt upp, lyfte henne från jorden och lät henne, högt över lagmännens huvuden, sväva fram genom rymden. Denna känsla uppfyllde henne med glädje och hopp och hon tänkte: "Förbannelsen kan då hävas för mig och mina systrar och vår del kan ännu bliva bland de frias!"
Ovillkorligt vände hon sig österut åt den trakt, där hon sett solen uppgå och såsom buren på osynliga vingar svävade hon fram över jorden. Men plötsligt kände hon sin flykt hämmas, och en barsk röst ropade:
"Halt! Wer da?"
Hertha svarade: "En själ, som söker frihet, liv och sällhet för sig och många systrar!"
"Vad för något?" sade rösten, "en själ? Och du är ett fruntimmer? Bort därmed. Här i landet få icke fruntimmer ha själar. De räknas ej med bland befolkningen. Du får icke komma hit. Vänster om, marsch!"
"Vem är du?" frågade Hertha, "och vad rätt har du att befalla mig?"
"Vad rätt?" dundrade rösten. "Jag är en kejserlig stor Ukas och står på post för att intet kontraband må inkomma i landet."
"Men jag är intet kontraband", sade Hertha, "jag är blott en själ, som ..."
"Resonera inte utan lyd", avbröt rösten, "eljest får du arbeta i Sibirien. En kvinnlig själ, som söker frihet, är det argaste kontraband i världen."
"Låt mig blott tåga fritt genom ditt land, o store Ukas; jag vill ej stanna där, jag vill längre österut, dit där solen uppgår!" bad Hertha.

"Du är en hövlig person", sade ukasen mildare, "och därför, fast du ej får fara fritt genom mitt land, så vill jag låta dig se en syn österut, som kan bota dina frihetssvärmerier." Och han lät henne se genom ett stort synglas öster ut ända till Kina, där icke blott kvinnornas själar men även deras fötter äro bundna, och överallt på jorden emot solens uppgång såg hon kvinnorna förtryckta och ringaktade, då de ej blevo fruktade såsom tyranniska och hämnande makter, vilket stundom hände, då de med våld brutit sina bojor.

"Vad hava de gjort?" frågade Hertha, "för att så behandlas."

"Vad går för nöd åt dem?" svarade ukasen, "de ha det så gott som de förtjäna och behöva. Ja, i mitt heliga land, ändå mycket bättre. Här ha fruntimren det riktigt överdådigt gott. De behöva ej skatta till kronan såsom själar, och de få ärva en fjortondedel i boet efter sina anhöriga. Därtill få de kläda sig granna och prata om lappri så mycket de behaga, blott att de äro lydiga och inte vilja flaxa för högt. Hör flicka! Du ser bra ut och jag tycker om dig; stanna här och du skall få bli en rik bojars trälinna. Kom, du skall få det gott!" Och den store ukasen fattade Herthas arm.

Stolt och förfärad slet hon sig lös och flydde, i det hon slungade en blick full av förakt på den store ukasen. Hon flydde norrut, ty hon såg ljus glimma och hörde glädjesånger ljuda vid ishavets stränder. Det var vilda nomadfolk, som drogo omkring på dess ödsliga tundror och genom dess stela urskogar. De höllo nu sina marknader och bröllop. Hertha såg männen tumla och slåss såsom under rus, till dess de föllo omkull på snön och somnade. I hyttan omringade kvinnorna bruden och gåvo henne dricka och drucko själva ur en bägare under skratt och stoj.

Hertha frågade dem: "Ären I fria och lyckliga?"

De svarade: "Vad är frihet? Är det något slags brännvin, så giv oss därav, att vi må ge åt våra fäder och män, så att de icke misshandla oss. Giv oss det, så att vi också må känna oss sälla. Eljest – lycklig den, som dör i sin tredje natt. Vi äro födda till träldom."

Nordanvinden brusade fram över fältet och bröllopsscenen försvann i ett moln av yrande snö. Sedan blev det lugnt och norrskenen dansade en fackeldans kring polkretsen, så där var ljust som den ljusaste dag. Och vid dess sken såg Hertha flockar av män och kvinnor, som drogo omkring klädda i skinn med sina renhjordar och hundar. Men överallt bland dessa vilda horder voro kvinnorna männens tjänarinnor och deras likar blott i stunder av rus och slagsmål. Stundom, likväl blevo de till häxor och kallades då "kloka" och blevo fruktade och åtlydda, ty deras kraft var stor i att tillfoga ont och hämnas, och deras blick, som kallades "den onda blicken", hade makt att slå med olycka både människor och kreatur.

Med en rysning vände Hertha sig bort från dessa folk och trakter, och åter svävade hon över jorden, men nu mot söderns varma länder.

Hon såg en annan himmel än nordens stränga, en skönare, yppigare jord full av blommor och frukter. Luften var ljuv som den ljuvaste godhet, källor sprungo, musik tonade, allt syntes svälla av levnadsfröjd. Det var i en stor trädgård nära en stor stad, som hon befann sig.

"O!" tänkte Hertha, "här måste människorna vara fria, goda och lyckliga, här torde jag finna frihet för mig och mina bundna systrar."

Då nalkades henne ur den stora staden några myndiga och mörka personer och sade: "Du talar om frihet. Du är en misstänkt person. Vad vill du här?"

Hon svarade: "Jag söker friheten för mig och mina systrar! – – "

De myndiga herrarna sågo på varandra och logo, som om de velat säga: "Hon är rubbad till sina sinnen." Och de sade åter till henne: "Vad är det du vill?" Hon upprepade sitt svar.

De frågade: "Är du rik?"

Hon svarade: "Nej. Min själ och min vilja äro min enda rikedom."
De svarade: "Då är du en toka. Gift dig, om du det kan, eller gå in i ett kloster."
Hertha svarade: "Nej, jag vill leva och arbeta i frihet och oskuld för det mål, mig är givet."
De sade: "Ingen frihet är oskyldig; minst hos kvinnor. Det vilar en gammal skuld på ditt släkte. Och i alla fall, du är en farlig person, ty du talar om frihet, och du kommer från ett land, där friheten av ålder slagit rot och vuxit till ett stort träd, som det säges, och där kvinnorna lära mer än en gång kämpat för landets frihet, alltså, du får ej gå lös här."
"Ack!" tänkte Hertha; "de veta ej, huru litet kvinnorna äro fria i mitt land!" Men hon sade intet, ty hon ville ej skämma ut sitt eget lands lagar.
På en gång hörde hon ett stort rop: "I kloster, i fängelse med tokan, med frihetssvärmerskan!" Och en flock svartklädda män fattade uti henne och drevo henne framåt mot en stor, mörk byggning med små förgallrade fönster. Fruktan och vrede gjorde henne stark, hon slet sig ur deras händer och flydde; lågan i hennes hjärta flammade högt och bar henne bort, bort till dess hon ej mera hörde de hotande, hånande ropen. Då stannade hon och såg, att hon kommit ut ur den stora staden, vars rök uppsteg på avstånd. Trött satte hon sig ned på en sten, men kände sig så ensam och övergiven, och så bedrövad över människors hårdhet och den förbannelse, som vilade över hennes kön, att hon begynte bittert gråta.
Då kom en grann, glittrande sky drivande från den stora stadens sida och sänkte sig mot jorden nära stället, där Hertha satt. Den var såsom en vävnad av fladdrande flor med silver och guldpaljetter; och ur den framkommo vackra unga flickor med lätta dräkter, levnadslustiga blickar och kransar på sina huvuden. De nalkades henne och sade:
"Varför gråter du?"
Hertha svarade: "Jag gråter emedan det vilar en förbannelse över mig och mitt kön, som bannlyser oss från de frias arbete och glädje."
Flickorna logo och sade: "Åh, vad, förbannelse? bannlysning? Bry dig ej om vad de sura säga. Var blott rätt djärv och yster, så får du vara så fri du vill. Du är för ung och vacker att gråta bort ditt liv. Kom med oss och gör som vi. Vi vilja upptaga dig i vårt samfund."
"Och vad gören I? Och vad ären I?" frågade Hertha med klappande hjärta, halvt tjusad av flickornas utseende och ord, halvt fruktande för något, som hon såg hos dem, men ej kunde giva namn.
De unga kvinnorna logo, sågo på varann och svarade:
"Man kallar oss glädjeflickor; ty vi leva för glädjen. Vi leka med männens hjärtan, och vi behärska dem. Om de än stundom leka grymt med oss, så kunna vi hämnas. Och komma de rätt in i våra garn, så bli de dem icke kvitt i all deras dar. Vi snärja dem och skratta åt dem, som trodde sig våra herrar."
"Och vad är ert mål, och för vad leven I?" frågade åter Hertha.
Flickorna skrattade och svarade: "Vi leva för ögonblicket. Vi fråga ej efter annat än att njuta dagen och roa oss på bästa vis. Vi äro de friaste väsen på jorden. Vi leva fritt eller på andras bekostnad i alla länder. Vi följa inga lagar utom våra nycker; vi lyda inga plikter. Vi taga män och övergiva dem, efter som det behagar oss. Vi kunna få barn som andra kvinnor, men binda oss ej som andra kvinnor att sitta och träla för dem; vi sköta blott våra nöjen!"
"Ni kunna få barn och vårda er ej om dem?" sade Hertha förvånad. "Vem vårdar sig om era små barn?"
"Det veta vi ej så noga", svarade flickorna; "det gör man på barnhusen; vi ha ej tid med sådant. Vi vilja vara fria kvinnor."

"O!" sade Hertha, "er frihet är icke den jag åtrår, er frihet är misstag! I tron er fria, men I ären slavinnor av ..."

"Vad, vi slavinnor!" utropade flickorna skrattande, "kom, vi skola visa dig huru vi äro bundna! ..."

Och de ryckte Hertha med sig i dansande ringar; fåfängt bad hon dem upphöra, fåfängt att lämna henne fri, de drogo henne med sig, svängande om i virvlande, yrande kretsar, till dess hennes sinnen ville förgå, och ångest betog hennes hjärta. Men glädjeflickorna dansade och drucko vin, ropande: "Så, så! till livets slut; så, så, in i evigheten! ..."

"O, det är förfärligt!" utropade Hertha, i det hon äntligen slet sig ur deras leder, "bort, bort ifrån mig, jag vill ej leva av er frihet!"

"Så lev av din dygd!" svarade glädjeflickorna hånskrattande, "vi andra vi leva av annat!" Och de höljde sig åter i det glittrande molnet, som nu liksom på miljoner par fjärillsvingar virvlade bort, drivet av vinden mot den stora staden tillbaka. Det var en grann syn, och länge hörde Hertha ljudet av deras glada prat och skratt.

Med djupt vemod såg Hertha efter dem och tänkte. "Dessa känna sig fria och lyckliga; och jag!" ... Lågan flammade i hennes hjärta och hon kände, att hon var född till något bättre än dessas lycka. Men till vad?

(...)

Och det syntes Hertha, att hennes själ förvandlades, och att den uppåt strävande, längtande lågan därinom antog en annan natur. Den hade längtat att värma och välgöra; nu ville den blott straffa. Hon själv var förvandlad till ett farligt väsen, som spridde omkring sig förstörelse. Lågan i hjärtat spridde sig genom alla hennes lemmar och allt, vad hon vidrörde, antändes därav. Hennes hand hade blivit en glödande brand. Hon lade den på sitt fädernehem och vilda flammor utbröto. Hon såg dem växa högt och sprida sig åt flera håll, antändande allt fler och fler hus. Hon hörde klockornas klämtande, larmtrummans virvlar, folkets rop och larm skränet av iskärror och eldsläckningsanstalter. Med vart ögonblick tilltog bullret, och hon hörde viskas i sitt öra: "Mordbrand! Mordbrand!" En onämnbar ångest bemäktigade sig henne, ty det tycktes henne, att detta allt var hennes verk. På gång uppstod hos henne så, som det ofta sker under svåra drömmar, tanken: "Det måtte vara dröm!" Hon sökte att vakna, kämpande häftigt med drömanden, som höll henne fången, lyckades slutligen och – vaknade.

Hertha's Dream

Chapter Five from *Hertha*

Translated by Ann-Charlotte Gavel Adams

It seemed to her that she was a soul, newly born on earth. She rested in the granite mountain, like in a cradle. She viewed herself as if the body was a transparent, an ethereal shell for her soul, and inside the soul she saw quite clearly the heart, with its wondrous system of ventricles and arteries, though which life throbbed in red, warm waves, and deep inside burned a flame, rising and sinking, now dimmer, now clearer, but it clearly strove upwards as if it was seeking a freer region.

It was morning, and the sun rose in red glow. She rejoiced in the light of the sun, and toasted it smilingly in little beaker-like lichens with purple edges standing around her cradle, filled with clear drops of dew. Her heart throbbed with longing for light and life. From her little nook in the granite rock, where she lay on a soft bed of moss, she saw the heaven bright above her head, and the hills and valleys of the earth all around her. She saw a tall gloriously verdant tree, whose branches reached far over the earth and all the way up to heaven; they were laden with beautiful, shining fruits and from the tree-top she heard voices whisper,

Listen to the whispering of the tree
By whose root your home is based!

A clear spring babbled forth not far from the foot of the tall tree. She saw three beautiful, earnest women fetching water from the spring and water the tree, which thereby seemed to grow more verdant and healthy. Swans with brilliant plumage swam singing in the spring water. Hertha saw people coming and going under the shade of the tree, picking its fruit and then exultantly bringing forth noble and beautiful works, which they called their creations. She saw glorious shapes, proud constructions, and the most tasteful ornamentations emerge from their hands; she saw them rejoice over their creations, and over and over empower themselves to new creations from the fruits from the magnificent tree. With a pounding heart she asked,

"Who are they?"

A voice answered, "They are the worshippers of the Sciences and the Liberal Arts, and they, who under the protection of the tree of life and freedom devote themselves to the professions which ennoble and gladden the hearts of the human beings". Several of these men seemed to pay special homage to woman. They portrayed her figure in many ways, they composed songs, they made beautiful speeches to her honor, calling upon her to beautify the earth and make it happy.

Hertha felt the flame in her heart burn higher and higher, and it inspired her to think, "Oh that I, like one of them, would be allowed to labor the shadow of the magnificent tree, to enjoy its fruits, and to gladden the hearts of my fellow human beings!"

While dreaming such, she saw looking down from the heaven above her a face of infinite majesty and infinite fatherly love, and involuntarily she looked up at it and prayed,

"Father: Allow me to work and rejoice, as these my brothers."

The glorious, mild face smiled and responded, "Go, my daughter!"

Hertha happily left her nook in the bosom of the granite rock and wandered towards the beautiful tree. But it was more distant than she had thought, and she encountered many obstacles on the way; but she overcame them all and hurried bravely forward, because she continued to hear the murmuring of the fresh spring, and the whispering from the crown of the mighty tree. When she now saw it up close, she became aware that it was surrounded by a wall, which prevented her from coming near it. There were several gates in the wall, each with a name of an academy or school. At a distance, the gates seemed to be open, but as soon as she approached to enter, she found them closed. Hertha knocked and asked to be let in. But the custodians answered her,

"Only men can freely enter and exit here. We do not have space for women in our halls of learning, and they have no business here!"

Hertha answered humbly, "I want to learn to create the noble and beautiful works like my brothers; I will not interfere with anyone, only work patiently and learn that I may one day be able to invigorate the hearts of human beings. Therefore – allow me also to pick the fruits of the large world tree."

Then they responded sternly, "Go away, the fruit is not for you. Return to your nook in the mountain, and learn to cook or spin. That is a benefiting occupation for you and your kind. You have no place among the free."

Now, she heard voices inside the gates, which said, "Let in the young woman, she should also be allowed to enjoy the fruits of the tree." But other voices said, "No!" And there was a commotion at the gates, as some wanted to open them and others opposed it. The latter were stronger and the gates remained closed.

Distressed but not discouraged, Hertha continued, looking for a gate through which she might enter.

(...) Through a tall iron gate she saw the clear spring and the beautiful women guarding it and pleaded,

"Give me a drink of water to refresh myself. I am perishing of thirst ..."

They looked at her, the beautiful earnest women, with eyes full of compassion and answered,

"We are forbidden to do that!" And the oldest of the Norns[1] added,

A doom has been spoken
A curse from olden times
Lies on your sex, o Woman
In the verdant home of Man.

Until this curse has been lifted
You are not allowed to drink
From Urd's spring;
The spring that gives new life!

The stern Norn Verdandi spoke now and said,
It is not for the meek.
It is only for *the courageous*,
The strong in willpower,
And for she who fights sincerely.
She alone is worthy.

But the youngest of the three looked with fiery eyes at Hertha and said,
Blessed are those who have *the vision*,
Who fight in faith and in hope!
They shall be welcome.
They shall win the victory!

Hertha did not understand the words of the Norns. She understood only that she was not worthy to drink from the life-giving spring, that they had rejected her.

(...) But she did not sit long like this. Her soul arose, she remembered the words of the Norns by the spring of Urd, "it is only for the courageous and for she who fights sincerely!" And a mighty desire arose in her to liberate herself and her captive sister-souls. (...) "I want to fight sincerely!"

The flame in her heart burst high, lifted her from the earth and made her soar through the air, high above the heads of the legislators. This feeling filled her with joy and hope and she thought, "The curse on me and my sisters shall be lifted, and our kind may after all be among the free!"

Involuntarily, she turned towards the east towards the region, where she had seen the sun rise, and borne as on invisible wings, she soared forth over the earth. But suddenly she felt flight impeded, and a harsh voice called out,

"Halt! Wer da?"

---

[1]   The three Norse goddesses of Fate are called Urd, Verdandi, and Skuld.

Hertha answered, "A soul who seeks freedom, life and happiness for herself and her many sisters!"

"What is that?" the voice said, "a soul? And you are a woman? Away you go! In this country women are not allowed to have souls. They are not counted among the population. You are not allowed to enter. About face! Forward march!"

"Who are you?" asked Hertha, "and what right do you have to command me?"

"What right?" thundered the voice. "I am the great Imperial Ukase[2] and I stand at my post to prevent any contraband from entering the country."

"But I am not contraband", said Hertha, "I am only a soul, who …"

"Don't argue, obey", interrupted the voice, "or you'll get shipped to Siberia. The soul of a woman, who is seeking freedom, that is the most dangerous contraband in the world."

"Allow me only to pass through your country, o great Ukase; I do not want to stay there, I am aiming to go further east, where the sun rises!" pleaded Hertha.

"You are a polite person," said the Ukase in a milder tone, "and although I will not allow you to pass freely through my country, I will let you catch a glimpse of the east, which will cure your infatuation with freedom." And he allowed her to peer through a large looking-glass all the way to China, where not only the souls of the women but also their feet are bound, and in all parts of the world where the sun rises, she saw the women oppressed and disregarded, except when they were feared as tyrannical and vengeful powers, which happened sometimes, when they had broken their chains by force.

"What have they done?" asked Hertha, "to be treated like that."

"Aren't they being well provided for?" answered the Ukase, "they have what they deserve and need. Yes, in my holy land, still much better. Here the women are outrageously well off. As souls, they are not required to pay taxes to the crown, and they are allowed to inherit one fourteenth part of the estate of their parents. In addition, they are allowed to dress gaudily and talk nonsense as much as they like, provided that they are obedient and do not want to fly too high. Listen, girl! You are good-looking and I like you; stay here and you can become a slave to a rich Bojar.[3] Come, you will have a good life!" And the great Ukase grabbed Hertha by the arm.

Proud and terrified, she broke loose and fled, hurling a glance full of contempt at the great Ukase. She fled towards the north, where she saw lights glimmer and heard joyful songs on the shores of Arctic Ocean. They were savage, nomadic people roaming the desolate tundra and through its icy primeval forests. They were now celebrating their fair and a wedding. Hertha saw the men tussle and fight as if drunk until they collapsed in the snow and fell asleep. In the hut, the women surrounded the bride and gave her to drink, while drinking themselves from a jug amid laughter and bantering.

Hertha asked them, "Are you free and happy?"

They answered, "What is freedom? Is it some kind of a brandy, then give us some so that we can give to our fathers and husbands that they will not abuse us. Give us some so that we may also feel happy. Otherwise – happy she who dies on her third night. We are born to bondage."

The north wind roared across the icy field and the wedding scene disappeared in the cloud of whirling snow. Then came the calm and the Aurora Borealis danced a torch dance around the arctic circle, and there was light like the brightest day. And in this light Hertha saw crowds of men and women, dressed in furs, moving about their reindeer and dogs. But everywhere among these wild hordes, the women were the servants of the men, and their equals only in times of drunkenness and fights. Sometimes, however, the women

---

[2]   Imperial Russian official who delivers a public edict.
[3]   A title of old Russian nobility.

turned into witches and were called "wise", and were then both feared and obeyed, because their power was great to do evil and to take revenge, and their glance, which were called "the evil eye" had the power to bring misfortune on both man and beast.

With a shudder, Hertha turn away from this region and its people, and again she soared over the earth, but now towards the warm countries of the south.

She saw a different sky than the severe sky of the north, a more beautiful and more fertile earth, abounding in flowers and fruits. The air was sweet like the goodness itself, water gushed from springs, music filled the air, everything seemed to swell with joy of life. She found herself in a large garden near a large city.

"Oh!" thought Hertha, "here people must be free, good and happy, here I will find freedom for myself and my captive sisters."

But then some solemn and magisterial looking persons from the big city approached her and said, "You speak of freedom. You are a suspicious person. What do you want here?"

She replied, "I am seeking freedom for myself and my sisters!   "

The official looking gentlemen looked at each other and smiled, as if they wanted to say, "She is out of her mind." And they said again to her, "What do you want?" She repeated her answer.

They asked, "Are you rich?"

"No," she replied, "my soul and my will are my only wealth."

"Then you are a foolish woman" they answered. "Get married, if you can, or go into a convent."

Hertha answered, "No, I want to live and work in freedom and innocence for the goals I have set for myself."

They said, "No freedom is innocent; least of all in women. An old curse rests upon your sex. And in any case, you are a dangerous person, because you speak of freedom and you come from a country, where freedom has struck deep roots since olden times and has grown into a large tree, they say, and where women have fought for the freedom of their country more than once; therefore, you may not roam free here."

"Oh," thought Hertha; "they do not know how little freedom the women in my country have." But she did not say anything, because she did not want to disgrace the laws of her land.

All at once, she heard a great clamor, "To the convent, to the dungeons with the foolish woman, the freedom fanatic!" And a flock of men dressed in black grabbed her and brought her by force to a large and sinister building with small grated windows. Fear and anger made her strong, she tore herself away from their hands and fled; the flame in her heart flared up, and carried her off, away until she could no longer hear the threatening and mocking voices. Then she stopped and saw that she had left the big city, the smoke of which rose in the distance. Tired, she sat down on a stone, but felt so alone and abandoned, and so distressed over the cruelty of men, and the curse that rested on her sex, that she began to weep bitterly.

At that, a brilliant, glittering cloud came floating from the big city, and settled down on the ground close to the place where Hertha was sitting. It was like it was woven of fluttering gauze, spangled with silver and gold; and from it emerged lovely young girls in airy attire, with eyes sparkling with joy and garlands on their heads. They approached her and said,

"Why do you weep?"

Hertha replied, "I weep because there is a curse on me and my sex, which banishes us from working in freedom and in joy."

The girls smiled and said, "Oh, what curse? What banishment? Don't worry about what those sourly people are saying. Be bold and merry, then you can be as free as you want. You are too young and beautiful to weep away your life. Come along with us and do what we do. We want to take you up into our society."

"And what do you do? And who are you?" asked Hertha with beating heart, half fascinated by the looks and words of the girls, half fearing something she saw in them, but could not name.

The young women smiled and looked at each other and answered,

"We are called ladies of pleasure; because we live for pleasure alone. We play with the hearts of men, and we rule them. If they sometimes play cruel games with us, we can take revenge. And if they get trapped in our nets, there is no escape for them in all their days. We ensnare them and laugh at those who fancy themselves as our masters."

"What is your intent with all this, and what do you live for?" asked Hertha again.

The girls laughed and answered, "We live for the moment. We ask for nothing more than to enjoy the day and to amuse ourselves as best we can. We are the freest of creatures on this earth. We live freely or at other people's expense in all countries. We follow no laws except our own fancy; we obey no duties. We take husbands and then desert them, as it pleases us. We might have children like other women, but do not bind ourselves like other women to sit and slave for them; we merely look after our own pleasures."

"You might have children and will not take care of them?" said Hertha astonished. "Who takes care of your children then?"

"We don't know exactly," answered the girls; the people at the orphanages; we do not have time for that. We want to be free women."

"Oh!" said Hertha, "your freedom is not the kind I yearn for, your freedom is a mistake! You believe that you are free, but you are slaves of ..."

"What, we slaves!" shouted the girls laughingly, "come, we will show you how we are bound! ..."

And they pulled Hertha along in dancing circles; in vain, she asked them to let her go, they dragged her along, whirling around in dizzy, bewildering circles until her senses seemed about to leave her, and anguish took hold of her heart. But the ladies of the night danced and drank wine, shouting, "This way, this way! Until the end of life; this way, this way until eternity! ..."

"Oh, this is horrible!" exclaimed Hertha, as she finally freed herself from their line, "get away from me. I will have no part of your freedom!"

"So go ahead and live by your virtue", the ladies of the night laughed contemptuously, "we live by other rules!" And they veiled themselves in the glittering cloud, which now, as if on millions of butterfly wings, floated back to the big city. It was a splendid sight, and Hertha continued to hear the sound of their merry voices and laughter for a long time.

With a profound melancholy, Hertha looked at the cloud and said to herself, "They feel free and happy; and I! ..." The flame in her heart flared up, and she felt that she was born for something better than their happiness. But for what?

(...)

It seemed to Hertha that her soul was transformed, and that the flame that strove and yearned thereby assumed another character. It had yearned to warm and do good; now it only wanted to punish. She had been transformed into a dangerous creature, who spread destruction around her. The flame in her heart spread all through her limbs and everything she touched was kindled by it. Her hand had become a flaming torch. She touched her paternal home and wild flames burst forth. She saw them grow higher and higher and spread to all sides, setting fire to more and more houses. She heard the bells tolling, the beating of the alarm-drum, the shouting and clamor of the people, the noise of the ice carts and the fire engines. For every minute, the tumult increased, and she heard some-body whisper in her ear: "Arson! Arson!" An unspeakable anguish overcame her, because it seemed to her that this was of her doing. All at once the thought occurred to her as it sometimes does in distressing dreams: "This must be a dream!" She tried to wake up, fighting violently with the dream spirit that held her captive and succeeded at last and – she woke up.

Primary Works

Teckningar utur Hvardagslivet:
   Axel och Anna; Tvillingarna; Förhoppningar, 1828.
   *Den ensamma; Tröstarinnan; Famillen H *** 1,* 1830.
   *Famillen H*** 2,* 1831. Eng. tr. *The H-Family,* 1844. Includes also *The Bondmaid and Other Tales.* Eng. tr. *The Colonel's Family,* 1995.
Nya teckningar utur hvardagslifvet:
   Presidentens döttrar: Berettelse af en guvernant, 1834. Eng. tr. *The President's Daughters* 1, 1843; *The President's Daughters* 2, 1844.
   Nina, 1835. Eng. tr., 1844.
   Grannarne, 1837. Eng. tr. *The Neighbours: A Story of Every-day Life,* 1843.
   Hemmet, eller familjesorger och fröjder 1-4, 1839. Eng. tr. *The Home: or Family Cares and Family Joys,* 1843.
   Strid och fred, eller några scener i Norge, 1840.
   En dagbok, 1843. Eng. tr. *A Diary,* 1850.
   I Dalarna, 1845. Eng. tr. *The Parsonage of Mora,* 1845.
   Syskonlif, 1848. Eng. tr. *Brothers and Sisters,* 1848.
Trälinnan, 1840.
Morgon-väckter, 1842. Eng. tr. *Morning Watches,* 1843.
Midsommarresan, 1848. Eng. tr. *The Midnight Sun: A Pilgrimage,* 1849.
Ett par blad från Rhenstranden, 1848.
Lif i Norden, 1849.
Hemmen i den nya verlden 1-3, 1853-54. Eng. tr. *Homes of the New World: Impressions of America* 1-2, 1854.
Hertha, 1856. Eng. tr., 1856.
Fader och dotter, 1858.
Lifvet i den gamla verlden 1-4, 1860-62.
Fredrika Bremers brev 1-4. Klara Johanson and Ellen Kleman, eds., 1915-20.
Brev. Ny följd, tidigare ej samlade och tryckta brev 1-2, Carina Burman, ed., 1996.

Selected Bibliography

Burman, Carina. *Bremer: En Biografi.* Stockholm: Albert Bonniers Förlag, 2001.

Rooth, Signe Alice. *Seeress of the Northland: Fredrika Bremer's American Journey 1849-1851.* Philadelphia: American Swedish Historical Foundation, 1955.

Sundell, Gunnar. *Med Fredrika Bremer i America.* Stockholm: Carlsson, 1993.

Stendahl, Brita K. *The Education of a Self-Made Woman: Fredrika Bremer 1801-1865.* Lewiston/Queenston/Lampeter: The Edwin Mellen Press, 1994.

Wendelius, Lars. *Fredrika Bremers Amerikabild: en studie i* Hemmen i den nya verlden. Stockholm: Almqvist & Wiksell International, 1985.

Wieselgren, Greta. *Fredika Bremer och verkligheten: romanen Herthas tillblivelse.* Stockholm: Norstedts, 1978.

Camilla Collett: Norway's First Feminist Writer[1]

SARAH J. PAULSON (NORWEGIAN UNIVERSITY OF TECHNOLOGY AND SCIENCE/NTNU)

Camilla Collett's (1813-95) authorship is groundbreaking in Norwegian literary history in several regards. Her literary breakthrough, *Amtmandens Døttre* (1854-55; Eng. tr. *The District Governor's Daughters*, 1992), which was published anonymously in two parts, created a sensation because of its revolutionary qualities.[2] Today *The District Governor's Daughters* is often referred to as Norway's first modern novel:[3] As well as being Norway's first socially critical piece of literature, it is also the first Norwegian work to focus on women's issues and on the conditions of women's lives. And it is the first Norwegian narrative to be told from a woman's point of view.

In *The District Governor's Daughters* Collett depicts bourgeois life and marriage and illustrates how the repressive bourgeois conventions of the *embetsstand*[4] affected women's lives and their happiness. According to these norms and conventions, a woman's lot is to marry. Thus, women are submitted to a *støpegodsoppdragelse*[5] which shapes them according to a feminine ideal that Collett insists is "based on the concepts tolerate – en-

---

[1] This essay is dedicated to the memory of Leslie Grove (1960-1997), who chose "Meeting Again" to represent Camilla Collett in this anthology and who began the translation, which she unfortunately was unable to complete before her sudden and unexpected death. The completion of the translation was generously sponsored by NORLA (the Norwegian information office for Norwegian Literature Abroad).

[2] See Aarnes (1977) for a presentation of the reception of *Amtmandens Døttre*.

[3] Bjørnstjerne Bjørnson's *Synnøve Solbakken* (1857) has also been given this title because of its groundbreaking language and style of narration. *Synnøve Solbakken*, named for its protagonist, is a bondefortelling, literally a "peasant's story", that can be described as a short novel depicting peasants and country life.

[4] Embetsstand refers to the bourgeoisie, the "ruling" class to which civil servants and government officials belonged.

[5] Støpegodsoppdragelse is a term Collett uses to criticize the way women are molded for marriage by their upbringing: Women are compared with støpegods, Norwegian for castings, which are identically formed in a mold.

dure – suffer – be silent, in short, on the most complete relinquishment of the self".[6] However, with *The District Governor's Daughters*, she argues for personal emancipation for women, the right of women to develop as free and happy individuals who have a voice in deciding their own futures and in choosing their own husbands. This early feminist stance is made explicit by Collett's later suggestion that *Et lands døtre* (A Nation's Daughters) might be a more fitting title for the book:[7] The four daughters of the district governor portrayed in the novel are to be understood as representatives of (bourgeois) women in general.

In her later critical essays, Collett continued to be a pioneer of women's rights, using her pen to fight for improved conditions for women. Not only was she Norway's first feminist writer, she was also Norway's first feminist literary critic, calling attention to literature's role in promoting conventional feminine ideals through depictions of passive, self-effacing women, and to what she saw as the role of the novel: to effect a change in attitude towards and among women through portrayals of strong, independent female heroes.

The focus of Camilla Collett's collected works is a woman's place in society. But her varied authorship also includes reflections on topics such as animal care, the monarchy, and famous people she met. She points out the virtues of taking walks in the fresh air, depicts nature and city life at home and abroad, and uses personal experiences and anecdotes to shed light on social and moral problems. Fiction dominates Collett's early authorship; in addition to *The District Governor's Daughters*, it includes a single volume of shorter prose pieces entitled *Fortællinger* (1861; Tales) and the autobiographical *I de lange Nætter* (1863; During the Long Nights). *Sidste Blade* (1868, 1872, 1873; Last Pages),[8] *Fra de Stummes Leir* (1877; From the Camp of the Mutes) and *Mod Strømmen* (1879, 1885; Against the Stream)[9] form the latter part of her authorship. In these six volumes additional genres are represented: non-fictional essays, travelogues, speeches, art and literary reviews, occasional poetry, and personal poems.

Seen in its entirety, Collett's authorship is significant because of her stylistic and linguistic mastery and because she placed women's problems on the agenda of the day. Her writings had an acknowledged influence on writers such as Bjørnstjerne Bjørnson (1832-1910), Henrik Ibsen (1828-1906), Jonas Lie (1833-1908), and Alexander Kielland (1849-1906). Thus,

---

[6]   *Samlede Verker* 2, 377.

[7]   See Collett's preface to the third edition of *Amtmandens Døttre* (1879).

[8]   *Sidste Blade*, subtitled "Memories and Confessions", was published in three volumes specified as "First Series" (1868), "Second and Third Series" (1872) and "Fourth and Fifth Series" (1873).

[9]   *Mod Strømmen* was published in two volumes specified as "First Series" (1879) and "Second Series" (1885).

Collett has a unique position in Norwegian cultural history; it is undoubt-edly her literary prestige and her influence on later feminist thought in Norway and Scandinavia that led to the placement of her image on the most commonly used bill of Norwegian currency, the hundred crown note.[10]

However, Camilla Collett is also a prominent figure in Norwegian cul-tural history through her family connections and circumstances of life. She was the daughter of Alette Thaulow and pastor Nicolai Wergeland, one of "Eidsvoll's men" who signed Norway's constitution at Eidsvoll in 1814, and the sister of the famous romantic poet Henrik Wergeland (1808-1845). At the age of seventeen Camilla Wergeland met and fell in love with her brother's political and literary rival Johan Sebastian Welhaven (1807-1873).[11] This doomed relationship provided the source of inspiration for *The District Governor's Daughters*, which Collett calls "my life's long repressed scream."[12] Because she dwelt upon her "lost love" for the rest of her life, this loss influenced her other work as well. Indeed, Collett indi-cates that her relationship to Welhaven gave a greater impetus to her under-standing of and work for women's issues than anything else.[13]

***

Camilla Collett began her writing career in the 1840s, writing stories and essays together with her husband Peter Jonas Collett.[14] These were pub-lished as serials in the conservative paper *Den Constitutionelle* until it folded in 1847. Her first solo publication, "Nogle Strikketøisbetragtninger" (Some Knitting Observations), was printed as a serial[15] here in 1842. Col-lett regarded this as her literary debut, later referring to the piece as "my first terrifying step on the path to becoming an author."[16] Two longer sto-

---

[10] The one hundred crown note depicting Camilla Collett, which was produced from 1979-1997, was replaced in 1997 by a new note bearing the picture of the famous singer Kirsten Flagstad (1895-1962).

[11] Both Wergeland and Welhaven were interested in building Norway as an independent nation, but they disagreed as to the means Norway should use to promote her inde-pendence. Wergeland, who saw nationalism as a political and constitutional concept, fought for a radical cultural and linguistic break from Denmark. For Welhaven, on the other hand, nationalism was culturally contingent, having to do with language and his-tory. Therefore, he maintained that Norway's cultural, literary and linguistic inheri-tance from Denmark should be an essential ingredient in building an independent Norwegian national identity.

[12] *Samlede Verker* 2, 63.

[13] See Alf Collett 1911, 62.

[14] In 1841 Camilla Wergeland married Peter Jonas Collett, a lawyer and writer who later became a university professor. They had four sons. Camilla Collett was widowed in 1851.

[15] A serial is a personal literary form including memories, observations and/or argumen-tation which make up a critical essay or prose piece.

[16] *Samlede Verker* 2, 295.

ries entitled "Kongsgaard" (The Neighbors' Estate[17]) and "Et Gjensyn" (Meeting Again) came out anonymously in 1847 and 1851 respectively.[18] In addition, she was not only a consultant for Peter Christian Asbjørnsen (1812-1885) and Jørgen Moe (1813-1882), but she also contributed to their folktale publications, writing, for instance, the realistic frame around the witch legends in "Graverens fortellinger" (The Grave-digger's Tales).[19]

In the 1840s and 1850s Collett wrote a number of prose pieces which she called stories, sketches or tales. These were inspired both by the realis-tic *Hverdagshistorier* (Everyday Stories) of the Danish writer Thomasine Gyllembourg (1773-1856) and by Maurits Hansen's (1794-1842) short stories. Liv Bliksrud (1998) has pointed out the fantastic element in these stories. She maintains fantasy breaks the illusion of the triviality and pre-dictability of reality; in these texts, life itself becomes a fantastic story. Indeed, magic tales, legends, dreams, superstitions and unbelievable occur-ances are woven within realistic frames depicting local and everyday events. While there are strictly speaking no supernatural or "fantastic" elements in "Meeting Again", it can nevertheless be seen to be a variation on the pattern. "Destiny" or "fate" is present in the chance and unlikely meeting between the middle-aged Mr. M. and the widowed Fredrikke, just as it was years earlier with the uncanny arrival of student Wilhelm Barth at the ball and the untimely interruptions of M.'s and Fredrikke's private conversations.

With its realistic elements and the "fantastic" presence of "fate", "Meet-ing Again" is representative of Collett's early prose pieces. The excerpts printed here exemplify how Collett wrote in dialogue with the romantic ideas and ideals that influenced the literary aesthetics of the time. The "commonplace and ordinary" event of being in love is portrayed in a poetic and extraordinary way through the eyes of young Mr. M. Thus, the realistic detail of the middle-aged Fredrikke is offset by Mr. M.'s romantic and

---

[17] Kongsgaard, which literally means "King's Farm", is both a place name and a family name. In this short story, it is the name of a large farm (estate) that is owned by a wealthy, noble family. Here the narrator tells of how she is fascinated and thrilled by this neighboring estaste as a child, of how she uncovers a secret about the estate and of how she later as a young woman finally hears the tragic story of love, jealousy and sorrow that "haunts" the estate.

[18] "Kongsgaard" was published in an anthology edited by Peter Christian Asbjørnsen entitled *Hjemmet og Vandringen – en Aarbog for 1847* (Home and Away – A Year-book for 1847), "Et Gjensyn" appeared in Asbjørnsen's "winter publication" *Ydale. Et vinterskrift* (1851; The Misty Valley; i.e. the wintery sky, the name of the dwelling of the Norse god Ull). Both were later published in *Fortællinger* (1861; Stories).

[19] Asbjørnsen and Moe, the most famous collectors and editors of Norwegian folktales and legends published in the mid-1800s, are the Norwegian equivalent of the German Brothers Grimm. "Graverens fortellinger" was published in Asbjørnsen's *Norsk Hul-dreeventyr og Folkesagn* (1845; Norwegian Huldre Tales and Folk Legends).

idealistic descriptions of her youthful, feminine beauty. In pointing out the suffering caused by romantic love as well as the harm done by societal norms and conventions regulating courtship and proper behavior, "Meeting Again" thematically foreshadows The District Governor's Daughters and prefigures the early feminist views found in much of Collett's work.

***

An undramatized third person narrator sets the stage in "Meeting Again", addressing the reader directly with comments, questions and sighs such as, "Who has not had occasion to see one of these dismal figures at one's door?" and "Ah, but what complexity can fully portray such a tragic life, so many-sided and substantial in its monotony, so lacking in poetry and trivial in its misery!" Today formal techniques such as these seem old-fashioned, but are common in texts from this period, functioning to make the story appear more probable and believable (i.e. realistic). Although modern readers have undoubtedly not seen "one of these dismal figures at one's door", these comments also steer the reader into an understanding and sympathetic role; the reader is to identify with Cabinet Minister M.'s response to the unfortunate woman who has sought his help. Since the narrator directs our attention toward her coarse appearance and hard life, it may seem that this woman is the central figure of this short story. However, Mr. M. is the protagonist of "Meeting Again"; his feelings for the young Rikke as well as his reaction to seeing her as the middle-aged woman described by the narrator constitute the focus of the text. Like so many of Collett's texts, the theme in "Meeting Again" is unhappy love; here the depiction of a ball, a metaphor for bourgeois relationships based on conventions and "rules for the 'acceptable and the appropriate'",[20] forms the background for the dramatic culmination of young M.'s and Rikke's "relationship". As with Sara Sandmark in "Eventyr-Sara og hendes Datter" (Fairy Tale-Sara and her Daughter; Eng. tr. *Storyteller Sara*, 1984),[21] M.'s hopes are dashed and his life is unexpectedly changed during the evening of the ball: Fredrikke is charmed by the dashingly handsome and persistent Mr. Barth, whose bold, self-important and shameless conduct is contrasted with M.'s shy, gentlemanly and "proper" behavior in Collett's descriptions of the ball at Storemoen.

In order to portray the characters' thoughts from a personal point of view at a time when techniques such as inner monologue and stream-of-consciousness were not yet in currency, Camilla Collett included excerpts

---

[20] *Samlede Verker* 3, 37. See the essay "Frisk Luft!" (1879; Fresh Air!) in which balls are contrasted with hikes in the fresh air.

[21] "Eventyr-Sara og hendes Datter" first appeared as a serial under the title "Badeliv og Fjeldliv" (Bathing Life and Mountain Life) in 1843. Published in its revised form in *Fortællinger* (1861), it was later incorporated into *I de lange Nætter* (1863).

of personal documents such as letters and diaries in her texts. In "Meeting Again", Mr. M. becomes absorbed in reading his personal account of the fateful evening of the ball that he has taken from "an old portfolio bound in leather". This portfolio is kept in a secret compartment of his desk; metaphorically speaking, this compartment is the innermost part of his soul. This way, the reader is allowed to "read" M.'s mind: "We will read it with him."

With the transition to M.'s account, we leave the (realistic) frame placed in the present and move to a related or parallel story that took place in the past. The use of this "Chinese box structure" was common at the time, and conventionally the frame begins and ends the narrative such that the narrative of the past is enclosed by the narrative of the present. In "Meeting Again", Collett deviates from this norm and reduces the frame to a brief introduction of the characters. Therefore, one might agree with Ellisiv Steen (1947) that it appears to function only as an excuse for turning to M.'s romantic account of the past. However, the frame plays a central role in the text. Since the second half of the frame is "missing," the narrative ends with M.'s account, dated December 28, 1832, of what happened exactly one year earlier. Thus, there is no return to the narrative's present which takes place "after so many years have passed." In this way, the structure of the text underlines how M.'s past has overtaken and merged with the present.

The reception of "Meeting Again" was positive. Reviewers such as Andreas Munch in the newspaper *Christiania-Posten* (December 22, 1850) praised the author's masterly command of language and style, characterizing the story as "well told" and "a striking genre painting".[22] A review in *Idun* (1/1851), subtitled "journal for literature and art", reads as follows:

> Such a true and moving episode is painted on these few pages that they contain more than most multi-volume novels. A heart's dream and disappointment is painted with the most elegant and lightest strokes, at times somewhat weak, but without being overwrought, without startling effects. The story is guided forward so surely and evenly that not one word is superfluous, merely a decoration.[23]

This reviewer also called attention to the text's realistic qualities in describing it as a "true episode" written "without being overwrought, without startling effects". Collett's contemporaries were, indeed, impressed by the realistic, believable and life-like dimensions of its characters. In the words of another reviewer, "The crude and vulgar are depicted with the same subtlety as the heartfelt, the graceful and the gentle, and yet it is real living people and not transparent novel characters who appear before us."[24]

---

[22]   Steen 1947, 219.
[23]   Ibid.
[24]   Ibid.

According to Ellisiv Steen (1947), "Meeting Again" is a "story about disappointed love (...) composed as a realistic description, with certain comic features that alleviate its tragic aspects."[25] While she agrees with Collett's contemporaries that "Meeting Again" is a linguistic masterpiece and points out the vitality and energy in the story, Steen's biographical approach forces her to conclude that this piece with its male protagonist is not as good as "The Neighbors' Estate", which "brought a message from the depths of her soul in a different way than 'Meeting Again'".[26] Liv Bliksrud (1998) does not compare and evaluate "Meeting Again" with "The Neighbors' Estate" as Steen does, but she otherwise agrees with Steen's comments about the text, suggesting that the fantastic element in "Meeting Again" lies in life itself, in destiny's tragi-comic play with people's lives.[27]

While the perspectives of Steen and Bliksrud offer certain insight into the text, I suggest that the key to understanding "Meeting Again" lies in the ironic juxtaposition of the "realistic description" with M.'s (and Rikke's) romantic ideals of love. The irony that permeates the entire narrative is closely connected with the role that destiny plays in M.'s and Fredrikke's lives. The frame functions to contrast and parallel M.'s account, visualizing and underlining the irony in his narrative: Here the irony of Fredrikke's situation is made perfectly clear. Not only does she choose an admirer who proves to be a brutal, lazy and thoughtless husband who gives her a life of worry and economic hardship, but she also asks M., whom she rejected, for financial assistance after widowhood accentuates her plight. M.'s important and lucrative position as cabinet minister, in addition to his resolve to be "a kind of gentle providence, one she shall never have cause to blush over," emphasize the irony of Fredrikke's choice.

The young M.'s naivité, blindness and lack of insight caused by his love for Rikke are also subjected to irony throughout his written account of "that evening's events." M.'s eyes are opened during the course of the evening of the ball and he sees Fredrikke for the first time as the deceitful, capricious girl she "really" is, "the heartless flirt, the twice breaker of promises." However, the focus in M.'s written account on his admiration for Fredrikke's beauty reveals that he still loves her a year later and that romantic dreams and ideals still cloud his vision. The irony in the text exposes the naivité in the young M.'s resolve to "recount this miserable story feature by feature with unadorned precision" so that "it will be over and done with for eternity." In fact, the irony in M.'s parting comment to Miss Lemvig ultimately seems to be directed at M. himself: "It is the first, but certainly also the last time that I have had the misfortune to intoxicate my-

---

[25] Ibid., 217-18.
[26] Ibid., 220.
[27] Both Bliksrud and Steen comment that Collett uses material from her childhood in Eidsvoll as background for this story.

self on bad liquor." M.'s first love is seemingly also his last: As a middle-aged man he can finally be a chivalric "knight in a fairy tale" who comes to Fredrikke's rescue even though "the prize of victory" is not as he envisioned it many years earlier on the night of ball.

While Collett plays on the metaphors of blindness and (in)sight throughout the text, the frame and Norwegian title explicitly contrast the characters in relation to these metaphors: Only M. is aware of the irony of their meeting since Fredrikke does not appear to recognise him. Thus, it is only his eyes that are opened and that "see again" [*gjen-syn*]. For M.'s romantic ideals, which were shaken during the evening of the ball and which have been hidden in the depths of his heart, locked up in his desk, "almost forgotten" during his existence as cabinet minister, are unearthed and shaken again when he is confronted with the middle-aged Fredrikke. His response to seeing Rikke, whose "mouth, the soul's unmistakeable mirror, (...) now appeared in all its discouraging coarseness", reflects his agitated state of mind: "He himself sat or rather threw himself onto a sofa, overwhelmed by an inner agitation while his hand flew over his high, balding forehead, as if to chase away a troubling memory." The emotion, discomfort and unwillingness with which M. reacts to seeing "the dream of his youth" in her "ruination" indicate that he has not changed as much as the glimpse of his trivial and prosaic life as cabinet minister would seem to imply. Thus, the irony in the frame draws attention to the unchanged quality of M.'s feelings and romantic dispositions even though "so many years have passed." Romantic ideals, the text implies, do not reflect or harmonize with reality.

While "Meeting Again" points out both M.'s and Rikke's lack of (in)sight in their choices in love, sympathy in the text for these unfortunate figures, victims of convention, the "rules of the ball," offsets the irony and adds elements of tragedy to the narrative. Camilla Collett[28] laments the tragedy visualized in "Meeting Again" in her essay "Frisk Luft!" (Fresh Air!),

> Ah, how many mistakes, how many bitter, erroneous assumptions have not been the result of cotillions[29] and chandeliers! How much unhappiness can not a well-placed garland of flowers in a few fluttering locks cause in only one evening... mistakes, errors, that it later takes a whole long, miserable, wasted life to atone for!

Thus, "Meeting Again" can also be read as a (feminist) critique of bourgeois norms and conventions of love and courtship as well as an acknowledgment of "the thousands, who have suffered irreparable damage at balls".[30]

---

[28] *Samlede Verker* 3, 38.
[29] The cotillion is a complex, formalized dance in which the head couple leads the other dancers through elaborate and stately figures.
[30] *Samlede Verker* 3, 37.

Et Gjensyn

Utdrag

Sind Sie Maria? fragt' ich voll Entsetzen.
Und steinern und metallos scholl eine Stimm':
So nennen mich die Leute.

Heine

Det var endnu tidlig Morgen i Statsraad M.s Arbeidsværelse. Hr. M. sad saa fordybet over sin Pult, at han ikke merkede Tjeneren, forinden denne stod lige ved hans Bord for at melde, at den Kone, der to Gange før forgjæves havde søgt ham, nu atter stod udenfor med indstændig Begjæring om at faa ham i Tale. Et Vink, og den anmeldte traadte ind.

Det var en middelaldrende Kone med et Ansigt, af hvilket kummerfuld Huslighed havde udslettet ethvert Ungdommens og Mildhedens Spor for at indgrave Lidelsens og Bitterhedens Merker istedet. Hun var iført en gammel sort Fløielshat, en brun Kaabe af et forældet Snit, kantet med slidte Frynser, og endelig en Krave, hvori hver Fold fortalte om Nød og Trang. Hvo har ikke havt Anledning til at se en af disse traurige Skikkelser indenfor sin Dør?

Hun lod ikke den, hun søgte, længe i Tvil om sit Erende. Med den Indledning, at hun vel ikke havde den Ære at kjende Hans Høivelbaarenhed, men at hun dog, saavel paa Grund af hans Ry for Velgjørenhed som paa Grund af hans formaaende Embedsstilling, vovede at henvende sig til ham om Hjælp, tog hun et sammenlagt Papir ud af et Bomuldstørkæde og præsenterede ham det.

M. kastede et flygtigt Blikk paa Papiret; det var en Liste, hvorpaa en del gavmilde Mennesker havde skrevet sine Navne. Han var bleven staaende foran hende og hørte venlig og taalmodig til, medens hun med kvindelig Vidtløftighed opramsede for ham den gamle velbekjendte Elendighedshistorie. Ak, hvilken Vidtløftighed kan tilfulde skildre en saadan Livstragedie, saa mangfoldig og indholdsrig i sin Ensformighed, saa poesiløs og triviel i sin Jammersfylde! Født af en god Familie, gift med en Mand, der var ligesaa brutal som letsindig, og som derhos manglede baade Evne og Vilje til at ernære hende og den voksende Barneflok, Enke uden Enkepension, efterladt i en af Landets afsides Kyststæder, hvor hendes Mand i de sidste Aar som Opsynsmand for en Skibsbygger havde havt et kummerligt Livsophold... dette var Grundtrækkene i den Skildring, hun udkastede af sit Liv.

Nu var hun taget ind til Christiania i Haab om at finde Hjælp hos en der bosat Broder; men ogsaa han var død og hans Enke trængende som hun.

"I hvilken Stilling var Deres Mand, før han modtog hin Opsynsbetjening?" spurgte M. deltagende.

"Ak, i slet ingen. Nu og da erhvervede han lidt ved Skriveri paa et Embedskontor. Det var bitre Aar; jeg syede Nat og Dag; men det forslaar lidet til at underholde en Mand og fem Børn med."

"Men hvor kunde da De, der, som De siger, var af god Familie, indlade Dem paa at egte en Mand, der intet var og intet vilde være?"

"Ak, Deres Høivelbaarenhed! Et Ungdoms Feiltrin..."

"Saa, saa, " afbrød M. hende og undveg et uanfegtet Blik af et Par hvasse, blaa Øine, der for længe siden havde tabt ethvert Udtryk af Sarthed og Blu.

"De var," tilføiede han, "en Datter af...?"

"Afdøde Foged Lemvig i Østerdalen."

"Hvordan! Foged Lemvig – Foged Lemvig, der kom i Kassemangel?"
"Ak ja, det var min ulykkelige Fader…"
"Virkelig! O virkelig! Saa… hm…" sagde M. med forandret Stemme –; "sæt Dem ned, jeg beder Dem! Vær saa god!"
Hun tog neiende Plads paa en Stol, som han med et noget keitet Galanteri tilbød hende. Selv satte han sig eller meget mer kastede sig overvældet af en indre Bevægelse ned paa Sofaen, medens hans Haand fór over den høie, skaldede Pande, som for at bortjage en trykkende Erindring. De opskudte Briller var igjen gledne ned over Øinene, og mod sin Vilje fikserede han den ligeoverfor ham siddende Kvinde.
"Ak, det er hende," sagde han ved sig selv, "det er hende – min Ungdoms Drøm. Er det hende?" gjentog han, medens han, tabt i den smertelige Beskuen, intet hørte af hendes Talestrøm. Han betragtede disse haarde Træk, disse spidse Omrids, denne mørke, galdeagtige Rødme, hvormed daglig Harme og en sjælløs, forbitret Kamp med Eksistencen langsomt inætser Huden, denne Mund, Sjælens ubedragelige Speil, der nu fremtraadte i sin hele, afskrækkende Simpelhed… Hvor godt havde ikke et Par smilende ungdommelige Læber fordum vidst at skjule den…! Kun de tykke Lokker af en smuk Askefarve og de mørke Øienhaar havde overlevet Ødelæggelsen, og syntes næsten at skamme sig i de Omgivelser, hvori de befandt sig.
"Deres Fader," tog han med Anstrengelse tilorde, "har jeg kjendt i mine yngre Dage. Han havde da Anledning til at vise mig nogle Tjenester. Det er mig kjært, at Skjæbnen tillader mig at gjøre Gjengjæld mod hans Datter. Giv mig Deres Adresse, og senest paa Søndag skal De høre fra mig… Fat Mod, gode Kone!" vedblev han og reiste sig. "Noget skal jeg med Guds Hjælp kunne udrette for Dem. Stol paa en Mands bedste Vilje, der var Deres… Deres Faders Ven."
"O, er det muligt! Saa megen Godhed!… Gud lønne og velsigne Deres Høivelbaarenhed derfor!" Hun greb hans Haand, som om hun vilde kysse den; han fór forskrækket tilbage.
"Det er godt, det er godt. Altsaa senest paa Søndag… Denne Dør, maa jeg be'… Adjø, adjø… Tag Dem iagt for Trappen." Og han stod endnu i Vinduet og fulgte hende med Øinene, indtil hun forsvandt om Hjørnet.
Denne Dags Aften vandrede M. tankefuld op og ned i Værelset. En ualmindelig Bevægelse stod malet i hans markerede Træk. "Hvilket Møde!" sagde han for sig selv. "For første Gang efter saa mange Aars Forløb erindres jeg om en Tildragelse, der næsten var svunden mig al Minde. Og paa hvilken Maade…! Hun kjendte mig ikke, nei gudskelov! I den Afkrog, hvori hun har henslæbt sin elendige Tilværelse, har hun ganske tabt mit Spor. Hun anede ikke, at den, hun anraabte om en Almisse, var den forskudte; og hun skal aldrig ane det. Jeg vil være hende et mildt Forsyn, uden at hun skal rødme derover… Hvor levende drages mine Tanker tilbage til hin Aftens Begivenheder!"
Han aabnede sin Pult og fremdrog af en hemmelig Skuffe en gammel Portefølje i Skindbind. Den indeholdt, hva en Students Portefølje almindeligvis vil indeholde; Brevskaber, Dagbogsblade, Reisenotiser, poetiske Forsøg, Skisser, Tegninger o.s.v. Han fandt snart det Hefte, han søgte, og fordybede sig i dets Læsning.
Vi vil læse det med ham.

28de December 1832.

I dag er det netop Aarsdagen, siden det passerede. Jeg vil nu nedskrive Historien, og dermed skal den være endt og afsluttet for evige Tider.

Fjerde Juledag holdtes det store Bal hos Proprietræren paa Storemoen. (…) Vi drog i flere Vendinger derhen. Først Fogden og Smaagutterne, derpaa Jomfru *Borre* og *Fredrikke*; og i sidste Vending skulde endelig den gamle Kontorbetjent *Svendsen* og jeg afsted. (…) Endelig var jeg færdig, og jeg maatte selv tilstaa, at jeg var upaaklagelig. Med denne dobbelt behagelige Følelse kastede jeg mig i Slæden; nu turde jeg igjen uforstyrret overlade mig til mine Drømmerier. (…) Jeg tilbagekaldte mig i Erindringen, hvad jeg havde oplevet siden Fredrikkes Hjemkomst fra Byen forrige Vinter, hvor hun havde været for at lære Musik og Skræddersøm; hvorledes jeg havde kjæmpet med Fortryllelsen og længe troet mig sikker, indtil jeg merkede, at hun despotisk beherskede mine Tanker Nat og Dag.

Min tause Monolog lød omtrent saaledes:

Ved hvilket sælsomt Spil er den Tilstaaelse, jeg ofte var i Begreb med at gjøre hende, hver Gang bleven afbrudt! Snart kom en af hendes smaa Brødre trampende ind og bad om en Forklaring paa et Sted i Leksen; snart kom Jomfru Borre, den fatale Jomfru Borre! Man skulde tro, hun havde det paa Veiret, hvergang der var noget, hun kunde forpurre. Altid plumpede noget parodierende ind i den lykkelige Stemning.

Undertiden var det ogsaa Fredrikkes egen Overgivenhed, der var Skyld deri. (…) Disse hurtige Overgange fra Alvor til Lystighed er eiendommelige hos hende; man kan aldrig være ganske sikker paa nogen Stemning, og hun vender de andres ganske efter sin egen. Det er ikke Mangel paa Gemyt; det er Kaprice, ungdommeligt Overmod. Naar hun bliver ældre, og Livets Alvor har brudt dette Overmod, vil hun maaske blive elskværdigere, men ikke fortrylle mig mer end nu, da hun saa ofte saarer mig. Hun mangler ikke Sjæl, men Dannelse, det vil sige den Dannelse, som Livet giver.

(…) Ved mere end ett Tegn, blot synlige for mig, har Fredrikke givet mig at forstaa, at jeg ikke er hende ligegyldig. Nu maa det komme til en Forklaring, nu eller aldrig… Jeg holder ikke længer Uvissheden ud; nu eller aldrig… Det skal briste eller bære. Ikke der hjemme i Dagliglivets Tvang kunde det ske, men i Baltummelen, i Menneskevrimmelens Ensomhed, der er netop Stedet for tvende Hjerter til at udtale sig for hinanden. Nu eller aldrig! Nu eller aldrig klinger det ogsaa i Djeldene uden Ophør.

Saaledes omtrent var Gangen i mine Betragtninger, da vi fik Gaarden isigte. Det skinnede langt udover Jorderne fra de mange oplyste Vinduer som fra et fortryllet Slot. Som en forvoven Ridder i Eventyret stevnede ogsaa jeg med Sverd og Skjold hen for at erobre Seirens Pris, endnu uvidende om, hvad Drager og Rædsler der kunde være at bekjæmpe. Mit Mod sank betydelig, og jeg blev mere og mere beklemt, jo nærmere jeg kom Gaarden; dog, min Beslutning stod fast. Nu eller aldrig. Iaften skal det afgjøres.

(…)

Vi traadte ind i Forstuen. Ved Hjælp af to Løgter, der var anbragte paa hver Side af Døren, fik jeg i Hast mit Tøi afkastet; – jeg merkede, at vi var af de sidste. (…) Efter at have passeret et Par tomme Værelser standsede jeg paa Terskelen af et større. Dette var ganske opfyldt af Damer. (…) Mit Øie fandt snart den, det søgte. O Himmel, hvor hun var deilig! Man saa det først ret, naar hun sad mellem alle de andre. En lyserød, klar Kjole omgav hende som en rosenrød Sky; hendes eneste Prydelse var en stor, hvid Rose paa Haaret. Jeg vil ikke bruge det ligesaa forslidte som usande Udtryk, at den falmede og syntes graa mod hendes Hud. Den lod slet ikke til at skamme sig paa sin Plads; men det er visst, at hendes Huds friske Hvidhed og Rosens mattere Bleghed gjensidig hævede hinanden paa den vidunderligste Maade. Der skulde en Dristighed til som Jomfru Borres for at sætte sig netop ved *hendes* Side. Jomfru Borre har den ubeskrivelige Teint, der

ligner Lungemos; det er en Blanding af brunrødt, graat og grønligt. Hendes Haar, af en
sodet Sorthed, de bevægelige, changeante Øine, de store hvide Tænder bag den haanlige
Mund, alt er karakteristisk i dette Ansigt; dertil har Naturen af Kaprice givet hende en
smuk Figur, som maaske gjør, at hun endnu har Fordring paa Courtoisie. Hun er mere
frygtet end afholdt i Bygden formedelst sin skarpe Tunge, der intet skaaner. Satire i den
gemytløses og udannedes Mund er afskyelig og udarter kun til raa Harcelleren. Dog ved
hun godt at insinuere sig hos dem, hun vil vinde.

(…)

Hvor har en (…) første Dans et eiendommeligt Præg, som den næste allerede tildels
har tabt, og som længere hen ganske forsvinder! (…) Og Fredrikke! Hendes Øie
straalede! Man sige, hvad man vil, til de sorte Øines Pris, men de kan ikke have den
fængslende Magt, dette ubeskrivelige, som et Par smukke blaa. Kun de forstaar paa én
Gang at saare og læge, at byde og bede, og naar de nu ovenikjøbet tilsløres af et Par
lange, mørke Øienhaar som Fredrikkes! Hun har en eiendommelig Maade at bære sig paa
i Valsen: Hun bøier Hovedet mod Siden med halvt tillukkede Øine og en Mine, som om
hun overgav sig paa Naade og Unaade til den lykkelige, som omslynger hende; men
pludselig, som vilde hun straffe denne forvovne Tanke, hæver hun Hovedet stolt i Veiret,
og hendes Blikke udsender Lyn til alle Sider.

Længere ud paa Aftenen erholdt jeg Løfte om en Vals af hende; jeg ventede den med
sitrende Utaalmodighed. Da jeg ilede hen for at byde hende op, stødte det unge
Menneske, der engang før var kommen mig i Forkjøbet, til og gjorde samme Paastand.
Fredrikke syntes et Øieblik forlegen og mente, at det var den følgende Vals, hun havde
lovet mig. Jeg forsikrede, at hun udtrykkelig havde lovet mig denne. Det samme paastod
han.

"Hvor er det muligt, at jeg kan beholde alle disse Engagements i Hovedet," utbrød
Fredrikke. "De maa virkelig undskylde mig, om jeg engang imellem bliver lidt konfus."

"Da ved jeg ikke bedre, end at Jomfru Lemvig vælger mellem os to," sagde Personen,
som jeg siden fik at vide hed Wilhelm Barth, med seiersviss Mine. "Jeg tænker, Hr. M. er
tilfreds dermed."

Jeg afventede ikke denne Dom, men bukkede og trak mig tilbage. (...)

Aftenen svandt; det lakkede mod Ballets Ende; Kotillonen skulde begynde. Jeg troede
selv neppe paa min Lykke, da jeg endelig ved hendes Haand stillede mig op i Dansen.
Neppe havde vi taget Plads, saa viste Hr. Barth sig paa den anden Side. (...) Jeg forstod
intet, jeg vilde intet forstaa, jeg var døv og blind, og al min Kval var glemt, da hun efter
Dansen trykkede min Haand og sagde med den sødeste Stemme:

"Vi har jo næsten ikke talt et Ord sammen."

"Det er ikke min Skyld, Jomfru Lemvig."

"Sandelig endnu mindre min," svarede hun. "Hvad skal en stakkels Dame gjøre? Hun
har ingen Vilje, men enhver paatrængende, som ikke ligefrem fornærmer hende, har Lov
til at falde hende besværlig. (...)"

"O, Fredrikke!" raabte jeg og greb hendes Haand, som hun ikke trak tilbage –
"Fredrikke… Jomfru Lemvig… maa jeg styre Dem hjem i Aften?..." Min Stemme skalv.

Hun bøiede Hovedet nærmere, saa længe paa mig med det samme forskende,
uudgrundelige Smil; derpaa sagde hun neppe hørlig: "Ja," og forsvandt i Vrimmelen. Jeg
stod bedøvet som i en Rus tilbage. Dette Ja, det var allerede en Tilstaaelse… det klang saa
dybt og høitideligt… Ballet er endt om faa Minutter… O dette Ja, det blev hvisket som
foran et Alter!

(…)

Kaffen var nydt, og man lavede sig til Hjemreisen. Fogden var allerede dragen afsted.
Inde i Sovekammeret var der en skrækkelig Tumult og Snadren, inden Damerne kom i

Reisetøiet, inden alle disse brogede Sommerfugle fik forpuppet sig igjen i den uformelige Indhylling og lidt efter lidt forsvandt. Jeg havde i skjælvende Hast hjulpet Fredrikke den røde Kaabe med Kræmerskindsbremmen paa og knyttet hendes Sokker og løb nu ud for at finde Slæden. Da jeg kom tilbage, mødte hun mig paa Trappen. I den snævre Indhylling kunde hun hverken se eller røre sig; jeg bar hende derfor ned i Slæden, tog Plads ved Siden af hende og jagede afsted.

(...)

Hva jeg sagde til Fredrikke, medens vi fór (...) hen under de hvidpudrede, lyttende Graner...? Jeg ved det neppe mere; jeg ved kun, at Ordet strømmede fra Hjertet som en længe og voldsomt tilbageholdt Strøm. Væk var al Keitethed og Frygtsomhed. Fredrikke sad taus, ligesom overvældet. Jeg forstod denne Taushed, disse halvthviskede Ord, som den sterke Indhylling gjorde endnu utydeligere. Engang gjorde hun en Bevægelse mod mig, som om hun vilde gribe min Haand. "O, sig intet," bad jeg hende; "at De hører mig og ikke afbryder mig, gjør mig allerede lyksalig. Lad mig tale, lad mig faa sagt Dem alt, hvad jeg saa længe har maattet fortie."

Da jeg begyndte at nedskrive denne Beretning, lovede jeg mig selv at være sand. Jeg vilde ikke skaane mig selv, men gjengive denne bedrøvelige Historie Træk for Træk med usminket Nøiagtighed. Det var en grusom Trang at mane dette min Sjæls Vrængebillede frem for mig, og jeg har hidtil holdt mit Løfte. Men jeg kan ikke længer dvæle ved denne Scene, jeg kan ikke nedskrive flere af disse Ord, de første og sidste, som nogensinde er kommet over mine Læber. Nei, jeg vil ikke haane dem mere, disse stakkels noksom haanede, foragtede Ord; men kunde jeg græde, vilde jeg udslette dem med mine brændende, bitreste Taarer. Jeg elskede hende dog saa høit! Paa mine Hænder vilde jeg have baaret hende gjennem Livet!

Det er snart fortalt, hvad en nogenlunde skarpsynt Læser maaske allerede vil have gjettet. Da vi stansede foran Døren, og jeg vilde løfte hende ud af Slæden, gled Tørklædet lidt tilside, og skjønt hun øieblikkelig drog det for igjen, kunde jeg ikke tvile paa, hvad jeg havde set. Det var intet djævelsk Blendverk. Under Sløret havde jeg set Jomfru Borre. Paa den spidse Næse og den haanlige Mund kjendte jeg hende straks. Et Øieblik stod jeg forstenet, som om en Slange havde stukket mig; men jeg fattede mig voldsomt igjen, og instinktmæssig lod jeg mig ikke merke med noget. Jeg fulgte hende indenfor Døren, bukkede for hende og sagde: "Godnat, Fredrikke, godnat, min Balprinsesse, min Eventyrfe i de mange Skikkelser, den *sidste* var den bedste..." og endel saadant Galmandssnak, jeg ved ikke selv hvad. Med jeg hørte en skjærende Latter, idet jeg stormede op ad Trappen. Det var mig selv.

Jeg vil ikke beskrive, hvordan jeg tilbragte den første Time paa mit Værelse. Den, der ikke har oplevet en saadan Time, vil ikke kunne fatte det alligevel. Nu blev det hele afskyelige Bedrageri mig klart... Det var et aftalt Spil mellem dem... Medens jeg var nede for at finde Slæden, havde de byttet Kaaber; de er omtrent ens Høide... Men hvortil dette? Blot til grusomme Løier? Ak, nu forstaar jeg alt. *Fredrikke skal ogsaa styres hjem!* "O Kvinde!" udbrød jeg med Fridthjof:

"Den förste tanke, som Loke hade,
Det var en lögn, och han sände den
I qvinnoskepnad till jordens mänd."

En hel Time efter hørte jeg Bjelder. Jeg saa ud; det var dem. Det var hende, den hjerteløse Flane, den dobbelte Ordbryderske. Maanen var gaaet ned, og Dagslyset begyndte at bryde frem, graat, nygternt og trist, ligesom det Lys, der gikk op i min Sjæl. Da jeg havde set Præliminaristen løfte hende ud af Slæden og jage afsted med den igjen, blev jeg roligere; min Forbitrelse gav Plads for en uendelig dyb Foragt.

Da jeg senere paa Dagen kom ned i Dagligstuden, var alle samlede.

"Nu, min kjære M., hvad synes De?" raabte Fogden mig venlig imøde. "Det gik lystig til. Det er bare Storemoen, der kan gjøre slige Baller. Der var ikke mange af Herrerne sikre paa sine Ben. Vor vise, høilærde Hr. M. var ogsaa en Smule paa Støvlerne, er jeg bange for, hvad? Ha, ha, ha!"

"Desværre, det la'r sig ikke negte," svarede jeg, "vi er alle skrøbelige. Men det er Jomfru Fredrikke, som jeg styrede hjem inat, hos hvem jeg har at atbede mine Synder."

"Jeg haaber, Jomfru Lemvig," sagde jeg og saa stivt paa hende, "at De *intet* erindrer af den daarlige Tale, hvormed jeg maaske har besværet Dem, ligesom jeg ikke vil erindre et Ord deraf. Saa meget kan jeg forsikre, at det aldrig skal hænde mere. Eftersmagen af en saadan Aften er altfor modbydelig. Det er første, men sikkert ogsaa sidste Gang, at jeg har havt den Ulykke at beruse mig i slet Spiritus."

Hun blegnede og slog Øiet ned.

Otte Dage senere forlod jeg Fogdens Hus.

Meeting Again

Excerpts

Translated by Leslie Grove and Diane Oatley
Footnotes by Sarah J. Paulson

> Are you Mary? I asked horrified.
> And a voice said stonely and dully:
> So I am called.
>
> Heine[31]

It was still early morning in Cabinet Minister M's study. Mr. M. sat with such concentration at his desk that he did not notice his servant until the man was standing right beside him. The servant announced that the woman who had sought his audience twice before in vain, was now outside his door again with a pressing need to engage him in conversation. A wave of the hand, and she stepped inside.

It was a middle-aged woman with a face from which miserable domesticity had erased every trace of youth and mildness in order to engrave the marks of suffering and bitterness instead. She wore an aging black velvet hat, a brown coat of an old-fashioned cut, edged with a worn fringe, and finally a collar, of which each fold attested to need and difficulty. Who has not had occasion to see one of these dismal figures at one's door?

She did not leave the man whose attention she sought, long in doubt about the nature of her errand. With the introduction that she of course did not have the honor of knowing

---

[31] Although it deviates slightly from the German original, the motto for "Meeting Again" is taken from Radcliff in Heinrich Heine's *Die Heimkehr* (1823-1824) in *Buch der Lieder* (1827). These lines in the German original are as follows:
"Sind Sie Maria?" – fragt' ich.
Erstaunt' ich selber ob der Festigkeit,
Womit ich sprach. Und steinern und metallos
Scholl eine Stimm': "So nennen mich die Leute."

the right honorable sir, but that she nevertheless, as much because of his reputation for beneficence as because of his influential government position, ventured to turn to him for help, she took a folded piece of paper out of a cotton handkerchief and presented him with it.

M. took a hasty look at the paper; it was a list, on which a number of generous people had written their names. He remained standing in front of her and listened in a friendly and patient manner while she with womanly complexity rattled off that old and well-known tale of woe. Ah, but what complexity can fully portray such a tragic life, so many-sided and substantial in its monotony, so lacking in poetry and trivial in its misery! Born to a good family, married to a man who was as brutal as he was heedless, someone who lacked both the capacity and the will to nourish her and the expanding flock of children; a widow without a widow's pension, left behind in one of the country's remote coastal spots, where her husband had lived his miserable existence, in his last years as inspector for a shipbuilder... These were the main features she sketched of her life.

Now she had come into Christiania in hopes of finding a brother who lived there, but he had also died and his widow was as much in need as she was herself.

"What position did your husband have, before he accepted service as an inspector?" asked M. sympathetically.

"Oh, none at all. Now and then he obtained a little scribbling at a government office. Those were bitter years; I sewed night and day, but it takes more than a little to maintain a husband and five children."

"But how could it be that you, who are, as you say, from a good family, agreed to marry a man who was nobody and never would be anybody?"

"Ah, your Excellency! A misstep of my youth..."

"There there," M. interrupted her, and evaded an unaffected glance from a pair of sharp blue eyes which long ago had lost every trace of delicacy and modesty.

"You were," he added, "a daughter of...?"

"The late Bailiff Lemvig in Østerdalen."

"What! Bailiff Lemvig – the same Bailiff Lemvig who experienced some financial difficulty?"

"Ah yes, that was my unhappy father..."

"Really! oh really! Well... hmm..." said M. with a changed voice – "Please, do sit down, please!"

She curtsied and took her place on a chair, which he offered her with a somewhat awkward gallantry. He himself sat or rather threw himself onto a sofa, overwhelmed by an inner agitation, while his hand flew over his high, balding forehead, as if to chase away a troubling memory. His glasses, which he had pushed up onto his head, had again slid down over his eyes, and against his will he stared hard at the woman sitting right across from him.

"Ah, it is she" he said to himself, "it is she, the dream of my youth. Is it she?" he repeated while lost in painful observance, hearing nothing of her stream of words. He contemplated these harsh features, these sharp contours, this dark, bilious flush, with which daily exasperation and a soulless, bitter struggle with existence had slowly etched into the skin; this mouth, the soul's unmistakable mirror, which now appeared in all its discouraging coarseness... How well a pair of smiling and youthful lips had known how to hide this in days gone by...! Only the thick locks of an ash blonde color and the dark eyelashes had survived the ruination and seemed almost ashamed of their present surroundings.

"Your father," he said with some effort, "is someone I have known in my younger days. At that time he had the opportunity to offer me some assistance. It is wonderful that fate gives me the chance to return the favor to his daughter. Give me your address, and you will hear from me on Sunday at the latest... Cheer up, good woman!" he said and rose from his seat. "I shall, God willing, be able to help you. Count on the good will of a man who was your... your father's friend."

"Oh, is it possible! So much goodness! God bless and reward your Excellency!" She grabbed his hand, as if to kiss it; he jumped back with fright.

"Good, good. Well, Sunday at the latest... this door, I beg of you... good-bye good-bye... mind the stairs." And he stood at the window, following her with his eyes until she vanished around the corner.

On the evening of this same day M. wandered thoughtfully up and down in his office. An unusual emotion could be read in his marked features. "What a meeting!" he said to himself. "For the first time, after so many years have passed, I am reminded of an event which had almost disappeared from my memory. And in such a way...! She did not know me, thank God! In that remote spot where she has dragged herself through a miserable existence, she has quite lost track of me. She had no idea that she had earlier rejected the man whom she begged for alms, and she shall never come to know it. I shall be a kind of gentle providence for her, one she shall never have cause to blush over... How vividly my thoughts go back to that evening's events!"

He opened his desk and drew an old portfolio bound in leather out of a secret compartment. It contained what a student's portfolio normally contains: letters, diary entries, travel notes, attempts at poems, sketches, drawings, etc. He soon found the folder he wanted, and became absorbed in reading it.

We will read it with him.

28th of December, 1832.

Today it has been exactly one year since it happened. I will now write down the story, and thus it will be over and done with for eternity.

On the fourth day of Christmas a huge ball was held by the proprietor at Storemoen. (...) We travelled there in several groups. First the bailiff and the little boys, then Miss *Borre* and *Fredrikke*; on the last leg the old office assistant *Svendsen* and I were finally to set off. (...) Finally I was ready, and I must admit to myself that I was impeccable. With this doubly pleasant feeling, I threw myself into the sleigh; once again I dared to lose myself in my dreams without fear of being disturbed. (...) In my memory I looked back upon what I had experienced since Fredrikke's return from town last winter, where she had been to learn music and tailoring; how I had fought against the magic spell and long thought myself safe, until I realized that she despotically controlled my thoughts night and day.

My silent monologue sounded about like this:

What a strange coincidence it has been that the confession I have frequently been about to make to her, has been interrupted each time! Sometimes one of her little brothers has come rushing in and asked for an explanation to part of his homework; other times it has been Miss Borre, the fatal Miss Borre! One would think she had some intuition, every time there was something she could spoil. Always stumbling in on the happy atmosphere in a somewhat ludicrous fashion.

Sometimes it was Fredrikke's own unrestrained nature that was also at fault. (...) These rapid transitions from gravity to merriment are remarkable in her; one can never be quite sure of any mood, and she changes the moods of others according to her own. This is no lack of character; rather it is caprice, youthful arrogance. When she is older, and the seriousness of life has broken this arrogance, she will perhaps be more lovable, but will not enchant me more than she does now when she so often wounds me. She does not lack soul, but breeding, that is to say, the breeding that life has to give.

(…) With more than one signal, barely visible to me, Fredrikke has given me to understand that she is not indifferent to me. Now the whole thing must be brought out into the light of day, now or never… I can no longer tolerate the uncertainty; it is now or never… I shall either sink or swim. Back there at home, in our daily life, it could not happen, but in the tumult of the ball, in the solitude of the crowded room, that is precisely the place for two hearts to speak to each other. Now or never! The bells too are ringing out, now or never, without ceasing.

Such was the train of my thoughts when we came into view of the farm. The lights shone far across the fields from the many lit up windows as if from an enchanted castle. Like a daring knight in a fairy tale I too met up with sword and shield to capture the prize of victory, still not knowing what dragons and fears[32] there might be to battle. My courage sank noticeably, and I became more and more uneasy the closer we got to the farm, but my decision was resolute. Now or never. Tonight it would be decided.

(…)

We entered the hall. In the light of two lanterns, which were placed on each side of the door, I was hastily quit of my clothing; – I noticed, that we were among the last to arrive. (…) After passing by several empty rooms I stopped at the threshold of a larger one. This one was quite filled with ladies. (…) My eye soon found the one it sought. Oh heavens how delightful she was! One really only saw this as she sat among all the others. A bright rose-colored dress surrounded her like a rosy red cloud; her only adornment was a large, white rose in her hair. I will not use that worn-out and untrue expression which finds the rose faded and gray against the hue of her skin. It was not at all put to shame in its present company, but it is certain that the fresh clarity of her skin and the more muted paleness of the rose each contributed to heightening the effect in the most marvellous way. Miss Borre showed her usual astonishing temerity in seating herself precisely next to *her*. Miss Borre has that indescribable tint to her skin which most resembles cooked liver; it is a blend of brown red, gray and green. Her hair, of a sooty black hue, the darting, changeable eyes, the large white teeth behind the contemptuous mouth, all this is characteristic of her face, but nature has in its caprice seen fit to give her a nice figure, which perhaps gives her a right to courtesy. She is more feared than admired in the village for her sharp tongue, which spares nothing and no one. Satire in the mouth of the uneducated and disagreeable is loathsome and can only deteriorate into raw sarcasm. Nevertheless, she knows very well how to insinuate herself with those she wishes to win over.

(…)

The first dance always has such an extraordinary character, which the next already partly has lost and which later on quite disappears! (…) And Fredrikke! How her eyes shone! Say what one will in favor of dark eyes, but they can not have the same indescribable power to enthrall as a pair of beautiful blue eyes. Only they can understand how both to wound and to heal, to offer and to plead, and when they in addition are veiled by long, dark lashes like Fredrikke's! She has an extraordinary way of carrying herself in the waltz: she tilts her head to the side with half-closed eyes and an expression which could be interpreted to mean that she was surrendering herself unconditionally to the happy man who was embracing her; but suddenly, as if to punish this rash thought, she raises her head proudly with lightning glances to all sides.

---

[32] The Norwegian original ("Rædsler") is ambiguous, encompassing both "fearful things" and "inner fears".

Later in the evening I obtained a promise of a waltz from her; I awaited this with trembling impatience. When I hastened over to ask her to dance, the young person who once before had stolen a march from me, pushed me aside and made the same assertion. Fredrikke seemed to be at a loss for a moment and thought that it might be the next waltz she had offered me. I assured her that she had most explicitly offered me this one. He contended the same.

"How is it possible for me to keep all these engagements in my head," exclaimed Fredrikke. "You must really excuse me if I occasionally become a little confused."

"Then I think it best that Miss Lemvig choose between us," said the person, whom I later discovered was named Wilhelm Barth, with a triumphant expression. "I think that Mr. M. will be satisfied with this."

I did not await this judgement, but bowed and withdrew. (…)

The evening faded; the end of the ball drew near; the cotillion was about to begin. I could not believe my own happiness when I finally took my place with her hand in mine. We had hardly taken our places when Mr. Barth showed himself on our other side. (…) I understood nothing. I did not want to understand anything. I was deaf and blind, and all my fear was forgotten when she pressed my hand after the dance and said in the sweetest voice:

"We have almost not said a word to each other."

"That is not my fault, Miss Lemvig."

"Surely much less mine," she answered. "What is a poor woman to do? She has no will, but any intruder who does not insult her, has permission to inconvenience her. (…)"

"Oh Fredrikke!" I cried and gripped her hand, which she did not withdraw – "Fredrikke… Miss Lemvig… may I take you home this evening?…" My voice shook.

She bent her head nearer and looked at me for a long time with that same searching, unfathomable smile. Then almost inaudibly she said: "Yes" and vanished in the crowd. I was left standing numb, as if I were intoxicated. This yes was already a confession… it rang so deeply and ceremoniously… the ball is over in a few minutes… oh, this yes was whispered as if in front of an alter!

(…)

We had enjoyed our coffee and began to prepare for the journey home. The bailiff had already made his departure. There was a horrible ruckus and chattering in the bedroom as the ladies donned their travel garments, as all of these gay butterflies cocooned themselves back into their shapeless wrappings and disappeared little by little. I had aided Fredrikke into her red coat with the Persian lamb fur piping and bound up her socks with trembling haste and now dashed out to find the sleigh. When I returned, she met me on the stairs. In her tightly wound bunting, she could neither see nor move: therefore, I carried her down to the sleigh, took my place beside her and dashed away.

(…)

What I said to Fredrikke while we raced (…) beneath the white powdered, listening fir trees…? I scarcely know anymore; I only know that the words flowed from my heart like a long repressed and violent stream. All my clumsiness and fearfulness were gone. Fredrikke sat in silence, as if overwhelmed. I understood this silence, these half-whispered words, which the heavy shrouding muffled even more. Once she made a movement towards me, as if she wanted to take hold of my hand. "Oh, please say nothing," I implored her. "That you listen to me and don't interrupt me already makes me blissful. Allow me to speak, allow me to tell you everything, everything that I have had to silence for so long."

When I began to write down this account, I promised myself that I would be truthful. I did not wish to spare myself, but to recount this miserable story feature by feature with unadorned precision. I had a terrible need to conjure up this mockery of my soul, and so far I have kept my word. But I can no longer dwell on this scene, I cannot write down any more of these words, the first and last which have ever passed through my lips. No, I do not want to scorn them any more, these pathetic, already scorned, despised words; but if I could cry, I would erase them with my burning, most bitter tears. I loved her so much! I would have carried her through life on the palms of my hands!

What a reasonably sharp-eyed reader must have already guessed is soon told. When we stopped before the door and I began to lift her out of the sleigh, her shawl slipped a little to one side and although she immediately drew it back into place, I could not doubt what I had seen. It was not a devilish mirage. Beneath the veil I had seen Miss Borre. I recognized her immediately by her pointy nose and derisive mouth. For a moment I stood as if turned to stone, as if a snake had bitten me, but I pulled myself together again with vehemence and instinctively did not reveal that I had noticed anything. I followed her to the door, bowed to her and said "Good night Fredrikke, good night my princess of the ball, my fairy tale nymph of many faces, the *last* was the best..." and more such madman's chatter, I don't know what myself. But I heard a piercing laughter as I stormed up the stairs. It was my own.

I do not want to describe how I spent the first hour in my room. He who has not experienced such an hour will not be able to understand it anyhow. The entire, disgusting deception became clear to me now... It was an arranged scheme between them... They had exchanged coats while I was down looking for the sleigh; they are approximately the same height... But to what end? Solely as cruel joke? Ah, now I understand everything. *Fredrikke is also to be driven home!* "Oh woman!" I burst out with Fridthjof:

> The first thought which Loki had
> Was a lie, and he sent it in the shape
> Of a woman to man on earth.[33]

A full hour later I heard bells. I looked out; it was them. It was her, the heartless flirt, the twice breaker of promises. The moon had gone down and the light of day began to break forth, gray, sober and sad, like the light which was emerging from my soul. When I had seen the student lift her out of the sleigh and dash away in it again, I grew calmer. My bitterness gave way to an infinitely deep contempt.

When I went down to the parlor later in the day, everyone was assembled.

"Now, my dear M, what do you think?" cried the bailiff amicably out to me, "It went off merrily. Only Storemoen can arrange such balls. Not many of the gentlemen were steady on their feet. Our wise, learned Mr. M. was also a bit tipsy, I fear, what? Ha, ha, ha!"

"Unfortunately, that can not be denied," I replied, "We are all weak. But it is Miss Fredrikke, whom I escorted home last night, whom I must ask for forgiveness for my sins."

"I hope Miss Lemvig," I said and regarded her stiffly, "that you have *no* recollection of that poor speech, with which I must have troubled you, but of which I do not wish to recall a word. I can assure you that it will never happen again. The aftertaste of such an

---

[33] M. quotes Frithiof in the Swedish author Esaias Tegner's (1782-1846) romantic masterpiece *Frithiofs saga* (1825; Frithiof's Saga), which has the form of an epic poem. Loki is a cunning figure in Old Norse mythology; he is of giant descent, but was raised among the gods and helps them in difficult situations. However, he also betrays the gods and is their enemy in the final battle.

evening is far too disgusting. It is the first, but certainly also the last time that I have had the misfortune to intoxicate myself on bad liquor."
She turned pale and lowered her eyes.
Eight days later I left the bailiff's house.

Primary Works

Amtmandens Døttre, 1854-55. Eng. tr. *The District Governor's Daughters*, 1992.
Fortællinger, 1861.
I de lange Nætter, 1863.
Sidste Blade, 1868, 1872, 1873.
Fra de Stummes Leir, 1877.
Mod Strømmen, 1879, 1885.
Samlede Verker, 1-3, 1912-13.
"Storyteller Sara." Eng. tr. *An Everyday Story: Norwegian Women's Fiction*, 1984, 17-26.

Selected Bibliography

Bliksrud, Liv. "Forord." *Camilla Collet. Fortellinger i utvalg.* Oslo: Aschehoug, 1996, 7-16.
–. "Fantastikk i Camilla Colletts fortellinger." *Skrift, kropp og selv. Nytt lys på Camilla Collett.* Jorunn Hareide, ed. Oslo: Emilia, 1998, 56-72.
Collett, Alf. *Camilla Colletts Livs Historie.* Oslo: Gyldendalske Boghandel/Nordisk Forlag, 1911.
Møller Jensen, Elisabeth. *Emancipation som lidenskab. Camilla Collett i liv og værk.* Copenhagen: Rosinante, 1987.
Steen, Ellisiv. *Diktning og virkelighet. En studie i Camilla Collett's forfatterskap.* Oslo: Gyldendal, 1947.
–. *Den lange strid. Camilla Collett og hennes senere forfatterskap.* Oslo: Gyldendal, 1954.
–. "Innleiing." *Amtmandens Døttre. Norges nasjonallitteratur,* 7. Oslo: Gyldendal, 1968.
Steinfeld, Torill. "'Gjør Sommeren blid for Svalerne'. Camilla Collett (1813-1895)". *Norsk kvinnelitteraturhistorie, 1: 1600-1900.* Irene Engelstad et.al., eds. Oslo: Pax, 1988, 77-83.
Østerud, Erik. "Kjerring mot strømmen. Camilla Colletts liv og forfatterskap." *Edda* 4 (1987), 291-314.
Aarnes, Sigurd Aa, ed. *Søkelys på Amtmandens Døtre.* Oslo: Universitetsforlaget, 1977.
Aarseth, Asbjørn. "Camilla Colletts virkelighet." *Realismen som myte. Tradisjonskritiske studier i norsk litteraturhistorie.* Oslo: Universitetsforlaget, 1981, 56-76.

Minna Canth:
Female Criminality and Social Conscience

The date of Minna Canth's (1844-97) birth, March 19, was established in
2003 as an official Finnish flag-raising day in honor of her bold voice for
equality, which resonates in her writings and as well as in the way she lived
her life. As the first woman to be endowed with such an honor, Minna
Canth endures today as a powerful and relevant symbol of a woman who
spoke to the social issues of her day, hosted an intellectual salon, produced
a fine body of literary and journalistic work, ran a successful business, and
raised a family with seven children. Minna Canth stands as the first major
Finnish woman writer and, with Aleksis Kivi, one of the greatest playwrights of Finnish literature.

Born in Tampere in 1844, young Ulrika Wilhelmina Johnsson moved
with her family to Kuopio as a child and began studies at the teacher's
seminary in Jyväskylä in 1863. After two years, she married one of her
teachers, Johan Ferdinand Canth, at age 21. We know little about her first
decade of marriage, but she remarked in her autobiography that once she
was married, there was one thing she understood clearly: that she was to be
subject to the will of her husband.

This idea, expressed almost verbatim in her play excerpted in this volume, *Työmiehen vaimo* (1885; A Workman's Wife), is a recurring theme in
her writings. Although she abandoned her formal studies after her marriage
in 1865, she engaged in intellectual pursuits the rest of her life. She cultivated her writing talent by assisting her husband doing editorial work for a
local newspaper and writing pieces on temperance and women's issues for
other regional publications. Widowed at 35 with seven children, she returned to Kuopio in 1880 to manage her father's fabric business. She became a successful businesswoman and continued her writing of articles,
prose fiction, and the plays for which she is most famous.

In Kuopio, Canth avidly studied Scandinavian and European intellectu-
als of the day. She names fellow Finnish writers Juhani Aho and Aleksis
Kivi, as well as Norwegian playwright Henrik Ibsen, as her favorite writers.

However, she studied the literature and ideas of many others. Ibsen's modern dramas and John Stuart Mill's *The Subjection of Women* (1869) reinforced her ideas on the woman question; Émile Zola gave a model for realistic-naturalistic style; and the deep faith and love of God in Leo Tolstoy and Fyodor Dostoevsky found their way into many of her works. She was a deeply religious woman who, nevertheless, saw no contradiction in her devotion to God in questioning established religious dogma. Canth also read the major contemporary scientists, philosophers, and psychologists, such as Charles Darwin, Ralph Waldo Emerson, Herbert Spencer, Hippolyte Taine, Ernest Renan, and Théodule Ribot. But her engagement with these thinkers and writers was not solitary. She hosted an intellectual salon – sometimes of women only, sometimes with a much wider group – which became a center in Finland for cultural and philosophical discussion until her death in 1897. Many of the most important artistic figures of Finland visited her here, including the composer Jean Sibelius, the painter Akseli Gallen-Kallela, and many Finnish writers and other cultural figures.

Canth was the first Finnish-speaking female journalist to work independently as an editor. Publishing some seventy pieces in over twenty journals and newspapers, Canth began writing either anonymously or with pseudonyms such as Wilja, Teppo, Airut, and X. Her interest in cultural issues was wide-ranging. She wrote not only about social problems but about politics, fashion and clothing, and the impact of new inventions such as the telephone. Many contemporary discussions from outside Finland she passed on in her own journal, *Vapaita aatteita* (Free Ideas), which she edited in collaboration with A.B. Mäkelä during 1889-1890. In addition to publishing her own radical ideas, she freely translated into Finnish selected writings by authors such as Georg Brandes, Tolstoy, and Knut Hamsun. But the journal was short-lived, due partly to financial problems, partly to the attention the journal drew from the censors.

Canth confronted the glaring social problems of her day in all her writings. She is most celebrated as a feminist ahead of her time, even influencing the forward-thinking of her time in regard to women's issues. When the *Suomen Naisyhdistys* (Finnish Women's Society) was founded in Finland in 1884, women of the intelligentsia in Kuopio immediately joined to support the aims for women's equal access to schools and universities, right of entry into all professions, equal pay for equal work, rights of women to keep and pass on the earnings of their own work, and other changes in laws regarding marriage and divorce. Minna Canth became the Finnish-language secretary of the Kuopio chapter – the first chapter created outside Helsinki – when it was established in 1886.

Minna Canth's writings persistently and ardently portray the suppression of women in the patriarchal order of religion and society. Her women are often creative and hard-working but held prisoner by circumstances, by chauvinistic men, and by the pressure of societal and religious expectations. Consistently sympathetic to the pressures upon women, her portrayals are varied in their treatment of moral dilemmas that these women face, which include issues of love and sexuality, jealousy, guilt, insanity, adultery, and even infanticide. Although women's issues dominate her writings and the reception of her work, she asserts her social conscience by addressing problems of the poor and working class, often positioning the plight of women as symptomatic of these other social, economic, and moral concerns. Her ideas about freedom of religion and equal rights for women were radical for her day. She actively worked toward transforming these ideas into policy, and many were implemented shortly after her death. Finland was the first European country to grant women the right to vote in 1906; and in 1922 a law was passed allowing citizens to choose which religion they would belong to – or to belong to no religion at all. Canth was a supporter of the temperance movement, a proponent for schools for girls, and vocal on improving assistance to the unemployed and mentally ill.

The selection from Canth's work included in this volume is from her third play and represents the energy and ideas expressed throughout her career. While most critics agree that *A Workman's Wife* is not Minna Canth's most artistic or sophisticated work, none can question the singular intensity and clarity of message of the drama. She describes it in her "Autobiographical Sketch" as being "filled with the sharpest satire from start to finish" but having "no deeper psychology or artistic ripeness either. Even so, it made a tremendous impact when ... it was performed for the first time at the Finnish Theater." The drama continues to make an impact today with its bold message and portrayal of harsh reality, despite significant advances in many of the social issues Canth addresses. *A Workman's Wife* represents Canth's first play that embraces a then radical agenda and signals a break from her two previous happy-ending plays. Canth wrote the play, as she explains, when she was "infected with reformist zeal" in order to lash out "boldly at all the injustices women were subjected to by the law, at preposterous religious notions, men's boozing and wantonness, women's stupidity, shallowness and disposition to be prejudiced – in short, all the evil and madness I had found in the world" (Canth, "Autobiographical Sketch", 149). Many were sympathetic to Canth's message. The drama was a great success, performed more than most in its day and a topic of conversation for theater-goers and non-theater-goers alike. It was performed immediately in Stockholm and St. Petersburg, and was even performed in the United States by Finnish immigrants before the end of the 19th century. Making Canth a well-known figure, the play also aroused criticism and caustic attacks for its sympathetic views of promiscuity, light-hearted portrayal of insobriety and biting censure of fundamental religion. In addition to its popularity and its importance in the literary career of Canth herself, the drama is important in Finnish literature for bringing to light domestic problems and gender issues and ushering in social realism in Finland.

Minna Canth started writing stories during 1877-1879. Though most celebrated as a dramatist, she wrote many prose works during her career, most notably "Köyhää kansaa" (1886; Poor Folk), *Hanna* (1886), and "Lain mukaan" (1889; According to the Law). "Poor Folk" and "According to the Law" carry many of the same social and familial concerns as well as the dramatic intensity of *A Workman's Wife*. *Hanna*, telling of a girl coming of age, is notable as a reaction to similar novels by male Finnish writers, namely, Juhani Aho's *Papin tytär* (1885; The Parson's Daughter) and Johan Ludvig Runeberg's *Hanna* (1836), written in Swedish. Canth's first play, *Murtovarkaus* (1883; The Burglary) was very successful, winning a prize from the Finnish Literature Society and appealing to the desire in Finland for plays in Finnish rather than in Swedish. *A Workman's Wife*, her third play, signaled a change in style – treating serious social issues in a bold and even radical manner. This style of unabashed portrayal of social ills and the expression of radical opinions reaches its peak with her play *Kovan onnen lapsia* (1888; Hard Luck's Children), which was banned after its first performance – not to be performed again until fifteen years later. From this point on, Canth, though retaining her focus on societal and familial issues, begins to soften the activist agenda and focus on the craft of characterization. *Kauppa-Lopo* (1889; Peddler Lopo) is a story focused on the dual natures of a cleptomanic woman and also represents, according to some, Canth's best achievement in the realist vein of portrayal. With *Sylvi* (1893), Canth writes for the Swedish-language stage about an unhappy marriage, very reminiscent of Ibsen's *Et Dukkehjem* (1879; A Doll's House).

Both Canth's prose works and most of her seven full-length plays thematize the law, touch on criminality and introduce images of imprisonment or captivity. A notable exception to this is Canth's well-known play *Papin perhe* (1891; The Parson's Family), though even here, one sees the children of the minister trying to escape from the constraining traditionalism of their father. Crime and law as a theme are more prominent in other of her works, from her first play, *The Burglary*, in which Helena stands accused of burglary, to her last, *Anna-Liisa* (1895), in which the eponymous character tries to conceal the infanticide which she had committed years earlier. Similar in its employment of themes of law and crime is *Kovan onnen lapsia* (1888; Hard Luck's Children), cancelled after its first performance because it was seen to condone murder, arson, and theft. Its main criminal character, Topra-Heikki, has been called Finnish literature's first anarchist and a modern Robin Hood.

Such issues of law and criminality, as well as the imagery of imprisonment, are used to powerful effect in the social commentary of *A Workman's Wife*. In a posture of capitulation (dropping "both her hands into Risto's hands"), Johanna submits to a marriage where her subservience to her husband is clear. Her no-account husband, Risto, robs and cheats not only his own wife but also his former fiancée, Homsantuu. Using the two opposite figures of Johanna and Homsantuu, a kind of outcast figure, Canth emphasizes the extreme injustices inflicted on women. Homsantuu, reacting violently, is jailed at the end of the play in her attempt to shoot Risto in retribution; and Johanna, in one of several bitterly ironic reversals in the play, is accused of the theft committed earlier by her husband. The theft underscores the significance of money in the play and, in particular, Johanna's inability, as a woman, to freely earn, spend, and preserve this valued medium of society. Both Johanna and Homsantuu reflect nineteenth-century discussion of marriage as institution – and, indeed, female relationships in general – as commercial or financial transactions. Maria Jotuni, another Finnish woman writer, continues to probe this theme in the early 20th century.

The following is from the first act of *A Workman's Wife*, which takes place at the wedding party of Risto and Johanna. At the party, Johanna suddenly learns of her new husband's dishonesty and states emphatically that she knows the two of them "do not belong together". Devastated by his lies and deception, yet forced to acknowledge the legal and religious power of the marriage vow that binds them, she realizes she is trapped in a marriage in which she must submit to her husband's will in everything. In Act One, we see her new husband's selfish concern for her money and beauty and his preoccupation with getting drunk. Canth uses stage direction and physical imagery to underscore the psychological context, as when Johanna asks the girls to help her out of her wedding gown. The symbolism of the gown – with pins that are too tight – and the anxiety she feels in trying to get out of her dress, is clear. Act One ends with an ironically festive dance, which stands in stark contrast to Johanna's solemn and constrained predicament. The rest of the play describes Johanna's trials as wife of a man who fritters away all her money with drink and as a mother struggling with poverty in a society in which all people and laws seem to be against her. The title of the play, *A Workman's Wife*, is poignantly ironic in its indication not only of the new bride as a possession of her husband but also in the identification of her husband as "a workman", for not once in the play do we see him work or exhibit any desire to provide for his family. Completely self-centered and insensitive, Risto siphons the life out of all women with whom he comes in contact. From beginning to end, Canth makes clear not only that Risto and his male companions display no feeling for women but that they cannot even understand or process the words of women that deviate from their own masculine discourse – such as Vappu's final words of condemnation in Act Five. Although criticized for being simplistic or improbable, this play depicts subtle psychological truths with literary finesse amid its plain characterization and dramatic – even melodramatic – plot elements. Canth's subsequent literary work shows continuity and consistency in the themes and emphasis on social issues found in *A Workman's Wife*; and in her later works, she develops these with a greater concentration on individual characterization amid these social concerns.

A Workman's Wife still draws large crowds in Finland when it is performed in amateur and professional theaters, attesting to its interest and relevance today. The play first appeared in English as *The Worker's Wife* in 1980, almost one hundred years after its premiere in Finland. This first English translation of 1980 was adapted for the American stage and performed in Duluth, Minnesota by the University of Minnesota. At least one other English translation by Hilja Karvonen exists in an 1987 manuscript.[1]

Työmiehen vaimo

Ensimmäinen näytös
Riston ja Johannan häähuone

(...)

Risto: Tahtoisinpa kuulla, mitä kuokkijat tuolla ulkona sanovat morsiamestani.

Yrjö: Kuulemattakin sen tietää, että he Johannaa siellä kiittelevät.

Risto: Ja minua kadehtivat. Niin, niin, Yrjö, kuinka lienee sinun laitasi. Monta vuotta kerrotaan sinun pitäneen Johannaa silmällä, mutta minä tulin ja sieppasin yks' kaks' sinulta tytön.

Yrjö: Mitä puhumme siitä. Hänellä oli valta ottaa kenet tahtoi. Sen toki sanon sinulle,

Risto: parhaimman kulta-aarteen sinä Johannasta omaksesi sait.

Risto: No, sinä et pane liikoja ollenkaan. Tiedättekö mitä? Kuusisataa markkaa hänellä on rahoja pankissa, ihan valehtelematta, ja korkoja vielä lisäksi. Jahkas teille näytän. Otin Johannalta pankin vastakirjan jo omaan huostaani. Katsokaapas tätä.

Kustaa: Kuusisataa on, totta maarin. Voi, miekkosta. Kelpaa sinun elää. Kunpa olisin minäkin yhtä onnellinen. Kuulitkos, Toppo? Kuusisataa markkaa tuo kullan poika sai vaimonsa myötäjäisiä. Emmekö lähde naimaan mekin.

Toppo: Helkkaria kanssa. Eihän niitä rikkaita tyttöjä kumminkaan joka miehelle riitä. Toiset saavat tyytyä köyhempiin taikka olla ilman. Ja minä puolestani olen ennemmin ilman, että saan elää niinkuin itse tahdon.

Kustaa: Älähän nyt! Köyhänkin kun ottaa, niin saapa yhtäkaikki sen, joka housut paikkaa, ettei tarvitse polvet ulkona käydä.

Risto: Niin, ja mikä siinä on, ettei mies saisi elää niinkuin itse tahtoo, vaikka akankin ottaa. Loruja? Tupakkaa piippuun, miehet.

Kustaa: Mutta kyllä minä sentään ennemmin rikkaan haluaisin, minäkin. Paha vain, ettei niitä ole juuri niin hyllyltä otettavissa, niillä kun tavallisesti on monta pyytäjää. Millähän mahdilla sinä, Risto, sait tuon Johannan taipumaan, olisipa hyvä tietää.

---

[1] A copy of it is located at the Kantillan Kulttuurikeskus in Kuopio, Finland. The following excerpt follows the text in *Valitut teokset* (Collected Works). Helsinki: Werner Söderström, 1954.

(...)

Risto: Älä, älä laske liikoja, Toppo. Minä en kuuna päivänä eukkoani pelkää, jos juoda tahdon. Ohoh, jopa jotakin.

Toppo: No, no, saadaan nähdä. Minkäpä sille taidat, kun eukkosi sanoo: rahat ovat minun, niitä et tuhlaakaan niin juuri niinkuin itse tahdot.

Risto: Minkä taidan? Heh, sepä kysymys. Kumpi omaisuutta hallitsee, mies vai vaimo? Tunnetkos sen verran Suomen lakia, veli veikkoseni?

Toppo: Kyllä minä tiedän, että laki antaa miehelle vallan, mutta näkyvät ne eukot koettavan puoliaan pitää kuitenkin.

Risto: Pahanilkisillä lienee jonkinlaisia konsteja ja koukkuja, mutta Johannapa ei ole semmoinen.

(*Toppo hyräilee pilkallisesti ja panee tupakkaa piippuun.*)

(...)

Johanna: Eihän täällä vain ruveta pitämään pahaa elämää tänä iltana? Minua jo alkaa pelottaa.

Risto: Pahaa elämää. Kissa vieköön! Sitäkö varten sinä noin totiseksi kävit. Älä turhia. Mitä pahaa elämää täällä pidettäisiin.

Johanna: Jos miehet ryyppäävät liiaksi ja humaltuvat.

Risto: Entä sitten. Kerrankos semmoista tapahtuu. Olletikin tällaisissa pidoissa. Eihän tuo niin kumma olisi.

Johanna: Se turmelisi meiltä koko hääilon. Risto kulta, olethan sinä ainakin varuillasi.

Risto: Niin minäkö? (*Hyräilee.*) Enkös minä häissäni sais' olla vähän päissäni? – Ei se ole mies eikä mikään, tiedätkös, joka ei koskaan uskalla edes väkeviä nauttia.

Johanna: Hiljaa, hiljaa, älä puhu niin kovasti. Sinä lasket leikkiä, Risto, et kai tarkoita, mitä sanot. Minä häpeäisinkin silmäni maalle, jos sinä joisit itsesi humalaan.

Risto: Kas vain! Näyttää siltä, kuin – Kuules, Johanna, älä sinä unohda, mitä pappi meille äsken lausui.

Johanna: Mitä niin?

Risto: Että mies on vaimon pää.

Toppo: Mies on vaimon pää, niinkuin kissa on hiiren pää.

Kustaa: Ja myöhä on hiiren haukotella, kun on puoliksi kissan suussa.

Risto: Oikein, Kustaa, oikein, ha, ha, ha. Myöhä on hiiren haukotella, kun on puoliksi kissan suussa. No, Johanna, jokos aloitamme?

Johanna (*Laskee molemmat kätensä Riston käsiin*): Aloitetaan!

(*Kaikki astuvat paikoilleen ja tanssivat polskaa. Tanssi käy yhä vilkkaammaksi, ilo nousee korkeimmilleen. Silloin aukeaa ovi ja Heikki raastaa sisään Homsantuuta, joka kaikin voimin panee vastaan. Tanssi taukoaa; itsekukin jää paikoilleen.*)

Homsantuu: Minä en tahdo tulla, kuuletkos, minä en tahdo! Laske minut irti, sinä pakanan pallinaama, taikka puren sormesi poikki.

Risto: Kerttu (*Vetäytyy syrjään.*) Mitä ihmettä tästä nyt tuleekaan.

(...)

Toppo: Mikä hiiden poropirkko tuo on?

(*Kaikki nauravat ja sipisevat; tytöt vetääntyvät kuiskutellen vasempaan.* – *Homsantuu seisoo jäykkänä, kädet nyrkissä kupeilla, ja katsele tuimasti ympärilleen.*)

Johanna: Tervetuloa, Kerttu!

Homsantuu: Tuli nyt nurkkihin nuhina sekä soppihin sohina.

Kustaa: Etkö kuule, Homsantuu, morsian puhuttelee sinua.

Homsantuu: Nimeni on Kerttu.

Johanna: Tervetultua häihimme, Kerttu!

Homsantuu: Pilkkapuikoksenneko minut tänne haetitte? (*Kädet puuskassa.*) Hyvä! Tässä olen nyt. Tehkää parastanne. Koettakaa saatteko minusta enemmän kuin minkä kirves kivestä saa.

Toppo: Ken on tuo satapaikkainen tytönhuitukka, jonka ikenet on irvallaan ja silmät kiljan kaljallaan.

Kustaa: Etkö sinä Homsantuuta ole ennen nähnyt? Hänet tuntee muuten koko maailma.

Homsantuu: Sama juuri, jota kilvan olette kiehuttaneet kielikattilassanne ja hautoneet hampaittenne välissä. Paljonko siitä työstänne lienette hyötyneet? Sanokaapa pilanpäin. Syntiä saitte sydämen täyden, mutta sitähän teillä oli kyllältä jo entuudelta.

Toppo: Voi, saksan pukki sitä sappea. Tohtiiko tuota ollenkaan likelle mennä, vai suihkuaako sen tuli suusta, lenteleekö kipinöitä kielen alta.

Johanna: Pois, Toppo! Kerttua ei saa kukaan pilkkanaan pitää, hän on kutsuttu vieras niinkuin kaikki muutkin. Ehkä tahtoisit tulla tuonne toisten tyttöjen luokse, Kerttu?

Homsantuu: En.

Johanna: Minä takaan, että he kohtelevat sinua hyvin, jos vain sinä puolestasi olet heille ystävällinen.

Homsantuu: Ennen minä kuusia kumarran kuin kumarran kunnottomia; ennen leppiä lepytän kuin lepytän lempoloita.

Laura: Tuo hävytön!

Katri: Kuinka hän uskaltaakin!

Kustaa: Emmeköhän sieppaa tyttöä uudelleen käsikynkästä ja vie häntä samaa tietä jälleen pois.

Heikki: Ja samaa hamppua, jolla hänen toimmekin.

Johanna: Hiljaa! Ei saa noin katkeroittaa hänen mieltään. Kuulettehan, että se on kyllin katkera jo ennestäänkin. Kerttu, lasi viiniä, jos saan tarjota.

Homsantuu: En huoli.

Toppo: Verkkasen tuli! Ei hän olekaan ruma, kun tarkemmin katson. Kaula on kuin kanervan varsi, huulet kuin hunajametsä ja poskipäät kuin kaksi puolikystä puolukkaa. Vähällä pita, etten rupea häntä rakastamaan.

Homsantuu: Tule vain likelleni, niin revin silmät päästäsi.

Toppo: No, no, ethän toki. Saapa kattikin kuningasta katsoa, ellei muualta niin uunin päältä.

Homsantuu: Pakenetko, koira!

Toppo (*peräytyy takaisin*): Älä, luojan luoma.

Homsantuu (*jälleen kylmänä ja tyynenä*): Lieneekö minut luoja luonut, vai synti synnyttänyt.

Johanna: Älä välitä heistä, Kerttu. He eivät saa tehdä sinulle mitään pahaa, niin kauan kuin olet minun turvissani.

Homsantuu: Sinun turvissasi? Olenko minä mikään vaivainen, että mina turvaa tarvitsen? Mene loitommalle minusta. Sinua vihaan vielä enemmän kuin noita toisia.

Johanna: Tyttö parka! Mikä sinun nuoren sydämesi noin on koventanut?

Homsantuu: Kysy sitä noilta kylän herjoilta. Ja kysy sitä ennen kaikkea omalta kurjalta sulhaseltasi, joka piileskelee tuolla toisten takana eikä uskalla näkyviini tulla.

Johanna: Ristoa et saa soimata. Hän ei ole sinulle mitään pahaa tehnyt.

Homsantuu: Enköhän sitä tiedä.

Johanna: Astu esiin, Risto. Älä anna hänen loukata kunniaasi ilkeillä syytöksillään.

(Risto tulee verkalleen esiin.)

Johanna: Näet, Homsantuu, että hän uskaltaa.

Homsantuu *(katselee hetken äänetönnä Ristoa, puhkeaa sitten raivosta tukahdutetulla äänellä puhumaan)*: Petit vaivainen valasi, söit kuin koira kunniasi.

Risto: Valehtelee, hi, hi, hi. Voi, peijakas, kuinka hän osaakin omiansa panna.

Johanna: Ja sitä sinä vain naurat, Risto.

Homsantuu *(astuu lähemmäksi Ristoa, kasi ojennettuna)*: Valehtelenko minä? Katso minua suoraan silmiin ja sano vielä kerran se sana, jos voit.

Johanna: Tee niin, Risto!

Risto *(naurahtelee hiukan hämillään, kääntyy pois ja lausuu puoliääneen miehille)*: Joutuu sitä johonkin tässä maailmassa, minkä sittaporrö seipääseen.

Johanna *(tukahduttaen heräävää tuskaa)*: Tee, niinkuin hän käskee, Risto. Minä tiedän, että voit.

(Hetkisen äänettömyys.)

Johanna: Katso häntä silmiin, Risto. Syytön sinä kumminkin olet.

Homsantuu: Käänny päin, jos uskallat, sinä kurja.

Johanna: Tuolla tavalla annat itseäsi herjata kaikkien kuullen. Jos olisin mies, kyllä häneltä suun tukkisin. En säälisi mokomaa ollenkaan.

Homsantuu: Joko paljastat kyntesi sinäkin, laupias samarialainen? Mainiota! Tuota juuri halusinkin. Tulkaa nyt kimppuuni jok'ainoa, mina en teitä pelkää. Minä huudan sittenkin, että kajahtaa korvissanne: Risto on sanansa syöjä, valansa rikkoja, kunnottomin konna, pahin petturi auringon alla.

Johanna: Suuri Jumala, etkö sinä puolusta itseäsi, Risto? Kiellä hanta jo viimeinkin; masenna tuo käärme, joka sylkee meihin myrkkyänsä.

Homsantuu: Kiellä? Masenna? Minutko? Oho! Kiven alla on kieltäjäni, maan alla masentajani.

Risto: Mitä sinä nyt joutavia pauhaat, Kerttu. Sovitaan pois kaikki vanhat vihat, syödään kissan kirppulihat. Ja sitten tanssimme polskaa, se on toista kuin tyhjästä riiteleminen. Minä vielä kaadan sinulle viiniäkin, Kerttu, tulepas juomaan.

Homsantuu: Kelvoton! Viinilläkö tahdot syntivelkaasi huuhtoa?

Risto: Olipa tämä nyt sitten hyvinkin suuri synti. Kantänka, sanoi ruotsalainen. Kerrankos nuori mies hiukan narailee kaunista tyttöä, ja olletikin tuollaista halvempaa naista, kuin sinä olet, Kerttu parka, vaikkei hänellä sen totisempia aikomuksia olekaan. Eikös ryypätä, miehet?

Homsantuu *(melkein mieletönnä)*: Seis! *(Tukahdutetulla äänellä)*: Minulla on vielä sana sanottavaa, ryyppää sitten vasta. Sinä teeskentelit rakkautta, kun petos asui mielessäsi, ehdollasi syöksit minut turmioon. Niinpä pitää sinun myös ansaittu palkkasi saaman. *(Ottaa povestaan sormuksen, jonka heittää Riston eteen.)* Tuon kihlasormukseni kanssa viskaan viimeisenkin hellän tunteen sydämestäni. Tästä hetkestä lähtien leimuaa siellä vain vihan ja kostonhimon liekki. Minun kiroukseni seuraa sinua aina kuolemaan saakka, vielä haudan tuolle puolenkin se ulottuu. Se painaa hartioitasi kuin vuori, se kalvaa rintaasi kuin mato, yötä päivää se sinulle muistuttaa kenen onnen ja elämän olet sortanut.

Johanna: Auttakaa – minä pyörryn.

Yrjö (*vie hänet tuolille istumaan*): Vettä, tuokaa vettä.

Vappu (*antaa Johannalle vettä ja hieroo hänen ohimoitaan.*)

Homsantuu: Joko nyt surkastuu tuo lemmen kukka? Joko lakastuu tuo kirkkokunnan kirkkain ja kansakunnan kaunein? Eihän ole vielä aika tullut. Nauti ensin sitä onnea, jonka toisen kadotukselle olet perustanut, nauti iloa ja lemmen ihanuutta niin kauan kuin voit. Minä sillä välin kiertelen kuin huuhkain teidän onnenne majaa ja huudan: kostoa, kostoa, kostoa! (*Syöksyy ulos.*)

(…)

Vappu: Onko sinun jo helpompi olla, Johanna?

Yrjö: Ehkä tahdotte vähän vettä vielä?

Johanna: En minä tarvitse enää mitään. Kun vain jaksaisin sen verran, että pääsisin täältä pois.

Risto: Johanna taisi säikähtyä vallan turhan takia. Älä ole milläsikään koko asiasta. Ei siitä semmoisesta kannata pahaa mieltä pitää. Kuuletkos! Ei, mutta katsokaa, kuinka hän on lapsellinen. Itkee nyt tuota.

Vappu: Onko se ihme? Menköön kukin itseensä. Ei mahtaisi olla niinkään hauskaa juuri hääiltana kuulla tuollaista sulhasestaan.

Risto: Minkälaista?

Vappu: Petoksesta.

Risto: Petoksesta! Kaikkia mun pitääkin kuulla. Vai petos! Olettepa hassuja. Petostako sekin on, jos tyttöjä hiukan narraa. Semmoista tapahtuu aina.

Toppo: Miesten narriksihan ne naiset on luotukin maailmaan. Eipä niillä mitä virkaa liene muuta.

Risto: Niinpä kyllä. Ja mitä pahaa siinä on, jos nuori mies rakastelee kauniita tyttöjä. Ei hän sentään voi kaikkien kanssa naimiseen mennä, ei mitenkään.

Vappu: Mutta olittehan kihlannut tuon tytön, ymmärsin. Minkätähden sitten jätitte hänet noin vain?

Risto: Minkätähden, minkätähden! Sepä kysymys. Tietysti sentähden että sain paremman. Tottahan Johanna on toista kuin Kerttu, jolla tyttöparalla ei ole kunnon hamettakaan, saatikka sitten rahoja pankissa niinkuin tällä. Ennemminhän minä toki sinut otin, Johanna, etkä suinkaan sinä minulle siitä vihaa kanna, vai kuinka, he he, he.

Johanna (*nousee*): Pois minun täytyy päästä, – pois, vaikka mikä olisi. Auttakaa minua, tytöt, irti näistä koristuksista.

Risto: Mitä nyt? Mihin sinä aiot? Kesken kaikkea. Sano, hyvä ihminen.

Johanna: En tiedä, kunhan vain pääsen pois. Tottapahan sitten selviää. Sen kumminkin tunnen, että me kaksi emme sovi yhteen.

Risto: Herra tule ja puserra, onko hän järkensä menettänyt?

Katri: Mitä sinä ajattelet, Johanna. Vallanhan sinä teet itsesi ihmisten naurunalaiseksi.

Laura: Vastikään vihiltä päässyt ja nyt jo tahtoisi erota miehestään. Ei semmoista ole vielä ikipäivinä kuultu.

Lotta: Ja mokomastakin syystä sitten. Hullun naikkosen tähden. Niin juuri; eihän Homsantuuta kukaan ihminen viisaana pidä.

Johanna: Kuinka kovaan nuo neulat panitttekaan. En saa niitä millään lähtemään.

(*Repii kruunut ja harsot päästään. — Leena-Kaisa ja Anna-Maija tulevat esiin ja asettuvat molemmin puolin Johannaa.*)

Leena-Kaisa: Katsokaahan tuota, kuinka paha henki ihmistä riivaa, kun hänet vain kerran pauloihinsa saa.

Johanna: Paha henki? Minua?

Risto: Niin kyllä. Pahan hengen yllytyksiä tuo on, ei muuta. Ei totisesti olekaan.

Vappu: Lienee, mitä lieneekin, mutta Johannan sijassa tekisin juuri samoin.

Laura: Toinen hyvä. Yllyttää vielä tuota hassua.

Katri: Mitäs Vapusta. Ei hän olekaan niinkuin muut. Ajattelee aina toisin kaikissa asioissa.

Leena-Kaisa: Vappu on maailman lapsi. Älä kuuntele häntä.

Vappu: Mutta ajatelkaa, hyvät ihmiset, pikkuisen. Kuinka saattaisi elää yhdessä semmoisen miehen kanssa, johon ei voi luottaa. Mahdotonta suorastaan. Ennemmin toden totta menisin kaivoon.

Johanna: Ennemmin kaivoon taikka sikoja paimentamaan. Älkää estelkö, vaan antakaa minun mennä.

Anna-Maija: Onneton, näinkö pian sinä pyhän vihkivalasi unohdat?

Johanna: Vihkivalani? (Painaa päänsä alas.)

Leena-Kaisa: Näinkö olet miehesi tahdolle alamainen? Näinkö häntä miehenäsi ja herranasi kunnioitat?

Anna-Maija: Emmekö kaikki olleet tässä todistajina äsken, kun sinut Riston omaksi annettiin, ollaksesi häneen elinkautesi sidottuna?

Leena-Kaisa: Ja käyttäytyäksesi kaikessa niin, että miehellesi kelpaisit.

Risto: Että miehellesi kelpaisit. – Niin papin sanat kuuluivat.

Anna-Maija: Kohta ensimmäisessä vastoinkäymisessä olet nyt kuitenkin valmis luopumaan hänestä, jonka tähden luotu olet, –

Risto: – sillä vaimo on luotu miehen tähden eikä mies vaimon tähden. – Senkin pappi luki virsikirjasta.

Anna-Maija: – olet valmis luopumaan hänestä, jonka tähden luotu olet, seurataksesi pahan hengen houkutuksia ja omaa lihallista mieltäsi. Voi sitä kadotuksen syvyyttä, jonka partaalla sinä ihmisparka, seisot.

Johanna: Taidatte olla oikeassa. En tullut tuota ajatelleeksi. Hyvä Jumala, mitä nyt teen?

Leena-Kaisa: Rukoile anteeksi mieheltäsi ja pyydä häntä kärsimään heikkouttasi, muistaen, että hänet on vahvemmalla luonnolla ja suuremmalla viisaudella varustettu.

Risto: Kyllä, – kyllä minä sen muistan. Ja että minun tulee vaimoa parhaakseni hallita. Kaikki se vihkimäkaavassa sanotaan. Enkä minä turhista vihaa kanna, vaan olen myöskin valmis antamaan Johannalle anteeksi.

Laura: Kuuletteko, kuinka hyväluontoinen hän on. Ei pahaa sanaa kaikesta tästä.

Katri: Noin ei olisi moni mies Riston sijassa tehnyt. Johanna saa kiittää onneaan.

Vappu: Lähde jo pois, Johanna. Minun luonani saat asunnon ensi aluksi.

Johanna: En minä voi erota miehestäni. Olisihan se suuri synti.

Vappu: Ja maarin mitä se olisi. Synti? Korjata erehdys, jonka huomaa tehneensä. En jaksa kuunnella.

Johanna: Sinä et muista, että pappi on meidät yhteen vihkinyt.

Vappu: Vaikka kohta, mitä se tähän kuuluu.

Laura: Siunaa ja varjele, minkälainen pakana hän on.

(…)

Vappu: Poispa minä täältä lähdenkin. – Jää hyvästi, Johanna!

Johanna: Nytkö jo? Viivy vielä hetkinen, Vappu!

Vappu: Ei, kiitos. Hääilosta olen tällä kertaa saanut tarpeekseni. Hyvästi vain kaikki.

(Menee.)

Risto: Olipa sillä helkkarin kiire. Hääilosta saanut tarpeekseen! Vastahan se, tiedämmä, oikein alkaakin. Panepas polskaa, Janne, taas, niin pääsemme tanssimaan.
Katri: Se oli hyvä sana. Tanssia meidän täytyy, että morsiamenkin poskille tulee puna. Näettekö, kuinka kalpea hän on?
Johanna: Jättäkää tanssi tänä iltana, ei se enää käy.
Risto: Mikäs sitä estää? Nyt se vasta käykin, kun on vähän lasia kallisteltu. Ota sinä, Toppo, Johanna pariksesi, minä tanssin tuon iloisen Liisan kanssa. (*Hyräilee*). Likka nätti ja sorea, poika potra ja korea, likka tanssivi somasti, poika polkevi kovasti. – Eikös niin Liisa?
Toppo (*kumartaa Johannalle*): Saanko luvan.
Johanna: Minä istun ennemmin tässä ja katselen.
Risto: Mitä nyt taas?
Johanna: En minä jaksa, Risto. Olen niin väsynyt ja aivan kuin kuumeessa. Varmaan kaadun, jos lattialle menen.
Risto: Vieläkös vain. Tule pois joukkoon. Tietysti sinun tanssia täytyy, kuinkas muuten.
Toppo: No, Johanna! Anna huolia honkasien, surra suuren suopetäjän ja tule sinä meidän kanssamme jalkoja heittelemään.
Risto: Joutuin, joutuin, Johanna. Kas niin. Ja te muut myöskin. Älkää viivytelkö noin, eihän tällä lailla ikinä pääse alkuun.

(*Janne soittaa; kaikki asettuvat paikoilleen.*)

Anna-Maija: Onneksi saimme Johannan järkiinsä sentään.
Leena-Kaisa: Jumalan kiitos, että kaikki näin hyvin päättyi. Minä jo pelkäsin, mitä tästä piti tulemankaan.

(*Tanssi alkaa.*)

A Workman's Wife

Act One

Risto and Johanna's wedding reception hall

Translated by Eric Schaad

(…)
Risto: I'd like to hear what those guys out there are saying about my bride.
Yrjö: You don't have to hear them to know they are over there praising Johanna.
Risto: And envying me. Yes, sirree, Yrjö, how about you? They say you had your eye on Johanna for years, but then I came along and snatched the girl away from you – just like that.
Yrjö: Why talk about that? She had the power to choose who she wanted. But I'll tell you this, Risto: in Johanna you got for yourself the finest treasure of gold.
Risto: You're not kidding! Do you know what? She's got six hundred marks in the bank – no lie – and interest on top of that! Here, I'll show you. I have already taken posses-sion of Johanna's bankbook. Take a look at this!

Kustaa: Six hundred it is, sure enough! You dog! It's certainly enough to live on. If only I were so lucky. Did you hear, Toppo? Six hundred marks this golden boy got from his wife's dowry. Why don't we get hitched as well?

Toppo: Hell's Bells! There aren't enough of those rich girls to go around anyway. The rest of us have to be happy with the poorer ones or do without. And for my part, I'd sooner be without so I can live how I want.

Kustaa: Come on! Say, even if you got a poor one, you would still have someone all of a sudden who can patch your trousers so you don't have to walk around with your knees poking out.

Risto: Yeah, and who's to say a man can't live how he wants even if he does tie the knot. Think I'm kiddin'? Lighten up, men!

Kustaa: Yeah, but I would still rather have a rich one, I would. With so many potential takers, it's just a shame you can't just grab one like goods on a shelf. By what power you got Johanna to consent, Risto, I'd sure like to know.

(…)

Risto: Quit kiddin' around, Toppo. If I decide to take a drink, I won't ever be fearing my old lady – you can count on that!

Toppo: Well, we'll see. What can you do if your old lady says: the money is mine, and I'm not going to let you just fritter it away how ever you want?

Risto: What can I do? Hey, that's the question. Who controls the property, the husband or the wife? Do you know enough of Finnish law, my friend, to answer that?

Toppo: Sure, I know the law gives the husband the power, but you'll see these women try to hold their own just the same.

Risto: The malicious ones might have some plots and schemes, but Johanna isn't like that.

(*Toppo hums with a sneer and fills his pipe with tobacco.*)

(…)

Johanna: You guys aren't going to start a ruckus this evening are you? I'm starting to get worried.

Risto: Ruckus? Sam hell! Is that why you are acting so serious? Don't worry. What kind of ruckus would we cause here?

Johanna: If the men drink too much and get intoxicated.

Risto: What if they do? Such things can happen – especially during an occasion like this. That's not so unusual, now is it?

Johanna: It would ruin our whole wedding night. Risto, darling, you'll watch yourself then at least?

Risto: You mean me? (*He hums*). Can't I get a little inebriated at my own wedding? It's not a man – or anything else – you know, that never has the guts to even take a drink.

Johanna: Quiet, quiet, don't speak so loudly. You're teasing, Risto. You don't mean what you're saying. I would have to hide my face in shame if you got yourself drunk.

Risto: Look here! It looks as if ... Listen, Johanna, don't you forget what the minister just said to us.

Johanna: What's that?

Risto: That the head of the wife is the husband.

Toppo: The head of the wife is the husband, just as the head of the mouse is the cat.

Kustaa: And too late awakes the mouse when it is halfway in the cat's mouth.

Risto: Right, Kustaa, right, ha, ha, ha. And too late awakes the mouse when it is halfway in the cat's mouth. Well, Johanna, shall we begin?

Johanna: (*Drops both her hands into Risto's hands.*) Let's begin!

(Everyone gets in their places and dances the polka. The dance grows more and more lively; the merriment increases more and more. Then a door opens and Heikki drags Homsantuu inside, who resists with all her might. The dance stops. Everyone remains in their places.)

Homsantuu: I don't want to come, you hear me, I don't want to! Let me go, you heathen mugface or I'll bite your finger in two.
Risto: Kerttu! *(Withdraws to the side.)* What on earth is going on here?
(...)

Toppo: Who is that rambunctious hellcat?

(Everyone laughs and whispers; the girls withdraw to the left speaking under their breath. Homsantuu stands rigidly, her fists clenched on her waist, and looks fiercely about her.)

Johanna: Welcome, Kerttu!
Homsantuu: Dawdling she danced into the corner, crashing into the cubbyhole.
Kustaa: Don't you hear, Homsantuu, the bride is speaking to you.
Homsantuu: My name is Kerttu.
Johanna: Welcome to our wedding party, Kerttu!
Homsantuu: So you brought me here to make a laughingstock out of me? *(Hands on her hips.)* Good! Here I am! Take your best shot! Try and see if you can get more from me than an axe can from a stone.
Toppo: Who is that immeasurable scatterbrain grimacing with her eyes wide open?
Kustaa: Haven't you seen Homsantuu before? Why, the whole world knows her.
Homsantuu: The very same, whom you cutthroats so vehemently cooked in your cauldron of words and seared with speech between your teeth. How much do you think you have benefited from your efforts? Tell me just for fun. You commit sin because of your heart, but you all certainly had plenty of that beforehand as well.
Toppo: Oh, Billy Goat Gruff, what bitterness! Do we dare go anywhere near her? Does fire spew from her mouth, or do sparks fly from beneath her tongue?
Johanna: Get away, Toppo! Kerttu is not to be made fun of; she is an invited guest, just like everyone else is. Maybe you'd like to go over there with the other girls, huh, Kerttu?
Homsantuu: No.
Johanna: I promise they will treat you well if you will just do your part to be friendly.
Homsantuu: Sooner will I bow before birch trees than before base and beggarly wenches; sooner will I submit to the spruce than submit to sulky she-devils.
Laura: That brazen infidel!
Katri: How dare she!
Kustaa: Why don't we just grab the girl again by the arm and take her right back out of here.
Heikki: And with the same gusto that we brought her here with.
Johanna: Quiet! We can't just rile her up like that. You can hear that she was plenty upset before this. Kerttu, could I offer you a glass of wine?
Homsantuu: Don't care for any.

Toppo: Hell's fire! She's not at all ugly when I take a closer look at her. Her neck is like a stem of heather, her lips like honey, and her cheekbones like two half-ripened lingonberries. Wouldn't take much for me to start falling in love with her.

Homsantuu: Come any closer, and I'll rip your eyes from your head.

Toppo: Well, well, no you don't. You can't stop a cat from gazing at the king, though he may do so from the top of the stove.

Homsantuu: Scram, you dog!

Toppo: (*Steps back.*) Stop – You're a human being created by God.

Homsantuu: (*Again cold and calm.*) I may have been created by God, or I may have been begotten by sin.

Johanna: Don't mind them, Kerttu. They won't be able to do anything bad to you as long as you're under my protection.

Homsantuu: Your protection? Am I such a wretch that I need protection? Get away from me! I hate you even more than those others.

Johanna: Poor girl! What made your young heart so hard?

Homsantuu: Ask those village gentlemen. And ask above all your own lousy husband, who's hiding there behind the others and doesn't dare show his face to me.

Johanna: You can't blame Risto. He hasn't done you any harm.

Homsantuu: I should know.

Johanna: Come out, Risto. Don't let her insult your honor with her malicious accusations.

(*Risto comes slowly out.*)

Johanna: You see, Homsantuu, he's not afraid.

Homsantuu: (*Looks silently at Risto for a moment, then bursts out, choking with rage, and speaks.*) You broke your valueless vow, devoured like a dog your honor.

Risto: She's lying, hee, hee, hee. Damn! – how she can talk through her hat!

Johanna: And you just laugh at it, Risto!

Homsantuu: (*Steps closer to Risto, arm stretched out.*) Am I lying? Look me straight in the eyes and say that one more time, if you can.

Johanna: Do it, Risto!

Risto: (*Laughs slightly embarrassed, turns away and speaks under his breath to the men.*) Sometimes in this world the shit is just gonna hit the fan.

Johanna: (*Suppressing a growing feeling of distress.*) Do what she says, Risto. I know you can.

(*A moment of silence.*)

Johanna: Look into her eyes, Risto. You're innocent after all.

Homsantuu: Turn over here, if you dare, you scoundrel.

Johanna: This is the way you let yourself be bad-mouthed for all to hear! If I were a man, you can bet I would shut her up. I wouldn't feel sorry for someone like that at all.

Homsantuu: So now you bare your claws as well, Good Samaritan? Great! That is exactly what I wanted. Come, and get me now, all of you – I'm not afraid of you. In any case, I'm going to yell so loud that your ears will ring: Risto is a double-talking two-timer, an oath-breaking bamboozler, the most wretched rat, the most damnable deceiver under the sun.

Johanna: Great God, aren't you going to defend yourself, Risto? Refute her already and be done with it; crush that snake who's spitting her poison on us.

Homsantuu: Refute? Crush? Me? Oh boy! Lower than a stone is he who refutes me; lower than the earth, he who crushes me.

Risto: What nonsense are you going on about now, Kerttu? Let's reconcile all past differences; let's bury the hatchet. And then we'll dance the polka – it's better than quarreling over nothing. And I'll even pour you some wine, Kerttu – come have a drink.

Homsantuu: Good-for-nothing! You want to wash away your sins with wine?

Risto: Now this was certainly a very big sin indeed! "I can imagine," said the Swede. Now is this really the first time a young man has tricked a beautiful girl – and a lowly woman at that, like you are – without his having the most honorable intentions? How about having a drink now, men?

Homsantuu (*Half crazed*): Stop! (*All choked-up.*) I still have something to say; you can drink in a minute. You feigned love, when deception resided in your heart; at your whim you thrust me into destruction. So you should get your just reward too. (*Takes a ring from her bosom, which she throws before Risto.*) With this engagement ring of yours I cast the last tender feeling from my heart. From this moment forward, in my heart will burn only a flame of hatred and desire for revenge. My curse will follow you all the way to death, and even beyond the grave it will pursue you. It will weigh upon your shoulders like a mountain; it will gnaw at your breast like a worm; day and night it will remind you of the woman whose joy and life you have destroyed.

Johanna: Help! – I am going to faint.

Yrjö (*Brings her to a chair to sit down*): Water, bring some water.

Vappu: (*Gives Johanna some water and rubs her temple.*)

Homsantuu: Is our love-flower already starting to wither away? Is the parish's brightest and the country's most beautiful flower already starting to fade? But the time has not come yet. First enjoy the happiness which you have established upon the destruction of another; enjoy the joy and splendor of love as long as you can. In the meantime I will circle around your cottage of joy like an eagle owl and yell: revenge, revenge, revenge! (*She storms out.*)

(…)

Vappu: So are you feeling any better yet, Johanna?

Yrjö: Maybe you'd like a little more water?

Johanna: I don't need anything else. If I can just manage enough to get myself out of here.

Risto: Johanna tends to get cold feet quite unnecessarily. Don't worry yourself at all about this. It's not worth getting upset about something like this. Listen! No, but look how childish she is. Now she's crying about it.

Vappu: Is it any wonder? Think about it – How would you feel? It can't be any fun to hear this kind of thing about her groom right on her wedding night.

Risto: What kind of thing?

Vappu: Lies, deception.

Risto: Lies? Deception? I've got to listen to everything! You say lies and deception. You two are silly. So it's deception to string along a few girls? That kind of thing always happens.

Toppo: After all, women were created into this world to be the dupes and playthings of men. They don't really have any other calling beyond that.

Risto: Yep, that's right. And what's wrong with a young man fooling around with beautiful girls? After all, he can't marry them all, now can he?

Vappu: But you were engaged with that girl – that's what I understood. So why then did you just leave her like that?

Risto: Why?! Why?! What a question! Naturally, because I got myself a better one. Johanna is obviously different than Kerttu, who, poor girl, doesn't even have a decent skirt, not to mention money in the bank like this one. I, of course, preferred to take you, Johanna; and you can't hold a grudge against me for that, can you? Ha, ha, ha.

Johanna (*Rises*): I've got to get away from here – away no matter what. Help me, girls, get out of these fineries.

Risto: What now? Where do you think you're going – in the middle of everything? Tell us, good woman.

Johanna: I don't know, as long as it is away from here. Then things will surely get better. But this I do know: that the two of us do not belong together.

Risto: Lord, take me now. Has she lost her mind?

Katri: What are you thinking, Johanna? You are really making a fool of yourself in front of everyone.

Laura: Just got out of the ceremony and already she wants to divorce her husband. Never heard of such a thing!

Lotta: And for such a reason as that. All because of a crazy shrew. Exactly – not one person thinks Homsantuu is sane.

Johanna: You put those pins on too tight. There is no way I can get these off.

(*She rips the bridal crown and veil from her head. Leena-Kaisa and Anna-Maija come forward and step to either side of Johanna.*)

Leena-Kaisa: Look how the evil spirit will possess a person as soon as he gets them just one time in his snares.

Johanna: Evil spirit? In me?

Risto: Yeah, that's right. It is the impulses of the evil spirit, nothing else – really, nothing else.

Vappu: Maybe so, but in Johanna's place I would do exactly the same thing.

Laura: There's another winner! Why she's actually encouraging that fool!

Katri: What's with that Vappu? She really is unlike the others. She always thinks differently about everything.

Leena-Kaisa: Vappu is a worldly girl. Don't listen to her!

Vappu: But think a minute, good people. How can someone possibly live together with a man who cannot be trusted. Absolutely impossible. I certainly would sooner jump in a well.

Johanna: Better to jump in a well or play sheppard to pigs. Don't stop me, just let me go.

Anna-Maija: Miserable soul, have you forgotten so soon your holy wedding vows?

Johanna: My wedding vows? (*She lowers her head.*)

Leena-Kaisa: Is this how you subject yourself to the will of your husband? Is this how you honor him as your husband and master?

Anna-Maija: Were we not all witnesses here a moment ago when you were given unto Risto to be bound to him for as long as you shall live?

Leena-Kaisa: And to act in everything so that you will be pleasing unto your husband.

Risto: So that you will be pleasing unto your husband – those were the words of the minister.

Anna-Maija: Right at the first sign of trouble you are ready to separate from the man, for whom you were created –

Risto: – For the woman was created for man and not man for the woman – that's what the minister read from his prayer book.

Anna-Maija: You are ready to leave the man, for whom you were created, in order to follow the temptations of the evil spirit and your own carnal desires. Oh, the depths of hell upon whose edge you are standing, poor creature!

Johanna: You may be right. I didn't think about that. Good Lord, what do I do now?

Leena-Kaisa: Pray for forgiveness from your husband and ask him to suffer your weakness, remembering that he has been equipped with a more robust nature and greater wisdom.

Risto: Indeed, indeed, I remember that – and that I should govern my wife to the best of my ability. It's all there in the wedding vows. And I am not one to hold a grudge – I am also ready to offer Johanna forgiveness.

Laura: Do you hear how good-natured he is? Not an evil word about any of this.

Katri: Not many men would have acted thus in Risto's place. Johanna should thank her lucky stars.

Vappu: Go ahead and take off, Johanna. You can stay with me for the time being.

Johanna: I cannot separate from my husband. It would be a great sin.

Vappu: What would it be – a sin? To correct the error you realize you've made. I can't listen to this anymore.

Johanna: You are forgetting that the minister has joined us together as one.

Vappu: Even so, what's that got to do with it?

Laura: God bless and protect us, what a heathen she is!

(…)

Vappu: I'm getting out of here anyway – Farewell, Johanna!

Johanna: Already? Wait a second longer, Vappu!

Vappu: No, thank you. I've had enough wedding merriment this time around! Good bye, all! (*She goes.*)

Risto: She was in a hell of a rush. Had enough wedding merriment! It's just getting started, far as I can tell. Crank up the polka again, Janne, and then we can get to dancing.

Katri: That's a great idea. We've got to dance 'til the bride's cheeks turn red. Do you see how pale she is?

Johanna: Forget dancing tonight – it's not a good time anymore.

Risto: What's preventing us? It's the perfect time now – now that we have tipped a few glasses. You, Toppo, take Johanna as your partner; I will dance with cheerful Liisa over there. (*He hums.*) Girl pretty and sweet, boy handsome and neat; the girl dances with grace, the boy stomps 'til red in the face – Isn't that right, Liisa?

Toppo (*Bows to Johanna*): May I?

Johanna: I would rather sit here and watch.

Risto: What's the matter now?

Johanna: I don't feel like it, Risto. I am so tired, and practically in a fever. I know I'll fall on my face if I go out on the dance floor.

Risto: Still with this? Come on and join the group. You definitely have got to dance, what else you gonna do?

Toppo: Well, Johanna! Let the fir trees fret, let pines trees lament and come with us to toss your feet around.

Risto: Quickly, quickly, Johanna. Indeed. And the rest of you as well. Don't just diddle-daddle, we'll never get rolling like that.

(*Janne plays; everyone gets into their places.*)

Anna-Maija: Luckily we got Johanna to finally come to her senses.

Leena-Kaisa: Thank God everything ended so well. I sure was afraid of how it was all going to turn out.

(*The dance begins.*)

Primary Works

Murtovarkaus, 1883; Eng. tr. *The Burglary*, 2001.
Roinilan talossa, 1885.
Työmiehen vaimo, 1885; Eng. tr. *The Worker's Wife*. Finnish Americana: *A Journal of Finnish American History and Culture 4* (1981), 1-71.
Köyhää kansaa, 1886.
Hanna, 1886.
Salakari, 1887.
Kovan onnen lapsia, 1888.
Lain mukaan, 1889.
Kauppa-Lopo, 1889.
Lehtori Hellmanin vaimo, 1890.
Papin perhe, 1891; Eng. tr. *The Parson's Family*, 2001.
Agnes, 1892.
Hän on Sysmästa, 1893.
Sylvi, 1893.
Spiritistinen istunto, 1894.
Anna Liisa, 1895; Eng. tr. *Anna-Liisa*, 1997.
Kotoa pois, 1895.

Selected Bibliography

Ahokas, Jaakko. *A History of Finnish Literature*. Bloomington: Indiana University Press, 1973.

Canth, Minna. "Autobiographical Sketch (Written for the Norwegian journal *Samtiden* in 1891)." Ritva Heikkilä, ed. and Paul Sjöblom, tr. *Sanoi Minna Canth – Pioneer Reformer: Extracts from Minna Canth's Works and Letters*. Porvoo: Werner Söderström, 1987, 143-52.[2]

Hermansson, Maarit. *Vapautumisen teema Minna Canthin kaunokirjallisuudessa: naisnäkökulma kirjallisuudentutkimukseen ja sosiaalihistoriaan*. Tampere: Tampere University Press, 1995.

Koskimies, Rafael. *Suomen kirjallisuus IV: Minna Canthista Eino Leinoon*. Helsinki: Suomalaisen Kirjallisuuden Seura & Otava, 1965.

Krogerus, Tellervo. "Minna Canth." *100 Faces from Finland. A Biographical Kaleidoscope*. Ulpu Marjomaa, ed. Roderick Fletcher, tr. Helsinki: Finnish Literature Society, 2000. (Also at: http://www.kansallisbiografia.fi/english.html).

Mäkinen, Kirsti and Tuula Uusi-Halila. *Minna Canth – Taiteilija ja taistelija*. Helsinki: Werner Söderström, 2003.

---

[2] Canth's original text in Swedish no longer exists. At the request of the editor of *Samtiden*, Harald Hansen, Canth sent him an autobiographical essay written in Swedish in the form of a letter. This original letter has been lost. Hansen translated the letter into Norwegian, and it appeared under the title "Selvbiografisk meddelelse" in *Samtiden* 2 (1891), 179-86. Subsequent to its publication in *Samtiden*, the autobiography was translated back into Swedish, and from the Swedish into Finnish as *Omaelämäkerta* (Autobiography).

Mehto, Katri. Introduction. *Anna-Liisa. Portraits of Courage: Plays by Finnish Women.*
    S. E. Wilmer, ed. Helsinki: Helsinki University Press, 1997, 4-108.
Schoolfield, George C., ed. *A History of Finland's Literature.* (*A History of Scandinavian
    Literatures*, 4. Sven H. Rossel, general ed.) Lincoln: University of Nebraska Press,
    1998.
Tiirakari, Leeni. *Taistelevat lukumallit: Minna Canthin teosten vastaanotto.* Helsinki:
    Suomalaisen Kirjallisuuden Seura, 1997.
Tiitinen, Ilpo. Introduction. *Minna Canth.* Ilpo Tiitinen, ed. Kodin Suuret Klassikot.
    Espoo: Weilin & Göös, 1987, 5-87.
Tuovinen, Elia, ed. *Taisteleva Minna: Minna Canthin lehtikirjoituksia ja puheita 1874-
    1896.* Helsinki: Suomalaisen Kirjallisuuden Seura, 1994.

Amalie Skram: A Norwegian Naturalist

JANET GARTON (UNIVERSITY OF EAST ANGLIA)

By the time Amalie Skram's (1846-1905) first novel was published in 1885, she was 39 years old and had a wide variety of experience from which to draw for her writing. Born Berthe Amalie Alver in Bergen in 1846, she had early on absorbed the atmosphere of that cosmopolitan town, fascinated by the street life and its colourful characters. When she was 17 her father went bankrupt and left for America. She promptly married a sea captain, August Müller, travelled the world with him, and bore him two sons. The marriage was unhappy and in 1878 they separated, a process which was so traumatic that she spent some time in Gaustad mental asylum to recuperate. She moved to the east of Norway, and in 1881 settled in Kristiania with her widowed brother and their joint children. In 1882 she was invited to Bjørnstjerne Bjørnson's anniversary celebrations at Aulestad, where she met the Danish author and journalist Erik Skram. They began a relationship – mostly by letter – which culminated in their marriage in 1884, when she moved to Copenhagen.

Amalie Müller's arrival in Kristiania in the early 1880s coincided with a time of cultural and political ferment, both in Norway and in Denmark. Following Georg Brandes' lectures in Copenhagen in the 1870s, the Modern Breakthrough was in full swing, with impassioned debates about the need for a literature which engaged with contemporary social issues such as poverty and inequality, eschewing the nostalgia for past glories and idealization of heroic figures characteristic of Romanticism. The "four greats" of Norwegian literature were producing their most socially engaged books: Henrik Ibsen's play *Et Dukkehjem* (1879; A Doll's House), Bjørnstjerne Bjørnson's play *En Hanske* (1883; A Gauntlet), Alexander Kielland's *Novelletter* (1879; Short Stories), Jonas Lie's novel *Familjen på Gilje* (1883; The Family at Gilje). Amalie Müller had ambitions to write, and had published her first criticism in 1877, a review of the Danish writer Jens Peter Jacobsen's novel *Fru Marie Grubbe* (1876); by 1881 she had also reviewed i.a. Bjørnson, Kielland, Lie, Collett, Ibsen, including a defence, courageous for its time, of Ibsen's play *Gengangere* (1881;

Ghosts) in the Kristiania newspaper *Dagbladet*. Her sympathies were very much with the radical left, and she had initiated a correspondence with Bjørnstjerne Bjørnson in 1878 and Georg Brandes in 1881, writing at first as a diffident apprentice, who soon turned into an outspoken debater as her confidence in her talent grew. Radicalism in the 1880s was very much a Scandinavian movement, with particularly close links between Norwegian and Danish writers, and she had become a member of the literary circle before she moved to Kristiania, even being proposed by Bjørnson as secretary of a Scandinavian literary journal he wished to start. She was attracted to Erik Skram not just as a lover, but because he had written a novel, *Gertrude Coldbjørnsen* (1879), in which the subject – the story of a young girl persuaded into a loveless marriage – echoed her own personal and literary preoccupations.

Skram's first fiction, a short story about a desperately poor family whose mother inadvertently kills her newborn twins, "Madam Høiers Leiefolk" (Madam Høier's Tenants), was published in the journal *Nyt Tidsskrift* in 1882. It demonstrates a passionate sympathy with the dispossessed and intimate knowledge of the details of their lives which informs so much of her writing. After moving to Copenhagen in 1884 she began writing in earnest, encouraged by her husband; they were a writing partnership, always hard up but never compromising their literary and political ideals. Over the next 16 years Amalie Skram published 15 books, mainly novels, but also short stories and plays, quite an achievement when one considers her many statements about what a torture it was to her to write, how desperately slowly the work progressed. Her fiction can be divided into two main groups, firstly what can loosely be termed her "novels of marriage" and secondly the tetralogy *Hellemyrsfolket* (The People of Hellemyr).

Novels of Marriage

Constance Ring (1885) tells of a young bourgeois girl whose ignorance of the facts of life has left her totally unprepared for her marriage to a well-meaning but insensitive older man. Her revulsion at physical contact drives him to seek solace in the bed of their maid, and when Constance discovers this she is determined to get a divorce. She is horrified when all the powers of society, in the shape of her pastor, her best friend and her worldly-wise aunt, unite to dissuade her from such a step. Her aunt explains that divorce is the worst possible option for a woman: "The world is arranged so that women must marry. We may be unhappy for a while, but an unmarried woman has far greater burdens to bear. We have to choose the lesser of two evils." (114-15)[1] Unable to resist this combination of forces, Constance returns home and passively endures until a timely shipwreck relieves her of her husband. Passivity has become a way of life, however, which changes only when imminent financial ruin persuades her to accept the proposal of an earlier admirer, Lorck. His passionate and considerate love does awaken a response in her, and for the first time she experiences sexual pleasure – but all is destroyed when she discovers that he had an affair with a maid before their marriage, who bore him a child. Her indignation is aroused at a society which accepts this exploitation of one class of women whilst idealizing another:

> By what right did men behave that way? They used up the youth, the health, the love of these women, as if they had been created for one purpose, used them until they had their fill. If they saw something more desirable, they cast them aside, leaving them to the fate their ruthless male egotism had prepared for them. She felt a strange compassion for this patient sufferer, who was so filled with goodness and resignation, and at the same time, a raging bitterness against the callous society that made it so safe and comfortable for men to indulge their sexual desires. (219)

In her bitterness she decides to take a lover herself, the ardent young Meier who worships her from afar. When she discovers that he too has a mistress – her own seamstress – her disillusion is complete and she kills herself.

The novel was published at the height of the pan-Scandinavian debate about sexual morality and the double standard, the so-called "Hanskefeide" (Gauntlet Feud) after Bjørnson's provocative play of that name. Social inequality was nowhere more apparent than between the prostitutes and the men who visited them, likewise gender inequality between sexually experienced men and the virgins they married. Georg Brandes and Bjørnstjerne Bjørnson were leaders in the debate, Brandes advocating equal sexual freedom for men and women, whereas Bjørnson believed that chastity for both sexes before marriage was the answer. The movement for women's rights in both countries was growing with the formation of the Norwegian Women's Liberation Organization in 1884 and the Danish equivalent, founded in 1871, becoming an active political force at that time. Public debate was however still mainly conducted by men, and censure was rife. Outspoken contributions to the discussion such as Christian Krohg's novel *Albertine* (1886) and Hans Jæger's *Fra Kristiania-Bohêmen* (1885; From the Kristiania Bohemia) were banned, and Jæger imprisoned.

It was even more difficult for women to speak out, as is demonstrated by the fate of *Constance Ring*. It was accepted for publication by Gyldendal,

---

[1] All quotes from Skram's novel are from the following edition: *Constance Ring*. Judith Messick and Katherine Hanson, trs. Seattle: Seal Press, 1988. The page reference is in parenthesis.

Copenhagen's main publishing house; but when its director Frederik Hegel read the book as it came off the presses he declared that he could not sanction the production of such a morally dubious text, and Amalie Skram had to pay for it to be published on commission in Norway. Like most of her work, it provoked a scandalized reaction from conservative critics.

The socially-sanctioned stifling of women's aspirations within marriage, and their socially-conditioned rejection of sexuality, is a recurring theme in Skram's fiction. It is the main theme of the long story "Fru Ines" (Mrs. Ines), printed in *Kjærlighed i Nord og Syd* (1891; Love in North and South) and of several short stories, and affects several characters in *Hellemyrsfolket* (1887-98; The People of Hellemyr). It appears again in the novel *Forraadt* (1892; Betrayed), in which the young Ory marries the older sea-captain Riber with no idea of what marriage means, and tries to run home in shock on her wedding night. Here, however, the narrative sympathy is more divided, as Riber is portrayed as being equally a victim of the double standard. Ory's revulsion turns into a horrified fascination with the details of his sexual history, which she insists on hearing over and over again whilst simultaneously refusing him sex, until his torment becomes so unbearable that he jumps overboard.

The play *Agnete* (1893), which remains a popular drama, focuses on the fate of the widow with no means, who is driven to lying and petty stealing in order to scrape by in genteel poverty. She dreams of a man who will love and marry her even when he knows her utterly, with all her faults – a dream which is destroyed when the man she loves admits he has not the courage to do so.

Lucie (1888) is also a novel about marriage, but with a very different slant. The protagonist Lucie is no shy young virgin trapped into marrying a roué, but a former musichall dancer and unmarried mother who is the mistress of Theodor Gerner, a lawyer captivated by her sensual charms. It is she who inveigles him into marriage in order to achieve the bourgeois respectability she covets. Once they are married, however, the balance of power shifts. What entranced Gerner as a lover affronts him as a husband, and he becomes increasingly harsh in his attempts to "educate" Lucie from being a high-spirited, spontaneous and flirtatious girl into a subdued and decorous wife. She rebels against this treatment and runs off, only to be raped and made pregnant by an escaped convict. She turns to religion in the hope that God will make the child be Gerner's, but when it is born and she sees from a mole on its cheek that it is the convict's, she loses the will to live and dies.

The society in which this drama is played out displays typical contemporary attitudes, as is demonstrated in the excerpt below. Bjørnson's *A Gauntlet* is a focus of debate, and reactions to suggestions of sexual permissiveness – and to Lucie herself – range from the conventional "moral rectitude" of Pastor Brandt, who upholds the double standard and abhors women's liberation, to the openmindedness of his sister Karen Reinertson. She is a woman of secure social standing and independent means who can afford to ignore petty conventions and put forward controversial opinions. She is also the only person amongst Gerner's acquaintances who makes a genuine effort to befriend Lucie; but even she cannot overcome social prejudice, and her interest is not enough to offer more than a glimpse of the way things could be.

The People of Hellemyr

Although she spent her writing life in Copenhagen, Amalie Skram always wrote in Norwegian and usually about Norway, where most of her novels are set. The series of novels called *Hellemyrsfolket*, (The People of Hellemyr) (which comprises *Sjur Gabriel* (1887), *To Venner* (1887; Two Friends), *S.G. Myre* (1890) and *Afkom* (1898; Descendants) draws on material from her native town of Bergen and from her early life. It is the story of a family from a poor coastal area near Bergen, and follows their development over several generations. The married couple in the first volume, Sjur Gabriel and Oline, eke out a living as subsistence farmers and fishers. Their life is so desperately wretched that they become brutalized, and Oline drinks when she can to numb the misery of existence. Sjur Gabriel's unhappiness is alleviated by the birth of his youngest son, whom he loves dearly; when the son dies he gives up the struggle to make a better life for the family, and the novel ends: "From that day on both the husband and the wife at Hellemyr drank."

The subsequent novels follow the fate of Sjur Gabriel and Oline's grandson, Sivert. He is a promising lad with many talents, and in *Two Friends* he goes to sea as a cabin boy. Here Amalie Skram drew on her experiences as a sailor to paint a realistic picture of life on board a sailing ship, and the exotic atmosphere of foreign ports, which was praised by many critics. Sivert is a good worker, and soon becomes a trusted crew member; but he cannot escape the burden of his inherited flaws, and is unable to resist telling tall stories of his own prowess, and finally stealing from two passengers who have befriended him. In *S.G. Myre* he has gone ashore in his native town, and found a good position as a store manager – but again he betrays the trust of his employer by stealing from the till. It is his fatal desire to impress other people which leads to him spending more money than he can afford; the psychology of a well-meaning young man who becomes embroiled in deceit against his will is convincingly observed. He is haunted by the figure of his grandmother Oline, now a local drunk whose presence continually reminds him of his family's shame; one day when he meets her on a lonely stretch of coast his frustration boils over, and he hits her and accidentally kills her. This novel also tells the story of Petra, Consul Smith's housekeeper, who is seduced by her employer and believes that he will marry her when his bedridden wife finally dies – only to be brutally disillusioned. The wealthy Smith buys his way out of the problem by paying Sivert's debts and setting him up in a business of his own, provided he marries Petra. This is a tenuous foundation for a marriage – and the result is predictable.

S.G. Myre presents a rich gallery of local characters around the two central figures. It is a study of a whole society, continued in *Descendants*. Skram's studies of street life bear fruit in an absorbing account of the sights, sounds and smells of the town. Sivert and Petra's marriage is miserable and he becomes indebted once more and goes to prison. Petra becomes a monster of a mother who takes out her misery on her children. They too cannot escape the burden of their inheritance: Severin becomes a student, but steals from a friend and then hangs himself in shame. The daughter Fie is sold in marriage to a rich older man to rescue her father from ruin. This tetralogy is one of the most sustained naturalist works in Scandinavian literature, demonstrating the inevitable downward spiral of a family unable to escape the inheritance of despair. Both Brandes and Bjørnson complained about Amalie Skram's depressing view of human nature. She replied that that was how she saw life around her, and how she had to reflect it in her writing.

The Final Years

Descendants did not appear until 1898, eight years after *S.G. Myre*, and cost Skram much torment to write. Her letters to Erik bear witness to the many hours she spent unable to write a line, and to the fact that when she did write, it was often in a flood of tears. Her own marriage was not free of conflict either, as she never quite believed that Erik was faithful. In 1894 her nervous state was such that she agreed to become a patient of the well-known psychiatric doctor Knud Pontoppidan in Kommunehospitalet (Copenhagen City Hospital) – and her experiences there were so devastating that on her release she wrote two lightly fictionalized novels about it, *Professor Hieronimus* (1895) and *På Sct. Jørgen* (1895; At St. Jørgen's). She was kept at the hospital against her will and in isolation from friends and family, and felt she was imprisoned in a madhouse and denied all autonomy. The novels present a strongly genderized picture of mental illness, where women are shut away, sometimes for no other reason than being awkward or inconvenient to their families.[2] Skram's novels caused a storm of debate and raised public awareness of the treatment of the mentally ill – although it was not until 1938 that a law was passed in Denmark guaranteeing them some minimal rights (whereas such a law had existed in Norway since 1848).

Amalie Skram continued writing novels and short stories for the rest of the decade, with increasing difficulty. Her marriage to Erik Skram finally foundered, and they separated in 1900. Often ill and with little money, she tried to earn money with her work while looking after her daughter Johanne, whom she called her only reason for living.

Julehelg (1900; Christmas Holiday) her last finished novel, tells of a young man's hopeless love for a married woman. She began another novel, *Mennesker* (1905; People), a dark tale of the relationships between a group of people in which sexuality has assumed grotesque forms and the only unsullied love is a spiritual one. She worked on the novel for many years, but it was unfinished when she died in March 1905 at the age of 58.

Amalie Skram struggled to be accepted as a writer. Her novels were bound to offend conservative critics, and early reviews were often dismissive or vituperative. As time went on, however, her work was taken seriously and reviewed more positively, particularly by Edvard Brandes, literary editor of the Copenhagen newpaper *Politiken*, who increasingly praised her writing. Other writers too, especially Herman Bang and Arne Garborg, supported her in private and in public. It was in Denmark rather than in Norway that she felt her work had eventually found a public and achieved critical recognition – so much so that in 1901 she published a pamphlet, *Landsforrædere* (Traitors), in which she proclaimed that she wished to be considered a Danish rather than a Norwegian author. It was *The People of Hellemyr* which was considered her most important work during her lifetime and after her death, but with the advent of feminist criticism in the 1970s and 1980s attention was focused more on her novels of marriage and their perceptive analysis of gender and society. With this interest came translations of several of her novels into English for the first time, so that her work is belatedly much more widely available. In 2005, the centenary of her death, interest in her is still growing.

---

[2] The foreword to the recent translation from 1992 of the novels, *Under Observation*, was written by Elaine Showalter, whose book *The Female Malady* (1985) is about just such a phenomenon.

Lucie[3]

Kapittel XIV

På Malmøen

„Er Frederik og bader?"
„Ja, det er han vist."
Henny og fru Rejnertson sad i et lidet grottelignende lysthus tilhøjre for den egefarvede trævilla i norsk schwejtserstil. Villaen lå højt over fjorden på en stejlt skrånende bakke med terrasseformige anlæg lige ned til den hvide grusvej ved dampskibsbryggen.

Begge damerne var i lyse morgendragter, og Hennys hår hang løst ned ad ryggen, fugtigt efter badet. Fru Rejnertson holdt et hækletøj mellem hænderne, som hvilte i skjødet, og hun så gjennem lysthusdøren ud over fjorden, der lå så glat og ubevægelig i det hvide sollys, at den syntes overtrukken med en ishinde.

„Se på skibene og bådene, Henny," sa fru Rejnertson. „Er det ikke livagtig, som om de var fastfrosne, endda de går. Jeg har aldrig set noget så rart."

„Det kommer af varmen og af, at det er så blikkende stille, vel," svarte Henny. – „Frederik ser trist ud, Du, Karen."

„Ja, stakker. Han har friet og fåt nej."

„Har han fortalt Dig det?" Henny så overrasket hen på Karen.

„Nej, men det kan jeg forstå på alting. Sidst han var her i byen for to år siden, gik han hele tiden og nynned:

Du spørger, hvem hun ligner, og hvorledes hun ser ud,
den kvinde jeg til brud mig haver kåret.

Nu holder han på med en sørgelig vise af Gluntarne[4] om brustne håb og verdens forfængelighed. Det er vist hende, Hilda Holm der nede i Arendal, som har forlovet sig med Marstrand."

„Jeg kan nok forstå, at hun ikke vilde ha ham, Du. Havde han endda ikke vært præst."

„Nej, for det passer han slet ikke til," sa Karen. „Men en kone måtte han da vel sagtens kunne få sig."

„Blir han her en tid?"

„Nej, han rejser op til Grefsen i eftermiddag alt."

Henny sad og pakked ud af en avis et par sko, som· var bleven repareret, og som stuepigen havde hentet inde i byen om morgenen.

Dampskibspibens fløjten, der i den stille, solmættede luft hørtes dobbel skinger og gjennemtrængende, lød op til dem.

„Se efter, om der er nogen med til os, Henny. Jeg er så mør af varmen."

„Venter Du nogen idag, da?" spurgte Henny og rejste sig.

„På landet er man jo aldrig sikker."

Henny gik op ad jordtrappetrinnene i en græsbevokset bakke tilvenstre for lysthuset, på hvis top der var en mægtig hængeask med tætte, løvfulde grener opbundne til staver, som var nedrammet i en runding. I midten var et rundt bord med bænker omkring, og

---

3   *Lucie*. Copenhagen: Schubothe, 1888.
4   A reference to the Swedish writer Gunnar Wennerberg's duets, depicting student life at Uppsala University in the 1840s.

asken ligned en opslåt kjæmpeparaply. På den side, som vendte mod fjorden, var der lavet et kighul mellem grenene, hvorfra man kunde overse dampskibsbryggen.

„Holms stuepige, Nissens husjomfru, Bertelsens strygebræt, en vattersottig slagtermadam, to opløbne gutunger!" råbte Henny deroppefra med ansigtet anbragt i åbningen. „En dame i grå spaserdragt og blå parasol. Hun må vist skulle til os, for hun går hen til lågen."

„Blond eller mørk," spurgte fru Rejnertson og kom op til søsteren.

„Knuden i nakken er lys. Der snur hun om, så har lågen vært stængt."

„Lad mig." Fru Rejnertson skjøv Henny tilside og keg ud gjennem hullet.

„Det er jo den små fru Gerner. Det er synd, hun skal traske omvejen gjennem skoven i denne varmen."

„Tivolifruen,"[5] sa Henny og trak på næsen. „Hvad skulde vi også med hende, Karen?"

„Å jo, for jeg har ondt af hende. Hun har jo ingen, stakker. Og med den tørpinden til mand."

„Ja, før jeg vilde være gift med Theodor Gerner," sa Henny og fulgte efter Karen ned over jordtrinene. „Så'n en sta og egenretfærdig herre. Og så har jeg engang som lidet barn set ham pille noe fælt noe ud af næsen sin. Det glemmer jeg aldrig."

„Ish da, Henny," sa fru Rejnertson.

„Liker Du hende virkelig, Karen, eller er det ikke bare fordi hun er en ,kvinde med fortid'?"

Henny udtalte de sidste ord med vrængende stemme.

„Å, jeg ved ikke. Jeg tænkte fra først af, at jeg kunde tat mig lidt af hende. Men hun er så forbeholden. Jeg får aldrig tag i hende."

„Har hun ikke vært så'n, ja slet og ret et offentligt fruentimmer?" spurgte Henny med en grimace.

„Nej da, Henny, så galt har det langtifra vært. Men selv som så var – vi gifter os jo allesammen med så at sige offentlige mandtimmere."

Karen gik hen til hjørnet af villaen og så ned ad stien langs skovkanten.

„Goddag, fru Gerner," råbte hun straks efter og gik hurtig nogle skridt nedover. „Det var da rigtig pent af Dem. Velkommen skal De være!" Hun tog begge Lucies hænder tiltrods for den opslåte parasol og kyssed hende.

„Her er min søster, frøken Brandt." Hun tørte Lucie hen til grotten, hvor Henny havde sat sig ned igjen." Og her er fru Gerner, Henny."

Lucie hilste og smilte og sa ingenting.

„Sæt Dem ned da." Fru Rejnertson trak en havestol frem. „Vi holder til her idag, for her er kjøligere. Siden skal De få bade. Nu må De hvile Dem lidt."

„Vil De ikke lægge hatten af, frue?" spurgte Henny, som gjerne vilde være venlig.

Lucie smilte og takked og tog hatten af.

„Så dejligt som her er," sa hun og drog vejret dybt. „En måtte næsten bli et bedre menneske af at bo her."

„Ja, her er bra," svarte fru Rejnertson. „Og så indelukket. Med fjorden foran og skoven klods op bagtil, kunde en gjerne tro, en var de eneste, som bode her, hvis en ikke vidste, der lå landsted på landsted som en krans rund om øen."

„Men hvad er det, Du har fundet i den gamle, fillede avisen, som optar Dig slig, Henny?" Hun vendte sig til søsteren, der sad og læste i bladet, skoene havde været svøbt i, med en mine og holdning, som om hun stjal sig til det.

„Det er om kvindesagsmødet fra i vinter. Nu har jeg bare to linjer tilbage."

---

5   Lucie used to be a dancer at Tivoli, a popular amusement park in Copenhagen. The other women often refer to her as "Tivolifruen", the Tivoli wife.

„Gud bevares, hvor hun blir overdænget, denne fru Asmundsen," Henny la avisen fra sig. „Hvad er det, hun egentlig har sagt for noe? Det kan jeg ikke finde ud af gjennem alle de skjældsord."

„Å, det var dette, at kvinderne ikke kunde tale med om sædeligheden, fordi så mange af dem var kjønsløse."

„Var det noe at bli så rasende for, da?" spurgte Henny.

„Jo, for nu da dette sædelighedsrabalder er rejst, har de forandret signaler. Det er ikke som før i tiden, da vilde kvinderne gjerne gjælde for angeliske naturer, som var rene og usanselige i sin kjærlighed, men nu er de ved gud ligeså sanselige som mændene, og derfor skal mændene værs'god tøjle sig liksom de selv har gjort."

„Men sig mig engang," sa Lucie ivrigt. „Tror De, det er sandt dette, at kvinderne –" hun stansed pludseligt, ramt af et agtpågivende blik fra Henny, og blev rød. „Ja, jeg mente bare – Nej, nå husker jeg ikke, hva' jeg mente."

„Hun må ha sagt mere end det," sa Henny efter nogen taushed. „For her i bladet står, at hvis hendes meninger gik igjennem, så blev det skamløsheden sat i system."

„Ja, hun sa noget om, at tilstanden var så slet, som den kunde være, og at det aldrig vilde bli anderledes, før det kom dertil, at det at tilfredsstille kjærlighedsdriften ikke længer kaldtes for usædelighed."

„Hvordan skulde det gå til da?" spurgte Henny og satte albuerne på bordet og kinderne i hænderne.

„Jo, for engang måtte vel menneskene ta fornuften fangen og rette sit arbejde på at omforme livet, istedetfor at spilde sine kræfter på at underkue driften. Og derfor burde alle alvorlige mennesker være socialdemokrater."

„Skulde der være noen hjælp i det, da?"

„Når samfundet blev ordnet socialdemokratisk, vilde alt det løses af sig selv. For det, det egentlig drejed sig om, var det økonomiske. I politik vidste vi, at magt var ret. På kjærlighedsområdet var det ligedan, og her vilde magt sige midler, både for mand og kvinde, til at ernære sig ordentlig."

„Men skulde vi da la sædeligheden gå i sin gamle gjænge?" sa Henny ivrigt. „Ja, for socialister kan vi dog vel ikke gå hen og bli."

„Kvinderne havde for tiden ingen anden opgave end at væbne og værge sig, mente fru Asmundsen. Ethvert ærligt og fornuftigt menneske vidste, at Hanskekravet[6] var noget, som hang løst i luften og altid vilde bli hængende der. Og derfor var der intet andet at gjøre, end såvidt muligt skaffe sig den samme fortid som mændene. Så vilde kvinderne ikke gå hen og lide kvaler i ægteskabet ved tanken på sin mands fortid. Så blev hun heller ikke så fortvilet over hans utroskab. Hun vilde da bedre kunne forstå, hvordan sligt gik til og også vide at trøste sig. Ægteskaberne vilde bli meget lykkeligere på den vis."

„Jeg begriber ikke, at De kan huske så mye af det," sa Lucie beundrende.

I det samme faldt en skygge hen over fru Rejnertsons ansigt, som Lucie sad og så på. Hun drejed hurtig hodet. Pastor Brandt i sort bonjour, pannamahat, hvidt slips og med den lange dameguldkjæde udenpå vesten stod midt i indgangen.

„Å, er Du der, Fredrik," sa Karen. „Du kjender jo fru Gerner."

Lucie letted sig halvt i sædet og hilste. Brandt bukked stift.

„Vil Du sætte Dig her hos os? eller hvad vil Du?" spurgte Karen.

„Hvis jeg ikke forstyrrer" – han satte sig på bænken ved siden af Henny og så åndsfraværende hen for sig. „Samtalen gik så kjapt da jeg kom," hans stemme lød tung og liksom kuet.

---

[6] A reference to Bjørnson's demand in his play *En Hanske* that both men and women should remain chaste until marriage.

„Vi talte om, hvad der må til for at et ægteskab skal bli lykkeligt," sa Henny. „Karen mener, at kvinderne bør slå sig løs."

Karen gjorde miner til Henny og så på Brandt med et blik, som om hun havde ondt af ham.

„Når kvinderne i de øvre samfundslag synker, så er det forbud på statens undergang," sa Brandt stille hen for sig.

Karen bed sig i læben, som for at ta ordet fra sig selv, men så kunde hun ikke dy sig og sa: „Det var sålænge kvinderne var engler, det. Når engler synker eller falder, så må jo enden være nær, men at det ikke varsler om nogen undergang, når talen er om mennesker, har mændenes eksempel længe nok bevist os. Da bruger man heller ikke ordet synke, da siger man „leve"."

„Du vilde altså rolig finde Dig i, at det onde sejred over det gode," sa Brandt sagtmodig og sukked.

„Godt er kun godt sålænge det kaldes således," svarte Karen. „I gamle dager var det godt og fortjenstfuldt at lemlæste uskyldige kvinder, indtil de svor de kunde hekse, og så brænde dem bagefter. Overhovedet eksisterer der ikke den forbrydelse i verden, som ikke har vært praktiseret til guds ære og menneskenes sande gavn."

„Ja, jeg skal ikke disputere med Dig, Karen," Brand slog mat ud med hånden. „Det var forresten en let sag at modsige Dig. Men jeg er ikke oplagt."

„Og er det ikke mændene, som tiltrods for sit liv har frembragt alt hvad vi agter og ærer og berømmer som stort og menneskeværdigt," vedblev Karen. „Og ernært os da! De har beholdt sin arbejdskraft usvækket. Mens kvinderne! – Jo, de har vært engler og glædespiger de, for det var deres mission og bestemmelse. Ser vi på frugterne, er der ikke noget afskrækkende i mændenes liv."

„Nej, kvinderne kan såmen gjerne stikke piben i sækken," sa Brandt livligere. „Vi går ud fra grundforskjellige præmisser, men i konklusionen er jeg enig. Og nu alt dette kjav om kvindernes rettigheder. Må jeg spørre, om de ikke besidder den største, den mest tyranniske af alle rettigheder: den at uddele kurve til sine offere. Hvad vil de mere?"

„Som om ikke mændene også gav kurver," sa Karen.

„Å de stakkerne! De går da ialtfald ikke hen og koketterer med en dame og bilder hende ind, de vil ha hende, bare for at ha den triumf at sige nej bagefter. Nej, kvinderne er samvittighedsløse nok i forvejen, om en ikke skulde gå hen og gjøre dem værre ved at gi dem endnu flere rettigheder." Brandt rejste sig.

„Jeg er så tørstig," sa han, „nej, bli' bare siddende," han vinked med hånden til Henny og Karen, der begge letted sig i sædet. „Jeg skal nok selv finde hvad jeg vil ha, og selters kan jeg be Lina om."

> „Ak hur vort liv er elendigt
> Det börjer med ståk
> Og det ender med gråt,
> Fins en sälhet som
> Vorre bestandigt,"

nynned han, mens han langsomt gik opover verandatrappen.

„Sig mig bare en ting," sa Henny, da Brandt var borte. „Hvad skal der gjøres med børnene i disse løse forbindelser?"

„Føde og klæde dem hver efter evne, naturligvis," svarte Karen. „Når det ikke længer var nogen skam at ha børn, så blev alt det lettere og anderledes. Og de, som ikke havde råd til at ha børn, behøved jo ikke at få nogen."

„Sa fru Asmundsen det?" råbte Henny.

„Ialtfald noget lignende."

„Så undrer det mig ikke, at de snakker om strafbare og pestbefængte lærdomme. For ved Du hvad, Karen!"

„Aa, den hykleriske idiotanstalten," råbte fru Rejnertson, og slog til bladet på bordet foran Henny. „Som om mændene ikke praktiserer det over en lav sko, just netop i de øvre lag, Fredrik snakked om, som om det ikke blir dem anbefalet af læger og sundhedspoliti her i vort sædelige, hanskesmykkede hyklersamfund."

Stuepigen kom og spurgte om hvad slags syltetøj, der skulde sættes på bordet. „Nu kommer jeg." Fru Rejnertson rejste sig. „Hvis Di vil bade, er der akkurat tid inden vi spiser," sa hun til Lucie.

„Så henter jeg nøglen," sa Henny og løb ind i huset.

Lucie var ganske fortumlet. Aldrig i sit liv havde hun følt sig så underlig tilmode. Hun var altså like go' som Theodor, og behøved ikke at skamme sig for hun havde vært sån. Å gud, kundskab og lærdom og en forstand som fru Rejnertson sin! Å for herlige gaver det var. Det var derfor hun havde det så lejt og vont og lod sig hundse af Theodor, fordi hun ingenting vidste og ingenting tænkte. – Tårerne kom styrtende. – Ja, også fordi Theodor heller ikke vidste om så'nt noe, som fru Rejnertson havde talt om.

Da Henny nærmed sig lysthuset, svingende badehusnøglen i et bånd på pegefingeren, så hun Lucie sidde og hulke med lommetørklædet for ansigtet. Hun stansed med et sæt og gik baglænds et stykke tilbage. Så gav hun sig til at nynne på en visestump og kom frem igjen, trampende alt hvad hun kunde med de tynde morgensko.

„Her er nøglen, fru Gerner," hun vendte halvt ryggen til indgangen og havde travlt med at fjerne fra en rosenbusk nogle makstukne blade, som hun omhyggelig la ned i sin hule hånd.

„Tak," sa Lucie og kremted for at klare stemmen.

„Jeg følger Dem ned over anlægget," sa Henny, da Lucie rakte hånden frem efter nøglen.

De gik forbi græsplænen og blomsterbedene på fladen foran huset nedover den skrånende bakke, hvor grusvejen delte sig i to, som begge førte ned til den lille låge i skigården. Dernede stak dampskibsbryggen ret frem i vandet, lang og hvid i solskinnet.

„En får lyst til at sætte sig her alle steder," sa Lucie og stansed ved en mosgroet bænk, hugget ud i et klippestykke, som var dækket af vild vin og havde nogle hængebirker på toppen."

„End her da," svarte Henny, som var nogle stentrappetrin længere nede. „Her under granen er den yndigste bænk en kan tænke sig. Men vi får nok skynde os, skal vi bli færdig til middagen.. Jeg skal jo også klæ mig om."

Udenfor den lille låge rakte Henny nøglen til Lucie. „De kjender jo badehuset. Den tredje brygge fra dampskibsbroen."

Lucie[7]

Chapter XIV

On Malmø

Translated by Katherine Hanson and Judith Messick

'Has Fredrik gone for a swim?'

'Yes, I think so.'

Henny and Mrs. Reinertson were sitting in a little summerhouse constructed like a grotto at the right of a large, dark-timbered house built in the Norwegian-Swiss style. The house lay high above the fjord on a steeply sloping hill, which was terraced all the way down to the white gravel road by the steamship wharf.

Both women were wearing light housecoats, and Henny's hair, still moist after her swim, hung loosely down her back. Mrs. Reinertson was holding a piece of crochet work in her hands, which were resting in her lap, and through the summerhouse door she gazed at the fjord, so bright and unmoving in the white sunshine that it seemed glazed with ice.

'Look at the ships and boats, Henny,' Mrs. Reinertson said. 'Isn't it striking the way they look like they're stuck in the ice, and yet they're moving? I've never seen anything so strange.'

'It must be the heat, and because it's so dead calm,' answered Henny. 'Fredrik seems sad, Karen.' 'Yes, the poor thing. He's proposed marriage and been turned down.'

'He told you that?' Henny looked at Karen in surprise.

'No, but I can tell in other ways. The last time he was in town two years ago, he went around the whole time singing to himself:

You ask who she favors, and if she is fair,
The woman I've chosen for my bride.

'Now it's a sad song from *Gluntarne*[8] about blasted hopes and the vanity of the world. I'm sure it's that Hilda Holm in Arendal who's engaged to marry Marstrand.'

'I can understand why she wouldn't accept him. If only he weren't a pastor.'

'No, he's not at all suited to it,' said Karen. 'But surely he must be able to find himself a wife.'

'Is he staying here awhile?'

'No, he's going up to Grefsen this afternoon.'

Henny removed the newspaper wrappings from a pair of shoes that been repaired in the city and that the housemaid had picked up that morning.

The steamship whistle reverberated up to them, doubly strident and piercing in the still, sun-drenched air.

'Look and see if it's brought someone to visit us, Henny. I'm so limp from this heat.'

'Are you expecting somebody today?' Henny asked, getting up.

'You never know in the country.'

Henny walked up the earthen steps of a grassy hill to the left of the summerhouse; at the top of the hill was a gigantic weeping ash whose thick, leafy branches, bound into

---

[7]   *Lucie*. Norwich: Norvik Press, 2001.

[8]   See footnote 4.

staves, were fastened around in a circle. With a round table encircled by benches in the centre, the ash looked like a giant open umbrella. On the side facing the fjord, a peephole had been made in the branches through which a person could look down at the steamship wharf.

'The Holms' housemaid, the Nissens' housekeeper, the Bertelsens' ironing board, a butcher's wife with dropsy, two gangly boys!' Henny called out, her face at the opening. 'A lady in a grey walking dress with a blue parasol. She must be coming here since she's going over to the gate.'

'Blond or dark?' asked Mrs. Reinertson, coming up to her sister.

'The knot at the back of her neck is blond. Now she's turning around, so the gate must be locked.'

'Let me see,' Mrs. Reinertson pushed Henny aside and peeked through the hole.

'Why, it's little Mrs. Gerner. What a pity that she'll have to tramp through the woods in this heat.'

'The Tivoli wife,'[9] said Henny, wrinkling her nose. 'What do we want with her, Karen?'

'You know, I feel sorry for her. She has nobody, the poor thing. And with that dried up old stick of a husband.'

'Yes, I can't imagine being married to Theodor Gerner,' said Henny following Karen down the earthen steps. 'Such an obstinate, self-righteous man. And once when I was little, I saw him pick something disgusting out of his nose. I'll never forget it.'

'Now really, Henny,' said Mrs. Reinertson.

'Do you truly like her, Karen? Isn't it just because she's 'a woman with a past'?' Henny pronounced the last words in a mocking tone.

'Oh I don't know. I thought at first that I could help her a little. But she's so reserved I can't get through to her.'

'Wasn't she one of those – well, not to mince words – a woman of easy virtue?' Henny asked with a grimace.

'No Henny, it wasn't as bad as that! But even if she were – *we* marry what can only be called men of easy virtue.' Karen walked over to the corner of the house and looked down the footpath along the edge of the forest.

'Good day, Mrs. Gerner,' she called out soon after, walking a few quick steps downhill. 'This is very kind of you. Welcome!' She took both of Lucie's hands, in spite of the open parasol, and kissed her.

'This is my sister, Miss Brandt.' She led Lucie over to the summerhouse, where Henny had seated herself again. 'And this is Mrs. Gerner, Henny.'

Lucie greeted her and smiled but said nothing more.

'Do sit down.' Mrs. Reinertson pulled over a garden chair. 'We're sitting out here today because it's cooler. You can take a swim later on. Now you must rest a little.'

'Won't you take off your hat, Mrs. Gerner?' Henny asked, wanting to be friendly.

Lucie smiled, thanked her, and took off her hat.

'It's so beautiful here,' she said taking a deep breath. 'Living out here would almost have to make you a better person.'

'Yes, it is beautiful,' Mrs. Reinertson replied. 'And so secluded. With the fjord in front and the forest close up in back, you could really believe you're the only one here if you didn't know the country houses make a wreath around the island.'

'But what have you found in that ragged old newspaper, Henny?' She turned toward her sister who was surreptitiously reading the sheet in which the shoes had been wrapped.

---

[9]   See footnote 5.

'It's about a women's rights meeting last winter. I just have two more lines.'

'My goodness, this Mrs. Asmundsen is certainly getting raked over the coals.' Henny put the newspaper down. 'What did she actually say? I can hardly tell through all the insults.'

'Oh, she said that women can't talk about sexual morality because so many of them are sexless.'

'Is *that* anything to get so worked up about?' Henny asked.

'Yes, because now that this ruckus about morality has come up, they've changed their tune. It's not like before, when women were pleased to be regarded as angelic beings, so pure and spiritual in their love. Now, by Heaven, they're just as sensual as the men, and therefore men must kindly restrain themselves, just the way women have done.'

'But tell me,' Lucie said eagerly, 'do you think it's really true that women …' She stopped suddenly, encountering an attentive look from Henny, and blushed. 'Well I just thought – oh now I don't remember what I thought.'

'She must have said more than that,' Henny said, after a silence. 'The newspaper says that if her ideas spread, indecency will be legitimized.'

'Something to the effect that the situation now couldn't be worse, and it would never be any different until satisfying love's urges was no longer regarded as immorality.'

'And how is that going to happen?' Henny asked, putting her elbows on the table and resting her cheeks on her hands.

'Well at some point people will have to come to their senses and direct their work toward reforming life, instead of wasting their energy repressing their desires. And that's why all serious people should be Social Democrats.'

'Do you think that would help?'

'If society were run by Social Democratic principles, all this would solve itself. Because the crux of the problem is economic. In politics we know that might makes right. In the domain of love it's the same, and here 'might' means the opportunity for both men and women to properly provide for themselves.'

'But are we just supposed to let morality follow the same old course?' Henny said heatedly. 'Because we can't all go off and become Socialists!'

'Mrs. Asmundsen says that right now women have no more important duty than to arm and defend themselves. Every honest and reasonable person knows that the *Gauntlet*-demand[10] is a pipe dream and it always will be. And so the only recourse, as far as possible, is to have the same past as the men. Then a woman wouldn't have to suffer agonies in marriage wondering about her husband's past. Nor would she be so upset about his infidelity. She'd be able to better understand how things like that happened, and how to console herself. Marriages would be much happier in this regard.'

'I can't imagine how you remember so much of that,' Lucie said admiringly.

As Lucie gazed at her, she saw a shadow momentarily cross Mrs. Reinertson's face. She quickly turned her head. Pastor Brandt was standing in the doorway wearing a black topcoat, panama hat, white cravat, and the long gold ladies' watch chain hanging outside his vest.

'Oh there you are, Fredrik,' said Karen. 'You know Mrs. Gerner, of course.'

Lucie half rose in her chair and greeted him. Brandt bowed stiffly.

'Won't you sit here with us? Or what would you like to do?' Karen asked.

'If I'm not intruding,' he answered. He sat down on the bench next to Henny and gazed around absent-mindedly. 'You were having such a lively talk when I came in.' His voice was heavy and subdued.

---

[10]   See footnote 6.

'We were talking about the requirements for a happy marriage,' said Henny. 'Karen thinks that women should let themselves go.'

Karen made a face at Henny and looked at Brandt as if she felt sorry for him.

'When women in the highest levels of society sink to that level, it's a sign that the collapse of the state is near,' Brandt said quietly.

Karen bit her lip, and looked as if she was trying to restrain herself, but then she couldn't resist saying, 'That's as long as women are angels. When angels rise or fall, then the end of the world must be near, but there's no warning about destruction when we're talking about human beings, as the example of men has demonstrated long enough. You don't use the word 'fall,' either, you say a man 'lives'.'

'So you would calmly accept evil triumphing over good?' Brandt said mildly, with a sigh.

'Good is only what people say it is,' Karen answered. 'In the old days, it was considered good and appropriate to mutilate innocent women until they swore they were witches, then burn them afterwards. There is absolutely no crime in the world that hasn't been committed for the glory of God and the good of mankind.'

'Well, I'm not going to argue with you, Karen,' Brandt waved his hand. 'It's easy enough to refute you, but I'm not in the mood.'

'And isn't it the men, who, in spite of the lives they've led, have produced everything we respect and honour?' Karen continued. 'And provided for us as well! They've kept their productive capacity undiminished. While women! – Well, they've been angels and women of pleasure – that's been their mission and their destiny. If we look at the results, there's nothing so horrifying about men's lives.'

'Indeed the women should really pipe down,' Brandt said with more animation. 'We're starting from fundamentally different premises, but I agree with your conclusion. And now all this fuss about women's rights. I ask you, don't they possess the greatest, the most tyrannical of all rights – handing out refusals to their victims? What more do they want?'

'As if men didn't refuse women, too,' Karen said.

'Oh the poor things! At least men don't start a flirtation with a woman, make her fancy they want to marry her, just to have the triumph of saying no afterwards. Oh no, women have little enough conscience to begin with, you shouldn't be so quick to give them even more rights.' Brandt got up.

'I'm so thirsty,' he said. 'No, don't get up.' He waved a hand at Henny and Karen, who both started to rise. 'I'll find what I want myself and I can ask Lina for seltzer water.'

> Oh, the misery of our life!
> Is there any joy on our earthly path
> That does not begin in glory
> And end in tears?
> There is no bliss that lasts forever!

He hummed as he slowly walked up the steps of the veranda.

'Tell me one thing,' said Henny after Brandt had left. 'What should be done with the children from these unsanctioned relationships?'

'Feed and clothe them according to one's ability, naturally,' answered Karen. 'If having children were no longer shameful, things would be simpler and different. And those who couldn't afford to have children wouldn't need to have any.'

'Did Mrs. Asmundsen say *that*?' cried Henny. 'Then I hardly wonder that they talk about criminal, pestilential doctrines. Really, Karen!'

'What a hypocritical, idiotic institution!' Mrs. Reinertson cried, waving at the paper on the table in front of Henny. 'As if men didn't practice it all the time, especially in the upper classes Fredrik talked about – if it weren't recommended by doctors and the health police here in our virtuous, *Gauntlet*-festooned, hypocritical society.'

The housemaid came in and asked what kind of jam should be put on the table.

'I'm coming,' said Mrs. Reinertson, getting up. 'If you want to take a swim, there's just enough time before we eat,' she said to Lucie.

'I'll go and get the key,' said Henny running into the house.

Lucie was quite dazed. Never in her life had she felt so unsettled. So she was just as good as Theodor, and didn't need to be ashamed because she'd been like *that*. Oh God, knowledge and book learning and a mind like Mrs. Reinertson's! Oh what wonderful gifts they were. That was the reason she was so miserable and let Theodor browbeat her – because she didn't know anything and didn't think about anything. – The tears came in a rush. – Yes, and because Theodor knew nothing about the things Mrs. Reinertson had talked about either.

When Henny approached the summerhouse, the bathhouse key swinging by a ribbon on her finger, she saw that Lucie was weeping with a handkerchief pressed to her face. She came to an abrupt stop and walked back a short distance the way she had come. Then she began humming a snatch of song, and advanced again, walking as heavily as she could in her thin slippers.

'Here's the key, Mrs. Gerner.' She was half-turned toward the entrance, busily clearing some worm-eaten leaves from a rosebush and collecting them in the palm of her hand.

'Thank you,' Lucie said, clearing her throat to steady her voice.

'I'll walk down with you through the grounds,' Henny said, when Lucie reached for the key.

They walked by the lawn and the flowerbeds on the level area in front of the house, down the diagonal slope to the place where the gravel path divided into two routes down to the little gate in the rail fence. Directly below lay the steamship wharf, gleaming long and white in the sunshine.

'You feel like sitting down every place you look,' Lucie said, stopping by a mossy bench carved out of the rock face and overhung by creeping vines and a weeping birch.

'How about here?' replied Henny, who was further down the stone steps. 'In here under the spruce is the most delightful bench you can imagine. But we really have to hurry if we're going to be ready for dinner. I have to change my clothes, too.'

Outside the little gate, Henny handed the key to Lucie. 'You know the bathhouse. The third dock from the steamship wharf.'

Primary Works

Constance Ring, 1885; Eng.tr. 1988.
Sjur Gabriel, 1887.
To Venner, 1887.
Lucie, 1888; Eng. tr. 2001.
Fjældmennesker, 1889 (with Erik Skram).
S.G. Myre, 1890.
Børnefortællinger, 1890.
Kjærlighed i Nord og Syd, 1891.
Forraadt, 1892; Eng. tr. *Betrayal*, 1986.

Agnete, 1893.
Professor Hieronimus, 1895. (In Eng. tr. *Under Observation*, 1992).
På Sct. Jørgen, 1895. (In Eng. tr. *Under Observation*, 1992).
Afkom, 1898.
Sommer, 1899.
Julehelg, 1900.
Mennesker, 1905.

Selected Bibliography

Bjerkelund, Ragni. *Amalie Skram. Dansk borger, norsk forfatter*. Oslo: Aschehoug, 1988.
Bjørby, Pål and Elisabeth Aasen, eds. *Amalie Skram – 150 år*. University of Bergen: Senter for humanistisk kvinneforskning 10, 1997.
Engelstad, Irene. *Amalie Skram om seg selv*. Oslo: Pax forlag, 1981.
–. *Sammenbrudd og gjennombrudd. Amalie Skrams romaner om ekteskap og sinnssykdom*. Oslo: Pax forlag, 1984.
–. Liv Køltzow, Gunnar Staalesen. *Amalie Skrams verden*. Oslo: Gyldendal. 1996.
Garton, Janet. *Norwegian Women's Writing 1850-1990*. London: Athlone Press, 1993.
–. ed. *Elskede Amalie. Brevvekslingen mellom Amalie og Erik Skram 1882-1899*. 1-3. Oslo: Gyldendal, 2002. (Selection of letters in *Caught in the Enchanter's Net. Amalie and Erik Skram's letters*. Norwich: Norvik Press, 2003.)
Haavet, Inger Elisabeth and Elisabeth Aasen, eds. *Amalie Skram – dikterliv i brytningstid*. University of Bergen: Senter for humanistisk kvinneforskning 6, 1993.
Kielland, Eugenia, ed. *Amalie Skram. Mellom slagene. Brev i utvalg*. Oslo: Aschehoug, 1976.
Køltzow, Liv. *Den unge Amalie Skram*. Oslo: Gyldendal, 1992.
Krane, Borghild. *Amalie Skrams diktning. Tema og variasjoner*. Oslo: Gyldendal, 1961.
Rasmussen, Janet E. "Amalie Skram as Literary Critic." *Edda* 1 (1981), 1-11.
Robinson, Michael and Janet Garton, eds. *Nordic Letters 1870-1910*. Norwich: Norvik Press, 1999.
Showalter, Elaine. *The Female Malady: Women, Madness and English Culture 1830-1980*. New York: Pantheon, 1985.
Tiberg, Antonie. *Amalie Skram som kunstner og menneske*. Kristiania: Aschehoug, 1910.
Aasen, Elisabeth, ed. *Amalie "Silkestrilen sin datter"*. Oslo and Bergen: Pax forlag and Amalie Skram Selskapet, 1996.
Årbok: Amalie Skram Selskapet. Bergen 1994-2005.

Victoria Benedictsson: The Problem of Female Artistry during the Modern Breakthrough

KATRIN ALAS (UNIVERSITY OF VIENNA)

Only a Woman

"Du kan aldrig bli annat än en kvinna." (You can never be anything but a woman.)[1] With this statement Victoria Benedictsson (1850-88) judged herself being nothing more than a woman and unable to produce real art, art in a man's fashion, the only way for her to get appreciation and men's approval. But why did she think so, when her books received good reviews and she, once her pseudonym was revealed, became well-known and was even considered to be the decade's greatest writer after none other than August Strindberg?

Victoria Benedictsson, born Victoria Bruzelius on March 6, 1850 near Trelleborg in the Swedish region of Skåne, dreamt as a young adult of becoming an artist. Her favorite subject was painting. But she did not dare to leave home against her father's will, although she regretted this decision. As soon as she found an opportunity to escape her status as a totally dependent daughter and the disharmony of her parent's marriage she took a chance and married Christian Benedictsson. He was the postmaster in the small town of Hörby and 30 years older than she, the widowed father of a flock of small children. Victoria now found herself in the position of being the mother of five children, with whom she soon had a very cordial relationship. Shortly, she was deeply sorry for her decision to marry.

After the first year of their marriage Benedictsson found she was pregnant, and she tried to kill herself. It was her first but not her last attempted suicide. She despised having sexual contacts but her hopes to escape having a sexual relationship with an aging husband were in vain. In 1873 her first daughter Hilma was born, followed by Ellen in 1876, who died within three

---

[1]   Victoria Benedictsson. *Stora Boken och Dagboken, 3. Dagbok 1886-1888.* Christina Sjöblad, ed. Lund: LiberFörlag, 1985, 298.

weeks after her birth, a fact that made Victoria feel guilty throughout her life, because during her pregnancy she had tried to get rid of this unwanted child.

Now, in the middle of the 1870s, Victoria Bernedictsson regularly began to write down her thoughts and experiences. With the chosen pseudonym Ivar F. Tardif she published her first romantic story entitled *Sirénen* (The Siren) in the newspaper *Sydsvenska Dagbladet* in 1875. She tried to find encouragement from different editors, but first after a persistent and protracted knee injury that confined her to her bed for several years, she had the possibility to intensely follow her passion to write and educate herself. Now, in the years 1881-83, when her annoying household duties were gone because of her injury, she devoted her time to reading and studying. It was also at this time that she began to write her diary, later called *Stora Boken* (The Great Book) – not published until 1985 – a collection of literary drafts and sketches, folk tales, anecdotes, studies and copies of her letters.

Finally, Victoria Benedictsson made her debut with the short story *En vilodag* (1883; A Day of Rest) in Uppsala's cultural magazine *Fyris*, edited by Franz von Schéele, who helped her to find a publisher for her first collection of short stories *Från Skåne* (1884; From Skåne). She established her literary reputation with this collection and at the same time introduced the pseudonym Ernst Ahlgren which she never gave up, although her true identity was soon known. It was now that Benedictsson adjusted her ideas according to the program of naturalism of the so-called Modern Breakthrough of the 1870s. As a result she developed her realistic style, and in 1884 established an intellectual friendship and teamed with Axel Lundegård (1861-1930), a later colleague and member of the group of writers who called themselves Det unga Sverige (Young Sweden) and a well-known realistic writer as well.

Victoria Benedictsson's first novel *Pengar* (Money) came out in 1885 and was received with much sympathy by the critics. As a result she received an invitation to visit Sophie Adlersparre in Stockholm, one of the leading members of the women's movement and woman editor of the *Dagny* magazine. Now it was obvious that Benedictsson, having access to the literary circles in the capital, belonged to the young and modern well-known authors of the country.

The following years show a hectic and astonishing productivity. To be economically independent, Benedictsson wrote numerous articles and short stories for various newspapers. Her annual income amounted to an average of 1,000 and 2,000 Swedish Kroner, results of her published books, newpaper fees and royalties of her plays.

A new period of her life began, when Benedictsson in 1886, in Copenhagen, fell in love with the leading Danish critic of the Modern Breakthrough, Georg Brandes (1842-1927). However, this unhappy relationship had no future, yet it labeled her as a tragic heroine in many literary histories to come. Victoria Benedictsson was deeply hurt, when her carefully written new novel *Mrs. Marianne* (Mrs. Marianne) was published in 1887 and was dismissed by Brandes as a "Dameroman" (a ladies' novel). All the other positive criticism and even the Swedish Academy's state-sponsored scholarship of 500 Kroner, which she received in 1887, did not give her any satisfaction; she felt herself generally rejected and condemned as a woman writer.

Her collection, *Folklif och småberättelser* (1887; Folk Life and Small Tales) was published the same year and the Kungliga Dramatiska Teatern in Stockholm successfully performed her play *I Telefon* (On the Telephone) on March 7, 1887. Still she felt her life was a failure, both as an artist and as a woman. On July 21, 1888 she committed suicide in Copenhagen, having left all her unpublished manuscripts to Axel Lundegård. Five days later she was quietly buried on Vestre Kirkegård in Copenhagen. On her gravestone one finds the name Ernst Ahlgren.

Woman and Artist

It is rather difficult to obtain more precise information about the personality of Victoria Benedictsson. Although she indulged herself in writing autobiographical documents, the wide range of the material shows, how much she wove fiction with autobiography. As early as in 1885 she decided to have her diaries published sooner or later, and with this in mind it is impossible to say how much of her writing was influenced by her wish to gloss things over and how much of it indeed gives a true account of her personality. She always had a tendency to play to the gallery and would willingly change her appearance in order to please her expected audience.

What appears from her diaries is the immense importance her writing had to her. In her work Benedictsson could find comfort, joy, happiness and the power to overcome all those dark periods of "weltschmerz" in her life which she regulary had to face. In her opinion work was the only possibility to find an identity and gain faith in one's self.

Of course, she felt different from women who found comfort only in marriage and children: "Hvad som gjorde skilnad på mig och andra qvinnor (...) vore att jag har hvad de nästan alla sakna: ett arbete." (What made a difference between me and other women [...] was that I had what all of them missed: work.)[2] She tried for herself to be acknowledged by men, especially by male artists – they were the only ones she granted any kind of genius and the faculty of judgment – and to be like one of them. While she

---

[2]   Benedictsson. *Stora Boken och Dagboken* 3, 194.

did not have many friends among women, she admired imputed male qualities like intellect and objectivity. The fulfilment of these postulates was
impossible for her – being a woman and experiencing herself as one. Thus
she suffered a kind of schizophrenia that split her into Victoria, the postmaster's wife, and Ernst Ahlgren, the writer. She clung to her pseudonym
till the very end. "Ernst" represented to her all the male parts in herself, her
ability to express herself in writing, the only abilities worth striving for.
But, being not male, she suffered the pressures and restrictions of women of
her time. In spite of protesting the female ideal of her society, self-
sacrificing motherhood, she felt herself as not being whole and needed a
male supplement.

When viewed from our perspective of the present, the life of Victoria
Benedictsson seems to have been more ambivalent about womanhood and
more complex in personality than has been acknowledged by many literary
histories. Critics were not interested in her art, but in her tragic fate and
suicide caused by her unhappy love for Georg Brandes. There is no doubt
about the painfulness of her relationship with Brandes, but she had already
endured the cultural stigmas of being an artist and a woman long before she
ever met him.

From the 1970s on the issue has been raised as to see Victoria Benedictsson as a feminist writer, both a heroine and a victim of the patriarchy.
She would not have known the meaning of "feminism", a word first used in
Sweden in the 1890s in the sense of "medvetenhet om kvinnoförtryck"
(awareness of women's suppression).[3] With a few exceptions Benedictsson
did not comment on the question of women's rights nor did she take part in
public discussion of socio- or sexual-political questions. Attitudes taken
from her diaries and letters, though changing throughout her lifetime,
clearly show her aim of being an objective portrayer of reality but never
taking sides in the "women's question", neither in favor of the conservative
women's movement with a positive attitude towards marriage, existing
since 1886 and lead by Sophie Adlersparre; nor in favor of the more radical
politico-cultural movement led by Georg Brandes, taking up the cause of
women's sexual liberation.

Benedictsson contradicted the women's movement with her convictions
of a general difference between female and male psyche, based on scientific
arguments of the theory of biological evolution of her time. She maintained
that in order to change outer circumstances in a sensible way you need an
inner liberation as well, otherwise the natural predispositions of men and
women would still go on producing different mental abilities.

After a visit to Stockholm in 1885, where she was asked to support
feminist requests, Victoria Benedictsson explained that she did not care

---

[3]   Claesson Pipping, 43.

more for women than for other humans. She strove for a balance between the sexes and rejected the idea of domination by one sex over the other. Nonetheless a monogamous marriage was the *non plus ultra* basis of Benedictsson's views on womanhood. However, she wished for new moral standards which to her meant a suppression of sexual desire through willpower. She never offered readers simple solutions. Her female figures show a range of possibilities to cope with life, from being self-sacrificing women to being artistically active women who get happiness from both work and love.

Victoria Benedictsson surely can not be considered a feminist in today's sense. She did not stand up for women's rights and expressed rather critical views concerning the radical developments in women's literature of her time. Throughout her life she depended on male authorities and their goodwill. Nonetheless, many of her matters of concern proved to be feminist: She knew of women's suppression, she knew of the sufferings of being female and their destroying effects on artistry. At the same time she looked for new alternatives for women's life, demanding better education and economical and social equality of the sexes.

Taking a closer look at the oeuvre of Victoria Benedictsson it becomes obvious that she primarily wrote short stories in her characteristic, realistic way. In addition, she wrote two well-known novels. The first, *Money*, deals with a young woman wanting to become an artist and ending in a conventional marriage. Here Benedictsson criticizes how young and uneducated women by way being fed romantic ideas, are pressed into lifelong marriages with economical dependence and sexual oppression. The novel ends with Selma, the main figure, breaking out of her marriage after having secured for herself some means to live on. Benedictsson's second novel, *Mrs. Marianne*, offers another point of view: the protagonist, Marianne, will not give up her marriage, although it faces severe difficulties. Rather, she finds a way of self-realization in motherhood and equal partnership, with the scene moved to a non industrial age in the countryside.

Scarcely known, however, is the fact that Benedictsson's oeuvre includes plays. From 1885 to 1888 she wrote five plays in different dramatic styles, beginning with *Final* (1885; Finale), the result of a team work with Axel Lundegård, followed by the staging of her one-act play *On the Telephone* in 1887. During the summer and fall of the same year she wrote a three-act comedy entitled *Teorier* (Theories) and in the last year of her life, in 1888, she wrote another one-act play *Romeos Julia* (Romeo's Juliet) (see below) and both a prose and dramatic version of a drama entitled *Den bergtagna* (The Spellbound). Yet, she was not as successful as a playwright as with her prose works.

Female dramatists made their first public appearances in Sweden during the Modern Breakthrough, a time of innovative literary activities from approximately 1870 to 1905 in Scandinavia. Initiated by Georg Brandes the task of this approach was now to debate social problems and discuss relevant questions of education and morality. The topics soon expanded to include the issues of women's rights and female sexuality, criticizing the sexual double moral standards. At the same time changes in the traditional images of women in the areas of culture, politics and art took place. More and more women wished to try to earn their own living by writing and publishing their own works.

One-Act Plays as a Female Domain

Until c. 1880 Swedish drama was a thoroughly male domain. Now female playwrights, including such well-known writers as Alfhild Agrell (1849-1923) and Anne Charlotte Leffler (1849-92) began to strive for professional acceptance. Their male critics feared they might change the literary quality of dramatic works for the worse, because they generally assumed that women were missing experience of life, never having had access to the big wide world and therefore had nothing of importance to tell. They were proved wrong: From 1880 to 1890 the plays of Anne Charlotte Leffler, for instance, were staged more often than the works of August Strindberg in Sweden. Many female writers did outstrip their male colleagues, because their precise and detailed knowledge of everyday home life, their ability to empathize with different persons and to show their inner life and problems of the human mind in general matched perfectly the demands of realism and the new drama. Their texts focused on women of the middle classes and their economical and social behavior concerning marriage, money, children and professional career.

Often female playwrights chose to publish one-act plays as a first attempt to establish a dramatical career. The one-act format was regarded as plain and simple. Usually these plays were performed before longer ones or several one-act plays followed one another. Personal data of the authors was not a requisite and thus helped to avoid public exposure. This ploy gained fairer reviews by male literary critics. These short plays lasted from fifteen minutes to one hour and represented a theatrical form that did not correspond with the Aristotelian drama, and was open to experimentation and did not employ the traditional sequence of conflict, climax and solution.

Romeo's Juliet

Romeo's Juliet, written in 1888, might not be the artistically most demanding work by Victoria Benedictsson, but it shows clearly how she felt about her artistry as a writer, expressed by the main protagonist Juliet, and emphasizes her female ideal of being an independent, successful artist and at the same time a loving woman in a fulfilling relationship. To work and to have a family was a dream many female writers shared. Benedictsson herself seemed pleased with what she had done, as she expressed it in a letter to Ellen Key: "En liten enaktspjäs, varm och mjuk som en fågelunge." (A little one-act play, warm and soft like a young bird.)[4]

The play itself was possibly staged at Svenska teatern in Stockholm, until 1888 called Nya teatern, which in 1925 burnt down together with its entire archives. Public performances took place in the Dutch city of Groningen and in Gothenburg in 1995; in the same year it was also played by the Gothenburg Radio Theatre.

In the course of the play, Stella Ramberg, a celebrated actress, is visited by young Arthur Zetterschöld, diplomat and poet, accompanied by Fritz Almquist, a famous writer. Almquist portrays Mrs. Ramberg, knowing her from a relationship from former days, in a bad light. Zetterschöld has hopes to seduce her. But in a conversation with her he becomes acquainted with and gains appreciation for her life story and views of life. The appearance of her children stress the atmosphere of a happy family life and Zetterschöld leaves with the realizisation that he has met a very special person.

The intimate tone of conversation in a home-like atmosphere brings about a personal relationship between Ramberg and Zetterschöld. This intimacy allows the discussion of very personal matters usually not brought into the public. When the men show their different opinions of Mrs. Ramberg, the audience may wonder whether the actress really is – stupid, as Almquist maintains, or yearning for a lover, as Zetterschöld thinks.

Now the perspective changes – Juliet herself appears and reduces both opinions offered to absurdity. She is more than a theater-Juliet, neither did she marry out of disappointment. The play takes advantage of the possibility of showing a very complex woman portrait. It deals, in addition, with the question of marriage and the debate of "free love", here being forcefully rejected: "Jag har aldrig känt frestelse att bli några veckors tidsfördrif för en annan." (I never felt tempted to be some weeks' pastime for another man.) Mrs. Ramberg talks quite naturally about her profession and her motherhood, giving new input to the discussion of female positions and status.

Juliet's former lover is characterized as being unkind and disapproving of female artists in general. He is neither grateful for her success with his

---

4   Sjögren, 242.

plays nor does he approve of her abilities. His cynical views have nothing to do with the "real" Juliet, as he calls her stupid and an idiot.

For Zetterschöld it is a question of courting and seducing. His dreams of conquest are shown in linguistic clichés. He regularly utters commonplace phrases like "De stränga äro de lidelsesfullaste" (Strict women are the most passionate) and "Konsten att vinna ett kvinna består i att gripa till" (The art to win a woman lies in seizing the opportunity). For him a woman means brainless beauty and passion. Whatever a woman may feel, he is sure to know that she will be unable to resist him. Mrs. Ramberg is nothing but a Juliet, in desperate need of a short passionate affair all the more because her youth is dwindling. That she is called honorable does not deter him. In their conversation Mrs. Ramberg makes him feel insecure because of her intelligence. Now, she has a chance to talk about herself and her work as an artist. In the end he alters his views about her and develops them into a more genuine and respectful relationship between man and woman.

Stella Ramberg turns out to be a strong, independent and intelligent woman. Her success did not come easily – and her account of her childhood and youth serves sociocritical means as well. Zetterschöld learns that she is anything but stupid, when she is referring to his poems and later in a most unconventional manner tells him that she did see through him.

Here Benedictsson paints a long cherished dream of the ideal marriage. There is no jealous husband who lays any claim on Mrs. Ramberg, she is "inte någon kufvad hustru, (...) bevakas inte som en mans egedom" (no suppressed wife (...) not guarded as any man's property) and conscious of her value as a human being and an artist. Stella Ramberg is a utopian figure, as is typical for the Modern Breakthrough and possible still is, who most successfully has combined private and professional happiness and found fulfilment through her children, her husband and her creative work.

Romeos Julia[5]

Dramatisk interiör

Utdrag

(...)
Almquist (*sätter sig*): Du kommer att bränna dina kol förgäfves. Fra Ramberg är (*med en axelryckning*) en "ärbar kvinna".

Zetterschöld: Så mycket bättre! De stränga äro de lidelsefullaste.

Almquist: Don Juan!

Zetterschöld: Också i kärlek gäller att lyckan står dem djärfvom bi. Konsten att vinna ett kvinna består i att gripa till.

(...)
Almquist: Jag vill inte såra din unga själfkänsla. Men jag kunde ha lust att upplysa dig om ännu en sak... (*Hviskar förtroligt.*) Stella Ramberg är – ja – hon är dum.

Zetterschöld: Det är inte något fel, att en vacker kvinna är... låt oss säga mindre begåfvat.

Almquist: Du ändrar kanske mening, när du lärt känna henne.

Zetterschöld: Man *skull* inte känna de kvinnor man älskar; det förtar illusionen. Tänk på Romeo och Julia; inte kände *de* hvarandra! Hela härligheten omfattar några dagar – men hur mycket lidelse rymma de inte!

Almquist: Lidelsen lockar dig – därför lockar hon dig, den poetiska Julia!

Zetterschöld: Jag har sällan sett något mer bedårande.

Almquist: Shaksperes Julia är härlig – men – hon var ingen grosshandlarfru.

Zetterschöld: Är Stella Ramberg inte vacker?

Almquist: Jag tycker inte om tulpaner. De skina på afstånd, men kommer man närmre och vill se ner i en av dem... är den tom och utan doft.

Zetterschöld: Du är ond på henne?

Almquist: Visst inte. (*Skrattar.*) I åtta år har tulpanen blommat för kassaskåpet, och tre gånger har hon satt frö.

Zetterschöld: Åtta år. Och ingen älskare?

Almquist: Nej.

Zetterschöld: (*upprepar långsamt, liksom för sig själf*): Åtta år med en grosshandlare! Hur måste den kvinnan kunna älska!

Almquist: Ja på scenen.

Zetterschöld: Kraften, innerligheten i hennes framställning tyda på en hemlig sträng, som vibrerar och ger de döda orden lif.

Almquist: Vad skulle det vara för en sträng?

Zetterschöld: Längtan! Hon drömmer om Romeo.

Almquist: Det vill säga om dig!

Zetterschöld: Om mig eller om någon annan – det kan bero på en slump!

Almquist: Romeo åt en kälkborgarfru! Åt den frökroppsligade dussinärbarheten! Väl bekomme!

Zetterschöld: Kan du inte förstå, att just en kvinna, som i sin ungdom aldrig har haft någon roman – eller låt oss säga: som levat "ärbart" – i sitt innersta *måste* ha en hopspard fond av lidelse, som aldrig kommit till användning i det så kallade äktenskapet – en institution som...

---

5   The original orthography has been retained.

Almquist (*avbryter*): ... en institution som jag tillhör – med hull och hår.

Zetterschöld (*småleende*): Romeo och Julia voro också gifta – "i hemlighet" säger den filuren Shakspere. – En ärbar kvinna kan under de flackaste yttre förhållanden gå och gömma på ett svärmiskt hopp om äfventyret, som en kvinna alltid drömmer om – *att bli älskad*. – Och i drömmen känner hon ungdomen glida undan – hur måste icke en sådan kvinna kunna älska!

Almquist: Men du, alla dårars dåre, förstår du då inte vad hela sta'n vet: att hon är nöjd med sin grosshandlare, att hon utom scenen bara lefver för grosshandlarn och för grosshandlarns barn.

Zetterschöld: Julia?

Almquist: Ja. Det är barockt, men Julia har funnit sin Romeo, och Romeo är ett kassaskåp. (*Tystnad.*) Den som söker smultron skall inte gräfva i ett potatisland! Men lycka till! Du tycks vara i stånd att njuta och beundra till och med ett jordpärons fullkomligheter!

Zetterschöld (*lägger händerna på hans axlar och ser honom i ögonen*): Det ligger agg i tonen.

Almquist: För det jag upplyser dig om att hon är dum!

Zetterschöld: Hon är en verklig konstnärinna.

Almquist: Rachel[6] var en *stor* konstnärinna – och kunde inte skrifva ett brev. Så är det oftast med skådespelerskor: deras röst och minspel ljuger fram en intelligens, som de alldeles sakna.

Zetterschöld: Inte hon! Den allmänna menningen om Fru Ramberg är...

Almquist (*avbryter*): Jag har aldrig känt mig solidarisk med den allmänna meningen. (*Tystnad.*)

Zetterschöld: Har du varit bekant med henne länge?

Almquist: Hon skapade titelrollen i mitt första skådespel.

Zetterschöld: Jag måtte ha varit utomlands den tiden. Hur gick det till? Berätta.

Almquist: Hon var ung, såg hyggligt ut och hade den gåfvan att kunna kackla vers. Naturligtvis föll det mig in, att hon var som klippt och skuren för skådespelet, som jag nyss fått färdigt. Jag studerade alltså in rollen med henne – där har du hela historien!

Zetterschöld: Hur spelade hon?

Almquist (*med en axelryckning*): Det blef succès!

Zetterschöld: Vad begär du mer?

Almquist: Men hon var en idiot!

Zetterschöld (*lyssnar*): Tst! Hon kommer! Du lämnar oss snart ensamma?

Almquist: Med största nöje!

(...)

Fru Ramberg: Tror ni inte, att jag förstått, varför ni kom? ... Jag skall gå era önskningar i förväg. Ni behöver inte förberedda någon lång belägring. Jag skall genast inviga er i allt.

(...)

Zetterschöld (*enkelt och varmt*): Jag har förnärmat er. Förlåt mig. (...) Ni har en underlig makt i er röst! Sluter jag ögonen och lyssnar, har jag stämmningen igen... en våldsam längtan att komma er närmre – närmre ... (*Buller utanför.*) Det är kanske er man?

Fru Ramberg: Han stör oss inte. Han är ett mönster för äkta man. Han känner sin plats. Han är kälkborgaren, och jag en konstnärinna, som tar emot beundrare. (*De lyssna båda.*) Ser ni! Där kom ingen svartsjuk äkta man in genom dörren. Jag är inte någon kufvad hustru, jag bevakas inte som en mans egedom; jag är en fri människa och kan

---

6   Rachel: the famous French actress Elisabeth Felix R. (1820-58).

göra allt vad jag vill. (*Går omkring och ordnar i rummet.*) Ni kan stanna så länge ni har lust.

Zetterschöld: Tack. Jag har redan uppehållit er alltför länge.

Fru Ramberg: Jag tycker om er.

Zetterschöld (*bugar stum, halft ironiskt*).

Fru Ramberg: Sätt er och låt oss tala uppriktigt. (...) Tror ni det finns mycket i mitt liv, som jag behöfver dölja?

Zetterschöld: Nej.

Fru Ramberg: Man menar, att det *måste* finnas – hos kvinnor som verkligen lefvat.

Zetterschöld: Det är naturligt. Med våra fördomar...

Fru Ramberg: Likafullt finns det människor så brett anlagda, att de tåla dagsljus öfver hela sitt liv. – Jag hör till dem. Och däri ligger min styrka.

Zetterschöld: Jag tror er.

Fru Ramberg: Det kommer också av vanan att äga en annans tillit, att bli trodd på sitt ord – alltid! – av denne ende. (*Tystnad.*)

Zetterschöld: Ni tänkte berätta mig något?

Fru Ramberg: Ja. Ni är diktare – – konstnär. Ni måsta känna människohjärtat, för det är människor ni skall skapa. Jag är också konstnär – ringare tycker ni – – bara en skådespelerska – – men också för mig är lifvet allt, också för mig är konsten att spela på det känsligaste strängarna i människornas sinnen. När vi äga makt öfver andra, makt att smälta och böja deras stämningar efter vår egen, då är det därför att vi känna starkare, mångsidigare än de, därför att lifvet griper djupare tag i oss än i hvardagsfolket. Bara det, som ligger inom räckvidden av vår egen natur, är äkta. – – – Ni såg, att Julias kärlek var det, därför sträckte ni ut er hand och sade: gif hit!

Zetterschöld (*sakta*): Den låg utanför min räckvidd.

Fru Ramberg: Ni vet inte vad det är att älska. (...) Det finns ett hemligt frimureri mellan oss. Märker ni det?

Zetterschöld (*nickar*): Ungdom, tror jag – den själens ungdom, som finns hos alla konstnärsnaturer.

Fru Ramberg: Ni har rätt. (*Räcker honom sin hand.*) Ni är god och ni är ung; ni får inte gå bort som en främling! Jag vill, att ni skall minnas mig och tänka: *sådan* var hon och inte sådan, som ... han kanske sagt er.

Zetterschöld: Hur kan ni tala om det?

Fru Ramberg: Det har gjort mig ont, det har gjort mig bitter och elak. Men nu är det förbi.

Zetterschöld: Ni ser lyckligt ut – Julia.

Fru Ramberg: Jag är lycklig – Romeo. Och för er, som skrifver vackra dikter, skall jag berätta min vackraste historia. Jag kom till elevskolan mycket ung. Så ung och så andligen omyndig, att jag var knappt mer än ett barn. Men ett barn med hundra lynnen, med skratt och sång och gråt i sin röst – allt som det bar till – och med hundra skiftningar i sin ansikte. Min minsta lilla tanke och min snabbaste stämning syntes strax; och vad jag, stackars toka, benämnde själ, bodde i ett glashus. Därför togs ansiktet i skola; det skulle lära att säga andras tankar och återge andras stämningar. Det var läraktigt, och jag kom snart på scenen. Men vad jag kallade själ tog inte jämna steg med mimiken. Jag spelade på instinkt – på outvecklade möjligheter. Intrigera kunde jag inte, men kom fram ändå. Jag, stackars fattiga unge från gränderna blef nästan rädd för applåder och hyllning, hade ingen tro på att det kunde räcka, darrade alltid för att nödgas vända tillbaka till kyffena.

Zettersköld: Stackare!

Fru Ramberg: Å, ja, ja! Ni kan inte veta, vad fattigdomen sätter för ett märke i en. Hur den jagar skräck genom märg och ben, gör en mjuk i rygg och knän. Det ryser i mig ännu, när jag tänker på att frysa och hungra. Det behöfver jag inte frukta för längre.

Zetterschöld: Det kom ångest i tonfallet bara för det ni talte om det. – Fortsätt!

Fru Ramberg: Ja. Hur var det? Jo... Så var det en ung, men redan känd författare, som skref ett historiskt skådespel, och jag utsås att skapa huvudrollen... Han instuderade den själf med mig.

Zetterschöld: Fritz Almquist!

Fru Ramberg: Han var en världsman, sedd i de finaste kretsar, son av en ansedd man, rikt gift, vacker. Ett snille, mente många; kvinnoeröfrare av smak och af fåfänga, granntyckt och fin, en bortskämd Adonis, som knappt vårdade sig om all den hyllning han fick. Vad visste jag om det! Jag kom aldrig i fina världen. För mig var han mer än världsman, han var skald – en gudarnas älskling: han blef min kejsare och kung.

Zetterschöld: Ofattbart!

Fru Ramberg: Jag talar, som jag kände det då. Det är länge se'n. Länge, länge!

Zetterschöld: Smärtar det er att berätta?

Fru Ramberg: A, nej. Det smärtar inte. Inte nu mer. Han tog min beundran som sin rättmätiga egendom. Varför skulle han inte? Han tycktes mig så stor och jag så ringa; jag var tacksam för det jag fick beundra honom. Jag vågade knappt svara, då han talte till mig, min tanke och handlingskraft förlamades i hans närhet, och det var som om hela min själ koncentrerats i två vidöppna ögon, med vilka jag betraktade honom – oafvändt – medan hvart hans ord ristade sig in i mitt minne som skuret med en diamant. (...) Vad jag var, var jag genom honom. Jag gick upp i hans verk, lefde i hans repliker. När han var god, då kändes det, som strålade solen öfver mig. Ännu – när jag tänker därpå – är det som dagen finge annan glans och blommorna finare doft. – – – Därom vet han ingenting annat att säga, än att jag var dum.

Zetterschöld: Älskade han då icke er?

Fru Ramberg (höjer på axlarna): Jag tror, somliga kalla det att älska ... Han fann behag i mig och lekte med mig.

Zetterschöld: Hur gick det?

Fru Ramberg: Det blef ett slags förhållande mellan oss. Inte brottsligt, men på gränsen.

Zetterschöld: Och hur slutade det?

Fru Ramberg: Han skulle göra en längre utrikes resa – bli borta ett par år. Jag tyckte det var, som om skolen skulle dö och gräs och blommor inte kunna växa... Och så kom han för att säga farväl. (Avbrutet och med ansträngning.) Det var en kväll. Vi voro alldeles ensamma – hemma hos mig. – Han var inte som vanligt, han var både mer varm och mer kall: – – – värmen var fordrande, och kylan – som låg under – gjorde mig rädd. – – – Ett enda ord av verklig känsla, och jag hade fallit; fem minuters tålamod och mitt lif skulle haft sitt benrangel att dölja ... Men ... han dröjde inte fem minuter, och det ordet ... det kom inte. (Efter en paus, med ett småleende.) Det var min lycka, att han den kvällen hade hjärta för andra än mig!

Zetterschöld: För vem mer?

Fru Ramberg: För sin hustru... Och alla de andra! Jag har förstått det sedan.

Zetterschöld: Och när han var borta?

Fru Ramberg: Då kom harmen, bitterheten, ärelystnaden, och min konstnärsindividualitet slog igenom. Den hade mognat i sol och vind; själen hade äntligen hunnit upp mimiken.

Zetterschöld: Ni gifte er sedan?

Fru Ramberg: Ja... När man känt, att ens bittraste själskval icke ens väcka medlidande, att man, med allt vad gott och ont som finns i ens varelse, med allt som kämpar i en för att forma sig till en karaktär – ändå inte är mer än ett nummer i en samling, och att den högsta ömhet man fick blott var samlarns stolthet, utan en skymt av annat – knappt ens av välvilja; då förstår man betydelsen av, att en man säger till en kvinna: blif min hustru.

Zetterschöld: Och ni är lycklig?

Fru Ramberg: Jag kan endast säga, att det inte finns en handling i mitt lif, inte en växling i mitt sinne, som jag behöfver ljuga bort för kälkborgarn, som ni kalla honom. Jag har aldrig känt frestelse att bli några veckors tidsfördrif för en annan.

Zetterschöld: Jag förstår er. (*Reser sig.*) Men det är på minnen av det andra, ni spelar?

Fru Ramberg (*reser sig också*): Nej. Sådant gör en människa gammal. Jag spelar på det som håller mig ung. (...) Jag har spelat Fritz Almquists kvinnoroller. Jag har gifvit dem vad de saknade: mänsklig värme – hjärta... Det har jag härifrån, från mitt hem.

Zetterschöld: Jag förstår!

Fru Ramberg: Förstår ni också, varför jag kunnat tala om allt detta utan bitterhet?

Zetterschöld: Ni äls...

Fru Ramberg: Säg inte ut. Det finns en känsla så sällsynt, att språket inte behövt skapa ord för den; den flammar inte vid första blick, den slocknar inte i en blink. Den växer av ett litet frö, näres av vissheten om en oinskränkt tillit – av tusen små värmeutstrålningar, av tusen små eftergifter. – – – Den växer som en planta och breder ut sig öfver ens liv. – Vid hvarje olycka, som hotar, varje missräkning, som möter, flyr man in under den: där är värme och trygghet. Och mot detta blir allt annat smått.

Zetterschöld (*bugar till afsked*): Jag gick att söka en konstnärinna och fann en människa. Jag ville bli bekant med en skådespelerska och lärde känna en fint tänkande kvinna... (*Sakta.*) Det är oändligt mycket mer!

(...)

Romeo's Juliet

Dramatic Interieur

Excerpts

Translated by Katrin Alas

(...)

Almquist (*sitting down*): You are going to waste your power. Mrs. Ramberg is (*shrugging his shoulders*) an "honorable woman".

Zetterschöld: So much the better! *Strict women are the most passionate ones.*

Almquist: Don Juan!

Zetterschöld: In love the luck is with the bold one. The art to win a woman *lies in seizing the opportunity.*

(...)

Almquist: I don't want to hurt your young self-confidence. But I could find myself in the mood to enlighten you of another thing ... (*Whispers confidential*) Stella Ramberg is – well – she is stupid.

Zetterschöld: There's nothing wrong with a beautiful woman being – let's say less talented.

Almquist: Maybe you'll make up your mind once you've come to know her.

Zetterschöld: One *should* not know the women one loves, it takes away illusions. Think of Romeo and Juliet, *they* didn't know each other! All the magnificence only takes some days – but how much passion don't they hold!

Almquist: Passion tempts you – therefore she tempts you, this poetic Juliet!

Zetterschöld: Seldomly I've seen something more enchanting.

Almquist: Shakespeare's Juliet is wonderful – but – she was no wholesaler's wife.

Zetterschöld: Is Stella Ramberg not beautiful?

Almquist: I don't like tulips. They shine from a long distance, but if you come closer and want to look down in one of them ... then they are empty and without any scent.

Zetterschöld: You are angry at her?

Almquist: 'course not! (*Laughs*) For eight years the tulip has blossomed for her safe, and three times she has given seed.

Zetterschöld: Eight years. And no lover?

Almquist: No.

Zetterschöld (*slowly repeating, as to himself*): Eight years with a wholesaler! How must this woman be able to love!

Almquist: Yes on the stage.

Zetterschöld: The power, the sensitivity in her performance point at a secret string, that vibrates and gives life to the dead words.

Almquist: What string should this be?

Zetterschöld: Longing! She dreams of Romeo.

Almquist: That is of you!

Zetterschöld: Of me or somebody else – that can depend on coincidence!

Almquist: Romeo for a petty bourgeois' wife! For the personified every-day respectability! Cheers!

Zetterschöld: Can't you understand, that just a woman not having had some romance in her youth – or let's say who lived "honorable" – in her innermost part ought to have a wealth of passion, which never was used in this so called marriage – an institution which...

Almquist (*interrupts*): ... an institution which I belong to completely.

Zetterschöld (*smiles*): Romeo and Juliet also were married – in "secrecy" says the rogue Shakespeare. – An honorable woman is able under the most superficial external conditions to hide an enthusiastic hope of adventure, which a woman always dreams of – *to be loved*. And in her dreams she feels how her youth slides away – how should not such a woman be able to love!

Almquist: But you, fool of all fools, don't you understand what the whole town knows: that she is satisfied to be with her wholesaler, that she off the stage lives only for her wholesaler and the wholesaler's children.

Zetterschöld: Juliet?

Almquist: Yes. It is grotesque, but Juliet has found her Romeo, and Romeo is a safe. (*Silence.*) He who looks for strawberries shall not dig in a field of potatoes! But good luck! You seem to be able to enjoy and adore even an potato's perfection!

Zetterschöld (*puts his hands on his shoulders and looks into his eyes*): There is resentment in your tone.

Almquist: Because I divulge to you that she is stupid!

Zetterschöld: She is a real artist.

Almquist: Rachel was a famous artist – and could not write a letter. So it is often with actresses: their voice and mimic art lie about an intelligence they lack completely.

Zetterschöld: Not she! The general opinion of Mrs. Ramberg is...

Almquist (*interrupting*): I never felt any solidarity with the general opinion. (*Silence.*)

Zetterschöld: Did you know her long?

Almquist: She performed the main part of my first play.

Zetterschöld: I must have been abroad then. How did it go? Tell me.

Almquist: She was young, nice looking and had the gift to cluck verses. Naturally it occured to me that she was born for the play I had but recently finished. I therefore rehearsed the part with her – that's the whole story!

Zetterschöld: How did she play?

Almquist (*shrugging his shoulders*): It was a success!

Zetterschöld: What more do you want?

Almquist: But she was an idiot!

Zetterschöld (*listening*): Shh! She is coming! You are going to leave us soon?

Almquist: With greatest pleasure!

(...)

Mrs. Ramberg: Don't you think I understood why you came to me? ... I shall fulfill your wishes in advance. You don't need to prepare for a long siege. I'll immediately open everything to you.

(...)

Zetterschöld (*simple and with warmth*): I did offend you. Forgive me. (...) There is such a strange power in your voice! If I close my eyes and listen, I'm in the mood again ... passionately longing to be closer to you – closer... (*noise outside.*) That may be your husband?

Mrs. Ramberg: He won't disturb us. He is a model of a husband. He knows his place. He is a petty bourgois and I am an artist, who receives her admirers. (*Both are listening.*) You see! No jealous husband came through the door. I'm no suppressed wife, I'm not guarded as any man's property; I am a free human being and can do whatever I want. (*Goes around in the room and puts things in order*)You can stay as long as you want!

Zetterschöld: Thank you. I've already detained you for too long.

Mrs. Ramberg: I like you.

Zetterschöld: (*Bows ironically.*)

Mrs. Ramberg: Sit down and let's talk frankly. (...) Do you think there is much in my life I need to conceal?

Zetterschöld: No.

Mrs. Ramberg: Everyone means, there *ought* to be something to conceal – in women who have really lived.

Zetterschöld: That's natural. With our prejudices...

Mrs. Ramberg: Yet there are people with so deep a disposition, they do endure daylight upon their whole life. – I belong to them. And that's my strength.

Zetterschöld: I believe you.

Mrs. Ramberg: That is also because of the habit of owning another person's confidence, to be believed implicitly – always! – by this one.

(*Silence.*)

Zetterschöld: You wanted to tell me something?

Mrs. Ramberg: I did. You are a poet. – – – An artist. You ought to know a person's heart, for it is human beings you shall create. I am an artist, too – you think less – – – only an actress – – – but for me, too, life is everything, for me, too, true art is to play on the most sensitive strings in the human mind. When we have power of others, the power to dissolve and bend their moods to our own, then it is because we feel more deeply, more complex as they do, because life touches us more deeply than ordinary people.

Only what lies within our own nature's reach is truly genuine. – – – You felt Juliet's love be genuine, that is why you reached out with your hand and said: Give it to me!

Zetterschöld (*slowly*): It was out of my reach.

Mrs. Ramberg: You don't know what it is to love. (...) There's a secret freemasonry between us. Do you notice?

Zetterschöld (*nods*): Youth, I think – the youth of our souls, which is to be found with all artists.

Mrs. Ramberg: You are right. (*Extends her hand to him.*) You are good and you are young, you must not go away like a stranger! I want you to remember and think of me: such like she was and not such as ... he maybe told you.

Zetterschöld: How can you talk about it?

Mrs. Ramberg: It has hurt me; it made me bitter and evil. But that is over now.

Zetterschöld: You look happy, Juliet.

Mrs. Ramberg: I am happy – Romeo. And for you who writes such beautiful poems I'll tell you my most beautiful story. I was still very young when I was schooled as a pupil. So young and mentally immature, I was but a mere child. But a child with verve, with laughter and song and weeping in its voice – as it so happened – and with hundreds of changes in its face. My tiniest thought and swiftest mood became immediately visible; and what I, poor fool, called soul, lived in a glass house. Therefore my face got trained to learn to tell other people's thoughts and to interpret their moods. It learnt well, and I was soon on the stage. But what I called soul didn't keep pace with my facial expressions. I played on instinct – on undeveloped possibilities. I could not plot and scheme, nevertheless I made progress. I, the poor youngster out of the lanes, got almost afraid of applause and honors, never believed it to be enough, always trembling of having to return to the hovels.

Zettersköld: Poor wretch!

Mrs. Ramberg: Oh yes! You can't know how poverty lefts its mark on you. How it frightens you to the quick, makes your knees tremble. I still shiver whenever I think of freezing and starving. I don't have to be afraid of it any more.

Zetterschöld: There was dread in your voice when only you were talking about it. Continue!

Mrs. Ramberg: Well. How has it been? Ah yes... There was a young but already famous writer who wrote historical plays, and I was chosen to create the main part... He himself rehearsed it with me.

Zetterschöld: Fritz Almquist!

Mrs. Ramberg: He was a man-of-the-world, to be seen in finest circles, son of a respected man, richly married, good looking. A genius, many said; a conqueror of women with taste and vanity, popular and elegant, a kind of spoilt Adonis who scarcely cared for all the honors he got. What did I know about it! I never came out into the elegant world. For me he was more than a man-of-the-world, he was a "poet" – favorite of the gods: He was my emperor and my king.

Zetterschöld: Incomprehensible!

Mrs. Ramberg: I tell you what I felt in those days. It was a long time ago. A long long time ago!

Zetterschöld: Does it hurt you to tell me?

Mrs. Ramberg: Oh no! It doesn't hurt. Not any more. He took my admiration as his legitimate property. Why shouldn't he? He seemed to me so great and I only so low, I was grateful I could admire him. I scarcely dared to answer when he talked to me, my thoughts and my capacity to act grew weary when he was present, and it seemed that my whole soul was concentrating into the two wide opened eyes, with which I looked at him – uninterrupted – and meanwhile every word of his got carved into my mind as if cut with a diamond. (...) Everything I was I was through him. I gave myself up into his work, I lived on his replicas. When he was nice to me, it felt as if the sun shone brightly over me. Even now – thinking of it – it is as if the day would get more lustre and the flowers sweeter flagrance. – – – Of that he doesn't know anything to say but I am stupid.

Zetterschöld: Did he not love you then?

Mrs. Ramberg (*raises her shoulders*): I suppose some would call it to love... He took pleasure in me and toyed with me.

Zetterschöld: How did it go?

Mrs. Ramberg: We had some kind of relationship. Nothing criminal, but on the border to it.

Zetterschöld: And how did it end?

Mrs. Ramberg: He was to go abroad for a longer journey – to stay away some years. It felt as if the sun should die and neither grass nor flowers grow again... And he came to say farewell. (*Breaking off and with effort.*) It was in the evening. We were just the two of us – at my home. – He was different, both warmer and colder: – – – his warmth more demanding, and his cold – beneath... – made me afraid. – – – One single word of true feeling, and I would have fallen; five minutes patience and my life should have had its smudge to hide. But... he didn't wait five more minutes, and this single word... it never came. (*After an interval, with a smile.*) It was my luck that this evening his heart was with others than with me!

Zetterschöld: With whom else?

Mrs. Ramberg: With his wife... And all these others! I've understood it since.

Zetterschöld: And after he was away?

Mrs. Ramberg: Then came a rage, and bitterness, ambition and I in my artistic individuality made a name for myself. I had matured in sun and wind; my soul had finally caught up with my mimics.

Zetterschöld: You did marry afterwards?

Mrs. Ramberg: Yes... When you have felt that your soul's most bitter anguish not so much as invoke any sympathy, that you, with everything that is good or bad in you, with all that struggle to mould character – are still not more than a number in a collection, and that the greatest tenderness ever received was nothing more but the collector's pride, without any trace of something else – hardly of goodwill; then you do understand the importance of a man's saying to a woman: become my wife.

Zetterschöld: And you are happy?

Mrs. Ramberg: I can only say that there is not a single action in my life, no vicissitudes in my mind, I have to tell a lie about for the petty bourgeois, as you call him. I never felt tempted to be some week's pastime for another man.

Zetterschöld: I understand. (*Gets up.*) But it is in memory of these other things you play?

Mrs. Ramberg (*gets up as well*): No. To do so I'd grow old soon. I play in memory of things that keep me young. (...) I've played the women's parts of Fritz Almquist's plays. I gave to them what they lacked: human warmth – a heart... That I've got from here, from within my home.

Zetterschöld: I see!

Mrs. Ramberg: Do you understand as well, why I could talk about this without any trace of bitterness?

Zetterschöld: You love...

Mrs. Ramberg: Don't say! There is a feeling so rare, that language didn't need to create a word for it; it is not aflame at first sight, it's not extinguished in any time. It grows

from small seed, nourished by the certainty of absolute trust – of radiating warmth, of thousands of small concessions. – – – It grows like a plant and extends itself over one's life. – At every misfortune threatening, every disappointment meeting you take shelter in it: It is warmth and protection. And by comparison everything else turns insignificant.
Zetterschöld (*bows in parting*): I came to seek an artist and I found a human being. I wanted to get acquainted with an actress and I got to know a noble thinking woman... (*Slowly.*) That is so infinitely much more!
(...)

Primary Works

Från Skåne, 1884.
Pengar, 1884.
Final, 1885.
Folkliv och småberättelser, 1887.
Mrs. Marianne, 1887.
I Telefon, 1887; performed in 1887.
Teorier, 1887; published 1980.
Berättelser och utkast, 1888.
Romeos Julia, 1888; performed in 1995.
Den Bergtagna, 1888; drama version published 1908; prose version published in *Samlade Skrifter* 7.
Stora boken and Dagboken, 1882-1888; published 1985.
Efterskörd, 1890.

Selected Bibliography

Böök, Fredrik. *Victoria Benedictsson och Georg Brandes*. Stockholm: Albert Bonniers Förlag, 1949.
Claesson Pipping, Git. *Könet som läsanvisning. George Eliot och Victoria Benedictsson i det svenska 1880-talet – en receptionsstudie*. Stockholm: Symposium Graduale, 1993.
Forsås-Scott, Helena. *Swedish Women's Writing 1850-1995*. London: The Athlone Press, 1997.
Heggestad, Eva. *Fången och fri. 1880-talets svenska kvinnliga författare om hemmet, yrkesliv och konstnärskapet*. Uppsala: Avdelningen för litteratursociologi vid Litteraturvetenskapliga institutionen, 1991.
Leffler, Yvonne, ed. *Bakom maskerna. Det dolda budskapet hos kvinnliga 1880-talsförfattare*. Stockholm: n.p., 1997.
Levy, Jette Lundbo. *Den dubbla blicken. Om att beskriva kvinnor. Ideologie och estetik i Victoria Benedictssons författarskap*. Enskede: Hammerström & Åberg, 1982.
Lyngfelt, Anna. "Att förena blidhet med skärpa. Enaktsformatet som möjlighet för kvinnliga pjäsförfattare vid 1800-tales slut." *Det glömda 1800-talet. Några populära genrer inom svensk prosa och dramatik*. Leffler, Yvonne, ed. Karlstad: Centrum för språk och litteratur 1993, 133-51.

–. *Den avväpnande förtroligheten. Enaktare i Sverige 1870-90.* Göteborgs Universitet: Litteraturvetenskapliga institutionen, 1996.

Sjöblad, Christina. *Benedictsson, Victoria: Stora Boken och Dagboken 3. Dagbok 1886-1888.* Lund: LiberFörlag, 1985.

Sjögren, Margareta. *Rep utan knutar. Victoria Benedictsson – en levnadsteckning.* Stockholm: Bonnier, 1979.

Tønnesen, Mette. *Identitet og arbejde. En læsning af Victoria Benedictssons forfatterskab.* Århus Universitet: n.p., 1983.

Selma Lagerlöf: A Modern Teller of Old Tales

ANN-SOFI LJUNG SVENSSON (LUND UNIVERSITY)

On March 16, 1990, the voluminous correspondence of Selma Lagerlöf (1858-1940) became accessible to the public at The Royal Library in Stockholm.[1] This deposit is the largest of its kind in Sweden and possibly one of the largest in the world. It contains 42,000 letters. Most are letters to Lagerlöf, but some are her letters to friends, acquaintances and readers.

The accessibility to such a collection of letters – four volumes of letters have been published so far – has triggered a wave of Lagerlöf scholarship, making a biographical perspective an unavoidable part of Lagerlöf studies. The letters exchanged with publishers, female friends, other writers and readers paint a portrait of an author who no longer hides behind her works. Instead, she is forward, outlining parts of her emotional and intellectual life with explanations, interpretations and keys to these texts.

The general reader is rewarded with Lagerlöf's biography. Lagerlöf herself was very aware of what she was doing. Not only did she toward the end of her life write a trilogy about her own childhood – the Mårbacka trilogy – but she did also constantly, during her nearly fifty years as a writer, draw upon the reality she had lived and the stories she had heard as a child.

Selma Lagerlöf was born November 20, 1858 on the moderately wealthy estate of Mårbacka in Värmland in central Sweden. Värmland has become closely associated with the literary history of Sweden through Selma Lagerlöf herself and poets like Esaias Tegnér (1782-1846), Erik Gustaf Geijer (1783-1847) and Gustaf Fröding (1860-1911). These writers are all originated from the typical Värmland culture of manors and rural industrial communities based on natural assets like forests, water power and iron ore.

Lagerlöf's childhood and home were a reality for her. Due to financial difficulties the family lost the estate in 1890, but she bought the manor back in 1907 when her literary accomplishments had brought her fame as well as fortune. Two years later, in 1909, she was the first woman, and the first Swede, to be awarded the Nobel Prize in literature. The prize money made

---

[1]   Lagerlöfsamlingen, Kungliga biblioteket, Stockholm.

it possible for her to buy back the landed property her family had lost. She died there, 81 years old, on March 16, 1940.

There are three biographies of Selma Lagerlöf, and each has merits. The oldest, written in German by Walter Berendsohn in 1927, was published in Swedish in connection with Lagerlöf's 70th birthday in 1928. Berendsohn stresses the imaginative power of her texts and the influences from traditional oral story telling, folklore and legends. He consolidated the established picture of her as "the naive provider of tales".[2] The second biography was published after Lagerlöf's death in 1940. It was commissioned by her publisher Albert Bonnier and written by the journalist and novelist Elin Wägner in 1942-43. For more than half a century it remained *the* Lagerlöf biography. Wägner's well-informed and extensive biography has distinct characteristics. It is written in an empathetic, if anything intuitive, way, heavily stamped by the biographer's wish to confirm and convey her own very personal conception of the author. Wägner shared Berendsohn's basic view of Selma Lagerlöf as an earth-bound and universal writer. The childhood memories are, according to Wägner, the driving force behind her literary work. Mårbacka becomes the metaphor for the ideas and ideals and the formative influence on Lagerlöf during her childhood, ideas and ideals which in her life worked as active agents in the creative process, enabling her to speak directly to a mythical, archaic and collective consciousness. Wägner's biography is considered a classic and has won great acclaim for its empathetic qualities. But over time it has also been criticized for its tendency to mold its subject to Wägner's own ideology of primitivist mysticism, de-intellectualizing Lagerlöf and turning her into a naive author out of touch with modernity.[3]

It took sixty years for the next and latest biographical work to materialize in 2002 – *Livets vågspel* by Vivi Edström. The atmosphere of intimacy, which permeates Wägner's, and to a certain extent also Berendsohn's works, is present also in Edström's biography, but it springs from different and new sources: the letters. Being the first biographer to use the large letter collection, Edström succeeded in establishing an indirect but far more penetrating relationship with the creative personality of Selma Lagerlöf. Edström draws attention to the fact that in the letters Lagerlöf, interestingly enough on several occasions, commented on her own relations with her texts. In a letter to her companion Sophie Elkan, who played a major role in Lagerlöf's life, she points out that "there is no better way to get to know

---

[2]   The representation of Lagerlöf as a naive provider of tales was already initiated by Sophie Adlersparre (the founder of the Swedish Fredrika Bremer-Society) in a review of *Gösta Berlings saga* in the magazine *Dagny* in May 1891 and was confirmed by Oscar Levertin in his essay collection *Svenska gestalter*. Stockholm: Bonniers, 1903.

[3]   An excellent discussion of Elin Wägner's biography of Lagerlöf can be found in Inger Larsson. *Text och tolkning i svenska författarbiografier*. Lund: Gidlunds, 2003.

yourself than to write books". And late in life she tells her newfound friend Henriette Coyet: "If you want to find out about me, you have my books".[4]

Selma Lagerlöf's life turned into text. She inscribed herself in her texts, and she did it, well aware that the reader would find her there. It is this "inscribed biography" Edström tries to depict. But Edström has no interest in re-presenting the image of Selma Lagerlöf in the construction of which her earlier biographers had played a vital role: the image of the divinely gifted, warm-hearted, always compassionate genius who had sprung directly from nature and therefore with supreme authority could tell tales about the blood, the soil and the soul. The great merit of Edström's work is that she quite deliberately and thoroughly refutes the one-sided image of Lagerlöf as the meek, soft spoken but inspired teller of tales.

Instead it is the "wild side" of Lagerlöf that Edström strives to bring to light. Not only her lust for life and imaginative power, but also her anger, vengefulness, and destructiveness. In her role as a writer Selma Lagerlöf was characterized by a strong sense of purpose and an iron will. She worked in a steadily more professional way, methodically developing her writing skills. Her conscious play with genres, style, point of views and language makes her a modern writer. That is partly a new image. In order to emphasize this, Vivi Edström chose a portrait of Lagerlöf for a bookcover made in 1917 by the Austrian expressionist Oskar Kokoschka.

The best introduction to Lagerlöf's own "life story" is her autobiographical trilogy based on childhood recollections: *Mårbacka* (1922), *Ett barns memoarer* (1930; The Memoirs of a Childhood) and *Dagbok för Selma Ottilia Lovisa Lagerlöf* (1932; Diary for Selma Ottilia Lovisa Lagerlöf). In an interesting move she manages to use both the retrospective perspective of an adult and a return to the child she once was, at the same time reliving and pondering the tales of her childhood. Fact blends with fiction in these, among themselves technically quite disparate books, but the keynote is one and the same and has a ring of authenticity. We are introduced to a young girl who claims to have already found her true vocation: to write books. The tales are her life. "[I]t is fun to keep a diary – almost more fun than reading novels."[5]

The idealization of the childhood home is, as Edström points out, a main feature of the autobiography.[6] It is a literary, enacted theme that reaches beyond Lagerlöf's own life. In spite of the cracks in the wall the image of the good home remains unshattered. The bourgeois home is a stage set for a spectacle of joy. Stagings of balls, birthday parties and outings to fairs and theaters are interwoven with the child's recollections of warmth and harmony.

---

[4] Edström, 10-11.
[5] Lagerlöf, *The Diary of Selma Lagerlöf*, 20.
[6] Edström, 52.

On a more profound level the three autobiographical works reflect the continuous decay of the Lagelöf family and estate as well as the general decline of the genteel Värmland culture of mills and manors. The hard economic times during the industrial revolution and the worsening alcoholism and premature death of Selma Lagerlöf's father drove the family away from the estate, which had been theirs for generations.

The loss of the childhood home was a traumatic experience for Lagerlöf. It made deep imprints on her literary production. Her first novel, *Gösta Berlings saga* (1891; Eng. tr. *Gösta Berling's Saga*, 1898), is not only an imagined story of decay, it also points back to Lagelöf's own childhood in an occasionally quite literal way. In the chapter "Auktionen på Björne" (The Auction at Björne) she re-enacts the fateful day in 1888 when the family goods were auctioned off. The loss of Mårbacka surfaces also in other novels. In *En herrgårdssägen* (1899; Eng. tr. *From a Swedish Homestead*, 1901) Gunnar Hede's fear of losing his childhood home Munkhyttan is the main theme.

Selma Lagerlöf regains Mårbacka – and she does it on several different levels. First of all, literally, by buying back the property and rebuilding the manor. She devoted the better part of her last thirty years to the reconstruction of Mårbacka.

It is possible to view her writings – constantly revolving around the legacy of the old tales of Värmland – as variations on the theme of the decline and fall of the feudally organized industrial society in which she had been raised, and as a continuous attempt to restore the lost world of her childhood. Nevertheless, Selma Lagerlöf is a modern writer, in whose works a developing modernity is portrayed in an ambivalent and non-prejudiced way. She never quite takes sides but depicts, both on a psychological and a symbolic level, the disruption of the individual caused by shattered social structures.

In spite of her attachment to her childhood province the young Lagerlöf also wanted to break out. She nurtured a strong yearning to become an independent and self-sufficient woman. In defiance of her father's wish she went to Stockholm where she attended *Högre Allmänna Lärarinneseminariet*, a training college for female teachers, one of very few educational institutions open to women at the time. Having graduated in 1885 she applied for, and got, a teaching job at a girls' school in Landskrona in southern Sweden.

Along with reconstruction, breaking away is an important theme in Lagerlöf's works. When Klara Gulla in *Kejsarn av Portugallien* (1914; Eng. tr. *The Emperor of Portugallia*, 1916) has climbed the mountain and sings out in joy because she is about to leave her childhood home and enter the real world, one can sense an affinity between the author and her fictional character.

The time Selma Lagerlöf spent away from home, studying in Stockholm, had a decisive impact on her writing in several ways. But her early literary efforts in different genres did not quite succeed. She wrote poetry on occasion and tried her hand with sonnets, but despite hard and dedicated work she only managed to have a handful of texts published.

But then something happened that gave Lagerlöf direction. Having attended a lecture in literary history she was strolling down Malmskillnadsgatan in central Stockholm one morning in the beginning of the 1880s and suddenly she has a vision of her *own* story: "The world you have been a part of down in Värmland is no less peculiar than the worlds of [Carl Michael] Bellman or [Johan Ludvig Runeberg's] *Fänrik Stål*. I dare say you have at least as good material to work on as those two provided if you can come to grips with it."[7]

Still, it took Lagerlöf quite a few years to get the tale of the wild cavaliers of Värmland "told and presented to the world".[8] Selma Lagerlöf was 32 years old when in February 1891 she made her real debut as a writer after having waited a long time for, as she herself puts it, her "spiritual clearing of ice".[9] In 1890 she won a literary contest in the magazine *Idun* she had entered with five chapters from her forthcoming novel. She then quickly and resolutely finished her first book, *Gösta Berling's Saga*. The result was a loosely composed novel, built on "tales from old Värmland".[10]

Together with works such as Gustav Fröding's poetry collection *Guitarr och dragharmonika* (1891; Eng. tr. *Guitar and Concertina*, 1925), Oscar Levertin's *Legender och visor* (1891; Legends and Songs) and Verner von Heidenstam's *Vallfart och vandringsår* (1888; Pilgrimage and Wander-Years) *Gösta Berling's Saga* marked the arrival of a new literary school in Sweden, called "nittiotalismen" (i.e. the literature of the nineties) after the decade, the 1890s, in which it came to a breakthrough, characterized by its radical shift from the realism and social commitment which had prevailed not only in Scandinavian literature but on the European literary scene as a whole during the 1880s.

But romanticism was not dead. Instead, it emerged as the main feature of the 1890s in Sweden and in Selma Lagerlöf's writings as a whole. Imagination, and idealism, were along with ethical and esthetic commitments once again regarded as vital literary virtues. The art of writing went through a phase of privatization giving birth to a modern subjective literature emphasizing personal and emotional experiences. The period's strong interest in local geography, history, and folklore mirrored a sense of loss and disorien-

---

[7] Lagerlöf. *En saga om en saga och andra sagor*. Stockholm: Bonniers, 1908.
[8] Ibid.
[9] Letter to Helena Nyblom, March 18, 1891. In Lagerlöf, *Brev* 1, 58.
[10] Lagerlöf wanted a subtitle to her first book, "Tales from the old Värmland". But she did not succeed in persuading her editor.

tation, created by ongoing economic, social and political changes in Sweden and can be regarded as a kind of collective soul searching, a way of finding and establishing a new identity, expressed in a new kind of nationalistic discourse. The concept of the nation used to be a concern only for the political few. Now it had turned into a question of identity on an individual level and called for an emotional commitment from every citizen.[11]

Selma Lagerlöf's romanticism was modern, in spite of its obvious connections to the saga genre and a tradition of oral story telling, and in spite of its ambition to "save our old legends".[12] Her supposedly "ancient" and "timeless" writing goes far beyond that formula.

Her debut novel was a bold departure from the literary norms that prevailed at the time. Using a vigorous, rhythmic and exuberant style, close to modern colloquial language, and directly addressing the reader, she enacted fragmentary and tableau-like scenes dealing with the individual's struggle with herself and her world. Gösta Berling, poet, drunkard and defrocked priest, is a splintered soul in a beautiful but decayed body and his changing fortunes take the reader on a winding, but vain hunt for understanding and coherence. Confidence and joy of living join hands with despair and destructiveness in a never-ending bacchanalian dance around the long lake of Löfven in Värmland.[13]

The Swedish reviewers were divided. The novel was received both with enthusiasm and harsh criticism. The overwhelming majority of the critics measured the novel with the yardstick of realism. The lack of interest in the immediate reality, as well as the lack of a tightly knit plot and a clear cut, coherent composition were regarded as flaws making the novel less convincing. But the subjective and imaginative power of the book and its ability to create compelling atmospheres were nevertheless recognized and Selma Lagerlöf was credited with being a writer of originality. It would be very wrong, however, to describe *Gösta Berling's Saga* as an instant success. It suffered quite a few attacks from Sweden's most prominent critics.

Denmark paved the way for Lagerlöf. On January 16, 1893, nearly two years after her debut, the influential Danish critic Georg Brandes published a review of *Gösta Berling's Saga* in the newspaper *Politiken*. It was Brandes' praise that opened the doors for Selma Lagerlöf not only in Denmark and the rest of continental Europe, but ironically enough, also in Sweden. Within a couple of years, in 1895, she was firmly established as a professional writer, who could live, and live well, by her pen.

---

[11] See further Staffan Björck. *Heidenstam och sekelskiftets Sverige. Studier i hans nationella och sociala författarskap.* Stockholm: Natur och kultur, 1946.
[12] Edström, 159.
[13] See Jenny Bergenmar's interpretation in her dissertation *Förvildade hjärtan* (2003) of *Gösta Berling's Saga* as a modern, norm-breaking novel.

Selma Lagerlöf's works are varied but at the same time characterized by a strong sense of unity. Her preferred form is the short narrative. She operates with a few recurring themes, places and historical periods. Her stories have rural settings. Urban settings, in particular big cities, are virtually nonexistent. Lagerlöf shunned them also in her private life.

Most of her texts are set in times past. The 1820s, a golden age for the culture and life style of the industrial estates in Värmland, are a key period, e.g. in her autobiographical works. But she also had an interest in Sweden's medieval period. Through visits and historical literature she became acquainted with the Swedish west coast and dramatic events that had taken place there in the past. She used some of these stories in works like *Drottningar i Kungahälla* (1899; The Queens of Kungahälla) and *Herr Arnes penningar* (1904; Eng. tr. *Herr Arne's Hoard*, 1923). The West Coast was also the setting for her contemporary novel *Bannlyst* (1918; Eng. tr. *The Outcast*, 1922), written during World War I and known as Lagerlöf's peace novel in reference to its "pacifist imperative".[14]

Lagerlöf traveled a lot and the world beyond Sweden was granted a limited but natural place in her writings. With her traveling companion Sophie Elkan she made long and inspiring voyages, particularly to southern Europe and the Middle East. Lagerlöf's Italian experiences are mirrored in a great number of legends and in her contemporary novel of ideas, *Antikrists mirakler* (1897; Eng. tr. *Miracles of Anti-Christ*, 1899) in which Lagerlöf in an ambiguous way portrays the main characters way of dealing with the two opposite poles that according to the novel rules the world, the heavenly and the earthly powers. In one of her most consistent and interesting works, *Jerusalem*, published in two volumes 1902 and 1903, she makes use of real life material in her description of how a religious revivalist movement gets a group of peasants to leave their homes in Dalecarlia and emigrate to the Holy Land. The conflict between the emigrants yearning to follow Christ and lead a righteous and self-sacrificing life and their consuming longing for the homeland they have left behind points right at the heart of Selma Lagerlöf's imaginary universe.

One of Lagerlöf's internationally best known books is *Nils Holgerssons underbara resa genom Sverige* (1906-1907; Eng. tr. *The Wonderful Adventure of Nils Holgersson*, 1911).[15] The story of the young boy Nils, who travels through Sweden, was originally published as a reader for the youngest pupils in the elementary school. The book was intended to depict Sweden as a success story and strengthen its readers sense of national belonging. Lagerlöf managed to write a pedagogical and an ideological book that bore all of her literary hallmarks. By letting Nils, transformed into a pixie,

---

[14] Ulla-Britta Lagerroth. *Körkarlen och Bannlyst*, 364ff.
[15] English translation 1911. Lagerlöf. *The wonderful adventures of Nils and further adventures of Nils.*

ride on the back of a goose from the southern tip of Sweden to the far north she treated herself to a narrative structure which allowed her to add story to story, image to image, scene to scene. Her basic literary form – short, episodic, cumulative – is used in an unsought and natural way.

Lagerlöf portrays Sweden as a vast, rich and varied but at the same time united and well defined country. Her descriptions of the Swedish nature, in all its variations, are accurate, elaborate and occasionally beautiful, but this is probably not the main reason behind Nils Holgersson's worldwide success. Due to the legends and tales that are woven into the narrative the book also offers gateways to the supernatural and miraculous. One can further more interpret the book as a novel of development and as a novel about rebellion, adjustment and socialization. As Nils travels through Sweden he grows – psychologically and symbolically – into a responsible, sensible and mature young man capable of acting morally right.[16]

Humankind is always at the center of Lagerlöf's writings. The individual's struggle with herself/himself and with her/his beliefs, the individual's aspirations for righteousness and peace of mind, constitutes the foundation for every novel, short story, legend, and tale: "O God! Vouchsafe that my soul may come to maturity ere it be reaped!" prays David Holm in *Körkarlen* (1912; The Coachman; Eng. tr. *Thy Soul Shall Bear Witness!*, 1921).[17] It is a prayer that every one of Lagerlöf's characters carries within themselves.

Righteousness and peace of mind are not to be taken for granted in Lagerlöf's writing. One must strive for them, timelessly, and in all ways. There are no ready answers, no fixed gospel and no church. Every individual has to find his or her own beliefs, peace of mind and state of righteousness. "Catholicism and whatever are fine with me as long as people can get themselves into interesting soul-searching moods", Lagerlöf stated to Sophie Elkan,[18] thereby touching upon the very core of her own literary manifesto. Man is the subject matter of her writings, not "the principles", those ready-mades that are brought into her texts only "to make something happen".

Lagerlöf was very distinctly "indifferent to the principles", as she puts it in a letter to Sophie Elkan in 1897 while working on *Miracles of Anti-Christ*. She was indifferent to ideologies and different manifestations of religion. It is characteristic for Lagerlöf that in her stories she avoided taking a clear stand on ethical and ideological issues. What is enacted is always human complexity, a complexity which makes it impossible to take a stand or take sides, a complexity which acknowledges the good in the bad

---

[16]   Louise Vinge has described Nils Holgerssons personal project as the wish "to become human again".

[17]   Lagerlöf. *Thy Soul Shall Bear Witness!*, 190.

[18]   *Du lär mig att bli fri*, 83.

and the bad in the good. This is the point of departure for the ambivalence and the ambiguity that Lagerlöf's literary characters are possessed by and for the elusive games they play. Is Gösta Berling a sweet poet or a slimy womanizer? Is Klara-Gulla a corrupted and lost daughter or a strong and independent woman? Is *Miracles of Anti-Christ* a book supporting or disputing socialism, supporting or disputing Christian beliefs? Lagerlöf's writings never question either-or. It is always both-and. And it is within the realm of the human soul this contest is found. That is what constitutes Selma Lagerlöf as a modern writer. Her early experiences of modernity gave birth to a human consciousness, which is present in her texts, an evolution into something more than talented variations on the old tradition of oral storytelling.

While portraying the young, beautiful and self-examining Marienne Sinclaire in *Gösta Berling's Saga* Lagerlöf arguably comes as close as she gets to the modern individual. In the chapter "The Auction at Björne" Marienne's father, the estate owner Melchior Sinclaire, chooses to disown his daughter since she has betrayed him by falling in love with the despised cavalier Gösta. By putting his entire household up for auction he is depriving Marienne of her heritage, home and father:

> She had been told that Melchior Sinclaire was going to have an auction at Björne and make away with all his possessions so that she would have nothing to inherit from him. They said he intended making the wreck as complete as possible. He would sell the furniture and household goods first, then the horse and cattle and farm implements, and lastly, the estate itself; and he intended putting the money in a bag and sinking it in the Löfven. Her inheritance would be ruin, dissipation, and dismay.[19]

One could argue that this feeling of being an heir to ruin probably was deeply rooted in Selma Lagerlöf herself. In the following excerpts from Lagerlöf's debut novel her own biography converges with the existential predicaments of modern life. Life, world and literary text merge into one.

It was with considerable purposefulness that Lagerlöf surrendered herself to her writings. With equal purposefulness she labored over Mårbacka. One can regard these two projects as different aspects of one and the same projects – restoring old Värmland in life and in literature.

In restoring Mårbacka Selma Lagerlöf created something more than an estate in Värmland, she created an icon, a living representation of her literary works and ambitions. Already in her lifetime Mårbacka had become a shrine, casting its spell over admirer who traveled to Värmlands to experience the landscape of Gösta Berling and his cavaliers, and maybe catch a glimpse of the world-famous author who used to wave to the visitors from her balcony.

---

[19] *Gösta Berling's Saga*, 169.

Gösta Berlings saga[20]

Landskapet

Nu måste jag beskriva den långa sjön, den rika slätten och de blåa bergen, eftersom de voro den skådeplats, där Gösta Berling och Ekebykavaljererna framlevde sin lustiga tillvaro.

Sjön har sin början ganska långt upp i norr, och där är ett härligt land för en sjö. Skogen och bergen upphöra aldrig att samla vatten åt den, strömmar och bäckar störta ned i den året om. Den har fin vit sand att sträcka ut sig på, uddar och holmar att avspegla och beskåda, näck och sjörå ha fritt spelrum där, och den växer sig hastigt stor och skön. Däruppe i norr är den glad och vänlig. Man skall bara se den en sommarmorgon, när den ligger yrvaken under dimslöjan, för att märka hur munter den är. Den gäckas först en stund, kryper sakta, sakta fram ur det lätta omhöljet, så trolskt vacker, att man knappt kan känna igen den, men så kastar den med ett ryck av sig hela täcket och ligger där blott och bar och rosig och glittrar i morgonljuset.

Men sjön nöjer sig inte med detta lekfulla liv, den snör ihop sig till ett smalt sund, bryter sig fram genom några sandkullar i söder och söker upp ett nytt rike åt sig. Ett sådant finner den också. Den blir större och väldigare, har bottenlösa djup att fylla och ett idogt landskap att pryda. Men nu blir även vattnet mörkare, stranden mindre omväxlande, vindarna skarpare, hela karaktären strängare. En ståtlig och härlig sjö är den. Många äro de fartyg och timmerflottar, som färdas där, sent får den tid att gå i vintervila, sällan förrän efter jul. Ofta är den också i vresigt lynne, den kan skumma vit av vrede och vräka omkull segelbåtar, men den kan också ligga i drömmande lugn och avspegla himlen

Men längre ut i världen vill sjön färdas, fastän bergen synas allt strävare och utrymmet blir allt trängre, ju längre ned den kommer, så att den än en gång måste som ett smalt sund krypa fram mellan sandstränderna. Sedan breder den ut sig för tredje gången, men inte mer med samma skönhet och värdighet.

Stränderna sjunka och bli enformiga, mildare vindar blåsa, sjön går i tidig vintervila. Alltjämt är den vacker, men den har mistat ungdomsyran och mannakraften, den är en sjö som alla andra. Med två armar famlar den efter vägen till Vänern, och när den är funnen, störtar den sig i ålderdomssvaghet utför stupade branter och går med en sista, dånande bragd in i vilan.

Lika lång som sjön är slätten. Men man må tro, att den har vanskligt med att komma fram mellan åsar och berg, alltifrån kitteldalen vid sjöns norra ändpunkt, där den först vågar breda ut sig och sedan allt framgent, tills den segrande lägger sig till maklig vila vid Vänerstranden. Det kan ju inte vara tal om annat, än att slätten helst skulle vilja följa sjöstranden, så lång den är, men bergen lämna den ingen ro. Bergen äro väldiga gråstensmurar, täckta av skog, fulla av klyftor, svåra att färdas i, rika på mossa och lav, i dessa gamla tider hem för massor av vilt. En sank myr eller en tjärn med mörkt vatten råkar man ofta mittuppe bland de långsträckta åsarna. Här och där finns också kolbotten eller en öppen plats, där timmer och ved ha tagits, eller ett svedjeland, och dessa vittna om att bergen också kunna tåla arbetet. Men vanligtvis ligga de i sorglös ro och nöja sig med att låta skuggor och dagrar leka sin eviga lek över deras sluttningar.

---

[20] From *Gösta Berlings saga*. Stockholm: Bonniers, 1934, 25-28 and 113-17. Published with permission from the Selma Lagerlöf heirs.

Och med dessa berg för slätten, som är from och rik och älskar arbetet, ett ständigt krig, i all vänlighet för resten.

Det är ju alldeles nog, säger slätten till bergen. om ni ställer upp era murar runtomkring mig, det är trygghet nog för mig.

Men bergen vilja inte lyssna till sådant tal. De sända ut långa räckor av kullar och kala högslätter ända ned till sjön. De resa härliga utsiktstorn på varje udde och lämna i själva verket sjöstranden så högst sällan, att slätten blott på några få ställen kan rulla sig i strandbräddens mjuka sand. Men det lönar sig inte, att den försöker beklaga sig.

Var du glad, att vi stå här! säga bergen. Tänk på tiden före jul, när de dödkalla dimmorna dag efter dag rulla fram över Löven! Vi gör god tjänst, där vi stå.

Slätten klagar över att den har liten plats och dålig utsikt.

Du är dum, svara bergen, du skulle bara känna hur det blåser härnere vid sjön. Det behövs, minst sagt, en gråstensrygg och en granpäls för att stå ut med sådant. Och för resten kan du var nöjd med att titta på oss.

Ja, titta på bergen, det är just vad slätten gör. Den känner väl alla de underliga skiftningar av ljus och skugga, som draga fram över dem. Den vet hur de i middagsbelysningen sjunka ned mot horisonten, låga och svagt ljusblå, och i morgon- eller aftonljus resa sig i vördnadsvärd höjd, klarblå som himlen i zenit. Stundom kan ljuset falla så skarpt över dem, att de bli gröna eller svartblå, och varje enskild fura, varje väg och klyfta syns på milslånga avstånd.

Det händer nog på sina ställen, att bergen maka sig åt sidan och låta slätten komma fram och titta på sjön. Men när den får se sjön i sin vrede, när den fräser och spottar som en vildkatt, eller ser den betäckt av den kalla röken, som kommer sig därav, att sjöråt sysslar med brygd och byk, då ger den snart bergen rätt och drar sig undan i sitt trånga fängelse igen.

Människor ha från urminnes tid odlat den härliga slätten, och där har blivit en stor bygd. Var helst en å med sin vitskummiga fors kastar sig utför strandsluttningen, där uppkommo bruk och kvarnar. På de ljusa, öppna platserna, där slätten kommer fram till sjön, blevo kyrkor och prästgårdar byggda, men i dalkanterna, halvvägs uppåt sluttningen, på stenbunden mark, där säden inte trivs, ligga böndernas gårdar och officersboställena och en och annan herrgård.

Dock må man märka, att på attonhundratjugotalet var inte trakten på långt när så uppodlad som nu. Skog och sjö och mosse var då mycket, som nu kan odlas. Folket var inte heller så talrikt och vann sitt uppehälle dels genom körslor och dagsverken vid de många bruken, dels genom att arbeta på främmande orter. Åkerbruket kunde inte föda dem. På den tiden klädde sig slättens invånare i hemvävda kläder, åto havrebröd och nöjde sig med en dagspenning av tolv skilling. Nöden var stor bland många av dem, men den blev ofta lindrad av ett lätt och glatt sinnelag och av en medfödd händighet och duglighet.

Men alla dessa tre, den långa sjön, den rika slätten och de blå bergen, bildade ett det vackraste landskap och göra så än, likaså är folket än idag kraftigt, modigt och väl begåvat. Nu har det ock gjort stora framsteg både i välmåga och bildning.

Må allt gå dem väl, som bo däruppe vid den långa sjön och de blå bergen! Det är några av deras minnen jag nu går att skildra.

(...)

Auktionen på Björne

Ofta måste vi unga mycket undra på de gamlas berättelser. Var det då bal varenda dag, så länge som er strålande ungdom varade?" frågade vi dem. Var livet då ett enda långt äventyr? Voro alla unga damer sköna och älskvärda på den tiden, och slutade vartenda gästabud därmed, att Gösta Berling enleverade en av dem?

Då skakade de gamla sina ärevördiga huvuden och gingo att berätta om spinnrockens surrande och vävstolens rassel, om köksbestyr, om slagors dunkande och yxans gång i skogen. Men det varade inte länge, förrän de åter voro inne på den gamla stråten. Då körde slädarna upp till förstutrappan, då ilade hästarna bort genom mörka skogar med de glada, unga människorna, då yrade dansen, och fiolsträngarna sprungo. Med dunder och brak brusade äventyrens vilda jakt runtom Lövens långa sjö. På långt håll hördes dess dån. Skogen sviktade och föll, alla ödeläggelsens makter sluppo lösa. Vårelden flammade, forsen härjade, vilddjuren ströko hungriga kring gårdarna. Under de åttafotade hästarnas hovar trampades all stilla lycka till stoft. Varhelst jakten brusade förbi, där lågade männens hjärtan upp i vildhet, och kvinnorna måste i blek förfäran fly från sina hem.

Och vi unga sutto undrande, tysta, hemska till mods och dock lycksaliga. "Sådana människor!" tänkte vi. "Vi ska aldrig se deras likar."

Tänkte aldrig den tidens människor på vad de gjorde? frågade vi.

Visste tänkte de, barn, svarade de gamla.

Men inte, som vi tänker, envisades vi.

Och så förstodo inte de gamla vad vi menade.

Men vi tänkte, vi, på självaktagelsens underliga ande, som redan hade hållit sitt intåg i vårt inre. Vi tänkte på honom med isögonen och de långa, krokiga fingrarna, han, som sitter därinne i själens mörkaste vrå och plockar sönder vår varelse, såsom gamla kvinnor plockar sönder lappar av siden och ylle.

Bit för bit hade de långa, hårda, krökta fingrarna plockat, tills vårt hela jag låg där som en hög trasor, och så hade våra bästa känslor, våra ursprungligaste tankar, allt, vad vi hade gjort och sagt, undersökts, genomforskats, sönderplockats, isögonen hade sett på, och den tandlösa munnen hade hånlett och viskat:

Se, det är trasor, bara trasor.

Det fanns väl ändå en av den tidens människor, som hade upplåtit sin själ för anden med isögonen. Hos en av dem satt han, vaktande vid handlingarnas källa, hånleende åt ont och gott, begripande allt, fördömande intet, undersökande, letande, sönderplockande, förlamande hjärtats rörelser och tankens kraft genom att hånle utan återvändo.

Den sköna Marianne bar självaktagelsens ande inom sig. Hon kände hans isögon och hånleenden följa varje steg, varje ord. Hennes liv hade blivit till ett skådespel, där han var den enda åskådaren. Hon var inte människa mer, hon led inte, gladdes inte, älskade inte, hon utförde den sköna Marianne Sinclaires roll, och självaktagelsen satt med stirrande isögon och flitiga, sönderplockande fingrar och såg henne uppträda.

Hon var delad i två hälfter. Blek, osympatisk och hånande, satt ena halvan av hennes jag och såg hur den andra halvan handlade, och aldrig ägde den underliga ande, som plockade sönder hennes varelse, ett ord av känsla och sympati.

Men var hade han då varit, den bleka väktaren vid handlingens källa, den natten, då hon lärt sig känna livets fullhet? Var var han, då hon, den kloka Marianne, kysste Gösta Berling inför hundra par ögon, och då hon i vredesmod kastade sig ned i snödrivan för att dö? Då voro isögonen förblindade, då voro hånlöjet förlamat, ty passionen hade stormat fram genom hennes själ. Bruset av äventyrens vilda jakt hade dånat i hennes öron. Hon hade varit en hel människa under denna enda förskräcklig natt.

O, du självförhånandets gud, då Marianne med oändlig möda lyckades lyfta sina förstenade armar och slå dem om Göstas hals, då måste du, som den gamle Beerencreutz, vända dina ögon bort från jorden och se på stjärnorna.

I den natten hade du ingen makt. Död var du, medan hon diktade sina kärlekshymner, död, medan hon skyndade ned till Sjö efter majoren, död, då hon såg lågorna färga himmelen röd ovan skogstopparna.

Se, de hade kommit, de starka stormfåglarna, de sönderslitande passionernas gripar. Med vingar av eld och klor av stål hade de kommit susande ned över dig, du ande med isögonen, de hade slagit sina klor i den nacke och slängt dig bort i det okända. Död och krossad hade du varit.

Men nu hade de susat vidare, de stolta, de väldiga, de, vilkas väg ingen beräkning känner och ingen iakttagare har följt, och ur det okändas djup var själviakttagelsens underliga ande återuppstånden och hade ännu en gång slagit sig ned i den sköna Mariannes själ.

Under hela februari månad låg Marianne sjuk på Ekeby. När hon uppsökte majoren på Sjö, hade hon blivit smittad av kopporna. Den förskräckliga sjukdomen hade med hela sin våldsamhet kastat sig över henne, som var förfärligt förkyld och utmattad. Döden hade varit henne nära, men mot slutet av månaden var hon dock återställd. Svag var hon alltjämt och mycket vanställd. Hon skulle aldrig mer kallas den sköna Marianne.

Detta var dock inte känt av någon mer än Marianne och hennes sköterska. Kavaljererna själva visste det inte ens. Det sjukrum, där smittkopporna härskade, stod inte öppet för var man.

Men när är själviakttagelsens makt större än under tillfrisknandets långa timmar? Då sitter den och stirrar och stirrar med sina isögon och plockar och plockar med de knotiga, hårda fingrarna. Och ser man rätt efter, så sitter bakom den en ännu gulblekare varelse, som stirrar och förlamar och hånler, och därbakom ännu en och ännu en, hånleende åt varandra och åt hela världen.

Och medan Marianne låg och såg på sig själv med alla de stirrande isögonen, dogo alla ursprungliga känslor inom henne.

Hon låg där och spelade sjuk, hon låg där och spelade olycklig, spelade förälskad, spelade hämndlysten.

Hon var allt detta, och dock var det blott spel. Allt blev till spel och overklighet under isögonen, som vaktade henne, under det att de återigen vaktades av ett par bakom dem, som vaktades av ett annat par i ett oändligt perspektiv.

Alla livets krafter voro inslumrade. Hon hade haft makt till glödande hat och hängiven kärlek under en enda natt, inte mer.

Hon visste inte ens om hon älskade Gösta Berling. Hon längtade efter att få se honom för att pröva om han kunde flytta henne utom sig själv.

Medan sjukdomens välde varade, hade hon haft bara en redig tanke, hon hade sörjt för att hennes sjukdom inte skulle bli känd. Hon ville inte se sina föräldrar, hon ville inte försoning med sin far, och hon visste, att han skulle ångra sig, om han finge veta hur sjuk hon var. Därför befallde hon, att hennes föräldrar och alla människor för övrigt skulle få veta, att den besvärande ögonsjukdom, som alltid överföll henne, när hon besökte hembygden, tvang henne att sitta inne bakom fällda gardiner. Hon förbjöd sin sköterska att tala om hur sjuk hon var, hon förbjöd kavaljererna att hämta läkare från Karlstad. Hon hade visserligen smittkopporna, men bara helt lindrigt, i husapoteket på Ekeby funnos läkemedel nog att rädda hennes liv.

Hon tänkte aldrig på att dö, hon låg blott och väntade på en hälsans dag för att få fara till prästen med Gösta och taga ut lysning.

Men nu voro sjukdomen och febern borta. Hon var åter kall och klok. Det var henne, som om hon ensam vore klok i denna värld av dårar. Hon varken hatade eller älskade. Hon förstod sin far; hon förstod dem alla. Den, som förstår, hatar inte.

Hon hade fått veta, att Melchior Sinclaire ämnade ställa till auktion på Björne och förstöra alla sina ägodelar, så att hon inte måtte få något arv efter honom. Man sade, att han skulle göra förödelsen så grundlig som möjligt. Först skulle han sälja möbler och husgeråd, så boskap och redskap och sist själva gården, och alla pengarna skulle han stoppa i en säck och sänka i Lövens djup. Förskingring, förvirring och förödelse skulle hennes arv heta. Marianne smålog gillande, när hon hörde detta, sådan var hans karaktär, så måste han handla.

Sällsamt tycktes det henne, att hon hade diktat den stora kärlekshymnen. Hon hade drömt om kolarhyddan, hon som andra. Nu syntes det henne underligt, att hon någonsin hade haft en dröm.

Hon suckade efter naturen. Hon var trött på detta ständiga spel. Aldrig hade hon en stark känsla. Hon sörjde knappt sin skönhet, men hon ryste för främlingars medömkan.

O, en sekund av glömska av sig själv! En åtbörd, ett ord, en handling som inte var beräknad!

En dag, då smittan hade blivit rensad bort ur rummet och hon låg klädd på en soffa, lät hon kalla Gösta Berling. Det svarades henne, att han var rest till auktionen på Björne.

Gösta Berling's Saga[21]

The Landscape

Translated by Lillie Tudeer

Now I must beg those of my readers who know this lake, this fertile plain, and those blue mountains, to skip a few pages. They can do this without compunction, for the story will be long enough without them. But you will understand that I must describe the country for those who do not know it, as it was the scene where Gösta Berling and the gay cavaliers of Ekeby spent their lives; and those who have seen it will understand too that the task surpasses the power of one who can only wield the pen.

I should have chosen to confine myself to saying that the name of the lake is the Löfven; that it is long and narrow, and that it stretches from the distant forests in the north of Värmland to the Vänern lowlands in the south; that a plain borders each side of the lake, and that a chain of undulating mountains surrounds the lake valley. But this is not sufficient, and I must try to picture in more graphic words the scene of my childhood's dreams, the home of my childhood's heroes.

The Löfven has its source far in the north, which is a glorious land for a lake, for the forests and hills gather water for it unceasingly, and streams and brooklets pour into it all the year round. It has fine white sand to recline upon; it has islands and promontories to admire and reflect; water-sprites and nixies make it their playground, and it soon grows strong and beautiful. Up in the north it is friendly and gay. You should see it on an early

---

[21] *Gösta Berling's Saga.* Lillie Tudeer, tr. New York: The American-Scandinavian Foundation; London: Humphrey Milford, Oxford University Press, 1918, 33-38 and 164-170. New edition Mineola, NY: Dover Publications, 2004.

summer morning, when it lies wide awake under its veil of mist, to understand how happy it can seem.

It seems as if it would coquette with you at first, so gently, so gradually does it creep out of its light covering; and so enchantingly beautiful is it that you hardly recognize it, till suddenly it flings its veil aside and lies there naked and rosy, glittering in the sunshine.

But the Löfven is not content with a life of pleasure alone. It pushes its way through the sand-hills on the south; it contracts to a narrow strait, and seeks a new kingdom for itself. It soon finds one, and here again grows strong and mighty; it falls a bottomless depth, and adorns a cultivated landscape. But now its waters grow darker, its shores are less changeful, the winds are bleak, and the whole character of the lake is more severe; yet it remains ever proud and stately. Numbers of vessels and rafts pass over its surface, and it is late before it can go to its winter rest – not until Christmas. It is often in angry mood, and, turning white with sudden fury, wrecks the sailing boats, but it can also lie in dreamy quiet and reflect the sky.

But once again it longs to make its way into the world, though the hills are pressing close around it; and it must contract again to a narrow strait, and creep between narrow sandy shores. Then it broadens out for the third time, but not with its former beauty and majesty. Its shores are lower and more monotonous, wilder winds blow, the lake goes early to its winter sleep. It is still beautiful, but it has lost the strength of its youth and manhood – it is a lake like any other. It throws out two arms to feel its way to the Vänern, and when it finds it casts itself in aged weakness down the steep slope, and, after this last thundering exploit, sinks to rest.

A plain follows the course of the Löfven, but it has a hard fight to hold its own between the lake and the hills, from the cauldron-like valley, which is the lake's most northerly point, to the Vänern lowlands, where it finally gains the mastery, and spreads itself wide in indolent ease. The plain would have unquestionably preferred to follow the lake shores, but the hills give it no peace.

These hills are mighty granite walls, covered with forest, full of chasms, abounding in moss and lichen, difficult to penetrate into, and, in the days we are speaking of, the home of numberless wild beasts. There is many a tarn of inky black water and many a quagmire in those long, far-reaching ridges. Here and there you find a coal mine, or an opening in the forest where the timber has been felled; now and again a burned clearing, which shows that the hills allow of a little cultivation; but for the most part they lie in placid calm, content to let the lights and shadows play their everlasting game over their slopes.

And the plain, which is good and fertile and loves cultivation, wages constant war against the hills – in all friendliness, be it understood.

"It is sufficient," says the plain to the hills, "if you raise your walls around me; then I shall be amply protected."

But the hills cannot be persuaded. They send out long stretches of tableland to the lake; they make lovely points from which to get a view; and, in fact, it is so seldom that they will leave the shore that the plain hardly ever has a chance of rolling itself down to the soft sand of the lake shore. But it is useless to complain.

"Be thankful we are here," answer the hills. "Remember the time before Christmas, when day after day the icy mists roll over Löfven. We are doing you a good turn by standing here."

The plane laments its want of room and that it has no view.

"You are stupid," reply the hills. "You should feel how it blows here near the water. At the least, it requires a granite back and a pine tree covering to bear it all. Besides which, you should be content with looking at us."

And that is what the plain does. You know what wonderful changes of light and shade and color pass over the hills. You have seen them in the midday light sinking to the horizon, pale blue and low, and at morning and evening rising majestic height, as deep a blue as the zenith of heaven. Sometimes the light falls so sharply upon them, they look green or blue-black, and every fir tree, every path and chasm, shows clearly at a great distance.

Sometimes the hills draw aside and allow the plain to approach and look at the lake, but when it sees it in its anger, hissing and spitting like a wild cat, or sees it covered with cold mist (the water witches being busy with washing and brewing), it soon acknowledges that the hills were right, and returns willingly to its narrow prison.

For many, many generations the plain has been cultivated, and great things have been done there. Wherever a stream, in its rapid course, has flung itself over the sloping shores, mills and foundries have sprung up. On the light, open places, where the plain comes down to the lake, churches and parsonages have been built; and in the corners of the valleys, half way up the hillsides, on the stony ground where the corn will not grow, stand the peasants' huts and the officers' buildings and here and there a gentleman's mansion.

But it must be remembered that in 1820-30 the land was not nearly so cultivated nor so populated as it now is. Much was forest and lake and marsh which is now reclaimed.

The population was scanty, and the people made their living partly by carting and day work at the many foundries; while many left their homes to find work at a distance, for agriculture alone would not pay them. In those days they dressed in homespun, ate oat cakes, and were content with a daily wage of a krona. The poverty was great, but it was mitigated by an easy-going temperament and an inborn aptitude for handicrafts, which greatly developed when those people had to make their way among strangers.

And as these – the lake, the fertile plain, and the blue hills – make a most beautiful landscape, so these people, even to-day, are strong, courageous, and talented. Great progress has been made in their well-being and education.

May they greatly prosper, the dwellers near the lake and the blue hills! It is some of their stories I will now tell you.

(…)

The Auction at Björne

We young people must often wonder at the stories told us by our elders. "Did you dance every night as long as your beautiful youth lasted?" "Was life for you one long adventure?" we asked them. "Were all girls lovely and amiable in those days, and did Gösta Berling elope with one of them after every ball?"

Then the old people shook their heads and told of the whirling if the spinning-wheels and the boom of the looms, of cooking, of the thunder and crash in the track of the axe through the forests; but before long they harked back again to the old stories. Sledges drove up to the hall door and races through the dark woods with their load of gay young people, the dancing grew wild, and the violin strings snapped. The wild wave of adventure rushed tumultuously along the shores of Lake Löfven, and its noise was heard afar. The forest swerved and fell, all the powers of destruction were loose, flames flared, the rapids swept away their prey, and wild beasts prowled hungrily round the homesteads. Under the hoofs of the eight-footed horses all quiet happiness was trampled in the dust. And wherever the wild hunt passed, men's hearts flamed up tempestuously, and the women fled from their homes in pale dismay. And we sat wondering, silent, frightened, and yet blissfully happy. "What people they were," we thought to ourselves; "we shall never see their like!"

"Did people in those days never *think* of what they were doing?" we asked.

"Certainly, they did," our elders answered.

"But not as we think," we persisted. Then our elders did not understand what we meant.

For we were thinking of the wonderful spirit of self-analysis which had already taken possession of our minds; we were thinking of him with the icy eyes and the long, knotted fingers – he, who sits in the darkest corner of our souls, and plucks our being to pieces as old woman pluck scraps of wool and silk. Piece by piece, the long, hard fingers have dissected us till our whole being lies there like a heap of rags – till all our best feelings, our innermost thoughts, all we have said and done is examined, ransacked, disintegrated, and the icy eyes have watched, and the toothless mouth has sneered and whispered, "See, it is but rags, nothing but rags."

Once of the people of those old days had opened her soul to spirit. He sat there watching at the font of all impulse, sneering both at the good and the evil, understanding all, judging nothing, examining, searching, and plucking to pieces and paralyzing all emotions of the heart and all strength if thought by smiling scornfully at everything.

Marienne Sinclaire bore the spirit of self-analysis within her. She felt his eyes follow every step, every word of hers. Her life had become a play, at which she was the only spectator. She was no longer a human being – she was neither wearied, nor did she rejoice, nor could she love. She played the part of the beautiful Marienne Sinclaire, and the spirit of self-analysis sat with staring eyes and busy fingers and watched her acting. She felt herself divided into two, and half of her being – pale, unfeeling, and scornful – watched the other half's transactions; and the spirit which thus plucked her asunder had never a word of kindness or sympathy for her.

But where had he been, the pale watcher beside the springs of impulse, on the night she had learned to feel life's fullness? Where was he, when she, the wise Marienne, kissed Gösta Berling before the eyes of two hundred people, and when she threw herself into the snowdrift to die in despair? The icy eyes were blinded, and the sneer was paralyzed, for passion had swept through her soul. The wild wave of adventure had thundered in her ears. She had been a whole being during that one awful night.

Oh, god of self-scorn, when Marienne lifted at last her frozen arms to Gösta's neck, then, like old Beerencreutz, thou wert compelled to turn thy eyes from earth and look at the stars! That night thou hadst no power. Thou wast dead while she sang her love hymns, dead when she hurried to Sjö for the Major, dead when she saw the flames reddening the sky over the treetops. See, they have come, the strong storm birds, the demon birds of passion. With wings of fire and claws of steel, they have swooped down upon thee, and flung thee out into the unknown. Thou hast been dead and destroyed. But they, the proud and mighty, they whose path is unknown and who cannot be followed – they have swept onward, and out of the depths of the unknown the spirit of self-observation has arisen again, and taken possession of Marienne's soul.

She lay ill at Ekeby all through February. She had taken smallpox at Sjö, when she went to find the Major, and the awful sickness had her completely at its mercy, for she had been frightfully chilled and wearied during that night. Death had been very near her, but toward the end of the month she grew better. She was still weak, and was greatly disfigured. She would never again be called beautiful Marienne. This misfortune, which was to bring sorrow over all Värmland as if one of its best treasures had been lost, was known, as yet, only to Marienne and her sick nurse. Even the cavaliers were not aware of it. The room in which the smallpox reigned was closed to all. But where is the spirit of self-analysis stronger than in the long hours of convalescence? There it sits and stares and stares with its icy eyes, and plucks and plucks to pieces our being with its knotted fingers. And if you look closely, you see behind him another pale being who stares and sneers and paralyzes, and behind him still another and another, all sneering at one another and the whole world. While Marienne lay there and stared at herself with those icy eyes, all feeling died within her. She lay there and played the part of being ill and being unhappy; she played at being in love and being revengeful. She was all this, and yet it was but acting a part. Everything became unreal under the gaze of those eyes watching her, which, again, were watched by another pair, and another, and another in an endless perspective. All life's powers were asleep; she had had strength for burning hate and overwhelming love for one night only. She did not even know if she loved Gösta Berling. She longed to see him to prove if he could carry her out of herself.

While the illness raged she had only one clear thought. She took care that the nature of the fever should remain unknown. She would not see her parents: she had no wish for reconciliation with her father. She knew he would repent if he heard how ill she was. So she commanded that her parents, and others too, in fact, were to be told that her eyes, which were always weak when she visited her native place, compelled her, for at time, to remain in a darkened room. She forbade her nurse to say how ill she was and forbade the cavaliers sending for a doctor from Karlstad. She certainly had the smallpox, but it was a mild case – the medicinechest at Ekeby contained all that was necessary to save her life. She never thought of dying: she only waited to be well enough to go with Gösta to the pastor and arrange for the banns to be published. But now the fever had left her. She was cool and prudent again. It seemed to her as if she alone was wise in this world of fools. She neither loved not hated; she understood her father, she understood them all. He that understands does not hate. She had been told that Melchior Sinclaire was going to have an auction at Björne and make away with all his possessions so that she would have nothing to inherit from him. They said he intended making the wreck as complete as possible. He would sell the furniture and household goods first, then the horse and cattle and farm implements, and lastly, the estate itself; and he intended putting the money in a bag and sinking it in the Löfven. Her inheritance would be ruin, dissipation, and dismay. Marienne smiled approvingly when she heard this. Such was his character; he was sure to act like this.

It seemed extraordinary to her that she should have poured forth that poem of love. She, too, had dreamed of the miner's hut – she, as well as others. It was wonderful to her that she had ever had a dream. She sighed for nature – she was weary of constantly acting a part. She had never had a strong feeling. She hardly mourned her lost beauty, but she shuddered at the thought of pity from strangers. Oh, a second of self-forgetfulness, a gesture, a word, an act which was not premeditated!

One day, when the room had been disinfected, and she lay dressed upon the sofa, she sent for Gösta Berling. They told her that he had gone to the auction at Björne.

Primary Works

Gösta Berlings saga, 1891; Eng. tr. *Gösta Berling's Saga*, 1918, 2004.
Osynliga länkar, 1894; Eng. tr. *Invisible Links*, 1899.
Antikrists mirakler, 1897; Eng. tr. *Miracles of Anti-Christ*, 1899.
En herrgårdssägen, 1899; Eng. tr. *From a Swedish Homestead*, 1901.
Jerusalem. I Dalarne, 1902; Eng. tr. *Jerusalem*, 1903.

Jerusalem. I det heliga landet, 1903; Eng. tr. *The Holy City: Jerusalem* 2, 1918.
Herr Arnes penningar, 1904; Eng. tr. *Herr Arne's Hoard*, 1923.
Nils Holgerssons underbara resa genom Sverige, 1906-1907; Eng. tr. *The wonderful adventures of Nils and further adventures of Nils*, 1911, 1999.
En saga om en saga och andra sagor, 1908.
Körkarlen, 1912; Eng. tr. *Thy Soul Shall Bear Witness!*, 1921.
Bannlyst, 1918; Eng. tr. *The Outcast*, 1922.
Kejsarn av Portugallien, 1914; Eng. tr. *The Emperor of Portugallia*, 1916.
Löwensköldska ringen, 1925; Eng. tr. *The General's Ring*, 1931.
Charlotte Löwensköld, 1925; Eng. tr. *Charlotte Löwensköld*, 1927.
Anna Svärd, 1928; Eng. tr. *Anna Svärd*, 1931.
Mårbacka, 1922; Eng. tr. *Mårbacka*, 1926, 1974.
Ett barns memoarer, 1930; Eng. tr. *Memories of my Childhood: Further Years at Mårbacka*, 1934.
Dagbok för Selma Ottilia Lovisa Lagerlöf, 1932; Eng. tr *The Diary of Selma Lagerlöf*, 1936, 1975.
Brev 1, 1871-1902.
Brev 2, 1903-1940, 1961.
Du lär mig att bli fri. Selma Lagerlöf skriver till Sophie Elkan, 1992.

Selected Bibliography

Berendsohn, Walter A. *Selma Lagerlöf: Heimat und Leben, Künstlerschaft, Werke, Wirkung und Wert*. München: Albert Langen, 1927. Eng. tr. *Selma Lagerlöf: Her Life and Work*. London: Ivor Nicholson & Watson, 1931, and Port Washington, N.Y.: Kennikat press, 1968. Swedish tr. *Selma Lagerlöf*. Stockholm: Bonnier, 1928.

Bergenmar, Jenny. *Förvildade hjärtan. Livets estetik och berättandets etik i Selma Lagerlöfs Gösta Berlings saga*. Eslov: B. Östlings bokförl. Symposion, 2003.

Bergman, Sven Arne. *Getabock och gravlilja. Selma Lagerlöfs En herrgårdssägen som konstnärlig text*. Gothenburg: Litteraturvetenskapliga institutionen, Univ., 1997.

Edström, Vivi. *Selma Lagerlöf. Livets vågspel*. Stockholm: Natur och kultur, 2002.

Holm, Birgitta. *Selma Lagerlöf och ursprungets roman*. Stockholm: Norstedt, 1984.

Karlsson, Maria. *Känslans röst. Det melodramatiska hos Selma Lagerlöf*. Eslöv: B. Östlings bokförl. Symposion, 2002.

Lagerroth, Ulla-Britta. *Körkarlen och Bannlyst. Motiv- och idéstudier i Selma Lagerlöfs 10-talsdiktning*. Stockholm: Bonnier, 1963.

Lagerroth, Erland. *Selma Lagerlöf och Bohuslän. En studie i hennes 90-talsdiktning*. Selma Lagerlöf-sällskapet. Lund: Gleerup, 1961.

Selma Lagerlöf i utlandsperspektiv. Louise Vinge, ed. Stockholm: Kungl. Vitterhets Historie och Antikvitets Akademien, 1998.

Stenberg, Lisbeth. *En genialisk lek. Kritik och överskridande i Selma Lagerlöfs tidiga författarskap*. Gothenburg: Litteraturvetenskapliga institutionen, Univ., 2001.

Ulvros, Eva Helen. *Sophie Elkan. Hennes liv och vänskap med Selma Lagerlöf*. Lund: Historiska media, 2001.

Weidel, Gunnel. *Helgon och gengångare. Gestaltningen av kärlek och rättvisa i Selma Lagerlöfs diktning*. Lund: Gleerup, 1964.

Wivel, Henrik. *Snedronningen: en bog om Selma Lagerlöfs kærlighed.* Copenhagen: Gad,
    1988. Swedish tr. *Snödrottningen. En bok om Selma Lagerlöf och kärleken.* Stock-
    holm: Bonnier, 1990.
Wägner, Elin. *Selma Lagerlöf* 1-2. Stockholm: Bonnier, 1942-43.

Cora Sandel's Fiction of Quiet Rebellion

ELLEN REES (UNIVERSITY OF OREGON)

Cora Sandel's (1880-1974) life and writing followed a lonely and circuitous path. She was born Sara Cecilia Margareta Görvell Fabricius on December 20, 1880 in Kristiania (today Oslo), Norway, the only daughter of a senior grade captain in the Norwegian Navy, Jens Schow Fabricius, and his eighteen-year younger wife, Anna Margareta Greger.

Her earliest years were spent in Kristiania in a pleasant, conventional apartment a few blocks from the royal palace, where family life was marked by her father's departures for and arrivals from exotic sea excursions. In 1893 Sara's father was granted a number of administrative military duties in the Tromsø district by royal decree. The move to Tromsø, a town of approximately 7,000 inhabitants at the time, was traumatic for the family, but it brought about a marked increase in their social status. Sara flourished in the environment, taking the Norwegian middle school exam (equivalent to a tenth grade education in the US) in 1897, and became one of a tight-knit circle of upper middle class girls whose talents and energies went unrecognized as their mothers groomed them for the marriage market. Her own interests lay in the direction of visual art and drama, and between 1897 and 1905 Sara stayed in Kristiania for a number of extended visits that included training at a painting academy for young ladies run by the Norwegian impressionist, Harriet Backer.

The decision to study painting marked her definitive move away from the bourgeois ideal of marriage and children as the only acceptable goal for young girls of the civil servant class and started her arduous transformation into the writer we today know as Cora Sandel. Provided by members of her extended family with the modest sum of 800 crowns, she departed for Paris in 1906 to paint, ostensibly for six months; but she remained there until 1921. By moving to Paris, Sara irrevocably broke with her class background and subjected herself to the harshest of living conditions on the fringes of the experimental art scene.

Sara Fabricius supported herself during these years any way she could, including writing pieces for Norwegian newspapers and magazines. However, she did not seriously turn to writing until the early 1920s. By then she had married the Swedish sculptor Anders Jönsson in 1913 with the hope of living with him in creative harmony. The birth of their first and only child, Erik, in 1917 brought about an abrupt reversion to traditional gender roles. The couple decided to return to Sweden in 1921 after having suffered through a great deal of physical and emotional hardship caused by the vagaries of the Great War. Their relationship deteriorated, ending in divorce in 1927, the year after Fabricius published her debut novel, *Alberte og Jakob* (Eng. tr. *Alberta and Jacob*, 1962) with Gyldendal Norsk Forlag under the pseudonym Cora Sandel.

Today Sandel is regarded as one of the most important and masterful Norwegian writers of the first half of the twentieth century. Her works continue to be read widely in Scandinavia, although they are less well-known in the rest of the world. Consequently, there are, unfortunately, very few critical sources about her writing available in English. During the 1970s, the feminist movement in Norway attempted to appropriate Sandel for their cause. However, from her earliest writing she made it very clear that she did not wish to be considered a feminist. Instead, she insisted that she wrote for and about humanity in its entirety. Initially, critics unambiguously categorized Sandel as a realist; however, recent scholarship has suggested a number of textual elements indicating the influence of modernist aesthetics and thought.

At the publication of *Alberta and Jacob*, Sandel was forty-six years old and had been living in France and Sweden in voluntary exile for nearly half of her life. The distances of time and space allowed her to explore the theme of alienation which predominates in her work, as well as an opportunity to take a critical look at the central premises of late nineteenth century Norwegian society. Sandel's first work exhibits a level of maturity and skill rare among debutantes and, in addition, subverts the genre of the popular novel of female development. Although the plot of *Alberta and Jacob* takes place within the narrow confines of a year in the life of an adolescent girl in a small northern Norwegian town, its author depicts an existential and nearly fatal foray into the no-man's-land of alienation. By nature Alberte is a profoundly modern character struggling to find a way to survive within the conventions of her bourgeois environment. Unlike many self-conscious modern protagonists, Alberte wants nothing more than to be loved and to please her family, yet even her simplest thoughts and actions subvert and threaten to shatter the façade her small town society hides behind. The novel was a critical and popular success, raising expectations of another volume about Alberte. Sandel's readers had to wait five years.

When *Alberte og friheten* (Eng. tr. *Alberta and Freedom*, 1963) finally appeared in 1931, everything had changed. In the opening scene the reader finds Alberte stripped naked – literally and figuratively – in a Paris atelier.

All ties with her past have been broken. *Alberta and Freedom* exults the cacophony and anonymity of the enormous, unknowable city and explores the treacheries of intimacy that desperation and the fear of loneliness provoke. Even more than in *Alberta and Jacob*, Sandel disassembles and subverts the formal conventions of the realist novel, in *Alberta and Freedom*.

The third and final book about Alberte, *Bare Alberte* (Eng. tr. *Alberta Alone*, 1965), appeared in 1939 just before World War II, and the book's central concern is the paradigm shift in art and human relations brought about by the trauma of World War I. Alberte's deep ambivalence about her role as mother brings her to a dispair which is never melodramatic, always self-aware and ironic. In the novel, the first signs of Sandel's doubts about literature as a meaningful human endeavor surface, although it is ultimately a self-reflective text about the writing and completion of a novel. Unfortunately, the novel was censored for political content by Sandel's publisher in a 1941 edition of the trilogy. Apparently Sandel was not informed, and all later editions up until 2002 as well as most translations – including Elizabeth Rokkan's English translation – were based on the censored edition. It was not until 1999 that Norwegian scholar Nina Evensen discovered the problem, and her 2002 unexpurgated edition of the Alberte trilogy is an important development.

In the years between the three volumes of the Alberte Trilogy, Sandel continued to struggle desperately to write and care for her son, publishing *En blå sofa og andre noveller* (1927; A Blue Sofa and Other Short Stories), *Carmen og Maja og andre noveller* (1932; Carmen and Maja and Other Short Stories), and *Mange takk, doktor og andre noveller* (1935; Many Thanks, Doctor and and Other Short Stories). Her letters to friends during this period witness her bitter struggle   she was reduced to pawning her typewriter at various times while trying to live off the little money she received from magazine publication of short stories. Sandel's attitude toward her own short stories is ambiguous. Although she crafted them as painstakingly as her longer prose pieces, she viewed them as inferior substitutes compromised by the constant need to get food on the table. In her stories, Sandel focuses her attention on a wider range of subversives – a prostitute, a mentally handicapped man, a psychotic woman, a child, a woman forced by her lover to undergo an abortion. Quite a few Sandel short stories and fragments written between the wars – among them a few outstanding texts – remained unpublished until the 1973 collection, *Barnet som elsket veier* (The Child Who Loved Roads).

Sandel's publisher, Harald Grieg at Gyldendal Norsk Forlag, pressured her to produce novels rather than short story collections which did not sell as well. When Sandel expressed interest in exploring dramatic forms Grieg actively discouraged her from doing so because there was no market for plays, particularly experimental plays. Pressured to stick with the more lucrative novel genre, Sandel found herself in a crisis exacerbated by her deep ambivalence toward literary pursuits in general. Her solution became a hybridization of drama and novel forms which she called "Interiør med figurer" (Interior with figures), a name borrowed from her painting past. This allowed her to dispense with many of the epic elements of the novel genre and pare it down, using the classic unities of time, space and action to focus more clearly on the existential crises of the subversive characters who continued to fascinate her.

In 1946 at the age of 65, Sandel published her most widely read work, *Kranes konditori. Interiør med figurer* (Eng. tr. *Krane's Café. An Interior with Figures*, 1968). This novel, which was has been staged and filmed numerous times, returns to the small northern Norwegian environment first introduced in *Alberta and Jakob*, albeit thirty years later. Sandel focuses on a female non-conformist, who in the course of one afternoon of drinking with a strange man, attempts to break all the ties that bind her to her miserable existence as the town's brilliant but unreliable seamstress. Rather than giving her misunderstood protagonist a dominant voice in the text, Sandel chooses to create a collective narrative voice representing the town and proper society at large. Sandel's narrative technique masterfully intensifies the reader's identification with the seamstress and the lonely world of the outsider.

Twelve years later, Sandel published her final prose text, *Kjøp ikke Dondi* (1958; Don't Buy Dondi; Eng. tr. *The Leech*, 1960), despite living on in good health for another sixteen years. Cora Sandel died on April 3, 1974 in Uppsala, Sweden. *Don't Buy Dondi* has troubled critics since its publication because they approach it as a realist text, rather than viewing it as a highly stylized and abstracted modernist text. As with *Krane's Café*, *Don't Buy Dondi* bears the subtitle *Interiør med figurer*. However, Sandel's final text is less a dramatic narrative than a symphony of different voices rising and falling, presenting major and minor themes in much the same way as a musical composition. Or perhaps more aptly, given the repeated references to jazz in the text, the characters function as jazz musicians improvising freely on a still recognizable jazz piece. Sandel also plays with her readers' expectations about her characters by creating a character, Dondi, who appears at first to be a typical Sandel heroine (a young, misunderstood female outsider). However, the reader soon recognizes that all the characters rework different elements of Sandel heroines. Of primary importance are Lagerta, worn down by age, self-denial and responsibility, but with a sharp edge and a profoundly subversive character underneath the façade, and the author of one good novel, Gregor, who is unable to produce more literature despite the urgings of his family, publisher and critics. The latter character appears to speak for Sandel in his ultimate renunciation of literature as a valid human endeavour.

In the short story "Armbåndet" (The Bracelet), which appeared in the 1932 collection *Carmen and Maja and Other Short Stories*, we find a number of Sandel's major themes and narrative strategies entertwined. The story has the light lyrical mood and subtle ironic turn that marks many of Sandel's texts. Her meticulous attention to details imbues the smallest gesture or change of expression with powerful significance. She deftly switches between points-of-view, representing the internal thoughts of both characters, which reveals to the reader an irony that remains hidden to her protagonists. Through this ironic tension, Sandel reveals some of the social issues that concerned her the most, including gender incquality, the economic and social marginalization of women, and the universal human desire for love and belonging.

Armbåndet

Hun la skjeen fra. Og med den siste rest is bitended kold mot ganen og en tiltagende eftersmak av vanilje i svelget, tok hun smilende en cigarett fra etuiet, han holdt åpent mot henne over bordet. Hennes håndledd med det nye armbåndet omkring kom inn i lyset fra bordlampen et øieblikk. Begge så på det, og derefter på hverandre. Hennes smil blev inderligere, øinene mørknet.

– Det er så nydelig, sa hun.

– Det er antikt, sa han.

– Jeg skjønner det. Det er noget av det peneste, jeg har sett. Jeg kan næsten ikke tro, det er mitt.

– Hh!

Genert over den tilfredshet med hennes svar, som han kjente i sitt ansikt og ikke straks kunde få bukt med, snudde han sig, så sig om efter kelneren og kaffen, dunket utålmodig med fyrstikkholderen i bordet. Skjenket så det siste av vinen op i glassene og løftet sitt: Skål!

– Skål!

Hun så ham mot en bakgrunn av ett balkongrekkverk, en mørk hekk og en flik grønn høsthimmel med en stjerne på. Den lille lampen under sin pergamentsskjerm belyste ham dempet og varmt. Hans ene arm lå et stykke innover bordet, så hånden kom frem i lysringen og lev med i stillebenet av frukt, blomster og gylne vinreflekser rundt en iskjøler. Den forekom henne fornemmere enn til hverdags, næsten forfinet. Fra cigaretten, han holdt, steg en smidig, lunefull, blå liten røk, som tegnet arabesker i luften.

Han tok sig ut nettop nå, hadde over sig noget, hun likte å se hos menn, noget avklaret rolig og selvfølelig. Kanskje hadde hun savnet det litt hos ham, funnet ham litt – ja, en tanke for anstrengt ungdommelig. Nå *var* han ung. Furene ved munnen var borte og pannen glatt.

Sån kunde han være, sån skulde han være herefter. Sån vilde hun ha ham.

Gjennem surret av stemmer og den ustanselige, lette slamren av porselen og sølvtøi, kom musikk i bølger til dem. De måtte bøie sig fremover bordet for å tale sammen. Mest tiet de, satt og lyttet efter melodistumper, nikket takt til kjente strofer. Så på menneskene omkring sig, vekslet blikk om dem og smilte.

Hun var litt ør. Det var godt. Det var å være nummen, uten tyngde, næsten ukropslig lett og ansvarløs. Nu syntes hun ikke annet enn, at alt var som det skulde være. Lettsinn? Langtfra. Det hele var godt og riktig. Det var godt og riktig å være to, komme og gå sammen med et mannfolk, bli sørget for og beskyttet igjen og få presenter, pene, gedigne presenter. Hun behøvde alt dette. Hun var ikke av disse freidige, som kan leve alene. Armbåndet? Noget iveien med armbåndet? Kunde han heller kommet med ett eller annet moderne nå, antikviteter ikke brukes videre? Det er slikt, menn ikke forstår, ikke menn av hans type iallfall. Hun skal se å få gitt ham ett lite vink en annen gang. Nydelig armbånd i og for sig, dyrt visst, gull og store topaser. Han er ikke redd for å spandere litt. Bra. God fornemmelse.

Har hun følt sig litt forundret, fått som et støkk et par ganger? Av ting han sa og gjorde? Bagateller, småting, en ikke får feste sig ved. Alle har vi våre sider, selv hun har sine. Der sitter han og gjør tilværelsen levelig og normal for henne igjen, er en å være hos. En pen, ungdommelig mann, som det er morsomt å vise sig sammen med. Det er ikke bare så at de har klamret sig til hverandre som to skibbrudne gjør. Hun kan være litt mere enn blott og bart takknemlig og varmt hengiven og sånn mot ham. Iaften kjenner hun det. Noget rører sig søtt og krevende i henne, noget rent legemlig, som våkner og går av hiet. Som hører til, som skal være der. Gudskjelov, det er der nu. Hun behøver ikke bare å late som – – –

Nogen måtte jo bli den, som ga henne øieblikk som disse, øieblikk av velvære og sorgløshet. Reddet henne fra pengemangel og kontorslaveri, to omstendigheter, som absolutt ikke ligger for henne. Og fra den pinlige, flaue, litt nakne fornemmelsen av å være dette mislykte, dette abnorme og vanføre, en kvinne uten mann. Fra den ørkenvandring, hun alt i alt befant sig på, da skilsmissens tumult og ståhei var over.

Fra nettenes bunnløse ensomhet.

En redningsmann måtte komme. Om ikke altfor lenge. En redningsmann kom.

I en underlig blandet stemning av lettelse og uro, av offervilje og spendt forventning og trossig lettsinn, lot hun sig redde.

Han var det, hun aller mest behøvde, at nogen var nettop da – op over ørene forelsket i henne. Han sa, at til han traff henne, hadde han vært som en drivende spån på havet, alene, misforstått, uten illusjoner, uten rød tråd i sitt liv. Alt var gått under, var tråkket ned i et trivielt og ulidelig ekteskap. Hun ga ham tilbake troen på det edle og gode i livet, gjorde ham ung på nytt, skulde og måtte bli hans. Litt umoderne og rare, men innlysende og begripelige ting, som styrket hjertet og fikk en til å kjenne sig som et kvinnemenneske og en person av betydning igjen, ikke bare som et gudsforglemt neutrum.

Og der sitter han nu og er pen!

I en plutselig munter og litt beveget stemning rekker hun ham hånden over bordet. Og det stikker til av glede i henne, da han bøier sig over den og kysser den. Hun er svak for sånt. Det gir livet farve og glans. La være, at det er litt gammeldags høitidelig.

– Hvad tenker du på?

– På – på ingenting spesielt. På oss to tror jeg. Atter engang må han snu sig for å skjule tilfredsheten i sitt ansikt. Det var så riktig svart. Han praier en forbiilende kelner og rekvirerer ett glass vann.

Så har han ansiktet iorden igjen og ser på henne, ser henne langt og megetsigende inn i øinene.

I sitt stille sinn tenker han: Vellykket med det armbåndet. Bra at jeg hadde det i tider som disse. Resikabelt? Nei. Amalie er i Rom, blir der sannsynligvis. Og Oslo er storby. Idiotisk om jeg bare hadde latt det ligge. Sitter hun ikke der som et lite, tillitsfullt barn og er gla i det og elsker mig? Ung og frisk, søt som pokker. *For* ung? Tøv. *Tøv!* Bra at det gikk som det gikk med Amalie og mig, bra at jeg fikk henne ut tilslutt. Sandelig på tide også efter tyve års ekteskap, rent biologisk sett. Livets lov simpelthen. Bra, hun var stor på det og lot efter sig tingene sine, greit. Noget må jeg jo komme med. Og nogen må jeg ha. Dette med frie forbindelser og uteliv ligger ikke for mig, ikke i lengden. Dyrt blir det også. Nei – en sånn liten hengiven sjel, som blindt og ukritisk ser op til en – jeg har da vært heldig –

Og han smiler til henne: Pen tango de spiller nå.

Plutselig ser hun ham bli anderledes i ansiktet, urolig, litt fortrukket, gammel. Også hans hånd, som ligger på bordet, får uro i sig, griper efter noget å ta i. Samtidig hilser han avmålt på en eller annen bak henne. Hun hører ham mumle: Faen.

– Hvem hilste du på?

– Ikke snu dig – ikke akkurat nå.

– Nei. Hvem er det?

– Hysj. Vil du endelig vite det, er det en gammel veninde av – av min forhenværende kone. Hennes beste veninde forresten.

En veninde? tenker hun: En veninde av –?

Hun ser for sig noget grått og farveløst. Som har eksistert og fremdeles skal eksistere etsteds. Noget litt gammelt, iført flate heler og fletteknute. En av disse naturens anomalier, som ikke forstår mennene, og som det ikke er morsomt for dem å være gift med. Som man dels synes litt synd i og dels at det er tilpass til. En utenfor.

Han har næsten ikke nevnt Amalie, bare talt om uoverensstemmelser og totalt forskjellige naturer, antydet, at han har lidt meget. Det har hun funnet pent og ridderlig av ham, korrekt og på alle måter tjenligst. Amalie er kjedelig.

– Å sitt litt stille, er du snild.

– Stille? Jeg sitter da stille. Jeg har ikke en eneste gang –

– Du fekter så med cigaretten. Ja, undskyld, jeg er nervøs, jeg –

– Fekter jeg? Jeg skjønner ikke, hvad du mener? Hvor sitter hun? Kom hun nå nettop?

– I dette øieblikk. Å nei, sitt stille da. Denne fektingen –

– Hvad er det du tøver om? sier hun litt ergerlig. Hun har ikke gjort en overflødig bevegelse og vet det. Hun er ikke sånn, er avmålt og rolig. Han behandler henne jo formelig, som om hun ikke hadde opdragelse. Skal hun ikke ha lov å røre sig, hvergang en gammel veninde av Amalie dukker op? Nei, denslags hensyn tenker hun ikke ta.

Men da hun snudde sig, så hun rett inn i ansiktet på en dame, som med optrukne øienbryn og ett lite smil satt og så på – på armen hennes – på armbåndet?

En pen, stilfull, ungdommelig dame. Svært pen. Var det sånne veninder Amalie hadde? Da var kanskje Amalie også –? Si mig, hvem du omgås –

– At du ikke kunde vente litt med å snu dig!

– Kjære, jeg er da ikke forpliktet til å vite –

Noget står innristet i hjernen på henne, en kombinasjon av to optrukne bryn, ett smil, armbåndet. Og av uttrykket i to øine. I løpet av ett sekund skiftet det fra ironi til – til medfølelse –?

Til noget i retning av "stakkars liten" –

Hun kjenner en ond rødme stige i ansiktet. Og en ond tanke i sinnet. En ekkel tanke. Noget, hun leste i et modekåseri forleden, om at det sist var moderne å gå med gamle ting omkring nittenhundre og ti, kommer for henne –

– Du må undskylde mig, hører hun ham si fra den andre siden bordet: men nettop henne der, har jeg aldri kunnet med –

– Betal er du snild, jeg fryser litt, jeg vil gå.

Han banker med fyrstikkholderen: Kelner!

Hun fryser virkelig. Alt er forandret, kveldshimmelen bak hekken mørk og død. Det trekker i verandaen, persiennene blaffer. Og menneskene rundt omkring er plutselig så uhyggelige. De griner umotivert og fjollet som figurer i onde drømmer, ler falsk og forsert. Om det så er lampen på bordet brender den med et forlorent og simpelt skinn. Ingenting er, hva det ga sig ut for å være.

Uten å se hverken tilhøire eller venstre, går hun fort foran mot utgangen. Noget, hun ikke vet, hvordan, hun skal ta, ligger som en lammelse i sinnet. Hun forfølges av ett medlidende ansikt, nei av to. Nede i kåpelommen har hun krenget av sig Amalies avlagte armånd. Det dingler mot benet, når hun går.

– Satan også, at dette mennesket skulde komme og ødelegge stemningen for oss. Stemmen hans prøver sig frem, litt usikker på hvad hun har skjønt og ikke skjønt. Litt forhåbningsfull også. Hun har sikkert ikke skjønt, at – – Han kommer med armen, vil ha den inn under hennes.

Hun ryster ham av sig, går fort foran.

The Bracelet

Translated by Ellen Rees

She laid the spoon aside. And with the last bit of ice cream bitingly cold on the roof of her mouth and an increasing taste of vanilla in her throat, she smilingly took a cigarette from the etui that he offered her across the table. Her wrist with the new bracelet around it entered the circle of light from the table lamp for a moment. Both looked at it, and then at each other. Her smile became more sincere, her eyes darkened.

– It's so lovely, she said.

– It's an antique, he said.

– I can tell. It's one of the prettiest I've seen. I almost can't believe it's mine.

– Hh!

Embarrassed over the satisfaction with her answer that he felt showing in his face and couldn't immediately control, he turned away, looked for the waiter and the coffee, thumped impatiently with the matchstick holder on the table. Then poured the last of the wine into the glasses and lifted his: Cheers!

– Cheers!

She saw him against the background of a balcony railing, a dark hedge and a sliver of green autumn sky with a star in it. The little lamp under its parchment shade illuminated him with a subdued and warm light. One of his arms lay on the table such that his hand came into the ring of light and joined the still life of fruit, flowers and golden wine reflections off the ice cooler. The hand appeared to her to be more refined than usual, almost delicate. From the cigarette he held arose lithe, temperamental blue smoke that inscribed an arabesque in the air.

He was at his best just now, had something about him that she liked to see in men, something clearly calm and self-assured. Perhaps she had missed that in him a little, found him a little – well, a notion too falsely youthful.

Now he *was* young. The lines at his mouth were gone and his forehead smooth.

This is how he could be, how he was, when life was a little kind to him. This is how he would be from here on. This is how she wanted him to be.

Through the buzz of voices and the unceasing, gentle clinking of porcelain and silverware, music came to them in waves. They had to lean over the table in order to converse. Mostly they were silent, sat and listened for the snatches of melody, nodded in time with verses they knew, exchanged glances about them and smiled.

She was a little light-headed. That was good. It was like being numb, without weight, almost incorporeally light and without responsibility. Now she felt nothing except that everything was as it should be.

Frivolous? Far from it. Everything was good and right. It was good and right to be two, come and go together with a man, be taken care of and protected again and get presents, pretty, magnificent presents. She needed all of this. She wasn't one of these bold women who can live alone.

The bracelet? Something wrong with the bracelet? Couldn't he have come up with something more modern instead, now that antiques aren't fashionable anymore? It's the kind of thing men don't understand, not men like him anyway. She'll make sure to give him a little hint another time. A lovely bracelet per se, expensive for sure, gold and large topazes. He's not afraid to spend a little. Good. Good sense.

Has she felt a little surprised, felt a little shocked a couple of times? Over things he said and did? Bagatelles, little things that one can't get hung up on. We all have our bad sides, even she has hers. There he sits and makes existence livable and normal for her again, is someone to be with. A handsome, youthful man who it's fun to be seen with. It's not as if they have just clung to each other like two shipwrecked people might do. She can be a little more than merely grateful and respectfully devoted and the like toward him. Tonight she feels it. Something warm and demanding moves inside her, something purely physical that awakens and leaves its lair. That is part of it, that is supposed to be there. Thank goodness it's there now. She doesn't have to just pretend that – – –

After all, someone had to be the one who gave her moments like these, moments of wellbeing and freedom from care. He had saved her from the shortage of money and office slavery, two situations that are absolutely not her kind of thing. And from the embarrassing, galling, almost naked sense of being the failure, this abnormal and disabled thing, a woman without a man. Saved her from the desert wandering that she, all things considered, found herself upon when the tumult and ado of the divorce was over.

From the bottomless loneliness of the night.

A rescuer *had* to come. And none too soon. A rescuer did come.

In a strangely mixed mood of relief and anxiety, of the will to sacrifice, of tense expectation and of contrary frivolity, she let herself be rescued.

He was what she needed most of all, that someone right then and there – was head over heels infatuated with her. He said that until he met her, he had been like wood adrift on the ocean, alone, misunderstood, without illusions, without the red thread that gives meaning in his life. Everything had gone under, was trampled down in a trivial and unbearable marriage. She gave him back the belief in the noble and good in life, made him young again, should and must become his. Slightly old fashioned and odd, but obvious and comprehensible things that strengthened her heart and made her feel like a woman and a person of consequence again, not just a godforsaken neuter.

And there he sits now and is handsome!

In a suddenly cheerful and slightly moved state of mind she reaches for his hand across the table. And she prickles with happiness when he bends over her hand and kisses it. She has a weakness for that kind of thing. It gives life color and radiance. Never mind that it's a little old fashioned and pompous.

– What are you thinking about?

– About – about nothing special. About the two of us, I think.

Yet again he has to turn away to hide the satisfaction in his face. That was such a perfect answer. He hails a waiter dashing past and commissions a glass of water.

Then he has his face back in order again and looks at her, looks her deeply and mean-ingfully in the eyes.

He thinks to himself: The bracelet was a success. Good thing that I had it in times like these. Risky? No. Amalie is in Rome, will probably stay there. And Oslo is a big city. It would have been idiotic to let it just lie there. And isn't she sitting there like a little, trusting child liking it and loving me? Young and healthy, sweet as can be. *Too* young? Nonsense. *Nonsense!* Good thing it ended up like it did with Amalie and me, good that I got rid of her at last. None too soon either after twenty years of marriage, biologically speaking. Simply the laws of life. Good thing she was big about it and left her things behind. I had to come up with something. And I have to have someone. This stuff about free love and nightlife is not my style, not in the long run. It gets expensive too. No – a devoted little soul like this one, who blindly and uncritically looks up to me – I really have been lucky.

And he smiles at her: That's a pretty tango they're playing now.

Suddenly she sees his face change, become anxious, a little distorted, old. And his hand lying on the table becomes uneasy, gropes for something to hold onto. At the same time he greets someone or another behind her back stiffly. She hears him mumble: Shit.

– Who did you say hello to?

– Don't turn around – not right now.

– No. Who is it?

– Shh. If you really want to know, it's an old friend of – my former wife. Her best friend, as it happens.

A friend? she thinks: A friend of – ?

She imagines something gray and colorless. Who has existed and will continue to exist someplace. Something a little old, wearing low heels and a braided bun. One of these anomalies of nature, who doesn't understand men and with whom it isn't enjoyable for them to be married. Whom one partly feels a little sorry for and partly feels fits the role. An outsider.

He has hardly mentioned Amalie, just talked about irreconcilable differences and completely different natures, implied that he has suffered a lot. She has found this proper and gentlemanly of him, correct and most suitable in every way. Amalie is boring.

– Oh, please would you sit still.

– Still? I'm sitting still. I haven't even once –

– You're waving your cigarette like crazy. Okay, I'm sorry, but I'm nervous –

– I'm *waving*? I don't understand what you're talking about? Where is she sitting? Did she just come in?

– Just this moment. Oh no, sit still, will you. This waving –

– What are you talking about? she says a little perturbed. She hasn't made a single un-necessary movement and knows it. She's not like that, she's measured and calm. He is literally treating her like she had no manners. So, she's not supposed to move any time an old friend of Amalie shows up? Nope, she's not going to take that kind of consideration.

– But when she turned, she looked right into a woman's face that with raised eyebrows and a little smile sat and looked at – at her arm – at the bracelet?

A pretty, stylish and youthful woman. Very pretty. Was that the kind of friends Ama-lie had? Then maybe Amalie was also –? One is known by the company one keeps –

– Couldn't you have waited to turn around?

– My dear, I'm not obligated to know –

Something has become engraved in her brain, a combination of two raised eyebrows, a smile, the bracelet. And the expression in two eyes. In the course of a second it shifted from irony to – to sympathy –?

To something along the lines of "poor little thing" –
She feels a wicked blush rising to her face. And a wicked thought rising in her mind. An unpleasant thought. Something that she read in a fashion report the other day, that the last time it was modern to wear old things was twenty years ago in nineteen-ten, comes to mind –
– Please excuse me, she hears him say from the other side of the table: but I have never been able to tolerate that woman –
– Please, would you just pay, I'm a little cold, I want to go.
He thumps the table with the matchstick holder: Waiter!
She really is cold. Everything has changed, the evening sky behind the hedge is dark and dead. There is a draft on the veranda, the venetian blinds flap. And the people around are suddenly so unpleasant. They grimace unprovoked and foolishly like figures in bad dreams, they laugh falsely and forced. Even the lamp on the table seems to burn with an artificial and vulgar light. Nothing is what it pretended to be.
Without looking to the right or left, she walks quickly ahead of him toward the exit. Something she doesn't know how she's going to face lies like a paralysis of the mind. She is haunted by a sympathizing face, no of two. Down in her coat pocket she has wrenched off Amalie's discarded bracelet. It dangles against her thigh as she walks.
– Damn it all, that that person had to come and destroy the atmosphere for us. His voice makes a tentative attempt, unsure of what she has and has not understood. He's a little hopeful too. Surely she hasn't understood that – – He reaches for her with his arm, wants to tuck it under hers.
She shakes him off, walks quickly ahead.

Primary Works

Alberte og Jakob, 1926; Eng. tr. *Alberta and Jacob*, 1962.
En blå sofa og andre noveller, 1927.
Alberte og friheten, 1931; Eng. tr. *Alberta and Freedom*, 1963.
Carmen og Maja og andre noveller, 1932.
Mange takk, doktor og andre noveller, 1935.
Bare Alberte, 1939; Eng. tr. Alberta Alone, 1939.
Dyr jeg har kjent. Historier for ung og gammel, 1945.
Kranes konditori. Interiør med figurer, 1946; Eng. tr. *Krane's Café. An Interior With Figures*, 1968.
Figurer på mørk bunn, 1949.
Samlede verk 1-6, 1950-51.
Kjøp ikke Dondi. Interiør med figurer, 1958; Eng. tr. *The Leech*, 1960.
Barnet som elsket veier. Steinar Gimnes, ed., 1973.
Selected Short Stories, 1985.
The Silken Thread – Stories and Sketches, 1986.

Selected Bibliography

Bale, Kjersti. *Friheten som utopi: En analyse av Cora Sandels Alberte-trilogi*. Oslo: Novus, 1989.

180   Ellen Rees

Billing, Anna Carin. *"Hvad er sannhet?"*: *Studier i Cora Sandels novellistik*. Oslo: Solum 2002.

Evensen, Nina. *Erindringens vev: En studie av fortidsdimensjonens betydning i Cora Sandels Albertetrilogi*. Tromsø: Universitetet i Tromsø, 1999.

Garton, Janet. "Cora Sandel," *Norwegian Women's Writing 1850-1990*. London: Athlone, 1993, 128-46.

Gimnes, Steinar. "Om fortolkningen av Cora Sandels *Kjøp ikke Dondi*." *Edda* 3 (1973): 163-71.

–. "'Tilværelsen kleber': Om kvinner og frigjering i nokre Cora Sandel-noveller." *Norsk litterær årbok* 1976. Oslo: Samlaget, 1976, 48-61.

Hunt, Linda. "The Alberte Trilogy: Cora Sandel's Norwegian Künstlerroman and American Feminist Literary Discourse." *Writing the Woman Artist: Esssays on Poetics, Politics and Portraiture*. Suzanne Whitmore Jones, ed. Philadelphia: University of Pennsylvania Press, 1991, 214-32.

Lervik, Åse Hiorth. *Menneske og miljø i Cora Sandels diktning: En studie over stil og motiv*. Oslo: Gyldendal, 1977.

Malm, Anne-Charlotte Leveau. "Det talande djuret: Kvinnan och hennes språk i Cora Sandels noveller." *Norsk litterær årbok* 1990. Oslo: Samlaget, 1990, 76-101.

Rees, Ellen. "Cora Sandel's *Kjøp ikke Dondi*: '...som de snakker, de menneskene'" *Scandinavica* 34:2 (1995), 221-35.

–. "Escape from the Novel: Cora Sandel's *Kranes konditori*." *Scandinavian Studies* 72:2 (2000), 181-98.

–. "På spor av modernismen i Cora Sandels Alberte-trilogi." *Edda* 2 (1997), 209-20.

–. "The Riddle Solved: Cora Sandel's 'En gåte.'" *Studies in Short Fiction* 31:1 (1994), 13-21.

Rokkan, Elizabeth. "Cora Sandel and the Second World War." *Scandinavica* 28:2 (1988): 155-58.

–. "Cora Sandel's War Story: 'Stort syn og smått syn.'" *Scandinavica* 26:1 (1987), 5-12.

Selboe, Tone. "Byvandringens betydning i Cora Sandels Alberte-trilogi." *Norsk litterær årbok* 2000. Oslo: Samlaget, 2000, 88-104.

Solumsmoen, Odd. *Cora Sandel: En dikter i ånd og sannhet*. Oslo: Aschehoug, 1957.

Zuck, Virpi. "Cora Sandel, a Norwegian Feminist," *Edda* 1 (1981), 23-33.

Øverland, Janneken. *Cora Sandel: En biografi*. Oslo: Gyldendal, 1995.

–. *Cora Sandel om seg selv*. Oslo: Den norske bokklubben, 1983.

Sigrid Undset: A Modern Medievalist

SHERRILL HARBISON (UNIVERSITY OF MASSACHUSETTS)

Sigrid Undset (1882-1949), Norway's most important female novelist, distinguished herself in the 1920s with two epic cycles of historical novels about medieval life in Norway, *Kristin Lavransdatter* (1920-22; Eng. tr. 1923-27, 1997-2000) and *Olav Audunssøn* (1925-27; Eng. tr. 1928-30). These massive works earned her the 1928 Nobel Prize for Literature.

The bulk of Undset's literary production – which includes novels, stories, poetry, children's books, memoirs, translations, criticism, hagiography, and hundreds of essays – occurred between 1907 and World War II. Much of her early fiction and most of the nonfiction has not been translated into English, though she did reiterate many of her previously published views on religion and politics for American publications during her World War II exile years in the United States.

Undset was one of Norway's so-called "epic novelists" (others in this category include Olav Duun, Kristofer Uppdal and Johan Falkberget), whose major works of historical fiction appeared in the 1920s. She broke new ground in the genre, both with her choice of subject matter and her method of developing it. While historical novels are usually built around a cataclysmic event such as war or revolution, what most interested Undset was Norway's gradual transition from a pagan blood-feud society to European Christian culture, a change that was mostly peaceful, but took centuries to accomplish. In her multi-volume works of the 1920s and the shorter *Fortællingen om Viga-Ljot og Vigdis* (1909; The Tale of Viga-Ljot and Vigdis; Eng. tr. *Gunnar's Daughter*, 1936) set at the turn of the 11th century, she focused on the momentous shift in cultural values that took place when Christianity arrived in the North at the end of the first millennium. Characters in her modern fiction register the effects of the same shift in reverse, as she observed faith in technology and secular science eclipsing Christian teachings at the second millennium's end.

The epic scale, psychological acuity, and irony that characterizes Undset's best work has drawn comparisons with Honoré de Balzac and Leo

Tolstoy, but her own models were the masterpieces from the Middle Ages, especially the Icelandic Sagas. She called *Njáls saga* (Njal's Saga) the 13th-century Icelandic saga that she first encountered at age ten, "a book that was a turning point in my life."[1] Her own work is deeply influenced by the salient features of the genre: a vigorous, sometimes brutal realism; a laconic style; close attention to details of domestic life; and vivid, individualized portraits, not only of strong-minded women but of men and children as well. The sagas were far from the only medieval influence on her work, however; her prose also consciously echoes the earthy lyricism of her favorite Danish ballads and the shimmering beauty of the medieval chivalric romances.

In addition, Undset was a devotee of English literature, and her narrative settings and human character types are Chaucerian in variety and range. Kristin's pilgrimage to St. Olaf's shrine at Nidaros in the company of a rich collection of dissimilar wayfarers is itself a tribute Chaucer's pilgrimage-as-travelogue in *The Canterbury Tales*. Undset's borrowings are also more explicit. For example, in a 1930 article about *The Canterbury Tales* for a Norwegian tourist publication, she notes that Chaucer's Wife of Bath had a dubious view of St. Paul's advice on chastity: while it was "good advice, it was not a Commandment," Undset wrote. The Wife had compared taking St. Paul's advice to "living on a diet of white bread," whereas it was "coarse bread that satisfies," adding that she herself was very happy to have eaten coarse bread with five husbands.[2] *Kristin Lavransdatter*'s Fru Aashild, whose scandalous sexual liaisons made her an outcast from polite society, is one of Undset's several tributes to Chaucer's lusty Wife. "I've had my glory days, Kristin," Aashild remarks about her life choices, "but I'm not foolish enough to complain because I have to be content with sour, watered down milk now that I've drunk up all my wine and ale" (*The Wreath* 49).

Undset's research in primary sources and her scrupulous accuracy of detail won her work unanimous praise from historians. Critics were divided, however, over whether her characterizations were medieval or modern, a question still debated today. What probably makes her portraits most convincing is her own sense of being contemporary with her characters. "I think the reason I understand our own time so well," she wrote to a friend in 1920, "is that ever since I was a child I've had a kind of living memory of an earlier time to compare with it."[3]

Sigrid Undset was born in Kalundborg, Denmark, on May 20, 1882, but her family moved permanently to Oslo (then Christiania) when she was

---

[1] "En bok som ble et vendepunkt i mitt liv," published in *Artikler og taler fra krigstiden*, 27-34.
[2] "Pilgrimmene." *Norsk turistforenings aarbok*, 1930, 65-71.
[3] Anker (1982), 57.

two. Her mother, Charlotte Gyth Undset, was an intelligent, cultivated Dane with literary interests and artistic talent; her father, Ingvald Undset, was a well-known Norwegian archeologist. It was apparent early that the child was precocious, and despite his failing health her father did his best to groom her for his own profession, introducing her to Old Norse and scientific method before she started school. For a time she wanted to be either a painter or a botanist, but when she was eleven her father died, leaving the family in straitened economic circumstances. Throughout adolescence Undset was withdrawn and depressed. At fifteen she quit school and went to work as a secretary to support her mother and two younger sisters.

During her ten years as an office worker Undset educated herself at night, reading widely in Scandinavian and European languages, history, and literature, particularly from the medieval period. In 1905, after working three years on a novel set in the Middle Ages, she received one of literature's more famous rejections: Historical fiction was "probably not [her] line," Gyldendal's publisher Peter Nansen advised, she should try her hand at "something modern."[4] Thus Undset made her literary debut in 1907 with a brief epistolary novel about modern-day adultery, *Fru Marta Oulie* (Mrs. Marta Oulie). Her second book, *Den lykkelig alder* (1908; The Happy Age) was a collection of stories about the emotional isolation of young working women like herself.

These successes won Undset an author's stipend, and in 1909 she was able to leave her secretarial job. Success also encouraged her to venture back to the Middle Ages with her third novel, *Gunnar's Daughter*, a shocking story of a female avenger from the Saga Age published in 1909. That same year, at age 27, Undset made her first journey abroad, where in Rome she met the painter Anders Castus Svarstad, a married man thirteen years her senior. For the next two years the couple conducted a "clandestine" affair in Christiania while waiting for his divorce. In 1911 Undset published *Jenny* (Eng. tr. 1921) a sensitive but overwrought novel about a fatherless, idealistic young painter who loses her moral compass while living among artists in Rome. The grisly story, which included frank descriptions of female eroticism, rape, incest, and suicide, caused a scandal and put Undset on the literary map.

Undset and Svarstad were married in Antwerp in 1912, and after spending six months in London returned to Rome for the birth of their first child. The idyll was short, as the infant boy nearly died, and Undset returned alone to Oslo to nurse him back to health. Later the couple set up housekeeping in Ski, near Christiania, where in 1915 a daughter was born. Shortly afterward Undset took in Svarstad's three older children, one of

---

[4]   Winsnes, 34.

whom was disabled. Before long it became clear that her own daughter, too, had developmental problems and was an epileptic.

During this period housekeeping and childcare were so demanding that Undset resorted to writing through the night, and in that manner she published seven volumes of fiction, translations, and essays between 1912-1919 – an average of one per year. These early modern stories treat variations of the same themes that appear in her historical works: the anarchic power of erotic desire, disappointments in romantic love, and the responsibilities of marriage and parenthood. The stories in *Fattige skjæbner* (1912, The Fates of the Poor; selected Eng.tr. "Simonsen," and "Selma Brøter" 1959,[5] "A Charity Ball" 1984,[6] "Første møte" 1994[7]) reflect the loss of dignity and family coherence that industrial capitalism imposed on the lower classes. In *Vaaren* (1914; Spring), *Splinten av troldspeilet* (1917; Splinters of a Magic Mirror; (selected Eng. tr. "Fru Hjelde," as *Images in a Mirror* 1938), and *De kloge jomfruer* (1918, The Wise Virgins, selected Eng.tr. "Thjødolf" 1959[8]) her characters engage in a futile search for love and erotic fulfillment in a society that cultivates the individual ego over communal responsibility.

The grueling all-night work regimen took a considerable toll on Undset's health, however. The couple was also growing apart: Svarstad was a non-participating parent who could not meet his wife's needs for domestic order and routine, and their political views had begun to diverge sharply. In 1919, while pregnant with her third child, Undset separated from Svarstad and moved with her own two children to Lillehammer.

While nursing her newborn that autumn, Undset issued *Et kvinnesyns-punkt* (1919; A Woman's Point of View, selected Eng. tr. "Reflections on the Suffragette Movement," 1993[9]), a collection of five essays written between 1914-19 that outlined her views on the status of women and of society in general. She deplored the replacement of spiritual values by a mechanistic world view and naïve scientific models of human behavior, and expressed skepticism that technology or social engineering could create a utopian society. Modern social problems had begun, she decided, when the Protestant Reformation turned nations away from the medieval ideal of an international community that recognized common spiritual leadership. Luther's denigration of Church authority and his insistence on the individual's direct relationship with God had inflated the ego, opening the way for

---

[5]   In *Four Stories* 199-245, 3-62.
[6]   Tr. Janet Garton, in *An Everyday Story*, ed. Katherine Hanson, Seattle: Seal Press, 1984, 76-96.
[7]   "First Encounter," Sherrill Harbison, tr. *Metamorphoses*, 3.1 (Dec. 1994) 69-73 and 3.2 (April 1995) 170.
[8]   In *Four Stories*, 63-146.
[9]   In Hudson, 187-205.

the cult of individualism and the aggressive nationalism that now rent the social fabric.

Undset's fiction in the next decade was devoted to portraying the Pre-Reformation society that accepted and accommodated itself – though not without vigorous struggle – to the earlier model of Christianity she admired. The drama in both *Kristin Lavransdatter* and *The Master of Hestviken* revolves around what medieval culture considered the worst of personal crises, a defiant individual who rebels against the social order and must pay the necessary cost. Undset's protagonists, who are guilty of serious legal and ethical transgressions, are ultimately restored to grace, not because they reform their social institutions (the modern solution) or become personally virtuous (in Undset's view "human perfection" was an oxymoron), but because they acknowledge their fallibility and are invested in a larger spiritual community which can absolve them.

In 1924 Sigrid Undset was herself received as a Roman Catholic, and her marriage to Svarstad was dissolved. In 1928 she joined the Dominicans, a teaching order, as a lay member. Throughout the 1930s she published an enormous quantity of educational essays and hagiography – which she ironically called her "Catholic propaganda" (Katholsk Propaganda 1927, Eng. tr. 1993[10]) – for the tiny, often persecuted Catholic population in suspicious Lutheran Scandinavia. Her fiction also reflected this preoccupation. In *Gymnadenia* (1929, Eng. tr. *The Wild Orchid*, 1931) and its sequel *Den brennende busk* (1930; Eng. tr. *The Burning Bush*, 1932), two related novels about the gradual, unspectacular conversion of the young Paul Selmer to Catholicism, Undset also explores what she regarded as the deluded individualism of Ibsen's generation in a sensitive portrait of Paul's mother Julie.

Undset viewed the German National Socialism developing in the 1930s as a direct descendant of Lutheran individualism, reinforced by sentimental German Romanticism, vulgar Darwinism, and Nietzschean *Übermensch* ideology. She did not hesitate to publish these opinions in the German press, and for this she was blacklisted there in 1933. As head of the Norwegian Authors' Union between 1935-1940 she used her platform to denounce the Nazi lackeyism of Union members, especially that of her long-time nemesis, Knut Hamsun, with whom she had tangled as early as 1914 over the human rights of the disabled and the elderly. In *Ida Elisabeth* (1932; Eng. tr. 1933) and *Den trofaste hustru* (1936; Eng. tr. *The Faithful Wife*, 1937) her heroines have no overt religious affiliation, but by electing to care for (rather than abandon) the mentally defective and physically weak, they embody the Christian values Undset believed were crucial to combat

---

[10]   In Hudson, 232-271.

the menacing "social hygiene" policies being promoted both by Hamsun and by the Nazi regime.

Early in 1939 Undset's ailing daughter died at age 23; her elderly mother's death followed a few months later. In November she published *Madame Dorthea*, the only volume she would complete of a planned trilogy about her own family, beginning in the 18th century. In February of 1940 Undset took in three Finnish children orphaned during Finland's 1939 Winter War, a costly and fruitless campaign to stop Russian expansion into Finnish territory, but when Germany invaded Norway in April 1940 she was forced to flee her own home and country. After arriving safely in Stockholm she learned that her oldest son had been killed in the first weeks of the Resistance. Her teenaged younger son – all that was left of her family – escaped to join her, and together they traveled to the United States via Siberia and Japan.

Between 1940-1945 Undset made her home in Brooklyn, and busied herself as a "soldier of the Resistance",[11] lecturing widely and writing prolifically in the anti-Nazi cause. While in the U.S. she published an account of her escape to America, *Return to the Future* (1942; Norw. version *Tilbake til fremtiden*, 1945) and two children's books, *Happy Times in Norway* (1942; Norw. version *Lykkelig dager*, 1947), and *Sigurd and his Brave Companions* (1943; Norw. version *Sigurd og hans tapre venner*, 1955).

After the war Undset returned to Lillehammer, exhausted, disillusioned, and in weakened health. She wrote no more fiction, but continued to warn her countrymen, some of whose collaboration with Hitler had stained the country's name, against smug complacency. She labored for some time on a biography of Catherine of Siena, which was published posthumously in 1951. She died in Lillehammer June 10, 1949, at age 67.

The critic Daniel Haakonsen used the term "ethical realism" to describe the spirit of the interwar period in Norway, in which novelists used straightforward storytelling to perform a symbolic mediation either between present and past or between individual and group.[12] Undset belongs in this frame of reference, but she also felt her own instinctive realism to be a form of truth-telling, and thus a moral responsibility. This concern with truth-telling, while striking, was not merely a personal idiosyncrasy, as lying had long been regarded as a cardinal sin in Norwegian culture. Undset liked to quote the recipe of an old farm woman: Never tell a lie. And never tell a truth unless it is necessary. But when it is necessary, tell the truth – even if it sounds unreasonable, disagreeable, or shocking.[13]

During the first two decades of the 20th century, Undset's conservative social and political views made many Norwegians uneasy, even more so

[11] Ørjasæter, 317.
[12] Naess, 205.
[13] Bliksrud (1997), 9.

when she converted to Catholicism. Feminists especially felt betrayed by her dismissive attitudes toward aspects of the women's movement that she saw as naive and misguided. Undset accepted these charges with studied irony, addressing her concluding essay in *A Woman's Point of View* to "likeminded reactionaries." By the 1930s, however, her fearlessness in speaking the truth as she saw it won Undset wide admiration and sympathy, and her wartime work made her a national hero. In 1947 she was awarded the nation's highest civilian honor, the St. Olaf Cross.

Although Undset is probably Norway's best-known writer after Ibsen and Hamsun, since her death she has suffered critical neglect in English-speaking countries. Outside Scandinavia she is studied most in France, where her insights into female eroticism are much admired, and in Russia, which has long had an affinity for the historical novel. Among her early works *Jenny* is the most powerful, while of those from her last productive decade the autobiographical novel of childhood, *Elleve Aar* (1934; Eleven Years; Eng. tr. *The Longest Years*, 1935) stands out for its delicate sensuality, ironic humor, and Undset's extraordinary grasp of child psychology. Of all her works, the writer herself preferred *The Master of Hestviken*, perhaps because she lived with it for so long – the book was a mature, rewritten version of her rejected first novel from 1905.

Most critics, however, agree that *Kristin Lavransdatter*, her ground-breaking domestic epic which combines the chivalric romance with the marriage novel, is her masterpiece, and public opinion seems to agree – it has been translated to nearly seventy languages and is still in print around the world. Written at a major transition in her life, the trilogy crystallizes much of the intellectual and emotional energy that Undset devoted to marriage, parenthood, and spiritual life during a period of crisis and commitment. Its pages are rich in intertextuality, rich in seasonal and botanical symbolism, and rich in sensuous and sensual experience – weather, food, smells, tenderness and lust, exhaustion and exhilaration, and the agonies of childbirth and death.

The selection printed here from the first volume, *The Wreath*, illustrates this mastery well. The text describes the break-point in a battle of wills between Lavrans Bjørgulfsøn and his seventeen year-old daughter Kristin, who has broken relations with the man to whom Lavrans had betrothed her. Instead, Kristin secretly committed herself to Erlend Nikulaussøn, an older man of dubious reputation whom Lavrans both dislikes and mistrusts. Unknown to her parents, Kristin has also been involved in the unsavory death of Erlend's former mistress, a mêlée in which Erlend received a serious knife-wound.

Kristin Lavransdatter

Bind 1, Kransen, 3. del, kapitel 4

Frosten ble stående. På hvert fjøs i bygden rautet og klaget de sulteforede dyr og led av kulden. Men folk sparte allerede nu på foret, det ytterste de kunne.

Det ble ikke meget til gjesting i julen dette året, men folk holdt seg hjemme hver ved sitt. I julen tok kulden til – det var som hver dag syntes kaldere enn den forrige. Folk kunne neppe minnes så hard en vinter – det falt ikke mere sne heller, selv ikke inne i fjellet, men den sneen som var kommet ned ved Klemensmesse, frøs hard som sten. Solen skinte fra klar himmel nu dagene tok til å lysne. Om nettene spraket og flakket vindlysene over fjellkammene i nord, de flakket over halve himmelen – men de bragte ikke værvending, en dag innimellom kunne det skye over, det drysset litt tørr sne, og så var det klarvær og brennkulde igjen. Lågen murret og klunket dovt under isbroene.

Hver morgen tenkte Kristin at nu orket hun ikke mere, hun holdt ikke ut denne dag tilende. For hver dag følte hun var som en tvekamp mellom faren og henne. Og skulle de stå slik mot hinannen nu, da hvert levende liv av folk og fe over bygdene led under *en* prøvelse. Men når kvelden kom, så hadde hun holdt ut.

Det var ikke slik at faren var uvennlig. De talte aldri om det som lå mellom dem, men hun følte bak alt han ikke sa, at han var ubøyelig fast besluttet på å holde ut i sin vegring.

Og det sved i henne av savn etter hans vennskap. Det sved så forferdelig hardt, fordi hun visste hvor meget annet faren hadde å bære på – og hadde det vært som før, da ville han talt med henne om det. – Det var så at de var bedre berget på Jørundgård enn de fleste steder ellers, men også her følte de uåret hver dag og hver stund. Ellers hadde Lavrans om vintrene brukt å ta opp og temme ungfolene sine, men dette året hadde han om høsten solgt dem alle sør i landet. Og datteren savnet å høre hans stemme ute i tunet, og se ham tumle med de smekre, raggete toåringene i den leken han elsket så meget. Det hadde jo ikke vært blankt der på gården i bur eller låver og binger etter forrige års host, men til Jørundgård kom også mange folk og bad om hjelp, til kjøps og til gave, og ingen bad forgjeves.

Sent en kveld kom en svær gammel skinnkledd mann på ski. Lavrans talte med ham ute i tunet, og Halvdan bar mat til ham i årestuen. Ingen på gården som hadde sett ham, visste hvem han var – saktens var han en av de folkene som levde inni fjellet; kanskje hadde Lavrans støtt på ham inni der. Men faren nevnte ikke besøket, og ikke Halvdan heller.

Men en kveld kom en mann som Lavrans Bjorgulfssøn hadde hatt noe utestående med i mange år. Lavrans gikk på boden med ham. Men da han kom inn i stuen igjen, sa han:

"Alle vil de ha hjelp hos meg. Men her i gården min er dere alle imot meg. Du og, hustru," sa han heftig til Ragnfrid.

Da for moren opp mot Kristin.

"Hører du hva far din sier til meg! Ikke er jeg imot deg, Lavrans. Du vet det jo, du og, Kristin, det som hendte her sør på Roaldstad senhøstes, da han for nedover dalen i følge med den annen horsmannen, frenden hans fra Haugen – hun tok sitt eget liv, den usalige konen som han hadde lokket fra alle hennes frender."

Stiv og hard svarte Kristin:

"Jeg skjønner at dere laster ham like meget for de årene han har strevd for å komme ut av synden som for de årene han levde i den."

"Jesus Maria," ropte Ragnfrid og slo sine hender sammen. "Hvordan er du blitt! Har enn ikke dette kunnet volde at du skiftet sinn."

"Nei," sa Kristin. "Jeg har ikke skiftet sinn."

Da så Lavrans opp fra benken hvor han satt hos Ulvhild: "Det har ikke jeg heller, Kristin," sa han dempet.

Men Kristin visste i sitt hjerte, på sett og vis hadde hun skiftet, om ikke sinn så syn. Hun hadde fått bud om hvordan den var løpt av, den ulykkesferden. Det hadde gått lettere enn en kunne vente. Om det var fordi det hadde satt seg kulde i såret eller hva det nu kom av, det knivhugget som Erlend hadde fået i brystet, hadde slått seg vrangt; han kom til å ligge syk en tid i herberget på Roaldstad. Herr Bjørn hadde pleid ham de dagene. Men ved det at Erlend var såret, hadde det falt lettere å forklare det annet og bli trodd.

Da han kunne fare videre, hadde han ført den døde med seg i en kiste helt til Oslo. Der hadde han nok ved Sira Jons mellomkomst fått gravplass til henne på kirkegården til den nedbrutte Nikulauskirke, og så hadde han skriftet for biskopen i Oslo selv, og denne hadde lagt på ham å fare til det hellige blod i Schwerin. Nu var han utdragen av landet.

Hun kunne ikke valfarte til noe sted og finne avløsning. For henne var det å sitte her, bie og tenke og friste å holde ut i sin motstand mot foreldrene. Det falt et underlig vinterkaldt lys over alle minnene om hennes møter med Erlend. Hun tenkte på hans voldsomhet – i elskov i sorg – og det bares henne for at hadde hun kunnet ta opp alle ting like så brått og storme slik med dem straks, da ville de kanskje baketter synes mindre og lettere å bære. Det hendte at hun tenkte, kanhende gir Erlend meg opp. Hun syntes hun hadde visst alltid hatt en liten frykt for at ble det for vanskelig for dem, så ville han gi opp. Men hun ville ikke oppgi ham, uten han selv løste henne fra alle eder.

Så led det fremover vinteren. Og Kristin kunne ikke lenger narre seg selv, men hun måtte se at nu ventet dem alle den hardeste prøvelse, for nu hadde ikke Ulvhild lenge igjen å leve. Og midt i sin bitre sorg over søsteren så hun med gru, at sannelig var hennes egen sjel forvillet og fortæret av synd. For med det døende barnet og foreldrenes usigelige sorg for øye tenkte hun enda på dette – hvis Ulvhild dør, hvordan skal jeg da kunne utholde å se på far og ikke kaste meg ned for ham, skrifte alt og be ham tilgi meg og råde over meg –.

De var ute i fasten. Folk hugget ned av de små buskaper de hadde håpet å kunne livberge, for at ikke feet skulle selvdø. Og menneskene ble syke av å leve på fisk og ha så lite og elendig melmat til. Sira Eirik løste hele bygden fra forbudet mot melkemat. Men folk hadde neppe melkedråpen.

Ulvhild lå tilsengs. Hun lå alene i søstersengen, og noen våket over henne hver natt. Det hendte at faren og Kristin satt over henne begge. Slik en natt sa Lavrans til datteren:

"Minnes du det som broder Edvin sa om Ulvhilds skjebne. Jeg tenkte det alt dengang at kanskje han mente dette. Men da skjøv jeg det fra meg."

I disse nettene talte han stundom om et og annet fra den tid barna var små. Kristin satt hvit og fortvilt og forstod at bak ordene tigget faren henne.

En dag var Lavrans gått ut med Kolbein for å hjemsøke et bjørnehi nord i fjellskogen. Hjem kom de med en binne pa en slede, og Lavrans hadde en levende bjørnunge i koftebarmen. Det mores Ulvhild litt da han synte den frem for henne. Men Ragnfrid sa dette var dog ikke en tid til å sette på et slikt dyr, og hva ville han med den nu?

"Jeg skal fø den opp til å binde foran buret til møene mine," sa Lavrans og lo barsk.

Men de kunne ikke skaffe bjørnungen fet melk, som den måtte ha, og så drepte Lavrans den noen dager etter.

Solen fikk så megen makt at det hendte det dryppet litt av takene midt pa dagen. Meisene klemte seg fast og klatret pa tømmerveggene til solsiden, de hakket så det klang, mens de søkte etter fluer som sov i stokkefarene. Utover vollene lyste sneen hard og blank som sølv.

Endelig en kveld tok det til å trekke med skyer over månen. Om morgnen våknet de på Jørundgørd i et gov av sne som de ikke kunne se ut av til noen kant.

Den dagen skjønte de Ulvhild skulle dø.

Hele huslyden var finne, og Sira Eirik kom over. Det brente mange lys i stuen. Tidlig på kvelden sloknet Ulvhild stille og rolig i morens armer.

Ragnfrid bar det bedre enn noen hadde ventet. Foreldrene satt hos hinannen, de gråt begge to ganske stille. Alle gråt som var i stuen. Da Kristin gikk bort til faren, la han armen om hennes skulder. Han kjente hvor hun rystet og skalv, og da tok han henne inn til seg. Men hun syntes selv at han måtte kjenne det som om hun var mere bortrykket fra ham enn den lille døde i sengen.

Hun skjønte ikke hvordan hun holdt ut. Hun husket neppe selv hva hun holdt ut for, men sløv og stum av smerte holdt hun seg oppe og falt ikke tilfote.

– Så ble etpar planker brutt opp i kirkegulvet foran Sankt Tomas' alter, og det ble hugget en grav i den stenharde jord under til Ulvhild Lavransdatter.

Det snedde tett og stilt alle de dagene barnet lå på likstrå; det snedde da hun ble ført til jorden, og det ble ved å sne, nesten uten stans, en hel måned til ende.

For folket som gikk og biet på vårens forløsning, syntes det som om den aldri ville komme. Dagene ble lange og lyse, og dalen lå i en damp av brånende sne, mens solen stod på. Men kulden holdt seg i luften, og varmen fikk ingen makt. Om nettene frøs det hardt – det smalt i is, det drønnet inne fra fjellene, og ulvene tutet og reven gjødde helt nede i bygden som ved midtvinter. Folk skavet bark til kreaturene, men de styrtet i hopetall på båsen. Ingen skjønte hvor dette skulle ende.

Kristin gikk ut en slik dag, da det sipret vann i veifarene og sneen glinste som sølv utover jordene. Mot solen var snefonnene ett innhule, så skarebremmens fine isgitter brast med sakte sølvklang når hun støtte til den med foten. Men overalt, i den minste skygge, var den skarpe kulden i luften og sneen hard.

Hun gikk oppover mot kirken – hun visste ikke selv hva hun skulle der, men hun droges dit. Faren var der – det var noen bønder, gildesbrødre, som hadde et stevne i svalen, visste hun.

Oppe i bakken møtte hun bondeflokken, som kom nedover. Sira Eirik var med dem. Mennene var tilfots alle, de gikk i en mørk, lodden klynge, dukket seg og snakket ikke sammen; de hilste tvert tilbake da hun hilste idet hun gikk forbi.

Kristin tenkte det var lenge siden den tiden da hvert menneske i bygden hadde vært hennes venn. Nu visste vel alle at hun var en ond datter. Kanskje visste de mere om henne og. Nu trodde de vel også alle at det hadde vært noe sant i den gamle snakken om henne og Arne og Bentein. Kanskje var hun i det verste vanry. Hun rettet opp sitt hode og gikk videre til kirken.

Døren stod på gløtt. Det var kaldt inne i kirken, men enda strømmet det som en lunhet mot hennes sinn fra det dunkle og brune rom med de høyt oppstrebende søylestammer, som løftet mørket opp mot takets sprengverk. Det var ikke tent på altrene, men litt sol falt inn av dørgløtten og glimtet svakt på billeder og kar.

Fremme ved Tomasalteret så hun faren lå på kne med hodet ned mot de foldede hender som krystet luen inn til barmen.

Sky og bedrøvet listet Kristin ut og stod i svalen. Rammet inn av buen mellom de to småsøyler hun stod og holdt om, så hun Jørundgård ligge, og bak hjemmet den blekgrå dis over dalen. I solen blikket elven hvit av vann og is utigjennom bygden. Men orekrattet langs dens løp var gulbrunt av blomme, granskogen var vårlig grønn allikevel heroppe ved kirken, og det pjutret og kvitret og fløytet av småfugl i lunden like ved. Åja, det hadde vært slik fuglesang hver kveld etter solnedgang.

Og hun kjente den lengselen hun hadde trodd måtte være pint ut av henne nu, lengselen i blodet og i kroppen, den rørte seg nu, spedt og svakt som den var ved å våkne av vinterdvale.

Lavrans Bjørgulfssøn kom ut og låste kirkedøren bak seg. Han gikk bort og stod nær datteren, så utover ved den neste hue. Hun så hvor denne vinteren hadde herjet faren. Hun skjønte ikke selv at hun kunne røre ved dette nu, men det for ut av henne allikevel.

"Er det sant som mor sa forleden dag, at du har sagt til henne – hadde det vært Arne Gyrdssøn, da ville du føyet meg?"

"Ja," sa Lavrans og så ikke på henne.

"Det sa du ikke mens Arne levde," svarte Kristin.

"Det kom aldri på tale. Jeg skjønte nok at gutten holdt av deg – men han sa intet og han var ung – og jeg merket aldri at du tenkte slik på ham. Du kunne vel ikke vente at jeg skulle by frem datteren min til en mann som intet eide." Han smilte flyktig. "Men jeg holdt av gutten," sa han sakte. "Og hadde jeg sett deg pines ut av kjærlighet til ham – "

De ble stående og se ut. Kristin følte at faren så på henne – hun strevde for å være rolig i ansiktet, men hun kjente hvor hvit hun ble. Da gikk faren bort til henne, la begge armene om henne og knuget henne i favn. Han bøyde hennes hode bakover, så ned i datterens ansikt, og gjemte det igjen ved sin skulder. Jesus Kristus, Kristin liten, er du da så ulykkelig –"

"Jeg tror jeg dør av det, far," sa hun inn til ham.

Hun brast i gråt. Men hun gråt fordi hun hadde følt i hans kjærtegn og sett i hans øyne, at nu var han så pint ut, så han orket ikke holde fast ved sin motstand longer. Hun hadde vunnet på ham.

Utpå natten våknet hun ved at faren rørte ved hennes skulder i mørket:

"Stå opp," sa han sakte, "hører du – ?"

Da hørte hun det sang om husnovene – den dype, fulle tone av vætemettet sønnenvind. Det strirant av takct, det vrisket av rugn som falt i bløt, tinende sne.

Kristin kastet kjolen på seg og gikk etter faren ut ytterdøren. Sammen stod de og så ut i den lyse mainatt – varm vind og regn slo imot dem – himmelen var et velte av flokete, drivende regnskyer, det bruste fra skogen, det fløytet mellom husene – og oppe fra fjellet hørte de dumpe drønn av sneen som skred utover.

Kristin søkte farens hånd og holdt den. Han hadde kalt på henne og villet vise henne dette. Slik hadde det vært mellom dem før, at han ville ha gjort det. Og nu var det slik igjen.

Da de gikk inn igjen for å legge seg, sa Lavrans:

"Den fremmede svennen som var her i uken, bar brev til meg fra herr Munan Bårdsson. Han akter seg oppover hit isommer for å se til mor sin, og da bad han om han måtte finne meg og få meg i tale."

"Hva vil I svare ham, far min," hvisket hun.

"Det kan jeg ikke si deg nu," svarte Lavrans. "Men jeg skal tale med ham, og så får jeg råde slik som jeg synes jeg kan svare for Gud, datter min."

Kristin krøp inn igjen til Ramborg, og Lavrans gikk og la seg ned ved siden av den sovende hustru. Han lå og tenkte på at hvis flommen kom stor og overbratt, da lå få gårder i bygden så utsatt som Jørundgård. Det skulle være en spådom om det, at engang ville elven ta den.

Kristin Lavransdatter[14]

Volume 1, *The Wreath*, Part 3, Chapter 4

Translated by Tiina Nunnally

The frost hung on. In every stable of the village the starving animals lowed and complained, suffering from the cold. But the people were already rationing the fodder as best they could.

There was not much visiting done during the Christmas season that year; everyone was staying at home.

At Christmas the cold grew worse; each day felt colder than the one before. People could hardly remember such a harsh winter. And while no more snow fell, even up in the mountains, the snow that had fallen on Saint Clement's Day froze as hard as stone. The sun shone in a clear sky, now that the days were growing lighter. At night the northern lights flickered and sputtered above the mountain ridges to the north; they flickered over half the sky, but they didn't bring a change in the weather. Once in a while it would cloud over, sprinkling a little dry snow, but then the clear skies and biting cold would return. The Laag murmured and gurgled lazily beneath the bridges of ice.

Each morning Kristin would think that now she could stand it no longer; that she wouldn't be able to make it through the day, because each day felt like a duel between her father and herself. And was it right for them to be so at odds with each other right now, when every living thing, every person and beast in the valleys, was enduring a common trial? But when evening came she had made it through after all.

It was not that her father was unfriendly. They never spoke of what lay between them, but Kristin could feel that in everything he left unsaid he was steadfastly determined to stand by his refusal.

And she burned with longing for his affection. Her anguish was even greater because she knew how much else her father had to bear; and if things had been as they were before, he would have talked to her about his concerns. It's true that at Jorundgaard they were better prepared than most other places, but even here they felt the effects of the bad year, every day and every hour. In the winter Lavrans usually spent time breaking and training his foals, but this year, during the autumn, he had sold all of them in the south. His daughter missed hearing his voice out in the courtyard and watching him tussle with the lanky, shaggy two-year-old horses in the game that he loved so much. The storerooms, barns, and bins on the farm had not been emptied after the harvest of the previous year, but many people came to Jorundgaard asking for help, either as a purchase or a gift, and no one asked in vain.

Late one evening a very old man, dressed in furs, arrived on skis. Lavrans spoke to him out in the courtyard, and Halvdan took food to him in the hearth room. No one on the farm who had seen him knew who he was, but it was assumed that he was one of the people who lived in the mountains; perhaps Lavrans had run into him out there. But Kristin's father didn't speak of the visit, nor did Halvdan.

Then one evening a man arrived with whom Lavrans Bjorgulfson had had a score to settle for many years. Lavrans went out to the storeroom with him. But when he returned to the house, he said, "Everyone wants me to help them. And yet here on my farm you're all against me. Even you, wife," he said angrily to Ragnfrid.

Then Ragnfrid lashed out at Kristin.

"Do you hear what your father is saying to me? I'm not against you, Lavrans. You know full well, Kristin, what happened south of here at Roaldstad late in the fall, when he traveled through the valley in the company of that other whoremonger, his kinsman from Haugen—she took her own life, that unfortunate woman he had enticed away from all her kinsmen."

Her face rigid, Kristin replied harshly, "I see that you blame him as much for the years when he was striving to get out of sin as for those when he was living in it."

"Jesus Maria," cried Ragnfrid, clasping her hands together. "Look what's become of you! Won't even this make you change your mind?"

"No," said Kristin. "I haven't changed my mind."

Then Lavrans looked up from the bench where he was sitting with Ulvhild.

"Nor have I, Kristin," he said quietly.

But Kristin knew in her heart that in some way she had changed – if not her decision, then her outlook. She had received word of the progress of that ill-fated journey. It had gone easier than anyone could have expected. Whether it was because the cold had settled in his wound or for some other reason, the knife injury which Erlend had received in his chest had become infected. He lay ill at the hostel in Roaldstad for a long time, and Herr Bjorn tended to him during those days. But because Erlend had been wounded, it was easier to explain everything else and to make others believe them.

When he was able to continue, he transported the dead woman in a coffin all the way to Oslo. There, with Sira Jon's intervention, he found a gravesite for her in the cemetery of Nikolaus Church, which lay in ruins. Then he had confessed to the Bishop of Oslo himself, who had enjoined him to travel to the Shrine of the Holy Blood in Schwerin. So now he had left the country.

There was no place to which *she* could make a pilgrimage to seek redemption. Her lot was to stay here, to wait and worry and try to endure her opposition to her parents. A strange, cold winter light fell over all her memories of her meetings with Erlend. She thought about his ardor—in love and in sorrow—and it occurred to her that if she had been able to seize on all things with equal abruptness and plunge ahead at once, then afterward they might seem of less consequence and easier to bear. Sometimes she thought that Erlend might give her up. She had always had a slight fear that it could become too difficult for them, and he would lose heart. But she would not give him up— not unless he released her from all promises.

And so the winter wore on. And Kristin could no longer fool herself; she had to admit that now the most difficult trial awaited all of them, for Ulvhild did not have long to live. And in the midst of her bitter sorrow over her sister, Kristin realized with horror that her own soul had been led astray and was corrupted by sin.

For as she witnessed the dying child and her parents' unspeakable grief, she thought of only one thing: if Ulvhild dies, how will I be able to endure facing my father without throwing myself down before him, to confess everything and to beg him to forgive me and to do with me what he will.

The Lenten fast was upon them. People were slaughtering the small animals they had hoped to save before the livestock perished on its own. And people were falling ill from living on fish and the scant and wretched portions of grain. Sira Eirik released the entire village from the ban against consuming milk. But no one had even a drop of milk.

Ulvhild was confined to bed. She slept alone in the sisters' bed, and someone watched over her every night. Sometimes Kristin and her father would both sit with her. On one such night Lavrans said to his daughter, "Do you remember what Brother Edvin said about Ulvhild's fate? I thought at the time that maybe this was what he meant. But I put it out of my mind."

During those nights he would occasionally talk about one thing or another from the time when the children were small. Kristin would sit there, pale and miserable, understanding that behind his words, her father was pleading with her.

One day Lavrans had gone out with Kolbein to seek out a bear's lair in the mountain forest to the north. They returned home with a female bear on a sled, and Lavrans was carrying a little bear cub, still alive, inside his tunic. Ulvhild smiled a little when he showed it to her. But Ragnfrid said that this was no time to take in that kind of animal, and what was he going to do with it now?

"I'm going to fatten it up and then tie it to the bedchamber of my maidens," said Lavrans, laughing harshly.

But they couldn't find the kind of rich milk that the bear cub needed, and so several days later Lavrans killed it.

The sun had grown so strong that occasionally, in the middle of the day, the eaves would begin to drip. The titmice clung to the timbered walls and hopped around on the sunny side; the pecking of their beaks resounded as they looked for flies asleep in the gaps between the wood. Out across the meadows the snow gleamed, hard and shiny like silver.

Finally one evening clouds began to gather in front of the moon. In the morning they woke up at Jorundgaard to a whirl of snow that blocked their view in all directions.

On that day it became clear that Ulvhild was going to die.

The entire household had gathered inside, and Sira Eirik had come. Many candles were burning in the room. Early that evening, Ulvhild passed on, calmly and peacefully, in her mother's arms.

Ragnfrid bore it better than anyone could have expected. The parents sat together, both of them weeping softly. Everyone in the room was crying. When Kristin went over to her father, he put his arm around her shoulders. He noticed how she was trembling and shaking, and then he pulled her close. But it seemed to her that he must have felt as if she had been snatched farther away from him than her dead little sister in the bed.

She didn't know how she had managed to endure. She hardly remembered why she was enduring, but, lethargic and mute with pain, she managed to stay on her feet and did not collapse.

Then a couple of planks were pulled up in the floor in front of the altar of Saint Thomas, and a grave was dug in the rock-hard earth underneath for Ulvhild Lavransdatter.

It snowed heavily and silently for all those days the child lay on the straw bier; it was snowing as she was laid in the earth; and it continued to snow, almost without stop, for an entire month.

For those who were waiting for the redemption of spring, it seemed as if it would never come. The days grew long and bright, and the valley lay in a haze of thawing snow while the sun shone. But frost was still in the air, and the heat had no power. At night it froze hard; great cracking sounds came from the ice, a rumbling issued from the mountains, and the wolves howled and the foxes yipped all the way down in the village, as if it were midwinter. People scraped off bark for the livestock, but they were perishing by the dozens in their stalls. No one knew when it would end.

Kristin went out on such a day, when the water was trickling in the furrows of the road and the snow glistened like silver across the fields. Facing the sun, the snowdrifts had become hollowed out so that the delicate ice lattice of the crusted snow broke with the gentle ring of silver when she pressed her foot against it. But wherever there was the slightest shadow, the air was sharp with frost and the snow was hard.

She walked up toward the church. She didn't know why she was going there, but she felt drawn to it. Her father was there. Several farmers – guild brothers – were holding a meeting in the gallery, that much she knew.

Up on the hill she met the group of farmers as they were leaving. Sira Eirik was with them. The men were all on foot, walking in a dark, fur-wrapped cluster, nodding and talking to each other; they returned her greeting in a surly manner as she passed.

Kristin thought to herself that it had been a long time since everyone in the village had been her friend. Everyone no doubt knew that she was a bad daughter. Perhaps they knew even more about her. Now they probably all thought that there must have been some truth to the old gossip about her and Arne and Bentein. Perhaps she was in terrible disrepute. She lifted her chin and walked on toward the church.

The door stood ajar. It was cold inside the church, and yet a certain warmth streamed toward her from this dim brown room, with the tall columns soaring upward, lifting the darkness up toward the crossbeams of the roof. There were no lit candles on the altars, but a little sunshine came in through the open door, casting a faint light on the paintings and vessels.

Up near the Saint Thomas altar she saw her father on his knees with his head resting on his folded hands, which were clutching his cap against his chest.

Shy and dispirited, Kristin tiptoed out and stood on the gallery. Framed by the arch of two small pillars, which she held on to, she saw Jorundgaard lying below, and beyond her home the pale blue haze over the valley. In the sun the river glinted white with water and ice all through the village. But the alder thicket along its bank was golden brown with blossoms, the spruce forest was spring-green even up by the church, and tiny birds chittered and chirped and trilled in the grove nearby. Oh yes, she had heard birdsong like that every evening after the sun set.

And now she felt the longing that she thought had been wrung out of her, the longing in her body and in her blood; it began to stir now, feeble and faint, as if it were waking up from a winter's hibernation.

Lavrans Bjorgulfson came outside and closed the church door behind him. He went over and stood .near his daughter, looking out from the next arch. She noticed how the winter had ravaged her father. She didn't think that she could bring this up now, but it tumbled out of her all the same.

"Is it true what Mother said the other day, that you told her ... if it had been Arne Gyrdson, then you would have relented?"

"Yes," said Lavrans without looking at her.

"You never said that while Arne was alive," replied Kristin.

"It was never discussed. I could see that the boy was fond of you, but he said nothing ... and he was young ... and I never noticed that you thought of him in that way. You couldn't expect me to *offer* my daughter to a man who owned no property." He smiled fleetingly. "But I was fond of the boy," he said softly. "And if I had seen that you were pining with love for him ..."

They remained standing there, staring straight ahead. Kristin sensed her father looking at her. She struggled to keep her expression calm, but she could feel how pale she was.

Then her father came over to her, put both arms around her, and hugged her tight. He tilted her head back, looked into his daughter's face, and then hid it against his shoulder.

"Jesus Christus, little Kristin, are you so unhappy?"

"I think I'm going to die from it, Father," she said against his chest.

She burst into tears. But she was crying because she had felt in his caress and seen in his eyes that now he was so worn out with anguish that he could no longer hold on to his opposition. She had won.

In the middle of the night she woke up when her father touched her shoulder in the dark.

"Get up," he said quietly. "Do you hear it?"

Then she heard the singing at the corners of the house – the deep, full tone of the moisture-laden south wind. Water was streaming off the roof, and the rain whispered as it fell on soft, melting snow.

Kristin threw on a dress and followed her father to the outer door. Together they stood and looked out into the bright May night. Warm wind and rain swept toward them. The sky was a heap of tangled, surging rain clouds; there was a seething from the woods, a whistling between the buildings. And up on the mountains they heard the hollow rumble of snow sliding down.

Kristin reached for her father's hand and held it. He had called her and wanted to show her this. It was the kind of thing he would have done in the past, before things changed between them. And now he was doing it again.

When they went back inside to lie down, Lavrans said, "The stranger who was here this week carried a letter to me from Sir Munan Baardson. He intends to come here this summer to visit his mother, and he asked whether he might seek me out and speak with me."

"How will you answer him, my father?" she whispered.

"I can't tell you that now," replied Lavrans. "But I will speak to him, and then I must act in such a way that I can answer for myself before God, my daughter."

Kristin crawled into bed beside Ramborg, and Lavrans went over and lay down next to his sleeping wife. He lay there, thinking that if the flood waters rose high and suddenly, then few farms in the village would be as vulnerable as Jorundgaard. There was supposed to be a prophecy about it – that one day the river would take the farm.

Primary Works

Fru Marta Oulie, 1907.

Den lykkelig alder, 1908.

Fortællingen om Viga-Ljot og Vigdis, 1909; Eng. tr. *Gunnar's Daughter*, 1936.

Ungdom. Digte, 1910.

Jenny, 1911; Eng. tr. 1921, 2001.

Fattige skjæbner, 1912.

Vaaren, 1914.

Fortællingen om Kong Artur og ridderne av det runde bord, 1915.

Splinten av troldspeilet, 1917; Eng. tr. (partial) *Images in a Mirror*, 1938.

De kloge jomfruer, 1918.

Et kvindesynspunkt, 1919.

Kransen (Kristin Lavransdatter 1), 1920; Eng. tr. *The Bridal Wreath*, 1923; *The Wreath*, 1997.

Husfrue (*Kristin Lavransdatter* 2), 1921; Eng. tr. *The Mistress of Husaby*, 1925; *The Wife*, 1999.

Korset (*Kristin Lavransdatter* 3), 1922; Eng. tr. *The Cross*, 1927; The Cross, 2000.

Kristin Lavransdatter. Combined Engl. ed. 1929, 2005.

Tre sagaer om islændinger, 1923.

Olav Audunssøn i Hestviken (*Olav Audunssøn* 1), 1925; Eng. tr. *The Axe* (1928), *The Snake Pit* (1929). Combined ed. *The Master of Hestviken*, 1932.

Olav Audunssøn og hans børn (*Olav Audunssøn* 2), 1927; Eng. tr. *In the Wilderness* (1929), *The Son Avenger* (1930). Combined ed. *The Master of Hestviken*, 1932.

Etapper, 1929.

Katholsk propaganda, 1927; Eng. tr. *Catholic Propaganda*, 1993.

Gymnadenia, 1929; Eng. tr. *The Wild Orchid*, 1931.

Den brændende busk, 1930; Eng. tr. *The Burning Bush*, 1932.

Begegnungen und Trennungen. Essays über Christentum und Germanentum, 1931.

Ida Ellsabeth, 1932; Eng. tr., 1933.

Christmas and Twelfth Night, 1932.

Etapper. Ny række, 1933; Eng. tr. *Stages on the Road*, 1934.

Elleve Aar, 1934; Eng. tr. *The Longest Years*, 1935.

Saga of Saints, 1934; Norw. ed. *Norske helgener*, 1937.

Fortschritt, rasse, religion, 1935.

Den trofaste hustru, 1936; Eng. tr. *The Faithful Wife*, 1937.

Selvportretter og landskapsbilleder, 1938; Eng. tr. *Men, Women, and Places*, 1939.

Madame Dorthea, 1939; Eng. tr. 1940.

Return to the Future, 1942; Norw. ed. *Tilbake til fremtiden*, 1945.

Happy Times in Norway, 1942; Norw. ed. *Lykkelige dager*, 1947.

Sigurd and his Brave Companions, 1943; Norw. tr. *Sigurd og hans tapre venner*, 1955.

True and Untrue and Other Norse Tales, 1945.

Catarina av Siena, 1951; Eng. tr. *Catherine of Siena*, 1954.

Artikler og taler fra krigstiden, 1952.

Four Stories, 1959.

Kjære Dea, 1979.

Tolv år, 1998.

Selected Bibliography

Aasen, Elisabeth. *Sigrid Undset*. Oslo: Aschehoug, 1982.

Amadou, Anne-Lisa. *Å gi kjærligheten et språk. Syv studier i Sigrid Undsets forfatterskap*. Oslo: Aschehoug, 1994.

Anderson, Gidske. *Sigrid Undset, et liv*. Oslo: Gyldendal, n.d.

Anker, Nini Roll. *Min venn Sigrid Undset*. Oslo: Aschehoug, 1946, 1982.

Bliksrud, Liv. *Natur og normer hos Sigrid Undset*. Oslo: Aschehoug, 1988.

–. *Sigrid Undset*. Oslo: Gyldendal, 1997.

Deschamps, Nicole. *Sigrid Undset, ou la morale de la passion*. Montreal: University of Montreal Press, 1966.

Engelstad, Carl Fredrik. *Mennesker og makter. Sigrid Undsets middelalderromaner*. Oslo: Aschehoug, 1940.

Fontander, Björn. *Undset, Hamsun, og krigen*. Stockholm: Aventura, 1991.

Heltoft, Bente. *Livssyn og digtning. Strukturgrundlaget i Sigrid Undsets romaner*. Oslo: Aschehoug, 1985.

Hudson, Deal W. *Sigrid Undset on Saints and Sinners, New Translations and Studies.* San Francisco: Ignatius Press, 1993

Johansen, Kristin. *Hvis kvinner vil være kvinner: Sigrid Undset, hennes samtid og kvinnespørsmålet.* Oslo: Aschehoug, 1998.

Krane, Borghild. *Sigrid Undset, Liv og meninger.* Oslo: Gyldendal, 1970.

Kvinnesyn-tvisyn. En antologi om Sigrid Undset. Oslo: Novus, 1985.

Lytle, Andrew. *Kristin, A Reading.* Columbia, University of Missouri Press, 1992.

Mørkhagen, Sverre. *Kristins verden: om norsk middelalder på Kristin Lavransdatters tid.* Oslo: Cappelen, 1995.

Naess, Harald, ed. *The History of Norwegian Literature.* Lincoln: University of Nebraska Press, 1993.

Oftestad, Bernt T. *Sigrid Undset, modernitet og katolisisme.* Oslo: Universitetsforlaget, 2003.

Ørjasæter, Tordis. *Menneskenes hjerter. Sigrid Undset, en livshistorie.* Oslo: Aschehoug, 1993.

Packness, Ida. *Sigrid Undset bibliografi.* Oslo: Universitetsforlaget, 1963.

Rieber-Mohn, Hallvard. *Sten på sten: fem blikk på Sigrid Undset.* Oslo: Aschehoug, 1982.

Sigrid Undset i dag. Foreword by Pål Espolin Johnson. Oslo: Aschehoug, 1982.

Skille, Nan Bentzen. *Innenfor gjerdet: Hos Sigrid Undset på Bjekebæk.* Oslo: Aschehoug, 2003.

Skouen, Arne. *Sigrid Undset skriver hjem: En vandring gjennom emigranårene i Amerika.* Oslo: Aschhoug, 1982.

Solberg, Olav. *Tekst møter tekst: Kristin Lavransdatter og mellomalderen.* Oslo: Aschehoug, 1997.

Steen, Ellisiv. *Kristin Lavransdatter, en estetisk studie.* Oslo: Aschehoug, 1969.

Thorn, Finn. *Sigrid Undset: Kristentro og kirkesyn.* Oslo: Aschehoug, 1975.

Winsnes, A. H. *Sigrid Undset: A Study in Christian Realism.* G. P. Foote, tr. London: Sheed & Ward, 1953.

Astrid Lindgren:
Tales of Rebellion and Compassion

EVA-MARIA METCALF (UNIVERSITY OF MISSISSIPPI)

With the exception of Hans Christian Andersen, no Scandinavian author writing for children has gained such popularity and fame around the world as has Astrid Lindgren (1907-2002). Her books have appeared in more than 80 countries and have so far been translated into more than 70 languages. Her most famous character, Pippi Longstocking, has joined the group of famous fictional children's literature characters that have taken on a life of her own, such as Alice in Wonderland, Pinocchio, Peter Pan, and Heidi.

In Sweden, Lindgren is still revered not only for her entertaining, engaging, and skillful storytelling in a variety of genres and media but just as much for her personal integrity, her great wit, and her equally great heart. Her deep compassion and unswerving commitment for the powerless, those in need, the suffering, and the unjustly treated – animals, the poor, and above all children – are a steady undercurrent in all of her works. Her passionate and lasting love of rural Sweden, the Swedish countryside, and especially Småland, where she grew up, has always resonated with Swedish readers. Her lively and detailed depiction of Swedish life at the beginning of the 20th century congeals into a regressive utopia to which not only Swedes respond. Her narrative perspective, reflecting the emotional and experiential horizon of children, further enhances Lindgren's universal appeal.

Especially in her fantastic novels, Lindgren's fictional landscapes transcend the specificity of time and place, assuming the quality of fairy tale-like universal fictional spaces of play and adventure where child characters play with abandon, and young heroes and heroines prove themselves and eventually succeed. Lindgren's striking ability to remember vividly and in great detail what it means to be a child and what her preferences and desires were at various ages gives her prose the freshness and intensity of a child discovering the world. When she wrote, Lindgren said repeatedly, she wrote for the child within, a child that had never lost touch with the smells, sights, sounds and feelings of childhood. As is apparent from letters

Lindgren received from her readers, her fictional landscape is a place that comes alive in their minds and for which they long. "Please tell me the way to get to Noisy Village. I would like to move there," is typical of the requests Lindgren received from her young readers.

Lindgren was born Astrid Anna Emilia Ericsson on November 14, 1907, the second of four children on Näs farm near Vimmerby in the province of Småland in southern Sweden. According to all accounts, her childhood was a happy one, filled with work and play on and around a farm much like the one she depicts in the fictionally enhanced stories about the Noisy Village children, in which children's play becomes the all-consuming activity. The original title *Alla vi barn i Bullerbyn* (1947; All of us Children in Noisy Village) and its sequels *Mera om oss barn i Bullerbyn* (1949; More about us Children in Noisy Village) and *Bara roligt i Bullerbyn* (1952; Having Fun in Noisy Village) were radically edited and combined into one volume in the American translation *The Children of Noisy Village* (1958).

Astrid Lindgren grew up in a culture replete with storytelling. Hearing, reading and later telling stories became Lindgren's great passion from the time she heard her first fairy tales through grade school, where her talent became obvious. In school, much to her dismay, she was called Vimmerby's Selma Lagerlöf, a reference to Sweden's famous Nobel Prize laureate and a designation that intimidated her at the time. Writing was to become her career, however. At the age of sixteen Astrid Ericsson became an apprentice journalist, writing for the local newspaper. This career was cut short less than two years later when Lindgren was forced to leave Vimmerby because of an unexpected pregnancy. A morally conservative climate in her provincial hometown made it impossible for her to stay. She left for Stockholm where she trained for and later worked as a secretary. The shorthand she learned as part of her training stayed with her throughout her professional life. All her manuscripts are written in shorthand.

In 1931, Astrid Ericsson married Sture Lindgren, and became a housewife taking care of her son Lars and her daughter Karin. During those years she wrote travelogues and published fairly conventional fairy tales in family magazines and Christmas almanacs. A letter Lindgren wrote to the editor of the newspaper *Dagens Nyheter* on December 7, 1939, using the name of her son, Lars, marked a change in her authorship. Written entirely from the child's point of view, the fictional letter to the editor promoted and defended the radical ideas carried forth by the new child-oriented pedagogy of the day, "(...) No, it's not easy being a child! What does it mean to be a child? It means that you have to go to bed, get up, get dressed, eat food, brush your teeth, and blow your nose when it suits the grown-ups, not when it suits you (...)."[1]

---

[1]   http://www.astridlindgren.se/eng/omastrid/dn.htm.

Reading this letter, it becomes a bit easier to understand how a fictional super-child character began to emerge in the Lindgren family lore in the early 1940s and soon reigned supreme. One day Lindgren's daughter Karin had asked her mother to tell her a story about Pippi Longstocking, a name she had invented on the spot. Her mother obliged and told her children, and later their friends, funny and exciting stories about the supergirl Pippi Longstocking, who never had to do as she was told. Pippi, who lived all alone in a big dilapidated house with her horse and her monkcy, could go to bed and get up whenever she pleased and even sleep upside down in her bed; she could eat where, when, and what she wanted and even talk back to grown-ups unpunished.

These stories eventually ended up in a manuscript that Lindgren submitted to Bonniers, the famous Stockholm publishing house. It was rejected Meanwhile Lindgren had entered a girl's book contest conducted by another publisher in Stockholm, Rabén & Sjögren. In 1944, Lindgren won second prize with *Britt-Mari lättar sitt hjärta* (Britt Mari Unburdens her Heart), a fairly conventional girl's book and teenage romance that launched her career as a writer. From then on, Rabén & Sjögren published all of her books and, from 1947 until her retirement in 1970, she worked for Rabén & Sjögren as an editor of children's literature.

While *Britt-Mari Unburdens her Heart* was a moderate success at the time, it was soon overshadowed by Lindgren's second book. Lindgren took the world of Swedish children's literature by storm in 1945 when a revised version of her second manuscript was published. *Pippi Longstocking* had won first prize in yet another Rabén & Sjögren competition. The hilariously funny, playfully imaginative, and quite provocative character of Pippi Longstocking took the readers by storm. Among critics, however, it caused quite a stir. Opinions differed as widely as might be expected over a watershed book. Parent organizations and educators were especially quick to condemn it, but child readers were enthralled with the wild redhead who responded to their dreams of omnipotence and their desire for power and independence. Reprinted and translated numerous times, and repeatedly adapted into plays and movies, *Pippi Longstocking* became a source of inspiration for feminist and anti-authoritarian children's literature in many countries around the world.

A long list of stories and tales followed through the 1970s up to Lindgren's last major work, the novel *Ronja rövardotter* (1981; Eng. tr. *Ronia, the Robber's Daughter*, 1983). Lindgren's productivity was especially astounding in the 1940s and 1950s. Between 1944 and 1950, she wrote *Pippi Longstocking* and its two sequels, two books about the Noisy Village children, three girl's books, a detective story, two collections of fairy tales, a collection of songs, four plays, and two picture books. The above list of publications also shows Lindgren's great versatility and her

willingness to experiment with a wide variety of genres. Whichever genre
Lindgren appropriated, however, she expanded and made her own, blending
literary elements and elements taken from oral story-telling tradition, including anecdotes, legends, sagas, and fairy tales.

Although Lindgren's most important contributions are to be found in her
children's books, she reached out to a variety of media almost from the
beginning of her career. She participated in quiz shows and read her own
stories on the radio, she wrote the scripts for the many filmed and televised
versions of her stories, and she even wrote scripts directly for film and
television. After the release of the film *Luffaren och Rasmus* (1955; The
Vagabond and Rasmus), Lindgren turned her script into the book *Rasmus
på luffen* (1956; Rasmus on the Road) published as *Rasmus and the Vagabond* in the USA in 1960. This merger of orphan and road story is, like
many of Lindgren's later stories, a story about friendship, love, and wish
fulfillment. After a sequence of adventures on the road with Paradise-
Oscar, Rasmus finally finds the home that he has longed for so long with
the very person he has grown to love during these travels. A subsistence
farmer with a hankering for the life of a vagabond, Paradise-Oscar provides
Rasmus with the ideal mix of freedom and security that Lindgren feels is
essential for a happy childhood.

Lindgren wrote many realistic and fantastic stories that touch on the
plight of lonely and neglected children, and that often nudge the edge of
sentimentality, while always being counterbalanced by humor. Above all,
Lindgren's fantastic tales could all be interpreted as tales of consolation and
escape that show a keen understanding of the psychology of children. In
Lillebror och Karlsson på taket (1955; Little Brother and Karlsson-on-the-
Roof) and its sequels *Karlsson på taket flyger igen* (1962; Karlsson-on-the-
Roof Flies again) and *Karlsson på taket smyger igen* (1968; Karlsson-on-
the-Roof Sneaks around again), translated and edited collectively in the
USA as *Karlsson-on-the-Roof* (1971), Karlsson, the hero, is a fantasy
playmate just like Pippi Longstocking, but he lacks her super-human qualities. This chubby, greedy, bragging, sulky, self-pitying and self-absorbed
yet charming and seductive little fellow, who lives in a shed on top of
Eric's apartment building, represents not only the ideal qualities of a child,
as does Pippi, but provides a much more balanced picture of childhood and
infantile desires.

Karlsson, whose only claim to fame rests on his ability to fly thanks to a
propeller strapped to his back, enters Eric's life through his window. The
youngest of three children in a perfectly ordinary upper middle-class
Stockholm family, Eric feels the need to resort to his fantasy playmate or
compensatory alter-ego at times when he feels left out, pushed aside, or
belittled. Karlsson, who is "the world's best" at everything, lets him act out
and forget his disappointments, and provides him with suitable excuses.

The two tease Eric's siblings and housekeeper, dress up as ghosts, and chase dim-witted robbers. Because of his ability to fly, Karlsson-on-the-Roof invites comparison with Peter Pan, another famous flying fictional character in children's literature. More profane than his predecessor, this human bumble bee or mini-helicopter is at most a distant relative of James Matthew Barrie's Peter Pan.

Karlsson did, however, have a predecessor in Lindgren's own writing who resembled Peter Pan more closely. This was Mr. Liljonkvast, the main character in Lindgren's fairy tale, "I Skymmningslandet" (In the Land of Twilight) from her collection *Nils Karlsson Pyssling* (1949; Little Nils Karlsson). Mr. Liljonkvast takes the paralyzed and seriously ill Göran into "The Land that is not," as he carries him off into the dusk that has fallen over Stockholm. Mr. Liljonkvast is an ambiguous character, befitting his name, which begins with "lily" and ends with "broomstick," the witch's favorite means of transportation. He is both upbeat and melancholy, and altogether bewitching. His lighter side reemerges as Karlsson-on-the-Roof, and his threatening and melancholy side, signifying existential loneliness and loss, as well as despair in the face of death, is echoed in *Mio, min Mio* (1954; Eng. tr. *Mio My Son*, 1956) and *Bröderna Lejonhjärta* (1973; Eng. tr. *The Brothers Lionheart*, 1975) two of the three adventure novels that crown Lindgren's authorship. Their heroes' excursions into the realm of fantasy are not a matter of whim or desire for entertainment, as is the case with Thommy and Annika in *Pippi Longstocking* and with Eric in *Karlsson-on-the-Roof*. Rather, they are necessary as ways to cope with loneliness, lovelessness, and impending death. These fictional children's heroic struggles in life are sublimated in the heroic tales about Mio and the Brothers Lionheart, which are drawn in stark images and powerful language.

Mio, My Son is written in highly poetic archaic prose, giving the novel mythic qualities befitting the novel's epic structure. An unloved and neglected foster-child, Karl Anders Nilsson is magically transported as Mio to Farawayland by a ghost who lives in a common beer bottle. There he is reunited with his real father, "Father, the King," and experiences warmth, love, beauty and friendship. But in true fairy tale and epic tradition the hero's valor and resolve must be tested. With the help of his magic sword, Mio fulfills his task by defeating evil incarnate in the form of Sir Kato from Outerland, who has a heart of stone. Although Karl Anders has overcome his own demons, the ending of the novel offers no other solution for him but to escape into the world of the imaginary and to remain in Farawayland as Mio.

Storytelling as therapy in the face of adversity is one of the basic themes of Lindgren's second adventure novel, *The Brothers Lionheart*. The sickly and dying Karl Lion is confined to his kitchen sofa-bed. He grieves the loss of his beloved brother Jonathan, who died while saving Karl when their apartment was engulfed in flames. Karl's fantasies carry him off to Nangi-yala, a place already familiar to him from Jonathan's stories. There the two brothers unite and eventually free Wild Rose Valley, which is ruled by the evil Lord Tengil. Like Sir Kato in *Mio, My Son*, Lord Tengil represents a threat to everything that is good, human, and alive. The battle with Lord Tengil and the elemental creature of evil, the dragon Katla, transposes Karl's battle with loneliness and death into the narrative imagery of the adventure tale. However, the Brothers Lionheart cannot remain victorious in their battle against death. Their plight matches that of Karl Anders Nils-son; the brothers have to seek refuge in yet another fantasy land, Nangilima, which they reach by jumping into a horrible abyss.

The double suicide that concludes this novel became quite controversial when the novel appeared in Sweden in 1973. What critics overlooked at that time are the novel's life-affirming qualities that are evident in its prominent themes of non-violence and love. Jonathan's adage and ethical guideline for Karl (and for readers) is quite simply to care about humanity and to muster the courage to fight for your convictions.

The jury for the German Bookseller's Peace Award recognized Lindgren's literary efforts on behalf of peaceful coexistence and a dignified way of life for all men and creatures on earth, in *The Brothers Lionheart* specifically and in her work in general, by awarding her the prestigious Peace Prize in 1978. "Never Violence" was the title of Lindgren's accept-ance speech in which she eloquently defended her pacifist ideas and her conviction that the seeds of violence are sown in childhood. Her arguments were made most effectively through a powerful little tale that illustrated the violence inflicted on children through corporal punishment.

In 1976 and again in 1985, Lindgren was able to show the power that can reside in tales and anecdotes told by a famous and respected writer. On each of these occasions, her open letters to Stockholm newspapers contrib-uted to a change in politics. In the first instance, her tale "Pomperipossa in Monismania," in which she revealed flaws in the Swedish tax codes and how power can corrupt, is said to have helped topple the Social Democrats in the subsequent election. The next time Lindgren spoke out publicly was in the spring of 1985, when she protested a widespread abuse of domestic animals in large animal farms in Sweden and other industrialized countries. At the age of 78, she wrote another open letter containing yet another little tale, illustrating that even cows are living creatures with feelings. In June 1988, "Lex Lindgren," a tougher Animal Protection Act, was enacted into law by the Swedish parliament.

Asked by a journalist once about her aspirations had she not become a famous writer, Lindgren answered without hesitation that she would wanted to have been a member of the early Social Democratic movement, envision-ing and fighting for a better society. Actually, she did become a visionary and fighter through her writing. All of Lindgren's characters from Pippi to Ronia reflect her idealism as well as her unmistakable humanitarianism.

Ronia, the Robber's Daughter is Lindgren's last grand tale of resistance and empowerment, and it is told with humor, drama, and deep emotion. Growing up in a thieves' fortress in a large forest, Ronia meets Birk, a boy from the enemy clan, and together they eventually renounce the ways of their fathers as they begin building a life together. Lindgren had told tales of resistance and empowerment many times and in many ways in her previous fantastic as well as realistic books, beginning with *Pippi Longstocking*. The characters of Pippi and Ronia mark the beginning and end of a string of strong and venturesome heroes and heroines, including Kajsa Kavat, Lisa, Bill, Rasmus, Meg, Jonathan Lionheart, and Emil. They all represent the new role model for children; no longer well-behaved and meek; they are curious children full of enterprising spirit and caring determination.

There are some obvious parallels between *Pippi Longstocking* and *Ronia, the Robber's Daughter*. In both books readers follow the adventures of strong-willed, courageous, caring, and self-assured girls whose fathers have taken the law in their own hands. Pippi's father, the captain of a pirate ship, and Ronia's father, the chief of a robbers' band, both teach their daughters independence early in life. This includes the ability to fight for their own rights, the rights of others, and the right to be themselves. But the stories Lindgren creates from this parallel set-up go in different directions.

Ronia, the Robber's Daughter continues where *Pippi Longstocking* leaves off. Both Pippi and Ronia at first admire their fathers and want to follow in their footsteps, but Pippi stunts her development, reverting to eternal childhood, and resigning herself to becoming "a small pirate." Pippi sees no other solution to her dilemma of retaining her freedom and independence in a society bent on domesticating and institutionalizing her. Ronia's development reflects the influence of feminist ideologies in the 1970s. Once she has learned to think for herself, she consciously chooses her own path, which brings her in conflict with her father. Realizing the cruelty and lack of social responsibility inherent in a robber's life, she renounces it and charts her own course with the son of the enemy clan, Birk. Whereas Pippi deconstructs calcified patterns of thought and behavior through her pranks, parody, and tall tales using trickster methods employed by the powerless throughout the ages, Ronia creates visions, builds relationships and claims new territory. *Ronia, the Robber's Daughter* is a novel about growing up, about conflicts and struggle, but above all about reconciliation and building bridges between genders and generations.

Pippi and Ronia are two strong female protagonists that bracket Lindgren's career as a children's author and provide important evidence of the continuity and change in Lindgren's authorship. The following excerpts exemplify her narrative style and give us a sense of her growth as author.

Astrid Lindgren won many awards during her lifetime, including the prestigious Hans Christian Andersen Medal, but perhaps the greatest tribute to her work is the love that children around the world continue to express for her books.

Pippi Långstrump[2]

Utdrag

I utkanten av den lilla, lilla staden låg en gammal förfallen trädgård. I trädgården låg ett gammalt hus, och i huset bodde Pippi Långstrump. Hon var nio år, och hon bodde där alldeles ensam. Ingen mamma eller pappa hade hon, och det var egentligen rätt skönt, för på det viset fanns det ingen som kunde säga till henne, att hon skulle gå och lägga sig, just när hon hade som allra roligast, och ingen som kunde tvinga henne att äta fiskleverolja, när hon hellre ville ha karameller.

En gang i tiden hade Pippi haft en pappa som hon tyckte förfärligt mycket om, ja, hon hade förstås haft en mamma också, men det var så länge sen, så det kom hon inte alls ihåg. Mamman hade dött, när Pippi bara var en liten, liten unge som låg i vaggan och skrek så förskräckligt, att ingen kunde vara i närheten. Pippi trodde, att hennes mamma nu satt uppe i himlen och kikade ner på sin flicka genom ett litet hål, och Pippi brukade ofta vinka upp till henne och saga:

"Var inte ängslig! Jag klarar mej alltid!"

Sin pappa hade Pippi inte glömt. Han var sjökapten och seglade på de stora haven, och Pippi hade seglat med honom på hans båt, ända tills pappan en gang under en storm blåste i sjön och försvann. Men Pippi var alldeles säker på att han en dag skulle komma tillbaka. Hon trodde inte alls, att han hade drunknat. Hon trodde, att han hade flutit i land på en ö, där det fanns fullt med neger, och att hennes pappa hade blivit kung over alla negrerna och gick omkring med en gullkrona på huvudet hela dagarna.

"Min mamma är en angel och min pappa är en negerkung, det är minsann inte alla barn som har så fina föräldrar", brukade Pippi saga så förnöjt. "Och när min pappa bara får bygga sej en båt, så kommer han och hämtar mej och då blir jag en negerprinsessa. Hej hopp, vad det ska bli livat!" (5-6)

***

Pippi var ett mycket märkvärdigt barn. Det allra märkvärdigaste med henne var, att hon var så stark. Hon var så gruvligt stark, att i hela världen fanns det ingen polis som var så stark som hon. Hon kunde lyfta en hel häst, om hon ville. Och det ville hon. Hon hade en egen häst som hon hade köpt för en av sina många gullpengar samma dag, hon kom hem till Villa Villekulla. Hon hade alltid längtat efter en egen häst. Och nu bodde han på verandan. Men när Pippi ville dricka sitt eftermiddagskaffe där, lyfte hon utan vidare ut honom i trädgården. (8)

***

Hennes hår hade samma färg som en morot och var flätat i två hårda flätor som stod rätt ut. Hennes näsa hade samma fason som en mycket liten potatis, och den var alldeles prickig av fräknar. Under näsan satt en verkligen mycket bred mun med friska, vita tänder. Hennes klänning var rätt egendomlig. Pippi hade själv sytt den. Det var meningen,

---

2   Astrid Lindgren: *Pippi Långstrump*. Stockholm: Rabén & Sjögren, 1947.

att den skulle bli blå, men det tyget räckte inte, så Pippi fick lov att sy dit lite röda tygbitar här och där. På hennes långa, smala ben satt ett par långa strumpor, den ena brun och den andra svart. Och så hade hon ett par svarta skor som var precis dubbelt så långa som hennes fötter. De skorna hade hennes pappa köpt åt henne i Sydamerika, för att hon skulle ha litet att växa i, och Pippi ville aldrig ha några andra. (9-10)

***

Pippi gick gatan fram. Hon gick med det ena benet på trottoaren och det andra i rännstenen. Tommy och Annika tittade efter henne så länge de kunde se henne. Om en stund kom hon tillbaka. Och nu gick hon baklänges. Det var för att hon skulle slippa vända sig om, när hon gick hem. Då hon kom mitt för Tommys och Annikas grind, stannade hon. Barnen tittade på varann under tystnad. Till sist sa Tommy:

"Varför gick du baklänges?"

"Varför jag gick baklänges?" sa Pippi. "Lever vi inte i ett fritt land kanske? Får man inte gå, hur man vill? Förresten ska jag säja dej, att i Egypten går alla människor på det viset, och ingen tycker, att det är det minsta konstigt."

"Hur vet du det", frågade Tommy. "Du har väl intge varit i Egypten."

"Om jag har varit i Egypten! Jo, det kan du skriva opp att jag har. Jag har varit överallt på hela jordklotet och sett mycket konstigare saker än folk som går baklänges. Jag undrar vad du skulle ha sagt, om jag hade gått på händerna som folk gör i Bortre Indien?"

"Nu ljuger du allt", sa Tommy.

Pippi funderade ett ögonblick.

"Ja, du har rätt. Jag ljuger", sa hon sorgset.

"Det är fult att ljuga", sa Annika, som nu äntligen vågade öppna munnen.

"Ja, det är *mycket* fult att ljuga", sa Pippi ännu mera sorgset. "Men jag glömmer bort det då och då, förstår du." (10-11)

Pippi Longstocking[3]

Excerpts

Translated by Florence Lamborn

Way out at the end of a tiny little town was an old overgrown garden, and in the garden was an old house, and in the house lived Pippi Longstocking. She was nine years old, and she lived there all alone. She had no mother and no father, and that was of course very nice because there was no one to tell her to go to bed just when she was having the most fun, and no one who could make her take cod liver oil when she much preferred caramel candy.

Once upon a time Pippi had had a father of whom she was extremely fond. Naturally she had had a mother too, but that was so long ago that Pippi didn't remember her at all.

Her mother had died when Pippi was just a tiny baby and lay in a cradle and howled so that nobody could go anywhere near her. Pippi was sure that her mother was now up in Heaven, watching her little girl through a peephole in the sky, and Pippi often waved up at her and called, "Don't you worry about me. I'll always come out on top."

Pippi had not forgotten her father. He was a sea captain who sailed on the great ocean, and Pippi had sailed with him in his ship until one day her father was blown overboard in a storm and disappeared. But Pippi was absolutely certain that he would come back. She would never believe that he had drowned; she was sure he had floated until he landed on an island inhabited by cannibals. And she thought he had become the king of all the cannibals and went around with a golden crown on his head all day long.

"My papa is a cannibal king; it certainly isn't every child who has such a stylish papa," Pippi used to say with satisfaction. "And as soon as my papa has built himself a boat he will come and get me, and I'll be a cannibal princess. Heigh-ho, won't that be exciting?" (11-12)

***

Pippi was indeed a remarkable child. The most remarkable thing about her was that she was so strong. She was so very strong that in the whole wide world there was not a single police officer as strong as she. Why, she could lift a whole horse if she wanted to! And she wanted to. She had a horse of her own that she had bought with one of her many gold pieces the day she came home to Villa Villekulla. She had always longed for a horse, and now here he was, living on the porch. When Pippi wanted to drink her afternoon coffee there, she simply lifted him down in the garden. (13-14)

***

Her hair, the color of a carrot, was braided in two tight braids that stuck straight out. Her nose was the shape of a very small potato and was dotted all over with freckles. It must be admitted that the mouth under this nose was a very wide one, with strong white teeth. Her dress was rather unusual. Pippi herself had made it. She had meant it to be blue, but there wasn't quite enough blue cloth, so Pippi had sewed little red pieces on it here and there. On her long thin legs she wore a pair of long stockings, one brown and the other black, and she had on a pair of black shoes that were exactly twice as long as her feet. These shoes her father had bought for her in South America so that Pippi would have something to grow into, and she never wanted to wear any others. (15-16)

***

Pippi walked along the street with one foot on the sidewalk and the other in the gutter. Tommy and Annika watched as long as they could see her. In a little while she came back, and now she was walking backward. That was because she didn't want to turn around to get home. When she reached Tommy's and Annika's gate she stopped.

The children looked at each other in silence. At last Tommy spoke. "Why did you walk backward?"

"Why did I walk backward?" said Pippi. "Isn't this a free country? Can't a person walk any way she wants to? For that matter, let me tell you that in Egypt everybody walks that way, and nobody thinks it's the least bit strange."

"How do you know?" asked Tommy. "You've never been in Egypt, have you?"

"I've never been in Egypt? Indeed I have. That's one thing you can be sure of. I have been all over the world and seen many things stranger than people walking backward. I wonder what you would have said if I had come along walking on my hands the way they do in Farthest India."

"Now you must be lying," said Tommy.

Pippi thought a moment. "You're right," she said sadly, "I am lying."

"It's wicked to lie," said Annika, who had at last gathered up enough courage to speak.

"Yes, it's very wicked to lie," said Pippi even more sadly. "But I forget it now and then." (16-18)

Ronja rövardotter[4]

Utdrag

Det gick en tid, och Skalle-Per blev allt svagare. Till sist kom där en natt, när de alla vakade over honom, Mattis och Lovis och Ronja och rövarna. Skalle-Per låg orörlig och med slutna ögon. Mattis sökte ängsligt efter något tecken till liv. Men det var skumt omkring bädden trots skenet från elden och talgljuset som Lovis hade tänt, nej, man kunde inte se något livstecken, och plötsligt skrek Mattis:

"Han är död!"

Då öppnade Skalle-Per ena ögat och tittade förebrående på honom.

"Det är jag visst inte! Tror du inte jag har folkvett så pass att jag tar avsked, innan jag ger mej iväg?"

Sedan blundade han igen en lång stund, och de stod där tysta och hörde bara några små pipande andetag.

"Men nu", sa Skalle-Per och slog upp ögonen, "nu, govänner, tar jag avsked av er alla! För nu dör jag."

Och så dog han.

Ronja hade aldrig sett någon dö, och hon grät en stund. Fast han var ändå så trött sista tiden, tänkte hon, nu får han kanske vila sej nån annan stans som inte jag vet om.

Men Mattis gick storgråtande fram och tillbaka i stensalen och skrek:

"Han har funnits jämt! Och nu finns han inte!"

Då sa Lovis:

"Mattis, du vet att ingen får finnas jämt. Vi föds och vi dör, så har det ju alltid varit, vad jämrar du om?"

"Men han fattas mej", skrek Mattis. "Han fattas mej så det skär i bröstet!"

"Vill du att jag ska hålla om dej ett slag", frågade Lovis.

"Ja, gör det för all del", skrek Mattis. "Och du Ronja också!"

Sedan satt han lutad ömsom mot Lovis och ömsom mot Ronja och grät ut sin sorg över Skalle-Per som hade funnits jämt i hans liv och nu inte fanns mer.

Nästa dag jordsatte de Skalle-Per nere vid älven. Vintern hade ryckt närmare, nu snöade det för första gången, och mjuka blöta flingor föll over Skalle-Pers kista, när Mattis och hans rövare bar den dit den skulle. Kistan hade Skalle-Per själv snickrat ihop åt sej under sin krafts dagar och genom alla år bevarat längst inne i klädkammaren.

"En rövare kan behöva sin kista när han minst anar det", så hade han sagt, Skalle-Per, och de sista åren hade han förundrat sej over att det dröjde så länge.

"Men förr eller senare kommer den till pass", sa han.

Nu hade den kommit till pass.

Saknaden efter Skalle-Per låg tung över borgen. Hela vintern var Mattis dyster. Rövarna var också nedslagna, eftersom Mattis humor bestämde både sorg och glädje i Mattisborgen.

---

4   Astrid Lindgren, *Ronja rövardotter*. Stockholm: Rabén & Sjögren, 1981.

Ronja flydde med Birk ut i skogen, där var det vinter nu, och när hon stod på skidor utför bergknallarna, glömde hon alla sorger. Men hon mindes dem så snart hon kom hem och såg Mattis sitta ruvande framför elden. "Trösta mej, Ronja", bad han. "Hjälp mej med min sorg!" "Snart är det vår igen, det blir bättre då", sa Ronja, men det tyckte inte Mattis. "Skalle-Per får inte se nån vår", sa han buttert. Och för detta kunde Ronja inte hitta någon tröst.

Men vintern gick. Och våren kom, det gjorde den ju alltid, vilka som än levde och dog. Mattis blev gladare, det blev han varje vår, och han visslade och sjöng när han i spetsen för sina rövare red ut genom Vargklämman. Där nedanför väntade redan Borka och hans män. Hoj, nu skulle rövarlivet äntligen komma igång igen efter den långa vintern! Det fröjdades de åt i sitt oförstånd bade Mattis och Borka, födda till rövare som de ju var.

Deras barn var vida klokare. De gladdes åt helt andra ting. Att snön var borta så att de kunde rida igen, och att de snart skulle flytta tillbaka till Björngrottan.

"Och så är jag glad för att du Birk aldrig vill bli nån rövare", sa Ronja.

Birk skrattade.

"Nej, det har jag ju svurit på. Men jag undrar vad vi ska leva av i vårt liv, du och jag?" "Det vet jag", sa Ronja. "Vi ska bli bergsmän, vad säjer du om det?"

Och så berättade hon för Birk sagan om Skalle-Pers silverberg, det som den lilla grådvärgen hade visat honom en gang för länge sedan till tack för sitt liv.

"Där finns det silverklumpar stora som bullerstenar", sa Ronja. "Och vem vet, det kanske inte är någon saga? Skalle-Per svor på att det var sant. Vi kan rida dit nån dag och titta efter, jag vet var det är."

"Men det är ingen brådska", sa Birk. "Håll det hemligt bara! Annars kommer alla rövare sättande och vill plocka silver!"

Då skrattade Ronja.

"Du är lika klok som Skalle-Per. Rövare är rovlystna som ormvråkar sa han, det var därför jag inte fick tala om det för nån annan än dej!" (203-234)

***

Tidig morgon är det. Som jordens första morgon så skön! Nybyggarna i Björngrottan, här kommer de vandrande genom sin skog, och runt om dem är all vårens härlighet. I alla träd och alla vatten och alla gröna snår lever det, det kvittrar och susar och brummar och sjunger och sorlar, överallt hörs vårens friska vilda sång.

Och de kommer till sin grotta, sitt hem i vildmarken. Och allt är som förr, tryggt och välbekant, älven som brusar där nere, skogarna i morgonljuset, allt är sej likt. Våren är ny, men allt är sej lik.

"Bli inte rädd, Birk", sa Ronja. "Nu kommer mitt vårskrik!"

Och hon skrek, gällt som en fågel, ett jubelskrik så att det hördes långt bort i skogen. (235-236)

Ronia, The Robber's Daughter[5]

Excerpts

Translated by Patricia Crampton

Time passed, and Noddle-Pete grew weaker and weaker. At last there came a night when they were all watching over him, Matt and Lovis and Ronia and the robbers. Noddle-Pete lay there unmoving, his eyes closed. Matt searched anxiously for any sign of life. But the bed was in shadow despite the light from the fire and the candle Lovis had lit. It was impossible to see any sign of life, and suddenly Matt bellowed, "He's dead!"

Then Noddle-Pete opened one eye and gave him a reproachful look. "I most certainly am not! Don't you think I have enough manners to say good-bye before I go away?"

Then he closed his eyes again for a long time, and they stood in silence, hearing only a few small, wheezing breaths.

"But now," said Noddle-Pete, opening his eyes, "now, my friends, I take leave of you all! Now I shall die."

And so he died.

Ronia had never seen anyone die, and she cried for some time. But after all, he has been so tired lately, she thought; now perhaps he can rest – somewhere that I don't know about.

But Matt walked up and down the stone hall weeping mightily and shouting, "He's always been here! And now he's not!"

Then Lovis said, "Matt, you know that no one can always be there. We are born and we die – that's how it's always been. What are you complaining about?"

"But I miss him," shouted Matt. "I miss him so much it cuts my heart!"

"Would you like me to hold you for a bit?" asked Lovis.

"Yes, you might as well," cried Matt. "And you too, Ronia."

So he sat leaning first against Lovis and then against Ronia and wept out his grief for Noddle-Pete, who had been there all his life and was not there any more.

Next day they buried Noddle-Pete down by the river. The winter had come closer; now it was snowing for the first time, and soft, wet flakes fell on Noddle-Pete's coffin as Matt and his robbers bore it to its place. Noddle-Pete had carved the coffin himself in the days of his strength and had kept it at the back of the costume chamber all through the years.

"A robber may need his coffin when he least expects it," Noddle-Pete had said, and in the last few years he had expressed surprise that it was taking so long.

"But sooner or later it will come to pass," he had said.

Now it had come to pass.

The loss of Noddle-Pete lay heavily on the fort. Matt was glum all winter long, and the robbers were downcast too, since it was Matt's mood that meant either sorrow or gladness in Matt's Fort.

Ronia took refuge with Birk in the woods, where it was now winter, and when she was skiing down the slopes she forgot all her sorrows. But she was reminded of them as soon as she came home and saw Matt brooding in front of the fire.

"Comfort me, Ronia," he begged her. "Help me in my grief."

"Soon it will be spring again. You'll feel better then," said Ronia, but Matt did not agree.

"Noddle-Pete won't see spring," he said grimly, and Ronia could find no comfort for him there.

But winter passed and spring came, as it always did, whoever lived or died. Matt began to cheer up, as he did every spring, and he whistled and sang when he rode out to the Wolf's Neck at the head of his robbers.

Borka and his men were already waiting down below. Hurrah, now their robbers' life was going to begin again at last, after a long winter! That delighted them, born to the robbers' life as they were.

Their children were much wiser. They delighted in quite different things, such as the disappearance of the snow, so they could ride again, and in the thought of soon moving back to the Bear's Cave.

"I'm glad you never want to be a robber, Birk," said Ronia.

Birk laughed. "No, I've taken an oath on it, haven't I? But I do wonder what we're going to live on, you and I."

"I know," said Ronia. "We'll be miners – what do you say to that?"

And then she told Birk the story of Noddle-Pete's silver mine, the one the little gray dwarf had shown him long ago in gratitude for his life.

"There are silver nuggets there as big as cobblestones," Ronia said. "And who knows, it may not be just a fairy tale! Noddle-Pete swore it was true. We can ride up there one day and have a look. I know where it is."

"But there's no hurry," said Birk. "Just make sure you keep it secret! Otherwise all the robbers will be in a rush to pick up the silver!"

Ronia laughed. "You're as wise as Noddle-Pete. Robbers are as eager as buzzards – that's what he said – and that is why I mustn't tell anyone but you!" (172-175)

***

It is early morning. As beautiful as the first morning of the world! The new inhabitants of the Bear's Cave come strolling through their woods, and all about them lies the splendor of springtime. Every tree, every stretch of water, and every green thicket is alive. There is twittering and rushing and buzzing and singing and murmuring. The fresh, wild song of spring can be heard everywhere.

And they come to their cave, their home in the wilderness. And everything is as before, safe and familiar. The river rushing down below, the woods in the morning light – everything is the same as ever. Spring is new, but it is still the same as ever.

"Don't be scared, Birk," says Ronia. "My spring yell is just coming!"

And she yells, shrill as a bird, a shout of joy that can be heard far away in the forest. (176)

Primary Works

Pippi Långstrump, 1945. Eng. tr. *Pippi Longstocking*, 1950, 1956.

Mästerdetektiven Blomkvist, 1946. Eng. tr. *Bill Bergson, Master Detective*, 1952.

Mästerdetektiven Blomkvist lever farligt, 1951. Eng. tr. *Bill Bergson Lives Dangerously*, 1954).

Pippi Långstrump går ombord, 1946. Eng. tr. *Pippi Goes Aboard*, 1956; *Pippi Goes on Board*, 1957.

Pippi Långstrump i Söderhavet, 1948. Eng. tr. *Pippi in the South Seas*, 1957, 1959.

Mio min Mio, 1954. Eng. tr. *Mio, My Son*, 1956.

Lillebror och Karlsson på taket, 1955. Eng. tr. *Karlson on the Roof*, 1958; *Karlsson-on-the-Roof*, 1963.

Rasmus på luffen, 1956. Eng. tr. *Rasmus and the Vagabond*, 1960, 1961.

Bullerbyboken, 1961. Eng. tr. *The Children of Noisy Village*, 1962); *All About the Bullerby Children*, 1964.

Madicken, 1960. Eng. tr. *Madicken*, 1963; *Mardie's Adventures*, 1979; *Mischievous Meg*, 1960.

Kalle Blomkvist och Rasmus, 1953. Eng. tr. *Bill Bergson and the White Rose Rescue*, 1965.

Emil i Lönneberga, 1963. Eng. tr. *Emil in the Soup Tureen*, 1970.

Nya hyss av Emil i Lönneberga, 1966. Eng. tr. *Emil's Pranks*, 1971; *Emil gets into Mischief*, 1973.

Än lever Emil i Lönneberga, 1970. Eng. tr. *Emil and Piggy Beast*, 1973; *Emil and his Clever Pig*, 1974.

Bröderna Lejonhjärta, 1973. Eng. tr. *The Brothers Lionheart*, 1975.

Ronja rövardotter, 1981. Eng. tr. *The Robber's Daughter*, 1983; *Ronia, the Robber's Daughter*, 1983.

Selected Bibliography

Allrakäraste Astrid: en vänbok till Astrid Lindgren. Stockholm: Rabén & Sjögren, 2001.

Byskov, Jonna. *Möt världens bästa Astrid*. Stockholm: Natur och kultur, 2002.

Edström, Vivi. *Astrid Lindgren: a critical study*. Eivor Cormack, tr. Stockholm: R&S books, 2000. (Skrifter utgivna av Svenska barnboksinstitutet, 70)

–. *Astrid Lindgren: vildtoring och lägereld*. Stockholm: Rabén & Sjögren, 1992 (Skrifter utgivna av Svenska barnboksinstitutet, 43)

–. *Kvällsdoppet i Katthult: essäer om Astrid Lindgren diktaren*. Stockholm: Natur & kultur, 2004. [Skrifter utgivna av Svenska barnboksinstitutet, 83)

Fellke, Jens. *Rebellen från Vimmerby: om Astrid Lindgren och hemstaden*.Vimmerby: Jens Fellke produktion, 2002.

Gaare, Jørgen. *Pippi och Sokrates: filosofiska vandringar i Astrid Lindgrens värld*. Stockholm: Natur och kultur, 2002.

–. *Världens bästa påhitt: nya filosofiska vandringar i Astrid Lindgrens värld*. Stockholm: Natur och kultur, 2004.

Hagerfors, Anna Maria. *Århundradets Astrid*. Stockholm: Rabén & Sjögren, 2002.

Karlsson, Petter. *Från snickerboa till Villa Villekulla: Astrid Lindgrens filmvärld*. Stockholm: Forum, 2004.

Kvint, Kerstin. *Astrid världen över: en selektiv bibliografi 1946-2002 = Astrid worldwide: a selective bibliography 1946-2002*, Martin Peterson, tr., Stockholm: Kvint, 2002.

Metcalf, Eva-Maria. *Astrid Lindgren*. New York: Twayne Publishers and Maxwell Macmillan International, 1995.

Strömstedt, Margareta. *Astrid Lindgren: en levnadsteckning*. 4th ed. Stockholm: Rabén & Sjögren, 2003.

Törnqvist, Lena. *Astrid från Vimmerby*. Vimmerby: Stift. Bevarandet av Astrid Lindgrens gärning, 1998.

Törnqvist, Lena. *Astrid from Vimmerby*. Patrick O'Malley, tr. Vimmerby: Stift. Bevarandet av Astrid Lindgrens gärning, 1999.

Tove Jansson: To Dive with Eyes Open

ULRIKA GUSTAFSSON (ÅBO AKADEMI UNIVERSITY)

Introduction

A list of Tove Jansson's (1914-2001) collected children's books, short stories and novels contains more than twenty titles. She also wrote for the stage, television and radio. She was born in Helsinki, in 1914, the daughter of the sculptor Viktor Jansson and the illustrator Signe Hammarsten-Jansson. She was educated in Helsinki, Stockholm and Paris as a painter and illustrator. In 1933 she made her debut as a writer. Her last book, *Meddelande* (Message), was published in 1998. Many of Tove Jansson's literary works are illustrated with her own sketches and paintings. All were written in Swedish. She died in 2001.

Message is an anthology of published short stories as well as several unpublished pieces. Among them there is a fragmentary short story built on short notes, written by close friends as well as unknown admirers. One, from Japan, says:

> Dear Jansson san
> I have collected money for a long time. I will come and sit at your feet to understand. Please when may I come there?[1]

This reader's letter indicates Tove Jansson's popularity, and also tells of the Japanese reader's striking fancy for her. Her Moomin books – she wrote the first one in 1945 – made her world famous. Today there is not only a range of Moomin books – available in more than thirty languages – but also Moomin cartoons, a TV series and an immense amount of other Moomin products such as household utensils, clothes and toys. The Moomin fan can even visit the Moomin land in Naantali, Finland. On a small island the Moomin house, the Moomins and their friends can be seen. As an author Tove Jansson has received numerous awards both in Finland and abroad. In her home country Jansson's work is very visible. For example, every day

---

[1] *Meddelande*, 287.

one can read a Moomin cartoon strip in the largest Finland-Swedish newspaper, *Hufvudstadsbladet*.

Apart from being the creator of the Moomins, Tove Jansson distinguished herself especially as a short story writer. However, to do justice to the corpus, one must understand the Moomin books as serious literature for children as well as for adults. The popularisation and commercialisation of the characters and stories jeopardize their kernels of meaning. Moreover, one has to state that the gap between the world of the Moomins and our own world is not wide.

The Sculptor's Daughter

Tove Jansson started her career as a writer of books for adults with *Bildhuggarens dotter* (1968; The Sculptor's Daughter). The title indicates its genre affiliation, namely the book is an autobiography. It is narrated from the child's perspective with a very entertaining voice. "It was a good story. – One more",[2] the child Tove says. She tells many stories. There is a certain effect when the child comes to conclusions which tend not to correspond to the adult readers' impression of the situations. For example, there is the case when the child tells about a glistening stone. She struggles all day to get the silver stone home. When she finally has the stone in the house, it has left ugly marks on the stairs – it then falls from the balcony. To the reader's relief it does not kill any passers-by on the sidewalk. The child, not reflecting on this risk, never tells her family how close it was that they could have been rich!

In this book the author portrays her parents, but the reader also gains insight into the milieus which characterize the whole textual corpus: the Finnish archipelago in the summer time and the Helsinki of the bourgeois artist circles in the winter.

When reading the collected works of Tove Jansson it is clear how close life and art can interact, i.e., how the author extracts material from a life experience to create literary worlds. The late *Anteckningar från en ö* (1996; Notes from an Island) is a collection of diary excerpts, notes and memories describing Tove Jansson's and her partner Tuulikki Pietilä's summertime life on the little island Klovharun in the southern archipelago of Finland. The texts are accompanied by Tuulikki's wash drawings and aquatints. In this autobiographical book the reader familiar with the earlier works of the author will recognize details and stories. Tove Jansson explains she loves stones because she is a sculptor's daughter. She describes the archipelago nature with its storms and birds as well as the boat "Victoria," known for

---

[2]   *Bildhuggarens dotter*, 57. Tr. by Ulrika Gustafsson.

instance from the short story "Victoria" in the volume *Rent spel* (1989; Fair Play). To be an artist is a central theme of this authorship; it is art about art. This theme is traced in the short story "Svart-vitt" (Black and White) from the collection *Lyssnerskan* (The Listener) written in 1971. The importance of the artist's milieu for his or her work – and *own* creativity – is pictured. Tove Jansson's life provides her works with certain themes, situations and milieus. On one hand this could be seen as a restriction, but on the other the insights of life recorded in the texts of this author no doubt are also more universally applicable. And there is certainly more than one central theme worthy of notice, such as travelling, nature and human relations, containing love, jealousy and friendship.

"If Tove Jansson had been born fifty or so years later, she would have ended up becoming a spokesperson for gay rights, now she was spared that", the literary critic Ann-Christine Snickars states in an article on Jansson and her colleague and contemporary, Astrid Lindgren, the great Swedish children's book writer. Homosexuality is both a theme and a motif in the corpus. Often there are single sex couples figuring in the novels and *Fair Play*, a collection of short stories which forms a kind of novel, illustrates the life shared by two women artists (see above). In 1990 the author was given an award for this book by Tupilak, the Nordic cultural worker's organization for homosexuals. The fact that homosexuality is put forward as a fact and not debated has the effect that it appears as a possible way of life and is not a spectacular circumstance. What is depicted are human relations as well as love in general. However, the fact that homosexuals live as minorities in heterosexual societies is a reminder of the possibility of the author's self censorship. In her book on Tove Jansson's later works from 1999, Birgit Antonsson states that it seems as if reviewers constantly have avoided this theme.[3]

The Complexity of Human Relations

In "Life in the Mist", an article on Tove Jansson's later writings, Maria Antas explains that the coldness in most of Jansson's short stories about artists and art makes her wonder. Because of the artists' "isolated solitude" she does not feel secure enough and does not know, if she can only respect the writer's work or also love it. "My respect for Tove Jansson's unique artistic achievement, including her visual art," she writes, "does not resem-

---

[3]   Snickars, 105; Antonsson, 189. For further discussion on this theme, see Barbro K. Gustafsson. It should be mentioned that Birgit Antonsson criticizes Gustafsson's analysis of Jansson's writings for overemphasizing the theme of homosexuality in Jansson.

ble love in the sense of love as feeling of warmth, of being touched."[4] Yes, there is coldness, but – as Antas also recognizes – there is warmth as well! One cannot take happy endings for granted, but they do occur.

The anger pictured in the short story "Dockhuset" (The Doll's House) from 1978, which is the name for a collection of short stories, is shocking in its primitiveness. The story deals with three men, Alexander, Erik and Boy. Alexander and Erik live together. Boy is a friend, who is soon engaged in an intense and time absorbing construction of a doll's house with Alexander. Jealousy, resulting in a violent outburst, grows in Erik. But in the end it is clear his reaction was not fully motivated:

> They heard the slam from the flat door. In a while Alexander came in, he stayed by the door and said: What the hell are you doing?
> He hit me, Boy said. Look. Blood.
> Erik? Alexander said. Why are you sitting on the floor? Where are your spectacles?
> In my pocket. I feel sick.
> What have you done?
> I do not know, Erik answered. But I have saved our tower. It is not destroyed.
> Alexander slowly opened a package of cigarettes. He took one out and lighted it. It really rotates, he said. Boy, you know your things. Now it is perfect. Never before has a house as mine and Erik's been built.[5]

There is a tower on the doll's house. But more important: Erik's and Alexander's relationship is as a tower, and obviously no one should visit it – or at least – no one should stay there too long. There is warmth in the relationship of Erik and Alexander, but at the same time insecurity which makes it dangerous, at least for outsiders.

This, the complexity of human relationships, is another major theme of the authorship. Jansson writes of people longing for company, but who are at the same time incapable of building solid human relationships. Some of them cannot trust others and isolate themselves from the social world, as does Vanda in the short story "Kvinnan som lånade minnen" (The Woman who Borrowed Memories) in *Resa med lätt bagage* (1987; Travelling with Light Luggage). In "Måsarna" (The Gulls), in the same collection, Arne is prevented from communing with anything, human or animal, because of his inner tensions. The story also thematizes a sickness of our modern society: the burnt-out syndrome.

In *Notes from an Island* the author narrates how she and Tuulikki, when they were younger, dreamt about the house they were about to build at Klovharun, the island far out in the sea:

> The room would have four windows, one in each wall. In the southeast we gave space to the heavy storms, which rave over the island, in the east the moon can be reflected in the

---

[4]   Antas, 254.
[5]   "Dockskåpet". *Dockskåpet och andra berättelser*, 29. Tr. by Ulrika Gustafsson.

black pool, and in the west there is a rock face with moss and polypody. Northwards one must be able to be on the lookout to see what comes and have time to get used to it.[6]

Strongly connected to the theme of artistry is the longing for peace and loneliness. To be famous has an anguished backside: To be put under the pressure of certain expectations and never to be left alone.

This theme had a particular relevance for the author herself, which, for example, is indicated in the excerpt from *Message* (see above). It is also, although not a main theme, relevant in the novel *Den ärliga bedragaren* (1982; The Honest Swindler). In this novel Anna, famous as an author of children's books, does not know how to cope with the letters from all the children who want to become friends with her and receive answers to their questions. The "honest traitor" Katri comes with a proposal how to put an end to the time and energy demanding correspondence. "I almost think you do not like them", Anna says to Katri. Katri smiles and says: "You do not either." Anna blushes but states that she could never betray the children by sending them ready made letters.[7]

This frankness, from the author's side, in regard to human relations also comes to show in Mrs Rubinstein's letter to her son. Mrs Rubinstein, a character in the novel *Solstaden* (1974; Sun City), is one of the old ladies and men living in a boarding house in St Petersburg, Florida. She writes:

Beloved Abrascha, my dreadful son, we are very much alike although the intelligence in a broader sense was not inherited by you. In any case, you should, after a long, strenuous and observing life together with your mother have understood that I detest banal messages more than silence, and half-hearted non-personal comments more than brutal truths.[8]

Mrs Rubinstein signs the letter with "Your beloved Rebecca Rubinstein", but it is never sent. She tears it into the smallest pieces she can.

The importance of seeing, both in the paintings and writings of Tove Jansson, is often emphasized in secondary literature. Seeing has to do both with seeing as a visual artist, as a painter, and with having insight into the meaning of things, the meaning of life. In the Moomin books, above all, it is obvious how pictures and texts accompany each other.[9] That does not only account for the picture books. The Moomin novels are also filled with drawings. And who does not recognize Tove Jansson's picture of the Moomin valley, once one has seen it!

The short story "Åttiårsdag" (Eightieth Anniversary), also found in *Travelling with Light Luggage*, is about desire, about the lust to see what is connected to the question of the meaning of life:

And to travel, I added. I have such a desire for travelling.

---

[6]   *Anteckningar från en ö*, 15. Tr. by Ulrika Gustafsson.
[7]   *Den ärliga bedragaren*, 112-13. Tr. by Ulrika Gustafsson.
[8]   *Solstaden*, 60-61. Tr. by Ulrika Gustafsson.
[9]   See further Westin, Stewen, and Antas.

Keke was silent for a while and then he said: Desire. As you see, I have lived for quite a long time, that is, worked quite a long time, it is the same thing. And do you know what, the single thing which is really important is desire.

A little further on it is said: "In fact, your grandmother never painted anything other than trees, and trees in exactly the same park. Finally she knew the idea of the tree. She is very strong. She never lost her desire." What you do – if you love, travel or paint – is not important, but how you do it is crucial. "My desire is maybe not spectacular, but it is at least mine", Jonne says.[10]

The View from Before and from After

In Tove Jansson's books the reader often comes to share a perspective with those who have a view on life from before adulthood, i.e. the children, and those who have a view on life from after adulthood, i.e. the elderly. Both are declared incapable of managing their own affairs by the grown-up majority, the society – but Jansson takes them seriously. In the novel *Sommarboken* (1972; The Summer Book) there are three persons living on a small island in the summertime, the child Sophia, her grandmother and father, but the focus is on the child and the old woman and their relationship. As in her other books, the author does not shut her eyes for personal and relational problems. Though, in this book, as in *Fair Play*, there is an apparent warmth. People care for each other, even if they occasionally quarrel. Both the dark and the bright sides of life are recognized and therefore the picture given is not utopian but quite close to life, although cute.

As in many short stories ageing is also a theme in *Sun City*. In this novel the omniscient narrator takes us with her into the minds and rooms of Mrs Rubinstein and her neighbours – enemies and friends, all living in a boarding house. This not only has the effect that events are narrated from different perspectives, but also that the house, filled with the elderly and their life stories, becomes as a real location in the reader's mind. When the book ends, one has the feeling that the story goes on.

In and Outside the Valley

With the Moomin books Tove Jansson renewed Finland-Swedish children's literature. The Moomins are found in picture books and novels. The picture book *Hur gick det sen?* (1952; What Happened then?) is a wonderfully

---

[10] "Åttiårsdag". *Resa med lätt bagage*, 24, 26, 28. Tr. by Ulrika Gustafsson.

colourful and creative piece of art, exciting not only for the child but also to the fantasy and eye of the adult reader.

It is not necessarily sensible to define the Moomin novels as children's books. In *Resa med Tove* (2002; Travelling with Tove), a book in memory of the author, Margareta Strömstedt writes: "I do not know anyone else who has illustrated existentialism as brilliantly simple as Tove Jansson in her last three Moomin books."[11] Especially the later ones – *Trollvinter* (1957; Eng. tr. *Moominland Midwinter*, 1958), *Pappan och havet* (1965; Eng. tr. *Moominpappa at Sea*, 1966) and *Sent i November* (1970; *Late in November*; Eng. tr. *Moominvalley in November*, 1971) – are often understood as directed towards an older audience. A development in the Moomin world – from a safe mythical one in the earlier books to one more like our own, the human reality, in the later ones – has been recognized. To connect to the discussion of warmth versus coldness in Jansson's work, one may say that the earlier Moomin books contain more warmth than the later. The later Moomin books are more realistic since in them coldness is recognized as part of life and expressed through insecurity and open ends. In her extensive work *Familjen i dalen* (1988; The Family in the Valley), Boel Westin identifies the tension between the idyllic and the chaotic as the central theme of the Moomin world. Thus, both *Moominland Midwinter* and *Moominvalley in November* have been read as concerned with a growing up problematic and sexual orientation.[12]

The family leaves the valley in *Moominpappa at Sea*. The independence of the family members bothers the father. He does not feel important and wants to go to the island where the light house is, to find his place in life – and to understand the sea. The novel is no fairy tale; the world in it is not a protected one with unchanged conditions. In a crucial scene of the book, the Moominmamma escapes into the garden, which she has painted on the wall when being lonely up in the light house. This old and famous motif of the artist disappearing into his or her own painting can also be found in e.g. Pamela Travers' books about Mary Poppins. Moominmamma's wall paint represents the garden back home in the Moomin valley:

> Moominmamma was standing on the table painting apples on the top of a tree with red lead paint. "If only I had these colours to paint with outside," she thought. "What lovely apples and roses I should have!"
> As she gazed at the sky, the evening light crept up the wall, lighting up the flowers in her garden. They seemed to be alive and shining. The garden opened out, and the gravel path with its curious perspective suddenly seemed quite right and to lead straight to the verandah. Moominmamma put her paws round the trunk of the tree; it was warm with sunshine and she felt that the lilac was in bloom.

---

[11] Margareta Strömstedt. "När muminmamman ställer ifrån sig väskan". *Resa med Tove*, 58. Tr. by Ulrika Gustafsson.

[12] See, for instance, Jones, Nikolajeva, and Gustafsson.

Like a flash of lightning a shadow passed across the wall. Something black had flown past the window. An enormous black bird was circling round and round the lighthouse, past one window after another, the west, the south, the east, the north… like a Fury, beating its wings relentlessly.

"We're surrounded!" Moominmamma thought in confusion. "It's a magic circle. I'm scared. I want to go home and leave this terrible, deserted island and the cruel sea…" She flung her arms round her apple tree and shut her eyes. The bark felt rough and warm, and the sound of the sea disappeared. Moominmamma was right inside her garden.

The room was empty. The paints were still on the table, and outside the window the black bird went on circling round the lighthouse. When the colours in the western sky disappeared, it flew away across the sea.

When it was time for tea, the family came home.

"Where's Mamma?" Moomintroll asked.

"Perhaps she's just out getting some water," Moominpappa said. "Look she's painted a new tree since we went out."[13]

The Moominfamily's trip in *Moominpappa at Sea* leads to another characteristic theme of this author: travelling. The bourgeois artist milieu of Helsinki and the Finland-Swedish summer archipelago are the primary milieus, where the stories by Jansson take place. However, during the trips, described in the books, new milieus are continually presented and confronted.

The title of the short story collection, *Travelling with Light Luggage*, signals the importance of travelling to Jansson, but there are also short travel stories in other books, for instance "Den stora resan" (The Big Trip) in *The Doll's House*, "Resa till Rivieran" (Travelling to the Riviera) in *Brev från Klara* (1991; Letter from Klara) and "Resa med Konika" (Travelling with Konika) in *Fair Game*. The title story "Travelling with Light Luggage" in the collection from 1987 is about a man's dream about free and careless travelling. "I sat and thought about the idea of travelling", the protagonist says, "that is being on the road, unbound, without responsibility for what one has left behind, without any possibility to plan what is in front of one. Just a big peace".[14] However, this dream seems to be impossible to fulfil. In "The Big Trip", to be on the road is synonymous with not to live in an automatized manner. As in "Travelling with Light Luggage", the big, long dreamt about trip can hardly be realized. Rosa, a protagonist, feels bound mostly to only imagined responsibilities. Rosa has a mother fixation. This is also the case in "Travelling to the Riviera", but in this short story the grown-up daughter is at least travelling with her mother. Ironically enough, the travellers' experiences, which should be excitingly "irrational", are standardized on the touristy Riviera. "Travelling with Konika" depicts with a comical effect the tourist who sees everything – if anything? – through the camera, which is, most of the time, next to her eye.

---

[13] *Moominpappa at Sea*, 161-62. Tr. by Kingsley Hart.
[14] *Resa med lätt bagage*, 73. Tr. by Ulrika Gustafsson.

Nature

In Jansson's works nature is not just a scene for events, but a force in itself. Heavy storms at sea awake fascination. In the first short story collection *Lyssnerskan* (1971; The Listener), a story entitled "Stormen" (The Storm) describes a storm of tropical strength which finds its way to "a safe, boring country where one lights Christmas trees to disarm the darkness".[15] A point often made is that everything that is perfect is too boring. The storm eases the boredom. It has the effect of release.

The storm is admired by the little Sophia in *The Summer Book*. "One thing that is strange with me", she says, "is that I always feel so good when there is a storm coming." In *The Sculptor's Daughter* there is "a hell of a weather" which makes the whole family excited and happy: "It was wonderful! The grass lay under the surface of the water and just rose up and the whole landscape was new with storm and night all over."[16]

Nature is alive. In *The Sculptor's Daughter* it is strenuous for the child to get the silver stone home, because it lays itself on its back, or on its stomach, and is hard to move. In *Moominpappa at Sea* the island is coming to life. It murmurs in its sleep, and about his object of investigation Moominpappa states: "The sea is sometimes in a good temper and sometimes in a bad temper, and nobody can possibly understand why."[17]

When discussing the importance of nature in this authorship, one must also mention the animals: among others the ape, the wolf and the squirrel, but maybe above all the birds. Relationships between humans and animals are often depicted. In *The Sculptor's Daughter* the child can not hide the fact that the attention that her father gives to the monkey "Poppolino" makes her jealous. Also in the above mentioned short story, "The Gulls", one person's relation to an animal, in this case the big sea gull, "Casimir", makes another person feel like an outsider. In *Moominpappa at Sea* the flying bird creates a magic circle. This scene may represent the fact that the nature and the world of the animals, in the realms of Tove Jansson, are not totally reachable and understandable to the humans.

***

Tove Jansson is foremost known as the mum of the Moomins. However, after a journey through her short stories and novels as undertaken in this essay, one can state that she is a many-faceted author. Nonetheless, it is possible to find connected tracks in this versatility. Maybe the most important conclusion to be drawn here is that Jansson's work is never cut out in

---

[15] *Lyssnerskan*, 96. Tr. by Ulrika Gustafsson.
[16] *Sommarboken*, 171 and *Bildhuggarens dotter*, 74. Tr. by Ulrika Gustafsson.
[17] *Moominpappa at Sea*, 195. Tr. by Kingsley Hart.

opposites. Even the idyll has dark spots. She dives into the human nature with her eyes open.

Badmorgon[18]

Sommarboken, första kapitlet

Det var en tidig mycket varm morgon i juli och det hade regnat på natten. Det nakna berget ångade men mossan och skrevorna var dränkta av fukt och alla färger hade fördjupats. Nedanför verandan var växtligheten en regnskog, ännu i morgonskugga, täta elaka blad och blommor och hon måste akta sig för att bryta dem medan hon letade, med handen för munnen och hela tiden rädd att tappa balansen.

Vad gör du? frågade den lilla Sophia.

Ingenting, svarade hennes farmor. Det vill säga, tillade hon argt, jag letar efter mina löständer.

Barnet kom ner från verandan och frågade sakligt: Var tappade du dem?

Här, sade hon. Jag stod just där och de föll nånstans mellan pionerna.

De sökte tillsammans.

Låt mig, sade Sophia. Du kan inte stå på benen. Maka på dig. Hon dök in under trädgårdens blommande tak och kröp mellan de gröna stammarna, härnere var det skönt och förbjudet, svart mjuk mark och där låg tänderna, vita och skära, en hel munfull av gamla tänder, jag har dem! skrek barnet och reste sig. Sätt in dem.

Men du får inte se på, sade farmorn. Det här är privat.

Sophia höll tänderna bakom ryggen. Jag vill se på, sade hon. Då satte hennes farmor in sina tänder med ett glapp, det gick helt behändigt och var egentligen ingenting att tala om.

När dör du? frågade barnet.

Och hon svarade: Snart. Men det angår dig inte det minsta.

Varför? frågade barnbarnet.

Hon svarade inte, hon gick ut på berget och vidare mot ravinen.

Detdär är förbjudet! skrek Sophia.

Den gamla svarade föraktfullt: Jag vet. Varken du eller jag får gå till ravinen men nu gör vi det i alla fall för din pappa sover och vet inte om det.

De gick över berget, mossan var hal, solen hade hunnit en bra bit upp och nu ångade allt, hela ön var full av soldimma och mycket vacker.

Gör de en grop? frågade barnet vänligt.

Jo, svarade hon. En stor grop. Och tillade lömskt: Så stor att vi allihop får rum.

Varför det? frågade barnet.

De gick vidare mot udden.

Såhär långt har jag aldrig varit, sade Sophia. Har du?

Nej, svarade hennes farmor.

De gick ända ut till udden där berget sjönk i mörkare och mörkare terrasser, varje steg ner mot mörkret var kantat av en ljusgrön frans av sjögräs, den svepte fram och tillbaka med vattnets rörelser.

---

[18]   Printed by permission of Schildts Förlags Ab, Helsingfors, Finland. Copyright (c) Tove Jansson, 1972.

Jag vill bada, sade barnet. Hon väntade på motstånd men det kom inte. Då klädde hon av sig, långsamt och ängsligt. Man kan inte lita på den som låter allting hända. Hon stack benen i vattnet och sade: Det är kallt.

Naturligtvis är det kallt, svarade den gamla kvinnan med tankarna på annat håll. Vad hade du väntat dig.

Barnet gled ner till midjan och väntade i spänning.

Simma, sade hennes farmor. Du kan ju simma.

Det är djupt, tänkte Sophia. Hon har glömt att jag aldrig har simmat på djupt vatten utan att ha nån med mig. Och därför steg hon upp igen och satte sig på berget och förklarade: Det blir tydligen fint väder idag.

Solen hade hunnit högre. Hela ön glimmade, och havet, luften var mycket lätt.

Jag kan dyka, sade Sophia. Vet du hur det är när man dyker?

Hennes farmor svarade: Visst vet jag. Man släpper allting och tar sats och bara dyker. Man känner tångruskorna utmed benen, de är bruna och vattnet är klart, ljusare uppåt, och bubblor. Man glider. Man håller andan och glider och vänder sig och stiger uppåt, låter sig stiga och andas ut. Och sen flyter man. Bara flyter.

Och hela tiden med öppna ögon, sade Sophia.

Naturligtvis. Ingen människa dyker utan att öppna ögonen.

Tror du på att jag kan det utan att jag visar dig? frågade barnet.

Jo, jo, svarade farmorn. Klä på dig nu så hinner vi hem innan han vaknar.

Den första tröttheten kom närmare. När vi är hemma, tänkte hon, när vi är inne igen så tror jag att jag sover ett tag. Och jag måste komma ihåg att säga åt honom att dethär barnet fortfarande är skrämt för djupt vatten.

The Morning Swim[19]

The Summer Book, first chapter

Translated by Thomas Teal

It was an early, very warm morning in July, and it had rained during the night. The bare granite steamed, the moss and crevices were drenched with moisture, and all the colours everywhere had deepened. Below the veranda, the vegetation in the morning shade was like a rain forest of lush, evil leaves and flowers, which she had to be careful not to break as she searched. She held one hand in front of her mouth and was constantly afraid of losing her balance.

'What are you doing?' asked little Sophia.

'Nothing,' her grandmother answered. 'That is to say,' she added angrily, 'I'm looking for my false teeth.'

The child came down from the veranda. 'Where did you lose them?' she asked.

'Here,' said her grandmother. 'I was standing right there and they fell somewhere in the peonies.' They looked together.

'Let me,' Sophia said. 'You can hardly walk. Move over.'

She dived beneath the flowering roof of the garden and crept among green stalks and stems. It was pretty and mysterious down on the soft black earth. And there were the

---

[19] Printed by permission of Sort of Books, London, UK. English translation by Thomas Teal (c) 1974 by Random House, Inc. USA.

teeth, white and pink, a whole mouthful of old teeth. 'I've got them!' the child cried, and stood up. 'Put them in.'

'But you can't watch,' Grandmother said. 'That's private.'

Sophia held the teeth behind her back.

'I want to watch,' she said.

So Grandmother put the teeth in, with a smacking noise. They went in very easily. It had really hardly been worth mentioning.

'When are you going to die?' the child asked.

And Grandmother answered, 'Soon. But that is not the least concern of yours.'

'Why?' her grandchild asked.

She didn't answer. She walked out on the rock and on toward the ravine.

'We're not allowed out there!' Sophia screamed.

'I know,' the old woman answered disdainfully. 'Your father won't let either of us go out to the ravine, but we're going anyway, because your father is asleep and he won't know.'

They walked across the granite. The moss was slippery. The sun had come up a good way now, and everything was steaming. The whole island was covered with a bright haze. It was very pretty.

'Will they dig a hole?' asked the child amiably.

'Yes,' she said. 'A big hole.' And she added, insidiously, 'Big enough for all of us.'

'How come?' the child asked.

They walked on toward the point.

'I've never been this far before,' Sophia said. 'Have you?'

'No,' her grandmother said.

They walked all the way out onto the little promontory, where the rock descended into the water in terraces that became fainter and fainter until there was total darkness. Each step down was edged with a light green seaweed fringe that swayed back and forth with the movement of the sea.

'I want to go swimming,' the child said. She waited for opposition, but none came. So she took off her clothes, slowly and nervously. She glanced at her grandmother – you can't depend on people who just let things happen. She put her legs in the water.

'It's cold,' she said.

'Of course it's cold,' the old woman said, her thoughts somewhere else. 'What did you expect?'

The child slid in up to her waist and waited anxiously.

'Swim,' her grandmother said. 'You can swim.'

It's deep, Sophia thought. She forgets I've never swum in deep water unless somebody was with me. And she climbed out again and sat down on the rock.

'It's going to be a nice day today,' she declared.

The sun had climbed higher. The whole island, and the sea, were glistening. The air seemed very light.

'I can dive,' Sophia said. 'Do you know what it feels like when you dive?'

'Of course I do,' her grandmother said. 'You let go of everything and get ready and just dive. You can feel the seaweed against your legs. It's brown, and the water's clear, lighter toward the top, with lots of bubbles. And you glide. You hold your breath and glide and turn and come up, let yourself rise and breathe out. And then you float. Just float.'

'And all the time with your eyes open,' Sophia said.

'Naturally. People don't dive with their eyes shut.'

'Do you believe I can dive without me showing you?' the child asked.

'Yes, of course,' Grandmother said. 'Now get dressed. We can get back before he wakes up.'
The first weariness came closer. When we get home, she thought, when we get back I think I'll take a little nap. And I must remember to tell him this child is still afraid of deep water.

Primary Works

Sara och Pelle och neckens bläckfiskar, 1933.
Småtrollen och den stora översvämningen, 1945; Eng. tr. *The Moomins and the Great Flood*, 2005.
Kometjakten, 1946; *Mumintrollet på kometjakt*, 1956; *Kometen kommer*, 1968, 1992 (revised ed.); Eng. tr. *Comet in Moominland*, 1951, 1967, 1973, 1986, 1991, 1992.
Trollkarlens hatt, 1948; Eng. tr. *Finn Family Moomintroll*, 1950, 1961, 1964, 1973, 1975, 1986, 1990, 1991 as *The Happy Moomins*, 1951.
Muminpappans bravader. Skrivna av honom själv, 1950; *Muminpappans memoarer* (revised ed.), 1968; Eng. tr. *The Exploits of Moominpappa. Described by himself*, 1952, 1966, 1968, 1969, 1972, 1991 as *Moominpappa's Memoirs*, 1994.
Hur gick det sen? Boken om Mymlan, Mumintrollet och Lilla My, 1952; Eng. tr. *(The Book About) Moomin, Mymble and Little My*, 1953, 1965, 1989, 1992, 1996, 1997, 2001, 2002.
Farlig midsommar, 1954; Eng. tr. *Moominsummer Madness*, 1955, 1971, 1973, 1991, 1992.
Trollvinter, 1957; Eng. tr. *Moominland Midwinter*, 1958, 1971, 1973, 1976, 1991, 1992.
Troll i kulisserna, 1958.
Mumintrollet 1-14, 1957-2004. Comics, with Lars Jansson; Eng tr. *Moomin* [1], 1957.
Vem skall trösta knyttet?, 1960; Eng. tr. *Who will comfort Toffle?*, 1960, 1969, 1989, 1992.
Det osynliga barnet och andra berättelser, 1962; Eng. tr. *Tales from Moominvalley*, 1963, 1964, 1973, 1974, 1976, 1991, 1995.
Pappan och havet, 1965; Eng. tr. *Moominpappa at Sea*, 1966, 1984, 1991, 1993.
Bildhuggarens dotter, 1968; Eng. tr. *The Sculptor's Daughter*, 1969, 1976.
Mumintrollen, 1969.
Sent i november, 1970; Eng. tr. *Moominvalley in November*, 1971, 1973, 1974, 1991.
Lyssnerskan. Noveller, 1971.
Sommarboken, 1972; Eng. tr. *The Summer Book*, 1974, 1975, 1976, 1977, 1988, 2003.
Solstaden, 1974; Eng. tr. *Sun City*, 1976, 1977.
Libretto för mumin-opera, 1974.
Fönstret, 1976.
Gymnastiklärarens död, 1976; Eng. tr. *Death of the gym teacher*, 1977.
Tio före fyra, 1977.
Den farliga resan, 1977; Eng. tr. *Dangerous Journey*, 1977, 1978.
Dottern, 1977.
Kvinnan som lånade minnen, 1977.
Orm i salongen, 1977.
Dockskåpet och andra berättelser, 1978.
Filifjonkan som trodde på katastrofer, 1978; Eng. tr. *The Fillyjonk Who Believed in Disasters*, 1990.

Skurken i muminhuset, 1980.
Den ärliga bedragaren, 1982.
Stenåkern, 1984.
Vinter i mumindalen, 1985.
Karin min vän, 1987 (facsimile).
Resa med lätt bagage. Noveller 1987.
Rent spel, 1989.
Brev från Klara och andra berättelser, 1991.
Visor från Mumindalen, 1993.
Anteckningar från en ö (with Tuulikki Pietilä), 1996.
Meddelande. Noveller i urval 1971-1997. Helen Svensson, ed., 1998.

Selected Bibliography

Antas, Maria. "Life in the Mist." *Books from Finland* 4, 2001, 252-54.

Antonsson, Birgit. *Det slutna och det öppna rummet. Om Tove Janssons senare författarskap*. Stockholm: Carlsson Bokförlag, 1999.

Gustafsson, Barbro K. *Stenåker och ängsmark. Erotiska motiv och homosexuella skildringar i Tove Janssons senare litteratur*. Diss., Uppsala University. Stockholm: Almqvist & Wiksell, 1992.

Jones, W. Glyn. *Tove Jansson*. Boston: Twayne Publishers, 1984.

Nikolajeva, Maria. "Barnlitteraturen efter kriget." *Finlands svenska litteraturhistoria* 2. Clas Zilliacus, ed. Helsingfors/Stockholm: Svenska litteratursällskapet i Finland/Bokförlaget Atlantis, 2000.

Snickars, Ann-Christine. "Astrid Lindgren and Tove Jansson. I want a Mum. And a Dad. And a Philosopher." *Nordisk litteratur/Nordic Literature* 2003, 102-5.

Stewen, Riikka. "The light of Seeing". *Books from Finland* 1, 1993, 21-24.

Svensson, Helen, ed. *Resa med Tove. En minnesbok om Tove Jansson*. Esbo: Schildts, 2002.

Westin, Boel. *Familjen i dalen. Tove Janssons muminvärld*. Stockholm: Bonniers, 1988.

Eeva Liisa Manner's Elemental Modernism

LOLA ROGERS (UNIVERSITY OF WASHINGTON)

Eeva Liisa Manner (1921-95) was one of the great Finnish writers of the 20th century. Her 1956 collection, *Tämä matka* (This Journey) has been called "[t]he most celebrated collection of Finnish-language poetry of the 1950s".[1] Manner published more than fifteen collections of poetry, numerous prose works, dramas, radio plays, and translations of world literature, but she is best known for her poetry.

Born in Helsinki in 1921, she was sent to live with grandparents in Viipuri, Karelia, then still a part of Finland, when her mother died shortly after her birth. The strict and pious household of her grandpartents may have been one source of the theme of loneliness that pervades much of Manner's writing. Manner described grandparents who seldom spoke to her as a child, and claimed that she herself took up writing because she didn't know how to speak. The loss of Viipuri to Russia during the Winter War of 1939-40 was an important event in Manner's life and in her writing. Her first collection of poems was written as a lament for the loss of Viipuri. In later life she made her home in both Tampere, Finland, and in Spanish Andalucia, where she found some of the beauty and peace she remembered from her early life in Karelia. Manner was the recipient of multiple literary awards, including the Finnish State Award for Literature, the Finnish State Award for Drama, the Translation Award, and the Aleksis Kivi Award. She died in Tampere in1995, at the age of 74.

Manner's poems are quintessentially lyric in their exploration of life's largest questions through examination of its most basic experiences, the interactions with the natural world that have shaped thought throughout human history. Most of her poems exist in a timeless, unspecified place, where the personality of the lyric voice is stripped to its human essence. Her poems are sometimes playful, sometimes solemn in tone, and contain a core of humility in their clear-eyed recognition of the inadequacy of human understanding faced with a fascinating but indifferent universe.

---

[1]   Envall, 189.

The First Finnish-Language Modernists

Following World War II, a large group of Finnish poets published in a breakthrough mode of modern verse, written without traditional rhythmic or metric forms. It was introduced to Finland by Swedish-language poets such as Edith Södergran and Elmer Diktonius in the 1920s, but their works were not widely known among Finnish-language writers and readers. A new Finnish translation, from 1942, of selected poems by Södergran was influential for many young Finnish-language poets, and particularly young women poets of the postwar period. Katri Vala and other members of the "Torch Bearers," a group of young writers who set out to reform Finnish literature and open Finnish culture to the rest of Europe, published a journal, *Tulenkantajat* in the 1920s and 30s and made a strong impression on the next generation of women poets, notably Helvi Hämäläinen (1907-98) and Kirsi Kunnas (b. 1924), who emulated the free verse and avant-garde approach of the Torch Bearers and were important contemporary influences for Manner's work.

Traditional folk poetry was also an important influence on Finnish-language modernists. While rhyming folk forms such as the ballad were a substantial portion of the base of pre-modern poetry in much of Europe, including parts of Finland, there was a founded tradition of non-rhyming poetry in many Finnish-speaking areas. The Karelian region, where Manner spent her childhood, is famous for its folk songs and poems, and was the primary source of poems for Elias Lönnrot's definitive edition from 1849 of the Finnish national epic, *Kalevala*, (Eng. tr. 1889 and later) Finland's most well-known collection of poetry. This traditional Finnish poetry, which is still a popular and productive creative medium, uses rhythm, repetition, assonance and alliteration, but does not rely on rhyme. It was thus a ready source of inspiration for young poets experimenting with form in the 1950s. Many of Manner's earliest poems echo Karelian folk poetry in their rhythms and alliteration.

Early Poems

Like Södergran, Manner lived in Karelia during World War II. Her first collection of poetry, *Mustaa ja punaista* (1944; Black and Red) deals mainly with her hometown of Viipuri, which was part of the Karelian region ceded to Russia during the Winter War. Manner was evacuated along with the more than 420,000 inhabitants of Karelia to the Finnish side of the new border when she was in her late teens. *Black and Red,* published when Manner was 23, used passionate and patriotic language to describe the sorrow of leaving home behind, and received critical acclaim. With her second collection, *Kuin tuuli tai pilvi* (1949; Like Wind or Cloud), Manner's distinct poetic voice began to emerge. While most of the poems of *Like Wind or Cloud* were written in rhyming meter, the flexibility of their metric forms, the plainspoken tone of the poems, and the sometimes parodic, sometimes plaintive juxtaposition of light and dark images and themes led at least one critic to hail them as "modernistic".[2]

The 1950s saw a rush of innovation and the publication of many new Finnish-language collections of free verse.With the publication of *Tämä matka* (This Journey) in 1956, Manner broke from metered verse, and joined Paavo Haavikko, Tuomas Anhava, and other young poets of the 1950s, bringing modernism to Finnish language poetry. With this Manner established her career with her distinct poetic voice and she continued to publish poetry into the 1980s.

Many of Manner's early poems, like the work of many young poets, are about loneliness, but they are also often funny and playful, while retaining a core of melancholy. Kai Laitinen has referred to the poems of *This Journey* as "games for the lonely".[3] Manner's loneliness is often expressed in relation to the natural world, the world of plants, animals, the cycles of nature, and physical sensation. Her early poems contain profound estrangement and separation, sometimes literally expressed as a physical distance, suspension in time and space, separation from nature as well as an estrangement from other people. In the poem "Maan huminan kuulen" (I Hear the Sigh of the Land), from the collection *Like Wind or Cloud*, the "I" of the poem is literally hanging in midair, disconnected from earthly life, but unable to ascend to "heaven's shaft". This idea of suspended animation and inability to take part in life continued to be a theme of Manner's work for many years. A prime example is the poem"Muiston pysyvyys" (Persistence of Memory) from her 1971 collection *Paetkaa purret kevein purjein* (Flee, Boats, with Light Sails) and the use of an image of a bridge the narrator is unable to cross. Watching life drift by, hearing snatches of music from shore, she is imprisoned aside from life, unable to reach either side of the water.

Though this idea of estrangement remained an important focus, over the course of her writing career Manner's poetry evolved from youthful themes of loneliness and an outsider's longing toward more complex and nuanced images examining larger questions of existence and the meaning, or lack of meaning, in human endeavor. In the beautiful seven-part series of "Cambrian" poems from *This Journey*, the narrative voice is separated not in space but in time from the scenes she describes, examining the evolution of life through the "writings" of the geological record and describing life forms in a graceful combination of scientific objectivity and vernacular

---

[2]   Wehanen, no pages.
[3]   Laitinen, 474.

immediacy that evades predictable stances toward the natural world, leaving the reader suspended between emotional and coldly intellectual responses.

Universal Poetry

Eeva-Liisa Manner was a writer of universal themes and an international scope. She lived a large and long part of her life in Spain, where she wrote many of her most acclaimed works, including *Kirjoitettu kivi* (1966; Inscribed Stone), *Fahrenheit 121* (1968), and *Jos suru savuisi* (1968; If Sorrow Smoked). Many of her poems from this period include Spanish titles and settings, others contain Arabian, Chinese, and German language and themes. Of her prolific works of criticism, the majority deal with non-Finnish literature, including such diverse authors as T.S. Eliot, Tasumari Kawabata, Kahlil Gibran, and Carlos Castaneda. Manner was also an active translator from the very beginning of her writing career. As a young writer in the 1940s, she translated popular and detective fiction, and continued to translate novels, plays and poems, including works by Shakespeare, Hermann Hesse, and Franz Kafka. She referred to her translations as the most important aspect of her "writer's education".

Unlike other early Finnish modernists such as Paavo Haavikko, whose poems often comment on modern phenomena in Finnish and European literature and life, Manner's most acclaimed poems, though modern in form, are timeless in content, and are not about Finland, or about Europe, specifically. Her poems rarely refer to specific times or places, but to more elemental settings: a lake shore, a forest, a nameless hillside. Often the traditional elements of earth, air, fire and water are stark environments from which the narrative voice speaks, giving her poems a timelessness and universality. Her poems describe experiences that almost any human being can recognize: a reflection of trees in the surface of a still lake, the sighing of the wind, the flicker of firelight. These ancient elemental ideas are used as rich signifiers of the substances from which human existence is constructed.

Nature and Intellect

The natural world is the focus of most of Eeva Liisa Manner's poetry, whether celebrated for its own sake, as in her 1964 collection *Niin vaihtuvat vuoden ajat* (Thus the Seasons Change), or examined philosophically. A central theme of many of Manner's poems can be described as a conflict between two worlds, the natural world, which is sensual, intuitive and irrational, and the world of human culture, which is intellectual, rational, and lifeless. She uses vivid sensory images as symbolic representations of these two worlds, the one full of textures, smells and subtle colors, the other geometric, vacuous, and colorless. Although the symbolic world of Manner's poems became more complex over time, the theme of life and absence of life, of human beings as intellect and human beings as animal, remained central throughout her work.

The juxtaposition between nature and reason in Manner's poetry is often an ironic one. She is, after all, an intellectual. As Envall has pointed out, "Manner is, paradoxically, a learned, cultured poet who opposes Western rationalism".[4] Over the course of her career, Manner incorporated diverse knowledge of music, visual art, psychoanalytical theory, natural science, eastern religion, and her own memories and impressions into a rich personal symbolism. She placed these ways of understanding in juxtaposition to that mystery, true reality, which, like the real world outside of Plato's cave, can be expressed in the poems only as flickering reflections or shadows. This idea is expressed in the elegant "Ranta ja heijastus" (Shore and Reflection) from *Orfiset laulut* (Orphic Songs; 1960), in which the touch of the tip of a bird's wing is enough to obliterate the image of reality that we create, leaving the real world unreflected, "member by member alone".

To become part of this real world, transcending the limits of human understanding, is an inherently paradoxical task in Manner's poetry. The natural end of our limited understanding is the end of our human life. The mystery and potential transcendence of death returns again and again in her poems, sometimes expressed as a rejoining with the natural world, when the "skin and hair fall away", and sometimes as a crossing over into mystery, spoken of by a voice that is "ready to travel" to the other side, if there is such a place. To be human, in Manner's vision, is to be between, to be an animal who cannot live and die like other animals but cannot, in spite of intellect and consciousness, transcend physical life. This paradox remains central to both the theme and the content of Manner's poetry, an uneasy truce between the purity of intuitive nature, and human reason, which is her best tool of communication. In the long run this bringing together of the real and the reflected, the act of creating the poems that bring these intellectual elements together, becomes an important theme in its own right, and is one of the great satisfactions of reading Eeva-Liisa Manner's work.

---

[4]   Envall, 152.

Kootut runot

Kokoelmasta *Kuin tuuli tai pilvi* (1949)

Maan huminan kuulen

Enää pyydä en mitään. Jo kaiken sain.
Ja mitä en saanut, sen aavistan minä kyllä.
Elämästä nyt itse aavistus olen vain.
Sinen siintoon en yllä, maan puoleen en enää yllä,
ne vaikka pään päällä ja kaukana allani nään.
Kuin pilvi ma jään
nyt keinumaan elämän yllä.

Kuin pilvi ma nään
hämyn, varjoni, maassa ja ylläni taivaan kuilun.
Enää takaisin tahdo en, kaipaa en elämää.
Kevyt kulkea on... Miten soi sävel ilmojen huilun,
miten soi urut tuulen...
Ja kaikki taas pois häviää.
Maan huminan kuulen,
maan ilon ja itkun ma kuulen,
mutta tunne en ikävää,
enää tunne en iloa, ikävää.

En itkeä voiskaan. Olen kuivempi poutaa.
Olen muotoa vailla ja vailla myös elämää.
Ajatuksetta keinua tahdo, vain keinua, soutaa
ja katsella maata allani kimmeltävää,
ikuisuuden kuilua katsella pääni päällä.
Vain katsella. Nähdä. Ja tietää ja ymmärtää,
miten kaunista kaikki on kaukaa katsoen täällä,
miten selvää ja kaunista, turhaa ja häviävää,
miten autius vitkaan tummuu mun pääni päällä
ja nousee ja kasvaa ja ylitse hulvahtaa,
miten vajoon ja hajoon ja hiljaisuudeksi muutun,
joka minussa, minusta merenä aaltoaa...

Hämyn, varjoni, maass' yhä nään ja ylläni kuilun,
ja mitään en tahdo, en kaipaa maailmaa.
Kevyt olla mun on... Miten soi sävel ilmojen huilu,
miten soi urut tuulen –
ja kaikki taas pois katoaa.
Minä huminaa kuulen,
minä kuilujen huminaa kuulen,
joka minussa, minusta merenä aaltoaa...

Post festum

Mä yksin kuljen iltaan himmeään.
Vain varjoni on saattajana mulla.
Hei varjo, nopsempaan siis kävellään.
On mulla ikävä ja ikävä on sulla.

Mut kulkiessa murheet unohtuu,
kun aatos tanssii menon rytmin mukaan.
Ja joka katulyhty, talo, puistoon puu
on outo tuttu, ystävä Ei-Kukaan.

Mut sentään ystävä. Ne meihin katsovat
kuin kaipaisivat ystäväänsä.
Ne vastaan käyvät, ohi kulkevat
ja unohtuvat omaan ikäväänsä.

Ne katsoo silmin kumman totisin.
Ne outoja – – kuin mekin – – ovat täällä.
Ja sateen murhe helmin särkyvin
soi niiden yllä, meidän päämme päällä.

Niin, muukalainen sade, itke vain.
Puun, lyhdyn, talon, varjon murhe soita.
Sun soittos rytmiin menon sovittain
näin seuraan lyhtyrivin auringoita.

Kuin hiili hehkuvat ne pimeyteen
ja varjoni mun tanssii niiden mukaan.
Mä niinkuin hiili sammun sateeseen.
Vain lyhty jää ja varjoni Ei-Kukaan.

Viimeinen laulu
jonka nimi on Sabishii

Tää ilta niin kuin runo on,
niin sairas, sabishii.
Käy tuuli yli nurmikon.
Sen laulu murheellinen on.
Ja kaunis. Sabishii.

Pään yli pilvet vaeltaa.
Ja sade. Sabishii.
Pois kulkee pilvet taivaan taa.
Ja niiden myötä vaeltaa
tää laulu – sabishii.

Ja alla askelten käy tie
niin outo, sabishii.

Se vaeltahan täältä vie
pois sinne missä lopuu tie
ja laulu – sabishii.

Kokoelmasta *Täma matka* (1956)

Kambri
sarja merestä ja eläimistä

I.

Kulkea yli vaihtelevien äärten,
mustien vesien, kuviteltujen porraspuiden,
läpäistä murtuvat solat, vuorten hitaat viivat,
vyörymät, lumiset pilvet, löytää valitut kivet
ja tulla seudulle
täynnä parillisia jälkiä, eläimellistä asutusta.

Nähdä taitettu tuonpuoeinen valo ja maan päälliset huolet,
syödä karvas hedelmä leipäpuun alla
ja tulla nälkäiseksi;
nousta ja kulkea, käudä punotut kengät loppuun,
etsiä virtaa ja tulla ihmisten tekemääle äyräälle,
pestä kädet ja hiukset ja juoda laskuvettä
ja nähdä raskaita unia viimeisestä tuomiosta:
saada aloittaa alusta rutaisesta lätäköstä
pientä alkeellista phuutta täynnä, kuten Dytiscus tai myöhäinen ihminen.

Kulkea, kulkea mihinkään tarttumatta
läpi lian ja lumen, vuorottelevan helteen
ja ankaran menneisyyden ja jääkeuden,
sen joka oli, ja sen joka tulee;
nukkua lumessa ja sulattaa ruumillaan pälvi
suuresta yhteisestä jäätiköstä,
oppia käsien taitoa, hidasta toivomista,
rakentaa tikuista talo ja antaa sateiden tulla,
löytää kulunut polku ja potkitut kivet,
kiven mykkä tiheys; myös ihmiset,
ja vihata lähimmäistään niin kuin itseään;
syödä käpyjä ja valittaa eläinten tähden,
jakaa ateriansa oravan ja näädän kanssa
ja oppia niiden vertaukset ja kieli ja nopeat jäljet.

Oppia vertaukset, ja sekoittaa ne ruumiillisiin asioihin,
oppia salaisuudet, ja unohtaa jälleen,
hukata tieto täällä vaelluksella
läpi ajan ja kerrostuneiden aikakirjain,
vaikeatajuisten kivikirjain ja puuttuvien dynastioiden.

Tulla tyhjäksi ja luopua taikauskosta, uskosta
joka on viisaus, peritty eläimiltä,
kaikilta ahdistetuilta sydämiltä
ja sidotuilta kasveilta ennen eläimeksi-tulemista.
Tulla tyhjäksi ja luopua – –
miten raskas on vaellu ilman taakkaa,
yksinäisyys ilman eläinten yhteisyyttä,
erilaisuus, jota sudet pakenevat ja pelkäävät.

Saapua viimein
kevyenä, väsyneenä,
ilman sanoja, telttaa ja eläinten myötätuntoa
meren tannalle, nähdä ruumiillaan tämä kaikki:
Hyytyvä valo ja pitkät ankarat aallot,
kova avaruus, joka kiertää, vingahtaa,
ja vitkaan jäätyvät tuulet;

lähettää tottumuksesta
tyhjä vene, huuto tuuleen
teitäen että vain sirpaleet pääsevät perille,
tai ei mitään.

II. (Kuoret)

Ei hengitystä.
Vain hiotut kivet
pitkin jäätikon reunaa.
Venheiden ruumiita, eläinten purjeita,
    trilobiitteja, kulkeutuneita luita,
pientä talletettua kuolemaa.
Musteettomia kaloja,
kalkkikirjoitusta,
kukkia jotka ovat eläimiä, tähtiä jotka ovat eläimiä,
eläimiä jotka ovat veneitä, koralleja jotka ovat aivoja,
liituun huolekkaasti painettuja,
uneksien, mikroskooppisesti
hitaita muistiinpanoja varten:

Miten lähellä ovat aikakaudet,
siluri, trias, jura, kuollut kambri,
miten kaukana tämä hetki, nykyisyys,
joka läsnäolevaa karttaa ja alas kurkottaa,
mesotsooisiin uniin,
jos ne ovat unta – –

Ovat kuoret hyljätyt, ja talot murtuneet.
Ovat kivet yksinäiset,
alkulinnut
ovat ylösnousseet,

hätääntyneet linnut laahautuvat
pitkin taivaan kuorta
ja huutavat kivettynein ennussäänin.
Maanpäälliset linnut
jäätyvät oksille,
nokat, luiset huilut ilman ääntä.

Ainoat muistot
järjestetyistä sävelistä
ovat sirot kuoret,
simpukat saranoin murtunein – –
pienet ovet ovat auki ja vievät tyhjiin
huoneisiin vailla mikroskooppista musiikkia,
tyhjät humisevat kammiot
eivät syö enää, eivät vaella pyhiin.
Poissa
on ryömivä lima ja henki.

III. (Myöhäiset Kirjat)

Kääntäkää kivinen lehti ja siinä
    ovat syvälle jäätyneet monimutkaiset silmut,
    silmien luvut.
Tuhatsilmäinen puu, kukan aihe ja kasvin ruumiin aihe,
aihe levitä ja humista ja täytää maa lihavuudella,
joka lahoaa tai ehkä korjataan
kuin saalis.
Kääntäkää lehtiä, niissä on värisevän joksijan aihe,
ravaavien sorkkien, sarvien, sarveissilmien aihe,
aihe paeta kuin kauris, kiitää tuulen mukaan,
kuulla koko ruumiillaan risahtava vaara,
haistaa se tuulesta ja maistaa
    asutuista lammikoista.
Nähdä tiheät kivet ja niissä sykkivä vaara,
joka viritetään, ja osuu,

sillä takana tulevat viekkaat eläimet, jotka
ovat vapauttaneet kädet ja nousseet kahdelle jalalle,
he ovat viisivarpaiset eläimet, heillä
on isot ja raskaat kallot ja raskaat aivot,
ja raajat venytetyt kuin gorillalla,
he ovat toimeliaat eläimet, ja säästäväiset,
he keräävät pieniä päitä vyötäisilleen,
ne kolisevat hauskasti tuulessa
ja tuottavat onnea, ei onnettomuutta
niin kauan kuin kolisevat, luiset korut,

he ovat ahkerat eläimet, ehillä on etevät sormet,
jotka osaavat laskea viiteen ja virittää kielen,

ei soittimeksi vaan surmaamista varten,
he koristavat itsensä tappamisen ja hyväntoivon luvuilla
ja teroittavat kivet tarkoiksi nuomenpäiksi,
joissa on tuhon tykyttävä aihe,
kivestä irrotettu,
nukkuva kiveen.

Kokoelmasta Orfiset laulut (1960)

Preludium

Kun ranta ja heijastus ovat aivan samat
ja ehyt ja tyyni on taivaan ja veden avioliitto,

kun syvä ja kirkas on peilin kuvitelma,
ja eläimet vaeltavat, ja pilvet, ja tumma metsä
humisee syvyydessä ilman tuulta,

tarvitaan vain veteen kastuvan linnun siipi särkemään harha:
valon ja veden ihastunut tunnustus maailmalle,
ohut kuin silkki; mutta se solmii liiton.

Ja maailma, tuore ja kaunis kuin sateen tai luomisen jälkeen,
tai meilenmuutoksen tai pitkän sairauden,
on ainoa, raskas, jäsen jäseneltä yksin.

Kun väsynyt länsi

Kun väsynyt länsi levolle lasketaan
ja punertuu ja tummuu, vuodatetaan
kypsä vuodenaika taivaan äärettömään maljaan,
kun miekat katkaistaan ja kirjat avataan
ja humina laskeutuu kuin siipien lepatus
ja esineet ansoistaan kuin henget kohoavat,
kirkkaampina, ehyet levon jälkeen,

luminen ratsu, aroilla kamppaillut,
pellolle kahlaa, otsalla toinen tähti,
seurassaan lapsi: alaston sotamies;
ja he juoksevat yli kukkivan maiseman
kuin madonnan helman, sinessä aaltoavan
ja äärettömään, valosta kudotun
ja tyhjyydestä.

Ja loppumaton
on kaikkien asioiden kauneus,
hellyys, ilo, leikki, ystävyys ja rauha.
Ja kuultava aamu aamun jälkeen nousee,
oksille linnut.

Kokoelmasta *Niin vaihtuvat vuoden ajat* (1964)

Heikentynyt syksy kuoli

Kujat tulevat punaisiksi, metsät keltaisiksi,
vuoret tummuvat kaukaisessa sateessa,
pihoilla palavat syyslehtien savut.

Kirves helähtää kaikuvammin kuin ennen,
metsän syvemmät äänet kertovat
puunhakkaajan matkan Haukkavuoren rinteellä.
Kaiku kulkee vastarannalla, terävä ja kirkas,
kuin joku näkymätön kaataisi tyhjällä rannalla luultuja puita.

Joskus he tervehtivät toisiaan,
tämä ja se toinen, kaikujen mies,
ja huutavat jotakin
tyynen metsäjärven yli, syvän ja kylmän.

Kokoelmasta *Paetkaa purret kevein purhein* (1971)

Muiston pysyvyys

En päässyt koskaan sen suuren sillan päähän asti.
Päivät lipuvat alitse, roskien ja heijastusten myötä,
jokin kaunis laiva tulee luo, taittaa savupiipunsa
ja katoaa. Toisella puolen on aina auerta,
laiva ui ilmassa tisella väreilevät talot
kuin peilien näyt, pukeutuen usvaan.
Laulua kuului avatusta ikkunasta: sydämeni kääntyy
puoleenne, mon coeur se recommande à vous (à vous à vous).

Hauraita muistoja; kadonneita ääniä, pitkiä kaikuja
            jotka litistyvät veteen
(olisin purjehtinut, jos olisit käskenyt),
kaikki säilöttynä laajenneeseen sekuntiin:

Sillä äkkiä mustiksi lakatut vaunut ajavat sillalle,
pyörä irtoaa, vaunut kaatuvat. Hevonen polvistuu ja vapisee
ja silta on punainen. "Ampukaa se, hyvä Jumala,
ampukaa se", sanoo joku, (ehkä se on) minun ääneni,
            mutta en tunne sitä.
Oliko se minun hevoseni, en tiedä, kai se on kuollut
ajat sitten, mutta muistin hylsyssä (siis minussa)
se yhä lankeaa, kuin tajuntani olisi syöpynyt
tähän halkaistuun hetkeen, joka on kuilu.
Ja irronnut pyörä tulee yhä hoippuen minua kohti
sillan rummun yli, joka sykkii taukoamatta.
En pääse koskaan pois tältä sillalta.

Kokoelmasta *Kuolleet vedet* (1977)

IV.

Sieluja on kaikkialla.
Kaada puu ja teet sen hengen kodittomaksi.
Tai se muuttaa taloosi ja tuo sinne surun,
humina täyttää pääsi.

Minulla on kolme sielua: uni, varjo ja aavistus.
Uni valvoo yöllä, kun minä nukun
ja näyttää heijastuksia tuelvaisuuden peileistä.
Varjo saattaa minut viimeiselle matkalle, joka on jo alkanut.
Se on veljeni, minun muotoiseni, äänetön, vieras,
ja avaa polun hukkakauraan,
jolla on hallan värit.

Se mittaa aironminta ja kääntyy,
kohtaamme veräjällä, vaatteeni putoavat pois,
tukkani irtoa, luuni pehmenevät,
minun pimeyteni lankeaa minun varjooni,
valoa reunat.
Hiljaisuus, ja revityn silkin ääni.

Nukuin kymmenen yötä savuavan tulen äärellä,
tunsin kamferipuun tuoksun.
Sananjaloille oli katettu parantava ateria,
söin, olin kuivasta ruohosta,
valmiina kulkemaan pimeän läpi,
pitkän tien pimeän läpi.

Luulin että kuistille oli heitetty kirje,
mutta se oli vain kuun kajoa.
Minä poimin valoa lattialta.
Miten kevyt se oli, kuun kirje,
ja kaikki taipui, kuin rauta, tuolla puolen.

Villisorsa huutaa
ja aamulla ruoho on kuurassa.
Kuin lasia: ohut hileinen ääni.
Ikävyyden huimaus.
On syksy. Minä palelen tulen loimussakin.
Kylmyys on ihon alla, ei katoa.

Tie on himmeä, kirkas, himmä, keltainen
ja rannalla vaeltavat kahlaaja sumuiset äänet.
Ne ovat lauseita. Ilta kokee verkkojaan.
Metsässä kehrääjän ääni: kutsu tai valitus.
Jokipajun tuoksu, ja kaislan ohut kaanon.

Selected Poems

Translated by Lola Rogers

From *Like Wind or Cloud* (1949)

I Hear the Sigh of the Land

I have it all. I ask nothing any more.
And what I don't have I can surely surmise.
I'm mere apprehension of actual life.
I can't reach the blue, I can't reach the shore,
I can only see them above me, and below, far away.
Like a cloud here I stay
above life, and dangle and sway.

Like a cloud I see twilight,
my shadow on the land, and above me heaven's shaft.
I don't want to go back now, I don't miss life.
It's light and easy to drift... How the flutes of the air their melody play,
how play the pipes of the wind...
And once again everything fades away.
I hear the sigh of the land,
I hear the tears and joy of the land,
but I don't feel sad,
I no longer feel happy or sad.

I can't even weep, I'm drier than drought.
without life and without design.
I want my thought to rock, just row and rock,
and to look down and watch the world shine,
watch eternity's shaft over my head.
Just watch. See. Know, and understand.
How beautiful it all is from far away here,
waste and dissolution, beautiful and clear,

overhead how the desolateness slowly darkens
rising and growing and welling,
how I sink and dissolve and become the silence,
inside me, outside me, a sea swelling...

Twilight, my shadow, is still on the land, above me I still see the shaft,
and I want nothing, I don't miss the world.
It's light and easy to drift... How the flutes of the air their melody play,
how the pipes of the wind are playing – –
and once again everything fades away.
I hear a sigh,
I hear the shaft sigh,
inside me, outside me, a sea swelling...

Post Festum

I walk alone into the evening dark,
with no one but my shadow for a twosome.
So, shadow, let's just liven up our walk.
Because I'm lonesome, and because you're lonesome.

But our troubles are forgotten as we walk,
as thoughts dance to our steps' velocity.
And every streetlamp, house, tree in the park,
is strangely known to us, friend, Nobody.

But anyway a friend. They gaze at us
like they could use some friendship of their own.
Approach us, come to meet us, and then pass,
forgotten in their languishing alone.

They're watching with such earnest, wondering eyes.
Just like us, they're strangers around here, too.
And the rainfall's sorrow rings in shattered pearls,
it rings beneath them, and on me and you.

Go ahead then, stranger rain, and weep.
Sing the sorrow of the tree, the lamp, house, shadow.
Your singing fitted to the rhythm of our step
the rhythm of the suns of the lamp-row.

Like glowing embers in the dark they burn,
my shadow dancing to their syncope.
I go out like an ember in the rain.
Just one lamp left, and my shadow, Nobody.

The Last Song
which is named Sabishii

This evening is like poetry,
so sickly, sabishii.
The wind blows through the greenery.
Sorrowful its melody.
And lovely. Sabishii.

Overhead the clouds drift by.
Also rain. Sabishii.
The clouds depart behind the sky.
And, drifting, are attended by
this song – sabishii.

And underfoot there is a road
so strange, sabishii.

It carries the traveler toward
the place where it will end, the road
and the song – sabishii.

From *This Journey* (1956)

Cambrian
a series about the sea and about animals

I.

To cross over the fluctuating edge,
the black waters, the flimsy footbridge,
to penetrate the crumbling passes, the slow lines of mountains,
the landslides, snow clouds, to find the chosen stones
and come to a region
filled with the even tracks of an animal colony.

To see the refracted, otherworldly light and the cares of the world,
to eat bitter fruit under a bread tree
and become hungry:
to arise and walk, to wear out woven shoes,
to search for a river and come to a man-made bank,
to wash your hands and hair and drink running water
and to have heavy dreams of the last judgment:
to be able to start at the beginning in a muddy puddle
full of small, primitive malevolence, like Dytiscus or a later human.

To walk, walk without clinging to anything
across dirt and snow, over alternating heat
and the harsh past and the ice age,
that which was, and that which will be;
to sleep in the snow and melt a hollow with your body
in the great common glacier,
to learn manual skill, to slow your desires,
to build a house out of sticks and let the rain come,
to find a beaten path and polished stones,
the mute denseness of stone: and people,
and to hate your neighbor as yourself:
to eat pine cones and complain for the animals' sake,
to share your meal with the squirrel and the marten
and learn their metaphors and language and swift feet.

To learn the metaphors, and confuse them with physical things,
to learn the secrets, and forget them again,
to lose the knowledge on this trek
across time and stratified chronicles,
abstruse stone tablets and failing dynasties.

To become empty and renounce belief in magic, belief
which is wisdom, inherited from the animals
from all the stricken hearts
and from earthbound plants before becoming an animal.
To become empty and to renounce – –
how heavy the trek is without a burden,
loneliness without animal communion,
difference, which the wolves flee and fear.

To finally arrive
light, tired,
without words, a tent, or animal compassion
at the edge of the sea, to see with your body all this:
Congealed light and long, pounding waves,
a harsh vastness that circles and creaks,
and slowly freezing winds,

to send, out of habit,
an empty boat, a yell into the wind
knowing that only fragments will reach their destination,
or nothing will.

II. (Husks)

No breath.
Just polished stones
along a glacier's edge.
Bodies of boats, animals' sails,
        trilobites, drifted bones,
small deposits of death.
Inkless fish,
white fresco writing,
flowers that are animals, stars that are animals,
animals that are boats, corals that are brains,
carefully pressed in chalk,
the microscopically
slow memoranda of dreams:

How close the ages are,
the Silurian, the Triassic, the Jurassic, the dead Cambrian,
how far away this moment, the Present,
which maps what is here and reaches down,
into Mesozoic dreams,
if they are a dream – –

The husks are discarded, the houses crushed.
The stones are lonely,
primitive birds
have arisen,

startled birds trail
along a husk of sky
and shout petrified prophesy.
Terrestrial birds
silently frozen, patient,
to windy branches,
their beaks, their bones soundless flutes.

The only memories
of the arranged melodies
are slender husks,
seashells with their hinges broken – –
their little doors are open and communicate
into empty rooms devoid of microscopic music
empty sighing chambers
no longer eat, make no pilgrimages.
Gone
is the creeping slime, and the spirit.

III. (Later Writings)

Turn the stone page and there
   are the deep-frozen, complex eyebuds,
   an account of the eyes.
A thousand-eyed tree, the origin of a flower and of plants' bodies,
origin of spreading and humming and filling the land with corpulence,
which decays or is perhaps retrieved
like spoils.
Turn the pages, here is the origin of quivering runners,
trotting hooves, horns, corneas,
the origin of fleeing like a goat, rushing with the wind,
hearing with your whole body the rustling danger,
smelling it in the wind and tasting it
   in the settled ponds.
Seeing the dense stones and their throbbing danger,
that lies in ambush, and strikes,

after them come the cunning animals, who
have freed their hands and risen on two feet,
they are five-toed animals, they have
large and cumbersome crania and cumbersome brains,
and elongated limbs like a gorilla,
they are industrious animals, and thrifty,
they collect little heads around their waists,
that rattle pleasantly in the wind
and bring luck, no misfortune
as long as they rattle, bony trinkets,

they are diligent animals, they have skillful fingers,

that know how to count to five and calibrate a string,
not for music but for murder's sake,
they adorn themselves with tallies of killing and with good hopes
and sharpen stones into keen arrowheads,
that hold the pulsing origin of destruction,
freed from the stone,
to sleep in the stone.

From *Orphic Songs* (1960)

Preludium

When shore and reflection are exactly the same
and the marriage of sky and water is smooth and complete,

when the mirror's image is deep and clear,
and animals roam, and clouds, and the dark forest
soughs in the depths without any wind,

it only takes a bird's wing dipped in the water to shatter the illusion:
the light's and the water's enraptured confession to the world,
thin as silk: but it binds the marriage.

And the world, fresh and beautiful as after rain or creation,
or a change of heart, or a long illness,
is solitary, heavy, member by member alone.

When At Last the Tired West

When at last the tired west
reddens, darkens, and is laid to rest,
ripe seasons are shed into sky's brimless cup,
and swords snapped in two, and books taken up,
and a humming descends like the flutter of wings,
and things from their cages like spirits ascend
brighter and whole after rest,

a snowy mount, victorious from the steppes,
wades into a field, another star on its forehead,
and with it a child: a naked soldier,
and they run over the blossoming landscape
as over the skirt of the Madonna, billowing in blue
and boundless, woven from light
and emptiness.

And the beauty of everything
is endless,
tenderness, joy, play, friendship, and peace.

And morning after glimmering morning ascends,
birds to the branches.

From *Thus the Seasons Change* (1964)

The Weakened Autumn Was Dying

The lanes turn red, the woods yellow,
the mountains darken in the faraway rain,
the smoke of autumn leaves burns in the yards.

An ax rings more echoing than before,
the woods' deeper voices report
the woodcutter's route over the crest of Hawk Mountain.
The echo travels to the opposite shore, sharp and clear,
as if someone unseen were felling, on the empty shore, imagined trees.

Sometimes they greet each other,
this man and the other one, the man of the echoes,
and yell something
across the still forest lake, deep and cold.

From *Flee, Boats, On Light Sails* (1971)

Persistence of Memory

I never made it to the other side of the great bridge.
The days glide by below, carrying trash and reflections,
some beautiful boat comes along, breaks off its smokestack,
and disappears. There's always a haze on the other side,
the boat swims in the air: on the other side are shimmering houses
as if seen in a mirror, dressed in mist.
A song can be heard from an open window: my heart is offered still
to you, mon coeur se recommande à vous (à vous à vous).
Brittle memories: vanished voices, long echoes that spread out over the water
(I would have sailed, if you had told me to),
everything preserved in the extended seconds:

In that instant the black-lacquered wagons drive onto the bridge,
a wheel comes loose, the wagons collapse. A horse kneels and trembles
and the bridge is red. "Shoot it, dear God,
shoot it", someone says, (maybe it's) my voice, but I don't recognize it.
Was it my horse? I don't know, it's probably dead
long ago, but in the capsule of memory (that is, in myself)
it still falls prostrate, as if my consciousness had engraved itself
into this cloven moment, this chasm.
And the unfastened wheel still comes staggering toward me

over the drum of the bridge, which pounds unceasingly.
I'll never get over this bridge.

From *Dead Waters* (1977)

IV.

There are spirits everywhere.
Fell a tree and you make its spirit homeless.
Or it will move into your house and bring its sorrow there,
the hum will fill your head.

I have three spirits: a dream, a shadow, and a dread.
The dream stays up at night, when I'm sleeping
and shows reflections of the future in the mirrors.
The shadow will take me on the final journey, which has already begun.
It is my brother, shaped like me, soundless, strange,
and opens a path into the oats of destruction,
which are the colors of the frost.

It measures the length of a paddle and turns,
we meet at the gate, my clothes fall away,
my hair comes off, my bones soften,
my darkness falls into my shadow,
the edges are made of light.
Silence, and the sound of torn silk.

I slept ten nights next to a smoking fire,
smelled the scent of camphor wood.
A healing repast was spread for the ferns,
I ate, I was light from the dry grass,
ready to travel across the dark,
across the dark of the long road.

I thought that a letter had been thrown on the porch,
but it was just the glow of the moon.
I gathered the light from the floor.
How light it was, the moon's letter,
and everything sagged, like iron, on the other side.

A wild duck cries
and in the morning the grass is covered in frost.
Like glass: a thin lamellar sound.
Vertigo of weariness.
It is autumn. I am chilled even in the glow of the fire.
The cold is under my skin, it won't go away.

The road is dim, bright, dim, yellow
and on the shore drift the calls of misty shorebirds.

They are sentences. The evening is checking its nets.
In the forest the call of a spinner: an invitation or a complaint.
The scent of river willow, and the thin canon of the bulrush.

Primary Works

Mustaa ja punaista, 1944.
Kuin tuuli tai pilvi, 1949.
Tyttö taivaan laiturilla; Pienoisromaani, 1951.
Tämä matka, 1956.
Kävelymusiikkia pienille virtahevoille ja muita harjoituksia, 1957.
Eros ja Psykhe; Runodraama, 1959.
Orfiset laulut, 1960.
Oliko murhaaja enkeli? Anna September, 1963.
Niin vaihtuivat vuoden ajat, 1964.
Uuden vuoden yö, 1964-65; Komedia, 1965.
Kirjoitettu kivi. Tammi: Helsinki, 1966.
Toukokuun lumi, 1966-67; 3-näytöksinen näytelmä, 1967.
Fahrenheit 121. Tammi: Helsinki, 1968.
Jos suru savuaisi. Tammi: Helsinki, 1968.
Poltettu oranssi; Balladi sanan ja veren ansoista, 1968. Eng. tr. *Burnt Orange*, 2001 (*Modern Women Playwrights of Europe*. Alan P. Barr, ed. New York: Oxford University Press, 123-59).
Paetkaa purret kevein purjein; Teema ja muunnelmia, 1971.
Kamala kissa; Pilakokoelma. Vanhoille lapsille laatinut, 1976.
Kuolleet vedet; Sarjoja yleisista ja yksityisistä mytologioista, 1977.
Santakujan Othello, 1987.
Ikäviä kirjailijoita, 1994.
Varokaa, voittajat. Rajatilanteita, eli kuusikymmentä aspektia erään mestitsiperheen-murhenäytelmään. Tammi: Helsinki, 1972.
Kauhukakara ja Superkissa. Kissaleikki; Prologi ja kaksi näytöstä. Kirjayhtymä: Tampere, 1982.

Selected Works in English Translation

Enchanting Beasts: an anthology of modern women poets of Finland. Kirsti Simonsuuri, ed. and tr. London: Forest Books, 1990.
Fog Horses. Ritva Poom, tr. New York: Merrick, 1986.
Selected Poems. Herbert Lomas, tr. Guildford: Making Waves, 1997.
Skating on the Sea: Poetry from Finland. Keith Bosley, tr. and ed. Newcastle upon Tyne/Helsinki: Bloodaxe Books/Suomalaisen kirjallisuuden seura, 1997.

Selected Bibliography

Ahokas, Jaakko. *A History of Finnish Literature*. Bloomington: Indiana University Publications, 1973.

Eeva Liisa Manner Database. Tampere University Department of Information Studies website. April, 2002. http://www.info.uta.fi/kurssit/a9/manner/mannerkehys.html.

Envall, Markku. *The Period of Independence I, 1917-1960*. Ritva Poom, tr.: *A History of Finland's Literature*. George C. Schoolfield, ed. (*A History of Scandinavian Literatures*, 4. Sven H. Rossel, general ed.) Lincoln & London: University of Nebraska Press, 1998.

Hökkä, Tuula. *Mullan kirjoitusta, auringon savua*. Helsinki: Suomalaisen Kirjallisuuden Seura, 1991.

Laitinen, Kai. *Suomen Kirjallisuuden Historia*. Helsinki: Otava, 1997.

Wehanen, Kyllikki. Eeva Liisa Manner; Kuin tuuli tai pilv (review). Tampere: Valvoja, February 1950.

Kerstin Ekman and the Necessity of Narrative

ROCHELLE WRIGHT (UNIVERSITY OF ILLINOIS)

The career of Swedish writer Kerstin Ekman (b. 1933) has undergone several transformations and realignments. Upon completing studies in languages and literatures at the University of Uppsala, Ekman worked as a documentary filmmaker and folk high school teacher. In the early 1960s she established herself as a skilled writer of crime fiction distinguished by insight into individual and group psychology and sensitive depiction of the natural world. By the mid-1970s, her realistic, socially conscious novels focusing on female characters had attracted significant critical attention as well as a large readership. Ekman's prominent position in Swedish letters was affirmed by her election in 1978 to the Swedish Academy and an increasingly public role in cultural discourse, a role she retains despite resigning from the Academy in 1989.

Since the 1980s Ekman's work has become increasingly complex, incorporating lyricism, fantasy, and intertextual references while continuing to highlight environmental and social concerns. Her novels have been translated into all the major European languages; seven are available in English.

After publishing six detective stories in quick succession, Ekman signaled a shift in orientation in *Pukehornet* (1967; Devil's Horn) by deliberately confounding the expectations of the genre. Rather than providing a resolution to the mystery posed in the plot, the author investigates the function of narrative itself, illustrating both its problematic relationship to the reality it attempts to portray and its crucial role in the creation of order, coherence, and meaning from random events. Ekman returns to this subject matter in several subsequent works, more tangentially in the historical novel *Menedarna* (1970; The Foresworn), where the actions and motives of Swedish-American labor organizer Joe Hill remain inscrutable, even in his own lifetime; it is the image promoted by stories, songs, and legends about him that survives.

Mörker och blåbärsris (1972; Darkness and Blueberry Sprigs), set in an isolated, impoverished area of northern Sweden, depicts the interactions of ordinary people and features a female protagonist, Helga Wedin. The major work that immediately followed, an interconnected series of four novels, expands on this gender and class perspective by tracing the growth and development of Katrineholm, Ekman's home town, through the lives of working-class women and children. The tetralogy – *Häxringarna* (1974; Eng. tr. *Witches' Rings*, 1997), *Springkällan* (1976; Eng. tr. *The Spring*, 2001), *Änglahuset* (1979; Eng. tr. *The Angel House*, 2002), and *En stad av ljus* (1983; Eng. tr. *A City of Light*, 2002) – encompasses about a century, from the arrival of the railroad in the 1870s to the present-day Welfare State. The series positioned Ekman in the epic, historically anchored and socially aware vein of Swedish literature that has been prominent since the 1930s, though her focus on female experience was relatively uncommon in that genre.

In *Witches' Rings* women's roles are constrained by biological as well as social and economic factors, but the picture is not entirely grim. In old age, the scrappy Sara Sabina Lans insists that her husband teach her to read and write, while her granddaughter, Tora, widowed with two young children, makes ends meet by selling home-baked bread at the square. The restaurant owner Mamsell Winlöf becomes a successful entrepreneur whose income exceeds that of the town's most prominent men. *The Spring* and *The Angel House* portray a society in transition as traditional patterns of behavior and modes of thought gradually give way to occupations and outlooks associated with industrialization, urbanization, and modernity. As the concerns of the fictional characters shift from mere survival to the search for self-realization and a meaningful life, the narrative becomes correspondingly interior.

A City of Light abandons the flexible third-person perspective of earlier volumes, employing instead a first-person point of view. External events recede into the background as the story centers on the narrator Ann-Marie Johannesson's psychological breakdown, convalescence, and recovery. Elaborating on the awareness formulated in *Devil's Horn*, Ekman demonstrates through Ann-Marie that the process of identity formation, the search for internal coherence, is intimately connected with the act of narration. By shaping her fragmented, sometimes faulty memories into a meaningful sequence, the protagonist is able to (re)construct both her past and a present-day persona. The prose poem *Knivkastarens kvinna* (1990; The Knife-thrower's Woman) recapitulates this account of disintegration and healing from a more personal perspective while interweaving allusions to myths about descent into the underworld, the Bible, and numerous works of Swedish literature.

Ekman's next novel, *Rövarna i Skuleskogen* (1988; The Outlaws of the Skule Forest; Eng. tr. *The Forest of Hours*, 1998), spans a broad chronological and geographic range, referring to selected events in Swedish and European history from medieval times to the early 19th century. Experience is filtered, however, through an alien consciousness, since the protagonist is a troll who learns to live among human beings. Once again Ekman establishes the significance of narration or story-telling for the development of self-awareness and an understanding of the world. Skord, the troll, learns about people by listening to their stories, gradually becoming aware of chronology and causality and deducing a connection between personal and historical narrative. History is many individual stories woven together, a way of shaping a shared past, yet this narrative inevitably is fragmentary, ambiguous, and contradictory. Skord, as fundamentally Other, nevertheless remains capable of perceiving the world in an intuitive and non-verbal way seldom accessible to human beings.

In *Händelser vid vatten* (1993; Events by Water; Eng. tr. *Blackwater*, 1997) Ekman closes the circle by incorporating some characteristics of the mystery genre. Like *Darkness and Blueberry Sprigs*, the novel takes place in a remote part of northern Sweden where the lumber industry has devastated the landscape and the local economy. Alternating between several narrative strands of approximately equal importance and between past and present, Ekman traces the repercussions of a brutal double murder committed twenty years earlier. The complex, interlocking plot is structured around various mythological patterns; appropriately enough, one of the characters is a professor of folklore.

Gör mig levande igen (1996; Revive Me) concentrates to an even greater degree than the Katrineholm series on female characters, in particular seven women of varying ages, backgrounds, and professions who meet regularly to debate issues of common interest. A similar discussion group, though composed entirely of men, is found in Eyvind Johnson's trilogy about Johannes Krilon (1941-43); Ekman's novel is in fact a multi-faceted intertextual response to that work, borrowing its polyphonic structure as well as many thematic concerns. Johnson, publishing during World War II, offered a ringing defense of humanistic principles and argued the necessity of taking a stand against tyranny and oppression. In present-day Stockholm, the political, social, and ethical issues are less clear-cut, but alienation and racially motivated violence appear to be on the rise. Like her predecessor, Ekman maintains that both action and debate – in real life and through the medium of fiction – are necessary.

Guds barmhärtighet (1999; God's Mercy), *Sista rompan* (2002; The Last String) and *Skraplotter* (2003; Scratch Cards) comprise a trilogy with the collective title *Vargskinnet* (The Wolf Skin) that is Ekman's latest work to date. The time frame of the three novels encompasses much of the 20th century, from 1916 to the late 1990s, with recollections of and allusions to events of the more distant past. In this regard *The Wolf Skin* calls to mind the historical scope of the Katrineholm series, which similarly focuses on successive generations in several interconnected families, reveals social change through the lives of individual characters, and underscores female experience. Set primarily in Jämtland in and around the village of Svart-vattnet, already familiar to Ekman readers from *Blackwater*, the trilogy intersects with that earlier work through shared characters and a similar structure, with several points of view and shifts between past and present. Ekman conveys different and occasionally contradictory perspectives in the trilogy by varying focalization in the third-person sections of the narrative, following, in turn, three generations of women in the same family: the midwife Hillevi in *God's Mercy*, her daughter Myrten in *The Last String*, and Myrten's daughter Ingefrid or Inga, a Lutheran minister, in *Scratch Cards*. In each of the volumes this point of view alternates with that of Elis Eriksson, a local boy who flees across the border, reinvents himself as the Norwegian artist Elias Elv, and returns permanently to Jämtland many decades later without revealing his true identity. The three volumes also share a single first-person narrator, Risten, the Sami foster daughter of Hillevi, who as an old woman in the 1990s tries to reconstruct events of the past, drawing both on written records, in particular journals left by Hillevi, and on her own recollected experience. Though the novels focus primarily on the lives of individual fictional characters, taken together, and especially when read along with *Blackwater*, they provide a paradigmatic history of social change in an isolated rural community.

The trilogy also reiterates and expands on certain thematic preoccupations central to other works of the author. A recurring motif, noted and remarked on periodically by all the major characters and particularly stressed in the final volume, is the capriciousness of memory and consequently of the versions of the past we regard as historically accurate, and more broadly, the inherent futility of attemptimng to convey complex emotional states through language. As in earlier works, recollection may be inaccurate and words may fail, but narration is necessary because it is our only way of creating coherence. In the excerpt from *Scratch Cards* provided here, that realization is present on several levels as Ingefrid tries to reconstruct and reinterpret the past and find words to describe a transcendent experience. Shifts from past to present tense and third to first person suggest the immediacy of remembered events.

The trilogy incorporates numerous instances of repetition and recapitulation, thus illustrating, as Risten notes, that "[b]erättelserna finns inte i en särskild tid. De händer och händer igen" (Stories don't exist in a particular time. They happen over and over again. *Scratch Cards*, 171). One such motif is a pattern of secrecy, loss, and disruption connected with out-of-wedlock childbirth that is reiterated with certain variations in all three novels. In *The Last String*, Myrten gives birth in secret to Elis's child, never informing him and going to great lengths to hide the situation from her mother and foster-sister. After reluctantly allowing her daughter to be adopted, Myrten makes herself known to Ingefrid only posthumously, through her will. Yet as the excerpt from *Scratch Cards* reveals, Myrten's anonymous gift of a concert ticket determined the future course of Ingefrid's life. Ingefrid discovers this connection by chance in the present time of the narrative, when her own adopted son, Anand, finds a copy of the concert program among Myrten's papers. Myrten herself presumably never knew her impact had been so profound.

Skraplotter[1]

Utdrag

Hon hade aldrig funderat mycket på vem det var som skickat biljetten till Johannespassionen i Engelbrektskyrkan. En tant, sa mamma. En som brukade komma hit förr.

Då hade det inte varit särskilt viktigt vem som sänt den. Värre var att mamma försökte smuggla undan den.

Hennes snabba fingrar tar ett av breven som flaxat ner på dörrmattan och stoppar det i förkläsfickan. Inga blir nyfiken och lite full i skratt. Har mamma hemligheter? Kommer det kärleksbrev till henne?

Om hon varit ett barn skulle tanken ha skrämt henne. Men hon ska snart fylla tjugoett.

Det ringer på dörren och när Linnea går för att öppna häktar hon av sig förklädet som är vått av diskvatten framtill. Hon hänger det på köksdörrens handtag. Inga kan inte låta bli att ta upp kuvertet och titta på det. Hon står fortfarande med det i handen när mamma kommer tillbaka.

> Fröken Ingefrid Fredriksson
> Parmmätargatan 7
> Stockholm

Någon hade strukit över adressen och skrivit dit *Mingus* och Pipersgatan 26 med kulspetspenna.

Hon vet mycket väl att hon är döpt till Ingefrid. Men ingen kallar henne någonsin så. Namnet ger henne en känsla av att brevet ändå inte är till henne och hon är tveksam när hon frågar:

Ar inte det här brevet till mig?

Äsch, säger mamma och försöker snappa åt sig det. Det där är bara nåt som kommer.

Nu, så många år efteråt, undrade hon om hon verkligen mindes orden rätt: *nåt som kommer*. Betydde det att det brukade komma brev till henne? Varje år?

Ge mig det där nu, det är ingenting.

Bara en biljett. Säger hon inte det? Att man inte kan minnas ens det viktigaste i sitt liv med den tydlighet som ger säkerhet. Men idiotiska småsaker minns man: mamma stod där med en våt fläck på magen.

Hon funderar nog inte på vem det var som skickat biljetten. Den där tanten som mamma talat om. Hon som brukade komma hit förr. Det är inte så viktigt. Det som

---

[1] Published by permission of Kerstin Ekman.

betyder något är att mamma försöker bestämma över henne. Vad hon ska göra och inte göra. Och mamma är vältalig: Jag trodde inte det där var nåt du skulle bry dig om. Du går väl inte i kyrkan. Då måste hon ju ha vetat vad det var i kuvertet. Det kom kanske varje år. Till jul också? En tant skickar biljetter och mamma kastar bort dem. Som om jag vore en femåring som inte kunde gå till kyrkan och höra på en konsert. En biljett som ligger ensam i ett kuvert. Inte en hälsning. Ingen avsändare. Och så går jag dit. Det måste vara några dar senare. En vecka eller ett par. Buss till Östermalm? Minns inte, Tjugotredje februari. Det betydde väl att påsken var tidig 1967.

Engelbrektskyrkan är stor och skrämmande. Inga förstår inte dess skönhet. Hon är van att lyssna till musik i trånga, rökiga lokaler. När hon hör stråkarnas trevande introduktion känner hon rädsla. Den springer genom kroppen. Trevande, vaggande är musiken. Ingång i ett meditationstillstånd. Så tänkte hon numera. Då kanske hon tänkte *modernt* och att det varit en sorts räddning i kaoset att hjärnan kunde forma ett ord. Hon hade naturligtvis mycket väl vetat att Johann Sebastian Bach verkade på 1700-talet, i dess första hälft. Men ett långt stycke in i musiken tror hon att verket blivit utbytt, att programbladet som hon håller i handen inte gäller längre utan att man spelar *nåt modernt*. Hon tänker på pappa och på den moderna jazzen som blev mer och mer sorglig. Ja, det tycker pappa också. Han menar inåtvänd och splittrad och utan melodi. Stjärnregnet faller inte över Alabama utan i rymder där det är glest mellan molekylerna. Här i Johannespassionens början ställer musiken ut människan i ödslighet och i väntan på en fruktansvärd fullbordan.

Det är Getsemane. Så tänkte hon nu. Sen kom den första kören. Då måste hon ha hört att det inte var modernt. Att det var Bach och 1700-tal, så som hon kanske hade hört det på radio utan att tänka så mycket på det.

Men förnedringen? Att lovsjunga förnedringen – hade hon förstått att det var vad kören gjorde?

Om hon hade gjort det så var det genom musiken, genom dess språng mellan underkastelse och jubel. Några ord kunde hon inte minnas från denna första gång. Hon hade gått in i ett ordlöst drama. Nu visste hon så väl att Jesus gick med sina lärjungar över bäcken Kidron in i örtagården där soldater med facklor och vapen skulle leta på dem och hota dem till livet. Men hon visste inte hur mycket av detta hon hade uppfattat då. Ett helt liv hade letat sig ner i den ursprungliga upplevelsen, många Johannespassioner i flera kyrkor.

Musiken sänker henne – långsamt? – i djup andakt. Fast vet hon vad andakt är? Annat än som ett ord: kvällsandakten i radio. Då stänger man snabbt av. I synnerhet om mamma är i närheten. Linnea är inte likgiltig för det religiösa. Hon hatar det. Men hon ser alltid till att skyla sitt hat med en ton sur förarglighet. Hon vill inte avslöja dess djup. Till vardags låtsas man att man inte har de känslor som skildrades i passioner och sorgespel.

Evangelisten, hans högspända stämma. Så hade hon hört den då och det mindes hon. Och att hans berättelse, vare sig hon förstått att Jesus och hans kära gick i örtagården eller inte, handlade om levande människor. Hon hade säkert vilat i körkoralen om den oerhörda, den måttlösa kärleken. Kanske behövt vila efter chocken då hon förstått att de var människor, de som gick över Kidron.

Nu mindes hon diffust hurdan tiden varit när hon hörde detta, 1967. Ryssarna hade ännu inte gått in i Tjeckoslovakien. Ungern var länge sen – 1956. Pansarvagnar. Människokroppar. Blod på asfalt. Allt det vanliga som nuförtiden gjorde henne slö av sorg. Då var det revoltens tid. Världsdörren stod öppen och slog. Det blåste rakt in i familjen Mingus tre rum och kök men bara Inga kände draget. Bensinen kostade inte ens en krona litern, allting var ju möjligt. Linnea for till bondauktioner i en Volkswagenbuss som hon lastade full med målade skänkar, spinnrockar och kopparsaker. Allt gick inte längre till nyinköp, hon hade börjat samla pengar på banken. Inga tyckte att man skulle spränga Världsbanken och dela ut pengarna till fattiga indianer. Numera revolterade de flesta med en inre kräkreflex och utan drömmar. Dörren var fortfarande vidöppen och de strömmade in – kurder, somalier, chilenare, kosovoalbaner – kanske indianer också. Men man gav dem fack som hette Rinkeby och Botkyrka och stängde om dem. Det stående skämtet på bjudningar var att det var en turkisk hjärnkirurg som hade kört en i taxi dit. Han påminde om en friboren men skuldsatt man i antikens romarrike, som varit tvungen att sälja sig till slav. Men innerst inne var man rädd för att han var en legosoldat från det sönderslagna Jugoslavien och man åkte inte långt ut i förorternas mörker med honom.

1967 hade hon haft en pojkvän som var en upprorets man. Pekkas känsliga bleka ansikte skiftade snabbt uttryck. Han frös mycket. Han skiftade tillhörighet också. Kom i ideologiska gräl och bytte ut bokstavskombinationen i sitt kommunistförbund mot en annan. Ett *l* eller ett *r* var avgörande för mänsklighetens framtid. Han brann blekt. Hon var rädd att han skulle ha stått bland Kaifas män och hetsat, om han varit i den där örtagården för nästan tvåtusen år sedan. Men kanske inte i turbakören. Döda ville han nog inte. Han hade haft förståelse för en del dödande i stor skala. En mycket abstrakt förståelse, hoppades hon.

Att ingenting var abstrakt i denna musikberättelse, det måste vara det som tagit henne så djupt? Örfilen på gården framför översteprästens palats. Men hade hon hört orden och vetat om den? Annat än musikaliskt, precis som Petrus bittra gråt efter det fega svaret. För då hade det redan börjat.

Det.

Så kallade hon det länge. Kanske säger kvinnor som börjar förstå att de är med barn så. De tänker på det och det är inte gott att säga om de menar tillståndet eller embryot.

Det börjar under sopranarian: *Ich folge dir gleichfalls mit freudigen Schritten.* Altarian har hon uppfattat som jämmer Och det är den väl också, den syndiga människans jämrande. Den hade säkert inte haft mycket att säga henne då, ett barn som hon var av sin tid som avskaffat individuell synd och skuld och höll på att göra deklarationsnummer av den kollektiva skulden. Ingen hade anat hur den hemliga skuldkänslan i ett jäktat liv skulle komma att avlösa föräldrarnas följeslagare, som bara varit enkel skam. Fattigskam. Kvinnoskam. Den kunde man kanske mota undan som en efterhängsen hund. Men skuld – den var *die Stricke meiner Sünden*. Den band och snärjde och trasslade in själen i härvor med hårdknut och löpsnara.

Kanske hade hon bara uppfattat altarian som musikalisk jämmer. Som när moster Lizzie hörde Birgit Nilsson på radio och sa:

Har människan ont i magen?

Det börjar med glädjen i sopranarian, med de snabba ivriga stegen. Hon springer in i sitt liv, springer på arians livliga sextondelsfigurer och avlägsnar sig från allt som hon hittills levat och stretat med, så snabbt som om hon faktiskt hade tagits upp till himlen. Eller som man skulle säga nu: till en annan dimension.

Hon tyckte inte om de där orden. Hon ville varken veta av himlar eller dimensioner. Därför hade hon egentligen aldrig talat med någon om vad som hände henne i Engelbrekts kyrka den 23 februari 1967. Hon ville inte låta någon applicera religionspsykologiska termer på det. Hon frös till när hon tänkte sig att Brita sa: Din *unio mystica*. Det skulle hon säkert göra om hon anförtrodde henne vad hänt den gången. Hon kanske skulle upprepa det, använda en term som omfattade alla möjliga människors konstiga upplevelser med en ljusvidgning som hotade att sära själen från kroppen som om de två verkligen varit två och inte bara orden för människa.

Han rörde vid mig.

Det var de enda ord hon tillät sig att tänka om detta och hon visste att de var bristfälliga och barnsliga. Han. Som om han var en man och hade händer. Men jag är en människa. Jag har inte annat än bristfälliga ord. Hon visste inte längre hur hon den gången hade genomlevt Pilatus obehag, hans hotande migrän, och lynchhopens hetsande. Judehatet som turbakören livade upp hade hon nog inte kunnat förstå eller ta ställning till även om hon varit sitt normala flickjag. Men hon var inte där. Hon kunde bara gissa hur musiken med varsamhet tagit henne till slutkörens *ruht wohl*.

Hon är i djup vila och vill inte resa sig i kyrkbänken när alla börjar gå ut efter slutkoralen. *Ruht wohl... ruht wohl... ihr heiligen Gebeine*. Ni var ben i en kropp som trasades sönder, nu är ni värda vilan och all den ömhet vi har att ge er. *Ruht wohl, ruht wohl...*

Hon hade varit med om någonting som hon inte förstod och inte kände igen. Förut hade hon alltid kunnat planera eller åtminstone förvänta sig det som hände henne. Det ingick inte i hennes livssyn och inte i någons som hon kände att det kunde förekomma okända upplevelser. Till och med förälskelsen var hormoniellt och kulturellt förberedd. Hon kände igen den när den kom. *They say that falling in love is wonderful* brukade pappa spela. Det var bara att fylla i med ett ansikte och *I've got you under my skin*.

Men hon hade nog inte förväntat sig mycket av livet. De flesta människor hade nertonade anspråk. De kände sitt samhälles och sina familjers ramar. Att väggarna skulle ramla in, det hade hon inte trott. Att en glädje kunde spränga dem. Och smärta. Tillsammans.

Glädjefylld smärta. Blod och tårar. Kyssa såret. Smeka korset. Hon avskydde det med hela sitt hjärta. Då hade hon inte kunnat något om teologi eller om kyrkohistoria men nu ansåg hon att pietismen hade förvridit kristendomen och gjort den kristne till en sentimental självbespeglare. Så hon hade velat finna andra ord än glädjefylld smärta eller smärtofylld glädje för det som stannade kvar i henne. Men de orden fanns inte. Bara detta: *han rörde vid mig.*

Jag visste ingenting om mitt ursprung. Att jag var avlad och född var lika avlägsen som ens inälvor är. När jag fick diagnosen colon irritabile i våras, tänkte jag ju inte precis på ett varmt tarmpaket som det kluckar och suger i och inte på lukten ur det. Lika overklig var min föreställning om mitt ursprung. Jag hade fötts av en fattig flicka från Jämtland. Min pappa var skidåkare. Det var blodlöst. Dessutom var det inte så.

När Anand hittade programmet till Johannespassionen bland Myrten Fjellströms papper fick jag veta att jag haft en tvillingcysta i mig. Vem skulle hon ha blivit? Och vem har gjort mig egentligen? Linnea har präglat mig, format, skulpterat, friserat och ansat mig. Hon har outtröttligt arbetat på mig i tjugoett år. Sen fick hon ge upp. Då inträdde Jesus Kristus.

Den första mamman födde mig ur sina inälvor, ur sitt blod och sina hinnor, ur slem och kroppsvarmt sekret. Hon stönade fram mig, kanske skrek hon också. När hon först upptäckte mig, förbannade hon mig säkert. Höll hon någonsin i mig? Då borde hon väl ha blivit rörd och velat behålla mig. Men jag var kanske obehaglig. Jag luktade intorkad sperma och tillbakahållna fjärtar och blodkvalm och smärtans kallsvett. Kanske bakfylla också.

Jag hade den kranka blekhet som eftertanken ger och den ofrivillige faderns stora kran. Jag var troll som Kristin Klementsen säger.

Ändå ville mamman frälsa trollet. Hon skickade biljetter. Hon ville att jag skulle gå i kyrkan.

Jag föddes då. Biljetten var ingen papperslapp som kom fladdrande i slumpvinden. Hon ville mig nånting. Till slut nådde hon fram. Den 23 februari 1967 gav mig det liv jag har.

Jag trodde det var Gud. Det var det också. (127-33)

Scratch Cards

Excerpt

Translated by Rochelle Wright[2]

She'd never given much thought to who had mailed her the ticket to the St. John Passion in Engelbrekt Church. A lady, Mother said. Someone who used to come visit.

Who had sent it didn't seem particularly important at the time. What mattered was that Mother tried to spirit it away.

Snapping up one of the letters that fluttered in through the mail slot, she quickly hides it in her apron pocket. Inga is curious and a bit amused. Does Mother have secrets? Is someone writing her love letters?

As a child the thought would have frightened her, but she'll soon be twenty-one.

The doorbell rings and when Linnea goes to answer she slips out of the apron, which is damp in front from dishwater, and hangs it on the handle of the kitchen door. Inga can't resist taking out the envelope and examining it. She's still holding it in her hand when Mother comes back.

> Miss Ingefrid Fredriksson
> 7 Parmmätar Street
> Stockholm

Someone had crossed out the address and written *Mingus* and 26 Piper Street with a ballpoint pen.

She knows perfectly well she was baptized Ingefrid, but no one ever calls her that. The name makes her feel the letter isn't for her after all and she asks hesitantly:

"Isn't this letter for me?"

"Pooh," says Mother, trying to snatch it back. "These things just come."

Now, many years later, Inga wondered if she really remembered the words correctly: *these things just come*. Did that mean she got other letters? Every year?

"Give it to me now, it's nothing.

"Just a ticket." Didn't she say that? Why can't we recall even the most important events in life clearly enough to be sure? Instead we remember silly, trivial things: Mother standing there with a wet patch on her stomach.

She probably wasn't wondering about the person who sent the ticket, the lady Mother had mentioned, the one who used to come visit. That didn't matter much. The issue was Mother trying to make decisions for her, tell her what to do or not do, and Mother knew what to say:

"I didn't think it was anything you'd care about. After all, you don't go to church."

So then she must have known what was in the envelope. Maybe something came every year, at Christmas, too? A lady sends tickets and mother throws them away, as if I were a

---

2   Published by permission of Bonniers Förlag.

five-year-old who couldn't go to a church concert. A solitary ticket in an envelope, no greeting, no name or return address.

And so I went. It must have been a few days later, a week or two. Bus to that part of town? Don't remember. February twenty-third probably means Easter came early in 1967.

Engelbrekt Church is vast and overwhelming. Inga doesn't appreciate its beauty. She's used to listening to music in crowded, smoky rooms. When she hears the tentative opening of the strings she's terrified. It runs right through her. The music is tentative, trance-like, the gateway to a meditative state. That's how she thought of it nowadays. Back then perhaps she'd thought *modern* and clung to the brain's ability to formulate the word as a reprieve from the chaos. Of course she was perfectly aware that Johann Sebastian Bach was an early eighteenth-century composer, but well into the piece she thinks it's something else, that the program in her hand no longer applies and they're playing something modern instead. She thinks about her father and modern jazz becoming more and more mournful. That's what Dad thinks, too. He means introverted and discordant and tuneless. Stars don't fall over Alabama, but in space, where molecules are far apart. Here, at the beginning of the St. John Passion, the music situates human beings in a state of abandonment, awaiting a terrible fulfillment.

It's Gethsemane. That's how she thought of it now. Then came the first chorus. At that point she must have recognized that it wasn't modern, that it was Bach and eighteenth-century after all, something she might have heard on the radio without thinking much about it.

But degradation? Praising degradation – had she realized that was what the chorus was doing?

If she had, it was through the music and its leap from submission to exultation. The text didn't make much of an impression this first time around. She'd become part of a drama without words. Nowadays she knew that Jesus was walking with his disciples over the brook Kidron into the garden where soldiers carrying weapons and torches would threaten their lives. But she wasn't sure how much of this she'd been aware of back then. A lifetime of experiences had superimposed themselves on the original one, many St. John Passions in other churches.

The music makes her drift – gradually? – into a deep, prayerful reverie. But does she actually know what prayer is, other than a word: the evening prayer on the radio? That's when you turn it off right away, especially if Mother is around. Linnea isn't indifferent to religion--she loathes it, but she always manages to disguise her loathing behind a tone of tart annoyance. She doesn't want to reveal how deep it goes. Ordinarily you didn't let on you could experience the emotions portrayed in passion plays and tragedies.

The evangelist, his high, piercing voice. That's how it had sounded then, she remembered. And whether or not she'd known that Jesus and his followers were walking in the garden, the story was about living human beings. No doubt she'd found respite in the chorale about mighty love without measure. Perhaps she'd needed that respite after the shock of realizing they were human beings, those figures who walked across the Kidron.

Now she recalled, somewhat hazily, how things had been back in 1967. The Russians hadn't yet invaded Czechoslovakia. Hungary was long ago, in 1956. Armored tanks. Human bodies. Blood on asphalt. All the familiar things that nowadays made her heavy with sorrow. Back then revolution was in the air. The door to the world had blown wide open and the wind whistled through the Mingus family's four-room apartment, though only Inga felt the draft. Gas cost less than one crown a liter; everything was possible. Linnea drove to auctions out in the country in a Volkswagen bus she loaded down with painted sideboards, spinning wheels, and copper pots. The revenue no longer went entirely toward new purchases; she'd opened up a savings account at the bank. Inga thought they should blow up the World Bank and distribute the money to needy Indians. Nowadays most revolutionaries had no illusions and suppressed a gag reflex. The door was still wide open and in they poured – Kurds, Somalians, Chileans, Kosovo Albanians – maybe Indians as well. They were sent to housing projects called Rinkeby and Botkyrka and the door slammed shut behind them. A standard party joke was that the cab driver who brought you there was a Turkish brain surgeon. He reminded you of a freeborn but debt-laden man in ancient Rome who was forced to sell himself as a slave, but deep inside you were afraid he was a mercenary from war-torn Yugoslavia and you didn't really feel comfortable riding into the darkness of the outlying suburbs with him behind the wheel.

In 1967 her boyfriend had been a revolutionary. The expression on Pekka's sensitive, pale face could shift rapidly. He was always shivering from the cold. His political allegiances shifted, too. He got into ideological arguments and the acronym of his communist splinter group changed. The difference of a letter could determine the fate of the human race. He burned with a pale fire. She was afraid that if he'd been in that garden nearly two thousand years ago he'd have joined Caiphas's men in the taunting. But maybe not in the turba choir. He probably wouldn't have killed anyone. He'd felt there was justification for a certain amount of large-scale killing, but in a very abstract sort of way, she hoped.

That nothing was abstract in this musical narrative must have been what affected her so deeply. The slap in the court yard of the high priest's palace. But had she heard the words and known this was happening, other than through the music, like the bitter tears of Peter after his cowardly response? By then it had already begun.

It.

She referred to it that way for a long time. A woman who's just realized she's pregnant might say that, thinking about it without knowing whether she means her condition or the embryo.

It begins during the soprano area, "Ich folge dir gleichfalls mit freudigen Schritten," I'll follow thee likewise with gladdening paces. The alto aria had seemed like wailing to her, and that's what it was, the wailing of the sinful. It couldn't have meant much to her then since she was a child of the times, which had abolished individual sin and guilt and made collective guilt an occasion for grandstanding. No one suspected that repressed guilt brought on by a stressful life could replace the shadow hovering over previous generations, which had been shame, pure and simple. Poor people's shame, women's shame – perhaps those could be brushed aside like a dog hanging at your heels. But guilt – that was "die Stricke meiner Sünden," the bondage of my sins. It fettered you and held you tight, tangling the soul into snarls with hard knots and snares.

Maybe the alto aria had only sounded like vocal wailing, as when Aunt Lizzie heard Birgit Nilsson on the radio and said, "Does the woman have a stomach ache?"

It begins with the soprano aria's joy, the quick, eager steps. She's running toward her life, running on the lively sixteenth-note figures of the aria, leaving behind everything she's lived and struggled with up till now, as quickly as if she'd actually ascended to heaven. Or as we'd put it now, to a different dimension.

She disliked those words. She wanted nothing to do with heaven or other dimensions, and for that reason she'd never actually told anyone what had happened to her in Engelbrekt Church on February 23, 1967. She didn't want anyone applying terminology from the psychology of religion to explain it. She shuddered thinking about Brita saying, "Your unio mystica" – which she surely would if Inga confided what had happened that day. Maybe she'd repeat it, using an expression that encompassed the bizarre experiences of all sorts of people, creating a wedge of enlightenment that threatened to separate soul from body, as if the two really were separate and not just words for human being.

He touched me.

Those were the only words of explanation she allowed herself, and she knew they were inadequate and childish. He. As if He were a man with hands.

But I'm a human being. Inadequate words are all I have.

She no longer knew how, back then, she'd gotten through Pilate's distress, his lurking migraine, the threats of the lynch mob. The anti-Semitism that the turba choir stirred up would have been difficult for her to understand or respond to even if she'd been her usual self. But she was beyond that. She could only guess how the music had gently transported her to the *ruht wohl* of the final chorus.

She's in a state of deep tranquility and doesn't want to rise from the pew when every-one else begins to leave after the final chorale. *Ruht wohl... ruht wohl... ihr heiligen Gebeine.* Rest well, ye holy bones. Once you were bones in a broken-down body; now you have earned peace and all the tenderness we can offer. *Ruht wohl.*

She'd experienced something she didn't understand or recognize. Previously she'd always been able to plan, or at least anticipate, what would happen to her. It wasn't part of her outlook on life, or the outlook of anyone she knew, that unfamiliar experiences could occur. Even falling in love had hormonal and cultural determinants. She recognized it when it happened. Dad used to play "They say that falling in love is wonderful." All you had to do was fill in a face and "I've got you under my skin."

But she hadn't really expected much from life. Most people's expectations were muted. They knew the parameters of their family and social class. She'd never imagined that walls could collapse, that joy could make them explode. And pain. Together.

Joyful pain. Blood and tears. Kissing the wound. Caressing the cross. She despised this with all her heart. At the time she'd known nothing about theology or church history, but now she was convinced that pietism had distorted Christianity, making Christians sentimental and self-involved. She'd have liked to find different words for what remained with her, not joyful pain or painful joy. But those words didn't exist. Just these: *He touched me.*

I knew nothing about my background. That I'd been conceived and born was just as vague as my internal organs. When I was diagnosed with irritable bowel syndrome last spring I didn't think about a bundle of warm intestines bubbling and contracting or the smell from them. The way I imagined my background was just as unreal. A poor girl from Jämtland had given birth to me. My father had been there for the skiing. It was abstract. Furthermore it wasn't true.

When Anand found the program for the St. John Passion among Myrten Fjellström's papers I discovered I'd had an unformed twin within me. Who would she have become? And who had actually made me the way I was? Linnea had marked me, molded me, shaped, improved, and groomed me. She'd worked on me tirelessly for twenty-one years. But she had to give up when Jesus Christ appeared.

My first mother gave birth to me physically, through blood and tissue, slime and warm secretions. Her moans brought me forth; maybe she cried out as well. When she first laid eyes on me no doubt she cursed me. Did she ever hold me in her arms? If so she should have felt something, wanted to keep me. But perhaps I was repugnant. I reminded her of dried semen and repressed farts and the queasiness of blood and the cold sweat of pain. Maybe of hangovers, too.

I had the pale sickliness of second thoughts and my reluctant father's big nose. As Kristen Klementsen said, I was a troll.

But that mother still wanted the troll to be redeemed. She sent tickets. She wanted me to go to church.

That's when I was born. The ticket wasn't just a piece of paper fluttering in on the wind of chance. She wanted something for me. Eventually she got through. On February 23, 1967 she gave me the life I lead.

I thought it was God. And it was.

Primary Works

30 meter mord, 1959.
Han rör på sig, 1960.
Kalla famnen, 1960.
De tre små mästarna 1961; Eng. tr. *Under the Snow,* 1988.
Den brinnande ugnen, 1962.
Dödsklockan, 1963.
Pukehornet, 1967.
Menedarna, 1970.
Mörker och blåbärsris, 1972.
Häxringarna, 1974; Eng. tr. *Witches' Rings,* 1997.
Springkällan. 1976; Eng. tr. *The Spring,* 2001.
Änglahuset, 1979; Eng. tr. *The Angel House,* 2002.
En stad av ljus, 1983; Eng. tr. *A City of Light,* 2002.
Hunden, 1986.
Mine herrar. . .: Om inträdestalen i Svenska Akademien, 1986.
Rövarna i Skuleskogen, 1988; Eng. tr. *The Forest of Hours,* 1998.
Knivkastarens kvinna, 1990.
Händelser vid vatten, 1993; Eng. tr. *Blackwater,* 1997.
Gör mig levande igen, 1996.
Guds barmhärtighet, 1999.
Urminnes tecken, 2000.
Sista rompan, 2002.
Skraplotter, 2003.

Selected Bibliography

Andersson, Lars. "Den som står bakom. En figur i Kerstin Ekmans rövarroman." *Skuggbilderna*. Stockholm: Nordstedts, 1995, 9-19.

Death, Sarah. "'They Can't Do This to Time': Women's and Men's Time in Kerstin Ekman's *Änglahuset*. *A Century of Swedish Narrative*, Sarah Death and Helena Forsås-Scott, eds. Norwich: Norvik Press, 1994, 267-80.

Forsås-Scott, Helena. "Kerstin Ekman." *Swedish Women's Writing 1850-1995*. London: Althone, 1997, 216-35.

Gruvaeus, Jonas. "Kerstin Ekman." *Svenska samtidsförfattare* 1. Lund: Bibliotekstjänst, 1997, 36-46.

Kerstin Ekman. Swedish Book Review Supplement, 1995.

Haverty Rugg, Linda. "Revenge of the Rats: The Cartesian Body in Kerstin Ekman's *Rövarna i Skuleskogen*." *Scandinavian Studies* 70:4 (1998), 425-39.

Röster om Kerstin Ekman. Från ABF Stockholms litteraturseminarium i oktober 1992. Stockholm: ABF, 1993.

Schottenius, Maria. *Den kvinnliga hemligheten. En studie i Kerstin Ekmans romankonst*. Stockholm: Bonnier, 1992.

–. "De underjordiska källorna." *På jorden: Nordisk kvinnolitteraturhistoria* 4. Höganäs: Bra Böcker, 1997, 412-19.

Wright, Rochelle. "Approaches to History in the Works of Kerstin Ekman." *Scandinavian Studies* 63 (1991), 293-304.

–. "Kerstin Ekman: Voice of the Vulnerable." *World Literature Today* 55 (1981), 204-09.

–. "Narration as Transformative Power: The Fiction of Kerstin Ekman." *Gender – Power – Text: Nordic Culture in the twentieth Century*. Helena Forsås-Scott, ed. Norwich: Norvik Press, 2004,155-68.

–. "Textual Dialogue and the Humanistic Tradition: Kerstin Ekman's *Gör mig levande igen*." *Scandinavian Studies* 72 (2000), 279-300.

–. "Theme, Imagery, and Narrative Perspective in Kerstin Ekman's *En stad av ljus*." *Scandinavian Studies* 59 (1987), 1-27.

Per Wästberg. "Kerstin Ekman i de gåtfulla tecknens rike." *Lovtal*. Stockholm: Wahlström & Widstrand, 1996, 227-51.

Märta Tikkanen:
Her Use of Alcoholism and Rape
as Literary Topics

ANNA LEPPÄNEN (FINLANDIA UNIVERSITY, MICHIGAN)

Märta Tikkanen (b. 1935) is one of the first women writers in the Nordic countries who has discussed feminism. She is a known contemporary Finnish writer and has received many literary prizes for her work: the prize of the Svenska Litteratur Sällskapet in 1972, 1979, 1982 and the Tollander Prize in 1999. She also received the Nordiska Kvinnors Litteraturpris in 1979, the Suomi-prize in 1996 and the Fredrika Runeberg-prize in 2001.

Tikkanen discusses in her works the problems of the working woman, wife and mother and how these roles combine in a patriarchal society. She exposes her own situation in her works and expresses the experiences and feelings common to many women of different nationalities around the world. Her works have been translated into many languages and have been transformed into plays, texts on television and radio, one work, *Män kan inte våldtas* (1975; Men Cannot Be Raped; Eng. tr. *Manrape*, 1977), even into a movie in 1978.

Märta Eleonora Tikkanen (née Cavonius) was born in Helsinki on 3 April, 1935 into a Swedish speaking Finnish family. Her father, Gösta Edwin Cavonius, was a university professor in pedagogy and psychology and her mother, Julia Margit Eleonora Stadius, an elementary school teacher. Tikkanen's family offered her the possibilities to receive an education and to become exposed to the capital's cultural life.

Tikkanen studied Swedish literature at Helsinki University. She received her master of arts-degree in 1961 and pursued a remarkable career. She worked as a journalist with the newspaper *Hufvudstadsbladet* (1956-1961), she was a teacher (1961-1966), the head of Svenska Arbetsinstitut (1972-1979) and has written columns and reviewed books for the newspapers *Ilta-Sanomat* and *Aftonbladet* as well as for the monthly supplement of the newspaper *Helsingin Sanomat* and various magazines. Tikkanen has worked as a freelancer with television and radio and has written children's plays and other plays.

Between 1958-1962 Märta Tikkanen was married to Leif Peter Ginman with whom she had one child. She met Georg Henrik Tikkanen, her second husband, at the Helsinki newspaper *Hufvudstadsbladet* where they were both working. Tikkanen (1924-1984) was a journalist, an author and a graphic artist. They began their relationship while both had other relationships in marriage. She decided to leave her husband and took her baby with her. Tikkanen came to live with her and they married in 1963 and had three children. Märta Tikkanen expected much from her marriage. Both she and her husband were able to work and write together and inspire each other. But Henrik's drinking became a problem as Märta was concerned with children and housework while proofreading her husband's texts. In 1969 she resumed her writing and took part in literary symposiums and meetings without receiving significant support from her husband.

Certain themes permeate Tikkanen's work: How to be a (working) woman, mother and wife. Another important theme is love: Love that seems impossible, love that cannot reasonably be explained. Tikkanen draws much from her own life in her writing. She openly exposes herself and her position. She does not hide anything from the reader and maybe that is why the reader finds it easy to identify him- or herself with the author and/or the text. Tikkanen belongs to a generation of women who openly transform their own lives into literature, who transform "private" into "public".

Tikkanen's works are often read (and not always rightly so) as a dialog with her husband's memoir novels, the "Address Suite": *Brändövägen 8 Brändö Tel. 35* (1975; Eng. tr. *A Winter's Day/Snob's Island*, 1980), *Bävervägen 11 Hertonäs Tel. 78035* (1976), *Mariegaten 26 Kronohagen* (1977), *Georgsgatan* (1980) and *Henriksgatan* (1982). In these *romans à clef* Henrik Tikkanen depicts alcoholism, love affairs and degeneration of his upper-class family. These novels aroused created a stir in Helsinki. The Swedish-speaking Finnish community tended to concentrate too much on the fact Märta Tikkanen was married to the well-known Henrik Tikkanen.

Märta Tikkanen's debut novel *Nu imorron* (Now Tomorrow) was published in 1970 and her second novel *Ingenmansland* (No Man's Land) in 1972. Between these two novels Tikkanen had read a great deal of Women's Liberation-literature (Kate Millett, Gloria Steinem, Betty Friedan, Robin Morgan and Valerie Solanas). This placed and connected her personal experiences to a larger picture, to the women's movement in the larger context of political movement and solidarity of women and also affected her work. *Now Tomorrow* is a first-person narrative but the same protagonist, Fredrika, in the second novel acts in the third person and is actively taking part in political meetings more consciously trying to solve her problems.

Her next novel *Vem bryr sig om Doris Mihailov* (Who Cares about Doris Mihailov) from 1974, is about loneliness and the exercise of power. Tikkanen describes it as her most pessimistic book, whereas her next novel *Manrape* from 1975 can be regarded as her most aggressive work. It became her international breakthrough. In 1978 the renowned Finland-Swedish director Jörn Donner made a movie, *Manrape*, based on the book. The novel tells a story about Tova Randers who is raped on her 40th birthday. She decides, after long consideration, to take matters into her own hands. She finds her rapist and rapes him in return, although in legal terms, a man cannot be raped. When Tova Randers reports her actions to the police, she is not taken seriously, since a man cannot be raped. The novel argues that women cannot fantasize about being raped. The myth that they all want to have sex, even though they say "no", is being passed down from father to son. The point is that men's and women's equality before the law is a precondition of fighting against subordination. Also, in her book Tikkanen discusses the relationship and the power roles between men and women.

The reception of *Manrape* in Finland was harsh. But in other Nordic countries, for example in Sweden, it gave rise to a lively debate. Sweden, at the time, was also changing its sexual legislation and the book with its rape issue made people react. Reactions in Finland were moralistic, condemnatory and indignant. This reception came as a shock to Tikkanen. It made her question her identity and she only came out of her crisis when a friend sent her Susan Brownmiller's *Against Our Will. About Men, Women and Rape* (1975). After reading Brownmiller's book Tikkanen realized to what degree her book was of current interest and rape is about power relations. But when Brownmiller's book was reviewed in *Hufvudstadsbladet*, there was no mention that a Finnish writer had written about the subject. In this book she raised rape as an issue in people's consciousness.

The Nordic Prize for Literature was established in 1962 but in the following seventeen years no woman writer received it. Responding, women critics and women writers in Scandinavia in 1979 established the alternate prize, Nordiska Kvinnors Litteraturpris. Tikkanen's *Århundradets Kärlekssaga* (Eng. tr. *The Love Story of the Century*, 1984), a collection of prose poems from 1978, received the first prize. Despite assumptions it was not an "answer" to one of Henrik's novels but was written at the same time. She did not write *Love Story of the Century* in response to her husband's writings and did not plan to publish it.

The Love Story of the Century is probably Tikkkanen's most outstanding work. It is strongly autobiographical, with stark realism and intense passion and a fierce outburst of emotions. It describes the alcoholism of the father of the family and its effects. But the poem also focuses on the problems of sexuality, love and trust between man and woman. The perspective is very subjective. Everything is seen through a woman's eyes as Tikkanen discusses woman's identity, hopes and disappointments. This work also deals with the question of how a woman can face aggression and anger, how she can fight and defend her children and win over a guilty conscience.

The discussion of alcoholism attracted much attention and caused a stir. Tikkanen touched a social issue in many people and reactions were strong. Alcoholism had never been so close in Finnish literature. Her point of view is that of the wife (or child), who has to bear the reality of alcoholism, with its violence, smells and vomiting. There is nothing pitiful in alcoholism.

The Love Story of the Century is dedicated to Henrik. It is in three parts and is direct, open and honest. In the first part Tikkanen writes about alcoholism, how it affects 'him' (Henrik), 'her' (Märta) and their children. The opening lines ask why she has not left him yet although the children can no longer endure the abuse. The answer is found in the poem. Tikkanen tells of her own childhood, her father, and how she could not have begun life in a more secure environment, whereas Henrik's childhood was an unhappy one with an alcoholic father. Tikkanen writes about Henrik and her children who are afraid of their father sitting with the gun all night long (when he is drunk he always talks about suicide). There is a child ten years old, drawing monsters who at night cannot go to sleep. Why does Henrik feel sorry for himself? Why is he lying there sobbing? Why is he not thinking of his children who dare not go to sleep? In fact, Henrik is a selfish child. His children are suddenly adults sooner than is necessary, protecting and comforting their father – the roles have been reversed. He has age and size. Yet, he represents the youth of his children and the fact they exist at all. He resents the spotlight does not shine on him alone. He is magnified only by alcohol and its power.

Märta Tikkanen is sarcastic about Henrik's drinking: The faster the better. It is not only practical, but also saves money because he gets drunk fast, vomits and passes out. When he is asleep the children have no need to be scared. They do not have to come home for dinner. Now she has time for herself, time to write, to have long telephone conversations with friends, without him listening to every word. She no longer is responsible for his drinking or talking about suicide. Märta Tikkanen is sarcastic about the book reviewers, who wrote about Henrik's honest account on alcoholism in his works. They forgot the smell of drink, vomiting and diarrhea. Tikkanen writes about her anger and hatred. She writes about how he would physically abuse her. Not for lack of love but because of love's despair.

In the second part Tikkanen writes about the relationship with Henrik and his cheating, love and jealousy of her work and how she finally found herself. In addition, she discusses her anger and hatred, which she grew up having to hide and suppress. Märta's and Henrik's love seems like a roller coaster with its ups and downs. Henrik doubts Märta's love. He loves Märta dearly but he loves his love more than her. But she wants him to love her less and respect her more. But, maybe, there is a chance if they dare to trust each other? Every day she lived with him she did so because she wanted to. Clearly Henrik was jealous of her work. Why should she work when he could earn her monthly salary in one afternoon? But Märta wanted to exist on her own terms, not his. She needed a social context to belong to, with friends and a place to be without him. Why does her job threaten him when his job does not bother her?

In the third part, Tikkanen addresses other women. She writes about women's position in a world of men and how hard it is to have time to sit and write. She begins with a portrait of her own mother's grandmother sitting at a white desk. Then she writes about her own mother who wanted and needed to have a desk but there was never a space for it although Märta's father had his own study and the children had their own desks. Tikkanen refers to all the mothers she would like to write about. She refers to Fredrika Runeberg and other women. Fredrika, the wife of Finnish national poet Johan Ludvig Runeberg (1804-1877), was also a writer and her husband was jealous of her work as well. Coincidentally a woman named Fredrika is the protagonist in Tikkanen's first two novels!

Again, Tikkanen mentions the deception. She can forgive all the other times but *not* the first time. She writes about the mornings when before breakfast with the family she had a poem in her head, but when she sits down, the poem is gone. Tikkanen writes about the importance of a woman having her own name and about how women should stop oppressing themselves and allow themselves the feelings of disappointment and hatred. But they must move, even though slowly creeping forward. There are so many different layers and themes in *The Love Story of the Century*: alcoholism with its many effects on the family life, difficulties in a relationship, children, deception, violence, women's work and free time. Tikkanen expected her work to open a dialogue between Henrik and her again and get to the root of their problems. But that did not happen.

Whereas *Mörkret som ger glädjen djup* (1981; The Darkness that Gives Happiness Depth) is a poetry collection dealing with two different mothers in two different centuries and their relationship with their mentally disturbed son, *Sofias egen bok* (1982; Sofia's Own Book) is a co-authored prose work about Tikkanen's own daughter Sofia who suffers from MBD (Minimal Brain Dysfunction) syndrome.

Also Märta Tikkanen's latest book, *Två – Scener ur ett konstnärsäktenskap* (2004; Two – Scenes from an Artist's Marriage) is autobiographical and has received considerable attention. Tikkanen writes about hers and Henrik's, two strong artists', marriage and life together and discusses what it was to be a woman and working mother in Scandinavia in the 1960s, 70s and 80s and what it means to be a woman writer in Scandinavia living together with an other artist. Overall *Två – Scener ur ett konstnärsäkten-skap* is a review of the everyday life in Märta's and Henrik's marriage but the work also offers valuable insights into the cultural life of the past decades and what it means to belong to a Swedish-speaking minority in Finland.

Henrik Tikkanen's voice is present in the book through his drawings and aphorisms. Why is he so strongly present in the book? It is as if Märta Tikkanen wants to say that she and Henrik are finally able to stand together complementing each other. On the last pages, Märta writes touchingly and truthfully about the last days of Henrik's life (Henrik Tikkanen died in 1984).

Tikkanen's last sentences in *Två – Scener ur ett konstnärsäktenskap* about her life with Henrik have gained a status of aphorism in Finland: "I miss him often. Not for a moment have I wished him back." The same paradox is also present in *The Love Story of the Century*: love and hate, the inability to be apart, the impossibility to live together. *Two – Scenes from an Artist's Marriage* makes it possible to understand why Märta's and Henrik's relationship might well indeed be "the love story of a century".

Århundradets kärlekksaga[1]
The Love Story of the Century[2]

Utvalda dikter
Selected Poems

Translated by Stina Katchadourian

Först känns det skönt	At first it feels good
rent svindlande och obegripligt	quite incredibly and tremendously good
skönt	that in spite of everything
att det trots allt också finns de som ser	there also are people who see
bakom fasaden	behind the façade
som vet	who know
och inser	and realize
Men sen blir allting	But then everything
bara ännu svarare	gets only more difficult
Sen kommer frågan:	Then the question comes:
Varför går du inte?	Why don't you leave?

---

[1] Published by permission of Märta Tikkanen.
[2] Published by permission of Stina Katchadourian.

Otaliga ganger har jag varit
på väg

Innumerable times I've been
on my way

om denhär perioden inte är
den sista
då går jag

if this drinking bout isn't
the last
then I'll leave

om elakheterna går ut over
barnen
då går jag

if his malice affects
the children
then I'll leave

om han dessutom börjar
ljuga
då går jag
och bär han nånsin hand
på mej
då går jag

if he also starts
to lie
then I'll leave
and if he ever uses force
on me
then I'll leave

när barnen inte längre
orkar
då bara måste jag gå

when the children can no longer
take it
then I'll simply have to

Och allting hände
Ändå gick jag inte

And all of it happened
Still, I didn't leave

Varför?
(...)

Why?
(...)

En så ärlig skildring
av alcoholism
säjer kultursidornas kloka män

Such an honest account
of alcoholism
say the wise men in the book review
sections

Hur kommer det sej
att ingen av dem
saknar
tillexempel lukterna?

Strange, that none of them
feel there's something missing –
like the smells,
for example

Den vassa genomträngande konjakslukten
som hugger en i mellangärdet
så fort man kommer inom dörren
Den ljumma runda stanken
av konjak utspädd med magsafter
när du har spytt opp alltsammans

The sharp penetrating brandy smell
that stabs you in the gut
as soon as you come through the door
The lukewarm bulging stench
of cognac diluted by gastric juices
when you've vomited it all up

(…)

(…)

Men allra vämjeligast
ölets humledrank
som du flåsar over mig

But most disgusting of all
the smell of putrid hops
you breathe over me

när du för femtusende gången
tror att öl är befrämjande för potensen, ha!
Mäsklukten som härsken lägger sej överallt

i sovrummet
när du har slocknat med kläderna på

tvärs över båda sängarna
saliven som ölbrun rinner over hakan

Diarrén som osvikligt
blir följden
känns i huset flera dar
tillsammans med det beska hemineurinet
som man kan får så vita tänder av

Bara en sån sak
Bara lukterna
(...)

Du berättar
om hur du somnade innanför dörren
med huvudet på din hund många nätter
hur du cyklade och grät
när din hund dog
att hunden betydde mer
för dej
än din pappa och din mamma
som aldrig var nyktra eller hemma
och som inte visste
vad de skulle ha dej till

Det är sorgligt
och du gråter

Jag sitter i stolen mittemot dej
och jag hinner tänka mycket
för historien är inte kort
och det är inte första gången
jag hör det

Du berättar
och jag sitter och undrar
varför du inte säjer nånting
om de kvällar när dina barn
inte har vågat somna
utan har slunkit runt hörnen
och lurpassat på dej –
pappa har väl inte börjat dricka igen
hur mår pappa

when for the five thousandth time
you think beer enhances your sexual power
The smell of rancid dregs hovering above
                                    everything
in the bedroom
after you've passed out with your clothes
                                    on
across both beds
the saliva that beerbrown runs down across
                                    your chin
The diarrhea that follows
without fail
can be felt in the house for several days
along with that drastic purge
which makes your teeth so white

Just that
Just the smells
(...)

You're telling me
how you fell asleep on the landing
resting your head on your dog many nights
how you biked around and cried
when your dog died
that the dog meant more
to you
than your father and your mother
who were never home or sober
and who did not know
what they wanted for you

It is sad
and you cry

I'm sitting in the chair opposite you
and I've got time to think a lot
because the story is not short
and it isn't the first time
I'm hearing it

You talk
and I sit and wonder
why you don't say anything
about the nights when your kids
haven't dared to go to sleep
but have sneaked around the corner
and spied on you –
Dad hasn't started drinking again, has he?
How's Dad?

här luktar väl inte
konjak
Han dricker väl säkert säkert inte
denhär natten?

Medan du gråter dej till sömns
för att det är så synd om dej
som hade en pappa som var
alkoholist

så sitter jag och undrar när
mitt hat
kommer att bränna dej till
vit aska

medan du ligger där och snyftar
utan en tanke på
att dina barn ju också har
en pappa
(...)

Ingen slog mej
nånsin

När jag var liten
knäppte de mej
på fingrarna och sa
Nej!
Då rörde jag inte deras böcker
på bokhyllan längre
(...)
När du var efter mej
med eldgaffeln engång
för många år sen
när du var full
var jag aldrig rädd för dej
för det var inte mitt namn
du skrek
när du höjde eldkaffeln
och du lugnade dej genast
när jag tog din hand
och talade med dej
så du hörde
att rösten var min

Ingen slog mej nånsin
och aldrig var jag
fysiskt rädd
för nån som kunde tänkas
slå mej

No smell of brandy
around?
Are you really sure he won't drink
tonight?

While you're crying yourself to sleep
because you feel sorry for yourself
who had a father who was
alcoholic

I sit wondering when
my hatred
will burn you
to white ashes

while you're lying there, sobbing
without thinking for one second
that your kids, too, have
a father
(...)

Nobody ever
hit me

When I was little
they slapped
my wrist and said
No!
After that I never touched
their books on the bookshelf
(...)
The time you were after me
with the fireplace poker once
many years ago
when you were drunk
I never feared you
because it wasn't my name
you shouted
when you lifted the poker
and soon you calmed down
when I took your hand
and spoke to you
so you heard
that the voice was mine

Nobody ever hit me
and never was I
physically afraid
that someone might
hit me

tills du slog mej	until you hit me
Du har all anledning	You have every reason now
att vara rädd	to be afraid
för mej	of me
(...)	(...)
I ultrarapid	In slow motion
lifter du din hand	you raise your hand
som ska slå mej	that will strike me
mycket hinner på	Many thoughts
genom min hjärna	pass through my mind
innan din hand	before your hand
är frame vid mej	reaches me
tanken	the thought
på alla kvinnor	of all women
i alla tider	in all times
som har upplevt denhär sekunden	who have known this second
sekunden innan handen slår	the one before the hand strikes
skräcken	the fear
som förlamar	that paralyzes
så jag inte förmår	making me unable
slita mej loss	to get away
bita sparka fly	bite kick free
jag kan inte öppna munnen	I can't open my mouth
jag skriker inte	I don't scream
känslan	the feeling
av att vara utlämnad	of being deserted
utan återvändo	with no turning back
utan möjligheter	with no options
inte rå på	not to have strength
inte ha kontroll over	not to have control
inte kunna nånting	not to be able to do anything
inte kunna nånting	not to be able to do anything
och slutligen	and finally
det otroliga i det	the incredible
som nu är over oss –	in what's happening to us –
det är inte tänkbart	it is inconceivable
det kommer inte att hända	it won't happen
det kan inte ske	it can't happen
du	you
kan inte slå	cannot hit
mej	me

Innan din hand
är framme vid mej
vet jag redan:
detta drabbar oss inte
av kärleks brist
utan av kärleks förtvivlan

ändå
är det svårt att fatta
omöjligt att glömma
(...)

Jag älskar dej så oerhört
sa du
ingen har nånsin kunnat älska som jag
Jag har byggt en pyramid av min kärlek
sa du
jag har placerat dej på en piedestal
högt ovanför molnen
Dethär är århundradets kärlekksaga
sa du
den kommer alltid att bestå
i evighet ska den beundras
sa du

För mej var det svårt att sova
de sjuhundratrettio första nätterna
sen jag insett
hur oerhört du älskar
din kärlek
(...)

Vi flyttade ihop
inte för att vi
ville det
utan för att vi låta bli

Vi flyttar inte
ifrån varannan
fast vi vill det
för att vi fortfarande
inte kan låta bli
varann

Om dethär är hat
hur ser då kärlek ut?
(...)

Noga kringgärdar du

Even before your hand
reaches me
I already know:
this comes to us not
from lack of love
but from love's despair

still
it is hard to comprehend
impossible to forget
(...)

I love you so immensely
you said
no one has ever been able to love like me
I have build a pyramid of my love
you said
I have placed you on a pedestal
high above the clouds
This is the love story of a century
you said
it will last forever
in eternity it will be admired
you said

I had difficulty sleeping
the first seven hundred and thirty nights
after I'd realized
how immensely you love
your love
( )

We moved in together
not because we
wanted to
but because we couldn't help it

We don't move
apart
although we want to
because we still can't leave
each other
alone

if this is hatred
what then does love look like?
(...)

Carefully you fence in

mitt liv	my life
När jag har startat från jobbet	When did I set out from the job
och när kommer jag hem	and when do I get home
och vad har jag gjort	and what have I done
en tom halvtimme	that extra half hour
mer än vägen rimligtvis	more than my return reasonably
kunnat ta	could have taken
ens i rusningstid?	even during the rush-hour
Mycket upprörd	Extremely upset
när jag har rakat mej	when I've just shaved
under armarna	my armpits
För vems skull	For whose sake
rakar jag mej egentligen	do I really shave
under armarna?	my armpits?
Vad är det förresten	And besides, what is it
som tvingar mej	that forces me
att jobba	to work
och göra mej onåbar	and make myself in accessible
när du kan	when you can
försörja mej	support me
så jag kan stanna	so I could stay
hemma och vänta på dej	home and wait for you
dagen lång?	all day long?
Det kan väl hända	It might well be
att du tycker	that you think
att friheten kan inte vara	my freedom can't be
så viktig	that important
för mej	to me
Men det beror ju bara på	But of course that's only because of
Din oerhörda	your enormous
kärlek	love
Varför uppskattar ja inte	Why don't I appreciate
din kärlek?	your love?
(...)	(...)
Hur ska jag kunna förklara	How can I explain
det paradoxala I	the paradoxical fact
att jag måste ha ett job	that I need my job
som tar för mycket av min tid	that takes too much of my time
för att jag har dej	because I have you
som tar resten av tiden	who take the rest of the time
(...)	(...)
Sjutton minuter i bussen	Seventeen minutes in the bus
när ja hinner läsa	when I have time to read
eller tvinna på en dikt i huvudet	or turn a poem over in my head
eller bara tänka på över nånting svårt	or just mull over something difficult

som hör ihop med det ställe
som just har krävt
hela mej
innan nästa ställe
som kräver hela mej
har slukat mej

Så länge jag har
mitt utslitande stimulerande
bedövande job
har jag iallafall nånstans
där jag kan vara
utan dej
så att jag orkar
komma hem igen
till dej
(...)

Behåll dina rosor
duka av bordet
istället

behåll dina rosor
ljug lite mindre
istället

behåll dina rosor
hör vad jag sager
istället

älska mej mindre
tro på mej mera

Behåll dina rosor!
(...)

Varje dag
jag levde tillsammans med dej
gjorde jag det
för att jag ville det

Varje gang
det var du
och ingen annan för mej
var det för att det var dej
jag ville ha

Alltid
när jag kommer tillbaka till dej
var det för att det var

connected with the place
that's just demanded
all of me
before the next place
that demands all of me
would have devoured me

As long as I've got
my demanding stimulating
numbing job
I've still got some place
where I can be
without you
so that I'll have the strength
to come home again
to you
(...)

Keep your roses
clear the table
instead

keep your roses
lie a little less
instead

keep your roses
listen to what I say
instead

love me less
respect me more

Keep your roses!
(...)

Every day
that I lived with you
I did so
because I wanted to

Every time
that it was you
and no one else for me
it was because it was you
I wanted

Always
when I came back to you
it was because it was

tillsammans med dej
och ingen annan
jag ville vara

together with you
and no one else
that I wanted to be

Först
när du vågar tro
att denhär dan
och alla andra dagar
är ett fritt val för mej
– du eller inte du –

Only
when you dare to believe
that this day
and all other days
are a free choice for me
– you or not you –

kan du och jag fortsätta
att leva
tillsammans
(...)

can you and I go on
living
together
(...)

Det är dags
för oss
att skrota ner
vårt dåliga samvete systrar

It is time
for us
to scrap
our guilty conscience, sisters

dethär samhället
lever
på vårt dåliga samvete

this society
lives
off our guilty conscience

man behöver inte alls
besvära sej med
att förtrycka oss
så länge vi nogsamt
förtrycker oss själva

no need at all
to bother about
oppressing us
as long as we
oppress ourselves

Det får räcka nu

This is enough

Nu är det dags
att skota ner
vårt dåliga samvete systrar

Now it is time
to scrap
our guilty conscience, sisters

Nu gäller det
för oss
att tillåta oss

Now we have
got to
allow ourselves

besvikelsen
ilskan
vreden
hatet

the disappointment
the anger
the rage
the hate

När vi har hatat färdigt
reser vi oss
och går

When we've done hating
we'll get up
and go

Primary Works

Eller vad tycker ni?, 1970.
En enda stor familj (together with Henrik Tikkanen and Kristin Olson), 1970.
Nu imorron, 1970.
Man borde, 1971.
Lunch med Beryl, 1971.
Ingenmansland, 1972.
Vem bryr sig om Doris Mihailov, 1974.
Hälsningar från Doris Mihailov, 1975.
Män kan inte våldtas, 1975; Eng. tr. *Manrape*, 1979.
Irtep, 1976.
Århundradets kärlekssaga, 1978; Eng. tr. *The Love Story of the Century*, 1984.
Våldsam kärlek, 1979.
Mörkret som ger glädjen djup, 1981.
Sofias egen bok, 1982.
Du tror du kuvar mig, liv? (edited with Tua Forsström), 1984.
Henrik, 1985.
Rödluvan, 1986.
Önskans träd, 1987.
Storfångaren, 1989.
Arnaia kastad i havet, 1992.
Bryta mot lagen, 1992.
Personliga anlägenheter, 1996.
Sofia vuxen med sitt MBD, 1998.
Kärlekens omöjlighet, 1999.
Arnaia, 2002.
Två – Scener ur ett konstnärsäktenskap, 2004.

Selected Bibliography

Linnér, Sven. Från Dagdrivare till Feminister. Studier i Finlanddsvensk 1900-tals litteratur. Helsingfors: Svenska Litteratursälsskapet i Finland, 1986.

Mazzarella, Merete. Från Fredrika Runeberg till Märta Tikkanen. Frihet och beroende på i Finlandssvensk kvinnolitteratur. Helsinki: Söderström, 1995.

Schoolfield, George C., ed. *A History of Finland's Literature*. (*A History of Scandinavian Literatures*, 4. Sven H. Rossel, general ed.) Lincoln: University of Nebraska Press, 1998.

Sundgren, Tatiana. Finlandssvenska kvinnor skriver. Helsingfors: Schildt, 1985.

Tuohimaa, Sinikka. Kapina kielessä: tutkimus feminiinisen ilmenemisestä kielessä. Helsinki: Gaudeamus, 1994.

Varpio, Yrjö. Suomen kirjallisuushistoria 1-3. Helsinki: Suomalaisen Kirjallisuuden Seura, 1999.

Katarina Frostenson:
Transforming Swedish Poetry

Ia Dübois (University of Washington)

Background

Since the early 1980s an increasing number of female voices have dominated Scandinavian poetry. Swedish poets like Katarina Frostenson, Ann
Jäderlund and Birgitta Lillpers seek a language that responds to the con-
flicted existence they experience in society today. Fragmentation, gender-
lessness and a focus on rhythm and sound rather than metaphors are emblematic characteristics of their poetry. The fragmentation affects the poems stylistically both with regards to form and content, the words are
spread across the page and unrelated images convey a feeling rather than a
meaning. The lack of a distinct speaking subject is common as is the often
present physical mutilation. The fragmented language and body convey
dramatically a female identity in a search for true expressions. By crossing
traditional boundaries these writers enter a new poetic reality often with
exceptional demands on the reader. In fact, Frostenson even claims she
does not write to create meaning, instead she strives to build texts that are
beautiful, texts that exist in the intersection of the sensual and the intellectual.

Today critics laude the postmodern women writers for their complex and
intellectual works. In fact, Åsa Beckman writes that this is the first time that
women poets have seriously stepped into Swedish poetry and transformed
it. (2002, 9) This is indeed a feat when considering that critics in the past
often dismissed female poets as they considered their works too personal or
trivial – in contrast to the universal themes they found in works by males.
Frostenson became the trendsetter with her distinct postmodern poetry in
the early 1980s and she rose to fame when she was elected to the Swedish
Academy in 1992. At that time, a critic suggested that her poetry appears
masculine because of the strong intellectual component, to which she responded that "a good author is genderless." (Svensson, 22)

Katarina Frostenson was born in 1953 in Hägersten, a suburb southwest of Stockholm. While poetry is her main genre, she has also written experimental plays and lyrical prose, introduced and translated several international writers and she wrote the libretto to the opera *Staden* (The City) to celebrate Stockholm as the cultural capital of Europe in 1998. The difficulty in Frostenson's style lies in her play with words and common references to popular Swedish songs and sayings. She often breaks the reader's anticipation by interjecting the unexpected while her affinity for tone and rhythm enhances the opposite, beautiful images and a sense of understanding. For example, when asked about her childhood in an interview, she stated that she played the violin and then remarked straightforwardly, "Den där jävla fiolen! Jag skulle ju ha haft ett piano att hamra på i stället! Skrivandet är som en lust att slå på ett piano, att upplösa språket i rytmer och klanger" (That damn violin! I should of course have had a piano to pound on instead! Writing is like a desire to pound away on a piano, to dissolve language into rhythms and tones). (Lundgren)

Frostenson is undoubtedly one of the most postmodern and innovative writers in Sweden, yet her works are also clearly influenced by canonical Swedish poets like Gunnar Ekelöf, Gustaf Fröding, Nils Ferlin and international poets like Rainer Maria Rilke and Friedrich Hölderlin. Apart from being a member of the Swedish Academy, she has received prestigious literary honors like the Great Prize of the Society of the Nine in 1989, The Bellman Prize in 1994 and the Swedish Radio Prize for Lyrical Poetry in 1996.

Poetry

Frostenson's first collection, *I mellan* (Be-tween), appeared in 1978. The title itself is symptomatic of postmodern poetics that became increasingly important in the 1980s and 1990s. To explore the in-between stage, the gap between the "I" and the world was the force that motivated postmodern poets. This theme is evident already in the title poem: "Ingenting mer osynligt / än ordens ledljus / I dig, i mig / i mellan / Möt mig i tystnad / I mellan" (Nothing more invisible / than the guiding light of the words / In you, in me / in between / Meet me in silence / In between). To make the invisible visible, to hear and understand silence, are dominant themes in Frostenson's writings. Her characters are formed in contrast to the other which is not only a "you" in the texts but also streets, buildings, nature and human body parts. To gain access to their hidden history and insights is at the nucleus of her works.

In 1981 Frostenson moved to Paris for a few years with her husband Jean-Claude Arnault, a French photographer and opera director. This sojourn became fertile ground for her later works as Boulevard de Sebastopol, Austerlitz Station and the Salpêtrière Hospital, for example, are places she particularly returns to in her writings. Here her affinity for making the city "talk," for giving it a soul that holds memories, becomes apparent. In her collection *I det gula: tavlor, resor, ras* (1985; In the Yellow: Images, Travels, Tumbles), for example, the poem "Paris Austerlitz – Salpêtrière" opens with the words "Vägg / vägg   kala talmur / svala order   kastrop / ekon   samlas / till en väv   Sov / stig   Mot väggen / svälj ner frågan   Res Till tysta / tunga frågorna. . . (Wall / wall   bare speech-wall / cool orders   pitch screams / echoes gather / in a weaving   Sleep / step   Toward the wall / consume the question   Travel To the silent / heavy questions . . .) The poem also communicates Frostenson's complex relation to language. Keenly aware of the pregnant silence of the hospital walls, she encourages that deeper silence. She trusts the human senses more than language itself as a means of communication.

The 1980s were extremely productive and creative years for Frostenson. She began writing experimental plays and published five volumes of poetry, *Rena land: dikter* (1980; Clean Lands: Poems), *Den andra: dikter* (1982; The Other: Poems), *I det gula: tavlor, resa, ras* (1985; In the Yellow: Pictures, Travel, Tumble), *Samtalet: dikter* (1987; The Conversation: Poems) and *Stränderna* (1989; The Seashores). In these collections Frostenson establishes her poetic language. In *Clean Lands* loneliness and sadness mix with childhood memories. However, while these expressions were easily comprehended in earlier poetry, they are here imbedded in fragmented articulations that become riddles to be solved. *In the Yellow* introduces the stark gender issues that culminate in the following decades. In the poem "Jungfrun" (The Maiden) Frostenson reacts to the patriarchy surrounding women writers: "Man talar sig ljummen / diktar sig varm, i försonliga cirklar / och skriver sig rakt in i kylan" (One speaks with a lukewarm voice / writes poetry to gain heat, in placable circles / and writes oneself straight into the cold). The poem ends with a wish to know what the maiden could have become. She accentuates the need to speak up, at the same time as the long breaks between words in the fragmented poems suggest a need for silence and contemplation. It is exactly these contrasts, speech-silence, beauty-vulgarity, the familiar-the unknown, that attracts the reader to Frostenson's poetry. It becomes an intellectual challenge to break "the code." Beckman writes that "[d]enna ambivalens till språket är ett grundtrauma i Katarina Frostensons författarskap. Det framstår inte som en kokett estetisk hållning, utan som ett djupt personligt drama." (This ambivalence to language is a basic trauma in Katarina Frostenson's writings. It does not appear as a coquettish aesthetic point of view, but as a deeply personal drama). (1997, 480) It is this inherent drama that propelled Frostenson's poetry to the forefront of Swedish cultural life in the 1880s.

The collection *Joner: tre sviter* (Ions: Three Suites) appeared in 1991 and must be seen both as a milestone in Frostenson's authorship and as a watershed in Swedish poetry. Here she refines her poetics by merging earlier motifs and expressions with intertextuality from three different sources – a Medieval Scandinavian ballad, a Greek myth and a horrible murder in Stockholm (in 1984 two doctors killed a prostitute whose dissected body was found in garbage bags). In the ballad, "Jungfrun i hindhamn" (The Maiden in Hind Skin), a knight shoots a hind only to discover that it is his beloved whom his stepmother had bewitched. The Greek myth describes how Artemis, the goddess of hunt, turns Actaeon into a stag when she realizes he has seen her naked. He is then killed by his own dogs that tear him apart. The gaze can be seen as the nexus of the collection while the killings, combined with androgynous elements, intensify the inherent ambiguous female identity – see poem "A" below. To see and be seen is a strong desire in the poems and Lena Malmberg suggests that Frostenson in fact perceives ambiguous desires particularly in the maiden. By desiring to both see and be seen she causes herself to be drawn to her own death. (106) She further compares the split speaking subject, the hunter and the victim, with the old traditional split of the woman into the whore and the Madonna. (108) Clearly, although Frostenson's works are difficult to fully understand, it is impossible to remain indifferent to them. Karl Vennberg, a canonical Swedish poet, actually stated: "Det är aldrig synd om den som skrivit en diktsamling som *Joner* . . . Det är inte sig själv och ännu mindre sina idéer hon torgför. Det verkligt dystra med henne är istället att hon hotar förvandla de allra flesta av oss andra till triviala propagandister." (The one who has written a poetry collection like *Joner* is never to be pitied . . . It is not herself and even less her ideas that she peddles. The sad thing is rather that she threatens to turn most of the rest of us into trivial propagandists). (Svensson, 20) The following year, in 1992, Frostenson was elected to the Swedish Academy as the youngest member, surpassing a whole generation of prospective male candidates.

While a collection like *Joner* exemplifies the complex poetics of the new generation women poets, Frostenson's next collection, *Tankarna* (1994; The Thoughts), illustrates the difference between these postmodern poets and their predecessors. The poem "Hägerstenen" (The Stone of the Heron) appears autobiographical as it presents images from a childhood in the suburb Hägersten where Frostenson grew up. The mutilated female body is absent in this collection but images of wounds and pain remain. The tongue, the mouth and the forehead recur in many different images that underscore the search for a true expression of feelings and thoughts. She writes, for example, "Med järnsmak i munnen. Med tungan mot ledstången / Med slitsåret och rotsaften / det var en sådan stränghet att lära /. . . tungan gnider sakta byråns sarg av värld är munnen brun / och skummig. Ut seglar vi på en matta av skrik / Ropet en silvergrå romb över fältet" (With a taste of iron in the mouth. With the tongue against the handrail / With the tear-wound and the sap of the root / it was so rigid to learn / . . . The tongue slowly rubs the edge of the cabinet from the world the mouth is brown / and foamy. Out we sail on a carpet of screams / The cry a silver grey rhomb over the field.) The poem is imbued by images of loneliness and sadness, by smells of fried fish and wet wool. While earlier women writers expressed their background in concrete terms, there is little in this poem that defines Hägersten to the uninitiated reader.

In the ensuing collection *Korallen* (1999; The Coral) Frostenson highlights the connection between nature, history and sound by recurring references to "korall-koral-klockklang" (cora-chora-chime) and to the goddess Echo. The poem "Salt" (Salt) is included below as an example of the more playful and ironic side of Frostenson. It is also an example of how she incorporates lines from folktales, nursery rhymes and old popular sayings. Here language is in focus and she questions the sincerity with which we treat it and our opinions. The italicized segment refers to fairytales and folklore. She warns against merely repeating the known and comfortable. If one does, one becomes nothing but a note taker. Another strong theme in the collection, like in her oeuvre on the whole, is our inability to truly communicate emotions and feelings. In the suite "Soliloque" (Soliloquy) she writes: "du sa   Jag skiljer / mig" (you said I want / a divorce) and the "I" responds," då blir / du nära" (then you / become close). Ironically, the person feels closer when absent. The distance between the individual and the other is accentuated in her works not only by the evident lack of meaningful communication but also by her acerbic frankness.

When *Karkas: fem linjer* (2004; Carcass: Five Lines) appeared as the first collection in the new millennium, one critic stated that he did not concur with the myth that Frostenson is incredibly difficult. In contrast, he found her work to be very concrete. The fourth "line" (suite), titled "Far fara (att utvinna ur sommarvak)" (Father fare [to extract from a summer wake]) – see below – is a powerful long poem in spite of her emblematic word play. It is a long monologue in which the "I" describes childhood memories and landscapes and tries to come to peace with the dying father, the "you" in the poem. Indeed, the poem hints at a new phase in Frostenson's poetry as now the emotions take precedence over the sophisticated imagery and word game. It conveys strongly the complex bond of love and frustration between an old parent and a grown child who still has questions unanswered. While the frustration lingers in the typical lack of communication and understanding, the new level of concreteness stems from the fact that the father figure is in focus and present throughout the poem. Interestingly, while earlier women writers were accused of being too personal in

their works, Frostenson becomes more accessible when she is raising the
level of the personal in her otherwise intellectual poetry.

Theatre and Literature

What Scandinavian women writers have done to poetry from the 1980s,
they have also done to drama. Frostenson started writing experimental plays
at the end of the 1980s when her husband opened Forum, a gallery and
multimedia stage in Stockholm. It became instrumental for her developing
into more interdisciplinary projects and experimental drama. For example,
she wrote lyrical texts to two books of paintings by the Swedish artists
Håkan Rehnberg and Jan Håfström. She also collaborated with her husband
in works such as *Överblivet* (1989; Remains) and, later, *Vägen till öarna*
(1996; The Road to the Islands). The books feature Arnault's photographs
and Frostenson's texts on themes from city scapes, nature, mythology,
music and folklore. Importantly, however, the stage Forum provided was
instrumental to Frostenson's development as a dramatist. Her first one-act
play, *Sebastopol* (1989) – see below – was written specifically for this
stage. Her exploration of urban streets and places in poetry continues in the
monodramas. The themes of her poetry become intensified in the plays:
buildings, streets and landscapes become symbolic characters; individuals
try in vain to connect. They merely exist as sounding boards for each other,
to build an identity in contrast to "the other."

Frostenson's monodramas established her as a dramatist in Sweden and
abroad. Four one-act plays are published as *4 monodramer* (1990; 4 Monodramas), including *Nilen* (The Nile), *Bro* (Bridge), *Sebastopol* and *För
sluttningen* (For the Hillside). *The Nile* and *Sebastopol* were performed in
Sweden in 1989 and in Oslo in 1995. If Frostenson's interest in theater was
kindled by Arnault, her own poetics and asceticism brought new dimensions to the genre. Like in her poetry the melodic and fragmented approach
appears also in her plays. Similarly, a host of references to other authors
(Swedish and foreign), to songs and hymns, and to common Swedish clichés, create an intriguing maze that leaves some perplexed, caught among
contrasting and exclusive images. While Frostenson has been lauded for her
poetry, her plays have received less notice. Audiences appear more as-
tounded than excited.

The Nile takes place in a park at night where a middle-aged woman is
reminiscing about a child; *Bro* describes a bridge and a man's efforts to find
his place in the city and the universe; *Sebastopol* is about the relationship
between the individual and the anonymity of the street and, finally, *For the
Hillside* depicts a man lying on a hillside singing as if trying to become one
with music and ascend to heaven as a musical tone. The latter was later

adapted into a libretto, *Mannen på sluttningen* (The Man on the Hillside) and performed as an opera on the Swedish Radio in 1991. Critics have not always been favorable to Frostenson's plays as some have found it difficult to accept her minimalist approach to stage settings and character presentations – only one character appears in each play. Others appreciate the lyrical dimension and her efforts to challenge the boundaries between poetry and drama. Per Arne Tjäder, for example, suggests that "Platserna – en park, en bro, en sliten gata – är ekogrottor av allt som hänt där, nyss eller för länge sedan. Monodramerna blir därmed stämningsbilder, där rösten, talet, språket möter platsen på ett eget sätt" (The places – a park, a bridge, a worn street – are echo-caves of everything that has happened there, recently or a long time ago. The monodramas become images of moods, where the voice, the speech, the language meet the place in their own ways). (15)

Frostenson's inclination to explore the soul of a landscape and to break apart language, "driva meningen ur meningen" (force the meaning out of sentences), reaches its heights in *Berättelser från dom* (1992; Tales from them). She calls the book a fairy tale in which "dom" (them) can be seen as elves or gnomes that flow from the ground and the walls of buildings. Words and things are transformed into an anonymous flow of *dom*, moving like a lemming migration, with one common consciousness, moving out of the ground and walls. The book is characteristic of literature of the 1990s which often describes a sense of homelessness and lack of identity. Maria Wennerström has pointed out that the work underscores Frostenson's view of language as a suffocating membrane between the human being and the world. In the book, the supernatural beings make words and things come alive. However, when a male human being enters the story at the end, he destroys harmony through his constant verbalizing. Again, the conflict between language and silence becomes the pivot point. *Berättelser från dom* is one of Frostenson's few works in prose and, like her plays, it is imbued with themes from her poetry.

In 1993 Frostenson returned to the Royal Theater in Stockholm with the production of her play *Traum*. The surrealism of the play is accentuated by the title which means "dream" in German and alludes internationally to "trauma". In fact, it seems that Frostenson looks to the dream as the place where concrete, constructive language exists. In this play a young couple is constantly redecorating their studio apartment in an effort to revitalize their lives. The absurdity of everyday life is underscored by the constant moving of things and by their dialogue which evolves through lyrical associations interwoven with allusions to well-known songs, nursery rhymes and fairy tales. The female character changes personalities in each act which creates a sense of a complex and provocative identity. Pia Forsgren, the director of the play, states that she enjoyed having a woman express complex, even demonic, sides of her personality on stage in contrast to the traditional either or personality – a Nora or a Medea. (Skawonius) Frostenson's ability to express a complex female psyche by combining fragmented incoherent images is remarkable. Note also, that while critics may have found her poetry to be *male*, here she is hailed for her *female* writing.

At the end of the 1990s, Frostenson's visionary approach to dramatization intensified in the play *Sal P* (1996; Ward P) and culminated in her libretto to the opera *Staden* (1998; The City). In *Sal P* she returns to the hospital La Salpêtrière in Paris, where about 5,000 mentally ill women were treated at the end of the 19th century. The hospital became renowned particularly for Jean Martin Charcot's efforts to treat female hysteria with hypnotism. Frostenson states in the introduction that La Salpêtrière was known as "smärtans Versaille" (the Versaille of suffering) and that her husband encouraged her to write *Sal P* as they discussed Charcot's research and methods during travels in Italy in 1988. The critical response to *Sal P* was split, like the response to her earlier plays. This time, feminist critics, who had perceived it as an historical feminist play, wished for more information about the women and for Charcot's presence on stage. Clearly, Frostenson's aesthetics are still problematic for critics who wish for more historicity. Other critics interpreted *Sal P* from a literary perspective and found the play closely linked to French postmodern thinkers of the 1990s, particularly Julia Kristeva who has written about the relationship between body and language. This interpretation reflects in fact Frostenson's own statement in the introduction, where she clarifies that this is not an historical play of the 1880s but a source of inspiration to explore the problems about how to give inner life physical expression.

In the fall of 1998 the opera *The City* was acclaimed as a great cultural event. Frostenson wrote the libretto to the opera which had been commissioned from the composer Sven-David Sandström. He chose Frostenson as the writer as he envisioned a complex lyrical text about the city rather than a historical story line. Indeed, there is no story line in *The City*, which is rather a symbol of intensified urbanization during the twentieth century. Sorl (Murmur) is the main character, a male personification that is mutilated in the second act and resurrected as a woman. Sorl's appearance as a male and a female character underscores Frostenson's inclination to write androgynous texts. In fact she has stated that "riktigt bra författare är androgyna, tvåkönade, det är därför de kan återskapa andra människors upplevelser" (really good authors are androgenous, both male and female, that is why they can recreate other people's experiences). (Svensson, 22) Her rhythmic poetry lends itself perfectly to the libretto, intensifying the visual aspects of what has been called a grandiose performance. One critic stated that the opera, through Frostenson's language, her symbolic themes and intuitive repetitions, has such a musical quality that it is unintelligible but it must be listened to. (Åhlén) What she communicates is a complex murmur of sorrow and suffering as well as desire and courage.

Conclusion

Women have waited for centuries to take their deserved space in the male dominated cultural sphere. In Sweden, the male poets of Modernism were declared to be intellectual and difficult. It is then remarkable that a woman, Katarina Frostenson, becomes the trendsetter among women poets and transforms Swedish poetry during Postmodernism. Indeed, Karl Vennberg's premonition that she "threatens to turn most of the rest of us into trivial propagandists" (Svensson, 20) seems to have come true as the postmodernist, multidimensional works often make others look too traditional and simplistic. The roles have changed. Now it is Frostenson who is deemed to be a difficult writer and she acknowledged, at the opening of the opera *The City,* that her works demand a great effort and she offered the advice "Jag tror inte mina texter går att följa, man måste möta dem" (I don't think one can follow my texts, one has to meet them). Critics might postulate that Frostenson's writing is male, because of its intellectual and stark imagery. Nonetheless, her influence within the cultural establishment as a female writer is steadily growing.

Dikter[1]

Överblivet[2]

nu kommer det där ljudet igen   en hes utdragen andning
i bild: en människa   ett fält november
en vindögd schäfer med fläckig nos   i de kala utmarker
                                        misstänkta
som din ort
                                    där, där man väntar ytterst
München   Paris Austerlitz   Stockholm Milano

            de kalla städernas hopp
            de fula platsernas kön   platser där skräp står
                                        fram som helighet

        smittande frånvänt   lockande bort

---

[1] Published by permission of Katarina Frostenson.
[2] From the collection *I det gula*, 1985.

Jag sitter i en väntsal
och äter kokt svart nos
Det är frukttider. Fall. Bakom glas
drar höga, blå djur sina klövar
genom alger och regn   Stiger
Störtar   Har aldrig bett
i halvhjärtat
i den avklippta frasen
den bara handen   ögats
stirrande fläck

och i saknaden   brinner ett ljus

A^3

(Artemis siktar på Aktaion)

Jag såg honom, i färd med att se mig
i vattenbrynet, källan –
: Och om han sett henne, gjort det: om han såg henne *utan*
att hon såg   Att han såg henne stå där i källan, naken –
ryggtavlan, axelns kant, det vita kogret   Om han såg henne
vända som av ett ljud och blottas ren, bli alldeles synlig
Döljas sen, med bara den vita ovalen högt över de andra   Men
sedd   Blicken som spreds, ilningen över kogret

Jag såg honom   när han såg mig   nu ser jag

Hon skjuter med båge
i sikte
ögonmåttet

Det börjar högst upp, med ett stänk, en brun fläck: rynkan,
bläsen   Den flyter ut till ett fält, fält över synen   Spetsörat
- Hela hans bruna, hans bruna osynlig nu   Inte bröstet,
manken, bogen, hovarna, klövarna   Ort högre upp – spädd. . . ut

(ljudet ur munnen)

SALT[4]

Den som hört det vet, det är öppet för alla
allmänt, att tala är bart

---

[3]   From the collection *Joner*, 1991.
[4]   From the collection *Korallen*, 1999.

det liknar bara tonen du nynnar högt i sömnen
då du rabblar, *torn och tinnar*

silvervatten, saltkristaller
slanka gråa hästar går och betar

det som inte går in i låten får vara, sånt
är språket: man vet vem Vire är

låten försvinner
och du blir saltskrivare

Far fara   *(att utvinna ur sommarvak)*

Utdrag[5]

Någon säger *ja*
ur luften   Observatoriekullen –

ljuset kommer   molnet går

>   *himmel, han andas*
>
>   Hänger du i trädet
>   i den stora eken
>   ur det gröna sorlet
>   ute där på gården, där det lyser gulvarmt
>
>   i den fläcken   gattet
>   solkattslöven
>   smörblomsfärgen under hakan

du är gul din
hand den faller ner för kanten
om och om igen

sängramen   den slår sig blå mot för att
jag skall fatta om det kala   i ett livsträd löper malva-
ådrorna ur huden
och därunder köttet   det som lever än

fläcken brun som snus och mylla

brun din färg den främmande jag aldrig kände
i det brunaste skall tanken samlas –

---

5   From the collection *Karkas*, 2004.

                              brunt det är
                              så uttrycksfullt – är sången
                              floden!

lär mig fatta
något av vart du skall gå

handens ryck i plädens bara
några strån är kvar   den vill dölja sig
den skäms för sina sår

                              när hjärta skäms för hjärta kommer
                              stunden   kommer du då äntligen ur
                              rummet –

far fara   kan jag göra något för dig

vara här

det är du som stavar mot mig nu
de bokstavsljuden   vara här

                              jag är inte här
                              jag är i solen
                              jag är solens barn den svarta, helios!

pappa stolpsäng
älgstudsare, gallan, stel-
krampen   lek inte med orden barn
Vaka

vaka över mig
du ber
. . .

                              är detta sanning   ät då
                              smulor ur min hand   vad är sanning

                              att vi lågande går bort

far   väl

dyker i orden
ner mot grundet
klyvs i synen   vattenvågen
gyttjebubblorna till ytan stiger
över dragen som det känns av årtagen
de tar i bruna vattenmassan, och far fram

en flicka röd ror över en sjö hon sjunger lågt
idag är det min födelsedag

Tanken på dig i övergången

Grönskan

Hur du sen fördes   svart   vitt

Ingens   forslad

mellan salar   fara   genom gångarna till

ljuset

Hängande i luften –

For sen genom staden   vad var det
för schäs du drogs i   bom bom
talade för sista gången kroppen

sade: kroppen

de där oberörda, männen
de på banken
i den vita hettan dallervågen
de skall bära fadern

Skådespel

Sebastopol[6]

PLATS

En rektangulär "gata". En nersliten och samtidigt skimrande plats, fläckvis lik en fäll.
Kanten på gatan, "stupet ner", kan t ex bekläs med vackra stenar: gatan är både reel och
irreell. En bild/avbild, en diabild av gatan kan projiceras bakom scenen.

---

[6]   From the volume *4 Monodramer*, 1990.

GESTALT

En ung kvinna, 20-25 år. Ingen "person" med skälvande inlevelse: hennes närmande till platsen är intensivt och samtidigt sakligt/främmande: ett avstånd hörs och känns.

PÅ BAND: KVINNANS RÖST I ETT SLUTET RUM:

Ta – ta gata Ta gatan, gå – över, gå – av . . . Gå över gatan, över gråstenen. Gå, tills gatan ansiktet tar . . .

(*Ljud tonar upp: tutor, bildörrar som slår igen, motorer, surranden, rop, ras av murbruk, klappor, vattenbrus – en röra av ljud och röst:*)

Taxi.		Taxi!			Vad var det jag sa? *Sa!*

		Vatten . . . vatten . . . Fröken!

		Du, du där, du dödar . . .	Ursäkta!

Stanna. Akta dig!

					Över, jag måste över nu –

		Vattnet, vattnet därnere, dit . . .

						Le monde!

Himmel!
		. . . men jag ville, ville dit . . .			NEJ!

	svarta, vita, likdelar . . .

Du, du där, du dödar mig om du inte köper mig

					Stanna!

				(*ljuden upphör tvärt*)

Jag går inte så långt idag. Bara dit, ditupp, bara till Gare de l'Est . . . de l'Est — det låter som en vind. En torr vind, en monsun . . . Luften här – är slut. Utandad. Alldeles still . . . alla lungor som har andats den. Som har dragit den igenom sig, som har sugit ut den, som har gjort den gul . . . Slut och full. Som gatan. Grå – stenen. Om jag kunde få ut det . . . Plocka ut allt. Leta, dela sönder, dissikera: skräpet, pisset, skiten, loskorna . . . Lägga upp allt. Allt, som trampats ner. Masserat, massakrerat, som har gjort den öm – om jag lägger mig ner kan jag kanske höra det, igen . . .

Nej. Nej: det är sant. Inte stå. Inte stanna. Aldrig stanna – det här är inte en plats där man står, där man stannar: rakt på bara. Gå, gå rakt fram, se rakt, ha en riktning . . . Där – där framme är den. Den är där. Det är sjunde dagen jag kommer hit.

Där. Stor. Grå – en fästning . . . Eller ett djur i sten. En hane där, i sten. Stora, fula tysta hus . . . Och ni – ni där? Ni, som går runt det där som runt ett totem: vart ska ni? Vart är ni på väg? Jag följer er! Efter er! Det här är ingen väg! Svara ! Har ni en plan, nån hemlig plan, en ordning, nån liten väg ut? Det här är ingen väg! Ingen väg säger jag! Här är bara . . .

Det finns inget tystare än platsen. Platsen som ligger där, dag efter dag, år efter år. Alla tider . . . Det är sjunde dagen jag kommer hit. Hit. Här. Jag är här. *Jag är här.*

. . . Allt kladd . . . de där ögonvitorna . . . som gulnat. Täppts igen . . . Som kläcks och kläcks och sprider sig och . . . Som bara fortsätter att gå. Uppsliten, förseglad. Vidöppen och stängd, på samma gång. Stirrar. Skelar. Vindar, tar sig fram, fram! Hit! Hit, men inte längre – inte längre, kom inte hit! Det är sjunde dagen jag kommer hit. Hit. *Jag är här.*

Här . . .

Sebastopol . . . boulevard Sebastopol . . . En raksträcka. Bara en rak, rak gata. Grå, som i ett ansikte . . . Man kokar asfalt, inte sant? Kokar den så att den stelnar, blir till guld. Det gråa, släta, tysta guldet. Fotsulorna gnider det. På kvällarna kan man rulla sig i askan och gnida ansiktet hårt, hårt, så att det skavs, skavs, sprids och stelnar och tar hela gatans färg. Tar gatans färg . . . Den färgen. Gatans färg! Jag gör det — jag har redan gjort det! Jag tar det! Jag ska göra det. Jag gör det! Jag är här. *Här!*

Löv, löv . . . ögon. I högar, i strömmar rasslar de, de drar sig över gatan, skavs . . . Uppsliten, förseglad. Vidöppen och stängd, på samma gång, drar en hel ström av ögon fram. Vit, den visar vitorna. Kastar med sina huvuden, kastar dem bak . . . Vindar, blänker, kisar, kläcks . . . Dag efter dag, natt efter natt. Ropen, rösterna huggs av, blir – obegripliga. Vita, svarta, gulnade ansikten . . .

Jag är här . . . I det här vattnet. Vadar fram . . . Snabbt, snabbt, drunkna inte! Snabbt, snabbt innan det fylls igen, innan det klibbas fast. Snabbt, skynda dig om du vill höra. Höra det – igen. Det är sjunde dagen jag kommer hit.

Men – det svarar inte . . . Det svarar inte, det bara – hörs . . .Vad är det som hörs och hörs, utan att tala? Som syns och syns, och bara ropar . . . Allt – allt är här. Allt är här och allt kan få komma –

"Men vad är det med dig. Sätt dig, sätt dig ned och var här – sluta säga att du är här, var här . . . var här . . ."

. . . vad det myllrar i ett ansikte . . . myllrar stilla . . . platsen — har ett ansikte. Nej. Nej! Nej, nej! Sluta säga ansikte. Inget ansikte. Det här är ingen väg. Ingen väg, en gata. Ga-ta-Se-bas-to-pol (*leker med ordet*) Försök stava fram det, staka ut det, ta hela gatan, här . . .

Jag är här . . . och jag vill . . . till – dig. Se samma sak, dag efter dag- Nöta bort färgerna tills allting grånar och tar gatans färg. Den färgen, gatans färg. Skava av mig, blandas, försvinna av ljuden, dövas, krossas till grus, gatsten, inget . . .

Gör mig grå. Grå, som det tillstånd där allting blandas, alla färger samlas, lös – upp – mig
. . . Asfalten är ett land, ett enda. Rösten, rösten där är en enda. Den kan svepa in mig,
sluta om mig, den kan lära mig tala. Tala. Jag ska tala! Jag ska lära mig tala. Tala, med
tungrotens yttersta tal – Det är sjunde dagen jag är här. Här. *Jag är här.*

Sebastopol . . . boulevard de Sebastopol – bara en rak, rak gata. En raksträcka, rak, som
varje dag. Ett myller, och stillhet. Myllret är stilla, jag vill ha ett svar. På allt som blandats
i dig, allt som du har fått ta emot. Hett, ja, det är hett, det sjuder . . .
Verklighet – vilken färg har ordet. Grå, det måste vara grått.
Grått, som i ett ansikte. Sebastopol . . .

Det finns ingenting att vara rädd för. Allt är här. Här. Allt är bara här och allt kan få
komma. Allt ska komma, kom!

*(En klockklang, svängande, sanslös, man hör också forsande vatten, efter ett tag går
klockan och vattnet över i gatubruset. Rösterna, gatans ljud tar över.)*

    Här, Här! Jag måste se. Se!   Taxi!

    Jag kan inte stanna, inte stanna . . . hennes ansikte . . .

vattnet . . .   Stanna. Akta dig!

    Hennes ansikte, hennes ansikte under vattnet . . .
                          Le monde!
    Över! Jag måste över. Försök fatta!

Du, du där, du dödar mig!
                     Solrosor!

Här. Här: ordet växer och blir en stod. Osynlig stod. Allt är här, jag är här, och allt kan få
komma
Allt är här . . . Det är sjunde dagen jag kommer hit. Vatten . . . Vatten? Små, små droppar?
. . . tunga massor, massor vatten . . . Men hur var det? Jag var här. Här, i det tunga.
Ingeting däruppe . . . fanns mer . . .

Det var klockan, det var klangen. . . den öppnade asfalten . . . Det var tonen som klöv
gatan med sin röst . . . Det ropade inne i den tunga klangen – först en spricka, som en
bräsch . . . Bräsch efter bräsch, lysande . . . Så gungade det i det grå, över mig, under mig,
överallt, vidöppet . . . Av och an, tungt. Tungt, vilken tyngd, vilken tyngd, äntligen . . .
Jag såg ner, ner under den milslånga skorpan . . . Väggarna – murarna – var av kroppar.
Levande, döda kroppar, leende, i aska, hela tiden . . . Så såg jag ner, ännu mer, längre ner
under de levande väggarna. Där var en dal. Djupt under öppnade sig en dal, jag ser det;
Rösten. Rösten var där, den fyllde rummet. Den *var* rummet. Den såg på mig med sitt
enda, sitt stora, sitt alldeles grå öga. Är du Där? Ja, jag är här. Har du kommit? Ja, jag har
kommit. Stannar du? Ja – jag stannar. Jag stannar, sa jag, jag lovar, jag stannar, jag
kommer tillbaka. Jag kommer tillbaka.

Det regnade. Asfalten var våt, grå, hal, vacker . . . Grå, grå asfalt, ett ansikte, inget
ansikte, ett land, inget land – grått, enhetligt, tyst, något – helt annat . . .

Gatan tar inga ansikten

Poetry

Translated by Ia Dübois[7]

Remains

now, there is the sound again   a hoarse   long breath

in view: a person   a field November
a cross-eyed German Shepard with a spotted nose   in the bare distant fields
                                                                                suspected
like your space
                                                                where, where one waits at the end
Munich   Paris Austerlitz   Stockholm Milan

             the cold cities' hope
             the ugly places' sex   places where garbage appear
                                       like holiness

             contaminating reversed   luring away

I'm sitting in a waiting room
eating boiled black nose
It's fruit season. Fall. Behind glass
high, blue animals pull their hoofs
through algae and rain   Step
Crash   Have never asked

in half-heartedness
in the clipped phrase
the naked hand   the eye's
staring spot

and in the regret   a candle is burning

---

7   It should be pointed out that it is nearly impossible to give credit to Frostenson's poetry in translation because of her intricate play with words. Many of her recurring words have multiple meanings in Swedish and change in the different contexts that she creates even within a poem. Besides, many expressions are derived from popular sayings and songs which are specific to Swedish culture but lack references in English. For example, the word "ras" in the collection *In the Yellow: Images, Travels, Tumbles*, is used as a noun and a verb, "rasa," in the poetry. As a noun it means either "tumble," "fall," "avalanche" or "collapse" while the verb also includes the meaning "to rage." In most contexts Frostenson seems to mean "tear down" and "rage," but she leaves the interpretation to the reader. Similarly, the words "far fara" in the title of the poem from *Karkas* can be present tense and the infinitive form of the verb "fara" = "to travel." As nouns "far" is also "father" and "fara" means "danger." I have interpreted the title to be about "father" and suggest "fare" as a compliment that could offer suggestive meanings and alliteration. Frostenson suggested herself, in a personal conversation, that her poetry sounds best and translates best into German; these are my efforts in English.

A

[Artemis aims at Actaeon]

I saw him, seeing me

At the water's edge, the spring –
: And if he'd seen her, done that: if he saw her *without*
her seeing   That he saw her standing there in the spring, naked –
the back, the shoulder's edge, the white quiver   If he saw her
turn around as from a sound and be all exposed, become completely visible
Then concealed, with just the white oval high above the others   But
seen   The gaze that spread, the thrill across the quiver

       I saw him   when he saw me   now I see

          She shoots with a bow
          in sight
          by the eye

It starts far up, with a splatter, a brown spot: the wrinkle,
the blaze   It flows out makes a field, field across the gaze   The pointed ear
- All his brown, his brown invisible now   Not the chest,
the withers, the shoulder, the hoofs, the cloven-hoofs   Space higher up – thinned . . .
out

                            [the sound from the mouth]

SALT

Those who have heard it know, it's open to all
generally, speaking is just

it's just like the tune you're humming loudly in your sleep
when you babble, *towers and turrets*

silver water, salt crystals
slender grey horses go grazing

what cannot get into the song is left, such
is language: you know who Thumbelina is

the song disappears
and you become a salt scribe

Father Fare (to wheedle from a summer wake)

Excerpts

Someone says *yes*
from the air   The Observatory Hill –

the light comes   the cloud leaves

   heavens, he's breathing

   Are you hanging in the tree
   in the big oak
   out of the green noise
   out there in the yard, where the light is yellow warm

   In that spot   the gut
   the sun bright leaves
   the buttercup color under the chin

you are yellow your
hand it falls down from the frame
over and over again

the bed frame   it beats itself blue against so
I will grab the bare   in a tree of life the lilac
veins run out of the skin
and there underneath the flesh   that which is still alive

the spot brown like snuff and humus

brown your color the odd one I never knew
in the brownest the thought will gather –

     brown it is
     so expressive – is the song
     the river!

teach me to understand
something of where you are going

your hand's pull in the blanket's bare
some hairs are left   it wants to hide
it's ashamed of its sores

     when heart's ashamed of heart the moment
     comes   will you then finally come out of
     the room –

father fare   can I do something for you

be here

it is you who spells to me now
those letter rhymes   be here

                              I am not here
                              I am in the sun
                              I am a child of the sun the black one, helios!

daddy post bed
rifle, bile, tet-
anus don't play with the words child
Watch

watch over me
you ask
. . .

                              Is this truth   then eat
                              crumbs from my hand   what is truth

                              that we pass away in flames

fare   well

diving in the words
down towards the shallows
split in my sight   the water wave
mud bubbles rise to the surface
across the currents as felt by the strokes of the oars
they grab the brown body of water, and fare forward

a girl in red rows out across a lake she sings softly
today is my birthday

The thought of you in transition

                    The verdure

How you then were brought   black   white

No one's   transported

between rooms   *fare*   through the corridors to

the light

Hanging in the air –

Drove then through town   in what kind of
chaise were you pulled   boom boom
the body spoke for the last time

said: the body

those unaffected, the men
those on the bench
in the white heat the trembling wave
they shall carry the father

Play

Sebastopol

PLACE

A rectangular "street." A worn and at the same time a shining place, like a skin at places.
The edge of the street, "the precipice," can for example be covered with beautiful stones:
the street is both real and unreal. An image/reproduction, a slide of the street can be
projected behind the stage.

CHARACTER

A young woman, 20-25 years old. Not a "person" with trembling sensibility: her arrival
to the place is intense and also matter of fact/strange: a distance is heard and felt.

ON A TAPE: THE WOMAN'S VOICE IN A CLOSED ROOM.

Take – take street Take the street, go – across, go – from ... Go across the street, across
the grey stones. Go, until the street takes the face . . .

(*The sound gets louder: horns, car doors are slammed, engines, buzzing, cries, falling
plaster, beaters, rush of water – a mixture of sound and voice:*)

Taxi.   Taxi!   What did I say? *Say!*

       Water . . . water . . . Miss!

         You, you over there, you are killing . . .   Sorry!

Stop. Watch out!

           Across, I must across now -

       The water, the water down there, there . . .

               Le monde!

Heaven!

           ...but I wanted, wanted to go there . . .   NO!

      black, white, parts of corpses . . .

You, you over there, you are killing me if you don't buy me

                      Stop!

                (*the sounds stop suddenly*)

I won't walk so far today. Just there, up there, just to Gare de l'Est . . . de l'Est – it sounds like a wind. A dry wind, a monsoon . . .The air here – is gone. Blown out. Completely still. . . all lungs that have breathed it. That have pulled it through themselves, that have sucked it out, that have made it yellow . . . Finnished and full. Like the street. The greystone. If I could get it out . . . Pull everything out. Search, pick apart, dissect: the junk, the piss, the shit, the spit . . . Display it all. Everything, that has been trampled down. Massaged, massacred, that has made it sore – if I lay down I can perhaps hear it, again . . .

No. No: it is not true. Don't stand. Don't stop. Never stop – this is not a place where you stand, where you stop: just go on. Go, go straight ahead, look straight, have a direction . . . There – up there it is. *It is there.* I come here for the seventh day.

There. Big. Grey – a fortress . . . Or an animal in stone. A male there, in stone. Big, ugly silent houses . . . And you – you over there? You, who walk around that like around a totem pole: where are you going? Where are you headed? I will follow you! After you! This is not a road! Answer! Do you have a plan, a secret plan, an order, some small escape out? This is not a road. Not a road I say! Here is just . . .

There is nothing more quiet than the place. The place that is there, day after day, year after year. Through time. . .
I come here for the seventh day. Hither. Here. I am here. *I am here.*

. . . All the mess . . . those whites of the eyes . . that have become yellow. Have become clogged . . . That cracks and cracks and spread . . . That just continue going. Torn up, sealed. Wide open and closed, at the same time. Staring. Cross-eyed. Winds, push forward, forward! Here! Here, but not further – not further, don't come here! I come here for the seventh day. *I am here.*

Here . . .

Sebastopol . . . Boulevard Sebastopol . . . A straight road. Just a straight, straight street. Grey, like in a face . . . You cook asphalt, don't you? Cook it so that it hardens, becomes gold. The grey, even, quiet gold. The soles of the feet rub it. In the evenings you can roll around in the ashes and rub your face hard, hard, so that it is chafed, chafed, spreads and hardens and takes the color of the whole street. Takes the color of the street. . . That color. The color of the street! I'll do it – I have already done it! I'll take it! I will do it. I will do it! I am here. *Here.*

Leaves, leaves . . . eyes. In heaps, in streams they rustle, they pull themselves across the street, become rubbed . . . torn open, sealed. Wide open and closed, at the same time, a whole stream of eyes are moving forward. White, it shows the white of the eyes. Throwing their heads, throwing them backwards . . . Winds, glisten, squint and hatch. . . Day after day, night after night. The cries, the voices are cut off, become – incomprehensible. White, black, yellowed faces . . .

I am here . . .in this water. Wade forward . . . fast, fast, don't drown. Fast, fast before it is filled again, before it gets stuck. Fast, hurry up if you want to hear. Hear it – again. I come here for the seventh day.

But – it doesn't answer . . . It doesn't answer, it is just – heard . . . What is heard and heard and never talks? What is seen and seen and just cries . . . Everything – everything is here. Everything is here and everything may come –

"But what is up with you. Sit down, sit down and be here –
stop saying that you are here, be here . . . be here. . ."

. . . how it swarms in a face. . .it swarms calmly. . .the place –
has a face. No. No! No, no! Stop saying face. No face. This is not a road. No road, a street. The-Street-Se-bas-to-pol (*playing with the word*) Try to spell it, mark it out, take the whole street, here . . .

I am here . . . and I want . . . to _ you. See the same thing, day after day. Wear the colors away until everything gets grey and takes the color of the street. That color, the color of the street. Rub it off me, be mixed, disappear from the sounds, be numbed, crushed into gravel, cobble stones, nothing . . .

Make me grey. Grey, like that state when everything is mixed, all colors collected, dis – solve – me . . . The asphalt is a country, only one. The voice, the voice there is only one. It can embrace me, close around me, it can teach me to talk. Talk. I will talk! I will learn to talk. Talk, with the last words of the root of my tongue – I am here for the seventh day. Here. *I am here.*

Sebastopol . . . boulevard de Sebastopol – just a straight, straight street. A straight stretch, straight, like every day. A swarm, and stillness. The swarm is still, I want an answer. On all that which is mixed in you, everything that you have received. Hot, yes, it is hot, it's simmering . . . Reality – what color has that word. Grey, it must be grey. Grey, like in a face. Sebastopol.

There is nothing to be afraid of. Everything is here. Here. Everything is only here and everything may come. Everything shall come, come!

(*A bell rings, swinging, senseless, one also hears rushing water, after a while the bell and the water merge with the sound of the street. The voices, the sound of the street takes over.*)

Here. Here! I must see. See!   Taxi

    I cannot stay, not stay . . .   her face . . .

the water . . .   Stop. Watch out!

    Her face, her face under the water . . .
                                 Le monde!

    Across! I have to get across. Try to understand!

  You, you there, you are killing me!

                       Sunflowers!

Here: Here: the word grows and becomes a statue. Invisible statue. Everything is here, I am here, and everything may come
Everything is here . . . I come here for the seventh day. Water . . . water? Small, small drops? . . . heavy volumes, volumes of water . . . But how was it? I was here. Here, in the heavy. Nothing up there . . . existed any more . . .

It was the bell, it was the sound . . . the opened asphalt . . . It was the tone that split the street with its voice . . . It cried inside the heavy sound – first a crack, like a breach . . . Breach after breach, shining . . . Then it swung in the grey, above me, under me, everywhere, wide open . . . To and fro, heavily. Heavily, what a weight, what a weight, finally . . . I looked down, down under the mile long crust . . . The partitions – the walls were of bodies. Living, dead bodies, smiling, in ashes, for long times . . . Then I looked down, still deeper, further down under the living walls. There was a valley. Deep below a valley opened up, I see it; The voice. The voice was there, it filled the room. It *was* the room. It looked at me with its only, its big, its completely grey eye. Are you There? Yes, I am here. Have you arrived? Yes, I have arrived. Will you stay? Yes – I will stay. I will stay, I said, I promise, I will stay, I will return. I will return.

It was raining. The asphalt was wet, grey, slippery, beautiful . . . Grey, grey asphalt, a face, no face, a land, no land – grey, uniform, quiet, something – completely different . . .

The street takes no faces.

Primary Works

I mellan: dikter, 1978.
Rena land: dikter, 1980.
Den andra: dikter, 1982.
I det gula: tavlor, resor, ras, 1985.
4 monodramer, 1990.
Joner: tre sviter, 1991.
Berättelser från dom: prosa, 1992.
Tankarna, 1994.
Traum; Sal P, 1996.
Korallen, 1999.
Kristallvägen; Safirgränd, 2000.
Staden: libretto, 2001.
Karkas, 2004.

Selected Bibliography

Beckman, Åsa. "Du som gör min ensamhet ännu större: Katarina Frostenson och vargmannen." *Jag själv ett hus av ljus: 10 kvinnliga poeter*. Stockholm: Bonniers, 2002: 128-142.

–. "Den herrelösa dikten: 1980-talets svenska lyrik." *Nordisk kvinnolitteraturhistoria* Volume IV. Stockholm: Bra Böcker, 1997: 478-484.

Bergsten, Staffan. *Klang och ater: tre röster I samtida svensk kvinnolyrik*. Stockholm: FIBs Lyrikklubb, 1997.

Lundgren, Kajsa. "Jag är ute efter det röriga och det grova." Interview with Katarina Frostenson (1983), retrieved 15 August 2001. http://hem.passagen.se/ingbjor/.

Malmberg, Lena. *Från Orfeus till Eurydike: En rörelse i samtida svensk lyrik*. Lund: Ellerströms, 2000.

Sigfridsson, Barbro. *Jagets Plats: Gestaltningen av det kvinnliga subjektet i Katarina Frostensons Nilen, Traum, Sal P och Staden*. Stockholm: Gidlunds, 2003.

Skawonius, Betty. "På jakt efter ett kvinnligt språk: 'Traum' – en poetisk dröm om inre världen." *Dagens Nyheter*, 12 February 1993.

Svensson, Per. "Mellan två stolar: Är Katarina Frostenson för svår för akademien?" *MånadsJournalen* 7 (1992): 18-25.

Tjäder, Per Arne. "Dramats återkomst." *Allt om böcker* 2 (1996), 13-15.

Wennerström, Maria. "Stilistisk åderlåtning: Språkliga teorier och strategier i Katarina Frostensons Berättelser från dom." *Horisont* 6 (1994): 59-67.

Åhlén, Carl-Gunnar. "Staden – Kungliga Operan." *Svenska Dagbladet*, 14 September 1998.

The Mad and the Irresponsible:
Rosa Liksom's "Ordinary" Women

SUSANNA MOLISKI (UNIVERSITY OF HELSINKI)

For the past 20 years Rosa Liksom (b. 1958), an author, a visual artist, a film maker and a Laplander, has been shouting from the edges of the Finnish literary scene. Her first collection of short stories, a collection called *Yhden yön pysäkki*, (One Night Stop) published in 1985, was also published in English as *One Night Stands* in 1993. There Liksom introduced her style, presenting a cavalcade of crazy, violent and irresponsible characters that did whatever they pleased. Liksom, who actually writes under a pseudonym, is a good example of a media oriented artist. For instance, she has a website where one can order online her designed collectibles. One of her latest projects includes designing a cow figure for the cover of a commercial milk container. In 1993 she stated her status in Finland in an interview with a Canadian journalist:

> I don't take part in any literary circles here, I don't give any interviews to journalists in Finland, and I don't go anywhere to read my stories or talk about myself. I stay outside the media. All they write about me is about my work, and that's the way I like it (Reynolds, 1993).

Liksom took her mission of shaking the fundamentalisms in the hierarchy of the Finnish society even further in her perhaps most valued and praised short story collection *Bamalama* (1993). Especially well-known characters from that collection are the police officers; sadomasochistic machos, ignorant and violent in their craze for power. Liksom is a writer of extremes. On one hand she is interested in describing fragmented moments of anonymous individuals, who seem to lack any attachment to any context. But, on the other hand, she can paint on a larger scale where the narrative stretches to include everything possible. This is a case of Liksom's first novel, *Kreisland* (1996; Crazeland[1]) where a good amount of Finnish his-

---

[1] The title is a combination of Elvis Presley's estate Graceland and Crazy Land.

tory, starting from the very myth of creation, is described following the actions of a female heroine, who is actually a pig (!). Also another 'symptom' of the insanity of her texts is their endless exaggeration. In her latest text *Reitari* (2002), a novel about a Northern artist Reidar Säreströniemi, everything is extreme. The elaboration extends to all the topics of the character's life: to violence, drinking, eating, partying, melancholy, hatred – and loving, too. Markku Soikkeli summarizes Liksom's philosophy in his review of *Reitari*, "Art has to be extravagance, an orgy of death that denies the *kaamos* (dark period of the winter in Lapland) and changes the night into day" (Soikkeli, 2002).

In her latest short story collection, *Perhe* (The Family) from 2000, Liksom continues to draw literary sketches of people who are sad, mad or at least a little bit melancholic. The four short stories which have been selected for this anthology are from the chapters *The Babyluck* and *Women*. None of Liksom's short stories have titles, which underlines their caricatured, comic-strip-like nature and the author's feeling of not belonging. The selected stories explore similar themes from various perspectives. Each story studies the problematic nature of womanhood, motherhood and relationships, but they do not do so, by any means, in a way that could be called ordinary or even probable. The stories are narrated in a woman's voice. The narrator is quite omniscient, and she is describes the incidents retrospectively.

In Liksom's stories women are not victims; if they are treated badly, they take justice into their own hands and punish those who have done them wrong. However, aspects of the grotesque, irony and mad satire step into the picture. The concept of what "doing wrong" actually means, transforms widely. For instance: a man can get himself killed just by being a slob or because the fun of summer is over. In these example stories one can find the Liksomian view of the world in the juxtapositions that place the characters into a broad dichotomy. On one hand there are the protagonists and those who share their twisted philosophies of life. On the other hand there are those, often silent, 'others'; the narrator's enemies, family members, friends, occasional acquaintances, in general those whom the main character feels superior to. The irony of these categorizations is that in most cases the narrator, who describes herself as a normal and ordinary person, and her actions, whether murder or child abandonment, somehow fit as perfectly normal actions. As Mervi Kantokorpi states in her review of *The Family* in the daily newspaper *Helsingin Sanomat*, a functional relationship in Liksom's world is just a joke (Kantokorpi, 2000a).

What is the world like, that these people inhabit? At first, it seems to be a brutal and loveless ecosystem, where everything has returned to the primitive struggle for survival; "kill or be killed". However, a closer look reveals soft spots and the evidence of humanity and even tenderness. This aspect is present for example in the story of the young mother who suffocates her baby daughter by accident as a result of her wild 21st birthday celebrations.

Perhaps one way of interpreting the meanings of Liksom's texts is to simply characterize them as irrational sketches. Anne Puumala has written about Liksom's anxious world of *The Family*: "In the end, *The Family* is about macabre laughter that can be silenced only by the meaninglessness of the story worlds" (Puumala, 2000). Perhaps Liksom's texts are meant to lack meaning, especially in her later work. This interpretation would place the texts less in the direction of sociopolitical anarchism, and more towards to the earlier mentioned, deliberate comic-style detachment from any context. Kantokorpi has described Liksom's style as *shortcut*, a literary subgenre that is similar to cartoons, TV-sitcoms, and many forms of visual arts (Kantokorpi, 2000b).

In the first story the narrator is a woman from northern Finland, who has moved to Helsinki. Her work as an accountant does not seem to go too well and in addition, she seems to have old quarrels with her sisters who still live in Lapland. The character sees her plan of having a baby also as a way to get back at her sisters, to show that she has the guts to do it, to achieve something that will remain after she herself is gone. The narrating-I sees herself somehow superior to the Southerners, who are not "outdoor persons" as she is. Still, the narrator refuses to go out and meet anyone, until she decides to have a baby. The ways she makes her first contacts with others after coming to the South seem quite radical: she has no problem standing on the street corner with Russian prostitutes, but still makes sure the father-candidates know that she is not one of them. This arrangement underlines the satiric paradox of a theme frequently met in Liksom's works. The narrator creates her own rules of being, thinking of herself as normal, and everyone else as insane. The narrator's misfortune continues, but does not depress her. Her viewpoint of her own maternal self and her self-image as a woman compares to an animal in the end of the text. In order to become pregnant she decides to see not a gynecologist, but a veterinarian. This illogical decision becomes even more absurd when the narrator's seeming ignorance of basic facts is compared to her use of Biblical metaphors. She knows her Rachels and Leahs, and is determined to show who she herself resembles.

The next story introduces a woman who is in a similar situation as the first narrator; she also needs a man. This time it is, however, not for making a baby, but apparently for the need of status. This claim is supported by the technique the narrator uses to choose her man. His name is not mentioned, just the things he owns. The narrator implies that the man is untruthful, when he is lying about his occupation. However, she is not shy to unmask herself to the reader: She does not tell the man she is a drug abusing doctor.

This lie brings the reader face to face with an important question that also becomes the main theme of the story; the unreliability of the narrator. The text continues with an ever accelerating speed towards to its climax in with the narrator and her colleague murder the man with a toxic cocktail. If the reader is familiar with Liksom's texts, she/he will know that murder is a favorite narrative and thus it is not a surprising outcome of a failed relationship. The surprising choice in the narrative comes after the murder: the offender regrets her act. She tries to confess, but in the Liksomian reality of the narrative she receives no solution. The attempt to pursue something that is generally accepted as an ethical value or as a virtue is meaningless in the text's world. Even the mental hospital receptionist seems to be just sympathetic toward her terrible Christmas stress. The criminal offender does not reach the longed-for catharsis; on the contrary, she begins to suspect the failure of her own memory. This likewise deflates the reader's hopes for some reasonable outcome or justice in the story. Now it seems that the narrator lied or imagined the whole story, and the reader is left empty-handed. And when even the myth of Santa Claus is drawn into the already shaky structure of the narration's reliability, it seems quite hard to believe a word the narrator has said.

In the next two stories the narrator's voice moves from that of a woman to a girl. Still, these girls are already having what the first narrator hopes for; they are mothers. Choosing these two entirely unsuitable teenagers as mother figures, Liksom's texts proceed to examine the subject of motherhood itself. In these texts the mothers are crazy, Marian inversions who still have their babies effortlessly. In both stories, the girls' mothers have threatened them with abortion, apparently aware of their daughters' immature personalities, thus representing the "sane and practical" mother, who cannot count on her daughter's ability to take care of an infant.

The narrator of the first story is calculating. She wants a child, but not just any child. She wants to have a summer baby. The main characteristics of the protagonist of the story are her inconceivably naïve understanding of motherhood, and her narcissistic views towards it. She still lives entirely in a teenagers' world, and looks at her surroundings from this vantage point. Again, the reader is misled. The beginning implies, at least to a certain extent that the narrator is willing to learn to take responsibility for her actions. But the real stage of her views is revealed already when she describes the current baby-world to her mother: "Nowadays babies survive on their own in life, fuck, modern babies don't need any fussing, they take care of themselves". She looks upon the baby as a living doll, she herself being the ten-year-old who gets the new toy for her birthday.

This story again evokes strong feelings in a reader, who probably has a strong image of how a decent mother should act like. The narrator's unbearable childishness and ignorance of her own inabilities as a mother are, of course, the main weapons of the text's satiric blade.

Ignoring the cutting edge of this blade can be surprisingly easy, especially when the text is read by an audience which matches the narrator's imagined age. When I introduced the text to my native Finnish speaking class of 15-year-old high school students, they could not stand the girl in the text. They called her idiotic and irresponsible. They understood her malfunctions as a mother. But most importantly, they could not cope with the paradox of the fictional nature of the story and, on the other hand, its realistic scenario. The subject came too close; the text's language was too realistic to be read purely as fiction. The students did not find the text funny, as I thought they might. This, again, tells us something about the seemingly easy settings of Liksom's texts, produced by their colloquialism and their casting of "ordinary" people. The test group's reactions prove that we need an understanding of certain definitions of basic concepts of literary techniques, if we want to read Liksom's texts as representatives of such styles. Naturally the sketches can be read in any other way, just like my students did, but perhaps then missing their essentially satiric nature.

A similar observation has been noted before, in another study of Liksom's earlier short stories, where a woman murders her husband without suffering any consequences. The story was used in a study (Eskola, 1996) of reader-reception theory. One set of responses was gathered by asking high school students and "new-middle-class" professionals about their opinions of the story. A second set of responses was gathered from university students in the social sciences. The respondents disliked the story on the grounds that the language was ugly and coarse. According to Jokinen, the reasons behind this response could be that the ideals to be seen behind the reception of Liksom's text are almost directly opposed to those Finnish readers usually use to characterise their favourite reading matter. (Jokinen, 2002)

The second story, in which Liksom deals with the multiples sides of motherhood, is the tale of the unfortunate mother who suffocates her baby by accident as a result of her birthday party. Even though one of the techniques used is the typically macabre juxtapositions of the innocent baby and her entirely careless mother, the main attention in this text focuses on the divided nature of the mother. The narrator speaks in two languages: A tough-tongued persona describes the craziness of the drinking gang, but when she talks about her baby, her tone changes entirely. The narrator uses expressions such as "oh, how sweet she was" or "a wave of tenderness washed over me". But in the end, the text switches back to the macabre reality of the young mother. Even the finality of death remains distant in her world, where the reality and fun of drunkenness is more familiar. In her child's funeral she just reads a poem where her late daughter is "waving happily at us from the top of a cloud". The story also carries side by side two entirely different conceptual worlds. On the other hand, there is the coarse world of the young drunks, where the value of fun is measured by the amount of alcohol, and the text is empty and cold in its violent self-abuse. But on the other hand, there is the poetic and romantic side of the narrator, who uses concepts such as the "goodness of God" and "wave of tenderness", to describe her perceptions. Still, the outcome is not one in which the protagonist grows and learns from her mistakes. Rather, the ending underlines even more the narrator's inability to take any responsibility for her actions.

What is Liksom's position in the Finnish literary scene? It is clear that she is the product of her own composition, an artist figure named Rosa Liksom. The popularity of her texts tells that there is a need for this kind of marginality in Finnish literary culture. Finnish literary scholar and critic Mervi Kantokorpi, who has studied Liksom's productions in depth, describes her texts as parodies that cultivate parallel, yet still relevant cultural texts. By these texts Kantokorpi does not only mean written texts, but also visual and spoken phenomena that tell stories about Finnish culture. (Kantokorpi, 1997, 20-21) Some other critics have, however, seen Liksom's texts as unsuccessful attempts to describe something *real*, and seeing her use of other art forms as an escapist way of deserting eschewing "serious" literature. (Jama, 1995) Perhaps the ambiguity of the interpretation in Liksom's artworks is their entire purpose.

Two things make translating Rosa Liksom's texts challenging. Firstly, Liksom often writes in a juicy and elaborate Northern dialect, her native language. The dialect is almost untranslatable without losing the atmosphere and the dialect's rich, specifically Northern vocabulary. Secondly, as a Laplander from a small village in Ylitornio, near the Swedish border, she represents the Northern moods and traditions, and the whole look at entire Northern worldview in her texts. Also this viewpoint is quite challenging to pass on in a translation. However, Liksom has proved of interest to a wider audience outside of Finland. She is currently one of the most translated Finnish contemporary writers, her texts being available in more than 15 languages.

Perhe

Novelli luvusta Lapsionni

Mie muutin Helsinkhiin kymmenen vuotta sitte ja asetin itteni asuhmaan tänne Kallion syähmeen. Molen kirjanpitäjä ja mulla on kotona oma virma. Tehen muutaman tilinpäätöksen vuessa, mutta enhän mie sillä elä, sosiaalihuolto minut maksaa niinko Roswitanki. Mie en ole pruukanu täälä pääkaupunkiseuvula käyä ulkona. Miekö olen semmonen aito luontoihminen ja ko täälä ei sitä luontoa ole niin molen aatelu pysyä sisälä. En ole solminu mikhäänlaisia suhteita näihin alkuperäisasukkhaissiin ko net tuntuva niinko kovasti ylpeiltä ihmisiltä. Soitan pohjosseen kerran päivässä. Mie ja sisko olema ko Jaakop ja Eessau, aina tukkanuottasilla. Mullehan kuuluu aina sitä sun tätä ko minun sisäneu elämä on niin rikasta. Mie säästän valtion rahoja ja porisen rapean tunnin. Kurkkuan oikein keuhkojen täyveltä ja sisko yrittää sanoa välhiin jotaki mullikoista ja siittä pörröstä äijästänsä, mutta eihän minua sen asiat juurikhaan kiinosta. Molen veikkosten niin helsinkiläistyny etten etes muista miten konheela lypsethään.

Molen semmonen kerrääjäihminen. Vuosikauet olen pannu kaikki valtionrahat kolphaan. Minun kortteeri oli niin täynä petsijoutsenia että jouvuin nukkuhmaan porstoan lattialla. Mieko olen aina ollu siisteyen perhään niin hyvinhän minun päivät kuluit siinä pölyrättiä heiluttaessa. Jos halvaa niin sanoa, olin vuosikauet oikein tytyväinen itheeni ja maaiilhmaan.

Viimikuussa mie heräsin keskelä yötä semmosecn vistoon vihlaukseen. Se nousi tuolta selkäpiistä ottalohkoon ja rävhäytti samala minun päähän semmosen ajatuksen, että mie halvan jättää ittestäni joku merkin tänne maanpinnale. Mietin, että mikä soon. Mulla ei ole ollu koskhaan lukupäätä niinko Veli-vaihnaala oli enkä mie ossaa verstää venheitä niinko Tyyne-täti. Valinanvarraa ei ollu. Hunteerasin, että vissiin soon minunki sitte pakko tehä kläppi. Mulle tuli kauhea hoppu jo hoksasin että hyänen aika molen jo pitkäle yli viiskymmentä.

Panin vaatheet pääle ja ajoin ratikalla Vuosaunkaule. Sielä mie seisoin kolmisen tiimaa ryssähuorien kanssa ja jo tuli miehenpuolikas kysyhmään, että mitä maksaa mitäki. Mie sanoin, että ei mithään, molen liikheelä tositarkotuksela. Vähän se siinä niinko empi mutta lähti kuitekki fölhjyyn. Menimä meile ja joima kahvit. Mie sanoin suohraan että halvaan maamerkin. Se nyökytteli, mutta justhiinsa ko meän olis pitäny laittaa siihen porstoan puolele, se pani ulsterin pääle ja käveli ovesta ulos.

Mie en antanu periksi. Aatelin, että molenko ko Raakkeli joka toivoo, pettyy ja taas toivoo. Panin pitkin toivon tietä asemalle ja sain sieltä houkuteltua yhen kevytpäisen Benonin matkhaan. Lorhautin samat praatit ja oikasimma pitkäksi. Mie siinä miettihmään, että mikä tälle panhaan nimeksi. Soli hiljaa pitkhään ja sano sitte, että sillä on hyppykuppa ja huulitippuri. Jo mie tipahtin hopusta ja korkealta. Mies keräsi vaatheensa porstoanlattialta ja meni pois, hyi olkhoon.

Mie siinä miettihmään että mikäs nyh etheen. Soithautin siskole, joka on tietekki ko Lea itte, kaetta täynä. Se oikein motkotti, että sie ja Eeva olettako kaks marjaa, molemat ahmitta syntiä ja halusitta ellää jotaki muuta elämää ko mitä Herra on teile määräny. Tietekki se aatteli, että minua ei ole luotu mihinkhään suuremphaan ko kolpaa jynssäähmään. Että aivanko minua ei olis koskhaan ollukhaan. En sanonu mithään. Maattelin, että vielä se saapi mainoa minun tekoja niin että tukehtuu siihen paikhaan.

Eilen mie sitte myin viimisen petsijoutsenen keltasessa pörssissä ja kävin ostamassa menolipun Tallihnaan. Sielä mie menen konitohtorille ja laitatan siemenen itähmään. Katothaan yheksänkuukauen päästä mihin asenthoon siskon naama sitte väänähtaa ko mie muutun Raakkelista Saaraksi.

Novelli luvusta *Lapsionni*

Lopetin Timin kanssa seukkaamisen elokuun viides ja syyskuun alussa mä olin raskaana. Ei se mikään vahinko ollu, mä laskin etä jos mä haluun kesävauvan niin se pitää panna itään syyskuussa. Mulla oli siis kiire. Mä menin kimmojen kanssa niin ku joka kesälauantai Kaivariin, join pääni täyteen ja kävin nussiin jonku espoolaisen lukiolaisen kanssa kallioilla. Ei siihen muuta tarvittu.

Mä en kertonu ekaan neljään kuukauteen kellekään, en edes Jannicalle vaikka se on mun bestis. Kelasin, että jos mutsi saa tietää niin se pakottaa mut abortiin. Mä siis venasin niin kauan ettei sitä pelkoa enää ollu. Ekaks mä kerroin mutsille ja sitten Jannicalle. Mutsi sekos totaalisesti. Se ei muuta ku itki ja hoki, ettei se enää jaksa hoitaa vauvaa. Mä sanoin että itsellenihän mä sen teen enkä sulle. Ei menny himaan. Jannica kohautti vain olkapäitä ja totesi että vittu sä oot tyhmä lehmä. Siinä koko saldo.

Sitä mukaa mun vatsa pyöristy, vanhat frendit kaikkos veke. Jannica lopetti soittelemisen ja aina kun mä ehdotin jotain niin sillä oli aina muuta. Eli se ei halunnu olla mun kaa enää missään tekemisissä. Mä purin hammasta että ookoo häipykää kaikki, mä haluun kesävauvan ja fuck off. Mutsi pysy mun messissä koska sen oli pakko. Se ei nimittäin luottanut pätkääkään mun selviytymiskykyyn. Se itki illat sitä, että mä en oo muka tajunnut sitä mieletöntä vastuuta, minkä skidi tuo mukanaan. Mä sanoin sille, että toi on jotain historiallista paskaa, että nykyään vauvat selviytyy itse elämässä eteenpäin, vittu modernit vauvat tarvii mitään hössötystä, ne huolehtii itsestään eikä niitä tarvi enää edes imettää kun tiede on kehitellyt kaikki tuttelit.

Mä ostelin vauvan vaatteita mutsin rahoilla, kävin kaikki kalukaupat läpi ja kannoin himaan miljoona lelua. Koko raskausaika oli älyttömän iisi. Mulla oli superolo, parempi ku koskaan aikaisemmin.

Toukokuun alussa se sit synty. Synnytys oli niin kaamee etten mä haluu puhuu siitä sen enempää, mut muuten kaikki skulas upeesti. Se oli vuosisadan hellekesä. Mä lojuin beibin kanssa kaiket päivät Uunisaaressa. Se ei duunannu mutta ku nukku, söi tuttelia ja ynähteli. Se oli terve ja helppo vauva. Mä hoidin sitä valtavalla innolla. Venasin malttamattomana että se pissaa ja kakkaa etä mä saan vaihtaa vaipat. Musta oli helvetin nastaa hoitaa sitä, ja siellä Uunisaaressa mä tutustuin Tiiaan ja Tuuliin, Mikaan ja Oskariin, Anjaan ja Johannaan. Otettiin brunaa ja meitä kaikki yhdisti yks juttu ja se oli tietysti vauva.

Syksy alko jo elokuun alussa, rupes sataan eikä me voitu mennä enää Uunisaareen. Anja ehdotti treffejä leikkipuistoon. Me mentiin sinne, mutta mikään ei ollu enää niinku ennen. Leikkipuisto tuntu tylsältä Uunisaaren aurinkoon verrattuna ja vähitellen mä jämähdin himaan ja mua rupes vituttaa koko vauva, vaikka se oli sairaan kiltti. Pari kuukautta mä siinä nähmäsin ja olo oli tosi kurja. Sit mä soitin mutsille ja sanoin, että sä olit oikeessa, tuu hakee tää beibi pois enneku muhun iskee ihan oikee depis. Mutsi tuli heti ja siitä saakka Elsa on asunut mutsin luona.

Mä rupesin riekkuun vanhojen frendien kaa ja Jannicaki rupes taas soitteleen. Me bailataan, relataan ja diggaillaan. Elsaa mä kutsun pikkusysteriks ja niin tekee kaikki muutki. Musta on paljon makeempaa olla isosisko ku äiti.

Oon mä kelannu, et sit ku mä olen viiskymppinen niinku mutsi nyt, mä hankin sellasen kesävauvan, josta mä pidän huolta myös talvella.

Novelli luvusta *Lapsionni*

Mulla oli synttärit lauantaina mutta me alettiin dokaamaan jo torstaina, heti kun äitiyspäivärahat tipahti tilille. Jartsa halus mennä Onnenmaahan vetään keskarin mutta mä sain sen pään kääntyyn ja me palattiin Alkon kautta himaan. Ostettiin kaksi neloskoria ja vielä viis Gambiinaa niinku juhlapäivän kunniaksi. Niissä oli ollu hirvee kantaminen, mutta lastenvaunujen alla ne kulki mukavasti. Mä olin hyvällä tuulella ja sanoin Jartsalle että kelaa nyt, nääki todistaa kuinka meidän kannatti tehdä vauva eikä abortti niinku mutsi ehdotti, vitun tappaja koko akka.

Okei, me mentiin meille, mä laitoin tuttelia pulloon ja heitin Jennan parvekkeelle. Se nukahti heti niinku aina. Isäänsä se on kai tullu, tuhisee ja nukkuu vaan. Me alotettiin bissellä ja mentiin siitä eteenpäin. Iltapäivällä meille tuli Jani ja Osku ja ne toi lisää viinaa. Me räkätettiin paskasesti ostarin hörhöille ja juttua riitti. Illansuussa mä muistin, että hitsi, mä olin unohtanut Jennan parvekkeelle. Mä ryntäsin sinne ja tietysti se itki. Naikahan silla ressulla oli ku ei ollu saanut koko päivänä ruokaa. Se oli ihan likomärkä ja mä kuivatin sen. Annoin sille kaks purkkia tuttelia ja hellin sitä ja vähitellen se rauhottu. Mä oon huomannut, et nousudokussa vauvanhoito on kaikista kivintä, laskuhumalassa taas tekee mieli heittää seinään koko paska.

Jartsa sammu jo kaheksalta ja mä ite puoleltaöin. Jani ja Osku jäi meille yöksi. Hyvä niin. Jani laittoi Jennan nukkumaan kun mä olin niin jurrissa että tiputin sen lattialle. Ei sille mitään tullu. Onneksi. Enkeli suojeli sitä niinku pikkuvauvoja aina, ei niille satu mitään, vaikka ne tippuu vaunuista tai rappuja alas.

Perjantaina piti skarpata, mutta heti kun Jani ja Osku lähtivät tuli Jartsan mutsi joka on kaamee puli. Se toi lisää viinaa ja me juotiin. Mä diggaan sitä muijaa koska se on nähnyt kaiken; se on saanut maistaa leipäveistä ja se on ollut Havajillaki viikon joskus nuorena, se muija ei jää ikinä toiseksi. Jartsa inhoaa sitä, koska se polttaa ketjussa. Jartsahan ei voi sietää röökinhajua. Siinä meni perjantai siihen malliin, että kolmen jälkeen mä en muista mitään. Jartsan mutsi oli hoitanu Jennaa, koska mä olin gone. Jartsa oli karannu jonku riidan jälkeen Onnenmaahan kostoksi ja niin edelleen. Tuttu juttu meidän perheessä.

Lauantai sarasti sitte saatanan sateisena ja mulla oli niin hirvee darra että mä tarvin kaks votkapaukkua ennenku mä pääsin edes sängystä ylös. Jartsan mutsi oli vielä meillä ja hyssytteli Jennaa, joka huus ihan ku sillä olis ollu puukko keuhkoissa. Voi vittu, mä kelasin. Jartsaa ei näkynyt. Makkarin lattialla loju parit sen paskaset sukat, siinä kaikki, vittu mikä jätkä. Mä olisin tappanu sen jos se olis tullu sillä hetkellä ovesta sisään. Se ties sen eikä uskaltanut tulla. Mä soitin Oskulle ja tottakai Jartsa oli siellä. Mä sanoin Oskulle, että potkase se saatanan paska pihalle. Se potkas ja Jartsa vääns ittensä himaan niin lutunen ilme naamalla. Me pussattiin, koska me rakastetaan niin toisiamme.

Okei, sit tuli tää Juhlapäivä, mä täytin kaksyks. Joskus aikaan, Jartsan mutsi sano, tää oli niinku täysikäsyyden raja, mä olis siis täysi-ikänen. Jartsan mutsi lähti himaan ja laitto Jennan parvekkeelle nukkuun. Mä kävin pussaan sitä. Voi miten sulonen se oli.

Me dokattiin koko lauantai. Naapuri soitti poliisit paikalle, kun sitä väkeä kertyi sieltä sun täältä ja desibelit nousivat suhteessa juhlakansan määrään. Jartsa osaa puhua ja pollarit häippäsivät vähin äänin.

Jenna kulki sylistä syliin ja kaikki paijas sitä kun se oli niin sulonen. Taija vaihto vaipat, Mari syötti, kuka mitäkin. Musta on hyvä, että vauva oppii jo nuorena sosiaaliseksi ja tottuu eri tyyppeihin, mä en ole ikinä ollu mustasukkanen. Mä vietin koko päivän lähinnä keittiössä Jartsan, Tuukan ja sen uuden kimmakaverin kanssa.

Kakut jäi tekemättä ja safkat kanssa, koska me oltiin koko helvetin jengi niin kauheessa pierussa. Jartsa sammu kymmeneltä, viimenen vieras lähti yhdeltä ja mä menin, vittu mä olin niin jurrissa, nukkuun heti sen jälkeen. Mä olin nukahtanut jo kun muistin että jumalauta missä Jenna on. Mä kompuroin lastenhuoneeseen ja mikä helpotus, siellä se tuhisi niin suloisena, että mut valtas se Ilanen kauhee helyyden puuska ja mä otin sen mun ja Jartsan viereen. Se ei edes herännyt kun mä siirsin sen. Mä kelasin, että voi ei kuinka Jumala on ollut hyvä, kun se anto meille tällasen vauvan, ja siihen mä nukahdin. Mä heräsin sunnuntai-aamuna 11.30 ja tuijotin hetken seinää. Ei kankkusta, ei mitään. Mä en edes muistanut mitään. Jartsa kuorsas tyytyväisenä ja mä käännyin ja ajattelin silittää sitä. Mutta jumalauta, siinä samassa kun mä käännyin mä muistin, että meillä on Jenna, kolmikuukautinen tyttö. Ja mitä vittua. se makas Siinä kuolemanvalkeana nyttynä. Mun ja Jartsan välissä. Mä hiffasin heti että se on kuollut. Tukehtunut jommankumman alle. Mä en uskaltanut koskea siihen. Mä herätin Jartsan ja se alko itkee. Mä soitin Jartsan mutsille, mutta se ei vastannut. Sitten mä soitin Oskulle, joka tuli samantien ja soitti poliisit paikalle.

Me haudattiin Jenna viime sunnuntaina. Hautajaisissa oli koko remmi, Oskut ja Janit sun muut. Se oli tosi kaunis tilaisuus. Mä luin sellasen runon, että siellä se Jenna vilkuttaa ilosena meille pilven päältä.

Novelli luvusta *Naiset*

Laitoin sanomalehteen ilmoituksen: tarvitsen kunnon miehen. Sain toistatuhatta vastausta, siivilöin kerman ja ehdotin tapaamista kolmelle. Kävin ehdokkaan läpi Café Esplanadilla saman päivän aikana., valinta oli helppo: turvatyynyllä varustettu Volvo, tilava moottorivene ja neljä vesiskootteria.

Hän sanoi olevansa viinaanmenevä toimistopäällikkö vaikka oli työtön autoradioasentaja. Minä sanoin olevani kampaaja vaikka olen lääkkeitä väärinkäyttävä lääkäri. Kesä meni kivasti pienessä pölyssä ja aina joko etupenkillä tai moottoriperseessä.

Tuli syksy ja olisi hänen pitänyt palata töihin. Se oli vaikeaa koska hänellä ei ollut työpaikkaa. Hän purki pahan olonsa minuun. Alamäki alkoi. Volvo seisoi pölyttyneenä parkkipaikalla, moottorivene upposi syyssateisiin ja nuorisorikolliset varastivat skootterit. Minä olin naistenklinikalla aina joko krapulassa, kännissä tai vähintään pahoinpideltynä.

Jouluaattona sanoin kollegalleni että nyt minä lopetan koko suhteen. Menimme minun kolmiooni ja missä tämä tapaus makasi hirveässä humalassa sohvalla. Ilmoitin hänelle ettei rakkautta enää olen. Hän katsoi minua hämmästynyt ilme kasvoilla ja sanoi laiskasti: "Älä viitti."

Minä poistuin kollegani kanssa keittokomeroon, pidimme palaverin, jonka aikana tyhjennettiin litran viskipullo. Ehdotin klassista tyynytapausta, mutta hän viittasi lääkekaappiin. Teimme cocktailin: sata grammaa pietarilaista vodkaa, kaksisataa viidenkymmenen gramman diapamia ja puolukka koristamaan joulujuomaan. Panin lasin jääkaappiin ja menin kollegani kanssa joulusaunaan. Kun olimme saunoneet palasimme olohuoneeseen. Siellä tämä piristynyt autoradioasentaja istui ja katseli televisiota. Kollegani sanoi hänelle, että joulun kunniaksi. Minä vilkaisin kelloa. Ruben tipahti ruutuun.

Hain juoman jääkaapista ja ojensin sen hänelle. Mies oli niin ahne, että imaisi sen pohjaan asti. Vatsalaukkuni väännähti. Tuntui samaan aikaan sekä hyvältä että pahalta.

Kollegani heitti lasin ikkunasta takapihalle ja minä vedin miehen omaisuuden vessanpöntöstä alas. Kaikki oli kuin häntä ei olisi koskaan ollutkaan. Paitse se ruumis, tietysti. Raahasimme sen kylpyhuoneeseen. Pesimme ja paketoimme. Hinasimme pakettia aamuyöllä Volvon takakonttiin ja ajoimme Salmisaareen. Työnsimme auton mereen.

Minä tilasin taksin. Ajoimme Tehtaankatua alas. Suurlähetystön kohdalla harhaili eksynyt joulupukki. Kollegani pysäytti taksin ja pyysi pukkia mukaan. Menimme kolmisin meille. Heräsin puolen päivän jälkeen olohuoneen sohvalta. Minut oli jätetty yksin. Join pullollisen vissyä ja muistin mitä olimme tehneet. Mietin soitanko ensin tappajien kriisikeskukseen ja sitten poliisille vai päinvastoin. Soitin poliisille. Kerroin päivystävälle yksityiskohtaisesti mitä oli tapahtunut. Hän kuunteli pari minuuttia aivan hiljaa, sitten hän keskeytti minut ja siirsi puhelun Hesperian päivystykseen. Siellä ystävällinen naisääni kehotti minua menemään nukkumaan. Hän puhui jotakin jouloustressistä joka laukeaa Tapanin jälkeen. Minä yritin selittää, ettei mistään sellaisesta ollut kyse, mutta nainen vain sanoi että minä voin tulla hakemaan päivystyksestä rauhoittavia, jos siltä tuntuu. Heilautin epätoivoisesti luurin paikoilleen, kävelin makuuhuoneeseen ja sujahdin viileään vuoteeseen. Annoin silmien painua kiinni ja vasta sitten minullekin heräsi epäilys. Olinko laittanut ilmoituksen lehteen vai olinko vain ajatellut laittaa? Olinko tavannut työttömän autoradionasentajan? Oliko mustaa Volvoa olemassa? Onko minulla yhtään kollegaa? Onko joulupukkia olemassa?

The Family[2]

Excerpts

Translated by Susanna Moliski

A short story from the chapter *The Babyluck*

I moved to Helsinki ten years ago and found myself right here at the heart of Kallio. I'm an accountant and have my own firm at home. I do a couple of balance sheets per year, but that really doesn't put the bread to the table. So I'm paid by the social support, just like Roswita.

I haven't gotten into the habit of going out here in the capital. You see, I'm a kind of an outdoor person myself, and since you don't have that here, nature I mean, I've decided to stay inside. Haven't had any relationships with these natives either: they seem so proud somehow.

I call North once a day. Me and my sister, we're like Jacob and Esau, always at each other's tails. I've always got something to report, you know, my inner life being so rich and all. I save the government's money and babble an hour or so. I rant and rave until my throat hurts and every now and then my sister tries to say something about the kettle and chat about her old man but couldn't care less. My goodness, I've turned into such a Helsinkian that I don't even remember how to use a milking machine anymore.

I'm a collector type. For years now, I've put all the government money aside. My place was so full of lacquered wooden swans that I had to sleep on the floor by the front door. And since I am such a tidy person, all my days went pretty much by whisking the duster. And let me put it this way; for years I was really satisfied with myself and my world.

---

[2]   Published by permission of Rosa Liksom.

Last month, in the middle of a night, I woke up to this nasty twinge. It shot up my spine to my forehead and jolted me with this idea that I really want to leave behind some kind of a mark of myself. I was wondering what that could be. I never was that clever in school like my late brother, and I can't carve boats either, like my Aunt Tyyne. I didn't have much of a choice. I thought that I too have to really have a kid. When I really started to panic, was when I noticed that I'm way over fifty already for God's sake.

I put my clothes on and left to the street where the hookers are on call. There I stood for about three hours with the Russian whores, and sure enough, one dude came to ask what I charge. I told him, nothing, and that I was there for the real thing. He looked kind of puzzled at first, but left with me anyway. We went to my place and drank a cup of coffee. I was straightforward about my wanting a landmark. He nodded but just when we should have gone to lie down by the floor, he took his coat and went out the front door.

I wouldn't give up. I thought that I'm like Rachel who hopes, gets disappointed, but then hopes again. Down the lane of hope I rambled to the station and luckily managed to seduce a guy to go with me. I put the usual on the table, and soon enough we were already lying down. I wondered to myself what to call this one. He was silent for a long time, but said then that he had syphilis and the gonorrhea on his lip. That surely brought me down from my dreams and fast. The man collected his clothes from the entrance floor and disappeared, for crying out loud.

There I am, wondering what the heck I'm going to do next. I rang my sis who is like Leah herself, so full of envy. She really started to whine like: "you and Eve are like a two peas in a pod, always gorging the sin, wanting to live in some other way than the one that the Lord has meant for you. Of course she thought that I was never created for anything better than scrubbing a kettle. Just like I was never even there. I didn't say anything. I was thinking to myself that one of these days she'll have to look up to my achievements so she'll drop dead right then and there.

So, yesterday I then sold my last lacquered wooden swan on eBay and went to buy a one way ticket to Tallinn. There I'll see a vet and have semen put in. After nine months let's see how my sister's face is going to look when I turn from Rachel into Sarah.

A short story from the chapter *The Babyluck*

I broke up with Timi on August 5th, and by the beginning of September, I was pregnant. It was no accident; I calculated that if I wanted a summer baby it had to get started in the fall. So I was in a hurry. I went with the girls to Kaivari Park, as every summer Saturday before, got wasted and fucked some high school kid from Espoo on the cliffs. That was about it.

I didn't tell anyone for the four first months, not even Jannica, who is my best friend. I figured that if mom gets to finds out she'll force me to have an abortion. So I waited until there was no fear of that. First I told mom and then Jannica. Mom totally flipped out. All she did was rant and rave about not being able to take care of another baby. I told her that I made this one for me, not for you. She just didn't get it. Jannica just shrugged her shoulders and claimed that you are one stupid fucking cow. That was the whole outcome.

As my belly got rounder all my old friends vanished. Jannica stopped calling and when I called she always had something else planned. I took it that she wanted nothing to do with me anymore. I grinded my teeth together like OK, go away you all, I want my summer baby and you can fuck off. Mom stuck with me because she didn't have a choice. She didn't trust in my survival skills whatsoever. Every night she would cry that somehow I didn't understand the responsibility that a kid comes with. I said that that's some pre-historic BS and that nowadays babies survive on their own in life, fuck, modern babies don't need any fussing, they take care of themselves and you don't even have to nurse anymore since science has developed formulas and all that.

I bought baby clothes with mom's money and I went through all stores and carried home about a million toys. The whole pregnancy was as easy as ever. I felt super good, better than ever.

Then, in the beginning of May it was born. The delivery was so awful that I don't want to say more about it, but otherwise everything went super smoothly. It was the hottest summer in the century. I spent every single day lying in Uunisaari Island with the baby. She did nothing else but slept, ate the formula and cooed. She was a healthy and easy baby. I took care of her with such enthusiasm. I couldn't wait for her to pee and pooh, so I could change the diaper. I thought it was so fucking cool to take care of her, and there in the island I also go to know Tiia and Tuuli, Mika and Oskari, Anja and Johanna. We lay in the sun and there was one common thing for us and that, of course, was a baby.

The Fall had begun already by the beginning of August, it began to rain and we couldn't go to the island anymore. Anja suggested a date in the park. We went there, but nothing was like it used to be. The park felt boring compared to the sun on the island, and little by little, I got stuck at home and the whole baby thing started to piss me off, even if she was so sweet. There I kind of hung on for a couple of months and I felt really lousy. Then I called mom and said that yeah you were right, come and get her away from me before I get really depressed. Mom came immediately and ever since, Elsa has lived with her.

I started to hang out with my old friends and even Jannica started to call me again. We party, hang out and dig stuff. I call Elsa my little sis and so does everyone else. I think it's so much cooler to be a big sis than a mom.

I've thought though that maybe when I'm like fifty or something like my mom is now, I'll get a kind of summer baby I'll take care in the winters, too.

A short story from the chapter *The Babyluck*

My birthday was on Saturday but we started to get wasted already on Thursday, right at the minute when the maternity welfare money dropped into my account. Jartsa wanted to go to a pub to suck down a pint, but I managed to change his mind and instead we returned home via the liquor store. We bought two cases of beer and also five Gambinas, just to celebrate, you know. It would have been a terrible gig to carry them but under the baby stroller they went on just fine. I was on a good mood and I said to Jartsa like, think about it, even this proves that the baby was really worth having, and not the abortion like mom suggested. That fucking killer bitch.

Okay, we went to our place and I put the formula into the bottle and took Jenna outside on the balcony. She slept immediately, like always. Comes after her father, I think, just sleeps and coos. So, we started with the beer and took it from there. In the afternoon Jani and Osku came and they brought more booze along. We laughed at the crazy bastards at the mall and babbled on and on. By the evening I remembered like, goddamn, I had forgotten Jenna out on the balcony. I rushed there and of course she was crying. She was hungry, the poor thing, having not eaten the whole day. She was like soaking wet and I dried her up. I gave her two carts of formula and comforted her and little by little she started to calm down. I have noticed that taking care of the baby is most fun when you're all tipsy but when you're going down, you feel like throwing the whole shitty thing to the wall.

Jartsa passed out already at eight and me about midnight. Jani and Osku slept over. That was good. Jani put Jenna to bed because I was so drunk that I dropped her on the floor. She was just fine, though. Thank God. An angel protected her like they always do protect little babies; nothing happens to them even if they would fall out from the stroller, or down the stairs.

On Friday I had to focus, but as soon as Jani and Osku left Jartsa's mom came, and she is as alcie as hell. She brought more booze and we drank. I dig that bitch because she has seen it all: She has got it from a knife and she's even been to Hawaii once for a week when she was young, that bitch is like never in the second place. Jartsa hates her because she smokes like a chimney. And you know that Jartsa can't deal with the smell of cigarettes. So the Friday went by so that after three I can't remember a thing. Jartsa's mom had taken care of Jenna, because I was so gone. Jartsa had vanished after some fight to the pub as a revenge and et cetera. Same ol' same ol' in our family.

The Saturday dawned rainy as hell, and I had such a terrible hang over that I needed two vodka shots just to get out of the bed. Jartsa's mom was still in our place she comforted Jenna who was screaming like she had a knife stuck in her lungs. Fucking fuck, I thought. Jartsa was nowhere around. On the living room floor was a pair of his dirty socks lying around, and that was all. That motherfucking douchebag. I would have killed him if he would have got in at that very moment. He knew that and wouldn't come. I called Osku and sure enough; Jartsa was there. I told Osku to kick that fucking loser out. He did, and Jartsa dragged his body home with such a cutie pie face on that I had to kiss him, because that's how much we love each other.

Okay, then came this big day of celebrations and I turned twenty-one. Once upon the time, Jartsa's mom said, it was like coming of age, and this made me of age, then. Jartsa's mom went home and put Jenna to sleep on the balcony. I went to give her a kiss. Oh, how sweet she was.

We drank booze all Saturday. The neighbor called the police when people started to gather around from all over the place, and decibels raised by the amount of folks partying. Jartsa can talk, and the cops disappeared without a whimper.

Jenna went from lap to lap and everyone was petting her because she was so adorable. Taija changed her, Mari fed her, everyone did something. I think it's good that the baby gets all these social skills already so young and gets used to all kinds of different people, and I was never a jealous type myself. I spend the whole day mostly in the kitchen with Jartsa and Tuukka, and with his new bitch.

We never got to the point of baking the cake or making the food, because the whole gang was so fucking wasted. Jartsa passed out about ten, the last guest left at one o'clock and I went, fuck, I was so wasted, to sleep right after that. I had already fallen asleep when I remember that fuck, where is Jenna. I staggered to the living room and to my relief, there she was, snuggling so sweetly that this sort of a wave of tenderness washed over me and I took her to the bed next to me and Jartsa. She didn't even wake up when I moved her. I thought like oh, how good God is that he gave us this kind of a baby, and I fell asleep to that thought.

I woke up about 11.30 am on the Sunday morning and stared at the wall for a while. No hang over, nothing. I didn't even remember anything. Jartsa was snoring happily and I turned to him and thought to pet him. But for crying out loud, as I turned I remembered that we have a girl, three months old. And for fuck's sake. There she lies still like a little baggy, white as a ghost. Between me and Jartsa. I figured out immediately that she was dead. I couldn't touch her. I woke Jartsa up and he started to cry. I called Jartsa's mom but she didn't pick up. Then I called Osku who came right away and called the police.

We buried Jenna last Sunday. The whole gang was at her funeral, Osku, Jani and everyone. It was a beautiful ceremony. I read a poem that said like, there she is, Jenna, waving happily at us from the top of the cloud.

A short story from the chapter *Women*

I put an ad in the newspaper: I need a decent man. I got close to two thousand replies, screened the *crème de la crème* from them and suggested a date for three. I went through the applicants at Starbucks that same day and the decision was easy: a Volvo with an airbag, a roomy motor boat and four water scooters.

He said that he was an office executive with a sweet tooth for booze, even though he was an unemployed car radio mechanic. I said I was a hairdresser even though I was a drug-abusive doctor. The summer went by on a nice high, and always either in the front seat or in the rear end by the engine.

The fall came and he should have returned to work. Well, that was hard since he didn't have a job. He took it out on me. It was all downhill from there. The Volvo got dusty in the parking lot, the autumn rains sank the boat, and young criminals stole the scooters. I personally was at the Women's Clinic always either hung over, wasted, or at least beaten up.

On Christmas Eve I said to my colleague that now I will end this relationship. We went to my condo, two bedrooms, and there this case was slouching on my couch, terribly wasted. I let him know that there was no love anymore. He looked at me with a surprised look on his face and said lazily: "C'mon."

I withdrew with my colleague to the kitchenette and we had a short briefing, during which we drank a gallon of vodka. I suggested the classic case with a pillow, but she pointed to the medicine cabinet. We made a cocktail: three ounces of vodka from St. Petersburg, two hundred pills of 50 mg Prozac, and a lingonberry to garnish the Christmas punch. I put the glass in the fridge and went to the Christmas sauna with my colleague. When we had bathed we returned to the living room. There the car radio mechanic was all brightened up, watching TV. My colleague suggested a Christmas toast. I peaked at my watch. Leno appeared on the screen.

I fetched the drink from the fridge and handed it to him. The man was so greedy that he sucked down the cocktail with one gulp. My heart sunk. I felt good and bad at the same time.

My colleague threw the glass out of the window to the backyard, and I flushed his possessions down the toilet. It was as if he had never existed. But there was the body, of course. We dragged it to the bathroom. Washed and wrapped it. We towed it to the back of the Volvo in the late night and drove to Salmisaari. We pushed the car into the sea.

I called a cab. We drove down Tehtaankatu. There was a lost Santa Claus wandering around the embassy. My colleague stopped the taxi and asked the Santa to come along. All the three of us went to my place.

I woke about noon on the living room couch. I had been left alone. I drank a bottle of sparkling water and remembered what we had done. I was considering whether to call first the hot line for killers or the police. I called the police.

I told the officer on duty a detailed version of what had happened. He listened silently for a couple of minutes, then interrupted me and switched the call to the ER of the mental hospital. There, a friendly woman's voice told me to go to get some sleep. She mentioned something about the Christmas stress that will ease after Boxing Day. I tried to explain it had nothing to do with that but she just said that I could come to the ER to get some sedatives if I felt like it. I swung the receiver back to its place with a desperate move, walked to the bedroom and slipped into the cool bed. I let my eyes close and it was only then that a suspicious thought came to me. Did I place an ad to the paper or did I only think about doing it? Had I even met an unemployed car radio mechanic? Was there a black Volvo? Do I have any colleagues? Does Santa Claus exist?

Primary Works

Yhden yön pysäkki, 1985; Eng. tr. *One Night Stands*, 1993.
Unohdettu vartti: stories, 1986.
Tyhjän tie paratiisit, 1989.
Väliasema Gagarin, 1987.
Go Moskova go, 1988.
Roskaa, 1991.
Bamalama, 1993.
Family affairs, 1993.
Kreisland, 1996.
Värityskirja, cartoons, 1998.
La famille terrible dans L'univers cybernetique, 2000.
Jepata Nastan lentomatka, 2000.
Perhe, 2000.
Reitari, 2002.

Selected Bibliography

Eskola, Katarina, ed. *Nainen, mies ja fileerausveitsi: miten Rosa Liksomia luetaan?*. Jyväskylä: Jyväskylän yliopisto (*Nykykulttuurintutkimusyksikön julkaisuja*, 49), 1996.

Jama, Olavi. "Haaparannan lukiosta sipirjaan. Tornionjokilaakson kirjallisuus kahden kansalliskirjallisuuden marginaalissa." Matti Savolainen, ed. *Marginalia ja kirjallisuus. Ääniä suomalaisen kirjallisuuden reunoilta*. Helsinki: Suomalaisen kirjallisuuden seura, 1995.

Jokinen, Kimmo. "Liksom's Short Story 'We Got Married' and (Finnish) Identity Construction." Comparative Literature and Culture: A WWWeb Journal. Purdue University, 2002. http://clcwebjournal.lib.purdue.edu/clcweb02-4/jokinen02.html.

Kantokorpi, Mervi. "Kymppi juksauksessa. Rosa Liksomia lukiessa." Mervi Kantokorpi, ed. Muodotonta menoa. Kirjoituksia nykykirjallisuudesta. Juva: WSOY, 1997.

–. "Hiljainen on kylätie. Rosa Liksom yhdistelee edelleen naurua ja kauhua." Helsingin sanomat, September 24, 2000.

–. "Pätkiksen kymmen vuotta." Helsingin sanomat, September 24, 2000.

Puumala, Anne. "Rosa Liksom kuvaa pimeää perhe-elämää." Ilkka, October 11, 2000.

Reynolds, Bill. "Lapland Cowgirl Goes Canada. Finnish writer Rosa Liksom gets a chance to demonstrate why her post-punk prose about losers is finding a large audience in Europe." Eye, October 21, 1993.

Soikkeli, Markku. "Taiteilijakuva Reitarista kaamoksen väreissä." Satakunnan kansa, November 13, 2002.

Inger-Mari Aikio-Arianiaick: From Mauritius and Ivalo

CHARLES PETERSON (NORTH PARK UNIVERSITY, CHICAGO)[1]

A Visit to Ima in Sápmi

Ivalo, Finland, is the northernmost airport served by the national airline Finnair. It is a small but international town. During a short stay at the Hotel Ivalo, one can hear Finnish, Norwegian, Russian, English, and Sámi spoken. A highway road sign points the way to Murmansk, Russia, 330 kilometers to the east. I flew to Ivalo in November 2004 to meet Inger-Mari Aikio-Arianiaick, a Sámi poet and journalist, who prefers to be called Ima. She had agreed to assist with the translation of her poems. Ima lives in Ivalo with her husband Sudhir and their son Áilu.

Inger Mari Aikio-Arianiaick (Ima) was born in 1961 near Lake Polmak, Norway, on the Finnish border. She attended boarding school in Nuorgam and Utsjoki, Finland, in the 1960s and 1970s. Most of her teachers were Finnish. Unlike teachers in boarding schools in earlier generations, Ima's instructors did not prevent her from speaking Sámi. She remembers how exciting it was when she had her first Sámi teacher, "Finally, someone like me!"

The textbooks, however, referred only to Finland and Finnish history. There was but one page about the Sámi: "Sámi live in the north, are short with black hair, black eyes, bowed legs and they herd reindeer," she recalls. (Aikio-Arianaick 2004)

Even today primary school textbooks do not include much Sámi history. Indeed, most Sámi language textbooks in Finland are translations of Finnish textbooks. Speaking of her young son's classroom experience during a

[1] I would like to acknowledge a travel and translation grant I received from FILI, the Finnish Literature Information Centre. I also appreciate the encouragement I received from the FILI staff to undertake this project and for their commitment to making Sámi literature in translation available to the English speaking reader.

break in the translation project, Ima stated, "Áilu learns about apple trees but not about the plants that grow around him." (Aikio-Arianaick 2004)

Ima was in the first group of students at the University of Oulu to study Sámi as a major subject area during the period 1980-82 but never finished her degree. Her first job was with *Sámi Aigi* (Sámi Times), a Sámi language newspaper in Karasjok, Norway. In 1988 she was employed by Sámi Radio in Inari, Finland, although she had no training in radio journalism. She began to travel for her own enjoyment and experience, visiting Asia, Africa, Central and South America, Australia and finally Mauritius where she arrived in 1993. "Magazines describe Mauritius as Paradise Island. Always warm, friendly people, good food, close family life," Ima recalls. (Aikio-Arianaick 2004) The island had been a Dutch, then French, and finally an English colony before winning independence in 1968. The inhabitants were former slaves and workers from Africa, India and Asia. The people have an international and multicultural worldview.

It was on Mauritius Ima met her husband, Sudhir, whose family migrated from India to Mauritius 150 years earlier. Her latest book *Máilmmis dása* (2001; From the World and Home) describes the difficulty of becoming a family when cultural and behavioral differences, different understandings and different religions collide in a small home. Their son, Áilu, was born in 1998. He was given that name in honor of the great Sámi cultural leader, Áillohaš (Áilu), known internationally by his Finnish name, Nils-Aslak Valkeapää (1943-2001). Valkeapää was not only active among the Sámi, but also was active in international organizations of indigenous peoples.

The family returned in April 2001 to Sápmi, the Sámi name for their region in Northern Scandinavia. Sudhir studied to become a cook and now works in the restaurant at the Hotel Ivalo, an interesting occupation for a Hindu vegetarian. He hopes to start his own restaurant some day. The family lived in a Sámi village before moving into Ivalo. "It was good for Áilu to be Sámi before we moved here to Ivalo. Now he admires the Finns. After three days in school, Áilu came home demanding, 'Don't always talk about the Sámi! We live in Finland,'" Ima recalls with some disappointment. (Aikio-Arianiaick 2004)

Ima has now finished a two-year time multi-media journalism program at ADULTA, one of Finland's largest educational centers. Her goal is to make Sámi films for theater and television. She also plans to return to Sámi Radio to produce radio and television. She is currently producing a children's CD featuring her own texts set to music by the best contemporary Sámi composers and performers including Niko Valkeapää, Mari Boine, Kai Somby, Sofia Jannok, Johan Kitti, Jiella, Mia Rasmus, Amoc&Aziz, Nicko Buljo, Catarina Utsi, and Tiina Aikio.

The significance of Sámi Cultural Production

Ima's books, CDs, and other media, are significant for two reasons. First, it is important to create new media in the Sámi language about the modern Sámi experience. The Sámi language requires new cultural products to encourage the consumption of Sámi language media by the Sámi people. Sámi literacy is now rebounding after generations of suppression and neglect by the dominant cultures. This come-back is the result of new media productions by Sámi authors, artists, musicians, journalists, and filmmakers. Second, it promotes an understanding of Sámi culture by the dominant cultural groups in Scandinavia and Europe.

The Sámi are the indigenous Nordic people of Northern Norway, Sweden, Finland and the Kola Peninsula of Russia. The total Sámi population is between 60,000 and 100,000 and a cautious estimate would be about 70,000. In Norway there are believed to be between 40,000 and 45,000 Sámi concentrated in the northern province of Finnmark, where there are about 25,000. Other Norwegian Sámi are distributed throughout Norway. Sweden has an estimated 17,000 Sámi, Finland has about 5,700. Most of the Swedish and Finnish Sámi live in Sápmi. About 2000 Russian Sámi live in the Kola Peninsula region.

The Sámi have suffered in ways similar to indigenous people the world over. In the past, dominant culture and national governments required that traditional ways of life (native languages, native dress, and native beliefs) be abandoned in favor of the dominant national culture. This was an effort to force the Sámi to become Norwegian, Swedish, Finnish, or Russian. Sápmi was invaded by settlers from the south. Rivers were dammed to provide electrical power needed by society in general. Borders were drawn and national identities were imposed upon them

Society in general considered the Sámi primitive and concluded they possessed no "culture." The Sámi language has survived because Sámi artists, poets, journalists, musicians, and authors have kept it alive through their dedication to Sámi culture. With a living language Sámi culture is not just a museum of traditional ways. In a sense Sámi culture has become a voice of encouragement for vibrant indigenous cultures throughout the world.

Over the centuries, anthropologists have been active in researching traditional Sámi culture. One very readable and enjoyable modern text by the American author, Hugh Beach, tells of his experience living with Sámi reindeer herders in Swedish Sápmi. His account reveals the great sense of humor that is typically Sámi and highlights the difficulty of maintaining the Sámi way of life. (Beach 2001)

A Review of Sámi Literature

A good introduction to the history of Sámi literature and other media is in the curriculum for the Bachelor of Circumpolar Studies at the Saami University College in Kautokeino, Norway. The section "Sámi Media, Arts, and Literature," an excellent review of the history of Sámi literature, was written by Vuokko Hirvonen. (Hirvonen 2004) Contemporary Sámi literature began in the 1960s with the work of several Sámi authors including the poet Paulus Utsi (1918-75) and the multi-media artist Áillohaš or Nils-Aslak Valkeapää (1943-2001). Áillohaš' pivotal role in the development of Sámi cultural production will be discussed here because his breakthrough as an artist was the major source of inspiration for Inger-Mari Aikio-Arianiaick and her entire generation.

Áillohaš began his cultural career as a yoiker. (A yoik is a traditional form of singing similar to the Native American chant, an intensely personal form of expression.) He expanded his cultural production as an author, composer, painter, sculptor, photographer and actor. His first book was first published in Finnish in 1971, *Terveisiä Lapista* (Eng. tr. *Greetings from Lapland*, 1983). The text was an introduction to the history and life of the Sámi, who in the book's subtitle are called "Europe's forgotten people." Even the Sámi's neighbors in the dominant Scandinavian culture knew very little about the Sámi when the book was written. This, unfortunately, is true even today.

Áillohaš' collection of poems *Beaivi, Áhčážan* (1988; Eng. tr. *The Sun, My Father*, (1997), was honored by the Nordic Council of Ministers with the Nordic Council Literature Prize in 1991. He was the only Sámi author to win the prize since the award was first presented in 1962. In 1994, Áillohaš was featured in the opening ceremony of the Olympic Games in Lillehammer, Norway. Arriving in the stadium on a sled pulled by a reindeer, he welcomed the world to Norway by performing a *yoik*. Áillohaš' international breakthrough as a poet came with the English language publication *Trekways of the Wind* (1994). The original Sámi edition, *Ruoktu Váimmus*, had been published by the Sámi publishing house DAT in 1985. Áillohaš toured the United States in 1995 to read from *Trekways of the Wind* meeting enthusiastic audiences as he performed his poetry in the original Sámi.

The similarities between Áillohaš' poetic style, layout, and artistic design and Ima's *Máilmmis dása* are readily apparent. They have on occasion co-operated. Áillohaš' books include his own drawings, photographs, and music notations. His poems are without individual titles and often use only lower case letters without punctuation. The individual lines may be indented in rhythmic patterns. Ima's Sámi language edition of *Máilmmis dása* features artwork by Áillohaš with photos by Ima and others. Her poems have no titles and use only lower case letters with very little punctuation. Individual lines may be indented.

A significant anthology of modern Sámi authors was published in an original English edition edited by the leading Sámi scholar, Harald Gaski from Tromsø University in Norway. *In the Shadow of the Midnight Sun* (1997) includes twenty-one short contributions from leading Sámi authors. Gaski has also edited a significant collection of essays on various aspects of Sámi culture in the volume entitled *Sami Culture in a New Era: The Norwegian Sami Experience* (1997). These two books provide an excellent introduction to the cultural context of Inger-Mari Aikio-Arianiaick.

Ima expresses not only the reality of Sámi women's experience but the experience of many women everywhere in the world. She reveals that all people, even the indigenous, face challenges in confronting multiculturalism. Ima shares with the reader her story of falling in love, getting married, being pregnant, giving birth and the first two years with her son. This is not an unusual story save that the couple comes from two cultures separated by many miles possessing many cultural differences. It is a long distance from Sápmi in Northern Europe to Mauritius in the Indian Ocean. The differences in life styles, foods, family life, and language proved to be a challenge to Ima even though she thought she would have no trouble with cultural differences.

I have found that female readers at my university, North Park University in Chicago, respond with appreciation and understanding to Ima's way of expressing her feelings. Her text is very female. It bravely describes the feelings of love, desire, uncertainty, wonder, anger, frustration and fear that are part of every parent's experience.

Máilmmis dása[2]   From the World and Home

Translated from Northern Sámi by Inger-Mari Aikio-Arianaick and
Charles Peterson

ájačáhci	spring water
honnet ja	honey and
silkeguobbara lákca	the silk mushroom's cream
ráhkesvuođa juhkamuš	the juice of love

---

[2]   (c) 2004 Nordic Studies Press, Chicago. Original book in Northern Sámi (c) 2001 Máilmmis dása DAT o.s, N-9520 Guovdageaidnu & Inger-Mari Aikio-Arianaick.

láđasmánnu	the full moon
munno lavttii	brought us together
oktii čanai	bound a band
ovttas doalai	held us fast
otnege munno guoddá	even today it bears us

láđasmánu šaldi mielde	over the full moon's bridge
lea álki	it is easy to walk
vázzit giehtalagaid	hand in hand

beaivi	sun
beaivvadat	sunshine

lihkku	happiness
lihkolaš	happily
lihkoleamos beaivi	the happiest day

munno heajat!	our wedding day!

dus čoaska čakča	a cold autumn for you
go dušše	when there was only

mu olbmot	my people
mu vierut	my ways
mu albmi	my sky

fáhkkestaga obbadálki	suddenly overcast

hoigadan čičči njálbmái	I lay a breast against your mouth

dat jeđđe	it comforts
olles albmáge	the entire man

ja go	and when
leaibeloddi seaivu	the redstart flies
váibmui	into the heart
vašši váidu	endured is the hate
erdos sánit goiket	insults silenced

iđitidja vizarda	the morning quits
beivviid njuolgut	the end of the day

go livččiimege guovttá	if we had only had peace
oahpahallamin eallit ovttas	to learn to live together
muht´ go dállu	but when the house is
dego márkanbáiki ja	like a marketplace and

juohkehaččas iežas ártetvuođat
muhtimin
nu dievva njálmmiid
čalmmiid, beljiid
aht´ buviha
ja doadjala čielggi

everyone has his ways
sometimes
so full of voices
eyes, ears
that I suffocate
and my back breaks

buorre dieđus
aht´ in astta doarrut isidiin
go anán buot fámuid
gierddahallat earáid

it is good, of course
that you don't fight
if all energy is used
to put up with the other

vuohpa garra jiena
vuotnáma sálmmaid
nuppi manji uksabeaškasa

the father-in-law's bitter voice
the mother-in-law's psalms
the sister-in-law's slamming of
                              doors

sivjjoha stoavkkuheami

the brother-in-law's lip smacking

gierddahallat
gierddahallat gierddahallamis

endure
endure enduring

ja gos mu eallin?
munno eallin?

and how about my life?
our life?

gökčon uvuuu duohken
lovttas 15 m² lanjas
ja doppege vel
vuotnáma lássaliinnit
vuotnáma addin seaŋgagovččas

behind the closed loft door
in 15 square meters
and in addition to
mother-in-law's curtains
mother-in-law's bedspread as a gift

botnis gal
iežan giehtasihkaldat
masa okta ja nubbige ain sihkasta

on the level below
my own hand towel
which everyone uses to dry
                              themselves

vieris gielat
vieris mielat

a strange language
a strange disposition

ja de mun
eallit dáppe?
ealestuddat?
gierddahallat?

and then I
live here?
survive?
endure?

ále gáttege
leat guhká lihkolaš!

just don't believe
in long-lasting joy!

biro nádđá
orbbeža gacca vuolde

the devil tempts
under the ring finger nail

ja huikkaša	and he rules there
čuohpan gacca	I clip the nail
ja dat ferte fárret	and he must surrender
ja máhccá fas	and he comes back
dalán go	as soon
gazza guhkku	as the nail grows
inhan mun	a well-traveled person
máilmme johtti	such as I
šat oaččo kulturšohka	surely won't suffer culture shock
gohan beare	if only
duot bahálačča krishnat	the damned Krishna
eaimmaskas liidneoaivvahat	the idiotic headscarves
ja dammalaš suoidneborrit	and the blasted cud chewers
eai boađe menddo lahka	don't come too near
bággu čuovvut	found it necessary
amas dábiid	to follow strange customs
vaši siepmanat	the seeds of hate
gahččet suttes eatnamii	fall in soft ground
čullet juovaid	you cleared the fields
čogget geđggiid	removed the stones
boldet guluid	burned the withered grass
vuollánkeahttá	without giving up
gilvet ja njuoskadit	you sowed and watered
jagis jahkái	year after year
ja de	and then
viimmat	finally
runiidii	green
ráhkesvuođainat	with your love
cahkkehit geasi	you ignited summer
mu sisa	in me
čohkkán uvjabeasis	I sit in my down nest
lállán ruškes mani	sitting a brown egg
soaját dolgi	your wing

njávkkasta njunnemáddagan	tickles the tip of my nose
beaivi báitá	the sun shines
eallin vizarda	life laughs
sáhkkiivuohta	curiosity
doalvu mánnui	carries to the moon
šaldi vuollái	to ruin
ja áhpeheapmin	and pregnancy
vissa vel	you will surely
earráneahkki!	divorce!
eanemustá	maximum
njeallje jagi!	four years!
na, eanemustá!	maximum!
čicža mánu	seven months
jo vádjolan	are already past
juohke beaivvis	and every day I
giittán vuollegaččat	most humbly give thanks
giittán lihkus	thanks for the joy
go ii dan	that nobody
goassige dieđe	ever can know
callimu	what life brings
ja olbmuid	and where humanity
gosa de	ends
gohčodit dán sullo paradiisan	this island is called paradise
beaivvádat	sunshine
pálbmamuorat	palms
turkosa mearra	turquoise blue ocean
muhto ásamat dáppe!	but try to live here!
guohca šaddomirkkohádja	stinking plant venom
goddá njuni ja	sticks in the nose and
gákkaha váimmu	I want to throw up
juohke nuppi beaivve	every other day
plastihkkaboahtalat	plastic bottles

plastihkkaseahkat	plastic bags
ruovdestobet	scrap iron
lihparat	diapers
báiddit	rags
gápmagat	shoes
báberkássat	paper bags
spáppat	soccer balls
sihkkelat	bicycles
don muora vuolde	under the tree
dán geaidnoguoras	in the ditch
duon mearragáttis	on the beach over there
dáthan lea duge ruoktu!	your home, this!
ii, ii agibeaivvesge	no, no never
nu guhká go	not so long as
in beasa málistit	I am not allowed to
maid háliidan	prepare the food I want to
in beasa válljet	not allowed to choose
lássaliinniid	the curtains
gohppaskáhpiid	the cupboard for the cups
ja gohpaid skáhpiide	and the cups for the cupboard
in beasa	not allowed to
giddet radio	turn off the radio
ja guldalit biekka	and hear the wind
dalle go háliidan	when I want to
nu guhká	not as long
go in beasa	as I don't have permission
manna ija	tonight I dreamed
niegadin málesbeavddi	four times
njealje geardde	of a lavish buffet table
ja guktii ovddit ija	and twice the night before
ja dan ovddit	and the night before that
inge beassan borrat	but I didn't get to eat
nugo in dáppege	like I don't get to eat here either
earágo suinniid	other than green fodder
lasttaid	leaves
rásiid	grass

amas dábit	strange customs
loktejit vaši	bring forth hate
dál ádden	now for the first time I understand
láttániid ja dážaid	the animosity
garra vuostehágu	that Finns and Norwegians
oahppat sámi	have towards everything Sámi
lihkus	luckily
beasan Sápmái	I am able to travel to Sápmi
eret dearvvaslaš ja nu	away from the wholesome
mirkkohuvvon šattuin	but poisonous plants
de fas	back to
bohccobiergu ja	reindeer meat and
čuovža, rávdu, luossa	whitefish, char, salmon

lean jo mannan	I have already left
vaikko	even if
vahku geažes easkka	I don't travel
vuolggán	for another week

skážas čohkánasta	a dragonfly sits
telefonstreaŋgga ala	on the telephone line

baksamiid bajábealde	sweat beads
laksi	on my lips

lea áigi	it is time
vuolgit	to go

nu don bázát	so you will remain
ja mun vuolggán	and I travel
ruđa maŋŋái	to where the money is

arvá	it is raining

olgun jo goalmmát vahku	for the third week
ja siste	and into
goalmmát beaivve	the third day

manin	why
máilbmi lea	is the world
álo nu guhkkin	always someplace else

manin	why
in mun	not I
ja don	and you

moai gehčče mánu	we gaze at the moon
mun dáppe	I here
don dieppe	you there

seamma mánu	the same moon

molssodan	I change my clothes

du čáhppes vuokta	I find your coal black hair
ain mu báiddis	on my blouse

boahtte ija	during the night
dat oađđá muinna	it sleeps with me

suorpmat	my fingers
čáŋadit vuovddis	in the bush
ohcet	look
ain du hája	for your scent
vaikko	even
jo máŋga mánu	after many months

vuosttas goaikkanasat	the first drops

šerres šearádat	shining clear
čižžegeažis	on my nipples

gullengo	I felt
su vuosttas čievččastagaid	the first kicks

vai buoskago dat	or was it only
dušše jođii?	a little fart?

son juhkagoahtá	he will begin to drink
don buohccát	you will get sick
doai earráneahkki	you will be divorced

šaddos du dáhttu!	thy will be done!

aiddo dál	right now
lean lihkolaš	I am happy

doppe son
čievččada

I feel a kick
there

jo dál
vuos su dárbbut

already now
the little one's needs

ja de
easkka mu

and then
before mine

reastalasat goikot
vuovdi šuvvá
soávll njuoskada
    gápmagiid

it drips from the roof
the forest sighs
I wander about
slush wet shoes

ja don
ainge nu guhkkin

and you
are still so far away

áhpehis nisu
galgá duhtadit háluidis
borrat justa dan maid háliida
ja dalle go háliida

she who expects a child
should heed the body's demands
eat what she desires
and when she desires

muđui
máná muođut rubbot

otherwise
the child will get a rash

chpet goittotge
suovvan mu
borrat bierggu!

in spite of this
you wouldn't let me
eat meat!

giehta
ohcala vuovdái

the hand
explores the bush

go don
leat nu guhkkin

when you are
so far away

vare son livččii nieida
    vare nieida
        nieida, nieida!
            nieida!

may it only be a girl
    be a girl
        girl, girl!
            girl!

gánda dušše morrašiid buktá
    láhtti ráigá
    seinniid njeaidá

boys only bring sorrow
    tear down the walls
    wear holes in the floor

lottiid báhčala
ovssiid doadjala

shoot birds
break branches

juhká ja doarru
eatni kámmárii nášđu

drink and fight
lays in bed with his mother

leage movtta
jurddaš beare čábbáid
balvvaid ja rásiid

keep your courage up
think about all the beauty
the flowers and the clouds

ále vašut geange
leage ráfálaš
amas mánás šaddat bahánihkkán

bear no grudge against anyone
keep the peace
so that your baby won't be naughty

dál jo
guhtta mánu ovdal riegádahttima
sii gilvet munnje sivalašvuođa

everything now
six months before birth
makes me feel guilty

olbmot
buorástahttet
mu čoavjji

people
greet
my stomach

ja de
easkka mu

and then
greet me

jus šat muitet

if they remember

geahčan speadjalis
njávkkadan čoavjji
in leat šat okto

look at me in the mirror
stroke my stomach
I am no longer alone

mánnu
laktá munno gieđaid
rastá ábi

the moon
clasps our hands
over the sea

biilalása sihkoniin
báhcá njođves luodda
mohtor gastá

after the windshield wipers
an obscure veil
the motor sputters

váimmu
šerres ádjagiin
goit illu basada

but in the heart's
clear spring water
bathes the joy

ja de
du hádja

in the redstart's chirping
in the whir from the wings

and then
your scent

leaibelotti civkasis
soajá rámškasis

du hádja
hádja
ja munno

your scent
scent
and ours

dovden du dalán
muhto
jáhldden easkka
go golbma dálvvi
ledje dápman mu

I recognized you immediately
but
was not able to believe it
before three winters
had tamed me

buađát
salastat maŋábeale

you come from behind
embrace me

gieđat
gávdnet

the hands
find

du soajá vuolde
havssán fas giđa
man mánnán láhppen

under your wings
I sense the scent of spring
that which was gone
when I still was a child

eai šleađggo násttit
eai libar guovssahasat

not a twinkling stars
a puff of northern lights

du gieđas
jaskes áhpi

in your hands
still ocean

otná iđit
fuomášin ruškes sárgá

early this morning
I could see a dark streak

mánná beahkimin
váimmu guvlui

the child crawls nearer
the heart

mu čiekŋalis
čáppa náhpi bukkada

my beautiful navel
bulges

viggágo son
dakko olggos?

are you trying
to come out there?

vuosttas geardi	the first time that
go in dárbbaš	I did not need
viggat čiehkat čoavjji	to hide my stomach

ránes šearpmas	on the gray screen
dego suoivanat	exactly like shadows

doavttir cuoigu	the doctor points
oaivi, váibmu	head, heart

iige mahká oainne	but he says he can't see
nieida vai gánda!	if it is a girl or a boy!

muht´ mun oainnán	I can even see
su unna suorpmažiid!	the small fingers!

čielgebávččas	pain in the back
suotnageasáhat	pulled ligaments
raddeboalddáhat	burning breasts

allet muital	but stay calm

aman bovdet daid	so it isn't caused
iežan baluiguin	by my anxiety

easkka 30 sentesaš	only 30 centimeters
ja dál jo earát	and already
dihtet buoremusat	the others know best
mii sutnje namman	what the baby should be named
gos skuvlla vázzit	and where it should go to school

go mun niegadan	when I dream of
čurrohiid ja vieksáid	flies and wasps
niegadago son	you dream then
njivnnaid?	of fleas?

ráhkisvuođas	love
šattai várri	became a mountain
váris duottar	the mountain became a plateau
duoddaris gáisá	the plateau peak

golmma mánu geažes	after three months
gáisá njiedjá leahkin	the peak flattens out

ođđa buolža   a new mountain range
lea riegádan   is born

bajándálki   a thunderstorm
vuojada mu siste   rages within me

ravddas ravdii   from edge to edge
miehtá almmiávgadasa   over the entire firmament of heaven

jietna joavdá easkka   first after three months
golmma mánu geažes   the sound comes forth

ále vel, mánazán   not yet, my child
astta vuordit   take your time
gal don vel   take it easy
gearggat oaidnit   you will soon enough see
boršu giđđajogaid   the rushing spring torrents

astta vuordit   take your time
boahtte giđa bievllaid   a new spring is coming
vuosstas beštoriid   with bare peaks and wagtails
astta vuordit   take your time
gal don vel   take it easy

bággu   no grace
dál   I have to go
dálán   soon

diibmu   one hour
75 minoha   75 minutes

smiehta   think
riŋge   call
viega   run
vuoje   drive
bádde   record
čuohpa   edit

ja de   and then
giehka guhkká   crazy cuckoos
jieŋat nálluluvvet   the ice becomes thinner
gollerássi moddjá stánže giettis   the buttercup smiles on newly
                                                          thawed earth

ii eerá go   nothing to do but
vuorddašit   wait
dassá go son lea   until the little one is ready

gárvvis boahtit
suorpmat
dego čárdnan njiččit

to come
the fingers
like milk-filled teats

vel
goittotge mánotbaji

still
one month more

suorpmat
ohcalit vuovdái

the fingers
explore the bush

gal dat ain doppe
vári duohken

it is still there
behind the mountain

30 diimmu ávttat
bákčasat, duski

30 hours with contractions
ache, pain

in álgage eanet
nissonolmmoš

more woman
I did not become

inge gal
ávdugasge

not pious
either

baicce galbmasut
earáid bákčasiidda

rather more unmoved
by others' needs

30 diimmu
dollet mu gieđas

for 30 hours
you held my hands

juohke ákta
bolddii duge siste

every contraction
like a fire also in you

gatnjaliiguin suoli

secretly you extinguished the worst
                                fires

jáddadit vearrámus dola

with tears

ja mu
don jeđđejit

and me
you gave comfort

geassemánnu
ii dohkken

June
was not good enough

ii idja
ii iđit
ii beaivi
ii eahket

not night
not morning
not day
not evening

iige suoidnemánu idja
iige iđitidja
iige árraiđit

not July evenings either
not dawn
not morning

vurddii beaivváža suotnjariid
jo bures ligget
ovdalgo de
viimmat

first when the sunbeams
made really warm
then
finally

buorre iđit
spábbáčiekči

good morning
soccer player

guhlkki
lei mátki

it was a long
trip

áhččát
sálte munno
gatnjaliiguin

your father
salts us down
with tears

čáhppes guhkes vuovttat
gánda
nuba dieđusge

long black hair
boy
naturally

ja goittotge
munno gánda

and, of course
our boy

makkár mánná?

what kind of child?

jierbmái
čáppis
čeahppi

wise
good-looking
clever

dieđusge!

naturally!

ja njuoskkas

and wet

gos alit soagit?
gos ruoná beaivváš?
gos fiskes johka?

where are the blue trees?
where the green sun?
where did the yellow river go?

eatni dovdduid
nu earát máidnon

the mother's emotions
others have told about

viimmat
beasan fas oađđit

finally
I can sleep

čoavjji alde!   on my stomach!

olles njeallje beaivve fal   four full days
ovdalgo   before my breasts swell
čiččit čárdne   into hard balls
spábbačiekčái spábban   for the soccer ball kicker

dál ádden   now for the first time
čárdnan bahččegusaid   I understand the cows
mat eahkedis   who with pressure in their udders
dopmet   hurry home
meahcis ruoktot   every evening

čoavján   my stomach
ain dego   still
bures geavvan   like a well-risen
nisoláibedáigi   wheat dough

hormonat   it is hormones
ráđđejit eadneolbmo miela   that govern a mother's disposition

na, jus olmmoš   well, if a human being is
dušše kemikálet   only made of chemicals

manin eai   why not
boahkot   vaccinate against

vaši   hate
gáđašvuođa   jealousy
birolašvuođa vuostá   devilry?

guokte vahku   two weeks
ráfálaš dego uvjabalva   calm as floating clouds
čuovgat dego fiskes lieđđegavja   bright as shining flower pollen
čieŋal dego ádjaga ruohtas   deep as the source of the spring

vihttanuppelogát beaivve   the fifteenth day
láiráuđas   a landslide

miehtá   as far as you can see
buot   endless
jalga   plains

guovttevahkkosažžan   at two weeks of age
álge eahketčierrát   the nighttime screaming started

beannot lihttera
ovccis gaskaidjii

one and a half liters
between nine and midnight

sus gatnjalat
munnos bivastagat

his tears
our sweat

bcakkán čeahpes musihkkár
guokte konseartta beaivvis
golbma diimmu hávil

like a famous musician
two concerts every day
three hours straight

guldaleaddjin dušše
eadni ja áhčči

with only two listeners
mother and father

beaivi beaivvi
idja ija mannjá

day after day
night after night

aiddo nohkai

barely asleep

ja dál jo
balan su lihkkat

and already
afraid he will awake

de duohta
maid golmma máná eadni
hoahkalii

it is true
what a three-time mother
once said

"lávejit čábbut
go nohkket"

"they are sweetest
when they sleep"

de duohta

it is true

27. beaivve
dan mannjá
go son riegádii
liegga guoika
šáviha fáhkka
dievva ratti

the 27th day
after
he was born
suddenly
a warm stream
through the breast

easska dál
vai
jo dál?

now first
or
all now?

mánotbajis
suoivanat leavvan
ládduid vuollái
bihci cieggan

in a month
the shadows have spread
under the water puddles
frost scratches on

ovssiid ala	the branches
jagi geažesgo	after a year
dievas skábma	full darkness
ja muhtton bovdna?	and no snowbound tufts?
guđavahkkosaš	six weeks old
su čalmmiin	in his eyes
oainnán jo	I already see
iežan oktonasvuođa	my own lonesomeness
dušše čiekŋaleappon	only deeper
mánná riehpu	poor child
buolli láva	burning lava
lahkana leavttuin	comes rolling in
farga gokčá	it will soon cover
min stobu	our house
alla sáttomielli	a steep sand ridge
luoitá merrii	rages out of the sea
mun lávkkun vulos	I hurry down
šávdon belohahkii	and am half buried
lossat	heavy
lossat	heavy
nu son deaddá	that is how he weighs
4-kilosaš	with his four kilos
6-vahkkosaš	six weeks
dán geasis	from that summer
muittán dušše	I remember nothing other
su čierráid	than his crying
cuigot	they say
ahte dát lea	that is how it is
náittosdili árga	in everyday married life
čierru mánná	crying child
girdi gavjjat	dust that drifts
skárton lihtit	dirty cups everywhere
guktot nu váiban	both of us
ahte oaivi	dizzy

dušše geasaša

from exhaustion

árga?
muhto
árgahan lea ránis!

everyday?
but
everyday is gray!

son bárgu
ja mun garrudan
son gillju
mun čierun

he cries
and I curse
he howls
I cry

son huká
   hálidan doaškkastit
   hávkadit guottáin
   bálkestit lássaráigge olggos

he bawls
   I want to hit him
   suffocate him with a pillow
   throw him out through the
                    window

snuđđu
čierru
bárgu
   báárgu
      bááááárguuuu

whimpers
cries
screams
   screeams
      screeeeeamsssss

holvu
   hooooooolvuuuuuuuuuuuuuuuuuu

howls
   hoooooowlsssssssšššššsssss

gillju
   giiiiiiiiiiiiiillllljuuuuuuuuuuuuuu

bawls
   baaaaaaaaaaawlssssssssssssss

gottášingo su
vai iežan?

shall I take his life
or mine?

lihkus vuot
okta beaivi meattá

thank goodness
another day is over

beaivi lagabus beaivvi
goas son vuolgá
eret ruovttus

one day closer
to the day he will leave
home

aiddo go
steampalasten gállosan
"meašttereadni"
son heittii njammamis
ja mcašttir seahkanii

right now
I stamped my forehead
"master mom"
he quits sucking
and the master goes crazy

oh go sáhtášinge
máhcahit su
dohko gos bođiige
bidjat fárrui báberstuhka
masa čálestan "vihki"
dahje "boasttu gálvu"

oh if I could only
send him back
where he came from
send him with a note
where I write either "defective"
or "wrong delivery"

manne ipmašis
son galgá
leat nu helvet váttis?!!

why of all days
must he be
so damned difficult?!!

jus ii leat
borranstreaika
de lea
njammanstreaika

if it isn't
an eating strike
it is
a sucking strike

muhto ii goassige
bárgunstreaika

but never
a crying strike

vuoi helvehiid helvet!

what the hell!

manin vávváahki
ii sáhte bistit
dušše mánotbaji?!?!?

why can't
infancy last
only a month?!?!?

gal livččii álki
vuolgit bargui
vuoiŋŋastit
ann´al earát
heibot suinna

it would have been so easy
to go to work
rest
let the others
deal with him

veallán

I lie

gulan go son bárgu
gulan
        gulan

hear that he cries
hear
        hear

rohpi
galggašii leat vielgat

the ceiling
should have been white

galggašii

should have been

gulan
        gulan

hear
        hear

sielu ija čađa

through the night of the soul

guohca joavdelas čižži!

the wretched suckling!

gánda bárgu
iige boađe mielki
doahtu ii fuola

the boy screams
not a drop of milk
and he doesn't want a bottle

čuohpašin rabas
lehkošin mielkerávssáid
divošin
vai fas

I could have cut
a hole in the mammaries
done anything
if only

gárta stuorru
su rattis

the map widens out
in him

ganjalgeađgi
čierráčoalbmi
bárggábákti

tear stone
complaint bay
crying mountain

bárut
stuorábut go
Buolbmatjávrris golggotmánus

waves
bigger than in
Buolbmatjávvri in October

oađekeahtes ijat
borre hálu
ja liikká
ferte

sleepless nights
kill desire
and even so
again

beivviid
áidna erohus
namma

every day
the only difference
the name

vuot ferte
čuohppat su gaccaid

time again
to clip his nails

áigi gollá
dattege

time passes
in spite of it all

guđamánnosačča oaivvis
čuovggáhallá jo násttáš

six months old
in his head a star twinkles

jierpmi čuovga

the light of intellect

fuones eadnige
lea buoret go

a lousy mother
is better than

áhčči	a father
gii lea	who is always
álo barggus	at work

gal olmmoš lea gáica	how dumb can one be

gádden náitalit duinna	I thought I married you
muhto náitalin suinna	but I am married to him
ja don bargguinat	and you with your work

dál son	now he tries
beahká ovddabealde	to move forward

ja mun	and I
heaŋgán	follow after
su lihparis	with his diaper

meattá	past
meattá	past

áigi	time
goas	when
ieš šaddadin	I myself created
iežan soajáid	my wings

son gaikkui mu	he brought me
eatnan ala	down toward earth

čanai muldii	bound me to a mold

in šat njuikko girdis	I don't skydive anymore
in gavcco Kilimanjaro	don't climb on Kilimanjaro

in šat smáhke cubbuid	I don't taste frogs anymore
ja guhkkin eret	and definitely not
vieksá suovssaid	wasp larvae

čievččadan	I squirm
dego boaru	like a gadfly
nállogeažis	on a needle point

vare beasašin	I wish
fáŋgan giddagassii	I were thrown in jail

doppege	even there
eanet friddjavuohta	more freedom
go ruovttus	than home
jahkásačča eadnin	as a one-year-old's mother

das son čohkká	here he sits
beaŋkka alde	on a chair
mieiggada	he rests
ruškes čalmmat	the brown-eyed
uhca albmáš	little man

áidna bargun	his only assignment
stuorrut	to grow

ja das mun geahčan	and here I sit
beavdguoras	at the end of the table and watch
mieiggadan	I rest
alit čalmmat	the blue-eyed
váiban eadni	tired mother

áidna bargun	my only assignment
stuorrut suinna	to grow with him

ja nu dáhpáhuvaige	and so it happened
ahte sturron	that I grew
ja son stuorui	and he grew
ju mii stuornimet	and we grew
guovtte jagis	for two years
guovtte guhkes jagis	two long years

ráhkis	dear
ráhkis uhca albmáš	dear little man

ja ráhkis	and dear
ráhkis stuorra almmái	dear big man of mine

mii!	we
MII!!!	WE!!!

Primary Works

Gollebiekkat almmi dievva (Golden Winds Fill the Sky), 1989.
Jiehki vuolde ruonas giđđa (Green Spring under the Glacier), 1993.
Silkeguobbara lákca (Silken Mushroom's Cream), 1995.
Máilmmis dása (From the World and Home), 2001.

Selected Bibliography

Aikio-Arianaick, Inger-Mari. Interview by the author, 13-14 November, 2004, Ivalo, Finland. Transcript in the hands of the author.

Beach, Hugh. *A Year in Lapland: Guest of the Reindeer Herders*. Seattle: University of Washington Press, 2001.

Gaski, Harald, ed. *In the Shadow of the Midnight Sun: Contemporary Sámi Prose and Poetry*. Karasjok: Davvi Girji, 1997.

–. *Sami Culture in a New Era: The Norwegian Sami Experience*. Karasjok: Davvi Girji, 1997.

Hirvonen, Vuokko. www.uarctic.org/bcs/BCS322/BCS322_mod9.pdf.

Valkeapää, Nils-Aslak. Terveis*iä Lapista*. Helsinki: Otava, 1971.

–. *Greetings from Lappland: The Sami – Europe's Forgotten People*. London: Zed Press, 1983.

–. *Ruoktu Váimmu*. Guovdageaidnu: DAT, 1985.

–. *Beaivi, Áhčážan*. Guovdageaidnu: DAT, 1988.

–. *The Sun, My Father*. Guovdageaidnu: DAT, 1997.

–. *Trekways of the Wind*. Guovdageaidnu: DAT, 1994.

Linn Ullmann: A Woman of Letters

MELISSA GJELLSTAD (INDIANA UNIVERSITY)

As a novelist, literary critic, and a journalist, Linn Ullmann distills the clamor of contemporary life to the purest elements in her writing. Her crisp and intense narrative voice probes intimate human relationships and reveals the fragility of their constructed nature. Her critical voice assesses the work of her peers with an even eye attuned to literature and society. Her inquisitive and informed journalistic voice asks difficult questions about Norwegian society and diplomatic relations abroad, especially with the United States. As a renowned woman of letters, Ullmann demands attention and provokes response in every aspect of her public life. She has established herself as a prominent literary voice in Norway, Europe, and North America, and her multifaceted publications reflect the broad scope of her literary and cultural knowledge. This talented writer is undoubtedly one of the most serious participants in Scandinavian literary life at the turn of the millennium, and this essay attempts to illuminate the complex variety in her work.

Born on August 9, 1966, to Liv Ullmann and Ingmar Bergman, Linn Ullmann grew up in New York with her mother. She attended The Julliard School as a dancer, but graduated in 1988 from New York University with a degree in English literature. Ullmann began work on a Ph.D.-degree in the United States, but chose to return to Norway to begin a career in journalism in 1990. When asked how she became an author, Ullmann responded thus: "Jeg ville egentlig bli operasanger, men jeg kan ikke synge. Så bestemte jeg meg for å bli skuespiller. Etter noen år på en teaterskole i New York, fortalte læreren meg at jeg var en elendig skuespiller. Min mor var helt enig. Dermed ble jeg journalist." (I actually wanted to be an opera singer, but I cannot sing. Then I decided to be an actor. After a few years at a theater school in New York, my teacher told me that I was a terrible actor. My mother agreed completely. Therefore I became a journalist.)[1] Currently Ullmann lives in Oslo with her husband, prominent Norwegian author Niels Fredrik Dahl, two children, two stepchildren, and a dog. Ullmann enjoys

---

[1] Author homepage, *Dagbladet*. http://www.dagbladet.no/kontekst/4085.html.

great popularity in her native Norway, and was awarded Den norske leser-
prisen (The Norwegian Reader's Prize) in 2002. Her novels have been
published in 30 countries in Europe and North America.

Linn Ullmann made her debut on the Norwegian literary scene in November 1998 with her novel *Før du sovner* (Eng. tr. *Before You Sleep*,
1999). Critics quickly pronounced the book as one of the best novels of the
year, an impressive label in its own right, but even more so considering her
relative inexperience and the high caliber of her fellow debutants that year.
Some of the other top-notch writers who joined Ullmann in 1998 include
Karl Ove Knausgård, Olaug Nielssen and Trude Marstein. Ullmann differ-
entiated herself from her colleagues with her striking narrative style, brisk
and unassuming, which reflected the attitudes and energy of 1990s Oslo.
Karin Blom, postmodern heroine and narrator of *Before You Sleep*, brilliantly blurs the lines between reality and fiction in everyday life and her
family history. One critic describes it thus: "Og sådan bruger Linn Ullmann
sin kvindelige fortællers fandenvoldske vilje til at gennemskue familien
som én stor livsløgn og fiktion, til at bevæge sig rundt i vort århundredes
syn på kærlighed og lykke." (And that's how Linn Ullmann uses her female
narrator's devil-may-care drive to skewer the family as one big life lie and
fiction, to concentrate on our century's views on love and happiness.)[2]
Although this quote was written in response to Ullmann's debut, the threads
of controversy, lies, love, and family run through her entire authorship.
Many critics have commented on her unique style and voice, describing the
tone as stark, chilly, and serious, descriptors foreign critics often associate
with "Scandinavian". Before continuing with a discussion of this novel and
the highly acclaimed subsequent works *Når jeg er hos deg* (2001; When I
Am With You; Eng. tr. *Stella Descending*, 2003) and *Nåde* (2002; Eng. tr.
Grace, 2005), it is helpful to locate Ullmann's authorship within the
charged literary scene in Norway at the millennium's end.

The breadth of 1990s Norwegian literature transcends one overarching
genre or form. Critical assessments of novels published during this time
cover the entire continuum of diversity in form and content. This said, some
characteristics that surfaced and gained credibility during the decade were
family, sincerity, intensity, truth, new moralism, ethics, and non-
existentialism. Traces of realism, modernism, romanticism, and postmodernism emerged in the plethora of the novels of the 1990s. Despite the
recirculation of older themes and styles, critics sensed that Norwegian
literature was on the cusp of something new. It was an energetic era and
critics disagreed heartily on the value and quality of the literature of the
times. The positive proponents of Norwegian contemporary literature made
these generalized comments about the 1990s: The new narratives turned

---

[2]   Jens Andersen. "Eventyrlig vellykket." *Dagbladet,* 23 November 1998.

inward to the personal, the emotional, and the intimate. Intensified emotion signaled a general expansion in the openness of text although the overall number of words was sparse in the favored terse narrative form. Yet the novels conveyed great depth of feeling.

The increased attention to local detail also manifested itself in a heightened concentration on realism and the everyday. Building on these factors, literary critic Tom Egil Hverven's controversial work postulated the family as the site of innovation between the individual and society in 1990s literature.[3] Hverven read this familial juncture as the nexus of meaning for authors at the turn of the millennium. His work altered the literary debates in Norway, and helped antagonists tighten their arguments against the prose of the 1990s. Some critics rallied against the moralizing and ethical turn of this body of literature, negating the value of the emotions surround these intimate familial affairs. Others read the pessimism and nihilism expressed therein as part of the fragmented nature of the narratives, lacking clear direction and purpose. Indeed, some authors rebelled against the "family" label, in fear that the sensitive subject matter would pigeonhole their work into a trivialized category of "women's literature" written by and for women only.

Ullmann stands amid this critical turmoil and voraciously confronts the tensions of familial and personal interactions, teasing out the intricacies of these relationships, and giving voice to women as mothers, wives, sisters, daughters and aunts. Under the guise of a feminist reading of the decade, especially regarding the notion of "family literature", the increased attention to detail and internal emotion is a positive trend that suggests a shift toward the realm of women, especially in their roles as mothers. This may or may not have been a conscious choice in her first three novels, but in an interview from 2004 Ullmann admitted that she was working on a fourth novel and searching for a definition of feminism in Simone de Beauvoir's *Le deuxième sexe* (1949): "I've been asking myself why female experiences are sort of absent from serious literature. Things such as birth, nursing, [and] pregnancy are either part of 1970s political literature or else they're trivial. It's always just 'get some hot water and towels'. What do they do with all that water and towels?"[4] Ullmann's narrative focus on and understanding of the contemporary female rank her as one of the principal authors of her generation, providing a powerful voice that contributes to the new third-wave feminist turn in 1990s Norwegian literature. The majority of mainstream Norwegian critics generally avoid feminism as a valid perspective for literary criticism and its absence is striking in the long list of labels stated above. Ullmann's thoughtful narrative allows that possibility

---

[3]   Tom Egil Hverven. *Å lese etter familien: Forsøk om norsk litteratur på 1990-tallet.* Oslo: Tiden, 1999.

[4]   Ninian Dunnett. "Light in the Darkness." *The Scotsman*, 19 August 2004.

and presents a serious alternative to the hegemonic masculinity so prevalent among her contemporaries. This does not mean Ullmann's male characters are weak or uninteresting. Her portrayal of Johan Sletten in the novel *Grace* led directly to the designation of The Norwegian Reader's Prize in 2002. Ullmann has a keen skill for capturing a character's spirit and creating a persuasive persona around it, especially for secondary characters.

Karin Blom, narrator of *Before You Sleep*, serves as a vivid example of the spirited and strident voice of Ullmann's female characters: the woman demanding recognition within her family and society. Karin tells the tale to her nephew Sander on the eve that his vacationing parents, Julie and Aleksander, should have reached their destination in Italy. Framed as a bedtime story, Karin recaps the history of the Blom family, weaving events from her days in Oslo in the 1990s to accounts of her grandparents' days in New York City in the 1930s. The story is matrifocal, comparing and contrasting three generations of sisters as they search for love and self-understanding in their relationships with men, their children, and each other. A refreshing element of this modern-day Scandinavian family saga is that there is hardly a traditional female archetype to be found among the cast of characters. Karin, her sister Julie, her mother Anni, her aunt Else, her grandmother June, and her great aunt Selma all come alive in Ullmann's creative prose and challenge stereotypes of the idealized woman and mother. This is due, in part, to the rogue nature of the narrator: Karin performs the role of the seducer and in so doing subverts the gender roles of the characteristically masculine image of the heartbreaker into an equally indifferent feminine version: "[Den lekende fortellerstemmen] er en lystløgnerske som på sett og vis kommer nærmere sannheten i sin familie enn andre av karakterene som etterstreber sannheten gjør." ([The playful narrative voice] is a life-liar who, in certain ways, comes closer to the truth in her own family than do other characters who strive for the truth.)[5] Karin's imagination and knack for storytelling combine to form splendid tales of sordid affairs with wedding guest Aaron, supermarket Billy, and cowboy Carl, among others. Her own sexual conquests stand in contrast to the settled lives of her sister, mother, and grandmother, and Karin recreates the intimate details of these women's relationships to their husbands Aleksander, her unnamed father, and Rikard Blom, respectively, as a way of investigating bigger questions of motherhood and marriage as societal icons of everyday life.

The publication of the second novel *Stella Descending* followed two years later, and the critical acclaim was slightly muted, perhaps because audiences were more confused by the unresolved questions in work. Loneliness is a central theme, and Ullmann describes the concentration thus, "Jeg håper boka ligger nær fargene til timen mellom 03-04. Alle søvnløse

---

kjenner denne timen, det er da skyggene er på sitt mest skremmende." (I hope the book nears the colors of the hour between 3-4 am. All insomniacs know this hour; it is when the shadows are at their scariest.)[6] The novel is a well-told family drama that describes isolation and love amid the slow unraveling of the marriage between Stella and Martin. Stella dies in the opening pages by falling from the roof of their apartment building, but it is unclear if she tripped, jumped, or was pushed. The remainder of the novel is an unchronological investigation into the death and life of the absent heroine, her family, and her friends. Viewed from all angles, motherhood is a central issue to the plot; Stella has a remarkable relationship with her mother, Edith Lind, and her daughters Amanda and Bi (Eng. Bee). Once again the female characters resonate with Ullmann's penchant for non-traditional images of women struggling to understand their lovers, their children, their parents and themselves. With one exception the unique narrators are female: Stella, Amanda, investigator Corinne, and three eyewitnesses Alma, Frederikke, and Ella. The exception is cantankerous Axel Grutt, Stella's neighbor and former patient in the hospital with whom Stella has formed a lasting friendship. Motive and intent for Stella's death are difficult to ascertain in the novel and Stella's fall from the rooftop mirrors the metaphorical fall that occurs when we lose our footing on life's path.

Building on the successful character sketch of grumpy widower Axel Grutt, Ullmann highlights another disgruntled older man in her third novel, *Grace*. The main character is 69-year old Johan Sletten, a retired cultural journalist for Oslo's third-largest newspaper. Sletten, happily married to his second wife Mai, a pediatrician seventeen years his junior, faces the terror and uncertainty of dying from cancer. With images of his father's disgraceful death burned into his memory Johan asks his wife to help him die. Children do not complicate the deep emotions in this love story; Johan is estranged from his son Andreas from a previous marriage, and Mai has chosen to remain childless. Details are sparse but emotions are deep; Ullmann intentionally pared down the external factors to create an isolated, non-glamorous character struggling with death, "Jeg hadde ikke lyst til å skrive om en helt, men om en helt vanlig man. Å lage en historie om en kjernekar som dør, det blir litt for amerikansk film-aktig." (I didn't want to write about a hero, but about an absolutely normal man. To create a story about an exceptional man who dies, that gets to be too American film-esque.)[7]

6   Veronica Karlsen. "Linn Ullmann: Lidenskap på stram line." TV2, 4 October 2001. TV2 is Norway's largest commercial television channel.
7   Ane Kolberg. "Døden er ikke vakker." NRK P2, 31 October 2002. NRK P2 is the cultural channel of Norway's major broadcasting institution, the Norwegian Broadcasting Corporation.

Even with the sour male protagonist, Ullmann stated that this is her most personal novel written to date.[8]

Departing sharply from buoyant language, cinematic style, and fantastic elements found in her previous novels, *Grace* retains the difficult honesty and soul-searching nature characteristic of the author, although it resembles a much more traditional narrative style. The gruesome question posed by the novel surprised most critics, prompting strong reactions to the investigation of the moral ambiguity of terminal illness and assisted suicide.

Ullmann's novels have been bestsellers in Norway and abroad, but she has also worked on a number of complementary projects. In addition to working as a literary critic and journalist for *Dagbladet*, one of Norway's leading newspapers, Ullmann has collaborated as a freelancer for various literary and cultural media. In 1998, she composed a thin volume celebrating the life and work of Norwegian film director Arne Skouen entitled *Om Arne Skouen og hans filmer* (Eng. tr. *Profession: Director. Arne Skouen and His Films*, 2001). In 1997, she co-authored an elementary school social studies textbook and edited a collection of contemporary Norwegian short stories. The latter volume, entitled *Men jeg bor her ennå* (But I Still Live Here), offers a snapshot of stories from the 1980s and 1990s that moved Ullmann as a reader, "Da mener jeg ikke den sentimentale bevegelsen, jeg mener at de beveget meg fra et punkt til et annet. (...) Forfatterne har funnet et språk og en form som uttrykker disse grunnleggende tingene på en slik måte at man blir sårbar i møte med dem." (By that I don't mean the sentimental movement, I mean that they moved me from one point to another. [...] The authors have found a language and a form that expresses these fundamental things in such a way that one becomes vulnerable meeting them.) This quote from the collection's introduction expresses Ullmann's desire as a reader, but it is also a projection of what her writing evokes in readers. Uncomfortable moments of longing, love, isolation, and loneliness that expose our vulnerability are paramount in Ullmann's work, and many of the selected stories by her contemporaries in this volume foreshadow and echo Linn Ullmann's thematic focus in her writing.

---

[8] Ullmann also admitted to starting the story with a female protagonist, which inhibited her creation of the narrative. It was only until she switched the protagonist to an old man that the story began to flow again. Ragnhild Plesner. "Finnes det en verdig død?" *Aftenposten*, 21 August 2002.

Før du sovner

Utdrag

I en krok i forstuen står tante Selma og regjerer for seg selv. Hun smatter på en sigarette og lytter med hevede øynebryn til et lite barn som har våget seg opp til henne.
Du ser ut som en heks, sier barnet.
Det er fordi jeg er en heks, sier Selma.
Men du er sikkert ikke en slem heks, sier barnet trøstende.
Er jeg visst det, sier Selma.
Hvordan slem da, spør barnet.
Det beste jeg vet er kokte pikelanker og stekte pikeører, sier hun mykt og griper etter barnets hals, og så spiser jeg gjerne litt deilig pikelungemos til dessert.
Jeg tror ikke på deg, hyler barnet og løper sin vei.
Selma himler med øynene.
Hei tante Selma, sier jeg.
Er det deg? sier hun surt.
Kan jeg bomme en sigarett? sier jeg.
Tante Selma gir meg pakken med sigaretter og sier: Jeg ser du driver og glor på en mann, han med den lyshårede kvinnen.
Ser du det, sier jeg.
Mora di er dum, søstera di er dum, mormora di var erkedum, mormora di var så dum at hun ikke forsto noen ting, men jeg er ikke dum. Det er klart jeg ser.
Jeg har tenkt å forføre ham, sier jeg.
Javel, sier Selma, det ser ikke ut som du gjør særlig framgang.
Nei, sier jeg. Har du noen gode råd?
Hun tar et drag av sigaretten.
Har du forsøkt med sjarm? sier hun.
Jeg tror det, sier jeg.
Har du forsøkt å se ham dypt inn i øynene?
Ja. Han enser meg ikke.
Har du forsøkt å snakke med ham?
Ja, for en stund siden. Det gikk ikke særlig bra.
Har du forsøkt å gå rett opp til ham og si at du vil ligge med ham, og at du ikke forventer mer fra ham enn at han stiller opp i et kvarters tid?
Nei. Men akkurat det tror jeg ikke har noen hensikt. Jeg tror ikke han er typen som faller for det.
Ikke det nei, sier hun. Det fungerte fint for meg da jeg var yngre og i samme ærend. Men jeg var penere enn deg, det hjalp.
Har du flere råd?
Har du forsøkt smiger? sier hun.
Smiger?
Ja, smiger. Det er en sikker vinner, slår aldri feil, sier hun.
Smiger, sier jeg.
Smiger, sier Selma.
Men hvordan? sier jeg. Hva skal jeg smigre ham med? Jeg kjenner ham ikke.
Det er hele poenget, sier hun, jo mindre du kjenner et menneske, jo lettere er det å smigre det.
Men hvordan? sier jeg.

Selma tar et nytt drag av sigaretten. Hun får røyken i vrangstrupen, blir rød i ansiktet, tungen fyker ut av munnen, tungen henger ut av munnen, hun krøker seg sammen. Selma krøker seg sammen og utstøter en surklende pipende rallende hostelyd som får alle i nærheten til å snu seg og tenke at nå dør hun, nå dør hun, nå er det helt sikkert over, ha det bra og takk for nå tante Selma, vi glemmer deg aldri, god tur og hils hjem. En sånn hoste, tenker jeg, som er så gammel og råtten at den har ligget og surklet i halsen hennes siden hun var ung og fabelaktig; en sånn hoste som kan dateres tilbake til en sigarett hun tente på en kafé i for eksempel New York i oktober 1929 da hun drakk om kapp med tre av finansverdenens gladeste spekulanter, drakk dem under bordet når sant skal sies, og tvang dem til å danse med henne etterpå, en etter en, og alle på en gang, enda så fulle de var; og alt etter skal visstnok ha bidratt til at de samme tre spekulantene fikk en forfedelig hodepine dagen etter og ikke kunne gjøre jobben sin ordentlig, og bedre ble det ikke da hele børsmarkedet kollapset, noe som forårsaket den økonomiske krisen i USA og store deler av Europa de neste ti årene. To av de tre spekulantene tok livet av seg samme kveld, konene deres klandret Selma.

Hun har aldri vært det man kaller en gledespreder, tenker jeg – og så slutter hun å hoste. Selma slutter å hoste. Hun reiser seg, løfter hodet, løfter blikket, smiler skjeløyd til alle samme, tar et nytt drag av sigaretten og lar røyken sive ut av neseborene: Dere trodde jeg skulle falle nå, dere trodde jeg var ferdig, dere trodde det var slutt. Men se! Jeg faller ikke, jeg står, jeg faller ikke. Selma ler og sier at du skal bare gjøre som jeg sier, Karin, og guttungen har ikke en sjanse. Den gutten der, sier hun og peker på Aaron med en lang gul pekefingernegl, den gutten der kan ikke motstå smiger. Det er ikke begjæret hans du skal stryke, men forfengeligheten, og da kommer alt det andre av seg selv.

Men hvordan, sier jeg.

Spill skuespill, Karin! Spill skuespill!

Selma hoster en gang til, så griper hun skulderen min og hvisker: Se på ham og la ham forstå at du ser den store hemmeligheten han bærer i sitt hjerte.

Hvilken stor hemmelighet?

Det er ikke poenget, sier hun. Det er godt mulig han ikke bærer på et skvatt i sitt hjerte, sannsynligvis gjør han ikke det. Poenget er at han gjerne vil *tro* at han gjør det, og at noen ser *at han gjør det*. Alle vil være mer enn de er, Karin, og gir du guttungen der borte et inntrykk av at du ser at han er mer enn han er, at du ser at han bærer på en stor hemmelighet i sitt hjerte, at han skiller seg ut, Karin, at han er annerledes, at han er kysset av Gud, ja så er det gjort, så er han din.

Jeg smyger meg inn i spisestuen, finner bordkortet med Aarons navn på, og plasserer det ved siden av mitt bordkort. Så tar jeg det overflødige bordkortet og plasserere det på Aarons opprinnelige plass, en Daniel K. leser jeg på kortet, en venn av Aleksander kanskje, jeg vet ikke.

Sånn! Nå er det gjort. Nå *må* han snakke med meg. Nå får han ikke lov til å la være å snakke med meg. Nå skal vi sitte ved siden av hverandre under hele den lange bryllupsmiddagen og det ville være uhøflig av ham ikke å snakke med meg. Han har ikke noe valg rett og slett. Han har ikke noe valg.

Jeg kjenner en hånd på skulderen min.

Hva er det du gjør, Karin?

Jeg snur meg. Det er far som spør.

Jeg bytter bordplasseringskort. Det er en person jeg har lyst til å sitte ved siden av, sier jeg.

Åja, sier far. Så sier han: Kan jeg gå min vei nå? Jeg vil ikke være på fest mer.

Nei, sier jeg.

Annis whisky er ikke god. Anni har *aldri* greid å kjøpe god whisky, sier han.
Nei vel, sier jeg.
Jeg liker Johnnie Walker, hun liker Upper Ten.
Ja, sier jeg.
Anni eier ikke smak.
Jeg vet ikke det, sier jeg.
Jeg retter på fars smokingsløyfe, er rød rose i knapphullet.

Aaron sitter alene i den pupurrøde sofaen med et glass i hånden, han drikker gin & tonic med en sitronskive i. På det runde steinbordet foran sofaen, en skål med saltstenger. Ved siden av Aaron sitter onkel Fritz, han har også et glass i hånden. Fritz drikker et eller annet rødt.
Jeg setter meg mellom dem i sofaen.
Dere er mine to bordkavalerer i kveld, stråler jeg.
Oj oj, sier onkel Fritz.
Så hyggelig, sier Aaron og blikket hans flakker rundt i rommet.
Blikket hans minner om en fugl som har forvillet seg inn i en stue.
Jeg snur meg mot Fritz. Hva er det du drikker, onkel Fritz?
Hva sa du Karin, mumler han.
Jeg spurte hva er det du drikker, det er rødt?
Sexy Sunrise, mumler han.
Åja, sier jeg.
Karin, sier han og stirrer ned i glasset sitt.
Ja, sier jeg.
Mamma har mistet en tann, sier han.
Jeg vet det.
Først mister hun tanna si, så mister hun ørene sine, så faller nesa av, så detter øynene ut – SE! sier han, SE HER! sier Fritz og peker på to grønne oliven som flyter rundt i drinken hans. Mamma! sier han, og plutselig en dag er mamma bare helt død.
Ja, men det er lenge til, sier jeg.
Karin, sier han.
Ja, sier jeg.
Jeg kjenner meg ikke riktig bra. Jeg er kvalm.
Da skal du ikke drikke mer av den drinken der, sier jeg.
Oj oj, sier han.
Fritz synker sammen i sofaen, kroppen hans siger framover, munnen åpner seg litt, i den ene hånden holder han glasset sitt.
Er alt i orden med han der, sier Aaron lavt.
Onkel Fritz ja. Alt er i orden, sier jeg.
Jeg ser på Aaron. Han møter blikket mitt.
Jeg legger hodet på skulderen hans. Jeg vet hva du tenker, sier jeg.
Aaron trekker seg unna.
Hva? sier han.
Jeg vet hva du tenker, sier jeg.
Javel? sier han.
Jeg snur meg mot ham, ansiktet mitt mot hans ansikt, pusten hans mot huden min: Jeg lyver, sier jeg. Jeg vet ikke hva du tenker. Jeg ville bare at du skulle legge merke til meg.
Aaron ser på meg et øyeblikk lenger enn han må. Så ler han litt. Jeg ser ned. Hendene hans er bleke, tynne, små, ganske hårete og samtidig pikeaktige, og under den høyre tommelneglen en flik av rød maling han ikke har greid å vaske bort.

En vinterkveld i begynnelsen av januar, det året Julie fylte tretten år og jeg ti: Jeg går oppover Jacob Aalls gate, skolesekken er tung, det er mørkt. Snøen glir sidelangs bortover gatene, virvler rundt ansiktet mitt, hvitt, gjennomsiktig, vått, nesten borte. Så ser jeg dem: Utenfor inngangsdøren hjemme står det en ungeflokk med armene strukket mot himmelen. På balkongen i fjerde etasjse står Julie, kledd i lang rød bomullsnattkjole med lange ermer. Det lyse lange håret hennes blåser i vinden, snøen faller rundt henne, ikke på henne, men rundt henne, snøen kapsler henne inn; en rød pike i snøslottet sitt, husker jeg at jeg tenkte.

Barnas ansikter blir tydeligere etter hvert som jeg kommer nærmere. Det er jenter og gutter fra nabolaget og fra klassen til Julie.

Julie står på balkongen, og med store rolige armbevegelser kaster hun tingene sine over kanten og ned til barna på gaten. Hun kaster den gamle dukken sin, den med øyelokk, øyevipper, og store blå glassøyne, dukken virvler gjennom luften og faller mykt på bakken, dukken sier au, og de store blå glassøynene blunker. Hun kaster den røde reiseradioen sin, alle grammofonplatene sine, bøkene, kjolene og genserne sine, selv det lille gullhjertet hun har rundt halsen, og som hun har fått av far, kaster hun.

Ungeflokken roper og heier og løper fra den ene siden til den andre og samler opp det de kan.
Mer Julie, roper de.
Snille snille Julie, roper de.
Mer, roper de.

Først står jeg stille og ser på. Jeg husker at jeg tenkte: Nå må du gjøre noe, Karin, nå må du gjøre noe. Julie kan ikke bare stå på balkongen og kaste fra seg alt hun eier.
Så går jeg opp de fire etasjene til leiligheten vår. Tre jenter og en tykk gutt med dunbart følger etter meg. Opp trappen, inn døren, inn på rommet til Julie.
De tre jentene og gutten ser seg rundt i rommet.

Hei, sier Julie.
Hei, sier barna.
Den ene jenta kikker i bokhyllen og finner Julies tegneseriepermer.
Skal du kaste disse, spør jenta og tar permene ut av hyllen og begynner å bla i dem.
Jeg vet ikke, sier Julie.
Vær så snill, sier jenta.
Jeg vet ikke, sier Julie.
Hvorfor ikke? sier jenta.
Okay da, sier Julie. Gå ned så skal jeg kaste dem til deg.
Okay, sier jenta.

Jeg går ut av rommet, ut av leiligheten, ned på gaten.
Julie er i full gang med å kaste igjen.
Barna løper fram og tilbake.

Nei, roper jeg.
Kan dere holde opp, roper jeg.
Kan dere være så snill å holde opp.

Det er ikke deres ting det er, det er Julies ting, roper jeg, og så forsøker jeg å rive en grammofonplate og en tøykanin ut av hendene på en stor bulkete jente. Jenta klamrer seg fast til tingene, og med den ene hånden sytter hun meg hardt i magen så jeg faller over ende.

Jeg reiser meg, vakler et øyeblikk, snapper etter pusten, og forsøker å dra henne ned i snøfonnene. Men jenta glipper ut av hendene mine og løper av gårde.

Vær så snill, roper jeg, og tråkker rundt i snøen. Snø i øynene. Snø på hendene. Snø i støvlene. Vær så snill. Kan dere være så snill å holde opp. Det der er Julies ting, ikke deres.

På gammeldags vis varsler Anni og Ingeborg at det er på tide å sette seg til bords. Ingeborg holder gongongen og Anni slår. Slik går de fra rom til rom.

Gir du meg armen din? sier jeg til Fritz, som sitter stille, helt stille i den purpurrøde sjeselongen

Jeg føler meg ikke riktig bra, sier Fritz.

Kan du i alle fall *forsøke* å føle deg bra? sier jeg.

Jeg forsøker, jeg forsøker, sier Fritz og holder seg rundt magen.

Det festdekkede langbordet strekker seg gjennom to store stuer, hvite duker, røde roser, nypusset gammelt sølv, Ingeborgs håndmalte porselen, asjetter, tallerkener, serveringsfat, alt sammen rødt i rødt. Vi er trettisju til bords, alle finner plassene sine, Aaron finner sin, ved siden av min, og nå går det riktig bra.

Kveldens toastmaster reiser seg, løfter gaffelen og klinger på glasset.

La meg presentere kveldens toastmaster: onkel Robert.

Onkel Robert er fars eldre bror, og den eneste i familien som betraktes som *lærd*. Det sies at han har lest forferdelig mange bøker, at han har lest så mange bøker at han kan svarene på nesten alt man kunne tenke seg å spørre om. Tante Selma sier selvfølgelig at det er bløff alt sammen, at han ikke har lest noe særlig i det hele tatt, bare et par sitatbøker og kultursidene i Dagbladet. Onkel Robert sier at dette kommer til å bli en minneverdig aften. Han forteller hva vi skal spise, og om noen har noe på hjertet er det bare å si fra til meg, så skal jeg notere det på talelisten, og husk, sier han: "Bordet er det eneste Sted, hvor man aldri kjeder sig den første Times Tid", for å sitere den franske gourmetfilosofen Brillat-Savarin som levde i Frankrike på 1700-tallet. Skål!

Jeg skåler med Fritz på den ene siden og jeg skåler med Aaron på den andre siden, og jeg tenker at innen desserten har vi en avtale du og jeg.

Dørene til kjøkkenet åpnes med et smell og to like høye magre unge kvinner i vakre røde kjoler kommer inn i stuen med hvert sitt store serveringsfat mellom hendene.

En forrett, sier onkel Robert og reiser seg igjen, samtidig som han smaker på ordet forrett. En forrett skal nytes, sier han, men ikke slukes; en forrett skal ikke mette sult, bare erte den, flørte med den. En forrett, mine venner, er det eneste måltid som faktisk tilfredsstiller et begjær uten å svekke det samtidig – noe som desverre ikke kan sies om ekteskap.

Onkel Robert kremter.

Jeg vil minne om min venn Lucullus, fortsetter han, romersk feltherre, kunstelsker og livsnyter. En gang, sies det, serverte han sine middagsgjester nittini lerketunger. En av gjestene, en kvinne, spurte bestyrtet om han ikke syntes det var for ille at alle lerkene måtte dø på grunn av et måltid. Men nei lerkene måtte ikke dø, svarte Lucullus, det var bare ikke mulig for dem å synge lenger. Skål!

Jeg skåler med Fritz og jeg skåler med Aaron en gang til. Så skåler jeg med Arvid som sitter rett overfor meg.

Arvid er høylytt og brautende.

Torild sitter et helt annet sted ved bordet, og sender Arvid engstelige blikk, *nå må du ikke drikke for mye Arvid vær så snill*, sier blikket hennes. Han løfter glasset og roper SKÅL! Skål Torild, ditt gamle ludder.

Alle ser på Arvid. Torild rømer og ser ned.

Skål Torild, sier Anni som sitter like ved.

Skål Anni, sier Torild.

Og nå må vi skåle for brudeparet, sier onkel Robert.

Skål, roper alle sammen, og så reiser onkel Robert seg og synger med høy, rungende stemme at dette skal være brudeparets skål hurra, og så synger alle at dette skal være brudeparets skål hurra, og skam på den som ikke brudeparets skål vil drikke! Skål!

Og så er forretten spist og hvitvinen drukket og første taler er Anni, brudens mor, fordi brudens far er altfor sjenert og forskrekket over å spille rollen som far i et stort gammeldags bryllup.

Anni reiser seg og sier: *Kjære Julie.*

Kjære Julie, sier hun, jeg skulle så gjerne lovet deg at alt går bra, at du og Aleksander skal bli lykkelige og få mange barn og leve godt og lenge. Men jeg kan ikke love deg noen ting. Det kan ingen. Det vet du like godt som jeg.

Anni holder talen sin. Den er lang.

Det var en fin tale, sier Aaron da hun er ferdig.

Jeg svarer ikke.

Din mor må ha vært en vakker kvinne, sier Aaron.

Jeg svarer ikke.

Before You Sleep

Excerpts

Translated by Tiina Nunnally[9]

In a corner of the entryway Aunt Selma is holding court with herself. She's puffing on a cigarette and listening with raised eyebrows to a small child who has ventured into her presence.

You look like a witch, says the child.

That's because I am a witch, says Selma.

But I bet you're not a mean witch, says the child, politely.

Oh yes I am, says Selma.

Mean in what way? asks the child.

My favorite dish is boiled little girl fists and fried little girl ears, she says softly, reaching for the child's throat, and then I like to have a dish of little girl stew to finish things off.

I don't believe you, howls the child and runs away.

Selma rolls her eyes.

Hi, Aunt Selma, I say.

Is that you? she says peevishly.

Can I bum a smoke? I ask.

Aunt Selma hands me her pack of cigarettes and says: I see you're wandering around staring at a man, the guy with the blonde woman.

You can see that? I say.

Your mother is stupid, your sister is stupid, your grandmother was as stupid as they get, your grandmother was so stupid that she didn't understand anything, but I'm not stupid. Of course I can see,

I'm planning to seduce him, I say.

I see, says Selma, it doesn't look like you're making much progress.

No, I say. Got any advice?

She takes a drag on her cigarette.

You try charm? she asks.

I think so, I say.

You try looking him deep in the eyes?

Yes. He doesn't pay any attention to me.

You try talking to him?

Yes, just a few minutes ago. It didn't go very well.

You try walking right up to him, telling him you want to sleep with him, and the only thing you expect from him is that he makes himself available for about fifteen minutes?

No. But I don't think that would do any good. I don't think he's the type to fall for that.

He's not, huh? She says. It worked fine for me when I was younger. But I was prettier than you, that helped.

You have any other advice?

You try flattery? she says.

Flattery?

Yes, flattery. It's a sure winner, never fails, she says.

Flattery, I say.

Flattery, says Selma.

But how? I ask. What should I flatter him about? I don't know him.

That's the whole point, she says, the less you know a person, the easier it is to flatter him.

But how? I ask.

Selma takes another drag on her cigarette. She chokes on the smoke, turns red in the face, her tongue shoots out of her mouth, her tongues hangs out of her mouth, she doubles over. Selma doubles over and lets out a gurgling squeaking rattling coughing sound that makes everybody in the vicinity turn around, thinking that she's had it, she's dying, it's definitely over, goodbye and thank you, Aunt Selma, we'll never forget you, bon voyage and give them all our best. A cough like that, I think, so old and so rotten that it's been gurgling in her throat ever since she was young and fabulous; a cough that might possibly date back to a cigarette she lit in a New York café, let's say, in October of 1929 when she was tossing back drinks with three of Wall Street's merriest speculators, drinking them under the table, if truth be told, and forcing them to dance with her afterwards, one after the other, and all three at once, in spite of how drunk they were; and no doubt this contributed to the fact that those same three speculators had terrible headaches the next day and couldn't do their jobs properly, and things didn't improve any when the entire stock market collapsed, bringing about the economic crisis in the U.S. and large parts of Europe for the next ten years. Two of the three speculators committed suicide that very evening; their wives blamed Selma.

She's never been what you might call a spreader of joy, I think—and then she stops coughing. Selma stops coughing. She straightens up, lifts her head, opens her eyes, gives everyone a cross-eyed smile, takes another drag on her cigarette, and lets the smoke seep out of her nostrils: You thought I was going to fall this time, didn't you, you thought I was done for, you thought it was all over. But look! I didn't fall, I'm still standing, I didn't fall. Selma laughs and says you just do what I tell you, Karin, and the boy won't have a chance. That boy there, she says, pointing at Aaron with the long yellow nail of her index finger, that boy there can't resist flattery. It's not his desire you need to stroke, but his vanity, and then all the rest will fall into place.

But how? I ask.

Be an actress, Karin! Act!

Selma coughs again, then she grips my shoulder and whispers: Look at him and make him understand that you can see the big secret he's carrying inside his heart.

What big secret?

That's not the point, she says. It's entirely possibly that he's not carrying a damn thing inside his heart, in all probability he isn't. The point is, he'd like to *believe* that he is and that *someone can see that he is.* Everybody wants to be more than they actually are, Karin, and if you give that boy over there the impression that you see he's more than he is, that you can see he's carrying a big secret inside his heart, that he's special, Karin, that he's different, that he has been kissed by God, well, then it's done, then he's yours.

I sneak into the dining room, find the place card with Aaron's name on it, and put it next to my own. Then I take the other place card and put it at Aaron's original place, a Daniel K. I read on the card, maybe one of Aleksander's friends, I don't know.

All right! Now it's done. Now he'll *have* to talk to me. Now he can't get out of talking to me. Now we'll sit side by side through the whole long wedding dinner and it would be rude of him not to talk to me. He has no choice, that's all there is to it. He has no choice.

I feel a hand on my shoulder.

What are you doing, Karin?

I turn around. It's Father talking to me.

I'm switching place cards. There's someone I want to sit next to, I say.

I see, says Father. Then he says: Can I leave now? I don't want to be at this party anymore.

No, I say.

Anni's whisky isn't any good. Anni never could tell the difference between good whisky and bad.

Whatever you say, I reply.

I like Johnny Walker, she likes Upper Ten.

Right, I say.

Anni has no taste.

I don't know about that, I say.

I straighten Father's bow tie, a red rose in his buttonhole.

Aaron is sitting alone on the purple couch with a glass in his hand, drinking a gin and tonic with a slice of lemon. On the round marble table in front of the couch there's a bowl of pretzels. Next to Aaron is Uncle Fritz, he also has a glass in his hand. Fritz is drinking something red.

I sit down on the couch between them.

You two are my dinner companions tonight, I beam.

Oh boy, says Uncle Fritz.

How nice, says Aaron and his eyes flit around the room.

His eyes remind me of a bird that strays into a living room.

I turn toward Fritz. What's that you're drinking, Uncle Fritz?

What did you say, Karin? he mumbles.

I asked you what you're drinking, it's red.

Sexy Sunrise, he mutters.

Sure, I say.

Karin, he says, staring into his glass.

Yes, I say.

Mamma just lost a tooth, he says.

I know.

First she loses her teeth, then she loses her ears, then her nose falls off, then her eyes fall out – LOOK! he says. LOOK AT THIS! says Fritz, pointing at the two green olives floating around in his drink. Mamma! he cries, and you know suddenly one day Mamma is … dead.

Yes, but that won't happen for a long time, I say.

Karin, he says.

Yes, I say.

I don't feel so good. I feel sick to my stomach.

Then you shouldn't have any more of that drink, I say.

Oh boy, he says.

Fritz huddles on the couch, his body bends forward, his lips open slightly, in one hand he's holding his glass.

Is everything all right with him? asks Aaron in a low voice.

Uncle Fritz, yes. Everything's all right, I say.

I look at Aaron. He looks back.

I lay my head on his shoulder. I know what you're thinking, I say.

Aaron pulls away.

What? he says.

I know what you're thinking, I say.

You do? he says.

I turn toward him, my face close to his face, his breath against my skin: I'm lying, I say. I don't know what you're thinking. I just wanted you to notice me.

Aaron looks at me for a moment longer than he should. Then he laughs a little. I look down. His hands are pale, thin, small, rather hairy, but at the same time girlish, and under his right thumbnail a speck of red paint that he hasn't washed off.

One winter night in early January, the year that Julie turned thirteen and I was ten: I'm walking up Jacob Aall Street, my schoolbag is heavy, it's dark. The snow is blowing sideways along the streets, swirling around my face, white, transparent, wet, almost gone.

Then I see them. Outside our building entrance there's a group of children with their hands stretched up to the sky. Standing on the balcony of the fourth floor is Julie, wearing a long red cotton nightgown with long sleeves. Her long blonde hair is blowing in the wind, the snow is encapsulating her; a red girl in her palace of snow, I remember thinking.

The children's faces grow clearer as I approach. They're boys and girls from the neighborhood and from Julie's class.

Julie is standing on the balcony, and with calm, sweeping movements of her hands she tosses all her things over the railing, down to the children in the street. She throws down her old doll, the one with the eyelids, eyelashes, and big blue glass eyes; the doll whirls through the air and falls softly onto the ground, the doll says Ow, and the big blue glass eyes blink. She throws down her red portable radio, all her records, books, dresses, and sweater; she even throws down the little gold heart she has around her neck, which was a gift from Father.

————————

The children all yell and cheer and run back and forth, gathering up whatever they can.
More, Julie, they shout.
Sweet, sweet Julie, they shout.
More, they shout.

At first I stand motionless and watch. I remember thinking: Now you've got to do something, Karin, now you've got to do something. Julie can't just stand up there on the balcony and toss out everything she owns.
Then I climb the four flights of stairs to our apartment. Three girls and a fat boy with a downy mustache follow me. Up the stairs, through the door, into Julie's room.
The three girls and the boy look around the room.

Hi, says Julie.
Hi, say the children.
One girl looks at the bookshelf and finds Julie's comic book collection.
Are you going to throw these out? asks the girl, pulling the comics off the shelf and starting to leaf through them.
I don't know, says Julie.
Oh please, says the girl.
I don't know, says Julie.
Why not? says the girl.
Well okay, says Julie. Go downstairs and I'll throw them down to you.
Okay, says the girl.

I leave the room, leave the apartment, go down to the street.
Julie is busy throwing things again.
The children run back and forth.

————————

No, I shout.
Stop it, I shout.
Please stop it.
These aren't your things, these are Julie's things, I shout, and then I try to tear a record and a stuffed rabbit out of the hands of a big hefty girl. The girl holds on tight to the things, and with one hand she punches me hard in the stomach so I fall to the ground.

I get up, tottering for a moment, catch my breath, and try to pull her down into the snowdrift. But the girl slips out of my hands and runs away.

Please, I shout, trudging around in the snow. Snow in my eyes. Snow on my hands. Snow in my boots. Please. Can't you please stop? These are Julie's things, not yours.

In the traditional manner Anni and Ingeborg signal that it's time for everyone to take their places. Ingeborg holds the gong and Anni strikes it. They walk from room to room doing this.

Are you going to offer me your arm? I ask Fritz, who's sitting motionless, completely motionless on the purple chaise longue.

I don't feel so good, says Fritz.

Can't you at least *try* to feel good? I say.

I'll try, I'll try, says Fritz, clutching his stomach with his hands.

The festively set long table stretched through two big rooms; white tablecloths, red roses, newly polished old silver, Ingeborg's hand-painted china: salad plates, dinner plates, service platters, all of them red. There are thirty-seven of us at the table, everyone find his place, Aaron finds his, next to mind, and now things are moving along just fine.

The evening's toastmaster gets up, picks up his fork, and clinks it against his glass.

Let me introduce this evening's toastmaster: Uncle Robert.

Uncle Robert is Father's older brother and the only one in the family who could be considered an intellectual. They say he's read an awful lot of books, he's read so many books that he knows the answer to practically everything you could think of to ask. Aunt Selma, of course, says it's all bluff, that he hasn't read much at all, only a couple of books of quotations and the cultural pages of the newspaper *Dagbladet*. Uncle Robert says this will be a memorable evening. He tells us what we're going to eat, and if anyone has anything they want to say, he declared, then just come to me and I'll make a note of it on the list of speakers, and remember: "The Table is the only Place where you are never bored during the first Hour," to quote the French gourmet philosopher Brillat-Savarin, who lived in France during the 1700s. Cheers!

I drink a toast with Fritz on one side of me and I drink a toast with Aaron on the other side, and I think that before dessert we'll have made a date, you and I.

The doors to the kitchen open with a bang and two skinny young women exactly the same height, wearing beautiful red dresses, come into the room, each carrying a large serving platter in her hands.

An appetizer, says Uncle Robert, standing up again, as he tastes the word appetizer. An appetizer should be savored, he says, but not gulped; an appetizer shouldn't quell your hunger, merely tease it, flirt with it. An appetizer, my friends is the only dish that actually satisfies your desire without weakening it at the same time—the same, unfortunately, cannot be said about marriage.

Uncle Robert clears his throat.

Let me remind you of my friend Lucullus, he continues, the Roman general, art lover, and hedonist. Once upon a time he served his dinner guests ninety-nine lark tongues. One of the guests, a woman, asked in dismay whether he didn't think it was a shame that all those larks had to die for the sake of one meal. But no, the larks didn't have to die, replied Lucullus, they just couldn't sing any more! Cheers!

I drink another toast with Fritz and I drink another toast with Aaron. Then I drink a toast with Arvid, who's sitting right across from me.
Arvid is loud and boisterous.
Torild is seated at the other end of the table, sending Arvid anxious looks, *now don't drink too much, Arvid, please,* her eyes say. He raises his glass and shouts CHEERS! Cheers, Torild, you old whore.
Everybody looks at Arvid. Torild blushes and looks down.
Cheers, Torild, says Anni, who's sitting nearby.
Cheers, Anni, says Torild.
And now we should drink a toast to the happy couple, says Uncle Robert.
Cheers, everyone shouts, and then Uncle Robert stands up and sings in a loud, re-sounding voice that this is a toast for the happy couple, Hurray! And shame on anyone who won't drink a toast to happy couple! Cheers!
And then we eat the appetizer and drink the white wine and the first speaker this evening is Anni, the bride's mother, because the bride's father is much too shy and embarrassed about playing the role of the father at such a big, traditional wedding.

Anni stands up and says: *Dear Julie.*
Dear Julie, she says, I want so much to promise you that everything will go well, that you and Aleksander will be happy and have lots of children and live a good, long life. But I can't promise you anything. Nobody can. You know that as well as I do.

Anni gives her speech. It's a long one.
That was a wonderful speech, says Aaron after she's done.
I don't say anything.
Your mother must have been a very beautiful woman, says Aaron.
I don't say anything.

Primary Works

Men jeg bor her ennå. Norsk samtid i prosa, 1997.
Om Arne Skouen og hans filmer, 1998; Eng. tr. *Profession: Director. Arne Skouen and His Films*, 2000.
Før du sovner, 1998; Eng. tr. *Before You Sleep*, 1999.
Når er jeg hos deg, 2001; Eng. tr. *Stella Descending*, 2003.
Nåde, 2002; Eng. tr. *Grace*, 2005.
Et velsignet barn, 2005.

Båsland, Harald, Grete Ertresvåg, Bjarne Hovland, and Linn Ullmann: *Terrella – Samfunnsfag for 5. klasse*, 1997.

Selected Bibliography

Andersen, Jens. "Eventyrlig vellykket." *Dagbladet*, 23 November 1998. 21 January 2005.
http://www.dagbladet.no/kultur/1998/11/23/143036.html.

Andersen, Per Thomas. "Spennende, men ujevn." *Dagbladet*, 4 October 2001. 21 January 2005. http://www.dagbladet.no/kultur/2001/10/04/285752.html.

Binding, Paul. "A leap in the dark that lasts a lifetime." *The Independent*, 23 January 2004. 21 January 2005. http://enjoyment.independent.co.uk/books/reviews/story.jsp?story=483780.

Brownrigg, Sylvia. "Long shots and close-ups seen through a glass, darkly." *The Independent*, 18 February 2000. 21 Jan 2005. http://enjoyment.independent.co.uk/low_res/story.jsp?story=46094&host=5&dir=207.

Dunnett, Ninian. "Light in the darkness." *The Scotsman*, 19 August 2004. 21 Jan 2005. http://news.scotsman.com/topics.cfm?tid=893&id=958802004.

Hagen, Gina Ingeborg. *Om Linn Ullmanns* Før du sovner. Hamar: Høgskolen i Hedmark, 2003.

Hverven, Tom Egil. "Åpning mot verden: Etterskrift om familien og litteraturen." *Å lese etter familien: Forsøk om norsk litteratur på 1990-tallet*. Oslo: Tiden, 1999, 80-95.

James, Caryn. "More Cries, More Whispers." *New York Times*, 10 October 1999. 21 January 2005. http://www.nytimes.com/books/99/10/10/reviews/991010.10jamest.html?oref=login.

Karlsen, Veronica. "Linn Ullmann: Lidenskap på stram line." TV2, 4 October 2001. 21 January 2005. http://pub.tv2.no/TV2/underholdning/bok/article3005.ece.

Kolberg, Ane. "Døden er ikke vakker." NRK P2 Kulturnytt, 31 October 2002. 21 January 2005. http://www.nrk.no/nyheter/kultur/2260367.html.

Mekjan, Sindre. "I don't know, and I don't care." *Morgenbladet*, 27 November 1998. 24 September 2002. http://morgenbladet.no/apps/pbcs.dll/article?AID=/19981127/ARKIV/811270333&SearchID=73201070911178.

Mørkedal, Marianne. *Et postmoderne samspill?: en undersøkelse av kjønn og identitet i romanene* Før du sovner *av Linn Ullmann og* The Blindfold *av Siri Hustvedt*. Dissertation. Bergen: Universitetet i Bergen, 2002.

Plesner, Ragnhild. "Finnes det en verdig død?" *Aftenposten*, 21 August 2002. 21 January 2005. http://tekst.aftenposten.no/forfindeks/fi.cgi?fiart+AFT2002+AFT2002082100 88&.

Skei, Hans H . "Glimt frå bokhausten 1998." *Norsk litterær årbok*. Oslo: Det Norske Samlaget, 1999.

–. "Roman i stort alvor." *Aftenposten*, 10 June 2001. 21 January 2005. http://tekst.aftenposten.no/forfindeks/fi.cgi?fiart+AFT2001+AFT200110060095&.

Stokke, Erle M. "Rapsodi ved århundrets slutt." *Morgenbladet*, 27 November 1998. 5 March 2005. http://morgenbladet.no/apps/pbcs.dll/article?AID=/19981127/ARKIV/811270323&SearchID=73201070911178.

–. Author homepage. *Dagbladet*, 21 January 2005. http://www.dagbladet.no/kontekst/4085.html.

The Contributors

Katrin Alas, born in Germany, received her MA-degree in Scandinavian Studies from Universität Wien, Austria, in 2003 with a thesis entitled "Das Frauenbild in den Dramen Victoria Benedictssons". Currently she is a PhD-candidate; her dissertation topic deals with the writings of the contemporary Swedish writer Marie Hermanson.

Petra Broomans is Associate Professor in Scandinavian Studies at the University of Groningen, the Netherlands, and has been a visiting professor at the University of Ghent, Belgium (2000-2003). Coordinator of the research project *Scandinavian Literature in Europe around 1900: the Influence of Language Politics, Gender and Aesthetics* at the Groningen Research School for the Study of the Humanities. Among her publications are: *"Detta är jag". Stina Aronsons litteraturhistoriska öde* (2001) as well as various articles on Scandinavian Literature.

Ia Dübois is Senior Lecturer at the Department of Scandinavian Studies at the University of Washington, Seattle, WA, USA, where she teaches undergraduate courses on Swedish literature and Scandinavian culture. She has published articles on Lars Gustafsson and Katarina Frostenson and is the co-editor of the anthology *Echo: Stories about Scandinavian Girls* (Women in Translation Press, 2000).

Janet Garton is Professor of European Literature at the University of East Anglia, Norwich, UK. She is also Managing Director of Norvik Press and editor of the journal *Scandinavica*. Her publications include *Jens Bjørneboe: Prophet without Honor* (1985), *Norwegian Women's Writing 1850-1990* (1993), *Elskede Amalie. Brevveksling mellom Amalie Skram og Erik Skram 1882-1899* (2002), and *Amalie Skrams brevveksling med andre nordiske forfattere* (2005). She is now working on an edition of Amalie Skram's novel *Constance Ring*. She is also active as a translator.

Ann-Charlotte Gavel Adams is Professor of Scandinavian Studies at the University of Washington, Seattle, WA, USA, where she teaches courses on August Strindberg, Scandinavian Women Writers, and Scandinavian

Children's Literature. She is the editor of *Inferno* and *Legender* in the National Edition of Strindberg's Collected Works and two volumes on 20th Century Swedish Writers in the series of *Dictionary of Literary Biography*.

Melissa Gjellstad is Coordinator of Norwegian Language and Culture and Lecturer of Germanic Studies and West European Studies at Indiana University, Bloomington, IN, USA. She received her PhD-degree from the University of Washington, Seattle, WA, USA, in 2004. She has published articles on Hanne Ørstavik and Tore Renberg. Her current projects focus on fatherhood and motherhood in contemporary Norwegian literature.

Leslie Grove (1960-1997) received her PhD-degree from the University of Washington, Seattle, WA, USA. She was Assistant Professor at St. Olaf College from 1992-1997 and led the Oslo Year Program in 1996-97. At the time of her death, she was the instructor for the SUST Program in Oslo, Norway.

Ulrika Gustafsson, born in Finland, has studied literature and folklore in Finland, Austria and Germany 1997-2002. She received her MA-degree from Åbo Akademi University, Finland, in 2002. At present she is a PhD-student at Åbo Akademi University and the Finnish Graduate School of Literary Studies writing a dissertation on the contemporary Finland-Swedish author Ulla-Lena Lundberg with focus on autobiography and anti-individualistic ideology.

Sherrill Harbison received her BA-degree from Oberlin College, Ohio, USA, in 1965 and her PhD-degree from the University of Massachusetts, Amherst, MA, USA, in 1996, where she is Lecturer in Scandinavian Studies. She has published numerous articles on Sigrid Undset, is the editor of the American Penguin edition of *Fortællingen om Viga-Ljot og Vigdis* (Eng. tr. *Gunnar's Daughter*, 1997), and has provided introductions to the volumes *Husfru* (Eng. tr. *The Wife*, 1999) and *Korset* (Eng. tr. *The Cross*, 2000) in the American Penguin edition of *Kristin Lavransdatter*. Her work on Undset has been supported by the Fulbright Foundation, the Norwegian Marshall Fund, and the National Endowment for the Humanities.

Anna Leppänen is born in Finland and has received her MA-degree in Comparative Literature from Tampere University, Finland, in 2002. She has taught Finnish at the University of Oregon, Eugene, USA, in 2003-04. Since 2004 she is working at Finlandia University, Michigan, USA, as a Finnish instructor.

Ann-Sofi Ljung Svensson is a PhD-student at the Department of Comparative Literature, Lund University, Sweden. She is working on a dissertation on the reception of Selma Lagerlöf's work in Germany at the turn of the 20th century.

Eva-Maria Metcalf teaches German and children's literature at The University of Mississippi, Oxford, MS, USA. She received her PhD-degree in German language and literature from the University of Minnesota, USA, in 1989, and publishes in the fields of German and Scandinavian children's literature.

Susanna Moliski received her MA-degree in 2001 from the University of Helsinki, Finland. Currently she is finishing her dissertation on Finnish contemporary fiction at the Department of Finnish Literature at the University of Helsinki: a study of the narratives of love in Pirjo Hassinen's work. In a wider prospect she is interested in creating connections between the scene of contemporary Finnish literary studies and the wider audience in the non-Finnish speaking academia and beyond. Currently she is a visiting PhD-student at the Department of Scandinavian Studies at the University of Wisconsin-Madison, USA.

Diane Oatley is originally from the United States, of Norwegian-American descent and a resident of Norway since 1982. She has a MA degree in Comparative Literature from the University of Oslo, Norway. Since the completion of her studies, she has worked with literature and dance as a lecturer, critic/essayist, translator, poet, consultant for dance productions, and performer/teacher of Oriental Dance. Expressions of the body represent an ongoing focus in her dance practice and writings, the latter in the form of essays, criticism and poetry published in newspapers, periodicals and anthologies in Norway, USA and Great Britain.

Inger M. Olsen is Adjunct Assistant Professor at Portland State University, Portland, OR, USA, where she has taught Danish since 1980. She was first educated in Denmark and then in the United States. She has presented papers and written various articles on Danish language and culture and translated articles on Ruth Berlau and Bertold Brecht as well as the story of an emigrant family's journey to Oregon. She is working on a translation of *Blåregnen*, an autobiography by former Danish Foreign Minister Kjeld Olesen.

Sarah J. Paulson is *førsteamanuensis* (Associate Professor) at the Norwegian University of Technology and Science (NTNU) in Trondheim, Norway, where she has taught Scandinavian literature and literary theory since

1994. Her publications include articles on Norwegian writers such as Herbjørg Wassmo, Cecilie Løveid, Cora Sandel, and Hanne Ørstavik. She is also a contributor to and editor of *Saklighet og sanselighet. Norsk prosamodernisme på 1930-tallet* (2000).

Charles Peterson received his BA-degree in music from North Park College, Chicago, IL, USA, in 1973, his MA-degree in communications from the University of Illinois at Chicago in 1980, and his PhD-degree in Radio-Television-Film from Northwestern University, IL, USA, in 1992. In 1988 he became Academic Dean and Professor of International Mass Media at Danvik Folkehøgskole in Drammen, Norway. In 1993 he returned to North Park University to become the Executive Director at the Center for Scandinavian Studies and Professor of Communication Arts. He is currently Academic Dean. His current research projects include Sámi and Eskimo Media, Culture, and Language.

Ellen Rees received her PhD-degree in Scandinavian Languages and Literature from the University of Washington, Seattle, WA, USA. She is Assistant Professor of Scandinavian Studies at the University of Oregon, and the author of *On the Margins: Nordic Women Modernists of the 1930s* (2005), as well as a number of articles on Scandinavian modernist prose fiction and Scandinavian cinema.

Lola Rogers is a language instructor, writer, and free-lance translator of Finnish poetry and prose. Her previous publications include original poems for *The Wire Harp* and *Syntax* literary magazines and translations for the *Journal of Finnish Studies* and *Books from Finland* magazine. She holds BA-degrees in Linguistics and Scandinavian Studies and a MA-degree in Scandinavian Languages and Literature from the University of Washington, Seattle, WA, USA. Her Master's thesis project was a translation of Eeva Liisa Manner's early poetry collection *Like Wind or Cloud.*

Sven Hakon Rossel is Professor and Chair of Scandinavian Literature at Universität Wien, Austria. He studied Comparative and Scandinavian Literature at the University of Copenhagen, has taught in Hamburg and Kiel, Germany, and at the University of Washington, Seattle, WA, USA. He has been a visiting professor at various European universities and has edited and/or written c. 40 books and published c. 100 articles and 250 reviews on Danish and Scandinavian literature. He is also active as a translator.

Eric Schaad received his PhD-degree in Comparative Literature from the University of Washington, Seattle, WA, USA. He lived for two years in Finland, studied at the University of Helsinki, and taught Finnish language at Brigham Young University, Utah, USA. His interest in 19th-century Finnish literature has included study of the *Kalevala*, Aleksis Kivi, Juhani Aho, and an unpublished partial translation of Aho's short novel *Rautatie* (1884; The Railroad). He currently works for a wireless company in Seattle and continues his academic projects, focusing on 18th and 19th-century literature, Icelandic sagas, Internet travel accounts, and the portrayal of law, criminals, and criminality in literature.

Monica Wenusch received her MA-degree in Scandinavian Languages and Literature from the Universität Wien, Austria in 2006 with a thesis on contemporary Danish writer Henning Mortensen entitled "Ud af fængslet: Henning Mortensens Ib-Zyklus" and is currently working on her dissertation, a translation and annotated edition of Johannes V. Jensen's novel *Kongens Fald* (1900-01). She is also active as a translator of Danish literature.

Rochelle Wright, Professor of Scandinavian and Comparative Literature, Cinema studies, and Gender and Women's studies at the University of Illinois, Urbana, USA, teaches courses in Scandinavian literature and Swedish film. Major publications include *Danish Emigrant Ballads and Songs* (1983), the chapter on "Literature since 1950" in *A History of Swedish Literature* (1996), and *The Visible Wall: Jews and Othe Ethnic Outsiders in Swedish Film* (1998). She has translated a number of Swedish novels. She is currently finishing a monograph on narrative strategies in the novels of Kerstin Ekman.

Wiener Texte zur Skandinavistik (WTS)

Herausgegeben von Robert Nedoma und Sven Hakon Rossel

BAND 1

Inger Olsen und Sven Hakon Rossel (eds.)

Female Voices of the North I. An Anthology

2002, ISBN 3-7069-0154-4, 339 Seiten, €-D 43,80 / €-A 45,00

Wiener Texte zur Skandinavistik (WTS)

Herausgegeben von Robert Nedoma und Sven Hakon Rossel

BAND 2

Johannes V. Jensen

„Ich habe deine wilde, unheilbare Sehnsucht gespürt ..."

Geschichten, Gedichte und Mythen. Eine Anthologie
übersetzt von Sven Hakon Rossel und Monica Wenusch

2005, ISBN 3-7069-0315-6, 246 Seiten, €-D 27,20 / €-A 28,00

Der dänische Nobelpreisträger Johannes V. Jensen (1873-1950) leitete mit seinen ersten Gedichten in freien Versen das 20. Jahrhundert in die dänische Literatur ein. Vor allem sind seine Texte von einer unüberhörbaren Begeisterung für die moderne Technologie, das Tempo und den Vereinigten Staaten durchdrungen – zumeist vermittelt durch die Konfrontation von scheinbar unvereinbaren Eindrücken. Alles was Jensen schrieb, ist von seiner Sehnsucht nach dem Fremden, nach dem Anderen geprägt, eine Sehnsucht, die aber von einer gleichzeitigen Liebe zur Heimat und den Traditionen in Gleichgewicht gehalten wird. Dies Erzeugt die enorme, modernistische Spannung in seinem Schaffen, die auch seine einmalige Kurzepik, die Erzählungen aus seiner Heimat und die Perspektiven sprengenden Fantasien, die Mythen, charakterisiert. Jensens Schaffen zeugt von einer einmaligen sprachliche Innovation und Intensität, die ihn auf die Stufe der Weltliteratur erheben.

Wiener Studien zur Skandinavistik (WSS)

Herausgegeben von Robert Nedoma und Sven Hakon Rossel

BAND 11

Friedrich E. Grünzweig

Runen auf Waffen
Inschriften vom 2. Jahrhundert n. Chr.
bis ins Hochmittelalter

2004, ISBN 3-7069-0227-3, 203 Seiten, € [D] 25,30 / € [A] 26,00

Die Runologie ist eine fächerübergreifende Disziplin, und ein gewisses Grundlagenwissen in vielen Wissenschaften stellt eine nicht zu vernachlässigende Hilfe dar. An erster Stelle stehen wohl Sprachwissenschaft und Archäologie. Über erstere muß nicht viel gesagt werden. Die Archäologie ist doch einige Erwähnungen wert. Ein wichtiges Detail für die Interpretation jeder Inschrift stellt die Datierung dar. Allzuoft wird diese in absoluten Zahlen angegeben, ohne in irgendeiner Form nachvollziehbar zu sein. Man muß sich etwas mit den Methoden der Datierung vertraut machen, um die von archäologischer Seite gebotenen Daten auch nachvollziehen und verwerten zu können. Es stellt für einen aus der philologischen Richtung kommenden Runologen keine Schande dar, die Ausführungen eines Archäologen eins zu eins zu übernehmen, doch sollten diese in ihren Grundzügen nachvollzogen werden können, um nicht in völlige Abhängigkeit zu geraten. Aber auch andere aus der Archäologie gewonnenen Erkenntnisse können wichtige Details liefern, wie sozialer Status, Beziehungen nach außerhalb etc. Man trifft immer wieder auf die landläufige Meinung, daß gerade Waffen einen typischen Träger für eine Runeninschrift darstellen. Dies ist auch von Zeit zu Zeit in der populärwissenschaftlichen Literatur zu finden. Waffeninschriften sind aber in vielen Schriftkulturen vertreten. Den ältesten mir bekannten Fall stellt ein goldener Dolch aus einem der Königsgräber von Ur mit dem Piktogramm ‚Vernichtung' dar, oder um ein "exotisches" Beispiel zu nennen, eine iberische Falcata trägt eine Inschrift. Die Fragestellung lautet: bilden die Runeninschriften auf Waffen eine besondere Gruppe innerhalb der gesamten runischen Überlieferung? Immerhin stellen sie doch einen beträchtlichen Anteil der ältesten Runeninschriften dar. Bleibt dieser hohe Prozentsatz im Laufe der Jahrhunderte gleich? Bereits der Aufsatz von Klaus DÜWEL 1981 zeigt, daß dem nicht so ist. Allerdings hat sich die Anzahl der Inschriften seitdem doch um einige erhöht, interessanterweise aber v.a. bei denen aus ältester Zeit. Eine andere Fragestellung ist, inwieweit Einflüsse aus anderen Schrifttraditionen (v.a. der lateinischen) zu verzeichnen sind. Diese und viele andere Fragen werden im vorliegenden Buch beantwortet.

PRAESENS VERLAG

Wiener Studien zur Skandinavistik (WSS)

Herausgegeben von Robert Nedoma und Sven Hakon Rossel

BAND 12

Roger Reidinger

Die Entwicklung der schwedischen Literatursprache im 19. Jahrhundert

Syntaktische und morphologische Untersuchungen zur neueren Sprachgeschichte des Schwedischen nebst einem kurzen Vergleich mit dem Dänischen

2005, ISBN 3-7069-0312-1, 346 Seiten, € [D] 31,10 / € [A] 32,00

Die skandinavischen Sprachen haben eine lange und bewegte Geschichte hinter sich, die von der Aufspaltung der ursprünglichen sprachlichen Einheit über die strukturellen Vereinfachungen im Verlauf des Mittelalters bis hin zur Entstehung der modernen Schriftsprachen führte. Die vorliegende Untersuchung beschäftigt sich mit einem eher jungen Kapitel der schwedischen Sprachgeschichte, nämlich mit den syntaktischen und morphologischen Veränderungen, die die schwedische Literatursprache im Laufe des 19. Jahrhunderts erfuhr. Die entsprechenden Entwicklungen werden in Überblickswerken üblicherweise nur als marginal dargestellt. Trotzdem gibt es zumindest einen Grund, aus dem es sich lohnen sollte, sich das 19. Jahrhundert genauer anzusehen, nämlich die gesellschaftlichen Umwälzungen (Verbürgerlichung, Proletarisierung), die diese Zeit kennzeichneten. Und tatsächlich erweist sich gerade das 19. Jahrhundert als eine Schnittstelle der schwedischen Sprachgeschichte, an der eine konservative, Gustavianisch geprägte Literatursprache durch eine lebendigere, dem mündlichen Sprachgebrauch etwas näher stehende Sprache ersetzt wurde. Diese Entwicklung verlief zwar nicht konsequent und stetig in eine Richtung, aber sie setzte sich durch und bereitete die moderne schwedische Literatursprache des 20. Jahrhunderts vor.

Wiener Studien zur Skandinavistik (WSS)

Herausgegeben von Robert Nedoma und Sven Hakon Rossel

BAND 13

Martina Chmelarz-Moswitzer

Mimesis und Auflösung der Form
Bildende Künstler und bildende Kunst in den Werken der skandinavischen Autoren Herman Bang, Henrik Ibsen und August Strindberg

2005, ISBN 3-7069-0335-0, 425 Seiten, € [D] 35,00 / € [A] 36,00

An Hand beispielhafter Werke der prominenten Autoren Herman Bang (1857-1912), Henrik Ibsen (1826-1908) und August Strindberg (1849-1912) wird in dieser interdisziplinär ausgerichteten Arbeit die Rolle bildender Künstler und bildender Kunst in der skandinavischen Literatur der 1870er bis 1910er Jahre einer eingehenden Untersuchung unterzogen. Neben literaturwissenschaftlichen und kunstgeschichtlichen Aspekten werden die Wechselbeziehungen zwischen fortschreitender Industrialisierung, einer erstarkten bürgerlich-kapitalistischen Gesellschaftsordnung, der Neuentwicklung von Medien und der Entstehung von Massenmedien beleuchtet. Alle drei genannten Autoren erklären in bedeutenden Werken innerhalb ihres Œuvres Künstler zu Hauptakteuren und räumen verschiedenen Kunstformen, von der Malerei und Skulptur über die Photographie bis hin zur Architektur, eine zentrale Stellung ein. Die Künstlerprotagonisten rekrutieren sich sowohl aus der ärmlichen Boheme als auch aus Kreisen gut situierter, erfolgreicher, ja sogar weltberühmter Künstler. Meist stehen diese Künstlerprotagonisten in einer kritischen Oppositionshaltung zur bürgerlich kapitalistischen Gesellschaft, die Kunst als gehobenes Konsumgut betrachtet oder wie Aktien zur Wertanlage nützt. Diese Oppositionshaltung ist Ausdruck einer tiefen Diskrepanz zwischen progressiven Künstlern und bürgerlicher Käuferschicht. Folglich beklagen Künstler das Unverständnis, das ihrer Arbeit entgegengebracht wird, und sind stets auf der Suche nach geistiger Heimat, die oft zum Verlust der geographisch-nationalen Heimat und ins Exil führt – eine Gemeinsamkeit der fiktiven Künstlerfiguren mit ihren Autoren.

Wiener Studien zur Skandinavistik (WSS)

Herausgegeben von Robert Nedoma und Sven Hakon Rossel

BAND 14

Matthias Langheiter-Tutschek

„…böcker säljer sig inte själva…"
Pär Lagerkvist und die deutschsprachigen Länder

2006, ISBN 3-7069-0283-4, ca. 240 Seiten, € [D] 25,30 / € [A] 26,00

„Inte syssla med mitt liv, utan med min diktning", also sich nicht mit dem Leben, sondern mit dem Werk zu beschäftigen, galt als dominierendes Paradigma innerhalb der Lagerkvist-Forschung des 20. Jahrhunderts. Der schwedische Literaturnobelpreisträger von 1951, Pär Fabian Lagerkvist (1891-1974), vermied Zeit seines Lebens öffentliche Auftritte, sieht man von den Sitzungen der Schwedischen Akademie ab, deren Mitglied Lagerkvist ab 1940 war. Die Aufarbeitung des Nachlasses, v.a. des in Form von Briefen im so genannten Lagerkvist-Archiv an der Kungliga Bibliioteket Stockholm vorliegenden Materials, förderte eine bislang wenig bekannte Fülle biographischer Fakten zu Tag. Durch die Auswertung von Lagerkvists Briefwechsel im Hinblick auf seine Auseinandersetzung mit den deutschsprachigen Ländern kann dem oben angeführten Diktum des Schweizer Skandinavisten, Übersetzers und Vermittlers Otto Oberholzer (1919-1986) entgegnet werden. „Böcker säljer sig inte själva" markiert um 1949 jene Trendwende in Lagerkvists 'Strategie' (LUHMANN), sein Werk auf dem deutschsprachigen Markt zu etablieren. Wenig erfolgreiche Vermittlungsversuche durch Heinrich Goebel (1870-1956) und die eindeutige Absage an den Nationalsozialismus durch Bödeln (1933; dt. „Der Henker", 1946), löste die in den deutschsprachigen Ländern ebenfalls geglückte Vermittlung des Romans Barabbas (1950; dt. 1950) ab, in dessen Zusammenhang auch die Verleihung des Nobelpreises gesehen werden muss. Das Alterswerk des Autors erschien seither im Schweizer Arche-Verlag (Peter Schifferli), Oberholzer zeichnet nach problematischen Übersetzungen sowohl von Barabbas als auch von Gäst hos verkligheten („Gast bei der Wirklichkeit", Übers. Edzard Schaper, 1952), sowie Sybillan („Die Sybille", Übers. Willi Reich, 1957) und Ahasverus död („Der Tod des Ahasver", Übers. Erich Furreg, 1959) für den Großteil der weiteren Arbeiten. Ein Anschlusserfolg an den Best- und Longseller Barabbas gelang nicht mehr, v.a. auf Grund der vertraglichen Bindung des Autors an den Bermann-Fischer-Verlag mit dem international erfolgreichen Dvärgen (1944; dt. „Der Zwerg", 1946). Lagerkvists Verhältnis zu den deutschsprachigen Ländern kann als problematisch angesehen werden, v.a. im Vergleich mit dem französischsprachigen Raum.

Wiener Studien zur Skandinavistik (WSS)

Herausgegeben von Robert Nedoma und Sven Hakon Rossel

BAND 15

Sven Hakon Rossel (Hg.)

Der Norden im Ausland – das Ausland im Norden

Formung und Transformation von Konzepten und Bildern des Anderen vom Mittelalter bis heute. 25. Tagung der IASS (International Association for Scandinavian Studies) in Wien, 2.-7.8.2004

2006, ISBN 3-7069-0371-7, ca. 700 Seiten, € [D] 38,90 / € [A] 40,00